Lamps and Lighting

Lamps and Lighting

A manual of lamps and lighting prepared by
members of staff of Thorn Lighting Ltd.

General Editors:

S. T. Henderson and
A. M. Marsden

EDWARD ARNOLD

© Thorn Lighting Ltd. 1972

First published 1966
by Edward Arnold (Publishers) Ltd.
25 Hill Street
London W1X 8LL

Second edition 1972

ISBN 0 7131 3267 1

Printed in Great Britain by
William Clowes & Sons, Limited, London, Beccles and Colchester

Preface

This new edition has been written, as before, by members of the staff of Thorn Lighting Ltd. (previously British Lighting Industries Ltd.): about half of the authors contributed to the first edition, but few of these have written on the same subject as they did previously. Although some of the figures and occasional paragraphs from the first edition have been used again, this edition is a completely new one: besides omitting obsolete material, information is included on many new developments.

The limited size of the book makes it necessary to omit some topics of interest, mainly minor ones, such as the history of lighting and the application of statistics to lamp measurements. With the needs of students of lighting in mind, more attention has been given to the theoretical aspects of the subject in the early chapters, without sacrificing practical detail in the later chapters, written as a reference source for engineers and designers in the lighting industry.

The internationally agreed system of metric units—Système International d'Unités (SI)—is used throughout, without excluding certain older units which are firmly established such as the electron-volt and the Torr. For terms and other conventions we have, where possible, used the documents of the International Electrotechnical Commission (IEC), the Commission Internationale de l'Eclairage (CIE), the British Standards Institution (BSI) and the Illuminating Engineering Society (IES), though we do not think that these always give the most convenient or logical descriptions. We have restricted the glossary in Appendix II mainly to units and terms which can be expressed by numerical values: many other terms have been omitted because they are adequately described in the text and can be located from the index.

We thank the authors for their contributions and for their patience with our editing of their manuscripts in the interest of saving space and making the book an integrated whole. The wives of our authors should also be thanked for their forbearance, and we are indebted to the many unnamed colleagues who have supplied material for inclusion in various parts of the book. Mr. L. C. Selwood of Edward Arnold (Publishers) Ltd. has given us help and guidance throughout.

Acknowledgments are due to the following for the use of copyright material:

Professor R. L. Gregory for Figs. 2.2 and 2.6 and the quotation on p. 44 ('Eye and Brain' published by Weidenfeld & Nicolson).

The Electrochemical Society for Fig. 8.2 (*J. Electrochem. Soc.*, Vol. 97, 1950, p. 266).

Applied Optics for Fig. 8.6 (*Appl. Opt.*, Vol. 5, 1966, p. 1467, published by the Optical Society of America).

Adam Hilger Ltd. for Fig. 11.3 ('Daylight and its Spectrum' by S. T. Henderson).

Dipl.-Phys. A. Dobrusskin of Osram GmbH, Munich, for Fig. 15.3 (*Ltg Res. & Tech.*, Vol. 3, 1971, p. 126).

The British Standards Institution for Table 11.1 (BS2833:1968), Fig. 31.1 (BS1376: 1953), Table 32.2 (CP1004:1963), and Table 32.3 (BS1788:1964).

The Optical Society of America for Fig. 15.16 (*J. Opt. Soc. Amer.,* Vol. 56, 1966, p. 91, J. H. Goncz & P. B. Newell).

The Marconi Company Ltd. for Fig. 17.3a and b.

Monsanto Chemicals Ltd. for Fig. 17.3c.

Manweb Electricity for Fig. 21.11.

The Electrical Review for Fig. 21.12 (*Elec. Rev.,* 7 Feb. 1969, p. 6).

NPL/HMSO for Fig. 21.1 (Symposium No. 12, Paper F5, Fig. 1).

Megatron Ltd. for Fig. 23.9.

BRS/HMSO for Fig. 23.14 ('BRS Daylight Protractors'), Tables 23.1 and 23.2 ('Architectural Physics—Lighting' by R. G. Hopkinson) and Table 23.3 (BRS Research Paper 72).

Rank Strand Electric (London) Ltd. for Figs. 29.2a, b and c.

Berkey Technical (U.K.) Ltd. for Fig. 29.2d.

British Railways Board for Fig. 31.4.

The Illuminating Engineering Society for many tables and figures extracted from its publications (Light and Lighting, Lighting Research and Technology, IES Technical Reports and the IES Code).

S. T. HENDERSON

A. M. MARSDEN

1972

Contents

PART ONE

Fundamentals

1 Light

The subject of this book is the modern technology involved in the production and utilization of light, the physical agency by which our sense of vision is stimulated. In the normal human being, the visual sense is the major channel through which information about the external world is received, hence the importance of adequate lighting in everyday life. Subjective visual sensations have given rise to concepts such as brightness and colour which are useful for qualitative comparisons of different light sources or lighting situations, but alone are not sufficient for technological purposes. It is therefore necessary to employ additional concepts based on an objective physical picture of light and amenable to measurement by means of instruments. This first chapter deals in the first two sections with the nature of light and its relation to the world of space, energy and matter. The second two sections introduce the fundamental concepts and the terminology used in later chapters for the quantitative treatment of practical lighting situations.

1.1 ELECTROMAGNETIC RADIATION AND LIGHT

Light is a form of energy that can pass from one material body to another without the need for any material substance in the intervening space. Such energy transfer has come to be called radiation, a term which implies that the energy flows out in straight lines in all directions from the source, although in fact straight line flow does not always occur when material substance is traversed. Some forms of radiation are known to consist of particles, for example those which are emitted by radioactive materials, and light was at one time thought to consist of a shower of particles but later it was found by experiments that the behaviour of a light ray could be better described in terms of waves, the ray direction being the direction in which the waves are travelling. Less than 100 years ago it was shown that light waves are electromagnetic in character, that is not material in the way that an alpha particle from radium or an electron are material, and since then it has become clear that light waves occupy only a very small part of a huge range of wavelengths in the spectrum of electromagnetic waves (Fig. 1.1). At the long wave end of this spectrum there are electromagnetic waves used for radio communications, with wavelengths ranging from tens of kilometres down to a few millimetres. At the other end of the electromagnetic spectrum there are X-rays and gamma rays, the latter being emitted during nuclear reactions and having wavelengths which are small even compared with atomic dimensions. The visible portion of the spectrum covers the wavelength range from approximately 380 nm to 760 nm (0·000 38 mm to 0·000 76 mm) and the eye discriminates between different wavelengths in this range by the sensation of colour. Blue and violet correspond to the short wavelengths and red to the long, yellow and green being in the middle of the visible range of wavelengths.

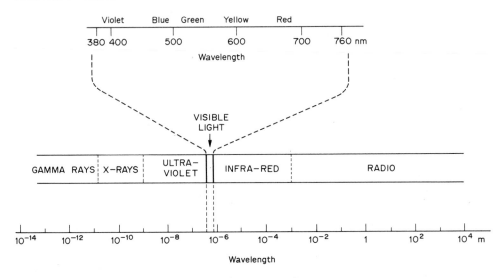

Fig. 1.1 The electromagnetic spectrum

1.1.1 The eye sensitivity curve

The sensitivity of the human eye is not uniform over the visible spectrum but varies with wavelength in the manner shown in Fig. 1.2. When adapted to medium and high illumination levels the eye has a maximum sensitivity in the yellow-green region of the spectrum at a wavelength of 555 nm. The visible spectrum falls in the middle of the range of wavelengths covered by solar radiation reaching the earth's surface. Radiation shorter than 290 nm in wavelength is absorbed by a layer of ozone in the upper levels of the earth's atmosphere and at wavelengths greater than 1400 nm there are strong absorptions due to water vapour and carbon dioxide in the lower atmosphere. It may be concluded, therefore, that the eye sensitivity curve is a result of evolutionary adaptation to the limits imposed by the transparency of the earth's atmosphere, though the maxima of eye sensitivity and daylight spectral emission do not coincide.

1.1.2 Ultra-violet and infra-red radiation

Electromagnetic radiations with wavelengths just beyond the violet and red ends of the visible spectrum are known respectively as ultra-violet and infra-red radiations. The ultra-violet is considered to extend down to a wavelength of 1 nm, below which the waves are regarded as X-rays, and the infra-red extends up to an arbitrary wavelength limit of 1 mm at which point the radio region begins. While not perceptible to the eye, both ultra-violet and infra-red radiation can be detected physiologically, if sufficiently intense, as a sensation of heat on the skin. This emphasises the fact that all radiation can degenerate to heat when absorbed, and there is no special heating effect associated with infra-red radiation, as is commonly supposed. In addition, ultra-violet radiation with wavelengths less than 320 nm can cause damage to living tissues, manifested on the skin as a delayed erythema (reddening) and blistering.

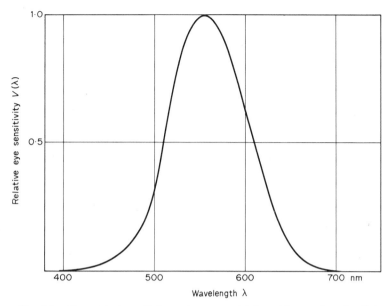

Fig. 1.2   The variation of photopic eye sensitivity with wavelength: $V(\lambda)$

1.2   PROPAGATION OF LIGHT

Light and all other electromagnetic radiations travel through a vacuum in straight lines at the same velocity which is close to 300 000 km/s. When passing through a material medium, such as air or glass, the velocity of propagation is less than in a vacuum by a factor known as the *refractive index* of the medium, for reasons which will become clear later. For any type of wave the velocity v is equal to the product of the wavelength λ and the frequency ν

$$v = \nu\lambda \tag{1.1}$$

where frequency is defined as the number of waves which pass a fixed point in one second. For example, the waves of violet light with a wavelength of 400 nm in vacuum have a frequency of $7{\cdot}5 \times 10^{14}$ Hz, and red light of 750 nm wavelength has a frequency of 4×10^{14} Hz. When waves pass from one medium to another the frequency does not change but any change in velocity will be accompanied by a proportional change in wavelength, since by Eq. 1.1 v/λ must be constant. When the wavelength of light is quoted without reference to a medium, it is normally taken to be the wavelength in air, which will be only very slightly shorter than that in a vacuum since the refractive index of air is close to unity.

At the boundary between two media of different refractive index incident light waves split into two groups, one of these is reflected back into the first medium, the other group is refracted into the second medium, as indicated by the ray diagram in Fig. 1.3. Laws governing the directions of the reflected and refracted rays can be deduced from the wave theory of light, with results as stated below.

5

1.2.1   Laws of specular reflection

At a bounding surface that is smooth compared with the wavelength of the incident light, specular reflection is said to occur. A single incident ray produces a single reflected ray and the following relations hold:

1. The incident ray, the reflected ray and the perpendicular to the bounding surface at the point of incidence all lie in one plane.

2. The incident ray and the reflected ray make equal angles with the perpendicular and are on opposite sides of it.

The proportion of light energy which appears in the reflected ray depends, among other things, on the ratio of the refractive indices of the two media and on the angle of incidence, that is, the angle between the incident ray and the perpendicular to the surface. As the angle of incidence approaches 90° the proportion of reflected light approaches 100%.

1.2.2   Laws of refraction

Light passing through a smooth boundary surface into the second medium suffers a change of direction according to the following laws:

1. The incident ray, the refracted ray and the perpendicular to the surface at the point of incidence all lie in one plane.

2. If the incident ray is in a medium of refractive index n_1 and makes an angle θ_1 with the perpendicular to the surface, and the refracted ray is in a medium of refractive index n_2 and makes an angle θ_2 with the perpendicular, then

$$n_1 \sin \theta_1 = n_2 \sin \theta_2 \tag{1.2}$$

where θ_1 and θ_2 lie on opposite sides of the perpendicular (Fig. 1.3).

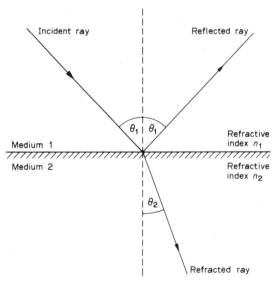

Fig. 1.3   Reflection and refraction at a boundary between two media

The above laws of refraction apply to most common materials such as glass, transparent plastics and liquids. In the case of certain crystals and transparent solids which are under strain these laws do not apply exactly, but the complicated effects which are observed under these conditions will not be discussed here.

1.2.3   Total reflection

When a ray passes from a high to a low refractive index medium, such as from glass to air, refracted rays exist only if the angle of incidence θ_1 is less than a certain critical value. If θ_1 exceeds this critical angle the refraction formula (Eq. 1.2) requires $\sin \theta_2$ to be greater than unity, which cannot be satisfied by a real value of θ_2. In practice it is found that no refracted ray is present under these conditions and all of the incident light energy appears in the reflected ray. This situation is referred to as total reflection. For glass of refractive index 1·5 the critical angle for total reflection at a glass to air surface is found by putting $n_1 = 1·5$, $n_2 = 1·0$ and $\sin \theta_2 = 1$ in the refraction formula to give a critical angle $\theta_1 = 41° \ 49'$.

Total reflection provides a means of obtaining a tarnish-free reflecting surface and is put to use in prismatic binoculars, reflective signs and some luminaires, also in fibre optics, where light is channelled along rods or fibres of glass which may take curved paths.

1.2.4   Dispersion

Refractive indices are dependent on the frequency of the light waves, an effect known as dispersion, and for common materials the refractive index increases as the frequency increases. For spectral violet the refraction is therefore greater than for red light. Dispersion effects are important in the study of colour (Chap. 3) and also in the design of optical instruments but are generally not large enough to require taking into account in the design of luminaires.

1.2.5   Absorption and scattering

A light ray passing through a perfect vacuum suffers no loss of total energy, although the energy may become more spread out as the ray progresses. In their passage through material media, however, light rays generally suffer energy losses due to absorption and scattering effects.

Absorption is caused by the conversion of light into some other form of energy, usually heat, but it could be changed into radiation of different wavelength (fluorescence), or into electrical energy as in photoelectric cells, or into chemical energy as in the photosynthesis carried out by plants. If the medium is homogeneous the loss in intensity of a parallel beam of light of a particular wavelength as it passes through follows an exponential decay curve of the form:

$$i = i_0 \exp{(-ax)} \tag{1.3}$$

where i_0 is the initial beam intensity, i is the intensity of the beam after travelling a distance x in the medium and a is the *linear absorption coefficient*, which usually depends on wavelength. For highly transparent materials a is very small so that i does not become appreciably less than i_0 until x is very large. In many materials a is large for all wavelengths, so large that i becomes virtually zero in very short distances; such materials are opaque to light except in very thin layers (for example metals). In some materials a is considerably different for different wavelengths of the visible spectrum; these materials change the spectral distribution of light passing through and form the basis for colour filters.

Under certain special conditions the absorption coefficient of a medium can be made negative, which means that light passing through it increases in intensity. This is the principle of the laser, a device which can be made to generate a light beam of extremely high intensity. The extra energy required for the light intensification must be supplied to the medium from some suitable source (Sect. 6.3.1).

Scattering occurs in non-homogenous media and is caused by multiple reflection and refraction at numerous, randomly orientated, boundary surfaces within the medium. Fog and cloud are examples of scattering conditions in air due to the presence of suspended water droplets. Much of the light entering a scattering medium may be scattered back out of it again without much absorption loss. Examples of this are the surfaces of white paper or cloth which consist of densely packed and almost transparent fibres. When light is strongly absorbed at scattering surfaces, such as carbon particles in dark smoke, very little scattered light finds its way out of the medium, which therefore appears black. If the scattering particles absorb selectively in the visible region a colour is imparted to the medium, as in the case of a paint in which coloured pigment particles are suspended in a transparent lacquer, absorbing some of the wavelengths from white light both on its path into the layer and also out of the layer after reflection. Scattering can be wavelength selective due to a contribution from diffracted light, and this also can impart a colour to a medium. All material media scatter light to some extent because of the molecular structure of matter. Scattering by very small particles, such as molecules, is greater for the shorter wavelengths of light; the blue of the sky is accounted for in this way (Sect. 23.1.3).

1.2.6   Diffuse reflection and transmission; the cosine law

When a light ray meets a surface which has irregularities comparable with or greater than the wavelength of the light, there is no longer a single reflected or refracted ray but the light energy spreads out in all directions from the point of incidence, just as in the case of scattering. The light which returns to the medium from which the incident ray came is said to be diffusely reflected, and that which passes through into the second medium is diffusely transmitted. In general, the precise angular distribution of the reflected and transmitted light depends on the angle of incidence of the ray to the surface and also on the nature of the surface roughness. With very fine grained surfaces the reflection may be almost specular at angles of incidence approaching $90°$.

To enable simple calculations to be made, the idea of a uniform diffuser is often used. A uniform diffuse reflector is one in which the reflected light distribution is independent of the angle of the incident light, and the intensity of reflected light in a direction making an angle θ with the perpendicular to the surface is proportional to $\cos \theta$. This cosine law can also be applied to uniform diffuse transmission. No real surface completely satisfies the conditions for a uniform diffuser but some surfaces are a good approximation to it, for example a layer of magnesium oxide powder.

1.2.7 Polarization

To understand the polarization of light it is necessary to form a suitable picture of an electromagnetic wave. This can be done by considering how such a wave may be generated by a vibrating electric charge. A stationary electric charge is surrounded by an electric field which may be thought of as lines of force radiating outwards in straight lines from the charge in all directions. If the charge is suddenly displaced a short distance, the lines of force remain attached to the charge and the displacement is propagated outwards along the lines of force at the speed of light. A vibrating charge in this way produces waves which travel along the lines of electric force much like waves on a stretched rope. Magnetic fields accompany these waves but the form of these magnetic fields need not be considered here. The foregoing picture of an electromagnetic wave is adequate to show that the electric component of the wave is in the plane defined by the direction of propagation and the direction of vibration of the charge. A ray of light is said to be linearly polarized when all the electric components of the waves lie in the same plane, the plane of vibration. The angle between the plane of vibration and some arbitrary direction, such as the vertical, is called the *angle of polarization*. Most sources emit unpolarized light, that is light consisting of waves with electric components randomly orientated. Linearly polarized light may be produced from unpolarized light by passing it through a polarizing filter, for example a suitable crystal or array of crystals (Polaroid), which selects the electric components of the waves in one plane only.

One property of linearly polarized light of particular interest is that the intensity of the ray reflected from a specular dielectric surface such as glass depends on the angle between the plane of vibration of the light and the plane of incidence, the latter being the plane defined by the incident ray and the perpendicular to the surface. When these two planes are coincident and the angle of incidence of the light is such that the refracted ray would be at right angles to the reflected ray, it is found that the reflected ray intensity is zero, that is, no reflection occurs. The angle of incidence in this case is known as the *Brewster angle*. The value of the Brewster angle is found from the laws of reflection and refraction to be equal to $\tan^{-1}(n_2/n_1)$; for a ray passing from air to glass ($n = 1.5$) this angle is found to be $56° 19'$. When unpolarized light is incident at the Brewster angle, the reflected light becomes linearly polarized in a plane at right angles to the plane of incidence. The calculation of light intensities after two or more specular reflections must take polarization into account and can therefore be quite a complicated process.

Polarization effects accompanying specular reflection may be used to reduce glare and improve contrast in a lighted scene. Horizontal surfaces such as polished table tops and glossy paper will give less specular reflection if the incident light is polarized in the vertical plane. Luminaires may be designed to take advantage of this fact, and one scheme is to use a number of plane parallel reflecting surfaces below the light source so that light transmitted at or near the Brewster angle will be depleted of the horizontally polarized component (Sect. 22.3.2).

In solids under strain and in certain crystals the refractive index is found to depend on the angle of polarization of the light relative to a strain direction or to an axis in the crystal. This finds application in the determination of strain in transparent materials and in crystallography.

1.2.8   Interference and diffraction

The wave nature of light does not produce any very obvious effects as far as general lighting is concerned, but there are two phenomena which have some technological application. The first is known as interference, and is exhibited when a screen is illuminated by two separate but mutually 'coherent' sources of light. Mutual coherence means that both sources are radiating light of exactly the same wavelength, and have a constant phase relation (Sect. 6.3). The result of combining the light from both sources is that at some places on the screen the light waves are in phase and add together, at other places the waves are out of phase and cancel each other. Interference between the two sets of waves is normally seen as a pattern of light and dark bands on the screen. In practice mutually coherent sources of light are produced by splitting a beam from a single source: this is usually achieved by using partially reflecting films on glass. One application of interference in present day lighting technology is in the 'dichroic' filters which are used to reflect or transmit certain selected parts of the spectrum (Sect. 9.2). These also make use of the fact that a beam of light, reflected at normal incidence from the surface of a medium of higher refractive index, suffers a phase change of 180°.

The second phenomenon resulting from the wave nature of light is known as diffraction and is the bending of light rays round the edges of obstacles. Diffraction effects are generally too small to be noticed by the unaided eye but are of considerable importance in optical instruments such as microscopes and telescopes operating at high magnifications. A combination of diffraction and interference occurs with the diffraction grating, a device used in instruments for examining the spectra of light sources.

1.2.9   Quantum phenomena

Although wave theory describes the propagation of light very well, it is not capable of explaining accurately the processes of emission and absorption. Experiments have shown that when light (or any other form of electromagnetic radiation) is emitted or absorbed, discrete amounts of energy called *quanta* are involved. One quantum of light energy is called a *photon* and the energy Q carried by one photon of light is given by Planck's relation:

$$Q = hv \qquad (1.4)$$

where v is the frequency and h is a constant, known as Planck's constant (Sect. 6.1.1). A photon of visible light carries only a very small amount of energy. At a wavelength of 500 nm, in the blue-green part of the spectrum, a single photon has an energy of 4×10^{-19} J, and a radiant power of 1 W at this wavelength is equivalent to $2 \cdot 5 \times 10^{18}$ photons per second. Using the quantum relation (Eq. 1.4) as a starting point, Planck in 1901 was able to derive theoretically the continuous spectral distribution of the radiation emitted by a full radiator or 'black body', the latter being defined as a body which completely absorbs all radiation falling upon it (Sect. 6.1.2). Incandescent solids, such as tungsten used for lamp filaments, give spectral distributions similar to that of the black body but with important differences (Sect. 7.2.1). Discontinuous spectral distributions are observed with electrically excited gases and are also explicable in terms of the quantum theory (Chap. 6).

1.3 RADIATION MEASURES

It is a common experience that the amount of detail in a scene that can be perceived by the eye is closely related to the amount of light available. At very subdued levels, all that can be seen are vague outlines of objects and in order to perceive fine detail or read small print it is necessary to have a relatively large amount of light, giving a 'high level of illumination'. Quantitative measures are therefore required and it is first necessary to establish a relationship between illumination and radiant power.

1.3.1 Radiant flux and radiant efficiency

Radiant flux (Φ_e) is equal to the total power in watts of electromagnetic radiation emitted or received. It may include both visible (luminous) and non-visible components. The radiant efficiency of a source (η_e) is the ratio of the radiant flux emitted to the power consumed.

1.3.2 Luminous flux, luminous efficiency and luminous efficacy

Before defining units of illumination it is necessary to refer to the spectral luminous efficiency curve (Fig. 1.2). An ordinate on this curve is denoted by $V(\lambda)$ and represents the relative sensitivity of the average human eye to radiation of the appropriate wavelength λ, the sensitivity at the peak of the curve being taken to be unity. For the normal eye adapted to medium and high light intensities (photopic vision) the peak of the $V(\lambda)$ curve occurs at a wavelength of 555 nm. Radiant flux containing wavelengths for which $V(\lambda)$ is greater than zero is considered to have associated with it a luminous flux Φ_v. The unit of luminous flux is the lumen (lm) and was originally defined in terms of a standard wax candle, which emitted 4π lm. Nowadays a more reliable standard light source is used (Sect. 1.4.4). As a measure of the ability of radiation to produce visual sensation the term luminous efficacy of radiation (K) is used, defined as the quotient of luminous flux in lumens by radiant flux in watts:

$$K = \frac{\Phi_v}{\Phi_e} \tag{1.5}$$

The maximum possible luminous efficacy of radiation, K_m, is for light of wavelength 555 nm, and is found by experiment to be about 680 lm/W. Radiation of any other wavelength or mixture of wavelengths has a lower efficacy: at a wavelength λ the efficacy $K(\lambda)$ is equal to $680 V(\lambda)$. The ratio K/K_m is the luminous efficiency of the radiation, denoted by V, which may be applied to complex radiation or a source by weighting according to $V(\lambda)$:

$$V = \frac{\int_0^\infty \Phi_{e,\lambda} V(\lambda) \, d\lambda}{\int_0^\infty \Phi_{e,\lambda} \, d\lambda} \tag{1.6}$$

When a source is considered, the luminous efficacy is the quotient of the luminous flux by the power consumed, again in lm/W, but with symbol η_v. Note the possible confusion between this unit and the dimensionless η_e in Sect. 1.3.1, also the differing treatments of radiation and a source. As an example, at a wavelength of 700 nm, corresponding to a visual sensation of deep red light, $V(\lambda)$ has the value 0·004 and the efficacy is approximately 3 lm/W.

To calculate the luminous flux or efficacy of radiation with a continuous spectrum it is necessary to perform an integration. If $\delta\Phi_e$ is the radiant flux over the wavelength range $\delta\lambda$, then $\delta\Phi_v$ the luminous flux over this range is given by

$$\delta\Phi_v = 680\ V(\lambda)\ \delta\Phi_e$$

Hence the total luminous flux Φ_v is given by integrating over the entire wavelength range:

$$\Phi_v = 680 \int_0^\infty V(\lambda)\ \mathrm{d}\Phi_e$$

$$= 680 \int_0^\infty V(\lambda) \left(\frac{\mathrm{d}\Phi_e}{\mathrm{d}\lambda}\right) \mathrm{d}\lambda \tag{1.7}$$

where $\mathrm{d}\Phi_e/\mathrm{d}\lambda$ is the spectral power per unit wavelength interval. The integration limits need not exceed the range of appreciable values of $V(\lambda)$, say 360 nm to 830 nm, and in practice 380 nm to 760 nm is usually adequate. Similarly, the total radiant flux is found from

$$\Phi_e = \int_0^\infty \left(\frac{\mathrm{d}\Phi_e}{\mathrm{d}\lambda}\right) \mathrm{d}\lambda \tag{1.8}$$

and the efficacy follows from Eq. 1.5.

In practice it is more usual to measure the total luminous flux directly by means of specially corrected photocells, and, if it is required, the radiant flux can be measured by means of a power sensing device such as a thermopile. Measurements of luminous and radiant flux are known respectively as photometry and radiometry (Chap. 4).

1.3.3   Ultra-violet flux

Natural daylight and light from many kinds of artificial source is accompanied by an appreciable amount of ultra-violet radiation. The intensity of ultra-violet radiation is normally measured in standard power units, namely watts for radiant flux and watts per square metre for irradiance. Calculations of ultra-violet irradiance are carried out in a similar fashion to those for illuminance (Sect. 1.4.1).

For convenience of reference, the CIE has distinguished three spectral ranges: UV-A from 400 nm to 315 nm, UV-B from 315 nm to 280 nm, and UV-C from 280 nm to 100 nm. In certain fields of application, where a particular property of ultra-violet radiation is of primary interest, some additional units have been introduced.

Erythemal radiation.   Exposure to ultra-violet radiation of wavelengths shorter than about 320 nm produces an erythema or reddening of the human skin. Although moderate exposure can have therapeutic effects (Sect. 6.2.2) prolonged exposure can produce painful and even dangerous results. The tissue (conjunctiva) of the eye is particularly sensitive to erythemal radiation, and protective goggles should always be worn if the eyes are likely to be exposed to this radiation.

The exact cause of erythema is not known but it has been shown to be dependent on the wavelength of the radiation. Erythemal efficacy rises to a maximum at a wavelength of 297 nm, declines to a minimum around 270 to 280 nm and increases again at shorter wavelengths. Where radiation covering a range of wavelengths is concerned, the erythemal efficacy can be related to the maximum for 297 nm wavelength. For convenience an erythemal unit the *E-viton* is introduced, one E-viton being the radiant flux required to produce the same erythemal effect as 10 μW of 297 nm radiation. A minimum perceptible erythema is produced on the average untanned white skin by an erythemal flux of 10^4 E-vitons per m^2 for a period of 2500 s; for 297 nm radiation this corresponds to a therapeutic *dose* of 250 J/m^2. The *dose rate*, or irradiance, in this example is 0·1 W/m^2 or 1 E-viton/cm^2, called a *Finsen*.

Bactericidal radiation. At wavelengths shorter than 320 nm, ultraviolet radiation has a lethal effect on micro-organisms. Bactericidal efficacy is at a maximum at about 260 nm, depending to some extent on the type of organism involved. An electrical discharge in mercury vapour at low pressure produces very intense radiation of wavelength 253·7 nm, close to the maximum for bactericidal efficacy, and this type of source is therefore frequently used for bactericidal (germicidal) purposes. A 'germicidal' unit (GU) of irradiance is sometimes used; it is defined as the irradiance required to produce the same bactericidal effect as 1 W/m^2 of 253·7 nm radiation.

Except at very low radiation intensities, the survival of organisms exposed to a constant intensity of radiation obeys an exponential decay law, which means that the number of organisms surviving decreases by the same factor for each consecutive unit of time. For example, when organisms of the type *Bacillus coli* are exposed to 1 GU of radiation for 15 s, 1% survive; a further 15 s exposure results in 0·01% survival, and so on. The sensitivity of various organisms to bactericidal radiation covers a wide range, and environmental conditions such as humidity can affect the sensitivity of any one type of organism.

1.3.4 Infra-red flux

The near infra-red part of the spectrum is represented in daylight and in many other light sources. For the latter this leads to a loss of luminous efficacy and appears as unwanted heat. As radiant flux it is measured in watts, as irradiance in W/m^2. The wavelength regions of most interest are classified by the CIE as IR-A, from 780 nm to 1400 nm, IR-B from 1·4 μm to 3 μm, and IR-C from 3 μm to 1 mm.

1.4 LIGHTING CONCEPTS AND UNITS

1.4.1 Illuminance

The illuminance E at a point on a plane is defined as being equal to the luminous flux

$\delta\Phi$ incident on an element of the surface containing the point, divided by the area δA of the element:

$$E = \frac{\delta\Phi}{\delta A} \qquad (1.9)$$

A corresponding quantity *irradiance* is similarly defined where radiant flux is concerned. The unit of illuminance is the lm/m^2 or *lux*: irradiance is expressed in W/m^2. Although illuminance is the preferred term, the words 'illumination' and 'illumination level' have been used in the past and are still widely used with the same meaning as illuminance.

It must be emphasized that illuminance, as defined here, refers to a point on a given plane; for this reason the term planar illuminance is sometimes used. The given plane is usually a horizontal one, but not necessarily so, and if the orientation of the plane is changed then in general the illuminance at a point on the plane also changes. Illuminance at a point in space has no meaning without further qualification (Sect. 1.4.9). The illuminance at a point on a curved surface must be taken to mean the illuminance referred to a plane which is a tangent to the surface at the point considered.

1.4.2 Luminous intensity of a point source

A frequent requirement in lighting engineering is the calculation of the illuminance produced on a surface by a given arrangement of light sources. The simplest example is the illumination of a plane surface by the theoretical 'point source', having an equal intensity in all directions. A more practical case is to consider a source whose dimensions are small compared with its distance from the surface. Referring to Fig. 1.4, a light source S, emitting luminous flux in various directions, illuminates a plane surface P. The flux $\delta\Phi$ intercepted by an element of area δA on P is the flux emitted within the solid angle $\delta\omega$ subtended at the source by the element δA: it is assumed that no absorption of light occurs in the space between the source and the surface. The quotient $\delta\Phi/\delta\omega$ is called the luminous intensity (I) of the source in the particular direction considered; thus

$$I = \frac{\delta\Phi}{\delta\omega} \qquad (1.10)$$

The units of I are lumens per steradian (lm/sr) or *candelas* (cd): an earlier term used for this unit was candle-power. Luminous intensity is therefore the luminous flux per steradian emitted in a particular direction. Radiant intensity is similarly defined as radiant flux per steradian. Generally I will vary with the direction of the emitted light: in the case where the luminous intensity is the same for all directions, the source is said to be uniform. For a uniform point source of luminous intensity 1 cd, the total flux emitted is 4π lm: this is the flux emitted by the now obsolete standard candle.

1.4.3 The inverse square and cosine laws of illumination

The illuminance E on a surface of area δA subtending angle $\delta\omega$ at the point source is found by eliminating $\delta\Phi$ between Eq. 1.9 and 1.10, which gives

$$E = I\frac{\delta\omega}{\delta A} \qquad (1.11)$$

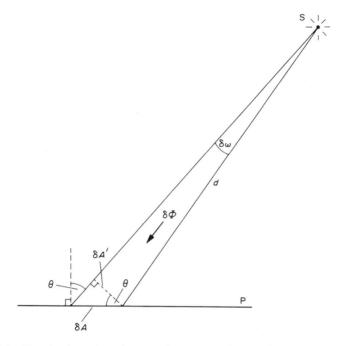

Fig. 1.4   Illumination of an element of area on a plane surface by a point source

From geometrical considerations (Fig. 1.4) $\delta\omega = \delta A'/d^2$ where d is the distance from surface to source and $\delta A'$ is the projection of the area δA on the plane perpendicular to the direction of the source.

Also we have the relation $\delta A' = \delta A \cos\theta$, θ being the angle between the direction of the source and the perpendicular to the surface. Eliminating $\delta\omega$ and δA from Eq. 1.11 leads to

$$E = \frac{I \cos\theta}{d^2} \tag{1.12}$$

Eq. 1.12 shows that the illuminance is proportional to the inverse square of the distance of the source and to the cosine of the angle of incidence of the light on the surface.

Multiple point sources.   The illuminance produced by a number of point sources is equal to the sum of the illuminances produced by each source separately. (This is not true for mutually coherent sources where interference effects are exhibited but for practical sources used in lighting the question of coherence does not arise.) The total illuminance may be expressed as

$$E = \sum \frac{I_k \cos\theta_k}{d_k^2} \tag{1.13}$$

The subscript k identifies the individual point sources.

15

Extended light sources. The illuminance produced by an extended light source can be calculated by dividing the source up into small areas, each of which can be considered to be a point source, and adding together the illuminance contributed by all the component point sources.

The illuminance δE produced by a single component point source of luminous intensity δI is given by

$$\delta E = \frac{\delta I \cos \theta}{d^2} \qquad (1.14)$$

and the total illuminance E due to the extended source can be expressed as an integral:

$$E = \int \frac{\cos \theta}{d^2} \, \mathrm{d}I \qquad (1.15)$$

The integral in Eq. 1.15 cannot be evaluated further unless something is known about how $\mathrm{d}I$ is determined. For this it is necessary to introduce the concept of luminance.

1.4.4 Luminance

If δA is an element of area of an extended source then the luminous intensity δI of the element viewed in a direction making an angle φ with the perpendicular to the surface of the source is given by

$$\delta I = L \, \delta A \cos \varphi \qquad (1.16)$$

where L is called the luminance of the source element, the unit of L being the candela per square metre ($\mathrm{cd/m^2}$). The corresponding radiation measure is radiance (L_e). Generally L will vary with angle φ and with the position of δA on the surface of the source.

The area of the projection of δA on to a plane perpendicular to the viewing direction is $\delta A'$, or $\delta A \cos \varphi$, and by substitution in Eq. 1.16 we obtain

$$L = \frac{\delta I}{\delta A'} \qquad (1.17)$$

From Eq. 1.17 it is seen that luminance can be defined as the luminous intensity per unit projected area of source. The substitution $\delta I = L \delta A'$ into Eq. 1.14 gives

$$\delta E = L \cos \theta \, \frac{\delta A'}{d^2}$$

Now, $\delta A'/d^2$ is equal to $\delta \omega$, the solid angle subtended by the source element at the illuminated surface (Fig. 1.5). Hence $\delta E = L \cos \theta \, \delta \omega$
and Eq. 1.15 can be written

$$E = \int L \cos \theta \, \mathrm{d}\omega \qquad (1.18)$$

Luminance standard. The concept of luminance is now used in the definition of a physically realizable standard light source which replaces the old standard candle. A

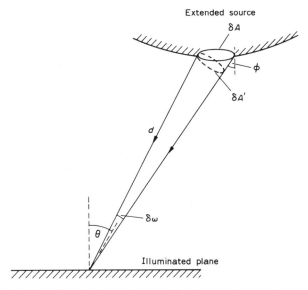

Fig. 1.5   Illumination of a point on a plane surface by an element of an extended source

black body at the temperature of solidification of platinum (2045 K) has a luminance of 6×10^5 cd/m² (60 candelas per cm²), when viewed perpendicularly to the surface.

1.4.5   Uniform diffuse sources

A uniform diffuse source is defined as one which has a constant luminance for all viewing directions. Real light sources rarely approach this ideal but the assumption of a uniform diffuse source is made in order to facilitate calculations.

If L is constant it can be taken outside the integral of Eq. 1.18 to give

$$E = L \int \cos \theta \, d\omega \tag{1.19}$$

The limits of the integral depend on the boundary of the light source as seen from the point at which the illuminance is to be calculated. It therefore follows that all uniform diffuse sources which have equal luminances and present the same outline as seen from a point will produce equal illuminance at that point (Sect. 5.3.2). For example, a spherical source produces the same illuminance as a flat disc of the same apparent diameter.

1.4.6   Luminous exitance

The luminous exitance at a point on a surface is equal to the total luminous flux emitted per unit area. An element of area δA emitting a total flux $\delta \Phi$ in all directions (over a solid angle 2π sr has a luminous exitance M_v given by

$$M_v = \frac{\delta \Phi}{\delta A} \tag{1.20}$$

17

The unit of luminous exitance is the lumen per square metre (lm/m^2). Radiant exitance M_e, with a unit of W/m^2 is defined in a similar way.

A relation exists between the luminance and the luminous exitance of a uniform diffuse source. Consider the illuminance E produced on the inner surface of a hemisphere of radius d by a small uniform diffuse source of luminance L and area S at its centre (Fig. 1.6). The light is incident perpendicularly to the surface, so by putting $\theta = 90°$ Eq. 1.12 becomes $E = I/d^2$. As the source is considered to be small, Eq. 1.16 may be

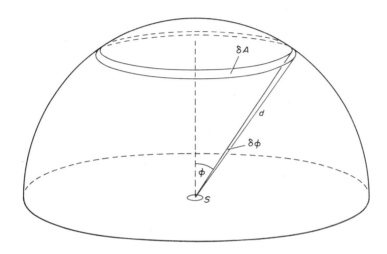

Fig. 1.6   Illumination of a hemisphere by a central uniform diffuse source

written $I = LS \cos \varphi$ so that $E = LS \cos \varphi/d^2$. The luminous flux $\delta\Phi$ falling on an element of surface δA of the hemisphere is therefore given by $\delta\Phi = E\,\delta A = LS \cos \varphi\,\delta A/d^2$. The total luminous flux falling on the hemisphere is given by

$$\Phi = \int d\Phi = LS \int \frac{\cos \varphi\,dA}{d^2}$$

The integral may be performed by replacing dA by $2\pi d^2 \sin \varphi\,d\varphi$, and

$$\Phi = 2\pi LS \int_0^{\pi/2} \sin \varphi \cos \varphi\,d\varphi = \pi LS$$

Also, as the hemisphere intercepts all the flux emitted by the source $\Phi = M_v S$, where M_v is the luminous exitance of the source. Hence for the uniform diffuse source

$$M_v = \pi L \tag{1.21}$$

1.4.7   Illuminated surfaces

An illuminated surface absorbs a portion of the light incident upon it and usually converts the energy into heat. Light which is not absorbed is either reflected or transmitted. A surface reflecting or transmitting light can be regarded as a secondary light source since the light it emits will add to the illumination of surrounding surfaces. The concept of luminance can be applied to a reflecting or transmitting surface and calculation of the illuminance it produces can be carried out in the way outlined in previous sections. The calculation of illuminance in a lighted interior can become a very complicated process since every surface may be reflecting light on to other surfaces and receiving reflected light from other surfaces (Sect. 5.4). As a result of this the total luminous flux falling on the surfaces in a room will be greater than the luminous flux emitted by the primary light sources in the room, and any small area, say of a wall, will appear of higher luminosity than if it were placed in isolation at the same place, with the light sources but without the rest of the room surfaces. This principle is used in the integrating sphere used in photometry (Sect. 4.2.2), and arises in calculations of reflected flux (Sect. 5.4). After many reflections the light from the primary sources will ultimately be absorbed in surfaces or will escape through an aperture such as a window. In the absence of any apertures the whole of the light eventually is absorbed. At any instant of time the total light flux being produced by the primary sources is then equal to the total flux being absorbed by the surfaces.

In order to perform calculations involving reflected light from surfaces use is made of a quantity known as the reflectance.

Reflectance (ρ).   The ratio of the total light flux reflected from a small area of surface to the total light flux incident upon it is called the reflectance. Alternatively, reflectance may be expressed by the relation

$$\rho = \frac{M_v}{E} \qquad (1.22)$$

where E is the illuminance on the surface and M_v is the luminous exitance, defined in the same way as for primary light sources. It must be pointed out that reflectance depends in general on the angular distribution, the spectral distribution and the polarization of the incident light. Only in the case of a uniform diffuse, white or neutral grey surface can the reflectance be regarded as a constant.

Reflectances can have values lying between zero and unity; $\rho = 0$ corresponds to the ideal 'black body' and $\rho = 1$ would be for a perfect reflector, but neither of these two extremes is met with in practice. Examples of real reflectances lying close to the extremes are $\rho = 0.01$ for black velvet and $\rho = 0.98$ for magnesium oxide.

Luminance of reflecting surfaces.   The directional distribution of light reflected from a surface depends in general on the directional distribution of the incident light. The luminance of the surface will therefore depend on the direction from which it is viewed. In the case of the uniform diffuse reflector which obeys the cosine law of reflection (Sect. 1.2.6), the luminance is the same for all viewing directions, just as for a uniform diffuse source. The proof is as follows.

The luminous intensity I of a uniformly illuminated area A of the surface viewed at and angle θ to the perpendicular is given by the cosine law $I = I_0 \cos \theta$, where I_0 is the intensity when viewing perpendicular to the surface. The projected area of the surface

19

on a plane perpendicular to the viewing direction is $A \cos \theta$. Therefore the luminance L (the luminous intensity per unit projected area) is given by

$$L = \frac{I}{A \cos \theta} = \frac{I_0}{A}$$

which shows that L is independent of θ. The luminance of a uniform diffuse reflector when subjected to an illuminance E is found by eliminating M_v between Eq. 1.21 and 1.22 to give

$$L = \frac{\rho E}{\pi} \qquad (1.23)$$

The occurrence of π in Eq. 1.23 may be inconvenient for some calculations but can be avoided by the use of an alternative unit for luminance, the *apostilb* (asb), defined by

$$1 \text{ asb} = \frac{1}{\pi} \text{ cd/m}^2$$

Eq. 1.23 can then be written

$$L_A = \rho E$$

where L_A is the luminance in asb. For a perfect diffuser ($\rho = 1$), L_A is numerically equal to the illuminance E or the exitance M_v (Eq. 1.21) in lm/m^2.

Transmittance (τ).   The transmittance of an illuminated surface is defined as the ratio of the total luminous flux transmitted by it to the total flux incident upon it.

The luminous exitance M_v of a surface transmitting light is related to the illuminance E on the other side of it by

$$M_v = \tau E \qquad (1.24)$$

The remarks regarding the influence of the character of the incident light on reflectance apply also to transmittance. The idea of uniformly diffuse transmission is exactly analogous to uniformly diffuse reflection; the cosine law and the constant luminance condition apply to both.

Since light incident on a surface is either transmitted, reflected or absorbed, the following relation holds:

$$\tau + \rho + \alpha = 1 \qquad (1.25)$$

where α is the absorptance, defined in an analogous way to the reflectance and transmittance.

1.4.8   The illumination vector

It is possible to use the concept of a vector when making calculations of the illuminance on a plane surface. A vector concept is applicable because the basic equation for the illuminance produced by a point source, $I \cos \theta / d^2$ (Eq. 1.12), shows that the illuminance E can be regarded as the component of a vector of magnitude I/d^2. The component is in the direction of the perpendicular into the plane on which the value of E is required, and

20

the vector is directed away from the point source and towards the plane (Fig. 1.7). The correct value of E is given only if θ is not greater than $90°$, that is, E is calculated on the side of the plane which is facing the source, otherwise a negative figure for illuminance is obtained because $\cos \theta$ is negative if θ lies between $90°$ and $180°$.

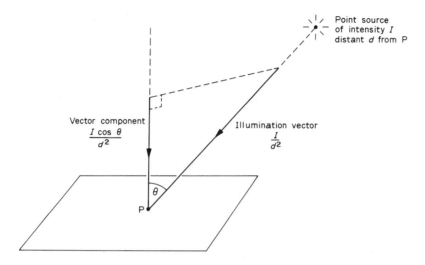

Fig. 1.7 Illumination vector due to a single point source

If there are many point sources, each source can be thought of as producing an illumination vector, and these can be combined into a single resultant vector. The resultant vector can be used to calculate the illuminance on a plane, but only if all the sources lie on the same side of the plane. If the latter restriction is ignored, then sources on one side of the plane have angles lying between $90°$ and $180°$ and their illuminance contribution is subtracted from the total. The net result is that if sources on both sides of a plane are taken into account, the vector method of calculation gives the difference in illuminance on opposite sides of the plane.

If the illumination vector at a point in space is zero, it does not necessarily mean that there is no light at that point but only that the illuminances on both sides of a plane placed there are equal for all orientations of the plane: an example of this would be a point midway between two point sources of equal luminous intensity.

1.4.9 Mean spherical illuminance

In order to give a measure of the amount of light available at a point in space without specifying a particular direction of the illuminated surface, a quantity known as the mean spherical or *scalar illuminance* can be used. It is defined as the mean illuminance over the surface of a small sphere placed at the point in question.

Calculation of scalar illuminance proceeds by first considering a point source of luminous intensity I at a distance d from a small sphere of radius r. The sphere intercepts the same luminous flux Φ as would a disc of radius r, and Φ is therefore given by $\Phi = \pi r^2 I/d^2$. The surface area of the sphere is $4\pi r^2$ so that the mean illuminance E_s on the sphere due to the point source is given by

$$E_s = \frac{\Phi}{4\pi r^2} = \frac{I}{4d^2} \tag{1.26}$$

which is therefore the scalar illuminance at the position of the sphere.

If the source is an extended one, a small element of surface with projected area $\delta A'$ is equivalent to a point source of luminous intensity $L\,\delta A'$, where L is the luminance of the source. The scalar illuminance δE_s at a distance d is therefore given by

$$\delta E_s = \frac{L\,\delta A'}{4d^2}$$

Now $\delta A'/d^2 = \delta\omega$ the solid angle subtended by the element of the source, therefore $\delta E_s = \frac{1}{4}L\delta\omega$. For the whole source, the scalar illuminance E_s is then $\frac{1}{4}\int L\,d\omega$.

For a uniform diffuse source L is constant so that

$$E_s = \tfrac{1}{4}L\omega \tag{1.27}$$

where ω is the solid angle subtended by the whole source.

1.4.10   Mean cylindrical illuminance

Although the mean spherical (scalar) illuminance gives a non-directional measure of illumination, it does not take into account the fact that a human observer is more conscious of light received from horizontal than from vertical directions. There is evidence that the subjective assessment of the general brightness of a building interior correlates better with the mean cylindrical illuminance, defined as the mean illuminance over the side of a small vertical cylinder placed in the interior. Calculation of the mean cylindrical illuminance proceeds in a manner similar to that of scalar illuminance except that a sine factor is involved.

With a point source of intensity I, at a distance d from a cylinder of radius r and length l, the flux Φ intercepted by the cylinder is given by

$$\Phi = 2lr\sin\psi\,\frac{I}{d^2}$$

where ψ is the angle between the axis of the cylinder and the direction of the light source (Fig. 1.8), and $2lr\sin\psi$ is the projected area of the cylinder; light incident on the ends of the cylinder is ignored. The surface area of the curved side of the cylinder is $2\pi lr$, so that the mean illuminance E_c on the side due to the point source is given by

$$E_c = \frac{I\sin\psi}{\pi d^2} \tag{1.28}$$

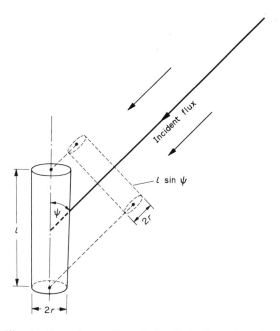

Fig. 1.8   Illumination of a small vertical cylinder by a distant point source

and for an extended source of luminance L this becomes

$$E_c = \frac{1}{\pi} \int L \sin \psi \; d\omega \qquad (1.29)$$

which for a uniform diffuse source becomes

$$E_c = \frac{L}{\pi} \int \sin \psi \; d\omega \qquad (1.30)$$

2 Vision

Without the eye the word 'light' would be meaningless: as has been indicated in the previous chapter there is a very small band of electromagnetic radiation which, when falling on the human eye, elicits a visual sensation. The eye and the brain work together to provide us with important information about the world around us, but only if that world directs appropriate radiation through the 'window' of the eye. The characteristics of this wonderful apparatus, fully appreciated by most of us only when its performance is impaired, are of obvious significance in the design of lighting systems, systems aimed at enabling us to see our environment. The object of this chapter is to outline the most important characteristics of vision from the viewpoint of lighting and its design.

2.1 THE VISUAL SYSTEM AND ITS OPERATION

Before examining the characteristics of vision, the apparatus itself must be described and some idea given as to how it works.

2.1.1 The structure of the eye

The human eyes, roughly spherical of diameter about 2·5 cm, are loosely embedded in fatty tissue within conical cavities in the skull, each eye being equipped with six external muscles which operate in pairs to position the eye. Two lateral muscles control sideways movement, upper and lower muscles upward and downward movements, and two oblique muscles provide primarily a rotational movement about the visual axis. The working of the external muscles of the two eyes is co-ordinated to maintain convergence of the visual axes of the two eyes whatever the distance away of the point of visual attention.

The outer layer of the eye is a protective fibrous material, some 1 mm thick, the *sclera*. Over an area of about one-sixth of the total surface, at the front of the eye, the fibres of this layer are uniform in size and regular in arrangement, resulting in this part of the layer being transparent: this area, the *cornea*, has a smaller radius of curvature than the rest of the outer layer.

Inside the sclera is a second layer, the *choroid*, a film of arteries and capillaries through which the eye in general and the nerves in particular receive nutrition. As the cornea is approached, the choroid is replaced by the ciliary body, out of which develop the interior muscles of the eye.

Within the choroid lies a third layer, the *retina*, which contains the nerve receptors which respond to light: that part of the retina which lies on the visual axis of the eye, the *fovea*, is of particular importance as it is here that the centre of visual attention is imaged.

The visual pathway.   Light enters the eye through the cornea (Fig. 2.1), and passes through a chamber filled with a transparent fluid, the aqueous humour, and through a coloured diaphragm, the iris, the hole in which is known as the *pupil*. The diameter of the pupil, varying between about 2 mm and 8 mm, depends on the brightness of the field of view, the brighter the field the smaller the pupil. Control of the iris, which is involuntary, is accomplished by the annular sphincter muscles and the radial dilator muscles which make up one of the two sets of interior eye muscles having their origin in the ciliary body.

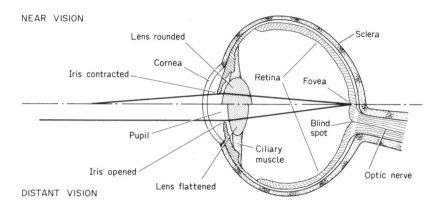

Fig. 2.1   Sectional diagram of human eye

Light then passes through a lens, an element made up onion-like of many layers of fibrous material contained within an elastic envelope: this envelope is normally held under tension by a membrane made up of radial suspensory ligaments, the zonule, making the lens relatively flat. The outer extremities of these radial ligaments end in the annular ciliary muscle, part of the ciliary body. This muscle contracts when near objects are to be viewed, reducing the radial tension in the zonule and allowing the lens to thicken: the process is known as *accommodation*. The space in the eye between the lens and the retina is filled with a clear jelly, the vitreous body.

The retina.   The end of the optical pathway in the eye is also the beginning of the nervous system which finishes up in the visual cortex, that part of the brain which mediates the sense of sight. The retina, Fig. 2.2, lining nearly two-thirds of the inner surface of the eye, consists of (a) a layer of nerve receptors of two types named by their general shape the *rods* and *cones*, adjacent to the choroid, (b) a layer of bipolar cells and (c) a layer of ganglion cells with their optic nerve fibres to the brain.

The cells and fibres are translucent, which they need to be as they are in front of the light-sensitive receptors. There are about 100 million receptors (6 to 7 million being cones) in the eye and about 1 million nerve fibres: most of the bipolar cells connect one or more receptors to the nerve fibre, but the connections are complex, as Fig. 2.2 indicates, and include inter-receptor linking by what are called horizontal bipolars.

25

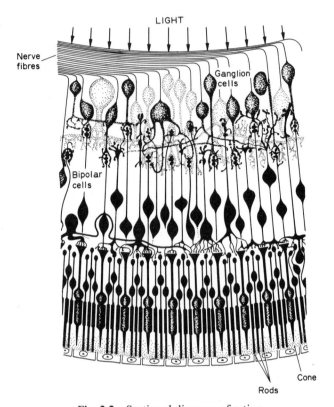

Fig. 2.2   Sectional diagram of retina

The distribution of receptors in the retina is by no means uniform but except for the blind spot, where the nerve fibres leave the eye and there are no receptors, the distribution is reasonably symmetrical about the visual axis of the eye. On the visual axis the cells and fibres are pulled to one side, producing a pit in the inner surface of the retina, the fovea, where there is a decreased obstruction to the passage of light.

The centre of the fovea is characterized by (a) a very dense concentration of fine cone receptors connected individually to nerve fibres, (b) the absence of rod receptors, and (c) a yellow colouring known as the *macular pigment*. Moving out from the centre the pigment gradually thins, the cones gradually thicken from their minimum diameter of 1 μm and fewer have a direct line to the brain: at somewhere between $\frac{1}{2}°$ and $1°$ from the axis the first rod receptors appear.

Increasing rod density and decreasing cone density characterize the remainder of the zone up to $2\frac{1}{2}°$ from the visual axis of the eye which defines the edge of the foveal pit. At about $20°$ off-axis the rod density reaches its maximum, about 160 000 per mm^2, and the cone density reaches its lowest value of about 5000 per mm^2 which is maintained over the periphery of the retina. The periphery is also characterized by each bipolar connecting a large number of receptors, rod and cones together, to one optical nerve fibre.

2.1.2   The process of seeing

The convex–concave cornea and the bi-convex lens of each eye result in crude real images of the visual scene of an observer being produced on each retina. These images are crude because of the spherical and chromatic aberrations of what by instrument standards are very poor optical elements. Each image is sharper the smaller the aperture of the optical system, which in the human eye results automatically from a brighter scene of view. The sharpest part of each image is the centre of visual attention, for which the lens is adjusted: this part of the image is on the fovea, where there is also the least obstruction to light and where the receptor structure is most finely divided.

Stereoscopy.   Images are produced on both retinae: the images are not identical because the two eyes look at the objects in the scene from slightly different angles. The brain is able to deduce from the difference in these images and from the degree of convergence of the two eyes a sense of depth in the visual scene, at least for distances of up to 6 m from the observer. The binocular field of view does not extend over the whole field of vision, being limited in the horizontal plane to the central 120° of the 190° total field. Monocular vision does not result in the complete loss of depth perception because the brain receives further cues from perspective, shadow and parallax: it also has stored experience of the size of common objects.

Receptor photochemistry.   The projection of an image of a visual scene on the retina implies the receptors receiving radiant power: the blackness of the pupil of the eye indicates that this light is absorbed, in fact by photochemical pigments contained within the receptors. These pigments undergo a chemical change on the receipt of light: a certain amount of 'bleached product' is produced depending on the wavelength of the light, the illumination and the duration of exposure. This chemical transformation is reversed in the absence of light stimulation, so that at any time the receptors contain a mixture of the original photopigment and the bleached product.

Retinal potential wave.   Associated with the photochemical process, and presumably a result of it, is the electric potential found to be developed across the retina: electroretinogram records, Fig. 2.3, show that a constant illumination gives rise to anything but a constant potential, large signals usually being associated with changes in the light falling on the receptor. Such potential waves have been analysed into components associated with retinal illumination, changes in that illumination and secondary feedback signals from optical nerve impulses.

Optical nerve discharge.   The third stage of the visual process is the production of electrical discharges in the optical nerve fibres, presumably initiated by the retinal potential wave. The discharge is in the form of pulses (Fig. 2.3) of constant amplitude but varying frequency: recorded discharges have been analysed into switch-on, switch-off and continuous signals. It is an attractive simplicity to see the nerve impulses as a coded form of the retinal potential wave, pulse frequency corresponding to potential magnitude.

Involuntary eye movements.   The production of nerve impulses from retinal images is further complicated by the fact that these images are not static on the retina. The eye is in a state of continuous movement even when an observer fixes his gaze. Three types of movement have been identified: (a) tremors of frequency 30 Hz to 80 Hz and amplitude corresponding to one or two receptor diameters, (b) irregular drifts of up to 1 s in duration and amplitude up to 40 receptor diameters, and (c) flicks at the end of each drift returning the image of the fixation point back towards the fovea. These movements add weight to the idea that vision is mediated more by changes in receptor illumination than by illumination itself.

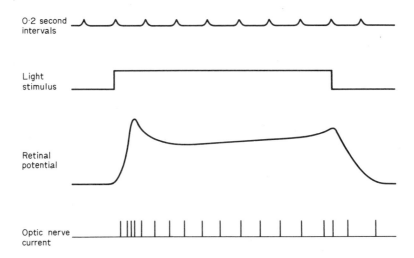

Fig. 2.3   Physiological effects of light stimulus

Visual cortex.   Vision resides ultimately in the visual cortex at the back of the brain. Here the two million or so electrical signals originating in the eye have to be sorted out. There is evidence of a general point-to-point projection of the retina on to a particular surface of cells in the visual cortex, but considerable integrative activity of the visual and other parts of the cortex is necessary to account for perception, as opposed to vision. Much still remains to be discovered about the logic processes underlying the inter-pretation of images and the recognition of colour.

Retinal illuminance.   To express the effectiveness of an external light stimulus when viewed through a pupil, either a natural pupil of the eye or an artificial pupil, vision scientists often use the unit of retinal illuminance, the *troland*. Allowance has to be made, in practice, for losses in the eye and for the fact that light passing through the centre of the pupil is more effective than light passing through nearer the periphery (the *Stiles-Crawford effect*), but for a large uniform field the retinal illuminance in trolands is equal to the product of the luminance of the external surface in cd/m^2 and the pupil area in mm^2.

2.2 CHARACTERISTICS OF VISION

2.2.1 Magnitude effects

Visual threshold. A fundamental question concerning vision is what is the smallest amount of light needed to evoke the sensation of light, given optimum seeing conditions for the observer. These conditions are that the observer shall have been in the dark for a sufficiently long time to be fully dark-adapted (Sect. 2.2.2). This matter involves the probability of seeing and the differences between individuals (Sect. 2.2.3), but values can be stated for a 50% chance of sensation being evoked for 50% of the population. A large object exposed for a long period can be seen when its luminance L is of the order of 10^{-6} cd/m². This is a useful value to quote in the context of lighting practice, with the general qualification that the smaller the object or the shorter the time it is exposed, the higher the luminance must be for visual sensation.

For small stimuli of short duration, up to 1° in size and up to 0·1 s in exposure time, threshold luminance values follow Ricco's law ($L \times$ area = constant) and the Bunsen–Roscoe law ($L \times$ time = constant), spatial and temporal summation being said to be complete. The threshold value of 10^{-6} cd/m² for a large object implies that several thousand quanta of light are absorbed per second by several million rod receptors: vision scientists have sought to define threshold in terms of quantum absorption by individual receptors.

Scotopic (rod) vision. Vision in a field with luminances between 10^{-6} and 10^{-2} cd/m² has an unusual characteristic: an object is seen less readily when it is made the centre of visual attention than when it is seen 'out of the corner of the eye'. Night lookouts are taught to scan the nightscape slowly rather than to fixate on specific outlines. The reason for this phenomenon is that vision at these levels, scotopic vision, is mediated primarily by the rod receptors, which are absent in the fovea: thus peripheral detection is superior to foveal detection.

It would be anticipated that the response of the dark-adapted eye to small amounts of light of different wavelengths would be related to the absorption versus wavelength characteristic of the rod photopigment rhodopsin, and this is the case. The relative sensitivity of the eye under scotopic conditions is shown by the left-hand curve of Fig. 2.4 where relative sensitivity is best interpreted as follows: $\frac{x}{10}$ W of light of wavelength 420 nm (relative sensitivity 10 appears as bright as $\frac{x}{100}$ W of light of wavelength 507 nm (relative sensitivity 100) where x is sufficiently small to ensure scotopic conditions.

There is no sensation of colour in scotopic vision: the world is grey.

Mesopic vision. As the illuminance of a scene is increased, with luminances from about 10^{-2} cd/m² upwards, three effects can be observed as well as a general increase in luminosity. Firstly, foveal detection becomes as easy as peripheral detection and then easier. Secondly, a sense of colour can be appreciated, feebly at first and then stronger. Thirdly, the relative luminosity of objects of different colours changes: in particular the luminosity of the reds increases more strongly than does that of the blues. This third effect is known as the Purkinje phenomenon and like the other two effects is due to the changing contributions of the rod and cone receptors to vision as the luminance changes

29

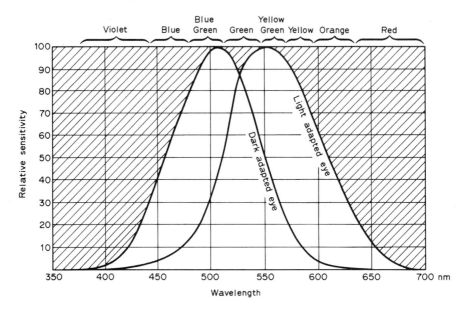

Fig. 2.4   Relative spectral sensitivity of human eye

in this mesopic range (10^{-2} cd/m^2 to 10 cd/m^2). The overall response to light of different wavelengths lies somewhere between the two curves of Fig. 2.4, moving from the left to the right as the prevailing luminance increases.

Photopic (cone) vision.   The response of the eye is not affected by luminance if the luminance is above about 10 cd/m^2, as vision is entirely mediated by cone receptors. This response, the right-hand curve in Fig. 2.4, was agreed internationally in 1924 after extensive experimental work requiring subjects to match the brightness of monochromatic stimuli of different wavelengths. With a maximum ordinate of 1·0 this function is known as $V(\lambda)$—the spectral luminous efficiency for photopic vision. It is of fundamental importance in photometric units (Chap. 1), colour (Chap. 3) and the measurement of light (Chap. 4), although some reservations are held currently about the short wavelength values.

Photopic vision is coloured and an indication is given at the top of Fig. 2.4 of the colour names likely to be ascribed to light of different wavelengths. Combining light of different wavelengths gives rise to less strong colours, even to colourlessness or 'achromatic colour'. The eye is unable to analyse the wavelength components in mixed radiation in the way the ear can detect the different frequency components in a musical sound. The colour characteristics of photopic vision are examined in Chap. 3.

Luminosity.   Luminance, like luminous flux, is a pseudo-physical quantity: it is different from a genuine physical quantity in that some allowance is made for its effect on people by weighting the different wavelength components it contains. Luminosity, commonly referred to as 'brightness', describes the sensation an observer experiences when subjected to the stimulus of luminance. In like manner heaviness is the sensation experienced by someone subjected to the stimulus of weight, electric shock the sensation experienced by someone subjected to the stimulus of electric current. While sensation would be expected to increase with stimulus, a little thought will show there is no reason to expect a doubling of stimulus to produce a doubling of sensation (consider luminances of $0.8\,\mu cd/m^2$ and $1.6\,\mu cd/m^2$ when $1.0\,\mu cd/m^2$ is the visual threshold). It has been found that most stimulus-sensation relationships are governed for a range of stimuli of several decades by a power law, sensation $\propto (stimulus)^n$. For electric shock, $n = 3.5$, for heaviness, $n = 1.5$. The value of the power index for the dark-adapted human eye subjected to brief flashes of light is about 0.3. When several stimuli are viewed simultaneously the phenomenon of induction (Sect. 2.2.2) produces a disordered luminosity–luminance relationship, but over a limited range of luminance a square-root law is approached. To double the luminosity of a surface or a source the luminance has to be increased somewhere between fourfold and eightfold.

2.2.2 Temporal and spatial effects

Adaptation. The eye is capable of functioning with stimuli ranging from about $10^{-6}\,cd/m^2$ to about $10^6\,cd/m^2$, the upper limit being defined by physical damage to the retina with excessive absorption of radiation. However, the eye cannot function efficiently with this complete range of stimuli visible at the same time: full information from a visual field can be extracted if the luminance range in the field is limited to about $10^4:1$. It would appear that the eye is a self-optimising device, automatically adjusting itself to ensure that it extracts the maximum available visual information, rather like an ammeter automatically choosing its own shunt to ensure that its needle lies at a readable position on its scale. This adjustment is known as the adaptation process and it takes time to be accomplished. Following a sudden transition of field luminance, vision is impaired while adaptation to the new conditions is taking place.

Adaptation has three components: (a) a rapid phase, which must be electrical in origin and presumably is a readjustment of cell or nerve behaviour, (b) a readjustment of pupil size, requiring the time appropriate for such a mechanical movement, (c) a slow phase, controlling the overall adaptation time, which is presumed to be necessary for the stabilization of the ratio of bleached to unbleached photopigment in the receptors following a luminance change.

A *dark-adapted* observer is one who has spent sufficient time in the dark for his eyes to be optimized for working in the dark: *light-adapted* is a looser term, usually implying the completion of the adaptation process to a visual field bright enough to guarantee photopic vision. The time required to adapt to a lower luminance is greater than that for adaptation to a correspondingly higher luminance, particularly if the former involves a transition from cone to rod vision. Such a transition can be seen in Fig. 2.5, which shows the time sequence of dark adaptation: the ordinate is the minimum illuminance required for a briefly-exposed white test object to be visible. Note that complete dark adaptation from photopic vision can take as long as an hour.

Flashes. A small brief flash of light has a luminosity equal to that of a steady source usually having a lower intensity, but a flash may be more conspicuous particularly when

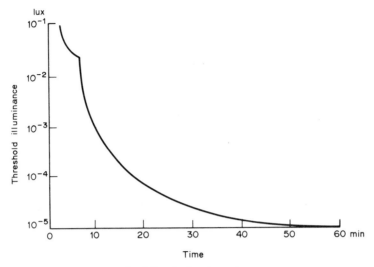

Fig. 2.5 Dark adaptation

viewed peripherally. The Blondel-Rey formula $I_e = It/(a + t)$ is a reasonable approximation for the equivalent intensity (I_e) of a visible flash of intensity (I) and duration (t) seconds, where a depends on viewing conditions but is of the order of 0·2.

After-images.   Associated with a flash of light, particularly if the luminance is high, is the phenomenon of after-images. Subsequent to the flash a succession of images may be seen, alternatively positive and negative of irregular strength and of decreasing frequency. The positive images are bright, of the same colour as the flash: the negative images are darker and have a colour which is approximately complementary to that of the flash. The effect is also experienced following a single change in retinal illumination.

Flicker.   As the frequency of a regular succession of flashes is increased, the appearance of a flickering light is produced. As the frequency is increased further the sensation of flicker disappears, and the light appears to be continuous: the frequency at which this occurs is called the *critical fusion frequency* (*CFF*). At this frequency or above it a flashing light can be matched to a steady light source and the Talbot-Plateau law states that the luminance or the intensity of the matching steady light will be found to equal the average luminance or intensity of the flashing light whatever the on/off time ratio of the latter.

    CFF is affected by both the luminance and the size of the flashing stimulus. At low luminances, with scotopic vision, *CFF* is below 10 Hz: it increases with increasing luminance to an asymptotic maximum of between 45 Hz and 60 Hz with a large field of luminance 1000 cd/m². *CFF* also increases with increasing size of field, but the relationship is complex because of the difference in *CFF* for rod and cone receptors: under photopic conditions *CFF* for a small stimulus falls from 40 Hz to 20 Hz when the flickering stimulus is imaged on the periphery instead of the fovea.

Phototropism and discomfort glare. The movements of plants towards the light is a well-recognized phenomenon, given the name phototropism. The human eye exhibits a similar effect, being drawn in the absence of other controls to fixate on bright spots in the field of view: this subject has not been studied extensively but it underlies the basic principle, long established for lighting visual tasks, that the task should ideally be the brightest part of the field of view. Luminaires in an interior lighting system are liable to be distracting, and there is at least an element of unfortunate phototropism in the phenomenon of discomfort glare.

This phenomenon has been studied by asking observers to rate the degree of discomfort they experience in an interior on a multiple-criterion scale (for example—just perceptible, just acceptable, just uncomfortable, just intolerable), enabling the physical parameters influencing this sensation to be identified. The Building Research Station formula is generally accepted in UK:

$$\text{Discomfort glare index} = 10 \log \Sigma \left(\frac{0 \cdot 48}{P^{1 \cdot 6}} \cdot \frac{L_s^{1 \cdot 6} \omega^{0 \cdot 8}}{L_b} \right)$$

In this formula L_s is the luminance of a luminaire in cd/m², ω its size in steradians, L_b is the luminance of the background to the luminaire and P is an index of position of the luminaire with respect to the observer's line of sight. The quantity in brackets is evaluated for each visible luminaire and then summed. Indices of 10, 16, 22 and 28 apply to the four criteria listed above. The use of this index in lighting design is described in Chap. 22.

Induction and disability glare. The influence of one part of the visual field on another is known as induction, also as simultaneous contrast. The difference in the apparent lightness of the two halves of the ring in Fig. 2.6, particularly if a dividing line is placed across the boundary, illustrates the sense of monochromatic inductive effects—stimulation of part of the retina reduces the sensation provided by stimuli in adjacent areas. There are also inductive colour effects: if the black and white areas in Fig. 2.6 were of different colours, the two halves of the ring would again appear different, taking on tinges of the complementary colours to their respective backgrounds. Induction is presumed to originate in the retina but the effect of a dividing line on Fig. 2.6 illustrates that cortical functioning plays a part in many real situations: when the dividing line is removed, the homogeneity of the ring is perceived and the difference in apparent lightness of the two halves of the ring is reduced, without any significant change taking place in the pattern of retinal illumination.

One possible consequence of induction is a reduction of foveal visual capability as the result of unwanted stimuli in the periphery. This does happen, and the phenomenon is given the name of disability glare: it is to be distinguished from discomfort glare by the effect of a loss of visibility as opposed to a loss of comfort. This difference is given point in the German terms for the two phenomena: they are translated as physiological glare (disability) and psychological glare (discomfort). By examining the visual capability of observers under glare conditions, it has been possible to find out, as with discomfort glare, how the physical parameters of glare stimuli influence the situation. It transpires that these operate in quite a different manner than for discomfort glare: the Stiles–Holladay principle states that a disability glare source acts as if a veiling luminance is added to the centre of the visual field, reducing the effective contrasts in the field. The

33

Fig. 2.6   Induction

veiling luminance is proportional to E/θ^2, whereas E is the illuminance produced by the glare source in the plane of the observer's pupil and θ is the angular separation of the glare source from the observer's line of sight. For a number of sources the principle of additivity applies.

2.2.3   Individual differences

The characteristics of vision outlined previously have not indicated the diversity in many of these characteristics across the population nor the variability in any one individual over a period of time. Some of the differences for a population or an individual are systematic: some are random. Two particular systematic variations, that due to age and that due to defective colour vision, are examined later in this section, but random variations also deserve attention.

Inconstancy in the visual capability of an individual arises partly from the quantum nature of light (particularly for visual threshold), partly from variability in the series of signal transformations in the receptor-cortex pathway and partly from involuntary and deliberate eye movements, to say nothing of variable motivation and effort while this capability is being measured. Diversity in the population at large would be expected to be at least as great as the inconstancy in individuals. Congenital differences between individuals exist and there is a systematic difference due to age, so the diversity is in fact greater than the inconstancy of one individual.

Individual inconstancy and population diversity imply that most visual characteristics should be defined by a range of values: most conveniently a value is given to the central tendency and to the spread. As an example, consider an experiment in which 35 observers are asked to adjust the illuminance of a pattern until it is just visible. The 35 illuminance values can be arranged in ascending order: the 18th value (the median) can be quoted as the central tendency and the 9th to the 27th values (the inter-quartile range) as the spread. If a large number of subjects are used, a frequency distribution histogram can be plotted, showing the number of subjects finding the pattern to be visible within different ranges of illuminance. Such a histogram is likely to be more symmetrical if plotted against the logarithm of illuminance than against illuminance. The curve drawn through the histogram (Fig. 2.7a, with 15 ranges of log illuminance) will then be a

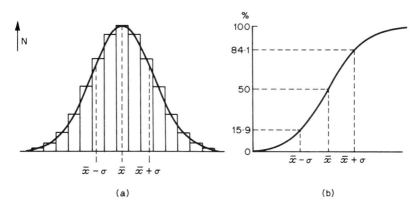

Fig. 2.7 Probability-of-seeing curves   (a) Histogram and Gaussian distribution   (b) Ogive

normal or Gaussian distribution: the central tendency of the distribution is the abscissa ($\bar{x}$) corresponding to the maximum ordinate, spread is identified by the standard deviation (σ) which is such that about 68% of the illuminance values lie within $\bar{x} - \sigma$ and $\bar{x} + \sigma$. Cumulative integration of the Gaussian distribution produces a sigmoid or ogive (Fig. 2.7b): with the maximum ordinate scaled to 100, this shows the percentage of the population who are able to see the pattern as a function of illuminance. Probability-of-seeing ogives are of importance in the specification of lighting levels for visual tasks (Sect. 2.3).

Effects of age.   It appears that age begins to take its toll on visual capability at an unfortunately early age, certainly below twenty years. The lens, growing with the child, yellows slightly as it grows, but of more significance is the accelerating degree of scatter of light with age in both cornea and lens after adolescence: this scattering is greater for light of short wavelengths than long. There is also a general reduction in the pupil size with age, particularly at low field luminance, due to a progressive weakening of the iris muscles. As a result of these two effects, retinal illuminance for a constant field luminance falls uniformly with increasing age between 20 and 60, the value at age 60 being about one-third of that at 20.

Some compensation can be given to the elderly by the provision of more light, but the effectiveness of this is reduced by (a) the extra luminance veil due to scattered light, particularly if the light has a significant blue component, and (b) the automatic functioning of the pupil, except at very high light levels. Age affects the operation of all the internal and external eye muscles, not only the iris muscles, and light certainly cannot compensate the elderly for the inevitable reduction of visual performance involving frequent eye rotation and accommodation.

Defective colour vision. Certain diseases lead to defective vision, including colour deficiencies, but there is an array of defects specifically in colour vision which are congenital. The basis of the inheritance of these defects is such that females are far less likely to acquire them than are males, though the deficiency is transmitted by the female: the frequency of congenital defective colour vision in males is of the order of 8%.

People with normal colour vision are described as normal trichromats (Sect. 3.1.2). It is believed that their cone receptors contain three different photopigments (erythrolabe, chlorolabe and cyanolabe) with different wavelength responses. This accounts for the well-established phenomenon of trichromatism, the ability of the eye to make a colour match over a wide range of colours by a mixture of not more than three lights (matching stimuli, Sect. 3.1.1). The photopigment rhodopsin is found in all rod receptors.

Anomalous trichromats, of whom there are three types, have a reduced capability of discriminating colours in some parts of the spectrum, in the red-green region in the case of protanomalous trichromats (about 1% of the male population) and deuteranomalous trichromats (about 5%), in the blue-green region in the case of tritanomalous trichromats (very rare). A reduced sensitivity to red light and to blue light respectively characterizes the first and the third of these: the $V(\lambda)$ characteristic of the second is normal. Dichromats, of which there are also three types, have no colour discrimination at all in some parts of the spectrum. Protanopes (about 1% of the male population) and deuteranopes (also about 1%) fail in the red-green, tritanopes (very rare) in the blue-green. Protanopes and tritanopes have the same form of reduced sensitivity as the respective anomalous trichromats. It is assumed that there is either weakness or failure of one or two cone photopigments in these six forms of defective colour vision. In the seventh form, rod monochromats (very rare), there is no cone functioning, no colour discrimination at all and a rod sensitivity characteristic for all values of field luminance.

It is clearly important that colour-defective people should not participate in activities where good colour discrimination is necessary: potential employees for such occupations can be checked by very simple tests such as being asked to read the specially-designed Ishihara colour plates.

2.3 VISUAL PERFORMANCE

2.3.1 The visibility of small detail

It has already been stated that the absolute visual threshold is a luminance of about 10^{-6} cd/m^2: this will apply to a large white object seen against a dark background with no restriction on viewing time. The smaller the size and the smaller the contrast with its background, the higher must the luminance be for it to be seen. Size in this context is defined by the angle the detail to be seen subtends at the eye, contrast by the ratio $|L_d - L_b|/L_b$ where L is luminance, the suffix d refers to the detail and the suffix b to the background. If the detail and its background are matt and uniformly illuminated, the contrast can be expressed in terms of reflectances $C=|\rho_d-\rho_b|/\rho_b$. The use of a modulus sign in these formulae implies a certain equivalence of visibility for details which are lighter or darker than their background: there is experimental evidence to support this for conditions of practical interest.

Threshold visibility. Luminance, contrast and size are three parameters defining the threshold visibility of small detail. In addition, there are spatial and temporal conditions (surround field, location of detail in space and time) and human parameters (adaptation, random and systematic individual differences) to complicate the issue. The interaction of the three major parameters can be demonstrated by a visual threshold surface, which is a three-dimensional plot of values of angular size α, contrast C, and luminance L of detail giving a 50% probability of seeing under the particular test conditions. Fig. 2.8a shows such a surface for a circular disc exposed for 0·2 s under rather unusual conditions designed to make detection very easy.

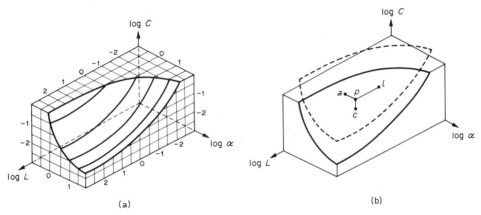

Fig. 2.8 (a) Visual threshold surface (b) Supra-threshold surface

There are three points to be noted immediately from Fig. 2.8a. Firstly, the near corner of the surface is almost horizontal, indicating that human vision has a limiting contrast sensitivity (the reciprocal of minimum detectable contrast) however much light is thrown on however large an object: for more usual viewing conditions this value is between 50 and 100. Secondly, the left-hand corner of the surface is approaching the vertical, indicating that human vision has a limiting visual acuity (the reciprocal of minimum detectable size in minutes of arc): maximum visual acuity is between 2 and 3 for objects such as discs. Thirdly, since the angles between the surface and the directions of each axis give an indication of the relative effectiveness of the three parameters in affecting visibility, it can be seen that the contribution of each parameter suffers from the law of diminishing returns: at low light levels a small percentage luminance change is very effective but at high levels contrast enhancement or optical magnification are more powerful tools for improving visibility.

The visual threshold surface of Fig. 2.8a is for 0·2 s exposure of disc targets: a different exposure time gives a different surface, skewed to that shown.

Supra-threshold visibility.   Threshold visibility is hardly a suitable target for the lighting of visual tasks. Supra-threshold conditions implies easier seeing: the most obvious way to express this is to quote a different probability, thus a range of practical seeing conditions can be expressed as a range of probabilities from something just over 50% to something just under 100%.

There are other ways of expressing practical seeing. It is possible to imagine on Fig. 2.8a a series of other surfaces, supra-threshold surfaces, for 60% probability of seeing disc targets, 70% probability, etc. A particular disc at a particular supra-threshold level can be represented by a point p in one of these surfaces identified by dashed lines in Fig. 2.8b. Lines pa, pl, pc are drawn parallel to the axes of size, luminance and contrast to cut the threshold surface in points a, l and c. The length pl in log units represents the fractional reduction in luminance necessary to reduce the supra-threshold task to threshold. Looked at from the threshold end, pl is a luminance multiplier expressing how much greater the luminance is than that needed for the task to be at threshold. Similarly, the length pc in log units is a contrast multiplier, another way of defining the degree of visibility: pa could also be used, a size multiplier.

As p is varied over the surface, in other words for a series of different discs at the same degree of supra-threshold visibility, it has been found that the most constant of the three spacings pa pc pl is pc: supra-threshold surfaces are approximately threshold surfaces displaced vertically. Contrast multipliers are therefore the best of these three possible alternatives to probability to define practical levels of visibility.

Easier seeing could imply quicker seeing, which suggests yet another way to express supra-threshold visibility. Visual threshold surfaces for different viewing times do not lie parallel to one another and so there is no consistent relationship between the speed of seeing and the probability of seeing.

2.3.2   The visibility of practical tasks

Early this century it was believed that the lighting requirements for practical visual tasks could be deduced by (a) analysing the size, contrast and exposure time of the critical detail in each task and (b) producing general data showing the inter-relation between these parameters and lighting for various levels of visual performance. Four or five decades of work in this field have shown up many limitations in this classical procedure.

Firstly, the contrast in practical visual tasks can hardly ever be defined by the reflectances of detail and background because perfectly matt surfaces are very rare. The luminance of a surface having any specularity depends to some extent on the way it is illuminated (direction and polarization) as well as on its illuminance. Thus the contrast of the print on this page depends on the particular lighting system under which it is read—it is not purely a parameter of the physical task (the paper and the print).

Secondly, the exposure time of many visual tasks is not externally controlled. Since many practical tasks (reading, for example) are self-paced, an observer will adjust the exposure time he allows to maintain a particular level of performance. Thus exposure time is not always purely a function of the task. To a lesser extent this also applies to size: an observer may elect to move nearer to a small detail, accepting the drawback of larger eye movements as he scans the task in order to perform better.

Thirdly, the hoped-for general data is somewhat of a myth. A series of visual threshold and supra-threshold surfaces can be produced, but their location depends on the method of extracting responses from observers and on the degree of detection involved—the presence of the test object or the recognition of its shape, for example.

Despite these limitations to the classical approach, the hope has persisted that a systematic method might eventually be devised for evaluating the visual performance of a range of practical tasks as a function of lighting conditions: without some systematic method the whole subject must become an empirical craft. Noteworthy contributions in this field have been made by H. C. Weston and H. R. Blackwell.

The Weston approach. A self-paced scanning task, such as reading, was simulated by blocks of Landolt rings with the gaps arranged randomly (Fig. 2.9a). Observers were

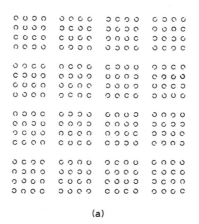

(a)

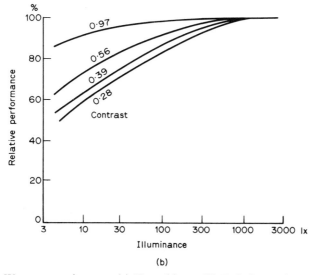

(b)

Fig. 2.9 Weston experiments (a) Test object (b) Relative performance curves

asked to work their way through a sheet of these rings, cancelling as many with a particular orientation of gap (say to the left) as they could in one minute. This was repeated with different values of illuminance, with different ring sizes, and with different contrasts between ring and background. Allowing for the time required for physically cancelling the rings it was possible to determine the rate of scanning the rings (speed): by noting the number of rings incorrectly cancelled and the number of appropriately-orientated rings that had not been cancelled, it was possible to determine the accuracy of working. Performance was defined as the product of accuracy and speed: this was found to increase with illuminance for each size and contrast of detail. Performance was then expressed as a function of the maximum obtained for a particular detail size and contrast, producing relative visual performance curves of the type shown in Fig. 2.9b.

Such characteristics were taken into account when illuminance levels for different tasks were recommended in the British IES Codes of 1955 and 1961, relative performances between 90% and 100% being the criterion used in 1961. This entailed some measurement of task contrast and size on the lines of the classical approach, but the Weston approach only overcomes to some extent the second of the three limitations previously listed.

The Blackwell approach. Fundamental experiments were carried out on the threshold detection of disc targets. A target appeared for a short period in the centre of a large field fixated by observers: it appeared during one of four time intervals and the observers had to indicate afterwards during which of the intervals the target had appeared, guessing if necessary. Allowing for guess-work, probability-of-seeing ogives were constructed after a series of tests with various target and background luminances. Visual threshold and supra-threshold surfaces could have been constructed akin to those in Fig. 2.8 for particular exposure times, but one particular contrast/luminance relationship was extracted as a reference—the 99% probability-of-seeing relationship for a 4′ disc exposed for 0·2 s.

A visual task simulator was constructed in which a series of plaques moved into and out of an observer's field at a controlled speed: some of the plaques contained 4′ discs in the centre having a slightly higher luminance than the plaque and the observer had

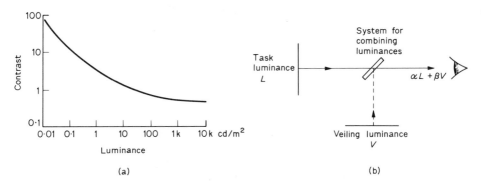

Fig. 2.10 Blackwell experiments   (a) Standard performance curve
(b) Principle of visibility meter

to signal whenever one of these was seen. It was found that the threshold contrast of these targets, dynamically presented, was a constant multiple of that found in the fundamental experiments over a 10 000:1 range of luminance. This contrast multiplier was regarded as a characteristic connecting laboratory conditions of detection with those of a practical task, and was applied to the particular curve extracted from the fundamental experiments to provide a standard visual performance curve (Fig. 2.10a).

The final element in the Blackwell approach was the development of an instrument called a visual task evaluator which evaluated the contrast of a 4′ disc equal in visual difficulty to any visual task under consideration. This evaluation was done by finding the disc needing the same reduction in contrast as the task to reduce it to threshold visibility, background luminance being equal. The principle of contrast reduction, by a superimposed light veil, is illustrated in Fig. 2.10b. The standard visual performance curve could be used to identify the luminance needed for the visual task to be performed to the selected standard of 99% probability-of-seeing under practical conditions. This approach, reputed to influence the illumination levels recommended in the American IES Lighting Handbook of 1959 and 1966, deals partly with the first and third limitations of the classical approach to the visibility of practical tasks.

The CIE approach. In 1971 the CIE circulated a draft of a proposed report No. 19, outlining the most promising systematic method to date for dealing with visual performance. It relies on the parallel nature of the intersection of any visual threshold or supra-threshold surface with any plane parallel to that containing the L–C axes (Fig. 2.8). This parallelism applies over the luminance range 1 to 10 000 cd/m², and gives rise to the concept of a universal *RCS* (*relative contrast sensitivity*) curve. This curve shows contrast sensitivity expressed as a percentage of the contrast sensitivity at 10 000 cd/m² versus luminance (Fig. 2.11a).

For the prescription of illuminance for a particular visual task, a development of the Blackwell approach is followed, a visibility meter being used in a rather similar way to

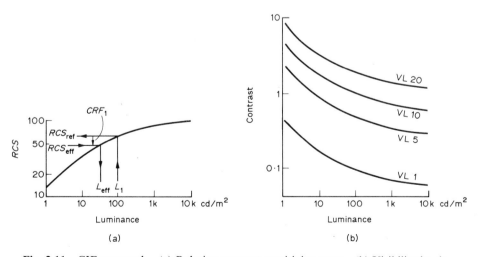

Fig. 2.11 CIE approach   (a) Relative contrast sensitivity curve   (b) Visibility levels

that of the visual task evaluator to evaluate the 4′ disc equivalent of a practical visual task. Instead of determining the required luminance from one standard visual performance curve (Fig. 2.10a), a set of parallel log C versus log L curves is used (Fig. 2.11b) labelled VL (visibility level) 1 to 20, the numbers being contrast multipliers from a reference curve VL1. Code makers are free to select the standard of visibility they wish to achieve: the effect on VL numbers of wanting to satisfy varying percentages of the population and populations of varying age is given in the CIE report. The relationship between visibility level and relative performance (Weston style) is also given, so code makers wishing to select their criteria on this latter basis are free to do so.

Illuminance levels emerging from this exercise are assumed to be provided by a reference lighting system equivalent to the conditions inside an integrating sphere, light arriving on the task from all directions. Assumptions similar to this are implied in both the original Blackwell and Weston approaches, but the CIE methodology allows for the reality of practical lighting systems to be taken into account.

The most potent influence of different lighting systems is the rendering of contrast, the first of the three limitations of the classical approach mentioned earlier. The *contrast rendering factor* (*CRF*) of a lighting system is defined as the ratio of the visibility of a particular task under that lighting system to the visibility under integrating sphere conditions, where visibility is expressed in terms of contrast. *CRF* can be measured using a visibility meter: the effective task luminance, from a visibility viewpoint, under a lighting system with a value of *CRF* not equal to 1, can be determined from the *RCS* curve. In Fig. 2.11a L_1 is the luminance of a task under integrating sphere conditions, implying a relative contrast sensitivity of RCS_{ref}: a particular lighting system, rendering contrast worse than an integrating sphere, has a contrast rendering factor CRF_1, providing an effective $RCS_{eff} = RCS_{ref} \times CRF_1$, implying an effective task luminance of L_{eff}.

CRF values for the 25° viewing of a pencil handwriting task under a variety of different lighting systems have been found to range from 0·83 to 1·08, implying L_{eff} values ranging from 35 cd/m² to 170 cd/m² when L_1 is 100 cd/m². The lowest value is for rows of overhead luminaires, the highest (giving better contrast rendering than reference integrating sphere conditions) for wall-mounted valances. In addition to the factors for contrast rendering, the CIE methodology introduces similar factors for the effect of disability glare and the transient effects of adaptation when operators glance away from their work. Both of these effects are realities in visual performance under practical lighting systems, although rarely as influential on visibility as contrast rendering effects.

2.3.3 Performance, preference and perception

For all the attempts to incorporate the reality of practical tasks into its methodology, the CIE approach to visual performances only scratches the surface of the subject of visual perception. It provides a necessary scientific basis for the provision of light to facilitate the seeing of two-dimensional detail which is not highly specular and which occupies the centre of the field of view.

There are many industrial visual tasks which are not two-dimensional, many which are highly specular and many which involve some detection in the periphery of the field of view: there are some tasks in which a colour difference accounts for most of the contrast between detail and background. In these cases the basis for the provision of lighting cannot yet be found within a general approach to visual performance, and solutions are based on experience (Chap. 24).

In all visual tasks a number of human factors influencing performance deserve attention—the visual skill or experience of the observer, the influence of fatigue and motivation on his work. Experience results in performance improving with time, fatigue the opposite. Fatigue may be visual or mental. Visual fatigue appears to be limited to the tiring of the interior or exterior eye muscles, and therefore performance drops only for tasks involving adaptation, accommodation or significant eye movements. Mental fatigue may be overcome for a considerable time by calling on reserves, which happens when motivation is high: motivation is influenced by all manner of stimuli ranging from financial inducement to the quality of the general working environment. Mental fatigue is also directly affected by environmental conditions.

A completely different approach to the specification of lighting from the analysis of performance is that derived from an analysis of subjective preference. In non-working environments this is wholly appropriate: it might be argued that in task situations workers would hardly prefer conditions which are unsympathetic to good performance and the influence of motivation must not be forgotten.

In Fig. 2.12 are shown the results of a number of studies in which observers have been

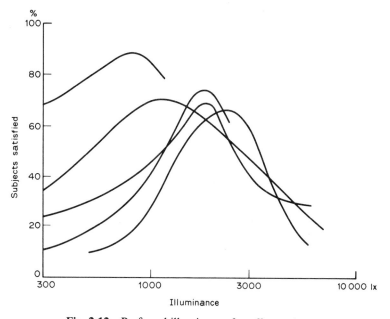

Fig. 2.12   Preferred illuminance for office tasks

asked to select the working illuminance they prefer for office tasks: the optimum values of 800 to 2500 lux correspond approximately to CIE visibility levels 9 to 11 for pencil handwriting tasks or 18 to 19 for good printed matter under integrating sphere lighting.

The question of the lighting of an environment as opposed to a task involves matters perceptual as well as visual. Some guide lines are beginning to emerge from research in this area, examined further in Chap. 22. These include the use of mean cylindrical or mean spherical illuminance as an indicator for the general brightness of an interior, the use of the ratio of the illuminance on a particular plane or the magnitude of the illumination vector to mean cylindrical or mean spherical illuminance as an indicator of the degree of modelling in an interior, the use of the direction of the illumination vector as an indicator of the flow of light: such indicators are attempting to express as simple quantities a very complex integrative activity of eye and brain, very much more complex than the visibility of a fixated two-dimensional detail. They are certainly useful as designers seek more meaningful criteria for interior lighting, but they are mere crutches in the general field of perception. To quote R. L. Gregory, 'we think of the brain as a computer and we believe that perceiving the world involves a series of computer-like tricks, which we should be able to duplicate, but some of the tricks remain to be discovered and, until they are, we cannot build a machine that will see or fully understand our own eyes and brain'.

3   Colour

The complicated mechanism of vision has been discussed in Chap. 2, and mention made of the fact that each wavelength of light gives rise to a certain sensation of colour. The components involved in the process of perception, that is, the light source, the object viewed, the eye and the brain, all affect the final sensation which consequently will be altered by a change in any of the components. These effects are complicated enough when dealing with black and white signals but when colour is introduced, the position becomes highly complex. In this chapter, some of the experimental facts of colour and the way in which they have been used as a basis for colour measurement are described, together with some of the subjective effects.

These subjective effects are many and various, and often seem to contradict the principles used in colour measurement. It must be admitted that colorimetry, though a convenient and necessary technique for communication between users of colour in many fields of work, is nevertheless built on a very simplified physical expression of the behaviour of the human eye and brain, and therefore cannot be expected to agree very closely with all subjective observations.

3.1   THE NATURE OF COLOUR

3.1.1   Historical experiments

Discussion of the subject of colour, particularly as evinced by the rainbow, has interested philosophers and scientists for many centuries but it is only in the last three hundred years that theories demonstrating the true relationship between the wavelength of light and sensation of colour have been developed.

In his famous experiments, Newton demonstrated that a beam of white light, obtained in his case from sunlight, could be dispersed by means of a prism into a spectrum. He identified seven distinct hues in the spectrum but observed that they merged into each other: 'so that there appeared as many degrees of colours, as there were sorts of rays differing in refrangibility.' At the same time, he recognized the subjective nature of colour as shown by the following quotation from his book on 'Opticks'. 'The rays to speak properly are not coloured. In them there is nothing else than a certain power and disposition to stir up a sensation of this or that colour.' The nature of surface colours was also studied by Newton; thus 'colours in the object are nothing but a disposition to reflect this or that sort of rays more copiously than the rest'.

Two other important facts which Newton discovered were that the properties of the rays, or wavelengths, were not altered by refraction or reflection and that the separate wavelengths could be recombined to give 'the same white light as before'. He also showed that colours produced by mixing separate wavelengths could give the same visual effect as an intermediate wavelength but emphasized that their spectral composi-tions would be different.

Newton attempted to devise a geometrical method for obtaining the colour of a mixture if the 'quantity and quality' of the primary colours were known. This he did by arranging the hues on a circle and assuming that the centre was the white point. However, his experimental mixtures of two primary colours never produced white probably because of the inferior quality of his optical components.

In these experiments, Newton laid the foundation of the modern science of colori-metry. Although he failed to produce white light by a mixture of two or three 'primaries', the laws of three colour mixing were well established by 1860 when Maxwell commenced his work on the quantities of red, green and blue light necessary to match the colours of different spectral wavelengths. Primaries are now known as matching or reference stimuli. In this chapter square brackets are used to distinguish them from other stimuli.

3.1.2   The experimental basis of trichromatism

The two fundamental experimental facts of colorimetry are (a) that any colour of light can be exactly imitated (or matched to visual observation) by a combination of not more than three pure spectral wavelengths of light, though not always the same three wave-lengths and sometimes with the necessary use of negative amounts, as discussed later; and (b) that additive relations in colour mixture are found to hold over a wide range of conditions. These basic principles may be formulated as follows, supposing that the *matching stimuli* are red, green and blue and the stimulus to be matched is (C_1).

$$c_1(C_1) \equiv R_1[R] + G_1[G] + B_1[B]$$

where $[R]$, $[G]$ and $[B]$ represent the *reference stimuli* (or physically defined selections of radiation) and have no numerical value, and the terms c_1, R_1, G_1 and B_1 represent the amounts of the stimuli. The equivalent sign, $\equiv$, means that a match exists between (C_1) and the mixture of $[R]$, $[G]$ and $[B]$ in respect of colour appearance only, not of spectral distribution. Similarly for colour (C_2),

$$c_2(C_2) \equiv R_2[R] + G_2[G] + B_2[B]$$

Suppose a new test colour is produced by mixing (C_1) and (C_2), then

$$c_1(C_1) + c_2(C_2) \equiv R_3[R] + G_3[G] + B_3[B]$$

If additivity holds, it would be expected that

$$R_3 = R_1 + R_2$$
$$G_3 = G_1 + G_2$$
and
$$B_3 = B_1 + B_2$$

It is also important that the colour match should hold if the luminance level of the field of view alters. Experimental evidence to date shows that these laws of additivity hold reasonably well for a viewing field of 2° angular subtense at the eye, at any rate for most practical purposes. This means that it is possible to build a visual trichromatic colori-meter in which a test colour is matched by an additive mixture of three matching stimuli, ideally narrow spectral bands of red, green and blue light. White can be obtained by mixing appropriate amounts of the three matching stimuli and adjustments of these amounts yield colours intermediate between white and the matching stimuli. The test colours are then specified in terms of the amounts of matching stimuli necessary for a match.

Certain assumptions have to be made for such a system of colorimetry to be widely applicable. They are that (a) most eyes have nearly the same colour response, (b) the match holds over a wide range of adaptation conditions, and (c) the viewing conditions under which the test colour is compared with the mixture of matching stimuli will not affect the match.

It is known that a certain number of people suffer from some degree of defective colour vision (Sect. 2.2.3), and obviously such observers will require different amounts of the matching stimuli compared with normal observers in order to match the test colour. 'Normal' observers also exhibit appreciable differences of colour vision but the practical consequences of these variations have been reduced by the adoption of the CIE Standard Observer data.

Concerning the second assumption, it has been found that a colour match is not disturbed by adaptation to white, coloured, or varying quantities of light, provided that the areas of the retina being used for matching are not affected differently in respect of adaptation.

The effects of viewing conditions on a colour match are complicated because the colour matching properties of the eye vary with field size due to the variation over the retina of the number of rods and cones (Sect. 2.1.1). Consequently a match made with the centre of the eye will hold for peripheral vision only if there is complete identity, both in colour appearance and spectral distribution, between the test and matching stimuli.

An interesting feature of a system of colorimetry designed in this way is that the actual sensation produced by the test colour is not defined; only the amounts of three known reference stimuli which cause the same visual sensation as that of the test colour are quoted.

3.1.3 The [RGB] system

As suggested in Sect. 3.1.2, the obvious basis of a practical system of colour measurement is the use of reference stimuli similar to those by which early experiments on colour matching were done. Continuing then with red, green and blue lights, we see that the colour equation represented by

$$c(C) \equiv R[R] + G[G] + B[B] \tag{3.1}$$

involves the colour quality as well as the quantity of (C). For a colour match, the quantities of light in the equation must be equal and so

$$c = R + G + B \tag{3.2}$$

Division of Eq. 3.1 by Eq. 3.2 gives

$$1 \cdot 0(C) \equiv r[R] + g[G] + b[B] \tag{3.3}$$

where

$$r = \frac{R}{R+G+B}, \qquad g = \frac{G}{R+G+B}, \qquad b = \frac{B}{R+G+B} \tag{3.4}$$

and hence

$$r+g+b = 1 \qquad (3.5)$$

Eq. 3.1 and 3.3 are *trichromatic equations*, *R*, *G* and *B* are the *tristimulus values*, and *r*, *g* and *b* are the *chromaticity co-ordinates* of (C) which can be plotted on a two-dimensional chart known as a *colour triangle* or *chromaticity diagram* (Fig. 3.1).

The method of mixing three stimuli is shown geometrically in Fig. 3.1 with different sets of reference stimuli at the corners of the triangles. The stimuli can be real light

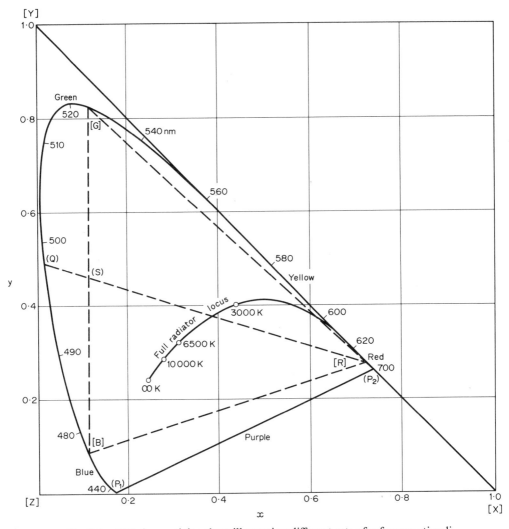

Fig. 3.1   CIE chromaticity chart illustrating different sets of reference stimuli

sources, for instance very narrow spectrum bands [R], [G] and [B], or sources such as [X], [Y] and [Z] which are not physically realizable. Because of the laws of additivity, the point representing a new colour formed by mixing two stimuli, for example reference stimuli [G] and [B], lies on the straight line joining [G] and [B], and the position of the new point can be determined using a simple centre of gravity calculation from the amounts of [G] and [B] used in the mixture. Extending this idea to mixtures of [R], [G] and [B], it will be seen that all colours situated within the triangle [RGB] can be produced by suitable mixtures of the three reference stimuli. Suppose, however, that the point (Q) represents a light source. It lies outside the [RGB] triangle and therefore cannot be obtained by mixing positive amounts of [R], [G] and [B]. If a small amount of [R], the stimulus of *complementary wavelength*, is added to (Q) (this process is known as desaturating), the colour (S) can be obtained and (S) can be matched by a mixture of [G] and [B]. Thus (Q) has been matched by positive amounts of [G] and [B] and a negative amount of [R].

It is an experimental fact, evident from the geometry of Fig. 3.1, that single spectral wavelengths cannot be matched by additive amounts of any three real matching stimuli but, if the desaturating technique is used, their colours can be matched and they lie on the curved line $(P_1)[B](Q)[G][R](P_2)$ which is called the *spectrum locus*. All real colours are contained within the area bounded by the spectrum locus and the chord $(P_1)(P_2)$ where purples are located. A considerable number of real colours lie outside any practicable [RGB] triangle, which results in their formulation in terms of negative amounts of other real colours. This is an unsatisfactory situation in practical colorimetry. Another difficulty is that the co-ordinates obtained from a particular colorimeter depend on the matching stimuli used in the instrument and consequently cannot be compared easily with results from other colorimeters. It was to resolve these difficulties that the CIE in 1931 adopted the Standard Observer and chromaticity system.

3.2 TRICHROMATIC COLORIMETRY

3.2.1 The CIE system of 1931: [RGB]

The first stage in the adoption of a standard observer for colour measurement had been the standardization in 1924 of the spectral luminous efficiency function, $V(\lambda)$, of the eye for a 2° field under photopic conditions (Sect. 2.2.1). By definition, the luminous flux, Φ_v, of a source is given by

$$\Phi_v = K_m \int \frac{d\Phi_e}{d\lambda} V(\lambda) \, d\lambda = K_m \int_{\lambda_1}^{\lambda_2} S(\lambda) V(\lambda) \, d\lambda \qquad (3.6)$$

since $(d\Phi_e/d\lambda)\delta\lambda$ is the radiant flux corresponding to the radiation between λ and $\lambda + \delta\lambda$. $S(\lambda)$ is the spectral power distribution of the radiation measured in watts per unit wavelength interval, λ_1 and λ_2 are the limits of the visible spectrum (Sect. 1.3.2) and K_m is the maximum spectral luminous efficacy, having the value 680 lm/W (Sect. 1.3.2).

The next step was the adoption by the CIE in 1931 of colour co-ordinates for wavelengths at 5 nm intervals throughout the visible spectrum in terms of an agreed set of reference stimuli. The values were based on investigations to determine the amounts of three spectral matching stimuli necessary to match each wavelength which yielded the chromaticity co-ordinates for each wavelength. Experiments had been carried out independently by Wright and Guild using different sets of matching stimuli and a number of observers. The observations were transformed to a system of reference stimuli at 700·0 nm, 546·1 nm and 435·8 nm, the units of the matching stimuli being adjusted so that equal quantities were required to match the NPL white then in use (of known spectral distribution corresponding to about 4800 K). The results from the two experiments were in good agreement and mean values of the chromaticity co-ordinates $r(\lambda)$, $g(\lambda)$ and $b(\lambda)$ for each wavelength were adopted. Fig. 3.2 shows these chromaticity co-ordinates plotted against wavelength: at each wavelength the co-ordinates add up to unity but one or other of them is always negative except at the wavelengths of the reference stimuli.

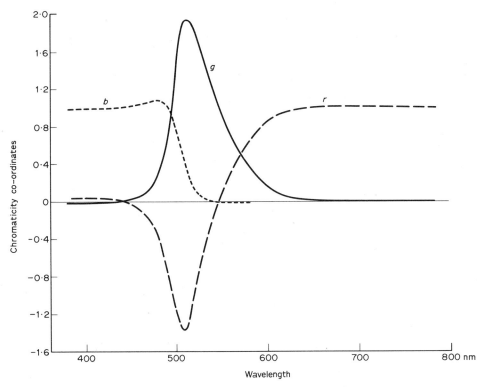

Fig. 3.2   Chromaticity co-ordinates of the spectrum for stimuli at 700·0 nm, 546·1 nm and 435·8 nm; the Standard Observer, CIE 1931

It is not possible to calculate the colour co-ordinates for a test source from its spectral power distribution if only the colour co-ordinates of the spectral wavelengths are known. It is also necessary to know the contribution of the energy of the source at each wavelength towards the tristimulus values *R*, *G* and *B*. This requires the definition of *colour matching functions* or *spectral tristimulus values* $\bar{r}(\lambda)$, $\bar{g}(\lambda)$, $\bar{b}(\lambda)$, which give the contribution of unit amount of energy at each wavelength towards the tristimulus values. With this device the tristimulus values for a source with a spectral power distribution $S(\lambda)$ may be calculated from

$$R = \int S(\lambda)\,\bar{r}(\lambda)\,d\lambda$$
$$G = \int S(\lambda)\,\bar{g}(\lambda)\,d\lambda \qquad (3.7)$$
$$B = \int S(\lambda)\,\bar{b}(\lambda)\,d\lambda$$

Now the measured colour co-ordinates of the spectral wavelengths $r(\lambda)$, etc., were not sufficient to define the spectral tristimulus values, since by Eq. 3.4, for unit amount of energy at each wavelength

$$r(\lambda) = \frac{\bar{r}(\lambda)}{\bar{r}(\lambda)+\bar{g}(\lambda)+\bar{b}(\lambda)}$$
$$g(\lambda) = \frac{\bar{g}(\lambda)}{\bar{r}(\lambda)+\bar{g}(\lambda)+\bar{b}(\lambda)}$$
$$b(\lambda) = \frac{\bar{b}(\lambda)}{\bar{r}(\lambda)+\bar{g}(\lambda)+\bar{b}(\lambda)}$$

These equations may be re-written as

$$\bar{r}(\lambda) = a(\lambda)\,r(\lambda)$$
$$\bar{g}(\lambda) = a(\lambda)\,g(\lambda)$$
$$\bar{b}(\lambda) = a(\lambda)\,b(\lambda)$$

where

$$a(\lambda) = \bar{r}(\lambda)+\bar{g}(\lambda)+\bar{b}(\lambda)$$

Therefore $a(\lambda)$ must be determined if the colour matching functions are to be derived from the known spectral colour co-ordinates.

The method used to determine $a(\lambda)$ involved the spectral luminous efficiency function, $V(\lambda)$. Since the laws of additivity seem to be valid, it was assumed that $V(\lambda)$ is a linear combination of the colour matching functions and

$$V(\lambda) = L_R\bar{r}(\lambda)+L_G\bar{g}(\lambda)+L_B\bar{b}(\lambda)$$
$$= a(\lambda)[L_R r(\lambda)+L_G g(\lambda)+L_B b(\lambda)]$$

where L_R, L_G and L_B are constants proportional to the relative luminous efficiencies of the reference stimuli, or the relative luminous flux in unit quantities of the reference stimuli of the system. The relative values of L_R, L_G and L_B were found by experiment to be $1:4\cdot5907:0\cdot0601$; these were then used to obtain the values of $a(\lambda)$. Finally the spectral tristimulus values $\bar{r}(\lambda)$, $\bar{g}(\lambda)$, $\bar{b}(\lambda)$ were derived (Fig. 3.3), the units of [R], [G] and [B] having been made equal for the equi-energy spectrum (Sect. 3.2.2).

3.2.2 The CIE system of 1931: [XYZ]

The [XYZ] reference system, chosen by the CIE to be independent of any set of real stimuli, was defined in terms of four *cardinal stimuli*, namely monochromatic light at

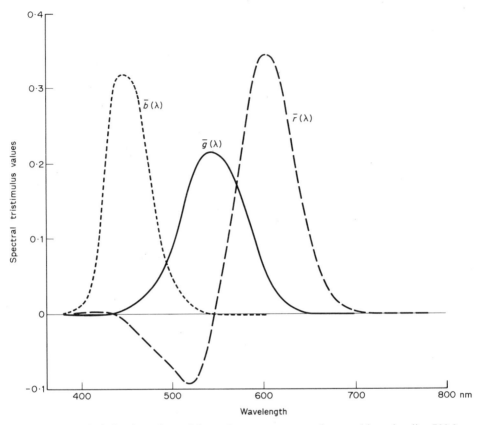

Fig. 3.3   Spectral tristimulus values of the equi-energy spectrum for matching stimuli at 700·0 nm, 546·1 nm and 435·8 nm; the Standard Observer, CIE 1931

wavelengths 700·0 nm, 546·1 nm, and 435·8 nm, and source B (Sect. 3.2.7). These four real sources were required so that calibration factors could be obtained experimentally for colorimeters. Tables of the colour co-ordinates, x, y, z (Fig. 3.1), and CIE spectral tristimulus values, $\bar{x}(\lambda)$, $\bar{y}(\lambda)$, $\bar{z}(\lambda)$ (Fig. 3.4) were given for wavelengths at 5 nm intervals from 380 nm to 780 nm. Recently values at 1 nm intervals have been interpolated and the range extended from 360 nm to 830 nm. The reference stimuli [X], [Y] and [Z] were those indicated in Fig. 3.1, and were not physically realizable since they lay outside the location of 'real' colours.

The system satisfied the following requirements.

(a) All numerical quantities used in chromaticity calculations are positive and thus all real colours have positive co-ordinates.

(b) The factors L_x, L_y, L_z for the standard observer were chosen to be 0:1:0 and so the $\bar{y}(\lambda)$ curve is identical with $V(\lambda)$ and Y is the exclusive measure of luminance.

(c) The primaries were also chosen to give the most convenient shape to the spectrum locus on the [XYZ] triangle and this resulted in the [Z] axis being coincident with the

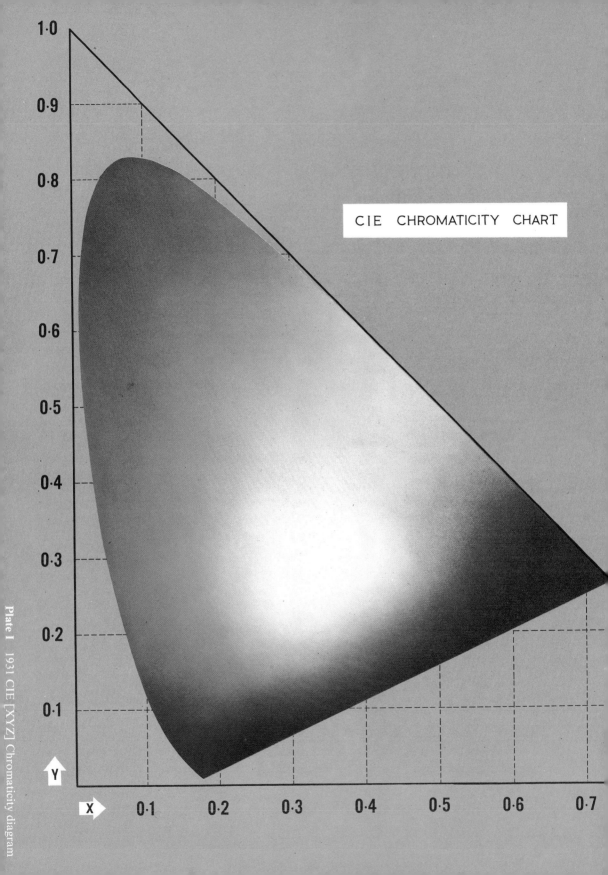

CIE CHROMATICITY CHART

Plate I 1931 CIE [XYZ] Chromaticity diagram

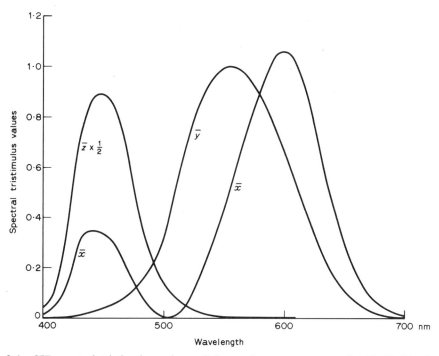

Fig. 3.4 CIE spectral tristimulus values of the equi-energy spectrum for X, Y, Z reference stimuli for 2° field

spectrum locus between about 630 nm and 770 nm and very close to it from 580 nm to 630 nm (Fig. 3.1).

(d) The units of [X], [Y] and [Z] were chosen such that the computed colour of the equi-energy source occupies the centre of the [XYZ] triangle. This (theoretical) source has a distribution of constant power per unit wavelength interval throughout the visible spectrum (S_E in Fig. 3.9).

The calculation of chromaticity co-ordinates x, y, z is described in Sect. 3.2.5. Plate I gives a general indication of the location of colours within the [XYZ] triangle.

3.2.3 The CIE 1964 supplementary standard colorimetric observer (10°)

The data standardized in 1931 applied to a 2° field of view; more recently, demand for colour matching functions for large field viewing resulted in the adoption by the CIE in 1964 of spectral tristimulus values, $\bar{x}_{10}(\lambda)$, $\bar{y}_{10}(\lambda)$, $\bar{z}_{10}(\lambda)$, for a 10° field, based on the work of Stiles and Burch, and Speranskaya. Sizeable differences exist between the 2° and 10° data and trials are still being made to test whether the use of the 10° data improves the correlations with visual observations for large field viewing conditions.

53

3.2.4   The CIE 1960 uniform chromaticity scale

A serious disadvantage of the x, y diagram was discovered during work on colour discrimination when Wright and MacAdam carried out experiments on the size of a 'noticeable difference' in colour in terms of x and y. Different techniques were used in these investigations but the results were similar and Fig. 3.5 shows MacAdam's results for loci of ten 'minimum perceptible colour differences' (mpcd) plotted on the x, y

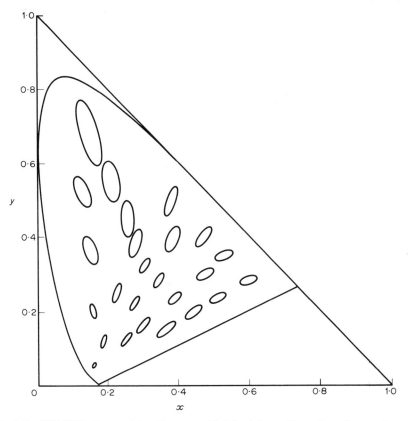

Fig. 3.5   CIE 1931 chromaticity diagram with MacAdam ellipses (ten times enlarged)

diagram. (Although usually so named, these are really differences of ten times the standard deviation in colour matching under the conditions used.) It will be seen that the size of the mpcd varies with its position on the chart and the direction in which the difference occurs—an ellipse represents equal visual steps in colour away from the centre point in any direction. This means that the x, y diagram is not uniform, that is, equal steps in x and y do not represent visually equal colour differences, and this is a serious disadvantage when measuring colour differences and specifying colour tolerances.

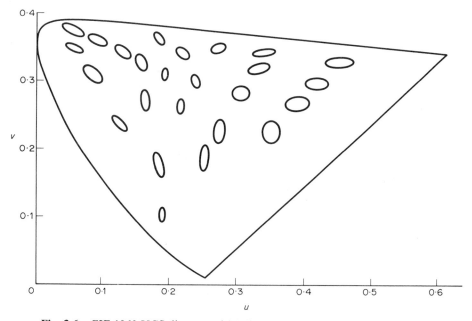

Fig. 3.6   CIE 1960 UCS diagram with MacAdam ellipses (ten times enlarged)

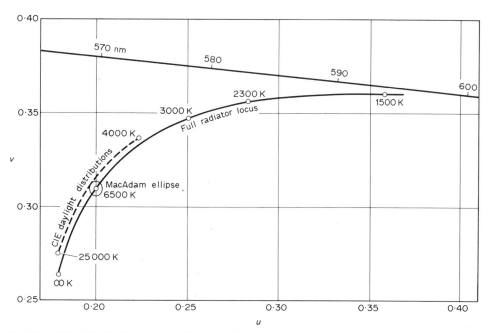

Fig. 3.7   CIE 1960 UCS diagram with the full radiator locus and the locus of the CIE daylight distributions

Various projections of the x, y diagram have been developed in an attempt to find a more uniform system but none of them has been completely satisfactory probably due to the fact that most of them involved linear transformations of the data. In 1960 the CIE recommended a transformation developed by MacAdam which appears to give a uniformity as good as any other transformation. The co-ordinates in the new system can be obtained by the following equations:

$$u = \frac{4X}{X+15Y+3Z} = \frac{4x}{-2x+12y+3}$$

$$v = \frac{6Y}{X+15Y+3Z} = \frac{6y}{-2x+12y+3}$$

$$(3.8)$$

The uniform chromaticity scale (UCS) diagram is shown in Fig. 3.6 where the ratios of the major to minor axes of the 10 mpcd ellipses are much more uniform than on the x, y diagram. In the centre of the diagram near the black body locus (Sect. 3.2.6) at 6500 K, the mpcd locus is almost a circle (Fig. 3.7).

3.2.5   Specification of colour

Colorimetry.   The measurement of hue in terms of x and y may be performed (a) by visual colorimetry in which the test light is matched by a mixture of three (or more) lights of known hue but arbitrary spectral composition; (b) by photocells used to measure several parts of the spectrum of the test source isolated by colour filters; or (c) by measurement of the complete spectrum of the light in energy (or power) units. Once the relative spectral power distribution, $S(\lambda)$ is known, the tristimulus values can be calculated from equations similar to Eq. 3.7:

$$X = \int S(\lambda)\beta(\lambda)\bar{x}(\lambda) \, d\lambda$$

$$Y = \int S(\lambda)\beta(\lambda)\bar{y}(\lambda) \, d\lambda$$

$$(3.9)$$

$$Z = \int S(\lambda)\beta(\lambda)\bar{z}(\lambda) \, d\lambda$$

where $\beta(\lambda)$ is the spectral luminance factor of a surface when this is the source of the coloured radiation, while for the determination of the chromaticity of a light source $\beta(\lambda)$ equals unity. Integrating limits include the whole visible spectrum. The chromaticity co-ordinates x, y, z, may then be calculated as before (Eq. 3.4), but using X, Y, Z in place of R, G, B.

In general only two of the chromaticity co-ordinates, usually x and y, are quoted since

$$x+y+z = 1$$

Very roughly, x, which is the fractional amount of the [X] stimulus, is associated with redness, y with greenness and z with blueness. It will be seen from Fig. 3.1 that an additive mixture of red and green gives yellow, green and blue produces blue-green (or cyan), and purple (or magenta) results from blue and red.

The luminous flux emitted by a source can also be calculated from Eq. 3.9 for Y if $S(\lambda)$ is known in absolute units (Sect. 3.2.1) since $\bar{y}(\lambda) = V(\lambda)$.

Luminous flux $$\Phi_v = K_m \int S(\lambda)\bar{y}(\lambda)\,\mathrm{d}\lambda$$

In all three methods of colorimetry, prior calibration of the instrument and some calculation subsequent to the measurements are required. Visual colorimetry, the foundation of the whole system, is now little used for practical measurement. The third method, spectrophotometry, is regarded as the fundamental one even though it is not the easiest method to operate and the measurements and calculations are more complicated than for the other two methods. Some instruments are described in Sect. 4.3.

Dominant wavelength.   An alternative method of specifying a colour using the chromaticity diagram is in terms of *dominant wavelength* and *purity*. The most 'saturated' colours which exist are those of spectrum wavelengths and as the colour moves towards the centre of the diagram it becomes less saturated. Considering Fig. 3.8, all the colours, for example C_1, that lie on a straight line joining the white point, W, to the spectrum locus are assumed to have the same hue, and the monochromatic stimulus is known as the dominant wavelength, λ_d, of that hue. For colours on the purple side of the white point, for example C_2, the dominant wavelength is that of the complementary wavelength λ_2.

Excitation purity.   The saturation of the colour is expressed by means of the *excitation purity* calculated according to one of the following equations

$$p_e = \frac{y - y_w}{y_d - y_w} \quad \text{or} \quad p_e = \frac{x - x_w}{x_d - x_w} \tag{3.10}$$

where x, y, x_w, y_w, x_d, y_d are the chromaticity co-ordinates of the test colour, the white point and the dominant wavelength respectively. For colours on the purple side of the white point, x_d and y_d are the chromaticity co-ordinates of the point P on the purple boundary (Fig. 3.8). The form of Eq. 3.10 which gives the greater value to the numerator is used for calculating the excitation purity. For self-luminous objects, the white point is usually taken as the chromaticity of the equi-energy spectrum ($x = y = z = 0.333$), but for illuminated samples ('surface colours'), the white point is that of the illuminant.

Metric purity.   If the CIE 1960 UCS diagram is used, the measure of saturation may be defined as the *metric purity* where

$$p_m = \frac{v - v_w}{v_d - v_w} \quad \text{or} \quad p_m = \frac{u - u_w}{u_d - u_w}$$

the subscripts having the same meaning as before.

Colorimetric purity.   An alternative method of specifying the saturation of a colour is given by the *colorimetric purity* where $p_c = p_e \cdot y_d/y$ but this measure is not widely used, though it has the advantage of including the luminance factor y_d/y.

57

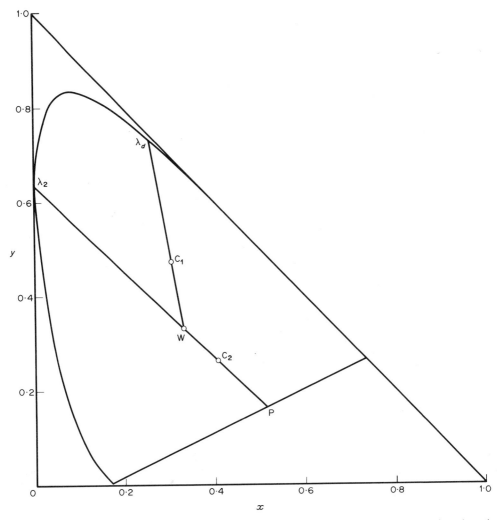

Fig. 3.8   CIE 1931 chromaticity diagram illustrating specification by dominant wavelength and purity

3.2.6   The Planckian radiator

It is well known that most bodies when heated to sufficiently high temperatures emit red light and as the temperature increases, the emitted light becomes whiter. The complete unifying principle which explains the phenomenon of thermal radiation was given by Planck in 1901 (Sect. 6.1.2). This allows the calculation of the power radiated throughout the spectrum by a black body (or full radiator) at a temperature $T(K)$ from the equation

$$M_{e,\lambda}(\lambda, T) = \frac{c_1 \lambda^{-5}}{e^{c_2/\lambda T} - 1}$$

where c_1 and c_2 are constants.

The spectral power distribution curves for black bodies at various temperatures are shown in Fig. 6.2. The colour co-ordinates calculated from such curves and plotted on the chromaticity diagram lie on a smooth curve called the *full radiator locus* (Figs 3.1 and 3.7).

If a light source has a chromaticity on the black body locus, it is said to have the same *colour temperature* as that particular full radiator even though their spectral power distributions may differ. A source not on the full radiator locus can be described by means of its *correlated colour temperature*, that is, the point on the locus which is closest to it on the UCS diagram. Lines of constant correlated colour temperature are thus perpendicular to the Planckian locus on the UCS diagram but inclined to it, except at $T = \infty$, on the x, y diagram. The use of correlated colour temperatures is perhaps justifiable for spectral power distributions of natural daylight but it has been much abused in the case of non-incandescent sources with chromaticities well away from the black body locus.

3.2.7 Standard illuminants and sources

In 1931 the CIE recognized the necessity for specifying internationally some standard sources particularly for calibration purposes in the colorimetry of surface colours. Three lamp or lamp and filter combinations were chosen. More recently the CIE decided to specify standard illuminants, not necessarily realizable in practice, in terms of their spectral power distributions and when possible will no doubt recommend practical standard sources which represent them.

Standard Illuminant A. The fact that the spectral power distribution for an incandescent lamp conforms closely to that of a full radiator makes such a lamp an immediate choice as *Source A* or S_A. The colour temperature originally chosen by the CIE was 2848 K and this distribution (Fig. 3.9) is now given by a full radiator at 2856 K due to subsequent revisions of the international practical temperature scale (Sect. 4.1.2). In practice this colour temperature is achieved by running a gas-filled (non-halogen) tungsten lamp at an applied voltage less than the nominal value. Since the spectral power distribution of the tungsten filament differs from that of the Planckian radiator of the same chromaticity owing to the varying spectral emissivity of the metal (Fig. 7.3), the filament and the black body are at somewhat different temperatures. For Source A at 2856 K the real temperature is approximately 2790 K: another example is that tungsten at 3000 K has a colour temperature of 3070 K.

Standard Illuminants B and C. For practical sources at temperatures higher than a tungsten filament could achieve, the CIE specified that S_A should be used in conjunction with liquid filters to produce sources at colour temperatures (on the present scale) of approximately 4874 K and 6774 K, S_B and S_C respectively. An appendix to the 1931

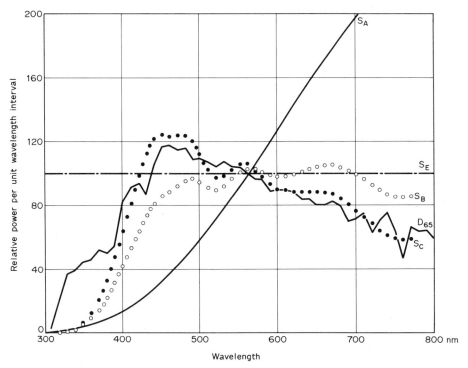

Fig. 3.9   Spectral power distribution curves for CIE Standard Illuminants A, B, C and D65, and the equi-energy spectrum

resolution contained the spectral power distributions for these sources (Fig. 3.9). Unfortunately the liquid filters were difficult to prepare and maintain and the sources were of no use where large area illumination was required.

Standard Daylight Illuminants D.   The best known and most widely used light source is natural daylight, and, variable though it is in intensity and spectral composition, it is a readily accepted standard for showing how objects 'ought' to look, north skylight especially being much used for visual colour matching purposes. In 1967, the CIE recommended a daylight distribution at 6500 K as a standard illuminant (D_{65}) together with a method for obtaining the spectral power distributions for daylight at other colour temperatures in the range 4000 K to 25 000 K. These distributions were based on several hundred measurements of natural skylight by Henderson and Hodgkiss, Condit and Grum, and Budde; the locus of the chromaticities fell on the green side of the full radiator locus (Fig. 3.7). It has proved impossible so far to produce sources which very closely imitate the standard daylight illuminants, though reasonable approximations can be obtained for less exacting requirements than those of colorimetry.

3.3   SURFACE COLOURS

3.3.1   Reflection and transmission

Single surfaces.   Colour considerations so far in this chapter have concentrated on light sources, as this approach is essential for establishing the principles of colour measurement. A more common problem is the evaluation of the colour of light either reflected from or transmitted by an illuminated sample. Restricting the discussion to reflection, since the same considerations apply to transmission, certain wavelengths will be reflected more strongly from a coloured surface than others, and the object will be colloquially called by the hue of the most strongly reflected wavelengths. The colour of a surface is mainly produced by subtracting wavelengths from the incident light, and it is important to remember that the perceived colour depends both on the spectral reflectance of the object and the spectral emission of the source. This can easily be demonstrated by illuminating a range of colours with a low pressure sodium lamp when most colours will appear to be brown or black. The colour co-ordinates of a sample can be calculated by inserting the values of the spectral luminance factor, $\beta(\lambda)$, in Eq. 3.9. The chromaticity does not completely define a colour and it is also necessary to know the luminance factor of the surface which may be calculated from

$$Y = \frac{\int S(\lambda)\beta(\lambda)\bar{y}(\lambda)\,\mathrm{d}\lambda}{\int S(\lambda)\bar{y}(\lambda)\,\mathrm{d}\lambda}$$

This is particularly important for surface colours as it is possible to have two samples, for example a yellow and a brown, with the same chromaticity co-ordinates but which look completely different because their luminance factors are not the same.

In general pigments and dyes reflect over a fairly wide band of wavelengths and consequently it is impossible to obtain saturated colours where the spectrum locus on the chromaticity diagram is curved because the colour depends on the integrated effect over the wavelength range which is reflected. Saturated reds and yellows with high luminance factor can be produced but not green and blue samples with high saturation and luminance factor.

Multiple reflections.   When a beam of light falls on a coloured surface some of the wavelengths are absorbed and if the reflected beam then falls on a similarly coloured surface, more of the same wavelengths will be absorbed. This will be repeated each time the reflected beam is incident on the surface and means that the saturation of a colour increases with multiple reflections. The effect accounts for the walls of a room being noticeably more saturated in colour than the small paint sample which was originally chosen.

3.3.2   Fluorescent pigments and dyes

In recent years a noticeable improvement in the luminosity (brightness) and saturation of surface colours has occurred with the development of fluorescent pigments and dyes. These materials absorb energy in the long wave ultra-violet or blue regions of the spectrum and convert it to light. The emission bands are fairly narrow and are superimposed on the reflection spectrum that the sample would have in the absence of fluorescence.

Similar materials emitting violet, blue or green light are used as 'optical brighteners' to overcome the natural yellowness of most 'white' materials.

3.3.3   Subtractive colour mixture

It has been shown that the colour of a surface, for example a pigment, is produced by a subtractive process, and therefore if two pigments are mixed, the resultant colour cannot be predicted by the principles of additive mixtures of lights (Sect. 3.1.2). Subtractive mixing can be illustrated by considering a mixture of blue and yellow pigments. Examination of their reflectance curves (Fig. 3.10) shows that the only region of the spectrum reflected by both pigments is the green. Hence a mixture of blue and yellow pigments produces green whereas the addition of blue and yellow lights yields white. The reflectance curve for a mixture of pigments is obtained by multiplying together the curves for the individual components. The low reflectance of the mixture is noticeable in this case.

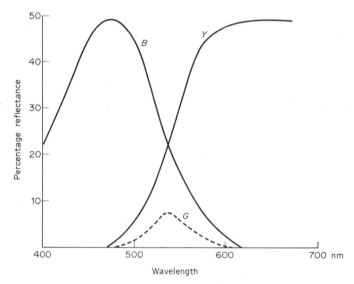

Fig. 3.10   Spectral reflectance curves for blue and yellow coloured pigments and their subtractive mixture

The most useful subtractive primaries are those which when added together produce the widest range of other colours; they also produce black when mixed in the correct amounts. They are cyan, magenta and yellow which are the complementaries of the additive primaries red, green and blue. In a subtractive mixture magenta and yellow give red, yellow and cyan produce green, and blue results from cyan and magenta. Colour printing and photography rely on these relations, and the Lovibond method of colour measurement uses subtractive effects on white light by means of calibrated glasses coloured red, yellow and blue.

Plate II Model of Munsell system, reflected in mirror

3.3.4 Colour space

CIE 1964 uniform colour space.   The complete specification of a surface colour comprises its chromaticity and luminance factor which, in the [XYZ] system, is usually plotted in the third dimension perpendicular to the plane of the *x, y* diagram. In 1964 the CIE extended the 1960 UCS system to colour space, but it was not satisfactory to make the third axis simply the luminance factor as the size of discrimination steps in this parameter varies considerably. It was also decided to relate the system to the achromatic colour, u_0, v_0, which in the case of surface colours is the illuminant. The three variables are defined as

$$U^* = 13W^*(u-u_0)$$
$$V^* = 13W^*(v-v_0) \tag{3.11}$$
$$W^* = 25Y^{1/3} - 17$$

Colour solids and atlases.   The practical concept underlying the previous section was the orderly arrangement of surface colours in colour space according to their measured colour parameters. It is also possible to arrange them systematically according to their subjective appearance and many atlases based on different arrangements have been developed. The best known is that due to Munsell in which the central vertical axis, called the *Value* scale, ranges from white at the top to black at the bottom with nine equally spaced shades of grey in between. The saturated colours are arranged on the equator of the solid into ten *Hues*, B, BG, G, GY, Y, YR, R, RP, P, PB each of which is divided into ten steps. The saturation, or *Chroma*, of the colour increases, also by visually equal steps, as it moves away from the central axis (Plate II). A colour is specified by a combination of three numbers, for example 5YR 6/8 where 5YR is the Hue, the Value is 6 and the Chroma is 8. In practice, the Munsell solid is not a sphere because it is not possible to produce saturated greens and blues with lightness (equivalent to Value) as high as for yellows and reds. The complete system contains approximately 1000 samples which are intended to be viewed under daylight. Their spectral luminance factors are known making it possible to calculate the chromaticities for any illumination. They were chosen so that the visual difference between adjacent samples was approximately the same throughout, though the uniformity is now considered to be far from perfect, especially between units of Value and Hue.

3.3.5 The CIE 1964 colour difference formula

The necessity to assess small colour differences has produced a large number of formulae for expressing colour differences in terms of a single number. Mostly these are very complicated and it is unlikely that any single formula will be satisfactory for the whole of colour space. The formula recommended by the CIE is in terms of the 1964 uniform colour space and the colour difference ΔE is given by

$$\Delta E = [(U_1^* - U_2^*)^2 + (V_1^* - V_2^*)^2 + (W_1^* - W_2^*)^2]^{\frac{1}{2}} \tag{3.12}$$

Another unit of ΔE is the NBS unit, devised by Judd, which is intended to be about five times the smallest difference which can just be detected under the best experimental conditions. In practice the CIE unit is approximately equal to the NBS unit.

3.4   COLOUR RENDERING

3.4.1   Objective assessments

During the last two decades the availability of a wide range of fluorescent lamps and the current advances in discharge lamp technology have emphasized the possible variations in the appearances of coloured surfaces due to different light sources. In general, it is unpractical to assess the colour rendering properties of light sources by direct observations, but two systems of measurement have been investigated. With the data available both appear to rank sources in the same order of performance. The problem of adaptation makes it difficult to compare two sources having different colour appearance (Sect. 3.4.3), and it is necessary to select a standard with a correlated colour temperature as close as possible to that of the test source.

Reference standards.   At colour temperatures below 3500 K, Planckian radiators were the obvious choice for reference standards as these are simulated by familiar incandescent lamps. The standardization by the CIE in 1967 of the daylight distributions provided a series of standards for colour temperatures higher than 5000 K. The intermediate region between 3500 K and 5000 K presents difficulties because no familiar natural source exists in this region, hence it was decided to adopt Planckian radiators up to 5000 K.

NPL-Crawford method.   The NPL-Crawford method depends on comparing the spectral power distribution of the test source with that of the reference, but this comparison is difficult to do point by point throughout the spectrum. Crawford divided the spectrum into six bands (Fig. 3.11), the luminance being integrated over each band and expressed as a percentage of the total luminance. This band system is superior to the previous system which employed eight bands since it gives less extreme variations of luminance between the centre and end bands.

   In calculating the Crawford index number, the percentage luminance in each band of the test lamp is compared with that of the appropriate reference and the percentage deviation of this ratio from unity is obtained. The excess of this deviation over a tolerance, 10%, determined statistically from Crawford's experimental observations, is then calculated. The effect of interactions between bands is considered by combining the deviations of adjacent bands if they differ from the standard in the same direction and the tolerance for such a double band is half that for a single band. The sum of the excesses of the deviations over the tolerances gives a demerit number which can be subtracted from an arbitrary number to give a figure of merit. A worked example of the method is shown in Fig. 3.11 for a fluorescent lamp: the demerit number is 114, a high value partly due to the fact that the chromaticity of the lamp (Natural fluorescent) lies well away from the black body locus.

CIE method: special colour rendering index R_i.   An alternative method of assessment was recommended by the CIE in 1965 based on the change in colour appearance of a surface colour which occurs when the illumination is altered. The colour shift in the u, v diagram caused by the replacement of the test source by the appropriate reference illuminant is determined. A correction has to be made to the chromaticity of the sample illuminated by the test source to allow for the fact that the chromaticities of the test source and reference standard are not usually exactly the same thus causing (in principle) different

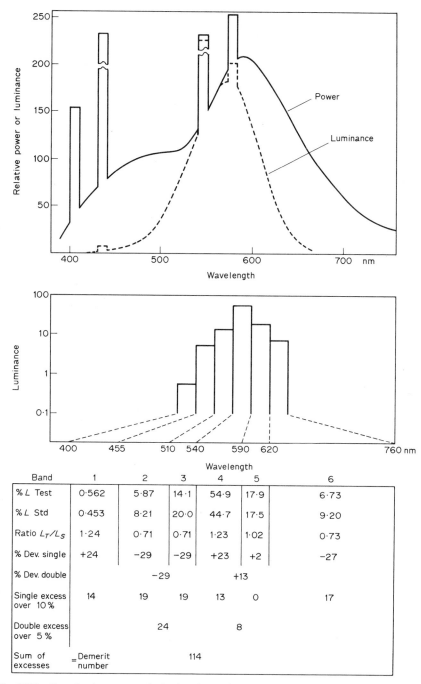

Band	1	2	3	4	5	6
%L Test	0·562	5·87	14·1	54·9	17·9	6·73
%L Std	0·453	8·21	20·0	44·7	17·5	9·20
Ratio L_T/L_S	1·24	0·71	0·71	1·23	1·02	0·73
% Dev. single	+24	−29	−29	+23	+2	−27
% Dev. double		−29		+13		
Single excess over 10%	14	19	19	13	0	17
Double excess over 5%		24		8		
Sum of excesses = Demerit number			114			

Fig. 3.11 NPL–Crawford system of six bands; calculation of demerit number for Natural fluorescent lamp

states of adaptation for the two illuminants. This correction is done by means of a von Kries transformation. The corrected chromaticity of the sample under the test source and the chromaticity of the sample under the reference illuminant are transformed into the 1964 UCS co-ordinates, $U^*V^*W^*$ (Eq. 3.11) and these values are inserted in the 1964 colour difference formula (Eq. 3.12) to give the colour shift ΔE_i. The CIE special colour rendering index is then obtained from

$$R_i = 100 - 4 \cdot 6\Delta E_i$$

where the factor 4·6 changes the scale so that a Warm White fluorescent lamp has a general colour rendering index of 50. There is no restriction on the choice of samples for the special colour rendering index provided that their descriptions are given with the index.

CIE method: general colour rendering index R_a.   The special index gives information only about one particular sample and to obtain information about the general colour rendering properties of a source it is necessary to assess a number of samples. The CIE selected a representative series of eight Munsell samples and the general colour rendering index is now defined as the mean of the special indices for these eight samples. Details of the method for calculating special and general indices are given in CIE Publication No. 13 (second edition). The index R_a for the lamp cited in Fig. 3.11 is 83.

Any system which describes the colour rendering properties of a source by means of a single number is bound to restrict the amount of information available. Equivalence of the CIE general index for two lamps will not guarantee interchangeability since the same mean may result from very different single values. The uncertainty regarding correction for adaptation makes comparison of sources with dissimilar colour appearance difficult, and leads to inaccuracies in the indices for lamps which are some distance from the full radiator locus in chromaticity. Because of these and other difficulties, such as the question of tolerances, the system has not as yet been widely adopted.

3.4.2   Metamerism

Light source metamerism.   In describing the principles of additive colour matching (Sect. 3.1.3) it was shown that a colour (S) (Fig. 3.1) can be matched by a mixture of [G] and [B] or (Q) and [R]. These two mixtures have the same colour appearance, but since their spectral power distributions are different, they possess different colour rendering properties and are said to be metameric. Normally such an extreme degree of metamerism is not shown by practical light sources but a pair of metameric lamps that can be produced fairly readily consists of a low pressure sodium lamp and an incandescent lamp with an appropriate yellow filter.

Surface colour metamerism.   Metamerism occurs more frequently for surface colours where a pair of samples may match under one illuminant but differ if the spectral emission of the light source alters. The degree of metamerism which is shown by a pair of samples can vary widely as it depends on the difference between the combined effects of the spectral reflectances of the samples and the spectral emissions of the illuminants. The phenomenon often poses serious problems in manufacturing industry where it may be desired to produce the same colour appearance in articles of different substrates, necessarily containing different colouring matters.

Observer metamerism.   A third form of metamerism is that due to differences between the colour vision of individual observers.

The three forms of metamerism are currently the subject of active work among colorimetrists, and various indices based on measurements of the colour differences involved are being investigated.

3.4.3 Subjective effects

Adaptation and constancy.   Adaptation to change in the quantity of illumination has been described previously (Sect. 2.2.2). In a similar way, the eye is affected by its previous exposure to a coloured field of view. If this is a saturated colour, then the colour receptor which is most highly stimulated will become fatigued and the perceived sensation will move towards the complementary colour of the fatiguing stimulus. For instance, suppose a white surface stimulates equal responses in the red, green and blue receptors. If the eye is then fatigued by exposure to green light, the white surface on re-examination will appear pink. Coloured after-images are also related to this effect.

The process of chromatic adaptation is the reason why large alterations in the colour rendering properties of light sources are often accepted without comment. For instance, a side-by-side comparison of natural daylight having a correlated colour temperature near 6500 K with a similar level of illumination of incandescent light at 2800 K reveals marked changes in the appearances of coloured samples. Yet these changes are accepted quite readily when the sources are viewed successively, the eye adapting in turn to the blueness of daylight and the yellowness of incandescent light. It might be said that the eye and its associated functions in the brain are always trying to establish a neutral or white reference point in the field of view, if this can be found; in other words, to maintain a state of colour constancy.

The objective assessment of the colour rendering properties of lamps is complicated by this constancy effect as no completely satisfactory method of making an allowance mathematically for chromatic adaptation has yet been developed. The von Kries transformation in the CIE method is an approximation which has some value.

Contrast.   Another effect which can cause large changes in the appearance of coloured surfaces is that of contrast between the object and its background. Any colour tends to induce a complementary colour in its background whether this is neutral or coloured, and existing hue or lightness differences between neighbouring colours will tend to increase. This has a practical significance as it tends to make objects more conspicuous against their backgrounds. Some of these contrast effects can be quite striking especially if a pattern is involved when the magnitudes of the apparent colour shifts become functions of the pattern size and detail. The effect may be partially explained by the fatiguing of receptors, the rapid involuntary movements which the eye makes continuously, and interactions between nerve impulses, but other factors in the eye and brain are also involved and the full explanation of all the phenomena of contrast has not yet been found.

Preference and memory.   The visual processes which cause the effects mentioned in the previous sections have either physical or physiological explanations. When questions of colour preference and memory are concerned, psychology and learning are involved.

Most people have preferences when considering single surface colours but these preferences may depend on the use to which the colour is put; for instance, the preference for a hue might be different for use as a paint than when used for clothes. Preferences may also be affected by the area of the colour and the surface texture of the sample, and this is particularly noticeable when combinations of colours are used.

When dealing with natural objects, such as human complexions and food, preferences are greatly affected by subconscious memory and conditioned responses. However, colour memory is unreliable as the tendency is to remember a colour as it is preferred. This has important applications in the food industry when artificial colorants may be added either to aid marketing, or in certain cases to replace natural colour lost during processing.

It is thus obvious that colour plays an important part in everyday life and consequently has a considerable bearing not only on the work of scientists and technologists, but also in the fields of design and marketing.

4 Photometry and colorimetry

The measurement of light and colour poses special problems in that, unlike purely physical measurements, it is concerned with the psycho-physical response to the very limited band of electromagnetic radiation which is perceived as light. The eye is incapable of measurement and can only adjudge equality, so it becomes necessary in visual instruments to make use of devices which use this property. However, it is now usual to use physical methods which are capable of providing quantitative measurements, and it is these and their use which will be chiefly described. While eliminating many subjective effects, these measurements depend on simplified physical relations which, though logical, only partly express the complication of the visual process.

4.1 EQUIPMENT AND STANDARDS

4.1.1 Standard lamps

All light quantities are related to the primary standard of light which is a full radiator at the freezing point of platinum having a temperature of 2045 K and a luminance of 60 cd/cm². This is maintained by national laboratories who provide suitable lamps calibrated to a high degree of accuracy for use by photometric laboratories as sub-standards of luminous flux or intensity. The responsible authority in UK is the National Physical Laboratory whose Division of Optical Metrology can provide this service. The degree of accuracy of measurement is determined by the type of lamp and the calibration is strictly correct only at the time of measurement. Such sub-standards should be used to calibrate a number of working standards which are subjected to periodic checks. In this way the sub-standards are used infrequently and will hold their calibration for a considerable time. Where standards are frequently used, as in routine measurements, it is good practice to calibrate a further set of lamps from the working standards and to use these for day to day calibration of photometers. When measurements of high precision are required, two sub-standard lamps should be used, one at the beginning and the other at the end of each series. The results against each standard should be calculated and the mean given. Both results should be in close agreement within the quoted tolerance and, if not, another sub-standard should be used to identify the faulty lamp.

A photometric laboratory should have a range of lamps calibrated for luminous flux covering the range over which it is desired to measure and of the different types to be covered, including tungsten filament, fluorescent, sodium, and mercury lamps. For measurements of luminous intensity it is usually sufficient to have calibrated a set of plane filament tungsten lamps in the range 2600 K to 2856 K. The ratings may conveniently be 100 W, 500 W and 1000 W providing intensities of approximately 100 cd, 700 cd and 1200 cd respectively.

For spectroradiometric and colorimetric measurements it is desirable to have lamps calibrated for both spectral power distribution and chromaticity in order to save some calculation. These lamps will in general be of the discharge type, especially fluorescent lamps, and should include some having chromaticities similar to those to be measured. For measurements in the ultra-violet region certain tungsten halogen lamps are useful, as they run at high temperatures and the envelope is of fused silica which transmits ultra-violet radiation (Sect. 10.2.5).

Lamps to be calibrated as standards should be of high quality and be aged to improve stability. Tungsten filament types should have their filaments mounted rigidly and be in large bulbs to militate against effects of blackening by tungsten deposition on the surface. They should be operated at rated voltage for 10 h and inspected for signs of deterioration like sagging filament and pinch discoloration. Discharge lamps should in general be aged for 750 h in a cycle, with 15 min off every 3 h for fluorescent tubes and every 6 h for mercury lamps. Periodic measurements should be made and lamps showing changes in luminous flux or current greater than 2% per 100 h should be rejected.

4.1.2 Colour temperature of radiators

The standard most commonly used for colour temperature (Sect. 3.2.6) and as a calibrating source for spectral power distribution measurements is Standard Illuminant A (S_A). This is a gas-filled tungsten lamp originally defined as operating at a colour temperature of 2848 K on the International Practical Temperature Scale (IPTS) of 1927, and its spectral power distribution was assumed to be that of a full radiator at 2848 K. By a change of the constant c_2 in Planck's law (Sect. 6.1.2) this colour temperature became 2854 K in the scale of 1948 and has so remained until recently, when by the IPTS of 1968 the value of c_2 has been altered again and a small change made in the gold (freezing) point. To convert from the IPTS of 1948, the colour temperature of a lamp is increased by

$$\Delta T = 5 \cdot 6 \times 10^{-4} T_{48} + 3 \cdot 8 \times 10^{-7} T_{48}^2 \tag{4.1}$$

The first term corrects for the change in c_2, the second for the change in the gold point. This empirical equation gives an accuracy of better than 0·1 K between 1900 K and 3500 K, and shows that a lamp previously calibrated at 2854 K (T_{48}) should now be assigned the colour temperature of 2858·7 K, the spectral power distribution for which must be obtained from the new tables of Planck's radiation function based on $c_2 = 1\cdot4388 \times 10^{-2}$ m.K instead of $1\cdot4380 \times 10^{-2}$ m.K.

If a lamp is recalibrated at 2858·7 K, its s.p.d. will be the same as it was for a lamp at 2854 K (more accurately 2853·95 K). The same computed spectrum arises from the Planck formula if T/c_2 is constant and for this purpose the changes in c_2 from 1·435 to 1·438 to 1·4388 in T_{27}, T_{48}, and T_{68} respectively require T to be successively 2848 K, 2854 K and 2855·5 K, which can also be calculated from the first term of Eq. 4.1. Each change gives a slight difference in the s.p.d. if a lamp is reset to the new temperature, but with a closer approximation to the original S_A distribution.

4.1.3 Radiation detectors

Two main kinds of photocell are in general use for the measurement of light, the *photoemissive* type and the *photovoltaic* type. In the former, electrons are emitted from a metallic surface by the action of radiation and are transferred to an anode which is maintained at a positive potential by an external voltage. A current dependent on the radiant intensity will flow. In the latter type, radiation causes a transfer of electrons across a rectifying boundary, usually of selenium and iron or aluminium, producing a current in an external circuit. Unlike the photoemissive cell, this requires no external voltage.

There are three main types of photoemissive cell, vacuum, gas-filled and photomultiplier. Of these only the first and last are used for measurement since, although an increased current is obtained from gas-filled cells, the performance is greatly affected by small changes in gas pressure and applied voltage.

Vacuum types are suitable because they are stable over a long period and the current for a given quantity of radiation is practically independent of the applied voltage. A well made cell can have a high degree of linearity of response over a range of the order of 50 000 to 1, with an accuracy of $0\cdot1\%$. It is advisable to keep the current below 10^{-7} A when fatigue effects will be negligible and to maintain the cell at a constant temperature near to the ambient to give maximum stability. It is customary to place a very high value of resistance in series with the cell and supply, and to measure the voltage drop due to the incident radiation. This voltage is amplified with one of many suitable circuits. The spectral response depends on the surface as shown in Fig. 4.1, and the cell should be selected with the most suitable response for the type of measurement required and the region of the spectrum to be investigated; cells are available which are sensitive to the ultra-violet and infra-red regions as well as to the visible part of the spectrum. Ultra-violet measurements are particularly important for some types of lamp (Sect. 12.4, 14.3.4, 15.1.5), though provision of the necessary standards is a difficult and specialized task. The basic requirement is that there shall be adequate response in the spectral bandwidth selected.

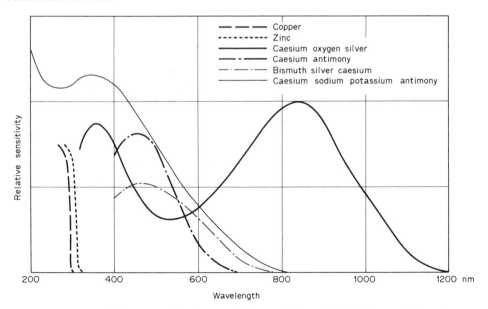

Fig. 4.1 Relative spectral response of photoemissive cells. (Ordinates arbitrary)

For photometric purposes it is essential that the spectral response approximates closely to the spectral luminous efficiency, $V(\lambda)$. No existing surface meets this requirement exactly and it is necessary to correct as closely as possible by means of liquid or coloured glass filters. A suitable photocell surface is bismuth-silver-caesium which covers the visible spectrum well (Fig. 4.1).

The *photomultiplier* uses intermediate electrodes, dynodes, each at a fixed potential above the next, typically 100 V. The number of stages is normally between 6 and 13: the greater the number the greater the amplification. It is customary to connect a resistor chain to a high voltage supply to obtain the dynode voltages, and because the amplification is dependent on the applied voltage it is important that the voltage be adjustable and stabilized. Sensitivities greater than 200 A/lm can be obtained whereas vacuum photo cells achieve only up to 35 µA/lm. This enormous increase makes photo-multipliers very useful for spectroradiometry where small quantities of power are to be measured in very narrow spectral bands. It is desirable to measure the current caused by incident radiation and a convenient method is to use a high-gain operational amplifier circuit designed to present zero resistance to the input and convert the current to a voltage. This voltage is best measured by a digital voltmeter although an indicating voltmeter can be used.

Where the highest degree of accuracy is not required, as in routine measurements, *photovoltaic cells* (usually selenium) are convenient to use, requiring only the connection of microammeter or galvanometer. However it is more convenient to use the measuring circuit described for the photomultiplier as, apart from the obvious advantage of digital presentation, the cell operates into a zero impedance circuit, under which condition the highest linearity is achieved. The spectral response compared with $V(\lambda)$ is shown in Fig. 4.2. Although it is higher in the blue and red regions and has some response in the ultra-violet region the peak is correctly placed for photometry. Suitable correction filters are available and certain cells are supplied already corrected. For illuminance

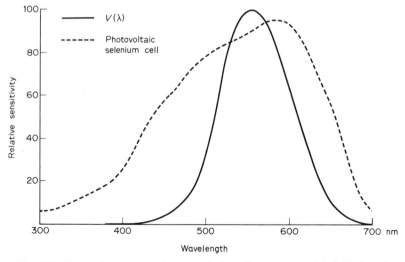

Fig. 4.2 Spectral response of photovoltaic cell compared with $V(\lambda)$ function

values above 10 lx, fatigue is a problem in precision measurement and can be 0·5% over 1 min. To overcome this, steady illumination or a regular sequence of dark and light exposure periods may be used. Typical sensitivity of the cell is 600 μA/lm. The smallest possible size of cell should be used as the linearity is a function of the ratio of the cell load resistance and the cell resistance which is itself inversely proportional to its area.

Photoconductive cells differ from the main types discussed above. They are of particular value for the detection of infra-red radiation as their response is mainly in that part of the spectrum. Those most useful for this purpose are the lead sulphide, lead telluride and indium antimonide types, although many other materials are known with similar properties. There is one which has a response in the visible region, the cadmium sulphide cell which is used in some designs of photographic light meter.

Silicon and germanium *semi-conductor photocells* generally have maximum response in the infra-red region but are also sensitive to visible radiation; they can give a current 10 to 20 times greater than a vacuum photoemissive cell for a given illuminance. They are similar in design and construction to other semi-conductor devices such as transistors, and have similar temperature characteristics.

A *thermopile* is essentially a device for converting radiation into heat and using this heat to produce an electric current by means of thermal junctions. A blackened surface is used which absorbs nearly all incident radiation and is therefore almost a full radiator (or black body) with a response nearly independent of the spectral composition of the incident power. The error due to selectivity is in general between 2% and 3%. Because it is a temperature-sensitive device the effects of ambient temperature must be considered especially when measuring small amounts of power. It is most suitable for measurement in the infra-red and there are vacuum thermopile designs with stable characteristics and high sensitivity. The use of a low frequency radiation chopping system has many advantages in this case, one of which is that high gain a.c. amplifiers can be used.

Bolometers and *Golay cells* are also used for radiation measurements. The former uses a Wheatstone bridge arrangement with a very small metal strip or semiconductor element whose resistance varies with temperature; and the latter is a pneumatic detector of very high sensitivity incorporating an aluminium film in an air or gas-filled cell, with an optical lever for amplification.

One general point must be made: it is of the highest importance to ensure that all of the radiation sensitive areas are exposed to the radiation to be measured. Failure to do this will lead to substantial inaccuracies in measurement, since in most cases these areas are not uniformly sensitive.

4.1.4 Illuminance and luminance meters

It is frequently necessary to make measurements of installations and portable meters are useful for this purpose. For illuminance measurements a variety of meters are available and these generally use a photovoltaic cell coupled to a microammeter scaled in lux or lm/ft^2. Ideally the photocell should be both $V(\lambda)$- and cosine-corrected, but if it is not the factors by which the reading is to be adjusted must be known for the lamps used and the angle of incidence of the light.

Luminance meters incorporate an optical system to project an image of the surface on the photocell. The illuminance on the photocell due to this image is proportional to the luminance L of the surface and to the aperture of the lens. The luminous flux on the lens is LSA/d^2, where S is the surface area, A is the lens area, and d the distance of the surface from the lens which must be large enough, compared with the dimensions of S and A, to allow the inverse square law to be applied. If τ is the transmittance of the lens, the image flux is $\tau LSA/d^2$. The image area is Sv^2/d^2, where v is the distance from lens to photocell, hence the illuminance is $\tau LA/v^2$. The surface to be measured is found by observation through the optical system, its size being usually between $0.5°$ and $1.5°$. The scale is usually calibrated by the makers; factors provide for different lens apertures or light of different spectral distribution where necessary.

4.2   PHOTOMETRY

4.2.1   Photometer bench methods

Where measurements involving distance and direction are concerned a photometric bench is required. Such a bench provides for mounting lamps at an adjustable and measurable distance from the photometer head. Because a bench makes use of the inverse square and cosine laws it is necessary that distances are measured to a high accuracy; for example, a photometric accuracy of 1% requires that the distance be measured to 0.5%. The photometer head may consist of either a photocell or a visual device such as the Lummer-Brodhun contrast head. In this the observer compares two adjacent fields each having a trapezoidal patch in the centre. At the point of balance equal contrast is perceived on both sides of the field with a difference in luminance of about 8% between each trapezoid and background. The contrast head is required however, only for the precise measurement of colour temperature.

The bench should be situated in a dark room, though if this is impossible it can be enclosed with curtains. The dark room should be light-proof and painted with matt black paint. The bench should be placed in the centre of the room to minimize the effect of reflections from the walls and for convenience of use. Screens should be placed between the lamps and photometer head to ensure that no stray light reaches the latter. These screens can conveniently be of aluminium painted matt black, with apertures of various sizes. The photocell should be mounted in a box, also painted matt black, with graded apertures to limit the field to the desired angle. It is of the highest importance to ensure that there is adequate screening and failure to do this will cause large errors.

Intensity measurements.   An appropriate calibrated lamp is selected and mounted on the photometer bench ensuring a correct alignment with the photometer head which should be mounted at one end of the bench. Two methods can be used. In the first the $V(\lambda)$-corrected photocell is maintained at a fixed distance from the lamp. A reading of the photocurrent is taken for the standard (R_s) and this serves to calibrate the photocell. The test lamp is substituted for the standard lamp and again the current is measured (R_t). If the luminous intensity of the standard is I_s and that of the test lamp I_t. Then

$$I_t = I_s \frac{R_t}{R_s} \tag{4.2}$$

In the second method the respective distances of the lamps, d_s and d_t, are adjusted until a convenient identical photocurrent is obtained in each case. The luminous intensities are then in the ratio of the distances squared, or

$$I_t = I_s \left(\frac{d_t}{d_s}\right)^2 \qquad\qquad (4.3)$$

This method has the advantage of eliminating errors due to non-linearity of the photocell and circuit and is convenient when there is a significant difference between the luminous intensity of the standard and test lamps.

Luminance measurements.   The luminous intensity can be measured as already described and the luminance found by dividing this value by the projected area of the surface in the given direction. It is often convenient to place an aperture of accurately known area in front of the surface particularly if there is variation in luminance across it. In this case the mean value will be determined.

Measurement of small sources of light, or of the luminance distribution over the area of a source, requires a different technique. One method is to use a lens to form an image of the source on a screen, the illuminance being measured at the desired part of the image. The relation between illuminance of the photometer and the luminance to be measured is described in Sect. 4.1.4.

Calibration of photocells and illumination photometers.   The photometric bench provides a convenient means of determining the relationship between illuminance and the photocurrent from photocells with their associated instruments, and of calibrating illumination photometers. The method is the same in both cases and consists of mounting the photocell on the bench and aligning it with a sub-standard lamp. The distance of the lamp is varied and noted for given instrument readings. It may be necessary to use a series of standard lamps of different luminous intensities in order to cover the range. The results should be plotted on a graph when departures from linearity can easily be seen. In the case of illumination photometers scaled in values of illuminance it is convenient to adjust the distances of the lamp such that the meter reads a series of convenient values.

When the photocells are not corrected to the CIE standard photometric observer, that is, to the $V(\lambda)$ function, it must be noted that such measurements are only correct for irradiance of similar spectral composition to that of the particular calibrating standard.

Colour temperature measurements.   It was mentioned earlier that a visual photometer is used in conjunction with a photometric bench to measure colour temperature. This is required to calibrate working standards, including tungsten lamps of the projector type operating at higher colour temperatures, against Standard Illuminant A, etc.

An appropriate calibrated lamp is mounted in correct alignment on the photometric bench together with the test lamp. The standard lamp should have the correct voltage applied to it and allowed time to stabilize, and the test lamp should also be stabilized at a voltage somewhere near its rated value. A series of readings should be taken by at least three observers in which they obtain a luminance balance of the head by adjusting the distance between the test lamp and head, also noting the colour difference, seen as a contrast between blue and red. If the test lamp appears too blue on the appropriate sections of the head then its temperature is too high and the voltage is reduced; conversely if it appears too red then the voltage should be increased. This procedure is repeated until no colour or luminance differences are observed. The mean of all readings is obtained. Such a measurement establishes equality with the standard only, so that if other colour temperatures are required it is necessary to use coloured filters especially designed for this purpose.

Where it is required to know the colour temperature at a prescribed voltage it is more convenient to use a red-blue ratio method. This relates the luminance ratio of a blue region of the emitted spectrum to that of a red region with the colour temperature, and is possible because the spectral distribution of a tungsten filament approximates to that of a full radiator. Colour temperature meters are available using this principle. They usually consist of a photovoltaic cell connected to a meter calibrated in colour temperature and having a fiducial mark on the scale. Two optical filters, red and blue, are so arranged in the instrument that they can be positioned in turn in front of the photocell together with an iris diaphragm. In use the instrument is mounted at a fixed distance before the test lamp with the red filter in position and the iris diaphragm adjusted until the meter pointer is coincident with the fiducial mark. The blue filter is then positioned and the reading of colour temperature noted on the scale. On the whole, measurements made without recourse to standard reference lamps are likely to be less accurate than the visual method described above.

A more reliable and precise method using photocell measurements requires a monochromator (Sect. 4.3.2). Two spectral bands of 5 or 10 nm width are chosen at, say, 450 nm and 700 nm. Using colour temperature standard lamps covering the range required, a series of photocurrent readings is made at 450 nm after setting the reading for 700 nm at some convenient value. A graph of colour temperature versus the 450 nm photocurrent gives a smooth curve on which the value for an unknown lamp may be interpolated.

It must be emphasized that these methods are suitable only for lamps having a nearly Planckian distribution. It sometimes happens that light sources whose spectral distributions depart widely from this distribution, such as fluorescent and metal halide lamps, are described by their correlated colour temperatures (Sect. 3.2.6). This practice is convenient but undesirable, especially when the chromaticity point is distant from the Planckian locus.

4.2.2   Flux measurements

Lamps designed for general lighting purposes are rated in terms of their total output of luminous flux so that this measurement is of the greatest importance. Luminous flux is measured fundamentally by a goniophotometer which, by a series of measurements, determines the average intensity of a lamp in all directions in space (Sect. 4.2.3). By definition this value when multiplied by 4π gives the luminous flux.

The integrating sphere.   For comparative measurements an integrating photometer is generally used in order to determine total flux by single measurements on test lamp and standard. If a lamp is placed within a sphere, the inner surface of which is painted with a non-selective uniformly diffusing paint the illumination on any one area is contributed to equally by the light reflected from all other equal areas.

Consider a sphere of a radius r which is large compared with the dimensions of the light source L at its centre, and has an internal surface which is uniformly diffusing and of reflectance ρ (Fig. 4.3a). A point P on the inner surface of the sphere, shielded from the direct light from the source by a small screen Q, receives light reflected from the whole of the remainder of the surface. The illuminance δE at P produced by an element δS of the surface at a distance d is given by

$$\delta E = \frac{L\,\delta S \cos\theta \cos\phi}{d^2}$$

obtained by combining Eq. 1.14 and 1.16, L being the luminance of the element δS. From the geometry of the sphere $\theta = \phi$ and $d = 2r\cos\theta$ so that $\delta E = L\,\delta S/4r^2$ and

$$E = \frac{1}{4r^2}\int L\,\mathrm{d}S \tag{4.4}$$

the integral being taken over the whole surface of the sphere, obstruction due to the screen being ignored. E is the illuminance at a point on the sphere due to the reflected light from the rest of the sphere and Eq. 4.4 shows that it is the same at all points on the sphere, regardless of how L varies over the surface. At any particular point on the sphere not in the shadow of the screen there is an additional illuminance E' due to the light coming directly from the source and the total illuminance E'' is therefore given by

$$E'' = E + E' \tag{4.5}$$

Now $L = \rho E''/\pi$ (Eq. 1.23), also $E' = \delta\Phi\,\delta S$ (Eq. 1.9). Hence from Eq. 4.5,

$$L = \frac{\rho}{\pi}\left(E + \frac{\delta\Phi}{\delta S}\right)$$

Substitution for L in Eq. 4.4 gives

$$E = \frac{1}{4r^2}\int\frac{\rho}{\pi}\left(E + \frac{\delta\Phi}{\delta S}\right)\mathrm{d}S$$

or, as E is constant over the surface

$$E = \frac{\rho E}{4\pi r^2}\int\mathrm{d}S + \frac{\rho}{4\pi r^2}\int\mathrm{d}\Phi$$

Now $\int\mathrm{d}S = S = 4\pi r^2$, the area of the sphere; also $\int\mathrm{d}\Phi = \Phi$, the total flux emitted by the source; therefore

$$E = \rho E + \frac{\rho\Phi}{S} = \frac{\rho\Phi}{(1-\rho)S} \tag{4.6}$$

which is the greater than the mean illuminance due to direct light from the source, Φ/S, if $\rho > 0.5$. Measurement of E, the illuminance of the surface shadowed by the screen, therefore enables Φ to be found if ρ and S are known, subject to errors due to obstruction of some light by the screen and the source itself. Illuminance E may be measured by a

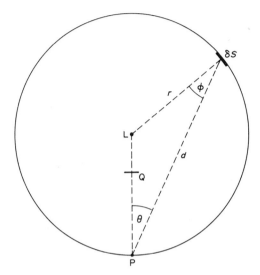

Fig. 4.3a The integrating sphere

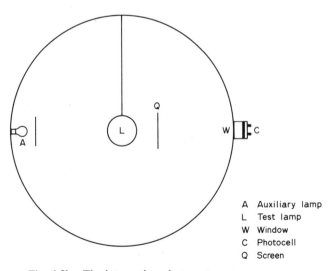

A Auxiliary lamp
L Test lamp
W Window
C Photocell
Q Screen

Fig. 4.3b The integrating photometer

cosine-corrected photocell placed at P and facing towards the centre of the sphere. Alternatively the luminance of the shadowed part of the sphere, equal to $\rho E/\pi$, may be measured by a photocell arranged to view only this shadowed area; this can be done from the outside by having a small uniformly diffusing opal glass window at P. For routine photometry the latter method is normally used, the integrating sphere providing comparisons of the total light flux from two different sources, one of which is taken as a standard of known lumen output. In this case the value of ρ does not need to be known, but if the sources have different spectral distributions it is essential that ρ should be the same at all wavelengths otherwise the light flux comparisons will not be correct; also the window diffuser needs to be non-selective. Regarding practical details, the screen should be as small as possible and be positioned one-third of the distance from the lamp to the window. All the internal surface and fittings should be painted with a special paint, though the requirements for this paint conflict in that the reduction of errors due to the effect of the screen demands a high reflectance whereas the reduction of absorption errors requires a low value. A compromise is achieved by using a paint of about 85% reflectivity. Suitable non-selective paint recipes are given in BS 354:1961, a barium sulphate suspension in a sodium carboxymethyl cellulose binder being recommended.

A lamp within an integrator will absorb a proportion of its own luminous flux. If the lamps to be measured are of similar type and size the self-absorption will be constant and can be neglected. If they differ it is necessary to determine the ratio of self-absorption. This is done by placing an auxiliary lamp A near the internal wall of the integrator together with a shield to prevent light falling on the window or on the test or standard lamp L (Fig. 4.3b). A reading is taken with the auxiliary lamp after which the standard lamp is placed in its normal position in the centre of the integrator but unlit and a second reading is taken. Let the ratio of these readings be R_s. This procedure is repeated with the test lamp substituted for the standard giving a ratio R_t. The ratio R_s/R_t is then used to correct the reading taken in the normal way.

A similar procedure can also be used to measure the light output ratio of a luminaire (Sect. 5.1), in which case readings are taken of the lamp or lamps and repeated with the lamp in the luminaire. The light output ratio is given by the readings corrected by the self-absorption ratio determined as above for the bare lamp and luminaire.

The photocell mounted behind the integrator window may have a $V(\lambda)$ response. It is useful to include an iris diaphragm or series of stops to control the amount of flux falling on the photocell, particularly when lamps of widely differing luminous flux are to be measured. It is necessary that the photocell be so positioned that it is fully illuminated under all conditions. Another useful feature of an iris diaphragm is that the measuring instrument can be made to give a direct reading of luminous flux without the need for factors.

The integrator should be as large as possible commensurate with acceptable sensitivity and convenience of handling. Its dimensions should be at least six times the overall length of the lamp. This requirement offers problems in the case of long fluorescent lamps where the desirable size becomes impracticable. Smaller integrators can be used successfully providing direct substitution is employed with a sub-standard lamp identical in all respects (except flux) to the lamps being measured; even so the major dimension of the integrator must not be less than $1\frac{1}{2}$ times the length of the lamp. An alternative method to that of direct substitution is to have the standard and test lamps simultaneously in the integrator and to take measurements of each in turn.

Although the ideal integrator shape is spherical it is possible to use other forms, such as cubes, rectangular boxes, or other symmetrical shapes, when the standard and test lamps are geometrically similar and have similar polar distributions.

Lamps should be mounted in the centre of the integrator and in the case of long lamps and luminaires the greatest dimension should be at right angles to the line passing through the centre of the integrator and the window. Adequate time must be allowed for the lamp to stabilize before measurements are taken. Special precautions are necessary when measuring fluorescent lamps because of their temperature dependence. The temperature should be held constant during test, preferably at 25 °C, and means for measuring this are required in the integrator.

Most lamp factories have facilities for measurement of their product. The accuracy of such measurements can be less than that of the standards laboratories, more attention being paid to speed of operation; for example, fluorescent lamps mounted on an endless belt may be fed successively into the integrator, and the measured data suitably recorded.

4.2.3   Intensity distribution measurements

The chief requirement for luminaires and directional light sources is knowledge of the distribution of luminous intensity with angular position. This is measured by a goniophotometer, or 'distribution photometer'. A simple instrument consists of a photocell mounted at the end of an arm or on a curved track, which is capable of being rotated about a luminaire to give a measurement of intensity at known angles. The luminaire is firmly attached to a rotatable platform enabling readings at any angle of azimuth to be taken. The length of the optical path from the fitting to the photocell should be at least five times the greatest dimension of the luminaire to be tested. Another requirement is that the luminaire should operate in its designed position. This is important because departures from this location will result in changes in light output, especially with fluorescent tubes where temperature changes may occur.

In order to reduce the size of the instrument it is possible to lengthen the optical path by using mirrors. The goniophotometer, shown diagrammatically in Fig. 4.4, should be situated in a dark room and great care taken to ensure that no stray light enters the photocell. Measurements are taken by reading the photocurrent for the required angles. These readings will give the relative luminous intensity and in order to calibrate them, the luminous flux is measured, as described above. An alternative method is to make a direct comparison with the distribution of a bare lamp. The calculations are described in Chap. 5. Such measurements are very lengthy and it is possible to make dramatic savings in time and attain increased accuracy by automation. Fig. 4.5 shows an example of a goniophotometer in which the optical path is 7·3 m, folded back by a mirror to reduce the arm length to half this value. The luminaire is tightly bolted to an arm which can be lowered for ease of mounting, as in the illustration. The light centre is set to the axis of rotation of the mirror by measuring its distance down the support bar and transferring this to an indicator on the gantry which when raised will stop at the desired position. The mirror arm and luminaire are rotated by motors and angular position is indicated by servo mechanisms. The photocurrent is recorded on punched tape by way of an amplifier, digital voltmeter and serialiser; a suitably programmed computer will read and process the tape and provide the information required.

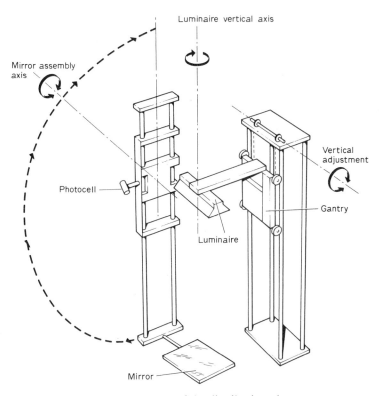

Luminaire vertical axis

Mirror assembly
axis

Vertical
adjustment

Photocell

Gantry

Luminaire

Mirror

Fig. 4.4   The structure of the distribution photometer

Luminaires emitting a concentrating beam such as spotlights and auto headlights must be tested at a greater distance than non-concentrating luminaires. Such luminaires usually have a parabolic reflector to control the light, a point source placed at the focus producing a parallel beam. In practice the finite size of the source will cause the beam to spread as shown in Fig. 20.4a, where the inner rays of the reflected cones of light cross over the axis. The point at which the rays from the edge of the reflector intersect the axis is called the cross-over point. If the reflector is viewed beyond this point it will appear fully 'flashed' except in areas where there are inaccuracies in the contour. The inverse square law only applies, even to a reasonable degree of approximation, beyond this point which therefore determines the shortest test distance. An optical path of 30 m is usually sufficient for floodlight projectors, but for auto headlamps an international agreement specifies 25 m. Measurements are carried out in a dark room with the luminaire mounted on a goniometer which allows precise adjustment of angle in both elevation and azimuth. In order to obtain the necessary path length it is sometimes convenient to locate the detector at the end of a light-tight tunnel which can pass through adjoining rooms. Where the size of dark room permits, it is useful to project the beam on to a screen which is painted black and on which is marked a grid so dimensioned that the lines subtend a known angle from the source to be measured. A small photocell

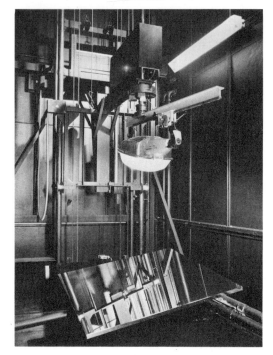

Fig. 4.5   A distribution photometer

mounted on a rod is used to measure the intensity or illuminance at known angles or in specific areas, and to trace points of equal intensity. Closed circuit television techniques may be used to automate this measurement, using a portable camera and video tape recorder to record an image of the illuminated screen.

Photometric test procedures for most types of luminaire are described in BS 3820:1964. BS 1788:1964 should be consulted for street lighting applications. Automobile headlamps may be required to meet national or international specifications.

4.3   COLORIMETRY AND RADIOMETRY

4.3.1   Colorimetry

Colour appearance, or *hue*, is generally stated in the chromaticity co-ordinates of the CIE system (Sect. 3.2.5). Before discussing the techniques of measuring these values it is necessary to consider the case of non-luminous surfaces whose colour depends on the illuminant. This statement is easily checked by observing, say, a piece of coloured material illuminated first by natural daylight then under a tungsten filament lamp. A more dramatic comparison can be made under low pressure sodium light where only the yellow hue is seen because the radiation is virtually monochromatic in this region of the spectrum. It is therefore important to specify the spectral composition of the illuminant to obtain reproducible results. There are several such sources, known as Standard Illuminants, or standard sources for colorimetry, and in 1931 the CIE specified three, Illuminants A, B and C (Sect. 3.2.7). These were intended to give incandescent filament, direct sunlight and average daylight distributions respectively, and were derived from a tungsten filament lamp at 2848 K, now 2856 K (Illuminant A) (Sect. 4.1.2). The required spectral distribution for Illuminants B and C was obtained subtractively from Illuminant A by means of liquid filters. In 1963 the CIE defined by spectral power distribution a further series of illuminants representing phases of daylight with correlated colour temperatures ranging from 4000 K to 25 000 K, known as the D series, a subscript defining the temperature. The one used most is D_{65} and it is hoped that it may replace Illuminant C (Fig. 3.9). At present it can be used only in calculations, not as a real source.

The most accurate method of colorimetry is to measure the spectral power distribution and from this calculate the chromaticity by multiplying the power at each wavelength interval by each of the three spectral tristimulus values, $\bar{x}$, $\bar{y}$ and $\bar{z}$, at the same interval and adding the products to obtain the tristimulus values X, Y and Z, equal to $\Sigma S(\lambda)\bar{x}(\lambda)\Delta\lambda$ etc., from which the chromaticity co-ordinates x, y and z are calculated (Sect. 3.2.5).

To obtain the UCS chromaticity co-ordinates, u, v, w, the transforms given in Eq. 3.8 are used. It is customary to take the wavelength interval at 5 nm or 10 nm. The calculation is lengthy and tedious but a computer programme is commonly used to derive the chromaticity as well as the spectral data.

Photo-electric tristimulus colorimeters provide a direct means of measuring colour. These instruments employ optical filter-photocell combinations having a close approximation to that of the spectral tristimulus functions. The photo-current for each is proportional to the tristimulus values X, Y, Z from which the chromaticity co-ordinates follow. For the highest accuracy the instrument should be calibrated with lamps of known chromaticity co-ordinates similar to the test lamp.

There are several photoelectric colorimeters available ranging from simple inexpensive instruments to those of considerable complexity at a much higher cost. One of the former type is the Harrison colorimeter. This incorporates two light sources; a 6 W fluorescent lamp having a spectral distribution similar to Illuminant D_{65}, and a fluorescent lamp with a filter transmitting power only in the ultra-violet region between 330 nm and 390 nm. The latter source is used for colour measurement of fluorescent materials. The filters are contained in a wheel which brings the required filter in position between the light diffused by the sample and the photocell. The instrument is calibrated against a white surface by reading the photocurrents for each filter. These readings are repeated with the test surface and the tristimulus values calculated by multiplying the known tristimulus values of the standard by the ratio of photocurrents. A measure of fluorescence is obtained with the aid of two filters, also mounted in the wheel. One filter transmits only ultra-violet radiation, the other only visible radiation. By measuring the photocurrents for each filter with the fluorescent sample in position it is possible to determine the effect of fluorescent dyes.

Two more complex instruments are the Colorcord (UK) and the Colormaster (USA). The Colorcord uses an integrating sphere to diffuse the light reflected from the sample with provision for measuring the specular component separately. The filters incorporate a mosaic of different coloured gelatines computed to give the best characteristics for a given photocell. The Colormaster splits the beam after passing through the chosen filter. One beam falls on a reference panel and the other on the sample. Two photocells are used differentially connected by means of a bridge circuit, and balance is obtained by adjusting the light gate which controls the intensity of the reference beam. The gate setting is shown on a counter. These instruments are essentially designed for the measurement of surface colours because the illumination of the sample is by a standard source of known spectral power distribution.

When light sources have to be measured the optics must be designed in such a way that direct viewing of the source is possible. The mask and dispersion type of colorimeter is a suitable instrument, capable of high accuracy. It has a lens and prism or grating system to disperse light incident on the slit into a spectrum, in the plane of which are masks cut to profiles which combine the shape of the distribution coefficients and the spectral response of the photocell which measures the integral light transmitted through the masks. The 'Physical Eye' instrument developed by G. T. Winch uses this technique, as does a colorimeter designed and used by the NPL.

Another type of colorimeter used for light sources was designed by H. A. S. Philippart (BBC Engineering Monograph No. 65, 1966). It is a tristimulus spot instrument of very high sensitivity used for colour television measurements, but also applicable to surface colours and light sources, the latter being measured by light reflected from a neutral surface. A spot is selected from the field of view and measured by the usual combination of alternative filters, a diffuser and an adjustable stop, a photomultiplier, amplifier and microammeter.

The perfect diffuser.   Mention has been made of the need for white diffusing surfaces both for calibration and measurement purposes. Ideally this should be perfect and reproducible but unfortunately these requirements are unrealizable. For many years the 'perfect diffuser' was prepared by burning clean magnesium ribbon and condensing the smoke on a surface, usually silver-plated brass or aluminium, but a perfect surface is difficult to produce, is very fragile and changes with exposure to air, and its reflectance is somewhat below 100% throughout the visible spectrum. The CIE recently defined the perfect diffuser on a theoretical basis stating that measurements should be related to a perfectly reflecting, perfectly diffusing surface. National laboratories are therefore engaged in the preparation of sub-standard surfaces for practical use, with correction factors to the perfect diffuser to enable measurements to be made on an absolute basis. The practical form of white surface can be smoked magnesium oxide, or pressed discs of the material with somewhat lower reflectivity but longer life and reproducibility. Specially prepared $BaSO_4$ is also an adequate standard of somewhat lower reflectance. For surface colour standards a set of ceramic tiles prepared by the British Ceramic Research Association is available from the NPL. There are 12 tiles covering a range of colours with 3 grey tiles for linearity checks. The calibrations of x, y and Y provided are related to the perfect diffuser and Standard Illuminant C.

4.3.2   Radiometry

This measurement is fundamental to the study of light sources because analysis of spectral power data can provide photometric and colorimetric quantities as well as information on the colour rendering properties of a lamp. The basic instrument required is a monochromator whose function is to separate the homogeneous radiation from a source into a spectrum, with provision for isolating discrete bands of known width. This is achieved by an adjustable entrance slit, a collimating mirror or lens, a dispersing device which may be either an optical prism or diffraction grating capable of angular adjustment, and an adjustable exit slit.

With prisms the dispersive power is a function of wavelength, resulting in non-linearity with greater dispersion the lower the wavelength; for a constant exit slit width the bandwidth will change through the spectrum. However only one spectrum is formed and the stray light can be lower than with a diffraction grating, which has a linear dispersion with wavelength, and is capable of better resolution than a prism. The main disadvantage of the grating is that several spectral orders are produced and optical filtering is necessary to remove unwanted ones. For example a discharge lamp spectrum extends from about 300 nm to the infra-red so that the second order will be added to visible radiation at 600 nm and longer wavelengths. A filter transmitting from 400 nm and upwards will remove the unwanted order from 800 nm onwards and enable measurements to be made in the visible region. This filter is inserted between the source and entrance slit at the same wavelength for both standardizing and test sources.

A property of the monochromator is to disperse on to the plane of the exit slit a series of monochromatic images of the entrance slit. If the entrance and exit slits are adjusted to pass a 5 nm band and centred on a wavelength λ nm, the image in the plane of the exit slit will extend from $(\lambda - 2 \cdot 5)$ nm to $(\lambda + 2 \cdot 5)$ nm. As the dispersing element is rotated this image moves past the exit slit, giving rise in an ideal instrument to a triangular slit function (ABC, Fig. 4.6). Similarly a wavelength of $(\lambda + \varDelta\lambda)$ will produce an image from

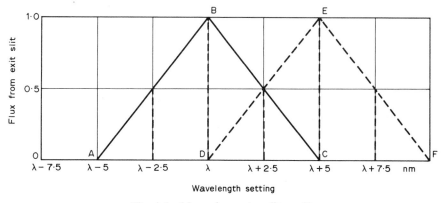

Fig. 4.6 Monochromator slit profile

$(\lambda + \varDelta\lambda - 2 \cdot 5)$ nm to $(\lambda + \varDelta\lambda + 2 \cdot 5)$ nm and placed at a distance $\varDelta\lambda$ from λ. If $\varDelta\lambda \geqslant 5$ nm the images may be resolved but if $\varDelta\lambda < 5$ nm they will overlap. Obviously if the spectrum is a continuum this overlapping is inevitable and the measurement does not accurately give power in the band $(\lambda - 2 \cdot 5)$ nm to $(\lambda + 2 \cdot 5)$ nm. In fact when the slit is centred at λ nm the detector measures only half the radiation at $(\lambda - 2 \cdot 5)$ nm and $(\lambda + 2 \cdot 5)$ nm and nothing at $(\lambda - 5)$ nm or $(\lambda + 5)$ nm. Hence only part of the total radiation in the band is

85

measured, but also some radiation over twice the bandwidth. If the slit is now centred on $(\lambda + 5)$ nm the profile is DEF and the proportion of radiation not measured with the slit at λ is included in the measurement at $(\lambda + 5)$ nm. Measurements must therefore be taken at intervals equal to the slit range if the total power is to be measured. Intervals smaller or larger than the range will result in some radiation either being measured twice or missed. The width of the slit determines the spectral resolution, but reducing the slit width reduces the amount of power and increases the number of measurements. A reasonable compromise is 5 nm (as in Fig. 15.3) or 10 nm. In practice the theoretical profile is not achieved due to diffraction at the slits, grating imperfections, etc., and these cause a rounding-off in the apex of the triangle and long tails at the feet. It is possible but complicated to correct for these deviations and they are usually ignored, the errors being included in the tolerance.

The combination of slits, optics and dispersing element is known as the mount and there are several in use such as Ebert-Fastie, Czerny-Turner, and Littrow. A major problem is that of stray light due to unwanted reflections within the instrument. This problem can be completely overcome by a double monochromator, which consists of two similar single monochromators so connected that the exit slit of the first is common with the entrance of the second. Instruments of this type are so arranged that both dispersing elements rotate together at precisely the same wavelength. Their drawback is the small amount of power transmitted compared with single dispersion instruments.

To ensure accurate and repeatable results it is necessary to irradiate the optical system and photocathode fully. For measurements in the near ultra-violet and visible region a magnesium oxide coated plate can be used as a secondary source, so mounted that the entrance slit is uniformly irradiated.

Calibration is carried out by measuring a lamp of known spectral distribution, usually a tungsten filament lamp, under the same conditions as the test lamp. For each point of measurement in the desired spectrum the ratio of the measured currents from the detector, due to the test lamp and the calibrating source respectively, multiplied by the known relative spectral power distribution factor for the calibrating source, gives a relative spectral power distribution term for the test lamp. The results may conveniently be plotted as a relative spectral power distribution curve for the lamp (Fig. 12.8).

In cases where the source emits a continuum with or without the addition of spectral lines it is possible to reduce the number of readings by taking measurements at wider intervals than the slit width, for example every 10 nm for a 3 nm slit width. Line contributions are omitted and the gaps filled by interpolation. Readings are then taken at each line wavelength and this value obviously includes the continuum contribution. To obtain line power, the interpolated value is subtracted from the total readings. Where the dispersing element is a prism it is necessary to correct the line readings for the bandwidth, as this will vary with wavelength. This method is of especial use for fluorescent lamps where it is customary to show the lines separated from the continuum.

For lamps having a large number of spectral lines such as metal halide and xenon a full exploration must be made preferably with a fairly small slit width.

When absolute values of power for each measured band are required, the further calculation is normally based on the luminous flux of the lamp and provides the radiated power in watts. It is assumed that the spectral measurements cover the whole spectrum without overlap, as discussed above, or that the values of $S(\lambda)$ are taken from a smoothed curve if fewer measurements are made with a narrower slit.

In order to obtain the factor F by which the relative values are multiplied to give absolute values it is necessary to solve the equation

$$F \sum S(\lambda)V(\lambda) = \frac{\Phi}{K_m} \qquad (4.7)$$

where $S(\lambda)$ = relative power
$V(\lambda)$ = the spectral luminous efficiency function
Φ = luminous flux in lm
K_m = the theoretical maximum conversion efficacy of electrical power into light (680 lm/W)

Summation is made over the whole visible spectrum.

The labour involved in these calculations can be considerably lessened by some degree of automation of the spectroradiometer. It is possible to correct the instrument response with respect to wavelength and to have the output punched on paper tape. A computer can then be used to process the data and provide it in the required format.

4.3.3 Measurement of CIE colour rendering index

The only measurement required is that of the spectral power distribution of the test lamp, all other data being provided in tables. Computations then determine u, v values, chromaticity shifts and index values for single samples (R_i) or a specified group (R_a): the use of a computer is almost indispensable.

5 Lighting data and computations

The principles of measurement of light and the units employed have been discussed in Chap. 1. In real installations, when large luminaires are enclosed in rooms with many partially-reflecting surfaces, complex calculations are required to determine illuminance and luminance, but these calculations are all based on the basic inverse square and cosine laws with the units already described.

The purpose of luminaires is to distribute light into an environment. Both the characteristics of the luminaire and the properties of the lighted space must be used in calculations to determine the distribution of the light in the space, but these two contributions to the final result can be separated. In this chapter the different methods of describing the distribution of luminous intensity from a luminaire are first considered, with the necessary further step of determining the relationship of this distribution to the luminous flux. Computational methods are introduced for determining direct illuminances produced by linear luminaires and large diffusing sources. The final distribution of light in the space depends on the direct flux from the luminaire, the reflected light from the surfaces enclosing the space, and the complex inter-reflections or flux transfer between the surfaces. This last process is analyzed and the necessary calculations explained.

5.1 DATA PRESENTATION

The form in which information is conveyed should depend on the use to which the information is to be put. Some information about luminaires can be expressed in the form of a single number; for example, the total luminous flux emitted, or the *light output ratio* of the luminaire which is the ratio of its light output to that of the lamps contained in it if measured outside the luminaire. Other data may be more complex, for example, the distribution of radiant flux as a function of wavelength. One obvious way of presenting an intensity distribution is by a table specifying the intensity for every 10° in azimuth and every 10° in elevation. Such a table does not have the immediate impact that a diagrammatic representation can have, although the latter may be less precise when examined in detail.

5.1.1 Distribution of luminous intensity

This must be considered the primary photometric specification for a luminaire. Since it is variable in three dimensions, it is necessary to select aspects of the distribution from which the whole can be assessed.

Polar curves. Many luminaires, particularly with small incandescent sources, have an axis of symmetry: this implies that the intensity distribution in any plane containing that axis is the same. One polar curve, a polar co-ordinate graph showing the luminous intensity in any axial plane as a function of angle, is adequate to describe the intensity distribution for such a luminaire. Polar curves for two axially-symmetrical luminaires are shown in Fig. 5.1: luminaire A emits all its light downwards in a cone subtending about 70°, whereas luminaire B emits much of its light in near horizontal directions.

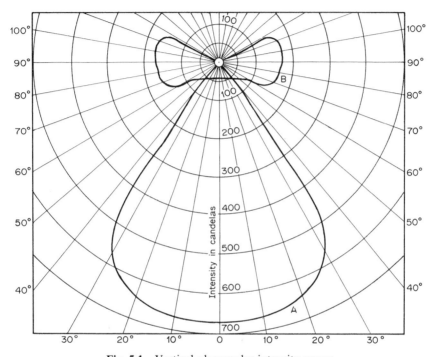

Fig. 5.1 Vertical plane polar intensity curves

It would appear from the curves that luminaire A emits more luminous flux than does luminaire B, but this is not the case. Luminaire A has certainly a higher maximum intensity, but the solid angle subtended by the beam is very much less than the solid angle subtended by the horizontal beam of luminaire B. This misleading impression is one disadvantage of the polar curve method of presenting an intensity distribution: a second disadvantage is the lack of precision when the intensity is changing very rapidly with angle, at 35° in luminaire A for example.

Despite these disadvantages the polar curve is the most common method of presenting intensity distributions for general lighting luminaires. For luminaires with concentrating beams, such as spotlights emitting all their luminous flux within a few degrees of solid angle, cartesian ordinates are preferred because of the need for more precision than a polar curve allows.

Interior luminaires for fluorescent lamps do not have an axially-symmetrical intensity distribution, but there is not the dramatic difference in the shape of the distribution for different vertical planes found in street lighting and floodlighting luminaires.

It is common practice to produce for fluorescent luminaires polar curves in the vertical plane containing the axis of the luminaire and the vertical plane at right angles to this, known as axial and transverse polar curves respectively.

BZ Classification.   General classification systems for luminaires have been in use for many years, using such terms as direct, semi-direct, semi-indirect and indirect to indicate the way that light reaches a horizontal working plane of a room from an array of luminaires mounted above: all the light from a luminaire classified as indirect reaches the working plane by way of the walls and ceiling.

The object of such classifications has been to simplify the determination of the *utilization factor* of a luminaire, which specifies the fraction of the flux from the lamps in the luminaire which eventually reaches the working plane (Sect. 22.2.1).

A more sophisticated system, known as the British Zonal (BZ) Classification, is described in IES Technical Report No. 2 (1961, revised 1971). Ten standard distributions (Fig. 5.2), known as BZ 1 to 10, have been selected; calculations have been made and

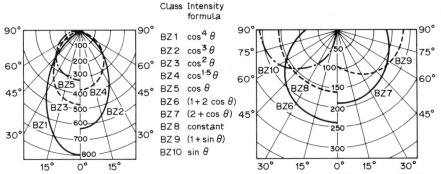

Fig. 5.2   British Zonal classification of luminaires, showing theoretical intensity distributions used

graphs drawn to show what fraction of the downward flux from a symmetrical array of luminaires of any given light distribution reaches a working plane directly (*the direct ratio*) as a function of room size and shape, assuming the luminaire spacing produces a reasonably uniform working plane illuminance. In order to classify a practical luminaire, similar calculations are carried out for this, and the resultant direct ratio graph is compared with those of the ten standard luminaires: the practical luminaire is then classified by the BZ number of the standard luminaire with the nearest direct ratio graph. An easier method of classification would be to compare polar curves, but as the classification is concerned with the utilization of emitted flux, polar curve comparisons can be erroneous.

The BZ classification is also used when the glare index of a lighting system is to be determined from tables (Sect. 22.2.2).

Isocandela diagram.   For luminaires which have no symmetry in their intensity distribution, the usual method of representing tables of intensity values is a diagram like that in Fig. 5.3, which shows the complete distribution of the luminaire in one hemisphere. A spherical surface surrounding the luminaire is plotted on a plane, as in maps of the

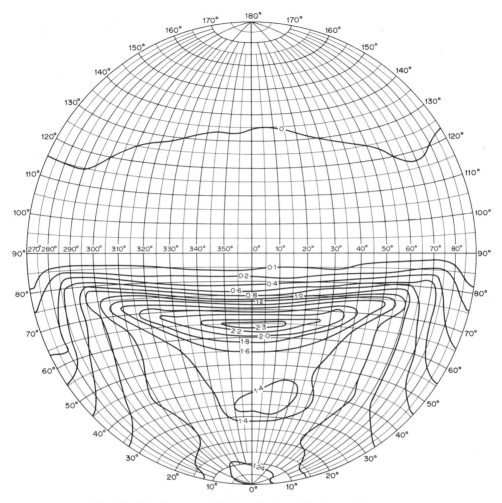

Fig. 5.3   Equal-area zenithal projection with isocandela contours

world, and lines are drawn joining points of equal luminous intensity (isocandela contours), akin to height contours on a map. Although it is not essential, it is useful to use a form of projection such that equal areas on the sphere surrounding the luminaire are represented by equal areas on the projection, a characteristic of most mapping projections currently used. A sinusoidal equal-area projection (Sanson's net) was formerly used for isocandela diagrams but the equal-area zenithal projection shown in Fig. 5.3 is now preferred, particularly for street lighting applications, because on this projection the edges of a straight road appear as straight lines instead of curves. Degrees along the equator of the diagram give azimuths from the road axis, while degrees round the circumference give angles measured from the downward vertical. Isocandela diagrams do not produce the misleading impression regarding flux given by polar curves. They have the disadvantage that they do not lend themselves to accurate interpolation between the contours.

5.1.2 Distribution of illuminance and luminance

It is not uncommon for photometric data for display and exterior floodlighting luminaires to be presented in the form of the illuminance distribution which will be provided on a specified plane some distance away from the luminaire. This may be in the form of a grid with specified illuminance values at the intersections or it may be in the form of illuminance contours: when illuminance contours are provided they are deduced by interpolation from an illuminance grid. Conversion factors may be supplied to indicate illuminance values on other planes parallel to the one specified.

It is an obvious step to extend this idea to provide luminance distributions for illuminated surfaces, always provided that the reflection characteristics of the surface are known. This extension is of particular interest in the case of street lighting, where CIE recommendations include values for average luminance and luminance uniformity (Sect. 32.4). The luminance of a surface which has a component of specular reflectance depends on the angle of view as well as on the geometry of the incident light. There is no problem in determining the luminance distribution with computers to hand, but the data even from a specific viewpoint are of questionable value unless both the specular and the diffuse reflectances of the surface are known with precision and are stable: in the case of street lighting this proviso is highly questionable owing to the continuous changes caused by wear and weather to the road surface. The luminance distribution of a surface such as a roadway, viewed at a large angle from the normal, is more appropriately presented on a perspective diagram of the surface than on a plan. Also, if an average value of luminance is required for the illuminated area, this is more reasonably determined by weighting the contribution from different areas as they appear in perspective.

5.2 RELATIONSHIPS OF LUMINOUS FLUX TO LUMINOUS INTENSITY

5.2.1 Zonal flux

The flux emitted by a luminaire within a given zone is equal to the average intensity in the zone multiplied by the solid angle the zone subtends at the luminaire. The term *zone factor* or zonal constant is used for the ratio of flux to intensity in a zone: it is in fact identical with the solid angle of the zone in steradians.

The solid angle subtended by a zone with boundaries at θ_1 and θ_2 from the downward vertical can be determined by integration: it is the area on a sphere divided by the square of the radius, r. Thus for an elementary zone at θ from the downward vertical, subtending a plane angle $\delta\theta$ (Fig. 5.4), the solid angle is

$$\delta\Omega = \frac{2\pi r \sin\theta . r\, \delta\theta}{r^2} = 2\pi \sin\theta\, \delta\theta \qquad (5.1)$$

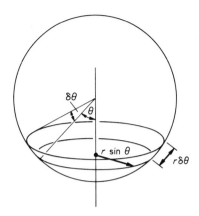

Fig. 5.4 Calculation of flux by zones on a sphere

For a zone extending from θ_1 to θ_2

$$\Omega = \int_{\theta_1}^{\theta_2} d\Omega = 2\pi(\cos\theta_1 - \cos\theta_2) \tag{5.2}$$

Values of zone factors for various sizes of zone are given in Table 5.1. The total for a hemisphere is 2π.

Of particular interest is the current CIE proposal to use as a significant specification for interior luminaires the flux in five zones, four of them making up the lower hemisphere having a solid angle of $\pi/2$ each, the fifth being the upper hemisphere. Eq. 5.2 shows

Table 5.1 Values of zone factors for 1°, 2°, 5° and 10° zones

1 Degree Zones		2 Degree Zones		5 Degree Zones			10 Degree Zones		
Zone limits (°)	Zone factor	Zone limits (°)	Zone factor	Zone limits (°)		Zone factor	Zone limits (°)		Zone factor
0–1	0·0009	0–2	0·0038	0–5	175–180	0·0239	0–10	170–180	0·095
1–2	0·0029	2–4	0·0115	5–10	170–175	0·0715	10–20	160–170	0·283
2–3	0·0048	4–6	0·0191	10–15	165–170	0·1186	20–30	150–160	0·463
3–4	0·0067	6–8	0·0267	15–20	160–165	0·1649	30–40	140–150	0·628
4–5	0·0086	8–10	0·0343	20–25	155–160	0·2097	40–50	130–140	0·774
5–6	0·0105	10–12	0·0418	25–30	150–155	0·2531	50–60	120–130	0·897
6–7	0·0124	12–14	0·0493	30–35	145–150	0·2946	60–70	110–120	0·993
7–8	0·0143	14–16	0·0568	35–40	140–145	0·3337	70–80	100–110	1·058
8–9	0·0162	16–18	0·0641	40–45	135–140	0·3703	80–90	90–100	1·091
9–10	0·0181	18–20	0·0714	45–50	130–135	0·4041			
				50–55	125–130	0·4349			
				55–60	120–125	0·4623			
				60–65	115–120	0·4862			
				65–70	110–115	0·5064			
				70–75	105–110	0·5228			
				75–80	100–105	0·5351			
				80–85	95–100	0·5434			
				85–90	90–95	0·5476			

that the upper boundaries of the three lowest zones will be given by cos $\theta = 0.75$, 0.50, 0.25. The boundary angles are therefore $41.4°$, $60°$, $75.5°$ from the downward vertical.

Average values of intensity within zones can be estimated from an intensity distribution, whether in polar or cartesian form, or from an isocandela diagram.

For floodlighting calculations (Sect. 33.3.2) these zones are subdivided in azimuth.

5.2.2   Total flux

For axially-symmetrical luminaires, the total flux Φ can be determined by summation of zonal fluxes: for most luminaires 10° zones are used.

The *Rousseau construction* from a polar intensity curve can also be used. The polar curve PQRS shown on the left of Fig. 5.5 is enclosed by a semicircle of radius OA $=r$, and is projected to the right so that A'O'B' corresponds to AOB and the distances A'P', O'Q', XR' ... are made equal to OP, OQ, OR ... (that is, values of I_θ). A small sector

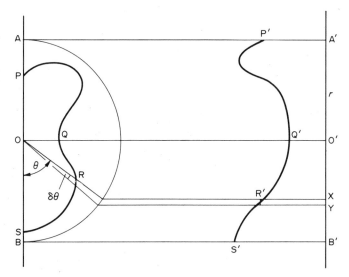

Fig. 5.5   Rousseau diagram for determining flux from polar intensity curve

OR of the polar curve subtending $\delta\theta$ at 0, when projected as shown on the Rousseau diagram gives an intercept XY on A'O'B'. The area of the element

$$R'XY = I_\theta r \sin \theta \, \delta\theta$$

and the total area of the figure P'Q'S'B'A'

$$= \int_0^\pi I_\theta r \sin \theta \, d\theta$$

But the total flux from an axially symmetrical luminaire

$$\Phi = \int I_\theta \, d\Omega$$

$$= \int_0^\pi 2\pi I_\theta \sin \theta \, d\theta \quad \text{from Eq. 5.1}$$

The area of the figure is therefore $\Phi r / 2\pi$ and its mean height

$$= \frac{\Phi r}{2\pi . \text{A}'\text{B}'}$$

$$= \frac{\Phi}{4\pi}$$

This mean height may be determined graphically by counting squares on the diagram, or by planimeter, or by dividing A′B′ into 10 or 20 equal intervals and averaging the values of I at the centre of each interval.

This last procedure is the basis of the *Russell angle* method of determining total flux: the critical values of I occur at angles given by $\sin \theta = $ odd multiples of $0 \cdot 1$ or $0 \cdot 05$. Values of Russell angles are given in Table 5.2. Polar photometers (Sect. 4.2.3) are often equipped with stops to enable the luminous intensity to be measured at Russell angles: summing these intensities enables the total flux to be determined.

Table 5.2   Russell angles for determining total luminaire flux

20 Angles (°)

18·2 31·8 41·4 49·5 56·6 63·3 69·5 75·5 81·4 87·1 92·9 98·6 104·5 110·5 116·7 123·4 130·5 138·6 148·2 161·8

10 Angles (°)

25·8 45·6 60·0 72·5 84·3 95·7 107·5 120·0 134·4 154·2

For fluorescent luminaires, the total flux is commonly determined from four vertical plane polar curves; the axial polar curve, the transverse polar curve and intermediate planes at 30° and 60°. The average intensity I_{av} in a particular zone is equal to

$$\tfrac{1}{12}(I_0 + I_{30} + I_{60} + \cdots + I_{330})$$

which by symmetry can be expressed as

$$I_{av} = \tfrac{1}{6}(I_0 + 2I_{30} + 2I_{60} + I_{90})$$

where the subscripts refer to azimuth angles. Either zone factors, the Rousseau construction, or Russell angles can be used to determine Φ.

The total flux from an asymmetric luminaire can be deduced from an isocandela diagram, provided this is on an equal-area projection, from $\Phi = 4\pi I_{av}$, where I_{av} is determined by measuring the areas between pairs of contours, multiplying each by the average intensity of the two contours, summing the result and dividing by the area of the diagram.

5.2.3   Direct flux on room surfaces

The obvious method of determining flux, by calculating illuminance values point by point for each luminaire and summing, is tedious. The BZ method provides a convenient but rough method:

(a) The ceiling flux is the product of lamp flux per luminaire, luminaire $ULOR$, and the number of luminaires.
(b) The working plane flux is the product of lamp flux per luminaire, luminaire $DLOR$. luminaire DR and the number of luminaires.
(c) The wall flux is the product of lamp flux per luminaire, luminaire $DLOR$, the factor $(1 - DR)$ and the number of luminaires.

In these expressions

$ULOR$ = upward light output ratio of luminaire, the flux emitted above the horizontal as a fraction of lamp flux.

$DLOR$ = downward light output ratio of luminaire, the flux emitted below the horizontal as a fraction of lamp flux.

DR = the direct ratio (Sect. 5.1.1)

Values of $ULOR$, $DLOR$ and DR are usually provided by luminaire manufacturers, but they can be determined from polar curves (IES Technical Report No. 2) and enable room flux values to be obtained more quickly than by point by point illuminance calculations.

5.3   ILLUMINANCE CALCULATIONS

The direct illuminance on a plane due to a small source (of maximum dimension less than five times its minimum distance from the plane) is shown by Eq. 1.12 to be $E = I \cos \theta / d^2$.

5.3.1   Linear sources

Fig. 5.6 represents a source of length l, at a vertical height h above the plane CD which is parallel to the luminaire; the normal N to the plane CD makes an angle ϕ with the plane of incident light APEB.

The illuminance at P on the plane CD due to the element δx of the source is

$$\delta E = \frac{\delta x}{l} I_{\alpha\theta} \frac{\cos \alpha \cos \phi}{(x/\sin \alpha)^2} \tag{5.3}$$

where $\cos \alpha \cos \phi$ is the cosine of the angle between N and δx at P.

Since
$$AP = \frac{h}{\cos \theta} = \frac{x}{\tan \alpha}$$

$$x = h \tan \alpha \sec \theta$$

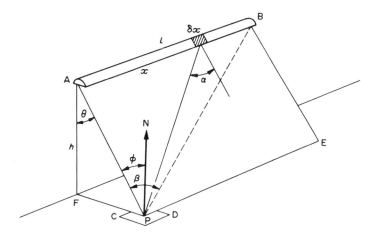

Fig. 5.6 Calculation of illuminance at a point due to a linear source

and

$$\delta x = h \sec^2 \alpha \sec \theta . \delta \alpha$$

From Eq. 5.3

$$\delta E = \frac{h \sec^2 \alpha \sec \theta . I_{\alpha\theta} \sin^2 \alpha \cos \alpha \cos \phi . \delta \alpha}{lh^2 \tan^2 \alpha \sec^2 \theta}$$

$$= \frac{I_{\alpha\theta}}{lh} \cos \theta \cos \phi \cos \alpha . \delta \alpha$$

and

$$E = \frac{I_{0\theta}}{lh} \cos \theta \cos \phi \int_0^\beta \frac{I_{\alpha\theta}}{I_{0\theta}} \cos \alpha . d\alpha \qquad (5.4)$$

where $I_{0\theta}$ is the intensity perpendicular to AB in the θ-plane.
Let

$$\int_0^\beta \frac{I_{\alpha\theta}}{I_{0\theta}} \cos \alpha . d\alpha = AF_\beta \qquad (5.5)$$

where AF_β is a function of (a) the intensity distribution in the θ axial plane and of (b) the angle β subtended by the luminaire at P in this plane.

It is found that for any practical fluorescent luminaire the shape of the intensity distribution is similar in any axial plane: thus for a given luminaire AF_β is independent of θ varying only with β. AF is known as the *parallel plane aspect factor* of the luminaire, and β as the *aspect angle*.

Different luminaires have different axial plane distributions and therefore different relationships of AF to β. A range of five theoretical distributions in functions of cos α covers the distributions found in practice, and AF versus β relationships have been calculated for each of these. The five theoretical distributions are defined in Fig. 5.7: the parallel plane aspect factors for each distribution are given as a function of aspect

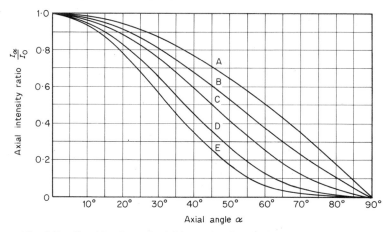

Fig. 5.7   Classification of axial intensity distributions, with I_α/I_0 equal to
(A) $\cos \alpha$ (B) $\frac{1}{2}(\cos \alpha + \cos^2 \alpha)$
(C) $\cos^2 \alpha$ (D) $\cos^3 \alpha$ (E) $\cos^4 \alpha$

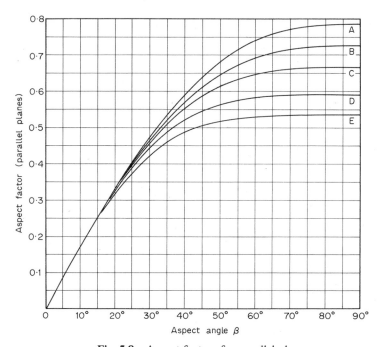

Fig. 5.8   Aspect factors for parallel planes

angle in Fig. 5.8. As an example of the calculation of these aspect factors, for the simple cosine distribution of type A, Eq. 5.5 gives

$$AF = \int_0^\beta \cos^2 \alpha \, d\alpha$$
$$= \tfrac{1}{2}(\beta + \sin \beta \cos \beta)$$

This defines curve A in Fig. 5.8.

To determine the illuminance produced at a point opposite the end of a luminaire on a plane parallel to the luminaire, (CD in Fig. 5.6), the axial plane distribution is plotted on Fig. 5.7 and compared with those given, enabling the luminaire to be classified. The aspect angle is determined and from Fig. 5.8 the value of AF is entered in the simplified version of Eq. 5.4,

$$E = \frac{I_{0\theta}}{lh} \cos \theta \cos \phi . AF \tag{5.6}$$

Should the point concerned not be opposite the end of the luminaire, the principle of superposition is applied. If it is opposite a point on the lamp then the illuminance due to the left and right parts of the luminaire are added: if it is beyond the lamp the illuminance due to a luminaire of extended length is reduced by the illuminance due to the imagined extension.

The same method is used for calculating the illuminance on a plane perpendicular to the luminaire (AFP in Fig. 5.6). The analysis followed above will apply with $\sin \alpha$ replacing $\cos \alpha \cos \phi$ in Eq. 5.3., resulting in a final expression for the illuminance at P:

$$E = \frac{I_{0\theta}}{lh} \cos \theta \int_0^\beta \frac{I_{\alpha\theta}}{I_{0\theta}} \sin \alpha . d\alpha \tag{5.7}$$

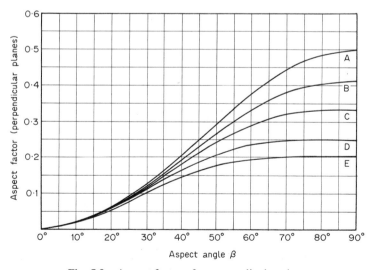

Fig. 5.9 Aspect factors for perpendicular planes

The integral expression is now the *perpendicular plane aspect factor* af_β. This is evaluated for the five standard distributions in Fig. 5.9, to be used in the equation

$$E = \frac{I_{o\theta}}{lh} \cos \theta \,.\, af \tag{5.8}$$

for determining the illuminance on a plane perpendicular to a linear luminaire.

Again, for the type A distribution,

$$af = \int_0^\beta \sin \alpha \cos \alpha \, d\alpha$$

$$= \tfrac{1}{2} \sin^2 \beta$$

This defines curve A in Fig. 5.9.

It is interesting to note that the illuminance due to a long linear source is inversely proportional to its distance from the measurement point, as opposed to the square of the distance in the case of a small source.

5.3.2 Area sources

An area source can be treated as the superposition of small sources or of linear sources, and illuminance calculations made using the inverse square law or the aspect factor method. Many practical large sources are uniform diffusers (Sect. 1.4.5) having the same luminance for all viewing directions: for such sources there are more convenient methods for calculating illuminance. The method described here is based on a formula for the illuminance due to a triangular diffuser.

Fig. 5.10a shows a horizontal triangular diffuser ABC, of luminance $L(\mathrm{cd/m^2})$. The point P lies at a distance h (m) vertically below one corner of the triangle.

The horizontal illuminance at P due to an element of length δx in the segment of length r and angular subtense δy can be deduced from the inverse square and cosine laws to be

$$\frac{Lx \, \delta y \, \delta x}{x^2 + h^2} \cdot \frac{h}{\sqrt{(x^2 + h^2)}} \cdot \frac{h}{\sqrt{(x^2 + h^2)}} \quad \text{(lux)}$$

For the whole segment

$$\delta E = \int_0^r \frac{L \, \delta y \,.\, h^2}{2} \cdot \frac{2x}{(x^2 + h^2)^2} \, dx = \tfrac{1}{2} L \, \delta y \,.\, h^2 \left(-\frac{1}{r^2 + h^2} + \frac{1}{h^2} \right)$$

$$= \tfrac{1}{2} L \frac{r^2}{r^2 + h^2} \, \delta y \tag{5.9}$$

For the whole triangle

$$E = \int_{\gamma = 0}^{\gamma = C} dE$$

In Eq. 5.9, r is related to γ from the properties of the triangle ACD by $r/\sin A = b/\sin (\gamma + B)$.

100

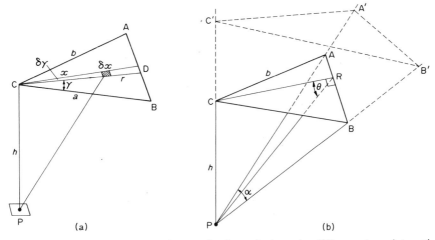

Fig. 5.10 Calculation of illuminance due to a horizontal triangular diffuser, at a point vertically below one corner

Hence

$$E = \tfrac{1}{2}L \int_0^C \frac{b^2 \sin^2 A \, \mathrm{cosec}^2 (\gamma+B)}{h^2 + b^2 \sin^2 A \, \mathrm{cosec}^2 (\gamma+B)} \, \mathrm{d}\gamma$$

$$= \tfrac{1}{2}L \, b \sin A \int_0^C \frac{b \sin A \, \mathrm{cosec}^2 (\gamma+B)}{h^2 + b^2 \sin^2 A + b^2 \sin^2 A \cot^2 (\gamma+B)} \, \mathrm{d}\gamma$$

Let

$$b \sin A \cot (\gamma+B) = x$$

then

$$\mathrm{d}x = -b \sin A \, \mathrm{cosec}^2 (\gamma+B) \, \mathrm{d}\gamma$$

and the integral is equal to

$$-\int \frac{\mathrm{d}x}{h^2 + b^2 \sin^2 A + x^2}$$

$$= -\frac{1}{\sqrt{(h^2 + b^2 \sin^2 A)}} \tan^{-1} \frac{x}{\sqrt{(h^2 + b^2 \sin^2 A)}}$$

Hence

$$E = \tfrac{1}{2}Lb \sin A \left[-\frac{1}{\sqrt{(h^2 + b^2 \sin^2 A)}} \tan^{-1} \frac{b \sin A \cot (\gamma+B)}{\sqrt{(h^2 + b^2 \sin^2 A)}} \right]_0^C$$

$$= \frac{\tfrac{1}{2}Lb \sin A}{\sqrt{(h^2 + b^2 \sin^2 A)}} \left[\tan^{-1} \frac{b \sin A \cot B}{\sqrt{(h^2 + b^2 \sin^2 A)}} - \tan^{-1} \frac{b \sin A \cot (B+C)}{\sqrt{(h^2 + b^2 \sin^2 A)}} \right] \quad (5.10)$$

In Fig. 5.10b, CR is drawn in the triangle ABC perpendicular to AB, and since ABC is in a plane perpendicular to CP,

$$b \sin A = CR$$
$$h^2 + b^2 \sin^2 A = PR^2$$
$$\cot B = BR/CR$$
$$-\cot (B+C) = \cot A = AR/CR$$

and Eq. 5.10 becomes

$$E = \tfrac{1}{2}L \frac{CR}{PR}\left[\tan^{-1}\frac{BR}{PR}+\tan^{-1}\frac{AR}{PR}\right]$$
$$= \tfrac{1}{2}L\alpha \cos \theta \quad \text{(lux)} \tag{5.11}$$

The angle α is measured in radians.

The boundaries of triangle A'B'C' in Fig. 5.10b have the same sight lines to P as the boundaries of triangle ABC. The formula given for the horizontal illuminance at P due to triangle ABC is therefore the same as that for triangle A'B'C' of the same luminance. This may not be obvious, but is proved by considering an element in ABC, which will produce an illuminance at P given by the product of its luminance, its projected area, and $\cos \phi/d^2$, where ϕ is the angle between CP and the line joining the element to P. The projected area divided by d^2 is the solid angle subtended by the element, thus $E = L\,\delta\Omega \cos \phi$, which depends only on angles, not distances. An element of luminance L in any plane with the same boundary sight lines to P will therefore give the same illuminance. Integrating the elements (Sect. 1.4.4) proves the equivalence of ABC and A'B'C': this also applies if A'B'C' is a curved surface, provided that inter-reflection (Sect. 5.4) is negligible.

Any diffuser can be considered to be the equivalent of a superposition of triangular diffusers each with an apex above the point where the illuminance is to be determined, allowing negative contributions if necessary. For example, in Fig. 5.11a, A'B'C' is equivalent, from the viewpoint of P, to the horizontal triangle ABC, which in turn is equivalent to two positive diffusers ABH and BCH and one 'negative diffuser' ACH.

Thus

$$E = \tfrac{1}{2}L(\alpha_{AB} \cos \theta_{AB}+\alpha_{BC} \cos \theta_{BC}-\alpha_{CA} \cos \theta_{CA})$$
$$= \tfrac{1}{2}L(\alpha_{A'B'} \cos \theta_{A'B'}+\alpha_{B'C'} \cos \theta_{B'C'}-\alpha_{C'A'} \cos \theta_{C'A'})$$

This means that the illuminance at P for any diffuser with corners A'B'C'D'... can be taken as that for its horizontal projection ABCD..., where the sides AB, BC, CD... subtend angles $\alpha_{AB}, \alpha_{BC}, \alpha_{CD}, \ldots$ at P, and the perpendiculars from P to AB, BC, CD... make angles $\theta_{AB}, \theta_{BC}, \theta_{CD}\ldots$ with the horizontal. The value of the illuminance is

$$E = \tfrac{1}{2}L \sum \alpha_{AB} \cos \theta_{AB} \tag{5.12}$$

Since θ may be $\gtrless 90°$, $\cos \theta$ may be positive or negative if $\cos \theta$ is defined for side AB as the angle between the top of the horizontal plane and that side of plane ABP which is not illuminated. In Fig. 5.11a, $\theta_{A'C'}$ is obtuse and $\cos \theta_{AC}$ is negative.

An example of the use of the triangular diffuser calculations is its application to the case of a circular disc. A horizontal disc of radius r (m) and luminance L (cd/m²) having its centre h (m) vertically above P can be considered as a number of elementary triangles,

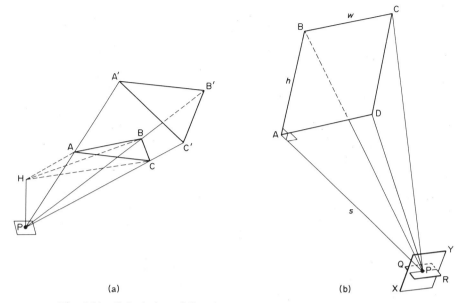

(a)   (b)

Fig. 5.11 Calculation of illuminance
(a) Due to an offset triangular diffuser
(b) Due to a rectangular diffuser, for parallel and perpendicular planes

each with $\cos\theta = r/\sqrt{(r^2 + h^2)}$, each element subtending an angle $r\,\delta\phi/\sqrt{(r^2 + h^2)}$ at P, where $\delta\phi$ is the angle of the triangle at the centre of the disc. Integrating this for $\Sigma\,\delta\phi = 2\pi$ gives the illuminance

$$E = \tfrac{1}{2}L\,\frac{2\pi r}{\sqrt{(r^2 + h^2)}}\,\frac{r}{\sqrt{(r^2 + h^2)}} = \frac{\pi r^2 L}{r^2 + h^2}\ \text{lux}$$

From this it can be deduced that a large diffusing area near to P provides an illuminance, as $h/r \to 0$, of πL lux.

Illuminances due to rectangular sources are of obvious importance in interior lighting with luminous ceilings or where walls act as secondary sources. In Fig. 5.11b, ABCD is a rectangular diffuser of luminance L and P is a point opposite corner A; that is, on the normal to ABCD at A. Formulae for the illuminance at P on the plane XY parallel to ABCD and on a plane QR normal to ABCD can be written down using $E = \Sigma\,\tfrac{1}{2}L\alpha\cos\theta$.

For the parallel plane XY, $\cos\theta_{AB}$ and $\cos\theta_{AD}$ are zero and

$$E = \tfrac{1}{2}L\left\{\left[\tan^{-1}\frac{w}{\sqrt{(h^2 + s^2)}}\right]\left[\frac{h}{\sqrt{(h^2 + s^2)}}\right] + \left[\tan^{-1}\frac{h}{\sqrt{(w^2 + s^2)}}\right]\left[\frac{w}{\sqrt{(w^2 + s^2)}}\right]\right\}$$

For the perpendicular plane QR, $\cos\theta_{AB}$ and $\cos\theta_{CD}$ are zero and

$$E = \tfrac{1}{2}L\left\{\left[\tan^{-1}\frac{w}{\sqrt{(h^2 + s^2)}}\right]\left[-\frac{s}{\sqrt{(h^2 + s^2)}}\right] + \left[\tan^{-1}\frac{w}{s}\right]\right\}$$

103

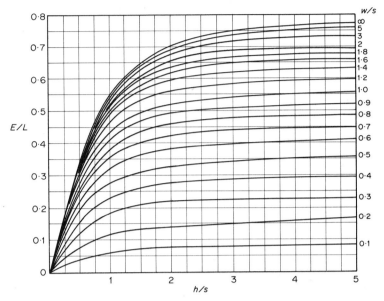

Fig. 5.12   Ratio of illuminance at a point on a plane parallel to the source to the luminance of the uniform rectangular source

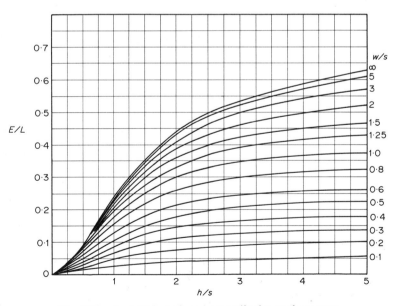

Fig. 5.13   As 5.12 but plane perpendicular to the source

In Figs. 5.12 and 5.13, E/L is shown as a function of h/s for different values of w/s, for parallel plane and perpendicular plane measurements. In each case the maximum value of E/L is $\pi/4 = 0.785$, which is a quarter of the value deduced for an infinite disc.

5.4   FLUX TRANSFER AND INTER-REFLECTION

5.4.1   Flux transfer

In an illuminated room, each surface will receive light reflected from any other surface on a line of sight, and the calculation of these effects is an important one in determining the total effect of a luminaire. The simplest theoretical case is that of a point source in an integrating sphere (Sect. 4.2.2), but a room offers a much more complicated problem.

In Fig. 5.14, suppose two uniformly diffusing surfaces A_1 and A_2 have luminances L_1 and L_2, and consider the light from an element of area δA_1 in A_1 directed towards δA_2 in A_2 at a distance d, the normals to the elements being NN. The luminous intensity of δA_1 is $L_1 \delta A_1 \cos \theta_1$ and the resulting illuminance at δA_2 is $L_1 \delta A_1 \cos \theta_1 \cos \theta_2/d^2$.

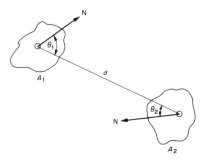

Fig. 5.14   Flux transfer between surfaces

The flux falling on δA_2 is $\delta \Phi_2 = L_1 \delta A_1 \delta A_2 \cos \theta_1 \cos \theta_2/d^2$. If M_1 is the luminous excitance of A_1 $(= \pi L_1)$ then

$$\frac{\delta \Phi_2}{M_1} = \frac{\delta A_1 \delta A_2 \cos \theta_1 \cos \theta_2}{\pi d^2}$$

If the surface A_2 has the same luminous excitance as A_1, it follows that the same expression for $\delta \Phi_1$ results for the flux received by A_1 from A_2: there is reciprocity in the flux transfer between the two surfaces if they have the same excitance.

The total flux received by A_2 from A_1 is given by

$$\frac{\Phi_2}{M_1} = \int \int \frac{\cos \theta_1 \cos \theta_2}{\pi d^2} \, dA_1 . \, dA_2 \tag{5.13}$$

The integral is known as the *mutual exchange coefficient* between the surfaces, g_{12}. It is equal to $g_{21} = \Phi_1/M_2$. In this case the order in which the surfaces are considered is immaterial.

There are two other ways of treating flux transfer in which the order of the surfaces is significant. The first uses the *flux fraction i* to specify the fraction of the flux emitted by one surface which is intercepted by the other, or Φ_2/Φ_1. Since $\Phi = MA$, the flux fraction $i_{12} = g_{21}/A_1$ and $A_1 i_{12} = A_2 i_{21}$.

The other term used specifies the ratio of illuminance of the receiving surface to the luminous excitance of the emitting surface, known as the *form factor f*. Since $E_2 = \Phi_2/A_2$, the form factor $f_{12} = g_{12}/A_2$ and $A_2 f_{12} = A_1 f_{21}$.

Hence
$$i_{12} = f_{21}$$

Mutual exchange coefficients, or the alternative quantities quoted, can be deduced from Eq. 5.13. Alternatively, use can be made of Eq. 5.12 for the illuminance due to area diffusers, and integration performed over the receiving area.

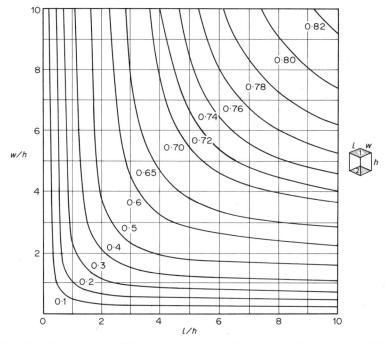

Fig. 5.15   Mutual exchange coefficient per unit area of emitting surface, for parallel surfaces

Tables and charts have been produced evaluating mutual exchange coefficients for parallel and perpendicular rectangles. Figs. 5.15 and 5.16 show the mutual exchange coefficient per unit area of emitting surface (or form factor) as a function of the geometry of the two surfaces. Mutual exchange coefficients for rectangles which are not adjacent or opposite can be deduced by positive and negative superposition as in determining illuminances due to linear and area sources.

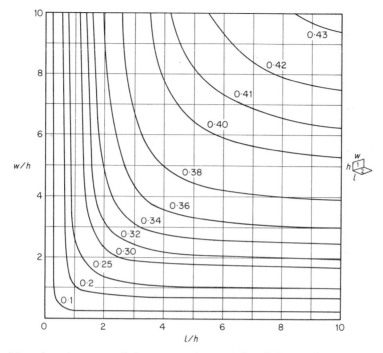

Fig. 5.16 Mutual exchange coefficient per unit area of emitting surface, for perpendicular surfaces

5.4.2 Inter-reflection

The series of flux transfers between the various surfaces of an enclosed space is known as inter-reflection. As in the integrating sphere, the process results in the luminances being greater than would have been predicted from the direct illuminances provided by a luminaire in the space, and the luminance distribution also becomes more uniform.

The final luminances $L_1, L_2, \ldots L_n$ in an enclosed space made up of n surfaces (allowing for inter-reflection) can be determined using mutual exchange coefficients, assuming that the initial luminances (due to direct light incident on the surfaces) $L_{01}, L_{02}, \ldots L_{0n}$ are known as well as the reflectances of the surfaces $\rho_1, \rho_2, \ldots \rho_n$. The initial excitances are $M_{01}, M_{02}, \ldots M_{0n}$.

The total flux leaving any surface is equal to the flux leaving it due to directly incident light plus the flux received from all the other surfaces multiplied by the reflectance of the surface.

Thus

$$M_1 A_1 = M_{01} A_1 + \rho_1 (g_{21} M_2 + g_{31} M_3 + \cdots g_{n1} M_n) \qquad (5.14)$$

$$M_2 A_2 = M_{02} A_2 + \rho_2 (g_{12} M_1 + g_{32} M_3 + \cdots g_{n2} M_n), \text{ etc.}$$

The solution of these n simultaneous equations produces the final luminous excitance values.

Strictly these equations apply only to diffusing surfaces. If one or more of the surfaces are essentially specular the method can still be used, but each specular surface has to be replaced by a mirror image of the rest of the space with initial luminances which are ρ_s times those of the real space, where ρ_s is the specular reflectance. For one specular surface there will then be $2n-1$ simultaneous equations to be solved.

The solution of many simultaneous equations presents no problem if a digital computer is to hand, but analogue computers have also been used to a limited extent. The best known electric analogue circuit for an n-surface space has n nodes interconnected through resistors of conductance g_{12}, g_{13}, g_{23}, etc. The voltages at nodes p and q will be M_p and M_q volts, the resistance joining them will be of $1/g_{pq}$ ohms and the current flow between these nodes will be $g_{pq}(M_p-M_q)$, which is the net flux transfer from surface p to surface q. The appropriate feeding network for each node has to be determined: it will be a generator of E volts with a resistance of R ohms, where E and R require calculation. Eq. 5.14 can be re-written

$$g_{12}M_2+g_{13}M_3+\cdots g_{1n}M_n = \frac{M_1A_1-M_{01}A_1}{\rho_1}$$

or

$$g_{12}(M_1-M_2)+g_{13}(M_1-M_3)+\cdots g_{1n}(M_1-M_n) =$$
$$\frac{M_{01}A_1}{\rho_1}-\frac{M_1A_1}{\rho_1}+M_1(g_{12}+g_{13}+\cdots g_{1n}) \quad (5.15)$$

But $g_{12}+g_{13}+\cdots g_{1n}$ is the total flux emitted by surface 1 when it has a luminous excitance of unity (1 lm/m²), which is equal to A_1. The right hand side of Eq. 5.15 is therefore equal to

$$\frac{A_1}{\rho_1}\left(M_{01}-M_1+\rho_1M_1\right) = \left(\frac{M_{01}}{1-\rho_1}-M_1\right)\frac{A_1(1-\rho_1)}{\rho_1}$$

when expressed in the form $(E-M_1)/R$, with $E=M_{01}/(1-\rho_1)$, and $R=(\rho_1/A_1(1-\rho_1))$;

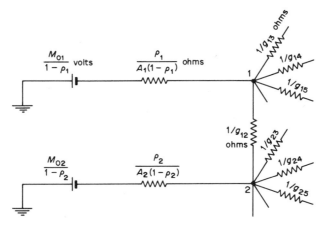

Fig. 5.17   Analogue circuit for determining luminous excitances of surfaces enclosing a space

and

$$g_{12}(M_1 - M_2) + g_{13}(M_1 - M_3) + \cdots g_{1n}(M_1 - M_n) = \left(\frac{M_{01}}{(1-\rho_1)} - M_1 \right) \frac{A_1(1-\rho_1)}{\rho_1}$$

This gives rise to the analogue circuit shown in Fig. 5.17. Final luminous excitances are determined by measuring the voltages at nodes 1, 2, 3, etc. Circuit components are usually scaled up or down by multiples of 10 from the actual values of luminous excitance and mutual exchange coefficient in order to limit power dissipation: a.c. circuits with variable transformer sources are sometimes used instead of the d.c. circuit shown.

6 Production and application of radiation

The preceding chapters have been concerned with the properties and measurement of light, while the remainder of the book deals with the production and utilization of light resulting from man-made processes, or 'artificial light'. The present chapter considers radiation more generally and the physical principles underlying its production. In the spectral range of 200 nm to 2000 nm there is a variety of applications which are not primarily for the purpose of illumination: these are discussed, as well as present uses of coherent light which is not yet applicable to conventional lighting methods. Succeeding chapters show how practical lamps have been developed from the basic principles of radiation production.

6.1 PRODUCTION OF RADIATION

6.1.1 Conversion of energy into radiation

All artificial light sources involve the conversion of some other form of energy into electromagnetic radiation. Looked at as a process in atomic physics, there are basically only two methods of doing this:

(a) the acceleration (or deceleration) of a charged particle, usually an electron;

(b) the excitation and subsequent de-excitation of atoms or molecules.

The first is the 'classical' process: it does occur in certain sources, and produces a continuous spectrum, but it is of little importance in practical lamps and will not be considered further.

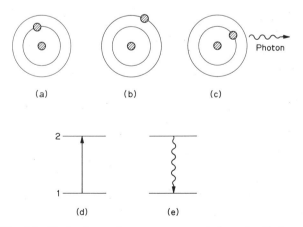

Fig. 6.1 Excitation and spontaneous emission of radiation

The second is the 'quantum' process, and by far the greatest proportion of all light is produced in this way. A very simplified representation of the process is given in Fig. 6.1a which shows an atom consisting of a nucleus with an electron in a stable orbit around it. This is 'excited' (e.g. by impact with another particle) so that the electron moves to another orbit with a higher energy, as at (b). Later the electron drops back 'spontaneously' to its original stable orbit, as at (c) and the excess energy is radiated as a photon or unit of light. This is known as the *spontaneous emission* of radiation. The frequency of the light radiated is given by *Planck's relation*:

$$Q = hv = hc/\lambda \tag{6.1}$$

where Q is the energy difference between the two states, v is the frequency, λ is the wavelength, c is the velocity of light, and h is Planck's constant ($c = 2 \cdot 998 \times 10^8$ m/s; $h = 6 \cdot 626 \times 10^{-34}$ J s). Discrete units of energy of this type are known as quanta: a photon is a quantum of light (Sect. 1.2.9).

It is customary to represent such transitions in the way shown in Fig. 6.1d which shows excitation from 'state 1' to 'state 2'; Fig. 6.1e shows the transition back to state 1, the wavy line indicating that it is a radiating transition. (Radiationless de-excitation transitions are also possible, in which the energy is removed in some other way.) The lowest stable state (1 in Fig. 6.1) is called the *ground state*.

Real atoms have many such energy levels or states, giving rise to a multiplicity of spectral lines of different frequencies, or wavelengths (Fig. 6.4). In atomic gases these may be quite sharp and distinct. In molecular gases there are so many levels that the lines merge together and form bands. In liquids and solids, the energy levels themselves are broadened and merge together, and the result is a continuous spectrum over a wide range of frequencies. Continuous spectra are also formed in other ways, for example when the atoms are ionized, and recombine with electrons, forming a 'recombination continuum'. When the atoms in a gas are compressed together, strongly heated, subjected to strong electric or magnetic fields, or otherwise disturbed, the energy levels become blurred, and the lines are broadened to a greater or lesser extent.

Let us now consider the source of energy. It may be thermal energy: heat from some external source. If this is great enough the atoms, and other particles present, collide vigorously and excite each other, so that they subsequently de-excite with the production of radiation. In the case of solids and liquids, this is the basic process of *incandescence*.

Electrical energy can only be converted into light indirectly. The electric field produced when a voltage is applied, say across the two ends of a wire, or between the electrodes of a discharge tube, is used to accelerate electrons: these collide with atoms, exciting them, ready for subsequent radiation. Usually there are many other processes occurring as well: the electrons collide and are scattered without causing excitation, the scattered atoms and electrons collide further, and so on. Frequently the collisions are so numerous that the motion of all particles becomes more or less random, with perhaps a 'drift velocity' in the direction of the field. This corresponds to heating, and we say that the motion has become thermalized. A solid or liquid body in this condition has become incandescent. If the heating is uniform, corresponding to a certain temperature T, then we say that there is *thermodynamic equilibrium*, and radiation is produced as described in the last paragraph. Sometimes the temperature varies gradually from one region to another, and we speak of *local thermodynamic equilibrium* (LTE). These are highly important concepts, which have been carefully analysed and precisely defined.

Chemical energy is converted into radiation when chemicals react together, as in the case of *combustion*, for example in a flame. Part of the radiation arises because the reaction produces heat, which in turn produces radiation as described above. In addition, however, the reaction itself often directly produces excited atoms (or other particles such as molecules or radicals), which can produce further radiation. So the radiation from a flame, for example, can exceed that to be expected from the heating of the gases alone. Another such process is chemiluminescence (Sect. 6.1.6).

Other energy sources which can produce radiation, either directly, or (more frequently) by means of heating, include radioactive materials, high energy charged particles, nuclear and thermonuclear reactions. The sun is the outstanding example of this last type. Thermonuclear reactions, in which hydrogen is converted into helium, release enormous quantities of thermal energy in the core of the sun, giving rise to the continuous spectrum: this is modified by absorption in the cooler outer layers producing, in particular, the dark Fraunhofer lines. This radiation is by far the most plentiful natural source available to us, providing our daylight (Chap. 23).

6.1.2   Incandescence

Thermal radiation.   We have seen how a body heated to a high temperature radiates as a result of its constituent particles becoming excited by numerous interactions and collisions. In general terms this process is extremely complex, and almost defies analysis. Fortunately, a great simplification can be made if the body is a perfect *black body*, that is, if it completely absorbs all radiation which falls on it when held at a uniform temperature T. An analysis of this situation shows that the power radiated at any wavelength from unit surface area of such a body is determined solely by its temperature in accordance with

$$M_{e\lambda} = \frac{c_1}{\lambda^5[\exp(c_2/\lambda T) - 1]} \tag{6.2}$$

where c_1 and c_2 are constants (if λ is in m, T in K, then $c_1 = 3 \cdot 7415 \times 10^{-16}$ W.m^2, $c_2 = 1 \cdot 4388 \times 10^{-2}$ m.K and $M_{e\lambda}$ is in W/m^3); $M_{e\lambda}$, formerly called the spectral radiant emittance, is now called the spectral radiant excitance. This is the celebrated law of Planck, the discovery of which not only revolutionized the theory of radiation, but the whole of modern science.

This relation is plotted in Fig. 6.2. Not only does the maximum power radiated increase rapidly with temperature, but the wavelength at which the maximum occurs gets shorter, corresponding to the simple observation that a heated body first glows red, then yellow and then bluish. Radiation of this form is called thermal radiation, or black body radiation. A perfect black body is also known as a *full radiator*.

Of course, no real material is perfectly black in this sense. However, if any body is held inside an enclosure at a uniform temperature T which completely surrounds it, then, whatever its nature, it will radiate thermal radiation in accordance with Planck's law. This may be observed, for example, through a small hole in the enclosure, and is therefore sometimes called cavity radiation. This is of considerable importance, for

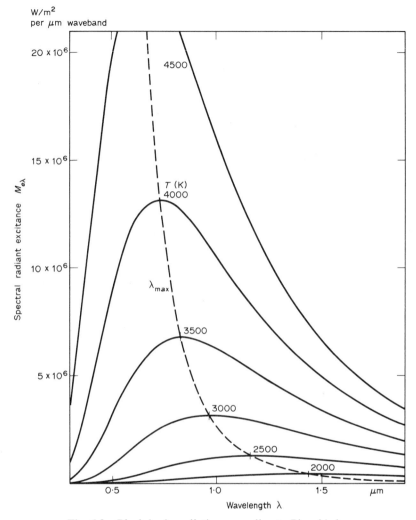

Fig. 6.2   Black body radiation according to Planck's law

example, in the determination of temperature, and certain standards of radiation such as the primary standard of light (Sect. 4.1.1). It represents of course a condition of thermodynamic equilibrium, as described in Sect. 6.1.1.

Selective radiators.   Any hot real material (e.g. wire or disc) not in such a cavity will radiate less than the thermal radiation corresponding to its temperature, and we define the *spectral emissivity* $\epsilon(\lambda)$ by

$$M_{e\lambda} = \epsilon(\lambda)M_{e\lambda}^{\text{th}}$$
(6.3)

113

where $M_{e\lambda}^{\text{th}}$ is the radiant excitance of a black body at the same temperature. Of course $\epsilon(\lambda) \leqslant 1$. An important relation is *Kirchhoff's Law* for a thermal radiator

$$\epsilon(\lambda) = \alpha(\lambda) \tag{6.4}$$

where $\alpha(\lambda)$ is the spectral absorptance for radiation incident on the same surface at the same temperature T. In other words, good radiators are good absorbers, and vice versa. Note that $\epsilon(\lambda) = \alpha(\lambda) = 1$ at all wavelengths for a full radiator, in accordance with its definition as a body which absorbs all incident radiation. If $\epsilon(\lambda)$ is less than 1 but constant for all wavelengths we speak of a *grey body*. This treatment has ignored the dependence of ϵ and α on angle, and the possibility that the radiation may be polarized. More detailed analysis yields corresponding relations for these cases also.

The emissivity $\epsilon(\lambda)$ varies greatly with the material and the wavelength. Many examples are given in Chap. 7. The carbon particles in a flame approximate quite closely to black bodies, and provide much of the light from a yellow 'sooty' flame. Tungsten has a lower emissivity in the infra-red than in the visible part of the spectrum (Fig. 7.3) so a tungsten filament lamp is a source of radiation which has a higher luminous efficiency than would otherwise be the case. The use of halogens in the envelopes of tungsten filament lamps does nothing to improve emissivity, but is merely a device to allow the use of higher filament temperatures without bulb blackening (Chap. 10). Ideally, of course, a source of visible light should have a high emissivity between 400 nm and 700 nm, and a low emissivity elsewhere, especially in the infra-red. Various attempts have been made to use other materials, such as tantalum carbide, or magnesium oxide, as lamp filaments for this reason. It is evident that a high temperature strongly favours high efficiency for the production of visible radiation (Fig. 6.2), so highly refractory materials have the greatest a priori advantage.

An example in which the opposite situation is advantageous is the Nernst filament. An extruded rod of a zirconium and yttrium oxide material is heated by an electric current to 1700 K to 2000 K to produce a source of infra-red radiation. In this case the emissivity is higher in the infra-red. Originally the filament was used as a source of visible light.

Enhanced radiation.   It was stated in the last section that the radiation from chemical sources can exceed the thermal radiation because of excitation of the constituent atoms by chemical processes. This can occur either in the body of the flame (say) or at some surface immersed in it: recombination and de-excitation occur more readily at surfaces than elsewhere, so the surface may glow more brightly than expected.

The *gas mantle* is an example: not only is the rare earth oxide mixture it is formed from an advantageous selective radiator, but additional radiation is formed by chemical interactions at the surface, and also by a slow burning away of the mantle itself. Another example is the *limelight*, in which calcium oxide is heated by a coal-gas or hydrogen flame. A more modern example is the photographer's flash bulb, in which aluminium or zirconium shreds are very rapidly burned under controlled conditions (Chap. 11). Most of the light comes from the white hot particles of oxide produced by the combustion, their thermal radiation being enhanced in this way.

6.1.3   Gas discharges

General features.   In order to understand the production of light by gas discharges, it is first necessary to consider the mechanism of electrical conduction. In a solid conductor the current is carried by the movement of free electrons through a tightly bound lattice of atoms or ions (atoms which have lost an electron and become positively charged) which, apart from thermal vibrations, are immobile. Metallic conductors contain about as many free electrons as fixed atoms or ions, hence their high electrical conductivity. The only direct effects of the passage of an electric current are the heating of the conductor and the appearance of a magnetic field around it. The emission of light occurs only if the heating is sufficient to excite the atoms and produce incandescence. In gases, by contrast, there are normally no free electrons, and conduction can only take place if the gas atoms are first ionized, to produce electrons and positive ions. In a discharge tube, across which there is an electric field, the electrons drift towards the anode and the positive ions towards the cathode, as illustrated in Fig. 6.3. The total current through the tube is thus the sum of the electron and ion currents. The ions, being larger and heavier than the electrons, move much more slowly, so the ion current is only a small fraction of the total current, usually between 0·1% and 1%.

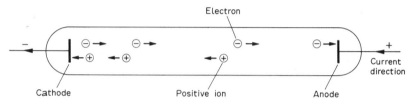

Fig. 6.3   Electric discharge through a tube of ionized gas

6.1.4   Low pressure discharges

Consider a discharge tube a few centimetres in diameter and a metre or so long, containing one or more gases at a total pressure not greater than a few Torr (1 Torr $= 133\cdot3$ N/m^2), say a hundredth of an atmosphere: a fluorescent lamp discharge is a typical example. With currents no larger than an ampere or two, there is negligible heating of the gas, and we speak of a low pressure discharge. Under these conditions, ionization is principally produced by electron impact.

Ionization by electron impact.   When a free electron collides with a neutral gas atom one of three things may happen:
(a) The electron may rebound with only a small loss in energy: an elastic collision.
(b) The atom may be excited, as illustrated in Fig. 6.1, with the electron sustaining a corresponding loss of kinetic energy.
(c) The atom may be ionized, releasing one of its own electrons completely. The incident electron again loses kinetic energy.
The relative probability of these processes depends on the energy of the colliding electron. Electron energies are usually expressed in electron volts (eV), 1 eV being the energy gained by an electron accelerated through a potential difference of one volt (1 eV $= 1\cdot602 \times 10^{-19}$ J). The ionizing energy for mercury is 10·4 eV and for argon 15·7 eV so that, in a mixture of mercury vapour and argon, mercury is preferentially ionized.

Thus in a fluorescent lamp discharge, which contains mercury and argon, most of the

115

ions are mercury ions produced by collisions of mercury atoms with the more energetic electrons in the discharge. Very few have sufficient energy to ionize or even excite argon, so most electron collisions with argon atoms are elastic collisions, which have the effect of slightly heating the gas.

Positive column and plasma.   The large uniform region of the discharge between the electrodes is called the positive column. This consists of a mixture of gas atoms, excited gas atoms, ions and electrons, all moving largely at random. The heavier particles form a gas at a temperature only slightly above the surroundings of the tube (typically 10 °C to 30 °C above, but sometimes a few hundred °C). The electrons require much more energy to cause ionization, however, and typically have energies corresponding to an *electron temperature* of 10 000 K to 20 000 K: this additional energy is derived from their acceleration by the electric field as they drift, with many collisions, in the direction of the anode.

The concept of electron temperature plays an important role in the treatment of low pressure discharges. It implies that the electrons behave substantially as a separate gas from the heavier particles, with an energy distribution corresponding to that of the atoms of a gas in thermodynamic equilibrium at a much higher temperature. This is termed the electron temperature, T_e, and implies a Maxwellian distribution of energies. At $T_e = 7737$ K the mean energy of the electrons is 1 eV, but there are a few electrons at many times this energy which produce excitation and ionization. Electrons with a non-Maxwellian distribution of energies are often represented as having an 'effective electron temperature' as an approximation, not usually very satisfactorily.

Most of the electrons are themselves the result of the ionization process, and throughout the positive column electrons and ions are present in almost exactly equal numbers. This equality is accentuated by the electrostatic attraction of the ions and electrons to each other, so that throughout the positive column there is practically no net space charge. Such a region of charge neutrality is called a *plasma*. The electron number density at any point is equal to the ion number density, and either is normally termed the *plasma density*.

As well as drifting towards the electrodes, the electrons and ions drift radially towards the wall, where they recombine to form neutral atoms. To preserve charge neutrality, they must do this in equal numbers, so the wall acquires a small negative potential (a few volts) which slows down the faster-moving electrons. This type of neutral charge drift is termed *ambipolar diffusion*, and is one of the sources of loss of energy in the discharge.

Electrical characteristics.   For the discharge to operate in a steady condition the rate of ionization must exactly balance the rate of loss of electrons and ions by ambipolar diffusion to the walls. The longitudinal electric field must therefore have such a value that the electrons acquire just enough energy (or electron temperature) to maintain this balance. The electrical conductivity of the discharge is proportional to the electron density, or plasma density, which increases with the discharge current. There is, therefore, no simple relationship between voltage and current, such as Ohm's law, and the voltage-current relationship, or electrical characteristic of the discharge is very complex, and dependent on all the constituents of the discharge and conditions of operation.

The increase in conductivity with current is normally so great that the voltage required to maintain the current falls as the current rises, and the discharge has a 'falling characteristic': the volt-ampere curve has a negative slope. Consequently most discharges are not current-limiting, and for stable operation from a constant voltage supply must include a current-limiting device such as a resistor or, for a.c. operation, an inductor, a capacitor, or some combination which minimizes power loss (Sect. 18.1.2). Voltage and current waveforms in a.c. circuits depart very substantially from the sinusoidal form, and simple r.m.s. relationships are not valid.

Electrodes and starting.   Since the electron current is much larger than the ion current, the cathode has the important function of supplying the electrons necessary to maintain the discharge; the anode is much less important, being mainly a receiver of the charged particles to complete the circuit.

Most lamps have hot cathodes which are heated either by a circulating current provided by the control gear, by the passage of the discharge current itself, or by bombardment by positive ions from the neighbouring region of the discharge called the *negative glow*. These provide electrons by thermionic emission, assisted by photoelectric emission, field emission and several other processes. Some form of electron emissive material is usually coated on the electrode, which is usually of a light construction which is easily heated (Chap. 7).

A few lamps have cold cathodes: these are larger in area and operate as 'glow discharge' cathodes. A voltage drop of 100–200 V, known as the *cathode fall*, separates the cathode from a surrounding *cathode glow*: this provides a copious supply of ions which are accelerated to the cathode to produce secondary electrons on impact which in turn produce more ions. The cathode fall in hot-cathode discharges is only about 10 V.

The electrodes play an important role in starting the discharge. On initially applying a voltage across the tube, there is practically no ionization and the gas behaves as an insulator. Once a few ions or electrons are present, a sufficiently high voltage accelerates these to provide more by electron impact ionization, and breakdown is achieved by a cumulative process or 'avalanche'. The initial electrons may be left from a previous discharge, may be provided by radioactive materials in the gas or on the tube, or from natural radioactivity, but suitable cathodes supply electrons at a very early stage in the breakdown process by field emission, photo-electric emission or thermionic emission, greatly reducing the excess voltage needed to strike the discharge. If the electrodes are pre-heated or if some arrangement such as an adjacent auxiliary electrode is provided, the voltage required is further reduced.

The control gear for the discharge has therefore not only to provide a stable limited-current supply for the steady operation of the discharge, but an excess voltage for striking and supplies for pre-heating electrodes, or auxiliary electrodes as required.

This striking voltage is often reduced by using what is known as a *Penning mixture* in place of a single inert gas. A small proportion of another gas is added which has an ionization energy slightly lower than the excitation energy of the main gas. Ions are then readily produced by electrons first exciting the major constituent which, in turn, ionizes the minor constituent by transferring its excitation energy on collision. A typical example is 99% Ne / 1% A (excitation and ionization energies 16·5 eV and 15·7 eV respectively); another is argon and mercury (11·6 eV and 10·4 eV respectively).

Production of radiation.   Most of the radiation from the majority of discharge lamps is from the uniform positive column. The energetic electrons which produce the ionization also produce excitation of the gas atoms, which subsequently radiate at their characteristic frequencies. Normally many energy levels are excited: Fig. 6.4 shows just a few of the excitation and radiating transitions of importance in lamps containing mercury vapour.

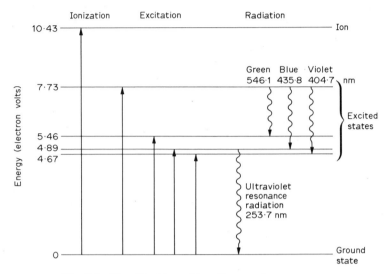

Fig. 6.4 Simplified transition diagram for mercury

The lowest excited state which can radiate produces what is called *resonance radiation*. This is important in low pressure discharges because it is usually very efficiently generated. In the case of mercury, ultra-violet resonance radiation at 253·7 nm is the principal source of radiation for exciting the phosphor on the wall of a fluorescent lamp, as well as being one of the principal sources available of short wave ultra-violet radiation. Mercury also has another resonance line at 185·0 nm, but this is of less importance in the present context. Certain states, such as those at 4·67 eV and 5·46 eV in mercury, cannot radiate: these are called *metastable states*. In the case of sodium the resonance radiation is in the yellow region at 589·3 nm (2·10 eV) near the wavelength for maximum visual response: hence the importance of the low pressure sodium vapour discharge.

One of the most important aspects of discharge lamp design is to ensure that as much as possible of the input power is directed into transitions producing the wavelengths desired. For example, by suitable choice of conditions, well over 50% of the input power to a fluorescent lamp type discharge can be radiated at 253·7 nm. By raising the pressure, however, and operating at a higher gas temperature, this can be almost entirely suppressed, and the power radiated from the other transitions which give visible radiation (Table 6.1, Fig. 6.4).

One of the characteristics of resonance radiation is that it is easily absorbed by other atoms in the ground state (compare Kirchhoff's law, Sect. 6.1.2, a form of which applies in this case also). Consequently it cannot reach the walls of the discharge tube without being repeatedly absorbed and re-emitted. This phenomenon is known as *resonance radiation imprisonment*: as well as limiting the efficiency of low pressure discharges, it becomes increasingly important in determining the spectrum emitted by high pressure discharges.

Table 6.1   Principal mercury lines emitted by discharge lamps. For the multiple lines indicated, the wavelength of the strongest is given

Wavelength (nm)	Colour	Type
185·0	Short ultra-violet	Resonance
253·7	Short ultra-violet	
296·7	Near ultra-violet	
312·6(2)	Near ultra-violet	Diffuse triplet
365·0(3)	Near ultra-violet	
404·7	Violet	
435·8	Blue	Sharp triplet
546·1	Green	
577·0(2)	Yellow	Combination
579·1	Yellow	Diffuse singlet
1014·0	Infra-red	Sharp singlet

Most practical discharge lamps contain one or more of the inert gases helium, neon, argon or krypton in addition to the metal vapour which produces the radiation. This gas performs the following functions:

(a) It reduces ion losses to the wall by ambipolar diffusion.
(b) It controls the mobility of the electrons, and hence the electrical conductivity.
(c) It provides easier breakdown at a lower striking voltage.
(d) It prolongs the life of the electrodes by reducing sputtering and evaporation.
(e) In the case of fluorescent lamps it forms some protection of the phosphor from mercury ions.

On the other hand the inert gas dissipates energy from the electrons by elastic collisions in the form of heat. This is least when the gas is heavy, so argon is used, for example, in fluorescent lamps to give maximum reduction of ion losses to the walls with minimum elastic collision losses. In sodium lamps, however, the tube must be heated to some 300 °C to provide an adequate vapour pressure of sodium, hence a relatively high pressure of neon is used to provide sufficient heat in this way. If sufficient thermal insulation can be provided in the form of vacuum jackets or infra-red reflecting layers (Chap. 13) the neon pressure can be reduced, to give a higher efficiency of radiation production.

Note that in the case of low pressure discharges, heating of the gas is incidental to radiation production, which arises directly from excitation of the gas atoms by the electrons, unlike the incandescence of solids and liquids, and high pressure discharges, in which a high temperature and radiation production are intimately related.

6.1.5   High pressure discharges

Comparison with low pressure discharges.   If we start with a low pressure discharge and gradually raise the pressure to a few atmospheres, two principal changes occur:

(a) The gas temperature is gradually increased by energy transfer by the increasing number of collisions (mainly elastic collisions) with the energetic electrons, and the mean electron energy, or electron temperature, is gradually decreased accordingly, until both are practically equal at some intermediate temperature, typically 4000 K to 6000 K.

(b) The high temperature becomes localized at the centre of the discharge, there being a temperature gradient towards the walls, which are much cooler: the discharge is now described as 'constricted'.

This situation is represented schematically in Fig. 6.5. In the high pressure region, when the gas and electron temperatures are practically equal throughout the discharge (although varying with position) there is essentially local thermodynamic equilibrium, LTE (Sect. 6.1.1). This greatly simplifies the analysis of the discharge, although other factors, such as the non-uniform temperature, complicate it.

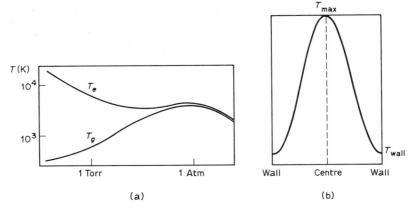

Fig. 6.5   Temperatures in a high pressure discharge (schematically)
(a) Transition from low to high pressure (T_e = electron temperature, T_g = gas temperature)
(b) Radial temperature distribution in a high pressure discharge

    The wall becomes much less important at high pressures, and not altogether essential: discharges can operate between two electrodes without any restraining wall, and are then referred to as arcs. There is no essential difference between an arc and a high pressure constricted discharge in a tube, which also is frequently called an arc. There is, however, a strong tendency to instability: the arc may either bow (as its name recalls) or writhe around, making it useless as a stable light source. A constraining wall, or electrodes which are not too far apart, are the principal means of preventing this, and we speak of wall-stabilized and electrode-stabilized arcs. Magnetic fields are also used sometimes. The longer types of lamp are usually wall-stabilized, and the shorter, compact-source types usually electrode-stabilized. There are also other factors necessary for good stability, the achievement of which is one of the major problems facing the lamp designer.

Like low pressure discharges, high pressure discharges generally have a falling characteristic, a volt-ampere curve of negative slope, over much of their range of operation. In some cases this levels off, and may actually rise again at high currents, especially if the vapour density continues to rise as the power is increased, as in the case of some types of mercury lamp. Nevertheless, they are inherently unstable characteristics, and a current-limiting device, such as a choke or high-reactance transformer, is still necessary to ensure stable operation at the required power.

Electrodes and starting.   The electrodes are more robust in construction than in a low pressure discharge, and are invariably self-heated by ion bombardment. Electron emission is essentially thermionic, with a cathode fall of only a few volts. In discharges containing a vaporizable material, such as mercury, sodium or metal halides, and an inert gas, only the gas (and a trace of mercury, when present) will be available for ionization on first striking. Three phases may be distinguished in establishing the discharge:

(a) Initial breakdown of the rare gas, as in a low pressure discharge. The discharge then operates as a glow discharge, with a high cathode fall, until the cathode has been sufficiently heated.
(b) Glow to arc transition. When there is sufficient thermionic emission from the cathode, the cathode fall suddenly collapses and (with normal circuitry) the current increases (Fig. 18.1).
(c) Run-up. The heat generated now vaporizes the condensed material and the pressure builds up to its operating value. The voltage gradually increases, and the emission of the characteristic radiation begins.

Sometimes (a) and (b) occur instantaneously and can hardly be distinguished; in other cases a few seconds may elapse. Run-up may take from 5 min to 15 min. If the discharge is extinguished, the pressure is too high for restriking until it has cooled sufficiently. In cases such as the xenon lamp, which contain a gas at a permanently high pressure, very high voltages are necessary for striking.

Local thermodynamic equilibrium.   Under conditions approaching LTE at a high temperature (several thousand K) the atoms and molecules of the gas are excited, dissociated and ionized by repeated collisions with each other, with the electrons already present, and by the absorption and re-emission of radiation. If conditions of LTE are fully met, then the number density of atoms excited to any state is completely determined by *Boltzmann's equation*

$$\frac{n_r}{n_g} = \frac{g_r}{g_g} \exp\left(-\frac{eV_r}{kT}\right) \tag{6.5}$$

where n_g and n_r are the number densities of atoms in the ground state g and excited state r, eV_r is the energy of r above g, $T(K)$ is the local temperature, k is Boltzmann's constant $(k = 8.62 \times 10^{-5}\,eV/K)$ and g_r and g_g are known small integers called the statistical weights of the states.

Similarly the number densities of (singly ionized) ions and electrons n_i and n_e (in m^{-3}) are given by *Saha's equation*

$$\frac{n_e n_i}{n_g} = 4.83 \times 10^{21} \frac{U_i}{U_g} T^{3/2} \exp\left(-\frac{eV_i}{kT}\right) \tag{6.6}$$

121

where eV_i is the ionization energy, and U_i and U_g are two small numbers called the partition functions of the ion and the atom. In a plasma $n_e = n_i$ if only singly-charged ions are present.

A full appreciation of these relations is vital to the understanding of high pressure discharges. If LTE is not fully established, they nevertheless give a good approximation to the degree of excitation and ionization in most high pressure radiation sources. Tables of the statistical weights and partition functions are available.

Production of radiation.   The atoms in the hot core of the discharge are excited thermally in this way, and then radiate exactly as in the case of low pressure discharges. As the pressure is increased, however, the wavelength of the lines becomes less precise, and the lines become increasingly broadened. There are two main causes of line broadening:

(a) Primary broadening: the wavelength of the radiation actually emitted by the excited atoms is broadened. This is mainly pressure broadening, caused by interactions between the atoms forced together by the high pressure. Electric fields and the motion of the particles can also contribute.
(b) Secondary broadening: this is produced mainly by repeated absorption and re-emission of the original radiation on its way through the cooler outer layers to the wall. This is the imprisonment process described in Sect. 6.1.4, but much intensified by the high pressure.

Both processes are strongest in the case of resonance radiation, where there is a special kind of pressure broadening called resonance broadening. The resonance lines therefore broaden first as the pressure is increased, and more so than the other lines. Since absorption in the cooler layers is strongest at the centre of the line, the line often becomes 'self-reversed', with a dark centre between two 'wings'.

In some cases self-absorption of the resonance line is so strong that the total radiation from it is much reduced, and the other non-resonance lines become the principal sources of radiation. This happens with the high pressure mercury discharge (Chap. 14), and in other cases when the basic transition probability of the resonance line is relatively low. When the transition probability is high, as in the case of sodium and the other alkali metals, the resonance line remains the principal source of radiation, but becomes very greatly broadened and self-reversed. This applies particularly to the high pressure sodium lamp (Sect. 13.2).

At higher pressures, the broadened lines merge together and form *continuum* radiation. Where there are self-reversed lines involved, these show as dark lines, or bands, against the background continuum (as in the case of the Fraunhofer lines in the sun's spectrum). Continua can also arise from transitions involving free electrons and ions. Undissociated molecules radiate very close groups of lines called bands: even at quite moderate pressures these merge together to form apparent continua.

In the limit, at the highest pressures and greatest currents, the radiation tends towards black body radiation of the same type as that emitted from solids, and the discharge is effectively an incandescent gas. Since the temperature can be much greater than that of any solid, a much greater radiant intensity can be obtained from a discharge. Note that even when these conditions are not reached, the maximum intensity at any wavelength cannot exceed that of a black body at the temperature of the discharge, and is normally well below that corresponding to the maximum temperature of the discharge in most sources at moderate pressure. There is, therefore, an absolute limit to the intensity which can be obtained at any given discharge temperature. In the case of low pressure discharges it is the electron temperature which establishes this limit: since this can be very high, the spectral intensity of a given line can also be very high, but since the lines are narrow, the total intensity from any transition is usually less than in a corresponding high pressure discharge.

6.1.6   Luminescence

Luminescence is the emission of light from a body in excess of its thermal radiation at the same temperature, or the temperature of the exciting source. It is characteristic of luminescence that the exciting source is often non-thermal in nature (as, for example, the energetic electrons in cathode-ray tubes) and it is therefore not limited by the same thermodynamic considerations as all the processes described so far. Frequently luminescent materials are near room temperature when operating. The alternative term *fluorescence* is sometimes applied to an instantaneous rise or decay of emission, in contrast to the visibly slow decay of *phosphorescence* occurring after the excitation process.

Physical principles.   Fig. 6.6a illustrates the simplest possible case: some atom or region of the body is raised by some non-thermal process to an excited state, from which it subsequently de-excites, with the emission of radiation. There may be intermediate changes (*relaxation*), as shown in Fig. 6.6b, producing a different wavelength of radiation; or there may be *traps*, as in Fig. 6.6c, either delaying the emission, as in phosphorescence, or requiring some form of *stimulation* to release the trapped energy, as in the various forms of image storage device (Chap. 16).

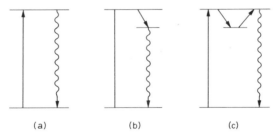

(a)   (b)   (c)

Fig. 6.6   Simplified representations of (a) luminescence (b) luminescence with relaxation (c) luminescence with trapping

Actual luminescent materials are usually much more complicated, with more levels and intermediate transitions. The levels may relate to single atoms or molecules, or they may be broad energy bands, which may extend throughout the material. Emission may take place at the same atom or centre as excitation, or the energy may be transferred to another region first. In zinc sulphide, for example, and similar materials, the upper level is a conduction band, through which the excited electrons may pass from one region to another before dropping to a lower level and radiating: these materials therefore behave as a type of semiconductor. Traps and other active centres, which are often produced by added impurity atoms or ions, thus play an important part in determining the properties of this type of material. In ionic materials energy can be transferred from one centre to another by a quantum process known as *resonance transfer* (no radiation is involved in this). Thus, in the halophosphates used in fluorescent lamps, excitation occurs in antimony ions: some of this is radiated from the same site, after relaxation, giving a blue radiation; but a proportion is transferred by this process to manganese ions some distance away, subsequently producing an orange radiation. In this case the manganese is considered to be the *activator*, while the antimony is called the primary activator or *sensitizer* (Sect. 8.3.1).

The following treatment classifies luminescence in terms of the method by which energy is supplied.

Chemical reactions.   Some chemical reactions, mostly slow oxidation of organic substances in living animals, give rise to feeble light emission (fireflies, glow-worms, plankton). Non-biological reactions between chemical substances are known which produce similar effects, for example the oxidation of phosphorus in air. A general term for these phenomena is *chemiluminescence*.

Charged particles.   High-energy protons and other charged particles can be detected in nuclear work by the luminescence they produce in plastics or crystal scintillators. Luminous paints are excited by the radiation (alpha or beta particles) emitted by long-lived radioactive materials such as radium, thorium or strontium 90. Some radioactive gases, such as tritium (^{3}H) and krypton 85, which emit beta particles (electrons) have been used, sealed in containers with a suitable phosphor, as long-lived but feeble light sources.

Electrons of lower energy are the exciting agent in cathode-ray tubes, used as indicators of many kinds and for television picture reception. Much more energy can be transferred to the phosphor in this way, to give a reasonable light yield, and its use as a light source has been seriously considered. This type of excitation is termed *cathodoluminescence*. Charged particles introduced in another way are considered later under the heading of junction electroluminescence.

Electromagnetic radiation.   By far the most important method of exciting luminescence is by electromagnetic radiation. This includes radio waves, infra-red, visible light, ultra-violet, X-rays and gamma rays. Nearly always the wavelength of the emitted radiation is longer than that of the absorbed radiation. This is known as *Stokes' law*, and is illustrated in Fig. 6.7a: evidently the energy of the emitted radiation must be less than that absorbed.

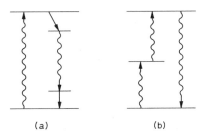

(a)   (b)

Fig. 6.7   Stokes' Law: (a) Conventional phosphor   (b) Anti-Stokes phosphor

All the phosphors used in fluorescent and discharge lamps for converting ultra-violet to visible light (Chap. 8), or for detecting X-rays or gamma rays (Chap. 16), obey Stokes' law.

Recently, however, certain types of phosphor have been developed which convert infra-red into visible radiation. This is only possible if two or more quanta of the exciting radiation are absorbed for each emitted quantum, for example as in Fig. 6.7b. These clearly violate Stokes' law, and are called anti-Stokes phosphors, or two-quantum phosphors. Since a double absorption is required they are only efficient under very intense incident radiation, and have mainly been of interest in junction electroluminescence: see below.

Electric field: electroluminescence. Certain luminescent materials when embedded as a powder in a dielectric material between two electrodes and subjected to an alternating electric field become luminescent. This was discovered by Destriau in 1936 with activated zinc sulphide, still the most widely used material, and is referred to as the Destriau effect, or simply as electroluminescence (Chap. 16).

Junction electroluminescence. Certain semiconductors, notably gallium arsenide and phosphide, emit radiation when recombination of charge carriers (electrons or holes) occurs after injection from a p–n junction. Since no thermal processes are involved in excitation, there are no direct thermodynamic limitations of the Planck radiator type, and very high luminances are theoretically possible: these are now beginning to be realized in practice as semiconductor lamps, or light-emitting diodes (Chap. 17).

6.2 CHARACTERISTICS AND APPLICATIONS OF RADIATION

Lamps are now used for many purposes other than as visual indicators or illuminants. The usefulness of any particular type depends largely on the suitability of its radiated power spectrum for the purpose intended. Since lamps are often used to reproduce the effects of natural radiation from the sun, quantitative data have been obtained on the intensity of solar radiation in various situations from outer space to the earth's surface (Fig. 23.6). This forms the basis for calculating the practical possibilities of performing similar functions by radiation from lamps.

6.2.1 Radiant power from lamps

Fig. 6.8 shows the radiated power distribution as a function of wavelength, and also as a proportion of total input power, for several of the principal lamp types. These are only a selection from the many types now available, and for which further information is available in later chapters. The diagrams are largely self-explanatory, but the following comments may be made.

The ordinary incandescent lamp (a) radiates most of its power in the near infra-red, and is thus very suitable for heating applications. Where a higher intensity is required, the higher power tungsten halogen lamps (Chap. 10) provide a similar spectral distribution at slightly shorter wavelengths. Still higher intensities are available from xenon lamps (b), and certain metal halide lamps (Chap. 15).

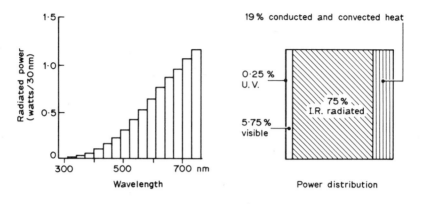

(a) 100 W incandescent tungsten lamp (12·6 lm/W)

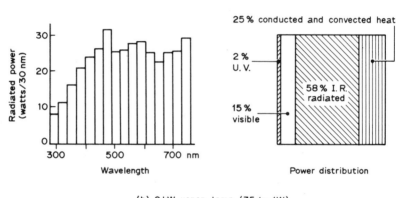

(b) 2 kW xenon lamp (35 lm/W)

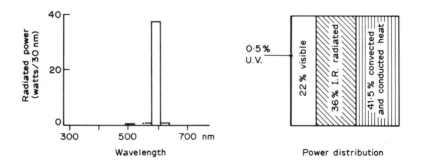

(c) 200 W linear low pressure sodium lamp (125 lm/W)

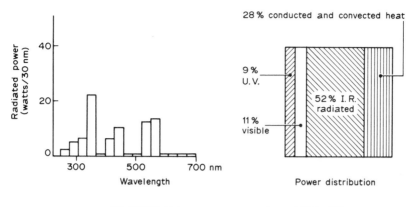

(d) 400 W high pressure mercury lamp (49 lm/W)

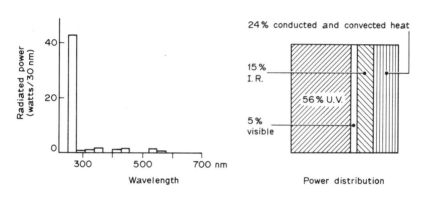

(e) 80 W low pressure mercury lamp (6·4 lm/W)

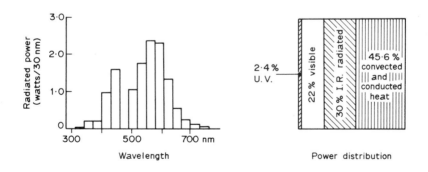

(f) 80 W tubular fluorescent lamp (Daylight) (62 lm/W)

Fig. 6.8   Power distributions of different lamp types, with typical efficacies

127

High and low pressure mercury lamps (d) and (e) are the principal sources of ultra-violet: envelopes of suitable transmittance are necessary for this purpose. Although the radiated power in the ultra-violet is higher for the low pressure lamp, the intensity of ultra-violet is lower than from the high pressure lamp, which is a much more concentrated source. Both types exist in a variety of forms modified by fluorescent coatings: many spectral distributions are available besides (f), giving a wide flexibility in practical distribution.

6.2.2   Applications

This section deals with applications of radiation other than for illumination or visual stimulation.

Heating.   This is the most easily appreciated effect of radiant power. Provided the material will absorb radiant energy at the appropriate wavelengths a body can be heated by radiation anywhere, including in a vacuum. Any wavelength which is absorbed can be used, even short wavelength ultra-violet, but generally high intensities of infra-red are most economically produced; tungsten filament lamps, especially halogen lamps, are usually most appropriate. For very high intensities, xenon arc lamps are useful. A particular example is the 'arc image' furnace in which the radiation from a xenon, or similar, arc is focussed into a small area to give temperatures in excess of 2000 °C. It is important to note that in no conceivable arrangement can a body be heated to a higher temperature than that of the source of the radiation, with a possible exception in the case of lasers (Sect. 6.3.1).

Photochemical.   The most obvious photochemical applications are photography and photoprinting (with which may be associated xerography, although not strictly a photochemical process). Many special lamps are available for these purposes, especially metal halide discharges (Sect. 15.1) and fluorescent lamps (Chap. 12) with spectral distributions in the visible and near ultra-violet designed to give optimum performance for specific processes. Flash photography is a particular case, and special photoflash bulbs (Chap. 11) and xenon flash tubes (Sect. 15.3) have been developed for this purpose.

When molecules are excited by the absorption of radiation, many chemical reactions occur which either do not occur otherwise, or only much more slowly. These form the extensive field of photochemistry: ultra-violet radiation is generally most effective. A technique using high speed flash tubes, flash photolysis, is proving a valuable means of investigating chemical reactions. High intensity radiation can be used for the polymerization or hardening of plastics and resins. Much interest has been aroused recently in the large scale use of radiation for the hardening of paints and varnishes, as an alternative to the evaporation of solvents, particularly with a view to reducing atmospheric pollution.

Photobiological.   Many biological processes are affected by natural radiation and can be reproduced or modified by the use of artificial sources. The most important plant processes controlled by light are photosynthesis (the synthesis by green plants of carbohydrates from water and oxygen, aided by light absorbed by the chlorophyll) and photoperiodism (the phenomenon whereby the length of the day controls the onset of flowering, or other stage of plant development). In general both require light of similar intensity, spectral quality and exposure time, as provided in their natural habitat.

For additional lighting in glasshouses high pressure discharge lamps, which are small and obstruct little daylight, are favoured. Where growth rooms without daylight are used, fluorescent lamps are preferred (Sect. 12.4). Radiation of different wavelengths produces different types of growth, and the spectral composition can be varied to produce desired characteristics.

The use of light for animal husbandry is increasing. In the case of poultry, white light at about 10 lux to 30 lux can promote egg production throughout the year. Low intensities of red light produce restful conditions, in which the birds gain weight rapidly. In addition, ultra-violet radiation is used, and both poultry and cattle are considered to benefit from its application. Some zoos provide artificial daylight for nocturnal animals during the night, so that their activities may be observed during the day under dim red light. Violet and ultra-violet light is used to attract insects into traps.

The bactericidal and erythemal properties of ultra-violet radiation are discussed in Sect. 1.3.3. The therapeutic use of this radiation requires high pressure mercury lamps with special outer envelopes to eliminate harmful wavelengths below 280 nm. Dosage at a lower level for recreational purposes may be applied by fluorescent lamps (Sect. 12.4). In USSR mild dosage of this kind is used extensively in schools, factories and hospitals. Excessive exposure is harmful not only for the short-term effects, but it may lead to cancer of the skin which is not uncommon in countries where there are sustained high levels of ultra-violet in sunlight. A known beneficial effect is the production of vitamin D in the skin, as well as the pigmentation which acts as a protection in subsequent exposure to the same radiation. Infra-red radiation provides comfortable heating, relieving muscular pain and nervous tension, since most of it is absorbed in the body tissues.

Scientific and technical. There are many scientific and technical applications of radiation, some requiring specialized sources, which can only be mentioned briefly. Photo-emission is, of course, widely used to initiate electronic circuitry when a light beam is intercepted, for example, by a person or vehicle. When visible light would be objectionable, or secrecy is required, infra-red radiation is used.

Many instruments require special sources of high stability, for calibration and as standards (Chap. 4), of a high degree of uniformity, and of particular spectral characteristics. Of the many sources developed particularly for spectroscopy, the wide range of 'hollow cathode' lamps, each emitting the radiation of a particular element as a very sharp line, and used in atomic absorption spectroscopy, is worth particular mention. Electrodeless discharge sources, in which vapours contained in a small glass bulb are excited by radiofrequency power, are used for similar purposes. Various sources of continuum radiation in all regions from the far ultra-violet to the far infra-red have been developed for absorption spectroscopy. Extreme cases are sources in the far ultra-violet (below 10 nm) which overlap with X-ray sources, and the far infra-red (above 10^5 nm) which overlap with microwave radio sources.

The simulation of extra-terrestrial solar radiation for investigations on space exploration requires high intensities and a close approximation to sunlight: xenon lamps are very suitable (Sect. 15.2). Very high intensities of radiation are needed for studies of the surface heating of fast high-flying aircraft and rockets in the upper atmosphere, and especially the 'ablation' of materials during nose-cone and satellite re-entry. This is not solely a matter of heating, but involves ionization, excitation and bombardment phenomena. Batteries of tungsten halogen or xenon lamps are adequate in some cases, but in others custom-built high power discharge sources are used.

Very high power flash discharge tubes and continuously running tungsten halogen lamps and discharge tubes have been developed specifically for laser pumping. The main requirement here is to maintain an optimum spectral distribution at the very high energies and powers required. These sources may be water-cooled, or as demountable units, sometimes constructed more as pieces of heavy engineering than as lamps.

6.3 COHERENT RADIATION

6.3.1 Lasers

Everything said in this chapter so far refers to what might be called 'ordinary radiation' generated from an 'ordinary source'. Until 1960 all the radiation at optical wavelengths (less than 10^4 nm) which had ever been produced was of this kind, known as *incoherent radiation*. Briefly, even though it may be monochromatic, of one particular wavelength, such radiation consists of a random superposition of many separate waves, each in a different phase, or part of its wave cycle: rather like the waves on a choppy sea.

In 1960, however, devices called lasers were first produced which generate radiation consisting of more regularly ordered waves, either in a single phase, or a number of phases superposed in a systematic and regular order: more like the waves from a single tuning fork dipped in a pool of mercury. Radiation of this type is called *coherent radiation*, and has properties not possessed by incoherent radiation. It shows much more readily the phenomena of interference and diffraction, it can be monochromatic to a much greater degree, and it is, at least potentially, capable of being modulated to convey information, as are ordinary radio waves. It is produced in lasers by a process known as *stimulated emission*. Unlike the spontaneous emission of radiation described in Sect. 6.1.1, stimulated emission is emitted as the result of interaction between excited atoms or molecules and incident radiation of the same wavelength.

There are several types of laser: solid state lasers which produce radiation mainly in the infra-red; gas lasers, which vary from small portable helium-neon lasers producing radiation in the visible or near infra-red, to very large carbon dioxide lasers producing radiation at 10·6 µm at powers up to 18 kW; and semiconductor lasers which are small and compact, similar to semiconductor lamps (Chap. 17).

6.3.2 Applications

The principal features distinguishing laser radiation from ordinary radiation are, in brief, that it is much more intense, directional, monochromatic and coherent. High intensity pulses of extremely short duration (10^{-11} s) can also be produced. These properties indicate its main applications and potential applications, of which there are so many that only a few can be mentioned.

The high degree of parallelism obtainable provides applications in surveying and optical alignment and, when pulsed, in ranging and tracking rockets, missiles and other military objects. Lenses or mirrors can focus the radiation into a very small area, providing localized sources of energy, or heat for melting, welding, drilling, etc., where special precision, special atmospheres or special materials are involved. Particular cases are micromachining and certain medical applications, such as retinal surgery on the eye. Extreme applications of this type are the focussing of giant pulses to produce very high temperatures, with a view to triggering thermonuclear devices, and for various military purposes.

There are many scientific applications in very high speed photography, spectroscopy and plasma diagnostics; also in the completely new field of non-linear optics, including frequency multiplication (for example the generation of ultra-violet radiation from red light) and frequency mixing (generation of sum and difference frequencies): these are phenomena which only occur at extremely high radiation densities.

Laser radiation has revolutionized optical interferometry, leading to much greater flexibility and refinement. Applications include precision mensuration of lengths, determination of translational and rotational velocities, and determination of refractive index variations.

A related development is *holography*, in which objects illuminated by coherent light are recorded as transformed images called holograms. These contain much more information than a conventional image, such as a photograph. For example, the three-dimensional properties of the object are included, and different views can be reconstructed from the same hologram by varying the viewing arrangement, again using coherent light. One important engineering application is to the study of small deformations arising, for example, from wear or thermal changes. The spatial structure of moving particles (as in smoke) or convection currents (as in lamps) can be studied by holography. Its possibilities for data storage and retrieval are also being investigated.

The coherent nature of laser radiation has led to much consideration of its possibilities in communication. The high frequencies available indicate enormous potential for the transmission of information, particularly in space. Many practical difficulties have to be resolved however: for terrestrial communication, at any rate, not the least of them is scattering by rain and fog.

PART TWO

Lamps

7 Lamp materials

Lamp-making materials can be broadly classified into three groups; (a) glasses and ceramics, (b) metals and (c) gases and vapours.

The common factor to most electric lamps is the need for a light transmitting bulb or envelope to isolate the inside of the lamp from the surrounding air, and maintain the necessary gaseous atmosphere. It must be compatible with the gas-filling and other lamp components and able to withstand the pressure and temperature of the device without interfering with its operation. Materials have gradually been developed to meet the needs of the industry, and a range now exists from low melting point glass to translucent re-fractory ceramic.

Of the lamp metals, tungsten is the most important because of its high melting point, low vapour pressure over the normal lamp operating temperatures and high mechanical strength. Its main use is for discharge lamp electrodes and incandescent lamp filaments, and while certain oxides and carbides have been proposed as alternatives to tungsten they have not been developed. Molybdenum is commonly used for internal components, such as filament supports, lead wires etc. Many others, including the less common metals, are also essential in lamp making.

Gas-filling has two distinct functions. The inert gas filling in a discharge lamp initiates the discharge and acts as a buffer, while a metal vapour provides the predominant component through which the discharge takes place (Sect. 6.1.4). Also the gas filling of an incandescent lamp suppresses filament evaporation and plays a predominant part in determining efficacy and life. It is essential therefore to have a knowledge of the physical properties of common lamp-making gases.

7.1 GLASSES AND CERAMICS

7.1.1 Glasses

The glass most commonly used in the lamp industry is the soda-lime silicate type. With only minor variations in batch composition it is used as envelope material for both general incandescent and fluorescent lamps. Relatively cheap batch materials are melted continuously in large furnaces capable of producing over 50 t of glass per day. In the high speed manufacture of incandescent lamp bulbs on the Corning ribbon machine, the glass flows from the furnace at a controlled rate, between water-cooled shaped rollers which form the glass into a thin ribbon having regularly spaced thicker 'biscuits' about 100 mm apart. The ribbon is picked up by a horizontal endless belt so positioned that each biscuit falls over a hole in the belt. As the belt travels on, the biscuit sags through the hole and begins to take on a bulbous shape which is then blown into rotating moulds which have been sprayed with water. The steam cushion thus formed between the glass and the mould leaves the bulb with a polished surface while the rotation eliminates mould seams.

The shaped bulb is finally cracked from the ribbon and dropped on to an annealing conveyor. This process will produce up to 60 000 bulbs per hour per machine depending upon bulb size. If pearl bulbs are required the interior of the bulb is treated (after annealing) with an etching fluid comprising mainly hydrofluoric acid, then washed and dried.

Tubing for fluorescent lamp envelopes is continuously drawn from the same type of furnace, the Danner process being commonly used. In this, glass flows from the furnace at a controlled rate on to the top of an inclined, rotating, hollow refractory mandrel. Air is blown down the centre of the mandrel as tubing is drawn from the bottom by a drawing machine which may be 50 m distant. The glass tube, as it solidifies, is supported between the mandrel and drawing machine by a series of shaped carbon rollers placed at regular intervals. The size of tubing drawn depends upon the diameter of the mandrel, drawing speed, amount of air blown through, glass temperature, and rate of cooling. Drawing speeds up to 75 m/min are achieved in the process.

The internal glass components of general lighting service (GLS) and fluorescent lamps are made from lead-alkali silicate glass, which is manufactured in the same way as soda-lime silicate material, although usually on a smaller scale. This is preferred to soda-lime silicate because of its higher electrical resistivity, which prevents electrolysis occurring in the pinch seal. The glass seals readily to the soda-lime silicate envelope and has a somewhat lower softening point and longer working temperature range than soda glass, all factors which assist in lamp making.

For lamps in which the operating temperature is too high for soda-lime silicate glass, such as envelopes for projector and high pressure discharge lamps, borosilicate glass is used. In addition to its ability to withstand higher operating temperatures, it also has a much lower thermal expansion coefficient and thus withstands greater changes in temperature. This leads to its use in sealed beam (Sect. 9.2) and other specialized types of lamps which may be subjected to sudden temperature variations. Where even higher service temperatures are required, aluminosilicate glass is used. This is the most refractory conventional glass in the lamp industry and it is produced in relatively small quantities using traditional hand methods.

Silica.   In the development of more compact and powerful light sources, conventional glasses became inadequate and led to the manufacture and use of transparent silica as an envelope material. This material is essentially pure silicon dioxide having only a fraction of 1% of other materials present as impurities (Table 7.1). It is colloquially known as 'quartz' in the lamp industry, though it is vitreous, not crystalline. Three main processes are used for manufacturing it for lamp making. The *vacuum melting process* uses Brazilian quartz crystal which has been sorted, acid-washed, crushed and screened. This is melted in a carbon mould by an induction-heated vacuum furnace. After cooling, the carbon mould is removed and broken away from the silica billet, which is then cleaned and placed in a second furnace having an orifice and mandrel. The silica is remelted in a reducing atmosphere and tubing is drawn through the orifice. This method produces extremely high quality tubing virtually free from airlines and having the lowest hydroxyl content of any type of fused silica. It is, however, extremely expensive. The *atmosphere furnace process* is a continuous process in which quartz crystal is fed into a resistance-heated refractory metal furnace having a protective atmosphere of forming gas (about 90% $N_2 + 10\%$ H_2). The level of the melt is maintained as the tubing is drawn over a mandrel and through an orifice at the base of the furnace. The tubing contains many air-

Table 7.1   Composition and physical properties of materials for lamp envelopes

	Soda-lime silicate	Lead-alkali silicate	Borosilicate	Alumino silicate	Vitreous silica	Vycor	Sodium resistant	Sodium resistant	Ceramic alumina
	GTC S.96	GTC L.92	GTC B.37 Tungsten sealing	GTC A.43 Molybdenum sealing		Corning 7913	GTC X.91	GTC X.93	
Composition, weight %									
SiO_2	73	56	76	54	100	96	8		
Na_2O	15	5	4				14		
K_2O	1	8	2					2	
CaO	7			14			6	8	
MgO	3								
Al_2O_3	1	1	2	21			24	26	99·9
PbO		30							
B_2O_3			16	8		3	48	22	
BaO				3				42	
Expansion coefficient (per °C × 10^{-7})	92	90	37	43	5	8			80/86[1]
Melting point °C									2050
Softening point °C	710	630	775	930	~1600	~1530			
Annealing point °C	530	435	525	750	~1150	~1020			
Log_{10} of d.c. resistivity at 250°C	6·5	9·6	8·7	12·6	11·7	>10			11·3[2]

Expansion coefficients are for 50 °C to 300 °C
Softening point corresponds to a dynamic viscosity of $10^{6·6}$ N s/m² [1 N s/m² = 10 poise]
Annealing point corresponds to a dynamic viscosity of 10^{12} N s/m²
(1) for 25 °C to 800 °C and 25 °C to 1200 °C respectively
(2) at 500 °C
GTC refers to material from Glass Tubes and Components Ltd.

lines caused by entrapped furnace gases and has a somewhat higher hydroxyl content and inferior optical quality to vacuum fused material. In the *flame fusion method,* the processed crystal is fed into a gas flame and is fused by the flame on to an inclined rotating refractory metal mandrel, from which tubing is drawn off from the lower end. This material contains numerous airlines and has a high hydroxyl content, but metallic impurities may be lower than in the other types because they are partially volatilized in the flame.

The hydroxyl content, that is the percentage by weight of OH^- groups present, is extremely important as far as envelope materials for tungsten halogen and metal halide lamps are concerned. Indeed, in certain critical designs, the hydroxyl content needs to be below 0·001% by weight.

The main advantages of fused silica are its transparency, resistance to thermal shock, and high operating temperature (up to 800 °C). Most of the lamps described in Chaps. 14 and 15 depend on it.

Vycor is a Corning Glass Works material increasingly used in the lamp industry as an alternative to vitreous silica, particularly where good optical quality or improved dimensional control is required. It begins as a borosilicate glass of general composition SiO_2 55–70%, Na_2O 6–10%, Al_2O_3 0·1–4% and the balance B_2O_3, and may also contain other elements such as Ca, Zn, Pb, Zr, V, Co, Fe, Cr. In this form it can be worked and shaped using standard equipment to normal glassworking tolerances. An acid leaching process then removes practically all the constituents except the silica and a little boric oxide and leaves the article filled with millions of tiny holes where the other constituents have been leached away. High temperature firing consolidates the porous structure and results in the article shrinking about 35% by volume. The amount of shrinkage can be predicted precisely and thus extremely good dimensional control can be achieved.

A glass having a small and very specialized application in the lamp industry is *sodium-resistant glass.* The powerful reducing properties of hot alkali vapours produce rapid blackening in normal silicate glass by reduction, and this can only be eliminated by using glasses which contain little or no silica or other readily reducible oxides. Of the two basic types shown in Table 7.1, the alumino-borate resists attack but stains slowly throughout life, while the glass modified by the addition of barium oxide does not discolour. Unfortunately both glasses are readily attacked by atmospheric moisture and are expensive and difficult to work. To produce a durable, economic material suitable for lamp fabrication, a thin layer (about 50 μm) of the resistant glass is flashed on the inside of a tube of standard soda-lime silicate glass (known as 'ply-tubing').

7.1.2   Translucent ceramics

The incompatibility of glasses containing silica with alkali metal vapours at high temperatures and pressures, has led to a demand for lamp envelope materials resistant to chemical attack under these conditions, particularly for the construction of high pressure sodium lamps. Modern developments in ceramic technology have made it possible to produce polycrystalline metal-oxide bodies of almost theoretical densities. Because of their essentially pore-free nature, articles produced from these materials are able to transmit a large proportion of any visible light incident upon them and this fact, together with their intrinsic refractoriness, makes them valuable materials for the construction of high temperature lamp envelopes. Oxides which may be produced in translucent or transparent form include alumina, common spinel, magnesia, beryllia, zirconia, thoria, and various rare-earth oxides.

At present, the most common polycrystalline oxide material used for the fabrication of lamp envelopes is alumina. In addition to its occurrence in various ores, alumina is found naturally in comparatively pure form as corundum and the gemstones sapphire and ruby. It crystallizes in two distinct forms. The poorly-defined cubic gamma alumina is stable only below about 1000 °C. Above this temperature the stable alpha alumina is formed, crystallizing in a close-packed hexagonal structure showing a small negative birefringence. Alpha alumina is one of the most stable of all compounds, being practically insoluble in strong mineral acids and resistant to attack by most metals (including sodium) and dry halogens; some reaction occurs with alkalis at high temperatures. It has a melting point of approximately 2050 °C and displays an adequate resistance to thermal shock. Alumina powder is normally relatively coarse and contains sodium, silicon, iron and calcium as major impurities. Powders of the highest purity are obtained by decomposition of purified organic or inorganic precursors like ammonium alum, and may have sub-micron particle diameters, according to the calcination technique. Such sub-micron powders typically contain up to 40 parts per million (ppm) each of sodium and silicon, 20 ppm iron and 10 ppm calcium as the main impurities, these levels being tolerable for the production of sintered alumina of high translucency. Sodium impurities are progressively injurious, leading to exaggerated grain-growth, entrapment of pores and hence loss of translucency during sintering. On sintering, silicon in any appreciable quantity diffuses to grain boundaries and would be readily attacked by the sodium in a high pressure lamp, leading to early failure.

Alumina was first sintered to translucency by R. L. Coble about 1957. The process involves the inclusion of a small quantity of a grain-growth inhibiting agent such as magnesia, which on sintering segregates at the boundaries of the alumina grains, reducing their high temperature mobility. Diffusion path lengths of gases entrapped in closed pores within the alumina grains are thus minimized, allowing the gases to diffuse away to grain boundaries during sintering. Since gases are then able to escape readily from the sintering body along grain boundaries, a polycrystalline mass of almost theoretical density results, as in a sapphire single crystal. In addition, the alumina is sintered in an atmosphere of hydrogen or oxygen, these gases being able to diffuse more readily through or dissolve in the alumina lattice. Hence the contents of any pores isolated from grain boundaries are also able to escape during sintering, leading to a finished body of the highest density (3980 kg/m^3).

Polycrystalline alumina tubes may be fabricated by normal ceramic methods. The starting powder is prepared by thoroughly admixing the grain growth regulating agents with pure alumina powder; it is then isostatically pressed into a rough tubular shape. After presintering the pressed shape at 1100 °C in air to increase its strength, tubes are ground to the required dimensions with due allowance for shrinkage during the final sintering. This is accomplished in a hydrogen atmosphere at a temperature of about 1800 °C for several hours, during which the tubing becomes translucent and dimensionally accurate.

Ceramic alumina made by this process is translucent because of the essential absence of porosity. Fig. 7.1 compares the pore-free microstructure of dense polycrystalline alumina with that of a conventional impervious ceramic. The mean grain diameter of the dense alumina is of the order of 40 µm. Although the straight line transmission or transparency in the visible region of a parallel-sided piece of material 1 mm thick is only of the order of 15%, the integrated transmission through a tube of 1 mm wall thickness exceeds 90%. Recent developments suggest that it should be possible to obtain polycrystalline alumina bodies of very high transparency by the addition of minimal amounts of grain growth controllers, since these diffuse to grain boundaries and may form second phases, acting as refraction sites within the material. The small optical anisotropy of alumina should not affect the transparency of a body of mean grain size of about 40 µm to any appreciable extent. Fig. 7.2 shows an example of a high density translucent sintered alumina tube.

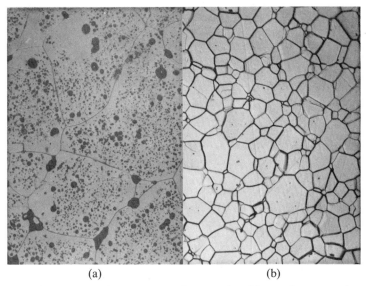

(a)   (b)

Fig. 7.1   (a) Porous microstructure of conventional impervious ceramic and (b) pore-free microstructure of translucent polycrystalline alumina (200 × magnification)

Fig. 7.2   Translucent polycrystalline alumina tubing

The latest development in alumina materials is the production of fully transparent alumina in tubular form, grown directly from molten alumina to the finished dimensions; these tubes are in fact pure single crystal sapphire. Although the material displays excellent thermal and chemical properties and good transparency, the total integrated transmission of visible light through a tube is at present no greater than that of a polycrystalline tube.

The other oxides mentioned are at present of little importance in the lamp industry owing to various drawbacks.

Common spinel, $MgAl_2O_4$, is the most stable of all spinels and having a melting point of approximately 2135 °C is more refractory than alumina, but it is mechanically weaker and more brittle than polycrystalline alumina and less resistant to thermal shock. It may be considered a reasonably good material for lamp envelopes.

Magnesia melts at approximately 2800 °C and has the greatest thermal expansion of all pure oxides. Its thermal shock resistance is less than that of alumina, and it is mechanically weaker, though transparent bodies may be prepared, particularly by hot pressing.

Beryllia melts at approximately 2550 °C, and has a very high resistance to thermal shock; the health hazard involved and its high cost render its use unlikely.

Zirconia melts at about 2700 °C and shows good thermal shock resistance, but difficulties exist concerning the long term stabilization of this polymorphic oxide in the cubic phase. Also, zirconia reacts with some metals, including sodium, at high temperatures. Although thoria is still more refractory, it is comparatively weak and sensitive to thermal shock, and reacts somewhat with alkali metals at comparatively low temperatures.

Recently rare earth oxides have aroused interest, since with suitable additions transparent polycrystalline bodies of good refractoriness may be produced. Such materials show severe discolouration and loss of transparency under certain operating conditions, and again there is no immediate application foreseen.

7.1.3 Glass metal seals

One of the major factors affecting the choice of vitreous material for a particular application is its ability to seal hermetically to other materials, particularly metals. The properties required of a glass to produce an ideal, stress-free seal to a metal are as follows:

(a) Its thermal expansion coefficient should match that of the metal over a wide range of temperature and particularly from the annealing temperature to room temperature.
(b) It must be readily workable in the sealing region.
(c) It must exhibit satisfactory chemical resistance to atmospheric attack.
(d) Its electrical resistivity, dielectric constant and dielectric loss must be satisfactory.
(e) It must be perfectly homogeneous and its properties must not fluctuate from batch to batch.

Where requirement (a) is met, a matched seal between the glass and metal is produced. Matched seals can be made between certain soda-lime and lead-alkali silicate glasses and alloys such as 50% nickel-iron, nickel-iron-chromium, nickel-iron-chromium-cobalt and iron-chromium. These combinations are little used however since a porous oxide layer tends to build up on the alloy surface during sealing, resulting in a high probability of leakage. In order to overcome this difficulty in sealing unprotected nickel-iron alloys, Dumet alloy is used almost exclusively throughout the industry for sealing to lead-alkali silicate glass. Dumet is a composite material consisting of a central core of 42–58%

nickel-iron alloy sheathed with copper which constitutes about 25% by weight of the complete wire. The surface of the wire is coated with sodium borate which prevents the formation of spongy cuprous oxide during sealing and also enables the wire to be more easily 'wetted' by the glass. Because of its composite structure the thermal expansion coefficient of the wire is different in the axial and radial directions. In the radial direction it matches that of the glass whilst in the axial direction it is less than that of the glass. Consequently to avoid axial tensile stress in the glass the seal is not completely annealed but cooled at a rate such that, at room temperature, it exhibits axial compressive stress. The stress is limited by keeping the wire diameter below 0·8 mm.

Matched seals can be made successfully between certain of the borosilicate and aluminosilicate glasses and nickel-iron-cobalt alloys and the refractory metals, tungsten and molybdenum. In many respects the two refractory metals behave in a similar manner but molybdenum is often preferred for use in seals because it is less expensive, has greater ductility and a lower brittle-ductile transition temperature. Both metals oxidize readily but excessive oxidation during sealing can be prevented by sleeving the wire with a thin coating of glass before it is sealed to the glass component proper.

A sleeving process is also carried out prior to sealing Dumet alloy into the ply-glass used for low pressure sodium vapour lamps. In this case the wires are sleeved with a glass of high electrical resistivity in order to prevent electrolysis occurring in the pinch during lamp operation. This glass must seal satisfactorily to the Dumet alloy and its expansion coefficient must not exceed that of the soda-lime silicate base glass.

A major problem exists when making seals between metals and fused silica or Vycor. This is because the thermal expansion coefficients of these materials are so low that there is no suitable metal with an expansion coefficient remotely matching them. The technique adopted in making seals to these materials is to use a length of feather-edged molybdenum foil about 0·025 mm thick and pinch-seal it into the vitreous material. The foil in this form is sufficiently ductile to deform but not fracture under the tensile stresses produced by the differences in expansion coefficient. Further refinements are mentioned in Sects. 10.2.3, 15.2.1.

7.2   METALS

7.2.1   Filament materials

As explained in Chap. 6 the power radiated by an incandescent body increases with temperature, as does the proportion of power radiated in the visible region until the temperature exceeds about 6000 K. The spectral emissivity is an important property of a filament material since it must so radiate that a large fraction of the radiated power is in the visible part of the spectrum. The variation of spectral emissivity with wavelength for a number of refractory materials at 2000 K is shown in Fig. 7.3. It is interesting to note that carbon is virtually a non-selective radiator whereas many of the other materials are selective in that their spectral emissivities are greater at the shorter wavelengths. As an example of the influence of spectral emissivity, a smooth surface of tungsten at 3000 K would have a luminous efficacy 40% greater than that of carbon at 3000 K, and the black body at the same temperature would also be considerably less efficient than tungsten. In real lamps there are power losses by conduction and convection which reduce the calculated advantages of tungsten. To achieve a high efficacy a filament must operate at as high a temperature as is consistent with satisfactory performance and therefore should possess a high melting point and preferably be a selective radiator. Other desirable properties include low vapour pressure, adequate strength and ductility at room and elevated temperature, good workability and suitable electrical resistance characteristics. Unfortunately, no material exists that satisfactorily meets all the requirements and the current choice of materials remains very limited.

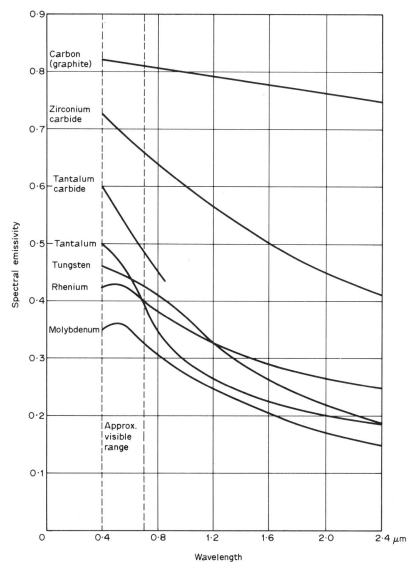

Fig. 7.3 Spectral emissivity of various materials at 2000 K

143

The first practical lamps made by Swan and Edison in 1879 contained filaments made from carbon which possesses a high spectral emissivity. Unfortunately, the high melting point of carbon (3600 °C) could not be fully exploited since its high evaporation rate caused excessive darkening of the lamp bulb and this necessitated lowering the operating temperatures with a concomitant reduction in lamp efficacy. Platinum (m.p. 1772 °C) and osmium (m.p. $\sim$ 3000 °C) have been used as lamp filaments but the low melting point of platinum together with the high cost of both these metals precluded their use on a commercial basis. Tantalum (m.p. 3000 °C) was used much more extensively as a filament material until the developments in the use of tungsten commenced in 1904. Since 1911 lamp filaments have been made almost exclusively from tungsten, a metal with a high melting point (3410 °C), low vapour pressure, selective emissivity and high strength at room and elevated temperatures. In recent years considerable effort has been applied to the development of materials having even greater thermal stability and more favourable spectral emission properties than tungsten. Materials investigated include compounds or composites based on the carbides of tantalum, tungsten, hafnium and zirconium, the hexaborides of the rare earth elements and some of the refractory ceramics, such as zirconia and thoria. Only limited success has been achieved in these investigations and so far no material has emerged that is likely to supersede tungsten in the foreseeable future.

The most important minerals containing tungsten are scheelite ($CaWO_4$) and wolframite (Fe, Mn) WO_4 which are found in many parts of the world, with particularly large deposits in China, Korea, Russia, South America and USA. In the extraction process the ores are treated chemically to produce pure tungsten trioxide from which pure tungsten powder is obtained by a high temperature reduction with hydrogen. Before reduction to the metallic state certain additives or 'dopants' are carefully mixed with the tungsten oxide in order to impart specific properties to tungsten metal required for lamp applications. After blending and reduction, the powders are compressed into bars and their density increased by carefully controlled sintering processes during which temperatures of 3000 °C are achieved. The sintered bars are then shaped into rods by swaging at temperatures of 1400 °C to 1600 °C during which a further increase of density occurs together with an improvement in the ductility of the metal. Finally, the tungsten is drawn into wire through tungsten carbide and diamond dies at progressively lower temperatures within the range 1000 °C to 400 °C. Tungsten wire for lamp filament applications may be drawn down to as low as 0·01 mm diameter and for special applications can be even further reduced by electrolytic etching.

In the shaping of coiled filaments the cleaned tungsten wire is wound on either an iron or molybdenum mandrel at slightly elevated temperatures while for coiled-coil configurations the primary coil is wound again on a second but larger mandrel. Extreme accuracy is essential in the coiling operation since the production of an irregular pitch can cause localized heating of the lamp filament, leading to early failure, or produce undue cooling by the filling gas with consequent loss in efficacy. The permissible variation of the space between the turns of filaments made from the fine wire is only a few millionths of a centimetre. After coiling, the filaments are heat-treated at approximately 1700 °C to remove the internal stresses generated in the wire during drawing and coiling and to provide the coils with a permanent set. Annealing conditions are selected to give maximum reduction in strain energy without promoting recrystallization in the tungsten, since this would embrittle the filaments and present difficulties in subsequent handling and lamp assembly operations.

In order to maintain the rated performance and efficacy it is important that the filament of an incandescent lamp retains its shape throughout the useful life of the lamp. The use of tungsten as a lamp filament presents numerous metallurgical difficulties since filaments operate at temperatures in excess of the recrystallization temperature of tungsten. Instabilities in the high temperature behaviour of metals are often associated with the physical processes of recrystallization and grain growth and in this respect tungsten is no exception. It is now well established that the production of filaments of high dimensional stability necessitates close control over the microstructures developed in the tungsten during and after recrystallization. In the drawn condition tungsten wire possesses a fibrous structure (Fig. 7.4a) and is sufficiently ductile to accommodate without failure the stresses imposed during coiling and lamp assembly. When wire in this condition is heated to the high temperatures common to lamp filaments, recrystallization occurs and new strain-free grains are nucleated within the tungsten and grow at the expense of the distorted fibrous grains. In pure tungsten these recrystallized grains grow quite rapidly and soon after reaching filament operating temperatures (2500 °C and above) many of them occupy the complete cross-section of the wire with the grain boundaries orientated perpendicular to the wire axis. In this type of structure progressive deformation of the wire tends to occur by shear along the grain boundaries ('off-setting') and this, together with the continuous grain growth, leads to filament distortion and premature lamp failure.

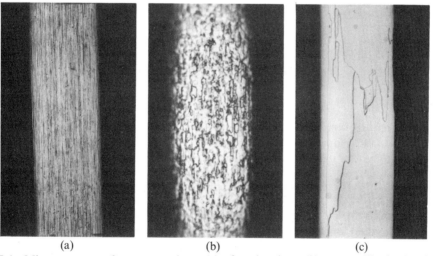

| (a) | (b) | (c) |

Fig. 7.4 Microstructure of tungsten wires (a) after drawing (b) recrystallized wire doped with thoria (c) recrystallized wire doped with alkali silicate (200 × magnification)

The attainment of a more stable and creep-resistant tungsten structure has been approached in two ways. Firstly, by producing a fine-grained recrystallized structure in which further grain growth is inhibited and secondly, by promoting extensive and rapid grain growth so that a very stable structure is quickly achieved. Both types of structure are produced by using small quantities of finely divided additives or dopants which are normally blended into the tungsten powder before pressing and sintering. The fine-grained structures are obtained by using additives, such as thoria, in quantities up to

145

about 4%. The oxide particles, which locate themselves at the tungsten grain boundaries, impede boundary movement and as a consequence not only increase the recrystallization temperature but also maintain a small grain size after recrystallization (Fig. 7.4b) thus improving the resistance to filament distortion and off-setting. After prolonged periods at normal filament temperatures the stability of the thoriated tungsten decreases due to the slow reduction of the thoria by tungsten. Additives of the second kind include potash, silica and alumina. In common with thoria these dopants increase the recrystallization temperature of tungsten but differ in that after recrystallization they promote rapid and extensive grain growth leading to large interlocking grains having many axially aligned boundaries (Fig. 7.4c). This type of structure has a high thermal stability, gives good high temperature creep strength and provides dimensionally stable lamp filaments. The mechanism by which these dopants delay the onset of recrystallization and influence the grain growth characteristics of tungsten is not fully understood. It should be emphasized that the production of non-sag tungsten wire is not only dependent upon the choice of dopant, but also relies upon very close control of the many stages involved in the production of tungsten metal and wire.

Most incandescent lamp filaments are now made from tungsten doped with potash, silica or alumina and only in special applications is use made of thoriated wire or tungsten wire containing between 3% and 5% rhenium. Additions of rhenium to tungsten result in a lowering of the brittle-ductile transition temperature, an increase in the recrystallization temperature, higher mechanical strength and ductility, better corrosion resistance and higher electrical resistance. This enhancement in the properties of tungsten wire makes the alloy particularly attractive for a wide range of filament applications but, unfortunately, the high cost of rhenium imposes severe restrictions on its use. Photoflash lamps commonly use it because of its mechanical advantages (Sect. 11.1.1).

7.2.2   Electrodes

Electrodes in discharge lamps have to conduct electrical power into the lamp and also provide a copious supply of electrons to maintain the discharge. Both the electrode design and the materials used in their construction are of considerable importance since lamp life is often determined primarily by electrode performance. The electrode material must be a good emitter of thermal electrons and must be capable of operating at high temperatures (1000 °C to 1800 °C) since the necessary electron emission densities can only then be achieved. The electrode must have a low evaporation rate to avoid excessive contamination of the lamp atmosphere and also to sustain its own life. In addition, the electrode material must resist attack by substances in the ionized state, possess adequate strength at elevated temperatures and resist sputtering. Few pure metals fulfil these requirements and only tungsten and, to a lesser extent, tantalum have found commercial importance in the lamp industry.

Tungsten is a copious emitter of electrons at temperatures in excess of 2000 °C but such high operating temperatures impose restrictions on electrode design and life. Electron emission can be considerably enhanced by coating the electrodes with one or more of the alkaline earth oxides. This electron-emissive coating provides an abundance of free electrons when hot so enabling the electrodes to operate at more moderate temperatures thus improving lamp performance and life.

The types of electrodes employed in hot cathode fluorescent lamps are coiled-coil, triple-coil and braided tungsten filaments. As with incandescent filaments a non-sag grade of doped tungsten wire is normally employed. In service conditions where the electrodes are likely to encounter vibration and shock, use is sometimes made of tungsten wire containing 3% to 5% rhenium.

In compact source mercury and xenon lamps, tungsten containing 0·5% to 3·0% thoria is sometimes used, particularly in highly rated lamps where an emitter coating would be sputtered off. Metal halide lamps also require thoriated tungsten electrodes since alkaline earth oxides react with halogens to form an involatile solid. In contrast, both thorium and tungsten react with the halogens to give a metal-halogen transport cycle in which these metal vapours are redeposited on the incandescent electrodes.

Occasionally, materials other than tungsten are used in the construction of electrodes. For example, in miniature low pressure mercury discharge lamps, operating on a low voltage d.c. supply, the cathode consists of an emitter-coated filament whereas the anode is made of nickel. Neon lamps, as used in advertising signs, contain cathodes whose shapes conform to the desired lettering or patterns. Such electrodes are of pure iron and are unheated ('cold cathodes').

7.2.3 Getter metals

Many of the materials used in lamp construction operate at high temperatures, in particular, filaments and supports, and in consequence their behaviour is sensitive to the lamp atmosphere. Gases such as oxygen, water vapour and hydrocarbons may contaminate the lamp atmosphere during processing and it is essential that these are removed or reduced to a low level if lamp performance is not to be adversely affected. Materials used to remove gaseous impurities after sealing are known as getters. These rely on the ability of certain solids, often metals, to collect free gases by adsorption, absorption, occlusion or chemical reaction. Getters, which often require some form of thermal activation, may be incorporated in lamps in the form of wire or sheet, or as surface deposits on selected components. The metals most commonly used include barium, tantalum, titanium, niobium, zirconium and some of their alloys, the choice of getter being dependent on the gases to be removed and the type of lamp. Since the temperature for maximum sorption of one gas may not coincide with that for another it may be necessary to employ more than one getter or operate a single getter at different temperatures. One non-metallic getter, which deserves a mention because of its extensive and long-continued use, includes red phosphorus as the active component in a mixture with cryolite.

7.2.4 Miscellaneous uses of metals

The property requirements of metals used in the manufacture of lamps are many and varied and this situation inevitably leads to the use of a wide variety of metals and alloys. Material properties that are of particular importance in lamp applications include melting point, mechanical strength, ductility, workability, weldability, vapour pressure, corrosion and oxidation resistance, thermal expansion and conduction, electrical resistance, surface finish and the sorption and desorption of gases. A number of factors have to be considered when selecting a metal or alloy for a particular application and the ultimate choice is usually based on a compromise involving material properties, cost and availability.

147

Metals used in lamp construction extend from the most refractory metal, tungsten, to the liquid metal, mercury. Table 7.2 summarizes the more commonly used metals and alloys and some of their more important applications. The preponderance of the more refractory metals is to be expected since many components of a lamp are required to operate at elevated temperatures for long periods of time.

Table 7.2   Metals and their applications in lamps

Metal	Application	Metal	Application
Aluminium	Internal reflector coatings, lamp caps	Molybdenum	Filament supports, mandrel wire, glass-metal seals, internal reflectors, lead wires
Barium	Getter		
Brass	Lamp caps		
Copper	Electrical leads	Mercury	Discharge lamps
Gold	Protective coating for lead wires	Niobium	Lamp caps
		Platinum	Joining of refractory metals, cladding material
Iron	Filament supports, electrodes, mandrel wire	Sodium	Discharge lamps
Nickel	Filament supports, internal reflectors, lead wires, electrodes, cladding materials	Tantalum	Filaments, filament supports, getter
		Tungsten	Filaments, filament supports, lead wires, electrodes
Nickel alloys	Glass-metal seals, bimetallic strips, filament supports	Zirconium	Getter, light source in photoflash lamp

Molybdenum, tungsten and nickel are three of the most common metals used in lamp manufacture, in particular, for components that are exposed to high temperatures. Both tungsten and molybdenum possess high melting points, 3410 °C and 2610 °C, respectively; also both metals exhibit high strength at elevated temperatures, high moduli of elasticity, high thermal conductivity, low specific heat and a low coefficient of expansion. Molybdenum has a somewhat greater ductility and a lower ductile-brittle transition temperature than tungsten and so lends itself more readily to applications such as filament supports and hooks, lead wires, internal reflectors and cathode supports. As previously mentioned, molybdenum has a coefficient of expansion that matches several grades of glass and is often used to form a glass to metal seal. Nickel, with a melting point of 1455 °C, is also extensively used for filament supports, lead wires and internal reflectors since it possesses good mechanical strength at high temperatures, resists oxidation and has good formability. In combination with other metals, in particular, copper, iron, chromium and manganese, nickel forms a range of alloys which find use in glass-metal seals, electrode supports and bimetallic strips. Pure copper is used for most current-carrying components although chromium-copper and beryllium-copper may be used in instances where it is necessary to combine high strength and electrical conductivity. Those alloys of copper which have good ductility and malleability are often used for making components that have to be formed by processes such as drawing and stamping. For example, brass is widely used for making lamp caps on account of its good malleability, although there is an increasing tendency to use aluminium as a substitute purely on account of lower material costs. Aluminium has some attractive properties in that it has a low density, good thermal and electrical conductivity and resists attack by air and water due to the formation of an invisible protective covering of aluminium oxide. This metal is used as a reflector surface when vapourized on to glass and plastic. In photoflash lamps where a continuous spectrum of intense white light is required, the radiation is produced by the ignition of zirconium foil.

Considerable use is made of clad metals in lamp manufacture so that specific properties of more than one metal can be exploited simultaneously thus affording economies in material. Examples of clad materials include iron clad with nickel, bronze clad with nickel, iron clad with brass and molybdenum clad with platinum. A particularly important composite wire is that known as Dumet (Sect. 7.1.3). Another form of composite is the bimetal strip used in flashing lamps and starter switches where thermally controlled deflections are obtained by exploiting differences in thermal expansion coefficients of nickel and nickel-iron alloys.

The various metals and alloys used in lamp manufacture have to be combined into complete structures and this often involves production of high-integrity joints. It is sufficient to state here that numerous metals and alloys are used in the joining of metals, glasses and ceramics to themselves and to each other.

7.3 GASES AND VAPOURS

The principal gases used for discharge and incandescent lamp fillings are found as naturally occurring constituents of air. They are separated by fractional distillation from liquified air; Table 7.3 gives details of their properties.

Table 7.3 Properties of atmospheric gases

Gas	Percentage by weight in air	Molecular weight	Boiling point °C	Melting point °C	Viscosity at 1000 K $\mu Ns/m^2$	Thermal conductivity at 1000 K mW/m. K
Nitrogen	78·0	28·0	− 195·8	− 210·0	37·2	83·0
Oxygen	20·95	32·0	− 183·0	− 218·8		
Argon	0·93	39·9	− 185·9	− 189·4	53·6	41·9
Neon	0·00182	20·2	− 246·1	− 248·6	69·5	107·3
Helium	0·00052	4·0	− 268·9	− 269·7	42·4	330·1
Krypton	0·00011	83·8	− 153·4	− 157·3	65·4	24·3
Xenon	0·000009	131·3	− 108·1	− 111·9	63·1	15·0

Other gases (CO_2, H_2, N_2O, O_3, etc.) are also present in small quantities

All types of electric lamps are sensitive to the presence of trace impurities, and the common lamp-making gases must not contain more than a few ppm of oxygen, carbon monoxide and dioxide, and hydrocarbons because these can react with the high temperature cathodes or filaments, to reduce efficacy and lamp life. The commonest and most destructive contaminant in lamps is water vapour, and whilst it is not difficult to detect, it is easily adsorbed on to surfaces at room temperature, making quantitative measurements in a small gas volume, such as the contents of a lamp, extremely difficult.

The most suitable instrument for measuring the percentage of major components and trace impurities in a bulk gas supply is the gas chromatograph; water vapour is usually measured separately by an electrolytic type water vapour meter. These techniques may be used to determine the gaseous contents of a lamp by breaking open the bulb, but mass spectroscopy is a more convenient method for handling a small volume sample.

With most lamp materials the applications are empirical, using the best available for the particular task, and little can be done by theoretical studies. In the case of tungsten it is possible to investigate its use more fundamentally. The case of energy exchange between gas and metal is an example where this approach has produced valuable results.

The gas filling in an incandescent lamp is crucial because in a vacuum the filament temperature and resulting efficacy are limited by the evaporation rate of tungsten; this can be greatly reduced (typically to 1/70th) by gas filling. There is a compensating disadvantage because the gas conducts heat from the filament, which reduces the lamp efficacy, but a change-over point, when gas filling gives an overall gain in efficacy and life, occurs at about 15 W for mains voltage lamps and 3 W for minature lamps such as torch bulbs. It is essential therefore to have some knowledge of the power loss to the gas filling so that the effect on efficacy may be calculated.

The Langmuir sheath model.   The power loss is determined by using the 'Langmuir model' which assumes that the viscous, low-density gas layer surrounding an incandescent surface is free from convention currents, and that heat flow from the filament is by conduction only. The diameter of the stationary sheath, b, surrounding a filament of diameter d, can be calculated from the following equation:

$$b \ln \left(\frac{b}{d}\right) = K_1 \left(\frac{\eta}{\rho}\right)^{2/3} \left\{\frac{T_1}{T_1 - T_2}\right\}^{1/3} \tag{7.1}$$

where η = gas viscosity at the average gas temperature
ρ = gas density at the average gas temperature
T_1 and T_2 are the temperatures at the filament surface and edge of the Langmuir sheath, respectively,
K_1 is a correlation coefficient approximately equal to 7·48 using SI units.

To evaluate Eq. 7.1, the gas viscosity must be known at the average gas temperature, and to calculate power loss thermal conductivity values must be integrated over the range of temperatures from T_1 to T_2. This calculation has recently been simplified by expressing the viscosity (η) and thermal conductivity (λ) of the common lamp-making gases in terms of the average gas temperature, a constant D and an exponent N:

$$\eta(T) = D(\eta)T^{N(\eta)} \quad \text{(in } \mu\text{Ns/m}^2\text{)} \tag{7.2}$$

$$\lambda(T) = D(\lambda)T^{N(\lambda)} \quad \text{(in mW/m.K)} \tag{7.3}$$

The equations hold good from 500 K to 3500 K. Values of $D(\eta)$, $N(\eta)$, $D(\lambda)$ and $N(\lambda)$ for the commonly used gases and mixtures (Table 7.4) are derived from the rigorous transport equations.

Power loss to the gas filling of a lamp (W) can now be calculated from the equation

$$W = \frac{2\pi L}{\ln (b/d)} \frac{D(\lambda)}{[1 + N(\lambda)]} \{T_1^{[1+N(\lambda)]} - T_2^{[1+N(\lambda)]}\} \quad \text{(in mW)} \tag{7.4}$$

where L is the filament length (in m). The precise influence that gas filling content and pressure have upon lamp life is rather complex. Filament life is inversely proportional to the mass evaporation rate, and it has been shown that the following approximate equation, relating the mass evaporation rate in vacuum (m_v) to the mass evaporation rate in gas (m_g), agrees well with earlier experimental results.

$$m_g = \frac{m_v}{1 + \left[\dfrac{d \ln (b/d) P_g M_g T_1}{K_2 \eta P_f M_f \overline{T}}\right] m_v} \tag{7.5}$$

where P_g and P_f are the gas filling pressure and equilibrium vapour pressure of tungsten, respectively

M_g and M_f are the molecular weights of the gas filling and tungsten, respectively
η is the gas viscosity at the average gas temperature of $\overline{T}$
K_2 is a correlation coefficient, approximately equal to 0·327 using SI units

Table 7.4   Thermal conductivity and viscosity constants and exponents for lamp gases

Component 1	Component 2	Thermal conductivity		Viscosity	
		$D(\lambda)$	$N(\lambda)$	$D(\eta)$	$N(\eta)$
100% A	—	0·476	0·648	0·610	0·648
95% A	5% N$_2$	0·459	0·657	0·603	0·648
90% A	10% N$_2$	0·444	0·665	0·596	0·648
80% A	20% N$_2$	0·418	0·680	0·582	0·648
70% A	30% N$_2$	0·397	0·694	0·568	0·648
—	100% N$_2$	0·342	0·763	0·460	0·648
100% Kr	—	0·277	0·648	0·743	0·648
90% Kr	10% N$_2$	0·270	0·670	0·727	0·648
80% Kr	20% N$_2$	0·269	0·687	0·710	0·648
50% Kr	50% N$_2$	0·282	0·720	0·644	0·648
100% Xe	—	0·170	0·648	0·717	0·648

Eqs. 7.4 and 7.5 can be used directly to calculate power loss and evaporation rate of tungsten from the filament of a conventional incandescent lamp. When applied to tubular tungsten halogen lamps with a central axially mounted filament, the value of b should be taken as the internal diameter of the cylindrical bulb. The reason is that the convection velocity is very low in a horizontal narrow bore tubular lamp, and the temperature gradient is not disturbed.

The required constants for pure gases are given in Table 7.3, and from this it can be seen that the heavier gases krypton and xenon, the most expensive and rare species, are more effective in suppressing filament evaporation and reducing power loss by their lower thermal conductivity. The choice of gas filling is usually a compromise between efficacy, life and the overall economics.

Gases in GLS lamps.   Generally, household lamps are filled with 90% argon and 10% nitrogen, but lamps containing 85% krypton and 15% nitrogen give a higher efficacy for the same lamp life (Sect. 9.3.5).

The nitrogen addition in mains voltage lamps, which are normally filled to just below atmospheric pressure, is absolutely essential to prevent a destructive arc forming through the high temperature low gas density zone adjacent to the filament. The arcing potential of a gas-filled lamp may be raised by increasing the gas pressure, or by introducing a small amount of non-reactive diatomic gas, usually nitrogen, which can absorb energy by molecular rotations or vibrations although its ionization potential (15·51 eV) is slightly below that of argon (15·76 eV). It is not practical to raise the pressure in a household lamp above atmospheric because this in itself would be a hazard. Tungsten halogen lamps are usually much smaller in volume with a bulb made from very strong and thick vitreous silica tubing, which permits the safe filling to high pressures without the risk of arcing or explosion; in these lamps pure argon or krypton may be used.

Other gases and vapours. Tungsten halogen incandescent lamps contain iodine or bromine to support a transport cycle which will keep the bulb wall free from tungsten (Sect. 10.1). Iodine is a solid at room temperature, with a melting point 113·6 °C, boiling point 183·0 °C and vapour pressure 0·375 Torr at 25 °C. It is mainly used in long life lamps, and is dried by sublimation in vacuum over phosphorus pentoxide to reduce the moisture content to a sufficiently low level for lamp use. Bromine is a liquid at room temperature, with a melting point −7·3 °C, boiling point 58·2 °C and vapour pressure of 234 Torr at 25 °C. The element is rarely used in lamps, and it is usually introduced as HBr, $CHBr_3$, CH_2Br_2 or CH_3Br to regulate the activity of the transport cycle. These vapours are dried by passing over conventional drying agents, such as calcium bromide or phosphorus pentoxide.

A recent innovation has been the introduction of the halogen together with phosphorus as a getter for oxygen and water vapour, in the form of a halophosphonitrile (Sect. 10.2.2). In this way bromine can be added as trimeric and tetrameric bromophosphonitrile, which are chemically inert solids of low vapour pressure. The melting point and vapour pressure of $(PNBr_2)_3$ and $(PNBr_2)_4$ are 192 °C and 202 °C; and 10^{-6} Torr and 4×10^{-10} Torr respectively at room temperature.

Discharge lamps usually have a low pressure of a monomolecular gas filling, neon, argon or xenon, to initiate the discharge and act as a buffer in the main discharge. In addition most lamps contain a metal vapour, such as mercury or sodium. These metals have a vapour pressure high enough to enable them to be volatilized into the arc, where they are excited to emit light of a characteristic spectrum (Chap. 6).

Mercury is one of the only two liquid metal elements (gallium has a melting point 29·5 °C); it is reasonably chemically inert at room temperature, and has a vapour pressure of $1·94 \times 10^{-3}$ Torr at 25 °C. These properties enable mercury to be dispensed into a lamp without interfering with the lamp processing after its introduction.

Sodium is a soft, silvery metal, having a melting point 97·8 °C. It is extremely reactive and difficult to handle and great care must be exercised to prevent reaction with oxygen and water vapour. Because of this reactivity special envelope materials have been developed to contain it, as previously described. Both of these metals are purified by a double distillation process under vacuum.

Other metals can be used to produce light, and those of low vapour pressure, such as scandium, thallium, gallium, etc., can be volatilized into the arc as their halides to give a variety of emission spectra (Sect. 15.1). These can be introduced as the metal halides with mercury, or as metals with mercuric halide. Being deliquescent, the halides are extremely difficult to handle. Since water vapour or the subsequent hydrogen produced will cause an increase in lamp striking voltage, it must be rigorously excluded, preferably to less than 1 ppm. To achieve this the materials must be handled in an atmosphere containing less than 1 ppm of water vapour.

8 Phosphors

This subject has been discussed from a theoretical standpoint in Sect. 6.1.6, but in view of its great importance in producing light a further treatment is necessary, adding practical details and examples to the basic principles previously outlined.

Historically, the term *phosphorescence* originates from the element phosphorus whose ability to glow in the dark was of great interest to the alchemists in the 17th and 18th centuries. Also derived from this is the term *phosphor* which is now widely used to describe materials, usually solids, which have the ability to *luminesce*. By coincidence many of the important phosphors used today are phosphorus compounds such as the phosphates, but whereas the luminescence of these compounds is brought about by the ability of the material to absorb one form of energy and re-emit part of it as visible light, in the case of the element phosphorus the glow is due to a chemical reaction which takes place when the element undergoes oxidation. The term 'fluorescence' is a general one covering many types of phenomenon, but in the past it has been restricted to describe very fast processes, as distinct from slow phosphorescence. It is more usual nowadays to use the term 'luminescence' for all similar processes in light emission.

8.1 METHODS OF EXCITATION

In order to differentiate between various types of luminescence, a prefix is often used, for example the glow of phosphorus is *chemiluminescence*, the luminescence caused by bombarding a phosphor with cathode rays is *cathodoluminescence*, and that excited by electromagnetic radiation is *photoluminescence*. The feeble light emission from certain living organisms such as fireflies, glow-worms and marine plankton is classed as *bioluminescence* which is a form of chemiluminescence. Similarly, there are other forms of luminescence bearing the prefixes electro-, tribo-, thermo-, etc., where the stimulating or exciting energy is an electric field, frictional energy, heat, etc.

8.1.1 Excitation by electromagnetic radiation

This type of excitation includes the action of the infra-red, visible light, ultra-violet, X-rays and gamma rays. By absorption in suitable material and partial re-emission as visible light, this source of energy is the most widely used in the excitation of luminescence: the emission is normally at a longer wavelength than that of the radiation absorbed (Stokes' law). For example, a most convenient way of exciting phosphors is by the use of the ultra-violet radiation which is produced in certain gas discharges. If an electrical discharge takes place in a low pressure of mercury vapour and argon, 50% or more of the energy applied to the discharge is converted into ultra-violet radiation at wavelengths of 253·7 nm and 185·0 nm. By using selected phosphors to convert this ultra-violet into visible light an efficient conversion of electrical energy into white light is obtained, and this is the basis of the fluorescent lamp. During the past 30 years the efficacy of generating white light in this way has risen to about 80 lm/W, which is higher than for any light source which depends on the emission of light by increasing the temperature of a solid to incandescence.

High pressure arcs in mercury although producing a high proportion of visible light also emit some ultra-violet wavelengths near 365 nm and different types of luminescent material are necessary to take advantage of this emission. Usually they are red-emitting phosphors which compensate for the lack of red wavelengths in the visible line spectrum of mercury. Phosphors can also be used with some metal halide lamps which have more extensive line spectra than mercury alone, in order to use the ultra-violet emission of mercury and of other metals in the discharge as well.

X-rays and gamma rays from radioactive materials are very short wavelength radiation, and they excite many materials to luminescence. However, their great penetrating power reduces the amount of energy which can be absorbed by a screen of reasonable thickness so that light outputs are small and are useful only for indicating purposes (for example in radiology, testing of materials, nuclear work, etc.).

Under very high excitation and precisely controlled optical conditions certain crystalline phosphors which have a line emission under normal conditions, will emit the same wavelength in a very powerful narrow beam of coherent light rather than their usual random and diffuse emission. This is laser action and is not normally considered as fluorescence though this is largely a question of definition (Sect. 6.3.1).

A source of infra-red radiation, normally of little interest because of its spectral location, is found in some semi-conductors excited by an electric field. There are a few *anti-Stokes phosphors* which can convert this infra-red radiation to useful visible light. They comprise certain fluorides and oxychlorides containing ytterbium and erbium, having their fluorescent emission mainly in the green spectral region (Sects. 6.1.6, 17.2). If a number of efficient phosphors of this type could be developed the range of colours available from light-emitting diodes would be usefully expanded. The more exciting application for phosphors of this type would be to convert the infra-red emission from incandescent filament lamps, at present 90% of the radiation, into useful visible light, and if this could be achieved it would be a tremendous advance.

8.1.2 Excitation by charged particles

Particles of high energy such as protons, alpha and beta particles are useful in the excitation of some phosphors, but they are of minor importance in lighting as distinct from giving indications by light (Sect. 6.1.6). *Beta lamps* are of some interest: these use tritium or krypton 85 in sealed glass bulbs with phosphor screens. They are finding wide application for illuminating telephone dials, marine compasses, marker buoys, and in other situations where a maintenance-free life of many years is required.

Beams of less energetic electrons are used to excite the phosphor screens in cathode-ray tubes, which are used as display devices and in particular for television pictures.

In contrast to radioactive sources where the energy of the particles is extremely high but unalterable and the incident density of radiation is normally very small, the usual cathode-ray source transfers more useful energy to a luminescent material. This is because many more particles but of smaller individual energy are involved, and this results in an

155

acceptable light yield with less deterioration of the luminescent material under bombardment. The efficacy of a 'black and white' cathode-ray tube screen for television reception is of the order of 40 lm/W when the bulb is of clear glass. Phosphors with very short afterglow (or fast decay) are necessary in most cathode-ray tubes used for television or display purposes, but in tubes used for radar some phosphorescence or persistence of emission is desirable to allow lengthy inspection of the traces.

8.1.3   Excitation by electric field

Electroluminescence is a form of light production which has been developed since 1950 to the point where it can be used to produce useful light levels for indicators and signs but is not suitable for general lighting purposes (Chap. 16). The luminescent material is used in a thin layer between plane electrodes one of which is transparent to allow the light to emerge. In this device, which is similar to a capacitor, the special phosphors used appear to be capable of locally enhancing the alternating field applied to them. The increased field strength can then excite electrons in the phosphor crystal to levels of energy from which they can make transitions which generate light. This is similar to the mechanism of light emission from a phosphor excited by ultra-violet radiation; but the manner of producing the free electrons is different. The efficacy is of the order of 0·5 lm/W.

The recombination of charge barriers at a p-n junction has been recognized as the cause of light production in silicon carbide in a powerful electric field, a phenomenon known for many years. Other binary compounds have now proved much more efficient in light production by *junction electroluminescence* (Sect. 6.1.6 and Chap. 17).

8.2   SOLID LUMINESCENT MATERIALS

8.2.1   Chemical composition

Although there are many interesting cases of luminescence in gases and liquids, only solid materials are of practical value for lighting purposes.

The first known solid luminescent materials were those which showed the emission of light after exposure to daylight or sunlight. These were sulphides of the alkaline earth metals. The artificial production of these materials was naturally very primitive and not until suitable ultra-violet sources and methods of experiment were available could any rational advances be made. It was then realized that a number of naturally occurring minerals are fluorescent and that by synthesizing them in a purer state but with the same crystalline form efficient phosphors could be obtained. Later, a multitude of phosphors in various crystal forms were synthesized, often having no known mineral counterpart or perhaps only a non-fluorescent one. A recognizable crystal structure is an almost indispensable property of solid inorganic phosphors, and X-rays have been used extensively in their investigation.

A feature common to a great many phosphors of the solid inorganic type, with which this chapter is largely concerned, is the presence of small quantities of foreign elements essential to the development of luminescence. These are called *activators*. One of particularly wide application is the transition metal manganese, found in many important phosphors described below.

Historically, the mineral willemite, which is a zinc orthosilicate containing a trace of manganese, is important because it is sometimes found in a fluorescent form which can convert short wavelength ultra-violet radiation into green light. This was one of the materials used by Crookes in his original work on discharge tubes. Synthetic zinc silicate containing a carefully controlled amount of manganese is obviously a more reliable source than random mineral specimens and it is still an important phosphor. During the latter half of the 1930's it was found that by incorporating small amounts of beryllium compounds during the preparation a range of fluorescent colours varying from green through yellow to yellow-orange and even to pink could be obtained. These manganese-activated zinc beryllium silicates were at one time very important for fluorescent lamp production.

In general terms, phosphors for lamps are almost exclusively oxygen-containing materials such as silicates, phosphates, borates, tungstates, vanadates, etc. Although certain of these are used for cathode-ray tubes and beta-lamps, some binary materials such as the sulphides, the related selenides and tellurides, and fluorides are also very important in these applications. Thus some manganese-activated phosphors based on magnesium fluoride have a sufficiently long afterglow to make them valuable for the radar presentations previously mentioned. Some sulphide types of phosphor have other uses; for example although a number of materials show electroluminescence, only the zinc sulphide types are of any great value: luminescent paints are also based mainly on sulphide materials.

X-rays were originally made visible for medical diagnostic purposes by screens of barium platinocyanide, but at present screens of zinc cadmium sulphide phosphor are widely used. The photographic action of X-rays may be increased by the use of blue fluorescent calcium tungstate screens in contact with the film.

Luminescent properties are not confined to inorganic solid materials, thus organic luminescent materials are familiar in the 'Day-Glo' type of poster paints. Some of these consist of organic dyestuffs like rhodamine deposited on synthetic plastics of a particle size suitable for making a paint, and operate by virtue of the violet and ultra-violet radiations present in natural daylight. Colourless organic dyes which show a blue fluorescence under ultra-violet are used as *fluorescent brighteners* in detergents and for white textiles and paper; their faint violet or blue fluorescence offsets the slightly yellowish colour of the fabric and so produces a 'brighter white'. Similar materials are also used for providing secret markings in papers and cards, and modern postage stamps incorporate stripes of luminescent dyes which enable mail to be sorted automatically by high speed machinery.

Very few luminescent materials are equally efficient under a number of different types of excitation and in general each phosphor needs to be adapted in composition or structure to the particular type of excitation for which it is required.

8.2.2 Emission spectra

Whereas the fluorescence of unrestricted atoms (in gases) consists of sharp spectral lines, the mutual interference which occurs in liquids and still more in crystalline solids, causes a widening of what are fundamentally lines into bands. Some of these are evidently broadened lines, others are so wide that they cover the whole of the visible spectrum. The widest bands arise from those phosphors with no apparent chemical impurity to provide an activator. The widest known single emission band is probably that of barium titanium phosphate, (Fig. 8.1a), extending from ultra-violet to infra-red with a peak in the blue-green. Fig. 8.1b shows the contrasting narrow emission band of a manganese-activated phosphor (Sect. 8.3.3).

Almost all these spectra, when measured as energy or power and plotted on a frequency or wave number scale, agree closely with one or more bands in the form of Gaussian error functions, and this approach is useful in the study of phosphors (Sect. 8.3.1).

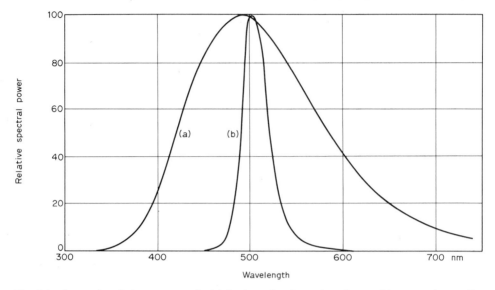

Fig. 8.1   Spectral emission curves of   (a) barium titanium phosphate   (b) magnesium gallate
Normalized at peak emission

By Gaussian band analysis of the emission from the sulphide phosphor series several independent bands can be isolated for each material and these show regular shifts through the visible spectrum with changes in composition, particularly with the substitution of zinc by cadmium. Less regularity is found in the oxygen-dominated materials, though if sensitization occurs (Sect. 6.1.6) it is easy to observe the decrease of the sensitizer band and the increase of the manganese band as the relative proportions of the two activators are varied (Figs. 8.2a and b). Another example is seen in calcium metasilicate activated by lead and manganese.

Emission bands may appear in the ultra-violet or the infra-red regions of the spectrum but naturally visible emission is most useful and most widely studied. Little use has been found for infra-red luminescence, though ultra-violet is valuable for special purposes ('black light' from fluorescent tubes or mercury lamps for display and theatrical effects, in artificial daylight sources, and in photocopying lamps, Sect. 12.4).

8.2.3   Temperature effects

The earlier distinction between fluorescence and phosphorescence has given way to a classification of the processes by which light output increases on excitation, or decays after it. If the light-emitting process of a phosphor depends on transitions of electrons

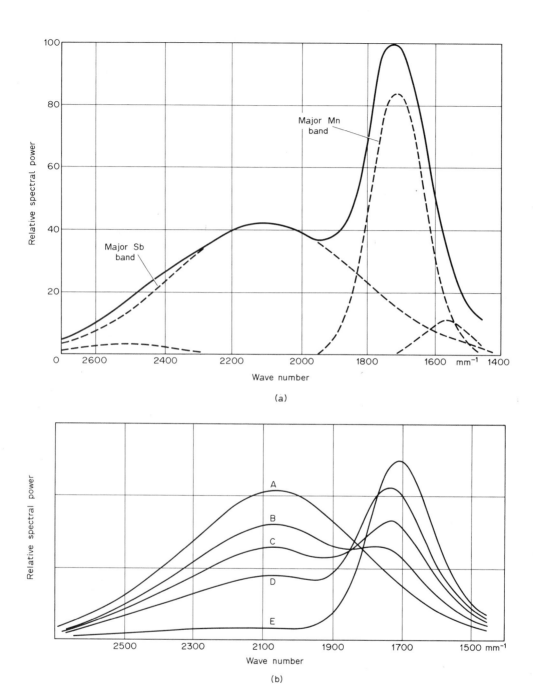

Fig. 8.2 (a) Gaussian analysis of fluorescent emission from calcium halophosphate: Sb, Mn. (b) Spectral power distribution of halophosphates with a 3:1 ratio of F:Cl and different Mn contents. Atoms of Mn per 3 atoms of P: A, 0; B, 0·025; C, 0·05; D, 0·1; E, 0·4

within the ions of the activator, without the intervention of free or 'conductivity' electrons, the processes of rise and fall of light are exponential and nearly independent of the temperature. However, if free electrons are involved, the processes resemble chemical reactions of the second order and are greatly accelerated by a rise of temperature or by more powerful excitation. To the first class belong most of the oxygen-dominated lamp and cathode-ray tube phosphors, with decay times varying from less than a millionth of a second to a few hundredths; cerium and manganese are typical activators in these respective speed groups. Sulphides are typical of the second class and their decay may last for hours, or days, especially when activated by copper. It is quite usual to find several independent decays with different time constants in the same phosphor.

For a given excitation most commercially useful phosphors have a maximum output of light at a particular temperature which is often near room temperature. As the temperature rises the efficiency falls to zero, with the increasing atomic vibrations in the crystal absorbing more and more of the power put in. This temperature quenching varies greatly in detail. Calcium tungstate loses all its luminescence at about 150 °C, whereas certain aluminates activated by chromium are still increasing in brightness up to 500 °C. Temperature resistance is necessary in phosphors used with mercury lamps since they may be operating in the region of 300 °C. When phosphorescing material is suddenly heated a burst of light will occur; followed by a fall to lower brightness. Part of the stored energy due to be given out as light in normal phosphorescence is prematurely released by the heating, but the total light output is likely to be less than it would have been if heating had not been applied to accelerate the process. Similar behaviour is observed if infra-red radiation is used instead of heating; this often acts as just described, by *stimulation*; sometimes it may decrease the total amount of phosphorescence by *quenching*. A similar kind of light emission occurs if there is stored energy but no visible phosphorescence, when *thermoluminescence* is produced on heating. Minerals subjected to radioactivity in past ages frequently show the effect, as have certain of the moon samples brought back by the recent Apollo missions; and some synthetic phosphors do so after excitation by ultra-violet or ionizing radiation.

8.3   PHOSPHORS FOR FLUORESCENT LAMPS

The fluorescent lamp has been an established light source for so many years that it is possible to describe in detail the properties which a useful fluorescent lamp phosphor must possess.

(a) It must be an inorganic material of a stable nature to withstand both processing and operating conditions.
(b) It must have a strong optical absorption band in the short ultra-violet region to absorb the 253·7 nm and 185 nm radiation with consequent fluorescence.
(c) It must have a minimum optical absorption in the visible part of the spectrum; that is, it should have no appreciable body colour.
(d) It must fluoresce in the required part of the visible spectrum with as little emission as possible in the near ultra-violet and infra-red regions.
(e) The optical absorption and fluorescence characteristics should be at a maximum at a temperature of 40 °C to 50 °C.

(f) The material must be capable of being prepared in a finely divided form or broken down to fine particles without loss of fluorescent efficiency.

(g) It must retain its fluorescent characteristics over long periods of operation in a lamp.

Although these are some of the more important general properties required of a lamp phosphor dictated by the conditions of its use, there are still the equally important practical considerations such as ease of preparation, availability of raw materials, and cost of manufacture. These latter features are of considerable importance because the manufacture of fluorescent lamps uses a greater quantity of inorganic phosphors than any other applications; it outstrips the consumption of phosphors for all other applications by an estimated 40 times.

It is not surprising therefore that only a few materials will satisfy all these highly specialized physical, chemical, economic and manufacturing requirements; in fact, of the hundreds of phosphors which have been discovered, less than 20 are of commercial significance for fluorescent lamp use.

The light output from a discharge lamp is of a pulsed nature because of the frequency of the electrical supply, consequently if the phosphor used in the lamp has some afterglow or phosphorescence this can help to suppress visible flicker of the lamp.

8.3.1 The halophosphates

Originally manganese-activated zinc silicate (willemite) and zinc beryllium silicate phosphors were used in fluorescent lamps, but the latter were subsequently replaced by a group of phosphors known as the halophosphates which are even more efficient in converting ultra-violet light into useful visible light, and in maintaining their luminescent characteristics over long periods of time. In addition, the halophosphates are more readily prepared in the form of the fine particles required for use in lamp coatings and have no known toxic properties. They were discovered in 1942 and since then increases in light output of fluorescent lamps containing halophosphates has been almost continuous, due to improvements in the physical characteristics of the phosphors by chemical means. Thus the 1200 mm 40 W White lamp has shown a fairly steady increase totalling about 33% in its initial efficacy in the past 20 years, and a still greater percentage increase after some thousands of hours' life due to improved maintenance.

The halophosphates are alkaline earth halogen-containing phosphates of the hexagonal apatite crystal structure with antimony and manganese activators; the alkali metal is usually calcium but strontium may be substituted in part. The fluorescence colour can be controlled by changing the ratio of fluorine to chlorine retained in the matrix and by adjusting the concentration of manganese.

Emission spectra of the halophosphates. Phosphors absorb ultra-violet radiation but only certain wavelengths of this absorption are effective in exciting luminescence and this is called the *excitation spectrum*; the absorbed energy which is not effective in producing luminescence is dissipated as heat within the material. High efficiency of a phosphor requires this spectrum to show high quantum conversion values at the wavelengths of the incident radiation.

The halophosphates absorb strongly in the ultra-violet and are effectively excited by the mercury lines at 253·7 nm and 185·0 nm, but not by the long wavelength mercury line at 365·0 nm. The excitation curve for the simplest of the halophosphates, calcium

161

fluorophosphate activated by antimony is shown in Fig. 8.3. It can be analysed into a number of Gaussian components which may be due to different activator sites, or different energy states of the antimony in the lattice. Excitation curves are difficult to measure, and the response of new phosphors is more often determined empirically than by consideration of their fluorescence yield or quantum efficiency through the spectrum.

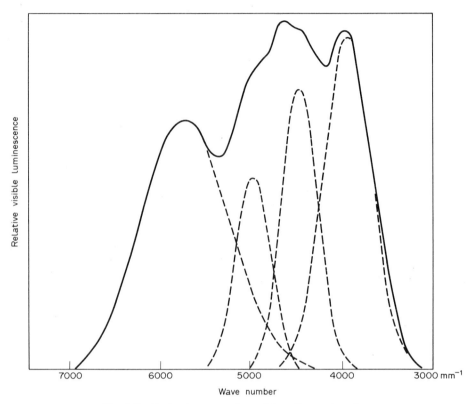

Fig. 8.3   Excitation curve for calcium fluorophosphate

Under normal conditions manganese-activated halophosphates do not show luminescence unless a primary activator or *sensitizer* such as antimony is present. This is because the excitation band for divalent manganese is too far in the ultra-violet and energy transfer is required between the primary activator antimony and the manganese by a radiationless process (Sect. 6.1.6).

The spectral power distribution of the fluorescence of some of these phosphors is shown in Fig. 8.2b. The blue emission due to antimony activation is a fairly broad band; when manganese is incorporated a new band appears at longer wavelengths, and the intensity of this band increases at the expense of the antimony band as the concentration of manganese increases. The result is a complex emission band extending over a wide spectral region. The fluorescence is shifted slightly towards longer wavelengths by replacing some of the matrix fluorine by chlorine.

Although the intensity of fluorescence of the halophosphates falls slightly with increasing temperature, the stability is reasonable over the temperature region in which a lamp normally operates (Fig. 8.4).

It should be borne in mind that the colour of the light from a fluorescent lamp is decided by both the phosphor emission and the visible emission from the mercury discharge so

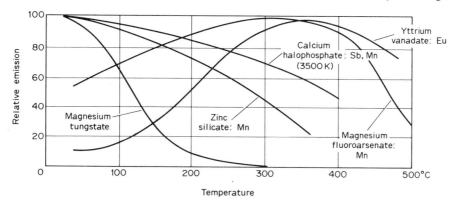

Fig. 8.4   Effect of temperature on fluorescence

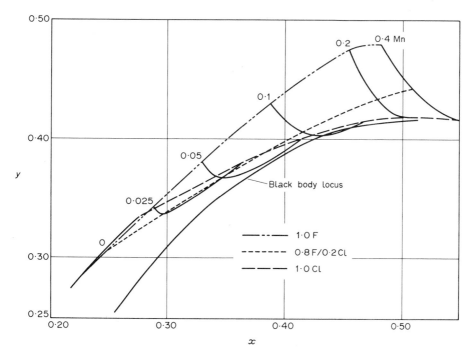

Fig. 8.5   Chromaticity diagram for calcium halophosphate system. Note that the usual effect of Cl addition is to increase the value of x, but this is reversed with no Mn present

163

that although the spectral energy distribution of most phosphors is a smooth curve, superimposed on this in the case of the fluorescent lamp are the strong lines from the mercury discharge (Fig. 12.8). The full range of colours obtained from lamps using antimony and manganese-activated halophosphates is shown in Fig. 8.5. It is a remarkable fact that the colours produced by fluorescent lamps with halophosphate phosphors are so conveniently placed within the range of acceptable 'whites'. It is however not always possible or economically best to obtain the exact colour required by using one phosphor alone. It is normal practice in manufacture to use a number of halophosphate phosphors of more or less constant colour, and then obtain the final colour required in a lamp by blending them together, or by the addition of relatively small quantities of other phosphors.

8.3.2 Other lamp phosphors

There are a number of inorganic phosphors which can be used in mixtures with halophosphates or alone in fluorescent lamps. The general properties required of these phosphors are the same as those previously discussed. The emission must be in a suitable spectral region and the phosphors must be compatible with one another during lamp manufacture, and not show any marked difference in light output during use. It is also of advantage if there is no great difference in the physical density of the phosphors so that when they are being applied to the glass tube in the form of a liquid suspension no separation takes place, otherwise there could be a colour difference from end to end of the finished lamp. Of these phosphors, the most important are given in Table 8.1.

Table 8.1 Some of the more important lamp phosphors

Matrix	Composition	Activator(s)	Emission
Zinc silicate	Zn_2SiO_4	Mn	Green
Calcium silicate	$CaSiO_3$	Pb, Mn	Pink
Calcium halophosphates	$Ca_5(PO_4)_3(F, Cl)$	Sb, Mn	Blue to pink
Cadmium borate	$Cd_2B_2O_5$	Mn	Red
Strontium magnesium phosphate	$(Sr, Mg)_3(PO_4)_2$	Sn	Pinkish white
Magnesium fluorogermanate	$Mg_4GeO_6 . MgF_2$	Mn	Deep red
Magnesium fluoroarsenate	$Mg_6As_2O_{11} . MgF_2$	Mn	Deep red
Barium silicate	$BaSi_2O_5$	Pb	Long ultra-violet
Magnesium gallate	$MgGa_2O_4$	Mn	Blue-green
Yttrium vanadate	YVO_4	Eu	Red
Magnesium tungstate	$MgWO_4$	—	Pale blue
Calcium tungstate	$CaWO_4$	—	Deep blue
Barium titanium phosphate	$Ba_4Ti(PO_4)_4$	—	Blue-white

One reason for the need for a variety of phosphors is the comparative lack of red emission in halophosphates, which as a result are highly efficient in light production but less so in colour rendering properties (Sect. 12.3.3). Calcium silicate, the alkaline earth phosphates and magnesium fluorogermanate are often used to provide this desirable red radiation. It is seen from Table 8.1 that, apart from phosphors with one or two activators, some useful materials, the so-called self-activated phosphors, require no foreign element at all for activation. There are numerous phosphors of this type, such as calcium and magnesium tungstates, barium titanium phosphate, magnesium titanium borate, and certain vanadates and molybdates. In this class of material the activator is not a foreign cation replacing a cation of the matrix, but is a complex anion forming an integral part of the matrix. Barium titanium phosphate is of this type and provides an example of a different type of emission. Whereas the fluorescence of the halophosphates can be varied over a wide range, the emission from self-activated barium titanium phosphate is a wide band of constant shape and position which cannot be usefully changed without causing a marked reduction in the brightness of the phosphor (Fig. 8.1a).

Despite the present importance of the halophosphates, the possibility of finding new and better phosphors must not be overlooked. A new replacement phosphor would require a brighter fluorescence, or a better maintenance of the light output when used in lamps, or give a better colour, or be cheaper to prepare. It should have a wide spectral emission to provide a near-white colour in fluorescent lamps.

If there were a number of bright phosphors whose emissions consisted of sharp narrow bands in different parts of the spectrum, these could be used together in a fluorescent lamp to give a high light output of better colour than conventional halophosphates because allowance could be made for the colour distortions produced by the mercury lines. A possibility in this direction is the use of europium-activated alkaline earth silicates. Although these phosphors were discovered before the halophosphates it was not until europium became plentifully available as a result of the demand for europium-activated yttrium vanadate that their potentialities were re-examined. It is now possible to prepare a number of highly efficient narrow band phosphors and there is the possibility of using blends of these; but whether the high costs involved in such an approach would provide serious competition to the halophosphates is at present doubtful.

8.3.3   Lamp phosphors for special applications

Although the majority of fluorescent lamps are used for general lighting purposes a surprisingly large number are used in photo-copying machines. Here the requirement is light of a fairly high intensity and of a carefully controlled spectral power distribution. Phosphors emitting in narrow bands are usually required and sometimes in regions of the spectrum of little interest for general lighting purposes, as in the near ultra-violet. One phosphor which has become of importance in this application is magnesium gallate activated with manganese (Fig. 8.1b). Other phosphors of this type which may become important are europium-activated silicates and phosphates. The characteristic of all these materials is the narrowness of their emission compared with that of other phosphors.

8.3.4   Luminous efficacy of lamp phosphors

Apart from its value in providing light in an immense variety of colours, luminescence has another main advantage in the high efficacy at which this light can be obtained from electric power by comparison with incandescent sources which necessarily emit so much energy in the invisible infra-red. Generally speaking, high efficacies are not reached with excitation of luminescence by high-energy particles or radiation, or by low-energy fields of electroluminescence, but are best seen with moderate energy cathode-rays, or ultra-violet radiation not far outside the visible region of the spectrum. Carrier injection luminescence in semiconductors is claimed to be highly efficient, but the optical conditions make it difficult for more than a small portion of the generated light to emerge.

The quantitative relations are best explained in the case of ultra-violet excitation. If a phosphor absorbs a beam of ultra-violet completely, and every quantum gives rise to a light quantum, the quantum efficiency is 100% and this state is nearly attained in suitable circumstances. Since by Stokes' law the absorbed ultra-violet quantum is greater than the emitted visible quantum, some energy is lost as heat and less than 100% reappears as useful light; though the quantum efficiency may be 100% the energy efficiency must be less and cannot exceed the wavelength ratio. In a fluorescent tube the main exciting agent is ultra-violet radiation of wavelength 253·7 nm. If the emitted light is at twice this wavelength in the blue-green region no more than half the energy in the ultra-violet line can be emitted as light. An early application for green-emitting zinc silicate was to use it on the walls of a neon tube in order to provide an amber coloured 'neon' sign. The peak of the phosphor emission is at 525 nm and the luminescence is excited by the ultra-violet of the neon discharge at 73·8 nm. Even if the quantum efficiency is 100% the conversion of energy from ultra-violet to visible light cannot be greater than the wavelength ratio, or one-seventh, and therefore the luminous efficacy of these tubes was low.

The highest possible efficacy of a light source is 680 lm/W for monochromatic yellow-green light of wavelength 555 nm. For a reasonable white, requiring a wide spectral distribution, no more than about 250 lm/W can be obtained. In practice moderate sized incandescent lamps give 12 lm/W and the fluorescence process in a tubular low-pressure lamp with a near white emission yields up to 80 lm/W. It must be observed that in the latter case the current-limiting control, not required in an incandescent lamp, dissipates appreciable power and may lower the overall efficacy to as little as 65 lm/W. In mercury lamps with phosphors for colour correction the fluorescence is a minor adjunct to the discharge instead of being the main light-emitting process as in a fluorescent lamp (Chap. 14).

Lumen maintenance.   Although the power dissipated at a point in the phosphor layer of a fluorescent lamp is less than on a television screen by a factor of 10 000 or more, exposure goes on for thousands of hours in an atmosphere which is not chemically inert. The gradual loss of brightness which occurs in the lamp is an appreciable drawback. Methods of phosphor manufacture leading to more complete chemical combination, and methods of lamp manufacture leading to tubes less contaminated by traces of air, water and other foreign materials have greatly improved the position, though the chemical and physical reactions responsible for phosphor deterioration are not fully understood. Physical absorption of the mercury on the surface layer of the phosphor grains and in the glass plays a large part, and different compositions of glass are also significant because of the migration of sodium from the glass into the phosphor, with damaging effects on the maintenance. Improvements in lamp performance can fairly be said to have resulted from empirical changes rather than a knowledge of the mechanism of deterioration. There is still a need to improve the performance, especially for lamps with power loadings above the normal ratings because here the phosphor deterioration is accelerated.

8.4   PHOSPHORS FOR MERCURY LAMPS

Improvement of the colour of mercury lamps has been an aim of lamp makers for many years. The considerable amount of ultra-violet emission near 365 nm by these lamps can be converted by fluorescence into visible light, given suitable phosphors excited by this wavelength. The first to be used in this way, coated inside the outer envelope of the lamp, were zinc cadmium sulphides. To minimize the serious fall in phosphor emission at elevated temperatures the envelopes had to be large and were 'isothermally' shaped. A phosphor capable of operating at high temperatures eliminates the need for such a large outer envelope and the first improvements in this direction were obtained by using either magnesium fluoroarsenate or magnesium fluorogermanate; both these phosphors are activated by manganese and emit deep red light; they are also used for colour improvement in ordinary fluorescent lamps. The spectral power distribution of a colour-corrected mercury lamp using magnesium fluorogermanate is shown in Fig. 14.9b.

When yttrium vanadate activated by europium became available in quantity for colour television tubes, its valuable qualities were recognized in the correction of mercury lamp spectra. It has a better temperature resistance than magnesium arsenate and germanate and its emission is at somewhat shorter wavelengths which produces greater lumen output (Figs. 8.4, 8.6 and 14.9c).

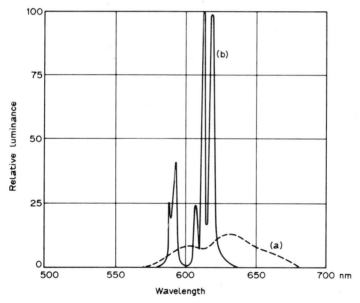

Fig. 8.6   Comparison of spectral luminance of (a) germanate and (b) vanadate phosphors. Ordinates of vanadate have been halved

The mercury lamp could be still further improved by similar phosphors compatible with the vanadate but emitting narrow bands in the blue and orange regions of the spectrum. Such materials would probably be activated by rare earths. One promising material of blue fluorescence is a europium-activated alkaline earth silicate.

In the conventional fluorescent lamp the phosphor is directly exposed to the mercury discharge and deterioration of the phosphor during use is understandable. The phosphor coating in a mercury lamp is not exposed to the discharge itself but can undergo deterioration by photolysis due to its exposure to ultra-violet. Yttrium vanadate suffers in this manner; a phosphor of improved durability retaining the temperature stability and fluorescence characteristics is yttrium phosphovanadate activated by europium, which although not quite as bright as the vanadate maintains its characteristics better in use.

8.5   PHOSPHORS FOR TELEVISION

Some of the most valuable phosphors are those where slight changes in their chemical composition made during their preparation produce marked changes in the colour of their emission; the zinc and zinc cadmium sulphides are such a system of phosphors. Their typical crystal structures are cubic or hexagonal. These materials are strongly excited by long wavelength ultra-violet but less so by the short wavelengths so that they are not used as lamp phosphors. They are readily excited by cathode-rays, and constitute the bulk of the phosphors used for television. Closely similar in characteristics, but not so extensively used as commercial phosphors, are selenides and tellurides.

The luminescent characteristics of the sulphides depend upon the presence of activators incorporated in the matrix during their preparation. For example, 0·01% of copper in zinc sulphide gives a product which has a strong green fluorescence; it also possesses a strong green afterglow. If instead of copper, a trace of silver is incorporated in the zinc sulphide, then it has a strong blue fluorescence, and a relatively short phosphorescence. When either copper or silver is used and some of the zinc is replaced by the equivalent amount of cadmium, the product still shows a strong fluorescence, but the emission is nearer the red end of the spectrum. In fact, with the sulphide phosphors, a complete range of fluorescent colours can be obtained depending on the ratio of zinc to cadmium in the sulphide matrix. Other activators than copper or silver and in particular gold or the halogens produce different fluorescent series but with the same general feature that the emission moves to the red as the proportion of the cadmium increases (Fig. 8.7).

Conventional 'black and white' television tubes have a screen which is composed of a mixture of minute crystals of a silver-activated blue zinc sulphide and a silver-activated yellow zinc cadmium sulphide, a blend which emits white light. The phosphors are operating in a high vacuum and any chemical deterioration is unlikely. Loss of emission may occur as a result of ion bombardment, but this is usually prevented by an ion trap in the electron gun and a film of aluminium over the phosphor. Generally the luminance of the television screen deteriorates by only 5% to 10% during 10 000 h.

8.5.1   Colour television phosphors

In colour television, the screen of the receiving tube is covered with very small dots of red, green, and blue phosphors. Between the sources of cathode-rays and the phosphor screen is a perforated sheet of metal called a *shadow mask*. The perforations in the shadow mask are very carefully engineered so that one hole corresponds to every three phosphor dots on the screen. The arrangement within the tube is that cathode-rays generated from one source pass through holes in the shadow mask and strike phosphor particles of only one type, say green phosphor; cathode-rays from an adjacent source similarly bombard only say blue phosphor dots, and from the third source only red phosphor dots. In this way, coloured television pictures are possible. The preparation of the phosphor screen is a process of extreme accuracy, and involves a photo-printing technique which imposes very close tolerances on the physical characteristics of the phosphor particles quite apart from their luminescent properties.

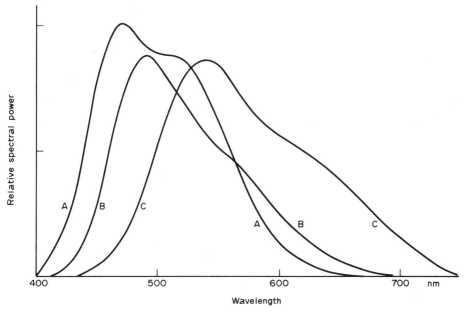

Fig. 8.7 Spectral emission of gold-activated zinc and zinc cadmium sulphide phosphors. Percentage CdS: A, 0; B, 7·1; C, 27·1.

From the point of view of the luminescent behaviour of the three phosphors, the intensity of fluorescence from each should be nearly equal if a correct colour balance is to be achieved. Until fairly recently, the green and blue phosphors were sulphide materials, and the red was a zinc phosphate activated by manganese. As the intensity of fluorescence from this latter material is relatively low, the full brightness of the green and blue materials could not be used, otherwise the colour of the pictures was deficient in red. Europium-activated yttrium vanadate phosphor is readily excited by cathode-rays and is very much brighter than the original red zinc phosphate. Consequently, by using this material for the red component the intensity of the blue and green phosphor does not have to be reduced and a high picture brightness is obtained.

As a result of this development other even better red phosphors such as europium-activated yttrium oxide or oxysulphide have been made and are being used in television tubes in place of the vanadate.

169

8.6 THE PREPARATION OF PHOSPHORS

In the preparation of phosphors very pure starting materials are necessary and a carefully controlled heating process is essential in order to develop the crystal structure required to produce the brightest luminescence. When a small amount of an activator must be incorporated in the matrix this is achieved during the thermal preparation process. In sulphide type phosphors, the quantity of activator may be less than 1 part in 10 000 of the whole, although the exact amount depends on the use for which the phosphor is intended; for example electroluminescent zinc sulphides require an activator concentration many times greater than sulphides used for television purposes. On the other hand, the proportion of activator required in oxygen-based phosphors is often as great as 1 part in 100.

The actual temperature to which a phosphor composition must be heated and the time required at that temperature in order to prepare the resultant phosphor depends on many factors such as the reactivity of solids, sintering and melting points, particle size and batch size. Depending on the particular system 800 °C to 1200 °C is the usual range of temperature required in the process.

8.6.1 Halophosphates

Some indications of the problems involved in the preparation of phosphors is shown by a consideration of the halophosphates. Here, as with other phosphors, a crystalline structure must be developed by a thermal process, and since some of the components from which these phosphors are prepared are volatile, due allowance for this must be made during the preparation.

A convenient method of preparation is to start with a mixture of calcium hydrogen orthophosphate, calcium carbonate, calcium fluoride, ammonium chloride, and as activators antimony oxide and a manganese compound such as the carbonate. Different starting materials can be used, but experience has shown these to be generally the most convenient. These materials should be as highly purified as possible, but it is not necessary to go to the exhaustive purification required for semi-conducting materials. The components are mixed together in the proportions found usually by previous experimentation to be the most suitable, and the aim is to prepare a product which contains no excess of any of the starting components, or of compounds formed as intermediates during the preparation, which has optimum particle size, and of course maximum fluorescence.

The basic reaction which has to be brought about during the preparation of the host material is:

$$6CaHPO_4 + (3+x)CaCO_3 + (1-x)CaF_2 + 2xNH_4Cl \longrightarrow$$
$$2Ca_5(PO_4)_3(F_{1-x}Cl_x) + (3+x)H_2O + (3+x)CO_2 + 2xNH_3$$

while at the same time the correct proportions of the activator compounds have to be incorporated in the crystal lattice.

The manganese activator required in the halophosphates is in the divalent condition, but manganese compounds are easily oxidized to higher valency states on heating. Therefore a strongly oxidizing atmosphere must be avoided in the phosphor preparation; but a reducing atmosphere will allow reduction of the antimony compounds, which is equally undesirable.

It is difficult to obtain exact figures for the world production of lamp phosphors, but it is estimated to be about 8 to 10 million kg per year of which about 80% is halophosphate phosphor.

8.6.2   Sulphides

In the preparation of sulphide phosphors the basic zinc and cadmium sulphide components are first prepared in a highly purified and carefully controlled condition. These are then mixed in the desired proportions with activators and fluxes and heated in a non-oxidizing atmosphere. By selection of the conditions, products are obtained which not only satisfy the stringent requirements for brightness, colour and absence of afterglow necessary for television receivers but also possess the phosphor particle characteristics required during the screen preparation. Minute quantities of activators are effective in the sulphides, and for a similar reason other impurities at very low concentration may have serious effects on the fluorescence colour and efficiency. This makes the preparation of sulphide phosphors a very exacting chemical process.

In the synthesis of other phosphor systems equally detailed considerations are necessary in order to prepare highly efficient materials.

9 Incandescent lamps

The filament lamp, developed nearly a century ago, has undergone many changes and improvements in design and manufacture to bring it to its present performance and convenience as a light source. In spite of more efficient competing types of source, it still accounts for a greater number made annually than any other kind of lamp has so far attained. In the home it is scarcely challenged as the universal light source, and while offices, factories, public buildings, shops and vehicles steadily adopt more and more fluorescent and other discharge lamps, the incandescent lamp seems to have an unlimited future. In this chapter the present state of the tungsten lamp is discussed, omitting developments in the tungsten halogen field which are treated in Chap. 10.

9.1 GENERAL LIGHTING SERVICE LAMPS

Incandescent lamps produce light as a result of the heating effect of an electric current flowing through a filament wire. Providing the temperature of the wire is raised above 500 °C, visible light is emitted in addition to the infra-red energy which is radiated appreciably at much lower temperatures than this.

Tungsten is particularly suitable for use as a filament material on account of its high melting point and relatively low rate of evaporation at high temperatures. It is because of these considerations that tungsten, in some cases with additives to achieve special characteristics, is used for the filaments of virtually all present-day incandescent lamps. In order to reduce thermal losses and to dispose the tungsten filament wire in a form which can be conveniently fitted inside a lamp envelope it is customary to coil the wire into either a single or double helix. On mains voltage lamps, this is usually achieved by winding the tungsten wire on a mandrel of either steel or molybdenum; this is then heat-treated in order to relieve coiling strain, and after removal of the mandrel by dissolving in acid, the filaments are, in some cases, furnaced again. On lower voltage lamps, particularly on those of 12 V and below, modern high speed manufacturing equipment produces filament coils by winding the tungsten on a retractable mandrel which withdraws after coiling; the filament is then cut off and automatically transferred to the lead wires of the inner lamp construction.

Fig. 9.1 illustrates a standard type of general lighting service (GLS) incandescent lamp with a coiled-coil tungsten filament A. The filament is supported at intermediate points by molybdenum wires B, the electrical connections to the filament are made through clamps on the end of nickel or nickel-plated wires C, which are part of a sub-assembly comprising usually three or more components. The inner wire C is welded to a section of a Dumet wire D, (Sect. 7.1.2). The lower end of the Dumet is connected to a protective fuse E, which is usually a small diameter copper-nickel alloy wire encapsulated inside a glass sleeve F. In some instances this glass sleeve is filled with small glass balls (ballotini)

172

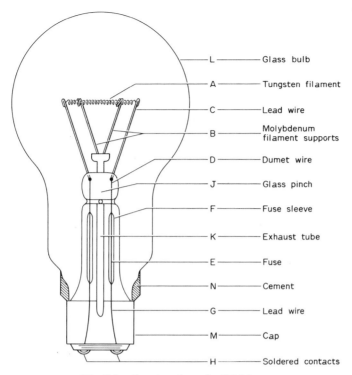

L	Glass bulb
A	Tungsten filament
C	Lead wire
B	Molybdenum filament supports
D	Dumet wire
J	Glass pinch
F	Fuse sleeve
K	Exhaust tube
E	Fuse
N	Cement
G	Lead wire
M	Cap
H	Soldered contacts

Fig. 9.1 Construction of a GLS lamp.

which have arc-quenching characteristics, providing adequate fusing by a single fuse per lamp, whereas otherwise two fuses are often required to achieve sufficiently long arc paths inside the lamp. An alternative technique uses bare wire fuses with specially insulated caps. The connection between the fuse and the soldered external connection is made by the lead wire G, which is terminated through an eyelet in the cap and electrically connected by solder at the contacts H. The molybdenum supports B are inserted into an inner glass member extending from the pinch J. The exhaust tube K is kept open at J to allow the air to be pumped from the bulb L after sealing, and for the introduction of the final filling gas. The metal lamp cap M is fixed to the bulb by a heat-curing cement shown at N. The lamp cap is usually constructed from either brass or aluminium.

Filaments The design of incandescent filaments is dictated to a large degree by the required operating parameters. The length of wire in the filament is primarily a function of the operating voltage and the wire diameter is determined by the operating current. These characteristics are modified somewhat by the running temperature which is in turn a function of the required life. The length of the wound coil is determined by (a) the control of mandrel to wire diameter ratio which is necessary to give the filament adequate stiffness and (b) the desire to make a coil as short as possible in order to reduce thermal losses from the filament. An extension of this principle is the use of secondary coiling (*coiled-coil*) which has the effect of reducing the finished coil length on a 40 W GLS lamp from 50 mm to 25 mm, so raising the filament efficacy by 20% for the same life. It should be recognized however that while the coiled-coil filament, with its greater light output, is perfectly suitable for normal domestic applications, it does not have the same robust character-istics as the single coil design recommended for any installations which have an environ-ment of shock or vibration.

A further range of heavy duty lamps is produced for service where vibration and shock are unavoidable. Improved lamp characteristics for such situations can be achieved by making filaments of small mandrel to wire ratios and by the inclusion of an increased number of intermediate filament supports. On certain types, particularly lamps for operation at low filament temperatures, improved vibration resistance can be achieved by the use of special grades of tungsten, with either rhenium or thoria additives which produce a more suitable metallurgical structure for this application (Sect. 7.2.1).

Bulbs.   The bulbs of GLS lamps are the long established pear-shaped bulb and, to an increasing extent, the mushroom bulb introduced in the late 1950's (Fig. 9.2a). The high speed manufacturing equipment on which these lamps are made is unsuitable for frequent changes in bulb dimensions, and economic advantages result from the reduction in the variety of shapes and sizes which has occurred over the past few years. At the present time the pear- and mushroom-shaped varieties of 40 W, 60 W and 100 W coiled-coil lamps are all made in a 60 mm diameter bulb. The minimum dimensions of a finished lamp are also limited by the acceptance by lamp manufacturers of a series of maximum levels for cap temperature rise during use. This, coupled with the fact that there is now a requirement for luminaires to be marked with the maximum acceptable wattage, should reduce problems of over-heating by the use of higher wattage lamps than those for which luminaires are designed.

The fundamental choice of a vacuum or a gaseous atmosphere within the bulb depends largely upon the current rating. Mains voltage lamps of 15 and 25 W, for instance, are normally of the vacuum type, lamps of 40 W and above would normally be made with a gas-filled atmosphere. Vacuum lamps enjoy the benefit of no thermal losses to a gas but carry the penalty that evaporation of the tungsten operating at incandescent tempera-tures is unrestrained, with the result that the bulb wall becomes blackened by tungsten deposition. The introduction of a gas into an incandescent lamp has the effect of reducing the evaporation rate of tungsten from the filament due to the presence of the gas molecules and this enables a filament to be run at higher temperatures for an equivalent life. The presence of the gas also causes heat to be conducted away from the filament, and causes

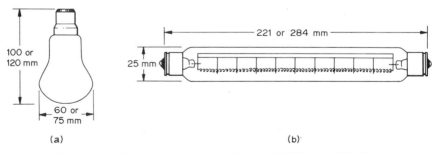

100 or 120 mm

60 or 75 mm

221 or 284 mm

25 mm

(a)

(b)

Fig. 9.2   (a) The mushroom-shaped lamp   (b) The striplight lamp

convection currents to be set up within the bulb, adding to the thermal losses. Gas filling is therefore used on lamp ratings which benefit more from the suppressed evaporation of tungsten than they lose by thermal losses to the gas. Sect. 7.3 describes the physical and electrical characteristics of the inert gases in the context of lamp filling and these factors, together with the economic considerations, determine the gas to be used.

GLS lamp life in UK has long been established at 1000h. This life was determined by calculations to evaluate the conditions for the minimum cost per unit of light, including the costs of lamps, power, and lamp replacement. Sect. 34.3.3 discusses the factors affecting lighting economics as they concern tungsten filament lamps.

9.2   DECORATIVE AND SPECIAL PURPOSE LAMPS

The incandescent filament lamp is, in its simplest form, purely a functional light source but the fact that an integral part of the lamp is a bulb fashioned from glass enables the designer to adapt and modify this envelope in order to give the product some aesthetic appeal.

One of the earliest attempts at decoration was the internal etching of the pear-shaped bulb to produce the 'pearl' lamp (Sect. 7.1.1). Internal coatings and finishes are now commonly applied to lamps of standard ratings, for example finely divided silica or titania on mushroom-shaped bulbs (Fig. 9.2a) where virtual obscuration of the filament and reduction of glare can be achieved with a light output loss as low as 4%. Coloured lamps are produced either by internally or externally coating the surface of the bulb with pigments. Perhaps the commonest of this type are the low wattage lamps with internally applied translucent colour coatings. Lamps coloured by the external application of a silicate suspension are especially suited, by virtue of their resistance to thermal shock, for use out-of-doors. It is necessary to ensure that the heating effect of the colour coatings neither raises the bulb wall to temperatures which release impurities nor the cap region to unacceptable levels. Transparent coloured lacquers find use on lamps for electric fires.

Perhaps the commonest form of decorative bulb is the candle lamp, which is produced in some quantity with either a smooth shape or in a twisted form. The finish may be clear, white or frosted.

In more recent years other lamps have been marketed which combine the roles of light source and decorative luminaire by virtue of their bulb shapes (Fig. 9.3). They are usually of larger dimensions than conventional lamps. Apart from their attractive shapes these lamps have the advantage that they are made with internal diffusing coatings, and are therefore rather more efficient as light-producing units than a combination of lamp and separate diffuser.

The 'striplight' range of incandescent filament lamps is another form which finds extensive domestic use. These lamps comprise a long tubular bulb of glass, either clear or white-coated, fitted with a small cap carrying an electrical connection point at either end of the bulb (Fig. 9.2b).

A lamp with a film of silicone-rubber applied to the outside of the bulb holds together the glass fragments in the event of breakage. Such lamps are intended for use in food preparation establishments, hospitals, garages, etc. The coating also makes the bulb resistant to breakage from thermal shock, as by water falling on a lit lamp.

175

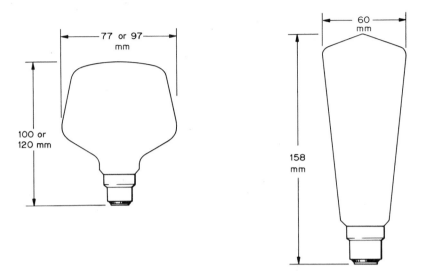

Fig. 9.3   Decorative lamps

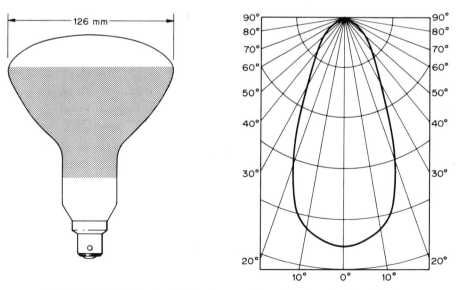

Fig. 9.4   150 W reflector display lamp and its polar intensity distribution

Directional beams.   A further range of special purpose lamps is made with directional beam properties for use in display and associated applications. These lamps are constructed with the filament at the focal point of a paraboloid, blown or pressed to form an integral part of the bulb surface and coated with a highly reflective material, usually vacuum-deposited aluminium. As the atmosphere within the bulb is inert, the condition of this coating is maintained to a high degree throughout the life of the lamp. Lamps in this category range from the 12 V 50 W screw cap type designed for use with a transformer and having a particularly high-intensity low-divergence beam, to the 150 W reflector display lamps (Fig. 9.4) which operate from mains voltage and are designed to produce the beam characteristic shown.

Sealed beam lamps.   A separate range of lamps of this type is made in the sealed beam (or pressed glass) construction. The manufacturing process for these lamps ensures that the filament is positioned relative to the reflector with a high degree of accuracy and this, together with the improved reflector profiles possible with this design, enables higher performance beam characteristics to be achieved. The sealed beam lamp is made in separate spotlight and floodlight designs (Fig. 9.5) and these are intended for a rather longer life than is normal for the blown glass type. Sealed beam lamps are also available in a mains voltage 300 W rating (Fig. 9.6), which is fitted with different lenses to produce a narrow, medium or wide beam. Apart from applications in studio and photographic work the necessity for high intensity beams arises from the increased levels of general illumination now being used in shops and commercial premises, where highlighting of specific items can only be achieved by powerful spotlights or floodlights.

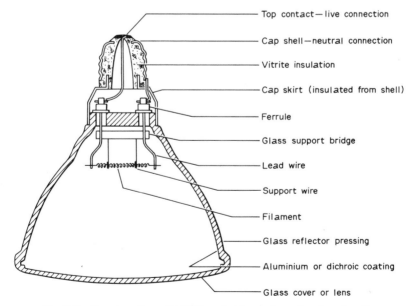

Top contact — live connection

Cap shell — neutral connection

Vitrite insulation

Cap skirt (insulated from shell)

Ferrule

Glass support bridge

Lead wire

Support wire

Filament

Glass reflector pressing

Aluminium or dichroic coating

Glass cover or lens

Fig. 9.5   Construction of 150 W sealed beam lamp (spot or flood)

177

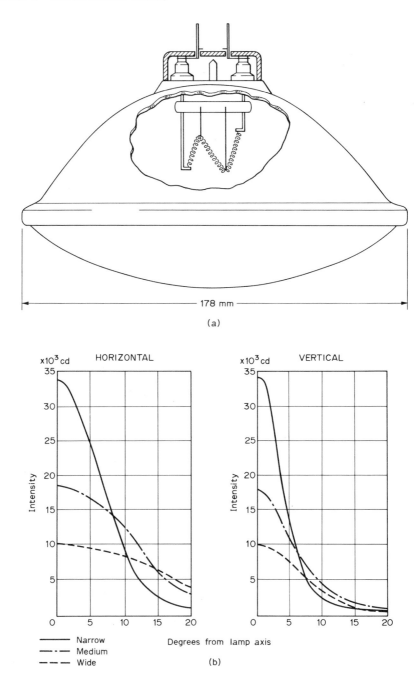

Fig. 9.6   300 W sealed beam reflector lamp   (a) Construction   (b) Intensity distributions for different beam widths

Sealed beam lamps are also produced with coloured front lenses to extend the field for these lamps. A 100 W rating is available having externally-applied transparent enamel colours on floodlight lenses, but the limits of temperature stability of enamels render them unsuitable for higher wattages. The colours available are red, blue, green, yellow and amber.

Dichroic coatings. A further type of coloured sealed beam reflector lamp of 150 W rating makes use of the selective optical properties of so-called dichroic coatings. Interference effects are achieved by coating the internal surface of the lens with a series of alternate layers of two different transparent materials, chosen for their respective refractive indices, which are required to have a specific relationship to the indices of air (1·00) and glass (1·52). Typical materials are magnesium fluoride and zinc sulphide, with refractive indices of 1·38 and 2·3 respectively. These are vacuum-deposited alternately on the glass surface, commencing with the material of higher refractive index. It is essential that the thickness of each layer is precisely controlled to make the product of thickness and refractive index equal to one-quarter of the wavelength of the light to be reflected. Thus each layer produces a phase difference of 180° between normally incident rays reflected from the upper and lower surfaces of the layer. In addition there is a 180° phase difference when the light is reflected at a layer of higher refractive index. Multi-layer coatings can be built up to transmit or reflect selected spectral wavelengths or narrow bands, and the colour of the residual light can be chosen over a wide range. For the filters used with lamps about 10 to 20 layers are used according to the effect desired, the outermost layer being of the high refractive index material. The absorption of light by these filters is very much lower than by pigmented coatings, and coloured light can therefore be produced much more efficiently. When curved surfaces are used, with variable angles of light incidence, as in lamps, it is of course not possible to achieve exact spectral selectivity.

The dichroic coating technique is also applied to the reflector surface in a range of lamps having clear lenses, known as Cool-ray lamps. These are based on the use of multi-layer coating to transmit the long wave-length (infra-red) radiation and to reflect the wavelengths in the visible spectrum. The effect of this is to produce an almost equivalent light output in the forward beam of these lamps but to reduce by about two-thirds the heating effect of the long wavelength radiation compared with lamps having aluminized reflectors. These lamps with 'cold mirrors' are particularly appropriate to illumination of refrigerated food displays, to the projection of film slides, and to any situation where it is felt necessary to reduce the heating effect for a given illuminance.

9.3 AUTOMOBILE AND MINIATURE LAMPS

9.3.1 Headlights

At the present time there are three convenient groups into which automobile headlamps may be sub-divided.

(a) Those having an assembly comprising a reflector formed from a metal pressing to which is affixed a glass lens, and in which the lamp is replaceable.

(b) Those which are constructed in the sealed beam, pressed glass design having a coated glass reflector and lens as a hermetically-sealed assembly, and usually containing two filaments in an inert atmosphere within this assembly.

(c) Lamps constructed either as (a) or (b) but fitted with a tungsten halogen lamp. These
   are discussed in Chap. 10.

Considering first the metal back assemblies, a typical example is illustrated in Fig. 9.7.
Headlights of this type have the primary merits of relatively low cost replacement value
of the inner lamp, and greater flexibility in shape than for sealed beam lamps. The latter

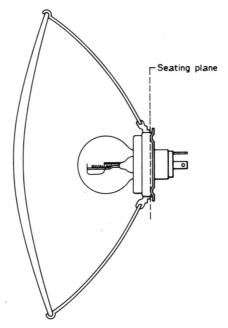

Fig. 9.7   Replaceable bulb headlight assembly

requirement has been particularly relevant over recent years where automobile styling
has dictated the use of headlamps of shapes other than circular in order to harmonize with
contemporary ideas of line and style. The use of these shapes inevitably incurs penalties in
optical efficiency but to some extent this can be compensated by an increase in dimensions of the reflector. One of the principal drawbacks of the replaceable bulb type of
assembly is that the unit cannot be completely sealed, and the almost unavoidable ingress
of moisture and dust gradually reduces the efficiency of the reflector surface.

A further significant consideration with the use of replaceable bulbs is that throughout
the life of the lamp evaporation of tungsten from the filament is deposited selectively on
the bulb wall above the filament. As it is the upper half of the reflector which makes the
largest contribution to the meeting (dipped) beam, the bulb blackening reduces the collection of light by this portion of the reflector; hence the performance of this type of unit
declines during the life of the lamp. The replaceable bulb assembly also suffers from the
additive effect of tolerances which are inevitable with this design. These tolerances are
incurred in several dimensions:

(a) Filament to reference plane of prefocus flange (cap type P45t–41: Fig. 9.14).
(b) Prefocus flange to seating plane mounted in the reflector.
(c) Seating plane to optical reference plane of reflector.

The effect of combinations of these tolerances is that the filaments can be located at some significant distance away from the designed position in the reflector, thus causing undesirable variability in the intensity and distribution of the headlight beam.

The European asymmetric E-type lamp. Standardizing activities in Europe over the past years have led to the acceptance of a single design of lamp for use in conventional metal-back reflector headlights. More recently the use of certain tungsten halogen lamps has been approved (Sect. 10.3.3). The majority of countries on the European mainland legislate to permit the use only of standardized E headlamps but such legislation is not applied in UK. The asymmetric lamp nevertheless finds wide application in UK on account of its compatibility with the special needs for light sources in rectangular head-lights. The lamp contains separate filaments for the meeting beam and the driving beam. The meeting beam filament A (Fig. 9.8) is mounted inside a hood or shield which is

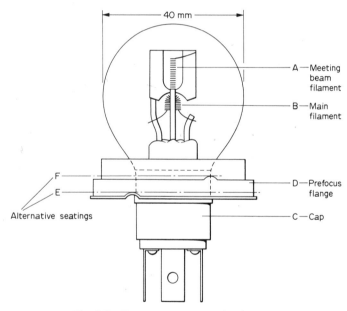

Fig. 9.8 European asymmetric E lamp

designed to produce a horizontal cut-off on the off side and a cut-off 15° above the horizontal on the near side. The main or driving filament B is mounted behind and slightly below the axis of the meeting beam filament and is usually formed into a bow-shape. The lamp has a straight-sided cap C (type P45t–41) carrying three lugs through the insulator. The prefocus flange D soldered to the barrel of the cap is of a standardized form with two separate reference sections E and F designed to accommodate the two standard types of seating used in European headlight designs. The 12 V lamp is rated at 45/40 W (driving/meeting) and the filaments have respectively 75 h and 150 h life, measured at 13·2 V.

Sealed beam headlights.   A typical sealed beam headlight is shown in Fig. 9.9. This type of lamp was originally designed to overcome the principal shortcomings of the metal-back reflector with replaceable bulb by ensuring that the reflector was protected from contamination by the inert gas filling and that the filament positioning relative to the

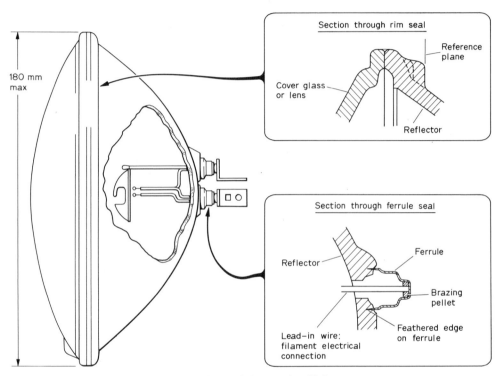

Fig. 9.9   Sealed beam headlight

reflector optics could be maintained to tolerances of about one-quarter of those occurring with the separate bulb system. The sealed beam type of lamp is normally constructed from low expansion borosilicate glass. The reflector portion is aluminized on the inner surface and is assembled with an inner mount construction which is brazed into three ferrules; these are sealed into bosses at the rear of the reflector and to them are fixed connection lugs for the external voltage supply. The assembly process is designed so that the filaments, mounted on the inner assembly, are accurately positioned with respect to the profile of the reflector before being mounted on the lead wires. The reflector pressing is made with an external flange or lip around the open end, and this lip is fitted with keys which locate in matching keyways on a similar flange on the lens pressing. The two pressings are sealed together around these flanges to produce an integral bulb in which the air is replaced by a filling of inert gas. The whole assembly operates in the same way as a conventional bulb with the exception that the large surface area greatly reduces the effect of blackening due to filament evaporation.

The commonest type of sealed beam lamp used in UK is the 180 mm diameter version which is made in a number of ratings.

The four headlight car is normally fitted with 145 mm diameter units, the inner pair of which contain one filament only for use as driving beams (referred to as No. 1 units), while the outer pair are each fitted with two filaments (No. 2 units), one which provides the meeting beam and the other serves as a secondary driving beam.

The third basic type of sealed beam headlight is that produced in a rectangular shape, developed to meet styling demands. Versions of both the 180 mm diameter and the rectangular types are made to comply with European beam requirements; all the standard ratings are made with or without a 'window' in the aluminized surface through which the side (or pilot) lamp may shine.

9.3.2 Auxiliary lamps

The lamps used for side lights, turn indicators, tail lights, brake lights and fog lights have been made the subject of European standardization; this has drastically reduced the number of ratings and types being used.

9.3.3 Panel lamps

The traditional system of panel illumination in automobiles was by use of lamps fitted with either miniature Edison screw or with miniature bayonet caps. Electrical contact to the lamps was made by wiring which terminated at the sockets, but this required a great deal of assembly time and increased the cost. The introduction of wedge base lamps allowed the use of printed circuit techniques and so made substantial reductions in assembly time and in cost.

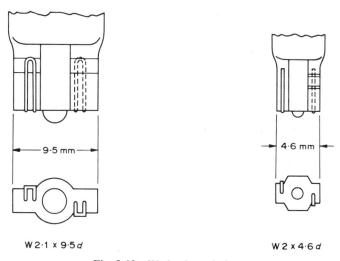

W 2·1 x 9·5 d   W 2 x 4·6 d

Fig. 9.10   Wedge base designs

The wedge base lamp is made without the usual metal cap and is retained in place by a specially designed socket with spring contacts locating in grooves moulded into the base of the bulb (Fig. 9.10). Electrical contact is achieved by means of hairpin-shaped lead wires from the lamp which are pressed between contacts in the socket and the glass of the base. The lamp has the advantage of simple assembly, and in use offers improved resistance to shock and vibration. There are gas-filled types for external use on vehicles, and vacuum types for panel applications. Panel assemblies based on a plastic moulding and using wedge base lamps in push-in sockets are used in conjunction with a flexible printed circuit in high volume production vehicles at the present time.

9.3.4   Sub-miniature lamps

Perhaps the most extensive use of sub-miniature lamps is to be found in aircraft applications. This results from the necessity to conserve space and weight, and these dual needs led to the development of special lamp types. Fig. 9.11a shows a typical aircraft panel indicator lamp made in a 5·6 mm diameter bulb with a midget flange cap. As the lighting system in aircraft is usually at 28 V the relatively long filament needs two intermediate filament supports in order to withstand the rigorous vibration conditions of service. In some instances voltage controls are introduced into the circuits in order to enable lamps of other voltages to be used, and accordingly lamps of a similar outline but with 6 V and 12 V filaments are also produced.

The need to conserve space is however not exclusive to aircraft and increasing use is being made of sub-miniature wedge base lamps. An international standard has been established for a 5 mm diameter wedge base design (Fig. 9.11b) and a 12 V 1·2 W version is now being used extensively in automobile panel illumination where the compact dimensions offer new design possibilities.

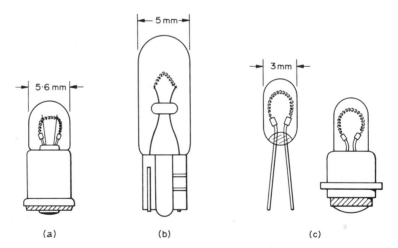

Fig. 9.11   (a) Aircraft panel indicator lamp
(b) 5 mm diameter wedge base lamp
(c) 3 mm diameter sub-miniature lamp

At the lower end of the sub-miniature lamp scale is a range of lamps in bulbs of 3 mm diameter and less. These are available either as wire-ended devices or with midget flanged caps (Fig. 9.11c). These lamps are often used in installations where replacement would be exceedingly difficult and for this reason the lamps are often designed to have indefinitely long life by virtue of low filament operating temperatures. Lamps of even smaller dimensions than those referred to have also been produced for incorporation in medical apparatus.

9.3.5 Miners' lamps

For many years now it has been standard practice to manufacture the lamps for use in mines as special high performance lamps. The basic requirement is for the miner to have a light beam of adequate intensity which will last for the duration of a shift and can be operated from a battery small and light enough not to hinder his manual operations. These considerations led to a specification for a lamp rated at 4 V with a current of 0·9A using krypton instead of argon filling, which yields an increase of 25% in light output for the same life and current rating. Different operating conditions in various parts of the world give rise to other requirements for current rating and life but the use of krypton in lamps of this type is a world-wide practice.

9.4 WORKING CHARACTERISTICS

The operating requirements of incandescent lamps in service lead to a great diversity of specifications in terms of life, light output and wattage. For example an automobile headlight filament is required to project a high intensity beam of light while dissipating power compatible with the capacity of the battery, and lasting perhaps 2 or 3 years. On the other hand a panel indicator lamp is required to produce a relatively low illuminance to facilitate night time instrument reading, to consume as little power as possible, and to operate virtually for the life of the vehicle. These two conflicting requirements result in the filament of the normal automobile headlight operating at a temperature of 2800 K while that of the panel lamp is of the order of 2400 K. The operating temperature of the filament has a direct influence on the evaporation rate and therefore on the life. If the voltage, current and life or alternatively the voltage, current and light output of a lamp are specified then the complete operating characteristics of the lamp are fixed. The influence of temperature on life can be transformed into a function of applied voltage. The relationship is that for moderate changes in voltage (say $\pm 25\%$) the lamp life is inversely proportional to the n-th power of the voltage, where $n = 13$ for vacuum lamps, 14 for gas-filled GLS lamps, and 11·2 for headlamps. This shows that for an increase of only 5% in operating voltage, the lamp life is halved, or on the other hand doubled by a 5% decrease. Thus photoflood lamps, which are overloaded in order to increase light output and efficacy, have as a result a very short life.

The dependence on voltage of other GLS lamp parameters may be described in similar terms. The exponents vary according to lamp type, but representative values may be quoted. The current is directly proportional to the square root of the voltage, the efficacy to the square, and the luminous flux to the 3·6 power.

185

The effect of frequent switching in life is quite marked on lamps designed to operate at high efficacy levels, such as projectors. Lamps of lower efficacy and longer life are less sensitive to intermittent operation.

9.5 MANUFACTURING METHODS

There are three methods of construction used in the standard ranges of incandescent lamps, the drop seal, the butt seal and the wedge base. As a rough guide, the drop seal technique is used on lamps rated in excess of 10 W, the butt seal on ratings below this level; the wedge base is also applied to ratings below 10 W but the principle may well be applied to lamps of higher wattage.

9.5.1 Drop seal construction

Lamps of the drop seal type are produced by sealing an inner sub-assembly comprising a flare tube, exhaust tube, lead wires, support wires where appropriate, and filament into a pre-formed bulb. Bulbs required in very large quantities are normally made on a machine which produces bulbs from a continuous ribbon of glass. Bulbs required in smaller quantities are normally made on machines which index and operate on quantities of glass collected individually from a furnace.

Fig. 9.12 illustrates the components of a drop seal incandescent lamp; sealing takes place between the flare of the inner assembly and the neck of the bulb which are progres-

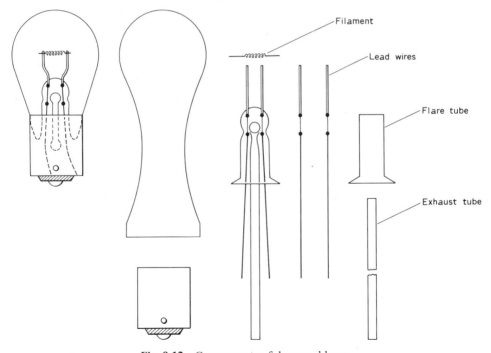

Fig. 9.12 Components of drop-seal lamp

sively melted together until the wall of the bulb drops on to the flare and fusion takes place. It is customary for this seal area while still molten to be blown into a mould to produce a regular shape ensuring good seating on the cap; the mould also forms keyways in the seal area to reduce the risk of torsional breakdown of the cap to bulb union.

After sealing the hot bulbs are evacuated through the exhaust tube which is held in a compression head on a rotating turret, and connected by pipes and a split valve plate to a series of vacuum pumps. Pumping normally takes place on each index of the machine and is sometimes accompanied by addition of quantities of inert gas between pumping stages for the purpose of flushing, until the final position on the machine at which the filling gas is introduced. The pressure of the filling gas is normally just below atmospheric so that, in the last position, where the exhaust tip is sealed off ('tipping-off'), the internal pressure of the gas does not tend to blow out the molten glass.

The lamp cap on GLS lamps is normally of the bayonet type in UK or the screw type in Europe and USA. It is fixed to the bulb by a heat-curing cement. The lead wires from the inner assembly are normally soldered to the two eyelets at the base of the bayonet caps but are sometimes welded to the contact points on screw caps.

In order to improve the atmosphere within the bulb it is common practice to include, on the lamp assembly, gettering materials which take up residual oxygen and hydrogen. Red phosphorus suspensions applied to the filament and zirconium-aluminium mixtures applied to the lead wires are typical of the getters used (Sect. 7.2.3). The initial lighting of a filament is often a critical operation in order to produce the optimum gettering effect, and to promote recrystallization of the tungsten filament wire, necessary to overcome sagging tendencies. It is customary to use a protective impedance in series with the lamp to avoid damage due to possible arcing.

9.5.2 Butt seal construction

Fig. 9.13 shows the basic components used in producing butt seal lamps. The bulbs for this type of lamp are often produced from 'sticks' of tubing held on rotating machines. The lowermost end of the tubing is progressively melted and blown from the upper end into an external mould. After shaping the bulbs are cracked off above the neck area to produce the shape shown.

The inner sub-assembly of this type of lamp is known as a bead-mount. This comprises two lengths of Dumet wire held by a bead of sintered glass and shaped into a form which seats on the open end of the bulb neck. At the other end it is splayed out and hooked around the tails of the filament, normally produced on a retractable mandrel coiling head on the bead-mount machine.

Assembly of this type of lamp is achieved by inserting the bead-mount into the neck of the upturned bulb and by sealing on a length of tubing of approximately the same diameter as the bulb neck. At a later stage this tubing is constricted above the area of the seal to facilitate the subsequent tipping-off process. The process of exhaust and gas-filling are largely as described for the drop seal technique.

9.5.3 Wedge base lamps

The bulbs are produced in the same way as for butt seal lamps, except that larger diameter tubing is used. The inner mount assembly is also produced as for butt seal mounts,

187

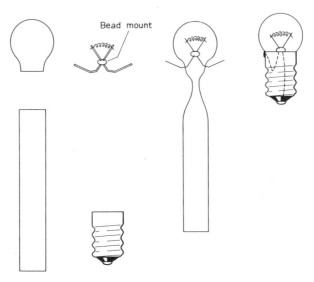

Fig. 9.13   Components of butt-seal lamp

but it is customary to use nickel-plated Dumet in order to reduce oxidation which may cause contact problems on the finished lamp where the lead wires themselves form the external contacts (Figs. 9.10 and 9.11b).

The lamp assembly is made by separately holding the exhaust tube, the bead-mount and the bulb in position while the neck of the bulb is heated until the base shape can be impressed upon it. Exhausting, gas filling where appropriate, and tipping-off follow the methods already described.

9.5.4   High-speed GLS manufacture

In order to keep down manufacturing costs it is necessary to use automated equipment operating at high speeds. One such type of equipment manufactures GLS lamps at a speed approaching 4000 per hour. Mounts, or completed internal lamp assemblies are produced by a linear (non-rotary) machine operating on a duplex indexing system whereby each process stage is duplicated. The rotary sealing and exhaust machines are also operated on the duplex principle and the capping process is fully automatic.

9.5.5   Caps and capping cement

The caps used on incandescent lamps fall into three main groups:

Bayonet (B) caps which have barrel diameters of 7 mm, 9 mm, 15 mm or 22 mm and are fitted into sockets by pushing inwards against springs and engaged by rotating, so that the pins seat in the closed end of a J-shaped slot or recess.

Screw (E) caps are available in diameters of 5 mm, 10 mm, 14 mm, 17 mm, 27 mm and 40 mm. Electrical contact is made when the contact in the base engages with the corresponding socket contact. The shell of the cap makes the other connection.

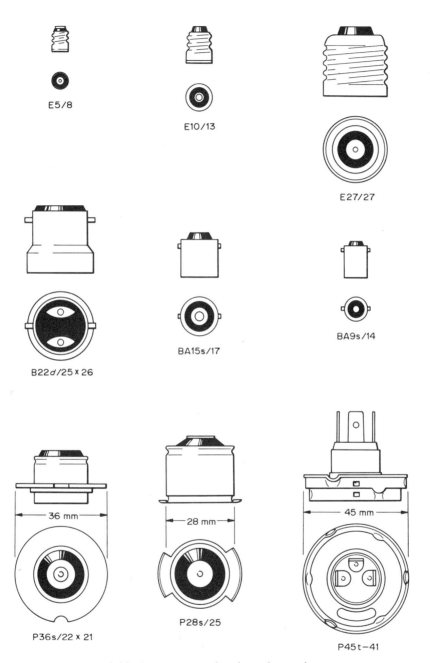

Fig. 9.14   Some caps used on incandescent lamps

Prefocus (P) caps are used on lamps where close control of filament position is essential, as in projection apparatus or headlights. This precision is achieved either by the attachment to the cap barrel of a flange which is accurately positioned relative to the filament, or by the use of construction processes which result in the filament being located with respect to some fixed feature of the cap or base. Prefocus lamps are generally made with filament height (light centre length) and axiality tolerances of ± 0.5 mm or closer.

Versions of prefocus caps range between the P13·5 s used on flashlight lamps to the P89 s for lighthouse lamps.

Wedge base (W) lamps have no caps but a moulded base, previously explained (Sect. 9.3.3). Versions of 4·6 mm and 9·5 mm diameter are standardized in IEC Publication No. 61, and larger sizes may be developed.

Fig. 9.14 illustrates some of the main cap types in use. They are standardized in the above IEC Publication. The relevant British specifications are BS 52, 98, 841, 1164 and 1298 (Appendix III). The numbers in the cap descriptions refer, in order, to shell or thread crest diameter in mm, overall length, and skirt diameter when appropriate. The letters s, d and t refer to single, double and triple contacts respectively.

Capping cements are usually mixtures of a thermo-setting resin and an inert inorganic filler applied to the inside of the cap rim, which attach the cap to the bulb on being heated. Improved adhesion under humid conditions can result from the inclusion of a small amount of silicone resin. Cements are available which will operate satisfactorily at temperatures up to 210 °C.

B22 and E27 caps are required to withstand torsion testing at 3 N m, and E40 caps at 5 N m both at the beginning and end of life testing.

9.5.6   Quality controls

In manufacture of all the foregoing lamp types it is essential that great attention is paid to the maintenance of material quality, filament characteristics, gas purity, pump effectiveness, temperature settings and all relevant processing schedules. The purity and precision required to produce lamps of good quality are such that only frequent checks of filament rating, exhaust quality and dimensional control can ensure consistent performance.

Statistical sampling techniques to monitor all specification requirements for physical, electrical and photometric characteristics are essential. Reliable photometric methods and the use of life test voltages stabilized to about 0·5% are necessary. Particularly on high voltage lamps such as GLS types it is usual to operate additional controls with high overload voltage tests which can produce extra information on lamp quality. It should perhaps be recorded that high overload voltage testing can lead to very misleading results unless correctly interpreted, owing to the fact that the lamp loadings and operating temperatures are substantially changed from normal. If any contaminants are present in lamps, the relations between voltage and life are altered and the trouble would be diagnosed in other ways.

Test conditions are laid down in IEC 64 and BS 161:1968, BS 555:1962 and BS 941: 1970 where details are given of selection, inspection, photometry and life testing (including burning position, regular switching, light output, maintenance through life and cap adhesion).

Environmental testing.   The service environments of many lamps impose special conditions of high temperature, humidity or vibration. Appropriate test equipment has been and is still being developed to simulate such service conditions in order that the performance of lamps may be assessed in the laboratory.

The effect of high humidity on capping cement is usually tested in a special cabinet which cycles humidity and temperature conditions, a typical cycle being to subject the lamps to a temperature of 60 °C at a relative humidity of 99% for a period of 16 h, followed by cooling to room temperature over 8 h. This cycle is repeated three times, after which the lamps are tested for cap adhesion.

There has been a tendency in the past to specify arbitrary tests for lamp resistance to shock and vibration, but more recently much greater emphasis has been placed on the necessity for accurate reproduction of the service environment so that lamps may be tested under strictly comparable conditions.

191

10 Tungsten halogen lamps

More than 90 years have passed since Swan made the first incandescent filament lamp consisting of a carbon wire in an evacuated bottle, operating at an efficacy of only a few lumens per watt and producing a very yellow light. The glowing wire vaporizing in vacuum soon caused the bulb wall to blacken. Attempts to increase the efficacy of the lamp and to reduce filament evaporation led eventually to the use of the more ductile tungsten filament wound into a close coil and operating at a higher temperature. This was followed by the gas-filled lamp in 1913 and finally in 1936 the coiled-coil filament was produced, raising the efficacy even further.

Some twelve years ago attention was once again brought to bear on the improvement of the performance of the incandescent lamp. Patents published as long ago as the beginning of this century showed that a chemical reaction between a halogen and tungsten could take place in a lamp, transferring evaporated tungsten back to the filament. At that time lack of effort, lack of proper understanding of the chemical mechanism, and lack of the necessary materials had prevented progress towards practical lamps. About 1959 it was found that by adding a halogen such as iodine to the gas filling of a specially designed lamp, having only tungsten components within the envelope and with the bulb wall temperature kept above 250 °C, a regenerative cycle could be achieved. A whole new range of lamps has resulted and active development is occurring in many directions.

10.1 THE REGENERATIVE CYCLE

The conventional incandescent gas-filled lamp loses filament material by evaporation; much of it is deposited on the bulb wall. When a halogen is added to the filling gas, and if certain temperature and design conditions are established, a reversible chemical reaction occurs between tungsten and halogen. In the simplest terms, tungsten is evaporated from the incandescent filament and some portion of this diffuses towards the bulb wall. Within a specific zone between the filament and bulb wall, where temperature conditions are favourable, the tungsten combines with the halogen. The tungsten halide molecules diffuse towards the filament where they dissociate, the tungsten being deposited back on the filament while the halogen is available for a further reaction cycle.

Expanding this to give further detail, consider an incandescent filament positioned along the axis of a closed tube containing an inert gas and one of the halogens (Fig. 10.1). The filament could normally operate at a temperature between 2600 °C and 3200 °C, the temperature being dependent on the desired life and applied voltage. Between the filament and the bulb wall there is a temperature gradient through the inert filling gas. This gradient can be divided into three zones, extending radially from filament to bulb wall, with limiting temperatures dividing them. Within the zone or layer immediately surrounding the filament there are no reactions, the inert filling gas and halogen atoms

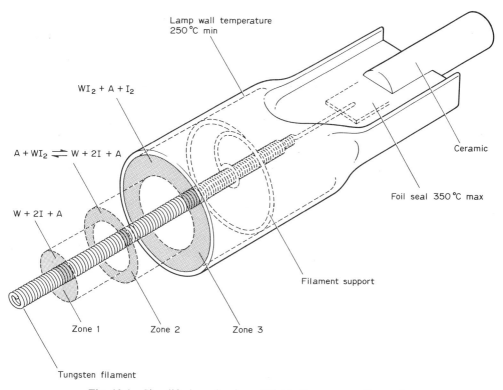

Lamp wall temperature
250 °C min

$WI_2 + A + I_2$

$A + WI_2 \rightleftharpoons W + 2I + A$

$W + 2I + A$

Ceramic

Foil seal 350 °C max

Filament support

Zone 1   Zone 2   Zone 3

Tungsten filament

Fig. 10.1 Simplified mechanism of the iodine regenerative cycle

being present as two separate components. The next outward zone contains halogen and tungsten atoms (with the filling gas), and both recombination of the halogen atoms and formation of tungsten halides will take place, with dissociation at the higher temperature side of this zone. Beyond the lower temperature side of this zone to the bulb wall, there is no thermal dissociation but recombination of halogen atoms and formation of tungsten halide is completed, mainly at the bulb wall. The tungsten halides formed in the two outer zones diffuse towards the filament, where they again dissociate into the halogen and tungsten, probably at about 0·5 mm to 2 mm from the surface.

The regenerated tungsten is not, in most cases, deposited directly back on the filament, but is liberated in the inner zone, where the tungsten vapour density is enhanced and the solid deposited on the filament. In the case of the iodine and bromine cycles it does not settle on the hot spots from where it was originally evaporated but on the cooler sections of the filament nearer the supports and tails.

All halogens are capable of supporting a regenerative cycle in a tungsten filament lamp, the main difference between them being the temperature at which the various reactions in the cycle may take place, and the extent to which they react with components and with impurities inside the lamp, especially oxygen and hydrogen. Fluorine dissociates at the running temperature of the filament and should theoretically give optimum performance

193

and a lamp life approaching infinity. There are, however, formidable practical problems in using fluorine owing to its corrosive nature; chlorine has not so far been found as useful as bromine and iodine.

10.2   DESIGN AND MANUFACTURE

10.2.1   Tungsten iodine lamps

Of all the tungsten halogen lamps, the iodine lamp was the first to become commercially available. This was due mainly to the fact that the temperatures required to maintain the regenerative cycle are well suited to many practical lamp designs, in particular lamps which have a life in excess of 1000 h where tungsten vaporizes at a moderate rate. The predominant reaction is $W + 2I \rightleftarrows WI_2$ and occurs at about 1000 °C. The boundary temperatures in the case of iodine and iodine compounds such as hydrogen iodide have been determined and for a successful regenerative cycle the filament must run at a minimum temperature of 1700 °C with the bulb wall at least 250 °C. Iodine quantity is variable and dependent upon the amount of tungsten to be regenerated, this in turn being related to filament temperature and overall lamp loading. The greater the proportion of iodine vapour in a lamp, the greater is the light loss due to the absorption by the characteristic pink vapour: this could be up to 5% in practical lamp designs.

10.2.2   Tungsten bromine lamps

The tungsten bromine cycle is very similar to the iodine cycle. The reaction in this case involves the formation of WBr_2 or higher bromides, and requires a temperature of about 1500 °C. Bromine is far more reactive than iodine and one of the disadvantages is that a small excess will cause erosion of the cooler parts of the filament (at 1500 °C). To some extent this has been overcome by the introduction of compounds such as HBr, CH_2Br_2, CH_3Br, which dissociate in the zone close to the filament releasing sufficient bromine to react with the evaporated tungsten. Most of the excess bromine remains in compound form as HBr, until during life some hydrogen diffuses through the bulb, leaving excess bromine which attacks the filament. Therefore bromine lamps are restricted to a short life of under 1000 h, and where the rate of evaporation of tungsten is greater than in the case of iodine lamps, with filament temperatures higher than 2800 °C. The advantage of these bromine compounds are that they can be introduced in gaseous form at room temperature, thus simplifying the manufacturing process. Bromine in the quantities used gives practically no light absorption and therefore a gain in efficacy over iodine. Also, the regenerative cycle operates over a somewhat wider range of bulb temperatures, approximately 200 °C to 1100 °C.

Gettering of bromine lamps.   In 1913 Langmuir discovered that small traces of water vapour could produce blackening of the lamp bulb by the formation of oxides on the hot tungsten filament, diffusion to the bulb wall and reduction of the oxides on the wall by residues of hydrogen. In addition, transport of tungsten can be produced along the filament if there is a temperature gradient along the coil and between the coil and supports. In the case of halogen lamps, traces of oxygen, hydrogen and water are frequently present.

These traces cause various transport cycles of the tungsten if they are not carefully regulated, with reactions involving WO_2, WO_2Br_2 and other compounds. These cycles occur in the vicinity of the temperature gradient in the filament, and may lead to early lamp failure due to thinning of the filament wire. It appears that the direction of tungsten transport along the temperature gradient varies according to the gas present. Excess oxygen in the lamp will produce transport of tungsten up the temperature gradient from the supports to the hotter filament, whereas water causes transport in the opposite direction towards the support, often building up dendritic growths in the form of spikes.

Quite recently a method has been found of reducing these traces of gas by a gettering action, using bromophosphonitrile $(PNBr_2)_n$. This chemically inert non-poisonous inorganic polymer makes it possible to administer into the lamp in solution an exact amount of a combination of phosphorus getter and halogen (Sect. 7.3). This will not dissociate until the filament is lit on ageing, after which the accurately controlled amount of bromine carries out its function in the halogen cycle and the phosphorus takes up the unwanted gases, thus achieving a longer and more controlled life, with less spread within a batch of lamps.

10.2.3   Bulb and seal

With very few exceptions these lamps are manufactured with bulbs of pure fused silica or similar materials with a silica content of greater than 96%, such as Vycor (Sect. 7.1.1).

This is the ideal material for lamps which have to operate at a high wall temperature and are subjected to violent thermal shock on switching. Unfortunately, there are no refractory metals available with similar low expansion which can withstand high temperatures and act as electrical conductors in the seals between the filament and the outside of the lamp. The technique, therefore, is to use very thin molybdenum foil, as described in Sect. 7.1.3. Molybdenum oxidizes in air above 350 °C and molybdenum lead wires may need protection by sheathing with a thin layer of platinum.

10.2.4   Filament and supports

The filaments of tungsten halogen lamps not only operate at higher temperatures, but they are often more closely wound to give greater luminous flux per unit area. Being in extremely small bulbs they must remain quite rigid, without sag, throughout life. A further demand is that the wire must be free from trace contaminants such as nickel and iron which would combine to form unwanted halides and condense on the bulb wall taking the halogen out of the cycle. This means that the tungsten wire has to be specially controlled from the powder stage throughout its processing. After it is coiled the wire structure of the filament is still fibrous and the filament is then held rigidly on a tungsten mandrel in a vacuum or hydrogen atmosphere and heated to about 2400 °C. During this operation the fibrous material is converted to a crystalline state; the crystals must interlock to prevent slip which would cause sagging of the filament (Fig. 10.2).

The supports holding the filament are normally made from tungsten. In some designs molybdenum supports are being used, but these lamps have a life of only a few hundred hours. If the design of the filament is complicated, having many limbs, then a silica bridge holding the various filament support wires can also be incorporated. As every lamp must have two conductors the designs include double-ended linear lamps where

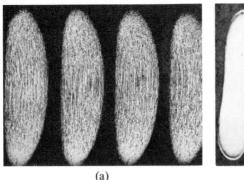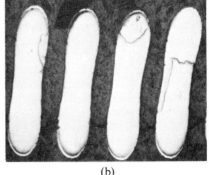

(a)   (b)

Fig. 10.2   Microphotographs of cross-sections of coiled tungsten filaments   (a) before and (b) after temperature treatment (127 × magnification)

there is one seal at each end, and single-ended lamps with both seals at one end. The double-ended lamps are mainly used for floodlight and general illumination purposes whereas the single-ended lamps have more compact filaments and are used in conjunction with precise optics.

10.2.5   Advantages of the tungsten halogen lamp

The improved efficacy and life of the tungsten halogen lamp over a conventional incandescent lamp do not in fact arise directly from the re-deposition of tungsten on the filament, for the regenerative cycle only prevents the accumulation of the tungsten on the bulb wall, giving virtually 100% lumen maintenance throughout life. This permits changes in the geometry and radical reduction in the size of the lamp, which in turn result in increased efficacy and life. The volume of a tungsten halogen lamp is very much less than the equivalent conventional lamp. For example, a 500 W tungsten halogen lamp is only 1% of the volume of its conventional counterpart (Fig. 10.3).

The respective diameters of the filament and of the lamp bulb are important design factors. Not only must the minimum temperature conditions be satisfied, but the bulb diameter should be designed so that there is virtually no gas convection which would cause heat losses and lower efficacy. Langmuir's 'sheath theory' shows that this absence of convection may apply to designs used in tungsten halogen lamps, and this is one reason for their increased efficacy over the conventional lamp when the sheath exceeds the lamp diameter (Sect. 7.3).

Another major contribution to the increase of efficacy and life is the possibility of filling these small and strong bulbs to a pressure well in excess of atmospheric, 1·5 atm. to 10 atm. according to type; this increases the gas density in the region of the filament and helps to suppress evaporation of tungsten. The gas filling is normally argon or argon-nitrogen.

The theoretical maximum efficacy of molten tungsten at 3410 °C is of the order of 53 lm/W. In practice such a temperature cannot be achieved as there are losses at the filament ends resulting in uneven temperature and other heat losses through the gas filling;

196

Fig. 10.3 Comparative sizes of 500 W GLS and 500 W tungsten halogen lamps

as a result the maximum efficacy of a lamp with a substantial filament carrying 10 A is about 40 lm/W but the life would be only a few minutes. Because of their design advantages, tungsten halogen lamps have efficacies up to 50% higher than those of conventional lamps. Depending on the life required in the particular application the efficacy varies from 15 lm/W to 35 lm/W with corresponding filament temperatures of 2400 °C to 3250 °C.

One feature of the lamp which needs to be mentioned is its larger emission of ultra-violet radiation than is the case for the ordinary tungsten lamp. This is due to the higher filament temperature and the ultra-violet-transmitting bulb. Usually the ultra-violet radiation is reduced to harmless proportions by a glass housing or shield. In spectroradiometry the lamp is useful as a source of long wave ultra-violet which may be standardized and used for calibration in measurements of spectral power distribution (Sects. 4.1.1, 4.3.2).

10.3   APPLICATIONS

The tungsten halogen lamp has a number of distinct performance and design merits over the conventional lamp. These include its near 100% lumen maintenance throughout life; its increased life or efficacy, with a filament of higher luminance; and its small, strong bulb with robust internal construction allowing luminaires and optics to be miniaturized and made less expensive, as the following applications show.

10.3.1   Floodlighting

This mainly uses double-ended mains voltage linear lamps ranging from the 117 mm long 300 W lamp to the 330 mm long 2000 W lamp. All are in tubular bulbs with diameters ranging from 8 mm to 10 mm. The 300 W and 500 W lamps have coiled-coil filaments whereas the 750 W, 1000 W, 1500 W and 2000 W lamps have single coil filaments. Floodlight lamps have mainly dish-shaped R7s end contacts held in a ceramic which can incorporate a fuse (Fig. 10.4).

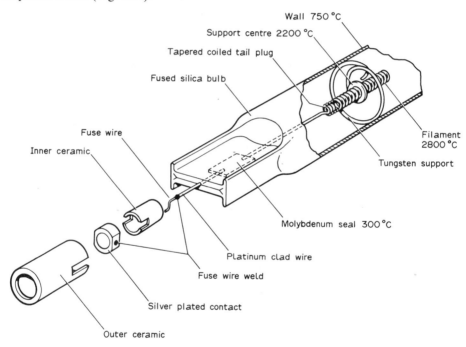

Fig. 10.4   Exploded view of end section of linear lamp and cap assembly

10.3.2   Projector and photographic lamps

Projector lamps are designed to have compact filaments and are used in conjunction with an optical system to concentrate the beam through a film gate and give maximum light on a screen. This is obtained by operating the filament at the highest possible temperature

198

compatible with an economic life which is normally 50 h. Voltage control can have a great influence on the life of these lamps which operate not far below the melting point of tungsten. Lamps operating below 30 V, requiring a transformer, normally have a flat mandrel filament whereas mains voltage lamps have coiled-coil single-plane or bi-plane filaments.

There are several film sizes for cine and still projection and these include 8 mm and 16 mm cine, and a variety of slide, microfilm and overhead projectors. More recently low voltage lamps have been developed which are used in conjunction with an ellipsoidal dichroic ('cold light') mirror, the latter either as a separate projector component or integral with the lamp (Fig. 10.5). These lamps give maximum light density on the film plane at the gate of the projector, but limiting by as much as 60% the unwanted infra-red radiation which passes through the mirror.

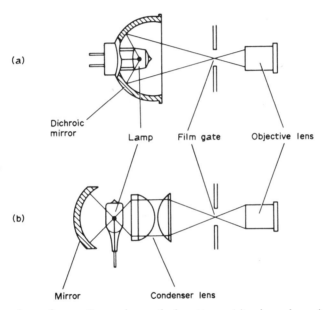

Fig. 10.5 Comparison of super 8 mm cine optical systems (a) using a lamp integral with the dichroic ellipsoidal mirror (b) using a single-ended halogen lamp with condenser lens

Photographic lamps are those designed for taking film and have a colour temperature of either 3400 K for amateur films or 3200 K for professional films. Those operating at 3400 K when designed for mains voltage have a life of about 15 h and are used in 'Sun Gun' lighting units, often mounted on a bar adjacent to the camera. For example, one 15 h life 1000 W U-shaped tungsten halogen lamp gives equivalent illumination to seven 275 W reflector photoflood lamps which have a life of only 4 h (Fig. 10.6).

10.3.3 Automobile lamps

The higher efficacy, compactness of filament and reduced bulb size of tungsten halogen lamps has created new possibilities for automobile lighting. Three lamps which have been

Fig. 10.6   'Sun Gun' lighting unit incorporating 1000 W U-shaped lamp

internationally standardized will find increasing use not only for spotlights and fog lights, but also for main headlight. Two of these are the single filament H1 12 V 55 W lamp with an axial filament and the single filament H3 lamp with a transverse filament of similar rating. Their simple design, incorporating a fixed prefocus cap which accurately aligns the filament in relation to a prefocus ring, has enabled these to be the first tungsten halogen lamps to be produced on automatic equipment.

The third type is the H4 twin filament lamp with one filament for the driving beam and another for the meeting beam, and incorporating a shield which, in conjunction with a specially designed front lens, gives an asymmetric beam of light with a sharp cut-off on the off-side of the road and allows an intensified beam on the kerb side. First developments showed that tungsten from the cold filament suffered chemical reaction resulting in transport of this tungsten to the hot filament. There are alternatives for the successful design of a twin filament lamp. Either (a) both filaments operate in close proximity in order that the cold filament is at a sufficiently high temperature from radiation or conduction to prevent chemical attack; or (b) the cold filament is substantially isolated from the running filament, being in an area of the bulb where there is insufficient free bromine to cause erosion. The latter design has been utilized in the H4 lamp (Fig. 10.7).

In Continental Europe it is general practice for headlights to have a metal-backed reflector with a bonded lens in front, but using a separate prefocussed lamp as in the case of the H4 tungsten halogen lamp.

Fig. 10.7 H4 twin filament lamp showing shield and frame construction

In UK the sealed beam lamp of all glass construction is in general use (Sect. 9.3.1). To improve this design a twin filament halogen lamp is used and prefocused on to the aluminized reflector; thus the merits of sealed beam and tungsten halogen lamps have been added with great advantage.

10.3.4 Studio lamps

The requirements for compact filament studio lamps ranging from 1 kW to 5 kW are somewhat different from those discussed so far. Conventional studio lamps are highly loaded and used in luminaires where operating temperatures are very high. Also, for colour television a constant colour temperature is required. Therefore the useful life of

(a)   (b)

Fig. 10.8 Comparison of centre line runway luminaires for   (a) tungsten halogen lamp   (b) conventional lamp

conventional lamps is determined not by filament failure, but by the degree of blackening which causes a reduction in light output, blistering of the bulb and a shift in colour temperature. All these drawbacks have been overcome in the tungsten halogen lamp, and with a considerable reduction in size.

10.3.5   Airfield lamps

Smaller luminaires giving greater accuracy of beam control and which can be embedded in runways and taxiways have been made possible by tungsten halogen lamps. In addition, they offer greater robustness to aircraft shock. With six times the lamp life the costly business of shutting down a runway for re-lamping has been considerably reduced. Fig. 10.8 compares the lamps and their housings for conventional and tungsten halogen sources.

11 Photoflash lamps

Expendable photoflash lamps emit a large light flux for a short and accurately controlled period of time by the combustion of finely shredded metals. They differ from all other lamps described in this book by the source of the energy which they convert into light: this is chemical and not electrical energy. Even the auxiliary use of an electric current to fire the photoflash lamp has been made unnecessary by a recent development. The lamps are primarily designed as a light source for the exposure of photographic materials and are mainly used in simple cameras with single speed shutters.

11.1 CONSTRUCTION AND OPERATION

11.1.1 Construction

A very fine tungsten or tungsten alloy filament (usually W-Re, Sect. 7.2.1) is mounted between a pair of contact wires which have similar expansion characteristics to that of the glass envelope. The filament assembly is sealed into the glass bulb or tube and a small moisture-sensitive spot is applied to the inside wall of glass for use as a leak detector.

A primer paste, made from very fine particles of combustible metals and powerful oxidizing materials is applied in accurately controlled quantities to the filament and tips of the contact wires. Finely shredded foil is introduced into the lamp in measured quantities. This is generally zirconium, replacing magnesium and aluminium formerly used. The lamp is heated and evacuated, which causes a colour change in the moisture-sensitive spot, usually from pink to blue. Sufficient oxygen to ensure complete combustion of the foil is introduced immediately prior to the completion of the final seal; in the case of the smaller lamps this results in a final oxygen pressure of several atmospheres, up to $800 \, \text{kN/m}^2$. To avoid the possibility of a lamp bursting during the combustion of the foil, the lamp is coated with a lacquer, usually a cellulose derivative in an organic solvent, sufficient in strength and thickness to withstand a possible explosive failure. A final coating of anti-static solution is applied to prevent inadvertent ignition due to the lamp being in contact with equipment or persons carrying a high charge of static electricity. The great majority of lamps now made are capless. Fig. 11.1 shows a typical design with a base construction originating in USA (Type AG). The European capless design (Type 1) has a larger base.

11.1.2 Operation

To fire the lamp an electric current is passed through the contact wires to the filament, which on heating causes the primer paste to ignite and explode. Burning particles of primer are scattered throughout the interior of the lamp and the foil ignites in several places simultaneously.

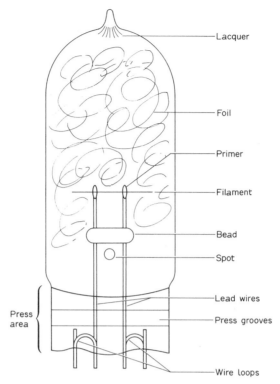

Fig. 11.1   Construction of AG1 photoflash lamp

Fig. 11.2 shows a typical photometric result, obtained by firing the lamp in an integrating sphere and displaying the output on an oscilloscope for direct measurement or photography. The following essential parameters may be derived from the curve.

(a) Time to peak (or half-peak). The time from initial closing of the firing circuit to the time at which the luminous flux reaches its maximum (or one-half of the maximum).
(b) Effective duration. The time during which the luminous flux is more than one-half of the maximum value.
(c) Peak light output. The maximum value of luminous flux.
(d) Total light output. The total light emitted from start to completion of flash, or the integrated area under the curve measured in lumen seconds. Compare Fig. 15.15.

To achieve an increase in total light output from a lamp of given volume an increase in combustible material and oxygen is necessary.

A change in peak output, time to peak or half-peak, and effective duration can be achieved by altering the cross sectional area of the foil strands: a lamp having twice as many strands as a standard lamp, but with the same weight and thickness of foil, will achieve a higher peak output in a shorter time with a shorter effective duration. The 'dark time', or time lag between the closing of the firing circuit and the start of the flash, may be altered without changing the general shape of the time versus light output curve. This

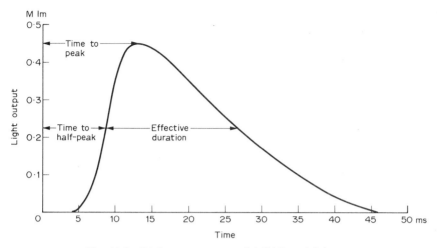

Fig. 11.2   Light output curve of AG1 B or 1 B lamp

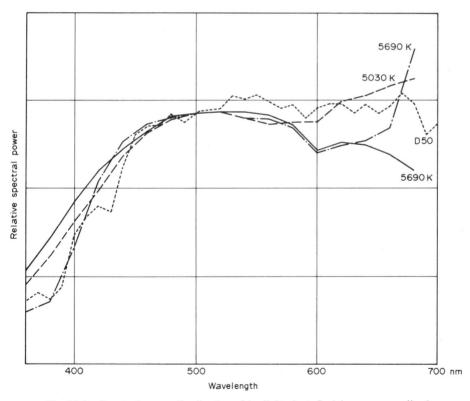

Fig. 11.3   Spectral power distribution of daylight photoflash lamps, normalized at 500 nm

control is usually effected by changing the composition of the primer paste and the geometry of the filament assembly.

11.1.3   Colour

Colour photography requires a correctly balanced spectrum of light to give acceptable results although it is rare to obtain exact reproduction of all colours in a photographed scene.

Colour films are usually designed for use with incandescent lighting or for use in natural daylight. The flash from an uncoated lamp has a colour appearance and spectral distribution similar to the 3800 K black body; when the bulb is coated with a clear protective lacquer coating it may be used with colour film intended for incandescent lighting. To enable daylight colour film to be used with photoflash lamps, either indoors or outside, a blue filter is necessary to give a light equivalent to 5500 K, usually by the addition of dyes to the lacquer coating. An alternative method of colour correction by a blue plastic flash-guard on a conventional flashgun, or a blue cover on a flashcube, enables clear photoflash lamps to be used. The trend is towards obsolescence of the clear lamp.

Fig. 11.3 shows the spectral power distribution of a number of daylight flashlamps from different makers, with their correlated colour temperatures, and the distribution of D_{50} for comparison (Sect. 3.2.7).

11.2   TYPES OF FLASHBULB

Types 1B and AG 1B are the blue-lacquered versions of the clear bulb Types 1 and AG1. Some manufacturers ensure that all four types have the same nominal peak light output and deliver the same quantity of light, typically 0·45 Mlm and 7500 lm.s respectively. Their names vary according to the maker concerned, but these most popular types all belong to the class MF in the BS classification given in Table 11.1.

Table   11.1   Flashbulb data

Class	Time to peak, ms	Time to half peak, ms	Effective duration, ms
MF	13 ± 3	8 ± 3	approx 12
M	20 ± 5	15 ± 5	approx 15
FP+		10 ± 4	min 25
FP		15 ± 6	min' 25
S	30 ± 3	20 ± 3	approx 20

11.2.1   Classification of lamps

It is necessary to produce several types of flashbulb because of the varied characteristics of camera shutters and the need to synchronize the flash and the opening of the shutter. Two types of synchronization are used for cameras with blade or iris shutters. Single speed cameras usually employ 'X-synchronization', whereas more sophisticated multi-speed cameras have 'X' and 'M' synchronized shutters.

With X-synchronization the camera shutter must be at least 80% open within 1 ms from the time of the initial closing of the firing circuit; class MF lamps may be used at shutter speeds up to 1/60 s, or class M lamps at shutter speeds up to 1/30 s. With M-synchronization a delay is incorporated so that the shutter must be fully open at 15 ms ± 2 ms from the time of the initial closing of the firing circuit. Class M or MF lamps may be used in this case at shutter speeds faster than 1/30 s.

Fig. 11.4 illustrates the necessity of M-synchronization when fast shutter speeds are required. It can be seen that at fast shutter speeds and using X-synchronization an MF photoflash lamp has only just started to ignite by the time the shutter has closed, but when M-synchronization is used the lamp remains above its half-peak value for the total time the shutter is open.

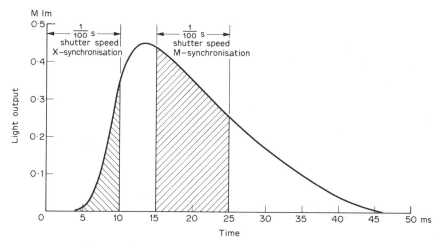

Fig. 11.4   Light output curve of type MF lamp related to synchronization

Class FP and FP+ lamps are designed for use with cameras having focal plane shutters. These usually consist of two flexible blinds mounted on spring-loaded rollers such that a slit between the two blinds passes horizontally or vertically across the frame of film. The shutter speed is usually changed by altering the width of this slit, and as it takes up to 25 ms for the slit to traverse the frame, the need for a photoflash lamp with an effective duration in excess of this time is apparent. Synchronization of this type of shutter for use with photoflash lamps usually incorporates a delay so that the slit does not start to travel across the frame until the lamp has reached half peak output.

Shutters of this type vary considerably in design and operation and for this reason it is necessary to have two classifications, FP and FP+. Class FP and FP+ lamps usually achieve a long effective duration by using strands of foil with two or more different cross-sections which burn at different speeds.

Class S lamps, usually with a large light flux, are mainly used by press and commercial photographers. To obtain maximum advantage from these lamps the whole output can be used by employing the open-flash technique. This requires the use of a camera with a setting that will allow the shutter to remain open and a flashgun in which a photoflash lamp can be fired independently. The necessary operations should be effected quickly and smoothly, opening the shutter, firing the lamp, and closing the shutter. Photographs of fast-moving subjects should not be attempted with this method, but the effective shutter speed can be estimated as this is approximately the effective duration of the photoflash lamp in use.

11.2.2 Lamp size

Recent development work utilizing new materials and improving production processes has enabled lamp performance to be improved and lamp sizes to be reduced. An example of this trend can be illustrated by comparing an early lamp having an internal volume of 8 ml and a total light output of 5500 lm s with the current version having an internal volume of 1·2 ml and a total light output of 7500 lm s.

This miniaturization of photoflash lamps not only makes them more convenient to store and carry, but also enables equipment manufacturers to reduce flashgun sizes and incorporate miniature flashguns within the camera body. The introduction of the AG and European capless photoflash lamps provided significant reductions in lamp size and cost, and with the increase in lamp performance these miniature types have sufficient light output for most amateur photographers and comprise a very large proportion of photoflash lamp sales.

Lamps with a higher light output, as used by commercial or press photographers, require larger quantities of foil and oxygen to produce this extra light. Whilst it might be possible to compact the foil sufficiently to utilize a small glass envelope, the oxygen would need to be at a pressure that could cause the lamp to explode. These lamps are therefore larger in size and are usually of the capped variety: they comprise only a small proportion of the total of photoflash lamps made.

11.2.3 Guide numbers

Manufacturers of photoflash lamps issue guide numbers for their products. These numbers are the product of the flash-to-subject distance and f-number or stop of the camera lens. They are only a guide to correct exposure and apply only to exposures made with the flash pointed directly at the subject. They are intended to be used with subjects and walls of medium colours in an average sized room. For photographs taken in a small room with light coloured walls a smaller aperture may be used whereas photographs taken out of doors in the dark, where there is little if any reflection, will require a larger aperture.

Metre guide numbers GN are calculated from a formula given in BS 4095:1970. For flash bulbs with separate reflectors,

$$GN = 0{\cdot}019 \, Lt . M . S_x$$

where Lt is the time integral of luminous flux in lm s

M is the 'reflector factor'

and S_x is the film speed.

If intensity I is measured for bulbs with integral reflectors, a similar formula is used, replacing $Lt . M$ by $4\pi It$.

Guide numbers should be rounded to the nearest figure in the following series, based on steps of approximately one-third of an f-stop:

10, 11, 12, 14, 16, 18, 20, 22, 25, 28, 32, 36, 40, 45, 56, 64, 72, 80, 90, 100, 110, 125, 140.

From this number either the flash distance or the camera stop can be found if the other is known. The guide number is based on a standard camera exposure of 1/30 s using X-synchronization, as this normally utilizes most of the light from class MF and class M lamps.

11.3 FLASH CIRCUITS

Photoflash lamps are designed to operate in the range of 3 V to 30 V and firing circuits fall into two categories.

Battery-capacitor systems. In the recommended battery capacitor circuit shown in Fig. 11.5 the capacitor is charged only when a bulb is fitted into the socket and therefore, provided the flashgun is stored without a lamp in the socket, the leakage current of the capacitor will not continuously discharge the battery.

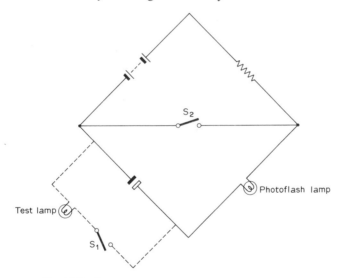

Fig. 11.5 Battery-capacitor testing and firing circuit

The resistor should be of sufficiently high value to ensure that the capacitor charging current will not fire the lamp, and of sufficiently low value to ensure that the capacitor is adequately charged in time for the user to take a photograph. The dotted lines indicate the connection of a test circuit which utilizes a test lamp drawing a sufficiently low current to ensure that the photoflash lamp will not fire. When switch S_1 is depressed, the test lamp will light if the photoflash lamp and its connection into the socket complete the firing circuit, which in turn is operated by switch S_2.

Battery circuits.   Most modern single speed cameras incorporating a flashgun in the camera body use a simple 3 V battery circuit to fire the lamp. This system, with two 1·5 V miniature batteries connected in series across the lamp, is favoured by camera manufacturers because of its space-saving advantages. As the open circuit voltage of new batteries is at the bottom limit of the normal operating voltage range for photoflash lamps, this system is very sensitive to battery condition. A small drop in e.m.f. due to use or excessive storage results in a comparatively large increase in the internal resistance of the battery and therefore insufficient current to ensure correct firing. The effects of failing battery condition are retarded ignition (increased time to peak), or fusion of the filament without ignition of the foil, and eventually the low voltage may be insufficient to fuse the filament.

As the 3 V battery circuit gained popularity with camera manufacturers it became necessary to control the 'flashability' of the lamps. This is defined as the ability of a lamp to fire with minimum energy input while still maintaining substantially the same luminous flux versus time characteristic. It is measured by the amount of deviation in the time to peak under conditions specified.

11.4   FLASHCUBES

The miniaturization of photoflash lamps resulted in a lamp having an internal volume of only 0·65 ml and a total light output only marginally less than for a Type 1 or AG1 lamp. Because these lamps were so small they became difficult to handle and fit correctly into the flashgun. To solve this problem and provide for rapid repetition of flashes, magazine units have been designed.

11.4.1   The flashcube

This resulted from the co-operative development by camera and flashbulb manufacturers of both the flashcube and a new range of cameras designed to use flashcubes exclusively as a source of additional illumination. The flashcube consists of four miniature photoflash lamps of conventional base construction, securely attached to a precisely constructed base moulding and accurately positioned within four aluminized, vacuum-formed plastic reflectors. The lamps and reflectors are encased in a transparent plastic cover sealed to the base moulding, forming a shape similar to a cube with sides of approximately 29 mm.

Although the lamps within a flashcube produce slightly less light than Type 1 or AG1 lamps, similar guide numbers are achieved by eliminating a large proportion of stray light that does not illuminate the subject. This is because a new highly polished reflector is used each time a lamp is fired, with the lamp positioned more accurately within the reflector. The types of cameras designed to accept flashcubes into a socket in the camera body range from simple versions where cube rotation is incorporated in the film advance mechanism or automatically after shutter release, to more sophisticated types where film advance and cube rotation is motor-driven so that it is possible to take four flash photographs in five seconds.

11.4.2   The Magicube

A recent analysis of photoflash lamp failures revealed that a high percentage were due to electrical faults in the firing circuit, usually caused by poor battery condition or high resistance contacts. A further common failure was an attempted flash photograph using flashcubes but with the inadvertent use of a previously fired face. As a result of this survey a mechanically fired flashcube known as a Magicube was developed for the latest range of Instamatic X cameras. This new flashcube requires no battery or external power source, and therefore eliminates failures associated with poor electrical contacts or weak batteries.

In the construction of lamps used in Magicubes, a thin walled metal tube containing an anvil wire coated with primer is sealed into the base of the lamp in place of the filament assembly used in conventional photoflash lamps. Each lamp is positioned in the base of the Magicube adjacent to its own securely mounted and cocked torsion spring (Fig. 11.6).

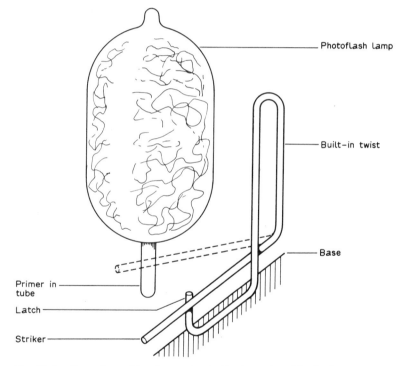

Fig. 11.6   Operation of torsion spring to fire lamp in a Magicube

As a Magicube is fitted to an Instamatic X camera a lightly sprung probe connected to the shutter release mechanism rests upon the striking end of the torsion spring through a hole in the cube base. This probe is inserted further into the base of the cube as the shutter button is depressed, releasing the striker from its retaining latch. This allows it to strike at high velocity on the metal tube protruding from the lamp. The impact causes the primer within the tube to ignite and send burning particles into the lamp to ignite the foil.

Less than 1·4 mJ of energy is required to release the striker from its latch, but the striker develops more than 21 mJ during the 0·3 ms it takes to travel from the latch to the tube. With synchronization achieved by the simultaneous action of the firing probe and shutter opening, aided by the fast spring movement, it has been possible to reduce the time to peak from the normal 13 ms achieved by conventional flashcubes to 7 ms, which has enabled the effective shutter speed of Instamatic X cameras to be speeded up to 1/50 s.

To avoid the inadvertent use of a fired face of a Magicube the firing probe is linked to a retractable shield within the viewfinder. With an unfired face the probe lightly rests upon the striker and vision through the viewfinder is unimpaired, but after a lamp has been fired the striker has moved away from the hole in the Magicube base allowing the probe to project further into the base, and this extra movement of the probe causes the shield to obscure vision through the viewfinder.

12 Fluorescent lamps

Of all the discharge lamps in use at the present time, the fluorescent lamp has proved by far the most successful and widely used. Its construction makes it very adaptable to mass production techniques and consequently it is relatively cheap. Also its performance in terms of its high conversion of electrical power to light, its flexibility in size, its colour rendering properties, together with its low surface brightness have made it a suitable light source for most applications. It is perhaps surprising that it has been used only to a limited extent for domestic lighting, though it has now been commercially available for over 30 years.

12.1 FLUORESCENT LAMP DESIGN

12.1.1 Lamp operation

A typical hot cathode fluorescent lamp consists of a glass tube with its inner surface coated with fluorescent powder, filled with argon gas at about 3 Torr ($1\,\text{Torr} = 133 \cdot 3\,\text{N/m}^2$) and containing a drop of mercury, and with tungsten wire electrodes coated with thermionic emitter sealed into each end of the tube (Fig. 12.1).

Light is mainly produced in the fluorescent lamp by conversion of short wavelength radiation to visible radiation by the phosphor coating on the tube (Sects. 6.1.4, 8.1.1).

Most of the radiation emitted from the arc in mercury vapour at a pressure of about $0 \cdot 01$ Torr is in the ultra-violet region at a wavelength of $253 \cdot 7$ nm, a resonance line. Other emissions occur in the ultra-violet and visible spectrum (Fig. 6.4). The lines in the visible spectrum have a considerable effect on the light emitted by the lamp.

The inert gas argon is added to the lamp primarily to assist starting since the vapour pressure of the mercury is very low. The gas pressure must be carefully controlled at the correct value to avoid difficult starting at high values, and shorter lamp life and worse lumen maintenance at low values of the pressure.

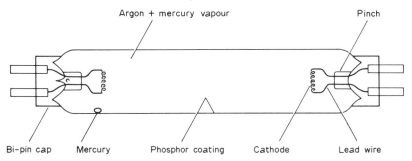

Fig. 12.1　Construction of a fluorescent lamp

213

The lamp is operated in conjunction with control gear which is necessary to heat the cathodes, provide sufficient voltage to start a discharge between them, and limit the current through the lamp (Sect. 18.2).

12.1.2   Lamp design

A number of requirements have to be considered when designing a fluorescent lamp for operation on mains voltage. These are the proposed lumen output and efficacy, the life, the colour and colour rendering, and the lamp's ability to light and remain alight under the conditions to be met in operation. The standard lamps so developed now range in length from 150 mm to 2400 mm, with diameters of 16 mm, 26 mm and 38 mm. Their ratings vary from 4 W to 125 W.

12.1.3   Cathodes

The cathode of a fluorescent lamp consists of (a) a tungsten wire which has been coiled and this primary coiling coiled again (the 'coiled-coil'), or (b) a braid made from 8 tungsten wires to form a tube and then coiled (the 'braided cathode'), or (c) a 'triple coil' made by over-winding a tungsten wire with a very fine wire and then coiling the composite wire twice, as in (a). The cathode is filled with an emissive material consisting mainly of carbonates of barium, strontium and calcium which are decomposed to the oxides during lamp manufacture. The design must be such that the cathode, under all conditions, is at a high enough temperature to produce sufficient electron emission, but not so high that excessive evaporation of barium is obtained. Also the cathode must hold the maximum amount of emitter in order to give a long life.

Fluorescent lamps were originally designed for use in switch-start circuits, in which the preheat current through the cathodes was controlled by a choke (Sect. 18.2.1). The cathodes were, therefore, made of comparatively high resistance (the 10 V cathode) in order to obtain long life. When circuits using transformers to preheat the cathodes were introduced in UK, the transformers were designed to match the cathode, and connected across the lamp in order to reduce the cathode voltage when the lamp struck. In USA the standard voltages of 110 V to 125 V necessitated the use of step-up transformers and it was convenient to put the cathode-heating windings on the same core, with the result that the cathode voltage was not reduced when the lamp struck. The low resistance or 3·5 V cathode was therefore introduced using the triple-coil construction to maintain adequate lamp life.

In some countries both high and low resistance cathodes are at present available in some sizes of lamps. The lamps are only interchangeable in circuits (switch-start and semi-resonant-start) in which the cathode heating current and not the voltage is controlled. In UK very few lamps with low resistance cathodes are in use, and the possibility of confusion exists only with 1500 mm lamps. The differences due to rating, cathode type and circuits are as follows:

80 W lamps with coiled-coil 10 V cathodes may be used in all 80 W circuits (switch-start and Quickstart); also in 65 W circuits (switch-start and resonant-start) though with slight loss of starting performance and with reduced lamp life.

214

65/80 W lamps with braided 10 V cathodes may be used in all 65 W and 80 W circuits (switch-start, resonant-start and Quickstart) without loss of starting performance. Life may vary slightly according to the type of circuit but minimum life will be at least as good as with 80 W lamps operating in 80 W circuits.

65 W lamps with triple-coil or coiled-coil 3·5 V cathodes may be used in 65 W circuits (switch-start and resonant-start), or in 80 W switch-start circuits without loss of starting performance and with normal lamp life. Performance and life of the control gear and lamp will suffer, however, in circuits designed with 10 V cathode heating windings (Quickstart or instant-start).

12.1.4 Lamp types

The different fluorescent lamp types available are shown in Table 12.1.

Standard fluorescent lamps are coated with a transparent water-repellent coating which prevents the formation of a continuous film of water on the glass (type MCFE/U). On starterless circuits (Sect. 18.2) the starting voltage of the lamp is partially dependent on the electrical resistance of the glass surface and is at a minimum when the resistance is either very low or very high: the silicone coating brings about this latter condition. The former condition is satisfied in the MCFA/U lamp which has a metal strip fitted to the outside of the lamp tube and connected to each cap. The strip is earthed through one of the lamp caps.

The MCFB/U lamp has an internal high resistance strip connected to one electrode. When a voltage is applied a glow discharge takes place between the unconnected end of the strip and the electrode nearest to it. There is then sufficient ionization to start the discharge between the two electrodes. These lamps may be operated on a choke ballast or tungsten lamp resistor. Special lamp caps are fitted to prevent exposure to full mains voltage if one end of the lamp is inserted in the holder and the pins at the other end are touched while the mains switch is on.

The TL-M lamp has an external conducting strip connected to one cathode through a 2 MΩ resistor in the cap. The lamp is not earthed but the high resistor value makes it safe if the strip is touched. This lamp is used in a starterless circuit and gives reliable starting at lower ambient temperatures.

The MCFR/U, amalgam and circular lamps are described in Sect. 12.4.

Slimline lamps, earlier so called because of their small diameter compared with their length, are now made in diameters up to 38 mm. They are instant-start lamps having single contact bases and are coated on the outside with a transparent silicone material. They are used on similar circuits to the normal bipin instant-start lamps.

The striking voltage of fluorescent lamps is at a minimum at about 20 °C, rising on either side of this value, most steeply below 5 °C and above 60 °C, although the starter switch and type of ballast influence it. Lamps are specially made for use in low ambient temperatures by reducing the argon filling pressure, but this has the disadvantage of reducing the lamp life.

Miniature lamps are standard types except for their low ratings (4 W, 6 W, 8 W and 13 W), narrow bulbs (16 mm) and miniature bipin caps. They have poor overall efficacy owing to control gear losses but are convenient in some applications (Chaps. 24, 26).

Table 12.1 Types of fluorescent lamps

British type reference	Other reference	Lamp description	Application
MCFE/U	Standard TL	Standard fluorescent lamp with transparent silicone varnish water-repellant on outside of glass tube. HR cathodes	Switch-start, resonant-start and Quick-start circuits
MCFA/U	Metal strip type	Fluorescent lamp with metal starting strip fitted to outside of tube and connected to both metal lamp caps. HR cathodes	Resonant-start and Quickstart circuits when metal strip is earthed
MCFB/U	TL-X or TL-S	Fluorescent lamp with internal metal starting strip, fitted with special single contact caps. IS cathodes	Division 2 luminaires on instant-start circuits
MCFR/U	Reflector TL-F	Fluorescent lamp with internal reflector. HR cathodes	As MCFE/U
Amalgam	TL-H	Fluorescent amalgam. HR cathodes	Hot surrounding temperatures on switch-start, resonant-start or Quickstart circuits
Rapidstart	RS	Fluorescent lamp. LR cathodes	Rapid-start circuits
Slimline		American type instant-start lamp with special single contact cap. IS cathodes	Instant-start circuits
Circular	Circline or TL-E	Circular tube. Usually with LR cathodes	Switch-start or rapid-start circuits
Low-Temperature	TL-B	Special MCFE/U lamp for low-temperature starting	Switch-start circuits
	TL-M	External metal strip connected to one electrode via 2 MΩ resistor. LR cathodes	Mainly resonant-start circuits

HR cathode (high resistance) requires preheat at $6\frac{1}{2}$ V–10 V which falls after the lamp has started.
LR cathode (low resistance) requires preheat at $3\frac{1}{2}$ V which is maintained after the lamp has started.
IS cathode is designed to withstand cold-starting without preheat.

12.2   MANUFACTURE, CONTROL AND TESTING

12.2.1   Manufacture

The phosphor, which may be a simple material or a blend of several (Sect. 8.2), is made into a suspension in either an organic solvent or water-based system with an appropriate binder. This process is carefully controlled so that the phosphor is dispersed with the minimum amount of crystal fracture as this reduces the light output of the phosphor. Glass tubes are thoroughly washed in hot demineralized water, dried and coated with phosphor suspension, either by allowing suspension delivered from a coating gun to run down the inside of the tubes, or by inserting the tubes in rubber heads and blowing the suspension up the tube from a stock tank by compressed air. In both cases the excess suspension is allowed to drain back into the stock tank.

The tubes are allowed to dry in a temperature- and humidity-controlled room under conditions to give as even a coating of phosphor from end to end as possible. It is important to control the amount of phosphor on the tube: too little will result in low light output due to some of the ultra-violet radiation not being converted into visible light, while with too much phosphor the same result will be obtained due to light absorption in the coating. The amount of phosphor on the tube is controlled by measurements of the phosphor weight and the optical density of the coating; adjustments are made in the specific gravity and viscosity of the phosphor suspension to give the optimum conditions.

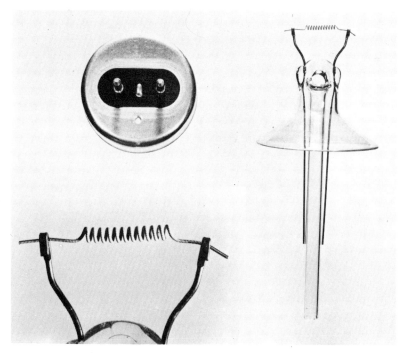

Fig. 12.2   Fluorescent lamp cap and cathode assembly

The dried phosphor-coated tubes are baked to remove the binder, and phosphor is removed from the ends to allow the cathode assemblies to be sealed into them, as small amounts of phosphor in the seals can give rise to cracks in the glass.

The cathode assemblies are made on automatic units by a series of operations which soften the glass of the flare and seal in the lead wires and exhaust tubes. The nickel ends of the leads are bent to shape and the cathode positioned and clamped. Finally the cathode is dipped in the suspension of emissive material and allowed to dry.

The cathode assemblies (Fig. 12.2) are sealed into the ends of the tubes either singly or at both ends simultaneously and the tube is then pumped. Two processes are in common use. One method is to pump all the air from the tube, and refill it with argon to the required pressure. This is between 1·8 Torr and 3·6 Torr depending on the lamp type and rating. The second method involves passing argon into the horizontal tube at one end after pumping out most of the air; the mixture of argon and remaining air is continuously removed from the other end. During this phase the cathodes are heated by controlled currents to convert the alkaline earth carbonates to oxides, the carbon dioxide being removed by the argon flow which is stopped shortly after addition of the required drop of mercury. The argon pressure is reduced to the correct value and the lamp sealed off.

The caps used on fluorescent lamps are of bipin construction (Fig. 12.2), specified in BS 1875:1952. Bayonet caps were formerly used on 1500 mm and 2500 mm lamps.

The next operation in lamp-making is the automatic threading of the lead wires from the tube through the pins of the lamp cap which has already been coated internally with a basing cement; the ends are baked to cure the cement (usually a phenolic resin). The excess lengths of the wires are cut off and either welded or soldered to the pins.

Fig. 12.3   A fluorescent lamp manufacturing unit

The lamp at this stage is unstable due to traces of gaseous impurities in it, and is aged by running it for some minutes during which time the impurities are 'cleaned-up' and the lamp stabilized.

Fig. 12.3 shows a typical view of a largely automatic unit using this process.

12.2.2 Control and testing

As fluorescent lamps are made at high speed and have very long life (making it impossible to test every batch of lamps before release to the market), it is necessary to have very efficient quality controls and inspection to maintain the quality of the finished product. These controls are applied both to the lamp-making equipment and to the product during manufacture.

All lamp components are checked before use in manufacture; for example, dimensional tests on the glass tubes, and performance checks on the phosphor for lumen output and colour, and on the emissive material for composition, impurities content and particle size distribution.

Quality controls during lamp manufacture are aimed at checking those conditions which are known to influence the final performance, namely light output and life. They include such inspections as the amount of phosphor on the glass tube, the amount of emissive material on the cathodes, and the pressure to which lamps are filled with argon.

Selections of lamps taken from those ready for despatch are checked for compliance with BS 1853:1967. The tests specified include adequate marking of the lamp, its dimensions, cap adhesion and insulation of the cap pins from the cap shell, attachment of the lead wires to the cap pins, starting voltage, colour, colour rendering, lumen output, lumen maintenance and life.

12.3 LAMP PERFORMANCE

12.3.1 Light output

The fluorescent lamp was introduced in UK at about the commencement of the second world war, and as 80 W control gear was available for use with mercury lamps and the total light output was considerably higher than with the 40 W lamp, the 1500 mm 80 W type in a tube of 38 mm diameter was adopted as standard in this country. In USA, where the supply voltages are 100 V to 125 V, the direct operation of the lamp on a simple choke ballast is limited to those operating at voltages not exceeding 60 V, which gives inadequate light output for general purposes. The 1200 mm 40 W lamp, with a running voltage of about 108 and controlled by an autotransformer ballast giving a step-up to 220 V, was adopted as standard in USA.

The light output of a fluorescent lamp depends largely on the lamp loading, or the amount of power dissipated per unit area of the tube. Lamps may be divided into three groups, the low loading group, operating at about $280 \, \text{W/m}^2$, for example, the 1200 mm 40 W lamp; the high loading group, operating at about $400 \, \text{W/m}^2$, for example, the 1500 mm 80 W lamp; and the American very high output group, operating at about $740 \, \text{W/m}^2$.

If the current in a given lamp is increased, it follows that the lamp voltage is lowered by reason of the negative volt-ampere characteristic of the discharge, while the wattage is

219

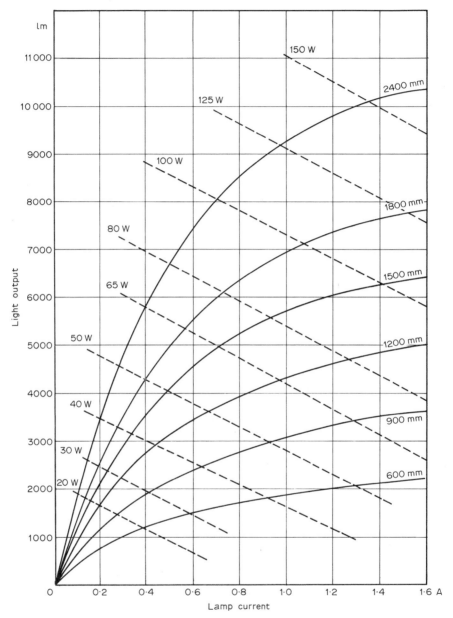

Fig. 12.4   Variation of light output with current for 38 mm diameter lamps of different lengths operated at different wattages. Data for 3500 K White lamps at 100 h

increased and with it the lumen output. However, the efficacy falls, partly from increased cathode losses, and partly on account of increased mercury vapour pressure caused by the higher bulb temperature, which results in increased self-absorption of the resonance radiation.

The advantages of low loading lamps are high efficacy and better lumen maintenance against which must be set the higher lumen output per unit length of the high loading types, even though they suffer the loss due to increased mercury vapour pressure.

The variation of light output with current, wattage and tube length is shown in Fig. 12.4. This diagram refers to lamps of 38 mm diameter which comprise the great majority now in use, and assumes the same gas filling pressure in all sizes.

A fluorescent lamp has its highest light output as soon as it reaches working temperature after switching on, but in the first 100 h of its life the light output falls by 2% to 4% and thereafter at a slower rate until at 2000 h it has fallen by only a further 5% to 10%, depending on the lamp rating and phosphor mixture. Due to this drop in lumen output in the early stages of life, the initial lumen output of a fluorescent lamp is never quoted. The usual value is the light output at 2000 h, which is known as the 'lighting design lumens' and is used by lighting engineers when designing installations.

The lumen maintenance improves slightly as the lamp loading decreases, but de luxe colours have a somewhat worse lumen maintenance than the standard colours. A typical lumen maintenance curve is shown in Fig. 12.5. Maintenance can be seriously affected by traces of impurities in the lamp, particularly by water vapour.

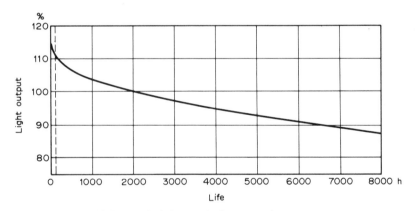

Fig. 12.5 Typical shape of a lumen maintenance curve

12.3.2 Life

The life of a fluorescent lamp normally ends when the emissive materials on one or both cathodes becomes exhausted.

When a lamp is running, a small amount of the emissive material is continuously consumed from the cathode, but when the lamp starts, particularly on switch-start circuits, a relatively large amount of emissive material is sputtered from the cathode and this shortens the life of the lamp. Since the actual lamp life is now so long, a lamp may be deemed to have had a useful life when the light output has decreased to a point where its output has ceased to be economical, perhaps at about 90% of the lighting design lumens.

The rated life of fluorescent lamps has been gradually increased from 2000 h through 3000 h and 5000 h until at the present time it is 7500 h for the 40 W, 65 W, 80 W and 125 W lamps. This life is based on a cycle of 8 switchings in 24h in a lagging switch-start circuit. A lamp which is switched less frequently will last considerably longer, in fact a continuously running lamp will last about $2\frac{1}{2}$ times the rated life (Fig. 12.6).

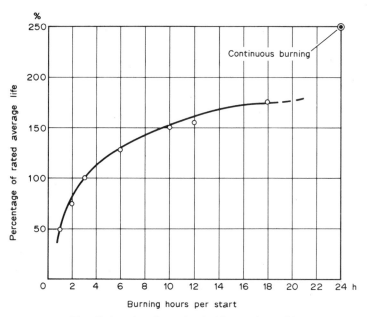

Fig. 12.6   The effect of switching on lamp life

12.3.3   Colour appearance and colour rendering

Fluorescent lamps comprise a large selection of near white colours, and may be divided into two groups: one which gives the highest attainable efficacy, and the other where some efficacy is sacrificed in order to provide a wider spectrum with better colour rendering.

It is necessary for the manufacturer to keep a close control over the colour of lamps produced. This could be done by colorimetry of sample lamps, but this is too lengthy and difficult for the control of high speed production. Lamps are made from a suspension of a new batch of phosphor and tested for colour by colorimetric methods before use: sample lamps are compared by visual inspection with existing standard lamps during the actual manufacture of the lamps, this checking being carried out by skilled observers.

It is possible to maintain the colour appearance of a lamp type within a very small tolerance over very long periods. BS 1853:1967 specifies the colour of the five main colours used in fluorescent lamps (Warm White, White, Daylight, Natural and Northlight/Colour Matching). The tolerances allowed by this specification are adequate to cover an appreciable spread between manufacturers, which would be considered much too large for lamps in one batch or even for successive quantities of phosphor. It is, therefore, often unsatisfactory to mix lamps of the same nominal colour in one installation if they comprise batches from different makers.

Fluorescent lamps are made in different loadings and consequently their operating temperatures differ. This affects the vapour pressure of the mercury and to a marked extent the combined colour of the mercury line emission. Hence there is a distinct difference in colour appearance as well as lamp luminance between, for example, 1200 mm 40 W and 1500 mm 80 W lamps. This is noticeable in installations where lamps of mixed loadings are used. It could be corrected by using phosphor suspensions of slightly different colour, but this is impracticable with present methods of production.

The tolerances in BS 1853 are 5 mpcd (minimum perceptible colour differences, Sect. 3.2.4) in any direction from the chromaticity point, as shown in Fig. 12.7.

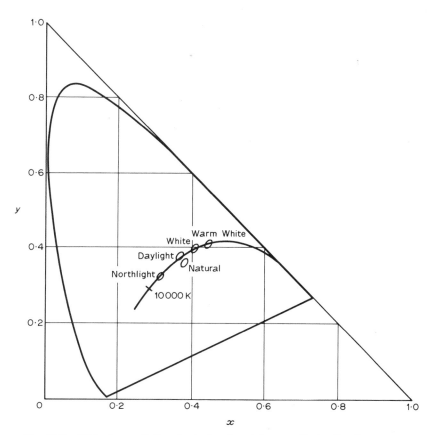

Fig. 12.7   CIE chromaticity chart showing tolerance limits for fluorescent lamps

Lamp	Colour temperature	Lighting design lumens (2000 h)	Spectral power distribution
De Luxe Warm White	3000 K	3100	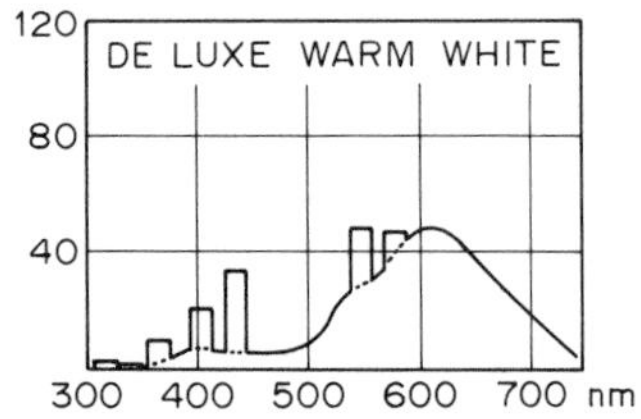 DE LUXE WARM WHITE
Warm White	3000 K	4600	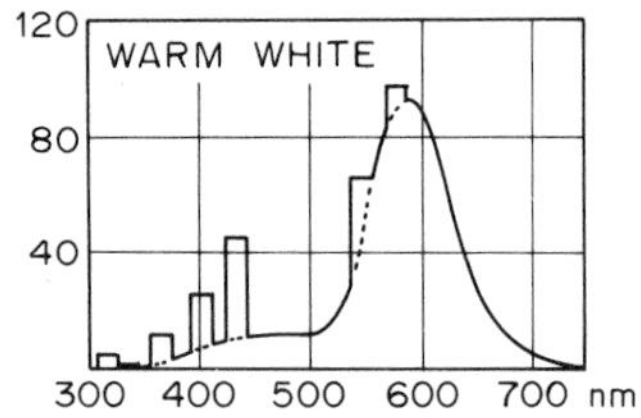 WARM WHITE
White	3400 K	4700	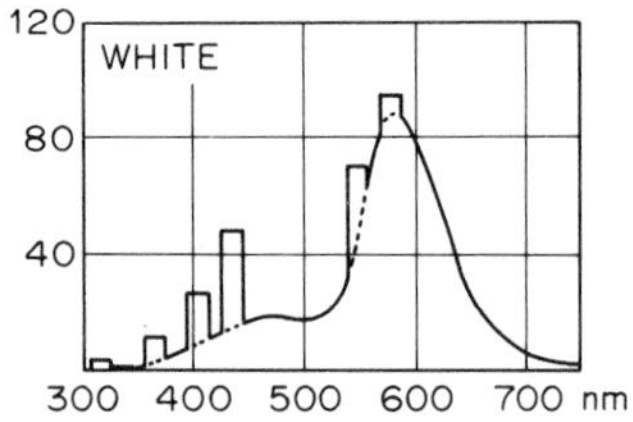 WHITE
De Luxe Natural	3600 K	2500	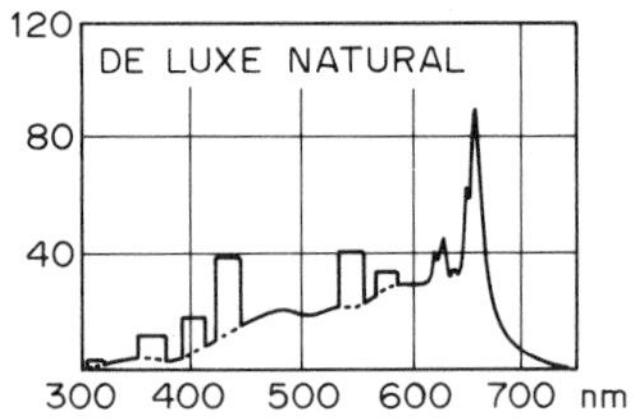 DE LUXE NATURAL
Natural	4000 K	3400	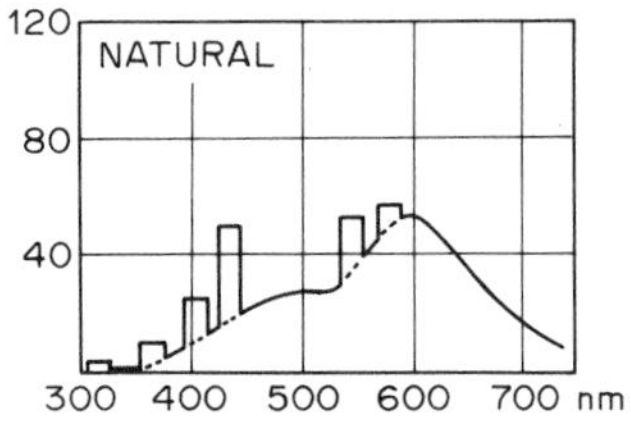 NATURAL

Fig. 12.8   Colour characteristics of the more common 1500 mm 65 W lamps.

224

Lamp	Colour temperature	Lighting design lumens (2000 h)	Spectral power distribution
°Kolor-rite	4000 K	3000	
Daylight	4300 K	4450	
Northlight Colour Matching	6500 K	2700	
Artificial Daylight	6500 K	2100	

Vertical scales are power in mW/nm bandwidth

The human eye is most sensitive to light at 555 nm in the yellow-green part of the spectrum (Sect. 1.1.1). Lamps of this colour would have the highest efficacy but this is impracticable with the fluorescent lamp, and in any case would be quite unacceptable for general lighting because of the colour and colour rendering properties. Since natural daylight is unconsciously used as a standard of 'correct' lighting, an ideal lamp would be expected to emit radiation over the whole visible spectrum without large contrasts in spectral concentration from wavelength to wavelength. The fluorescent lamps with the highest efficacy, using halophosphate phosphors, while producing acceptable 'white' light, are still lacking in the red end of the spectrum, and better colour rendering is often required. There are several such improved types of lamp, some of which are included in Fig. 12.8 together with the high efficacy types (Warm White, White and Daylight).

These de luxe lamps contain a mixture of phosphors in order to improve the balance of radiation over the range of the spectrum. De luxe lamps have a lower lumen output than standard lamps owing to the admixture of phosphors, usually with red emission, of lower lumen output than the standard phosphors, although there is some evidence that higher illuminance is needed for equal visual clarity when the standard colours are used.

Another cause of poor colour rendering from fluorescent lamps is the presence of the violet-blue mercury lines. It is possible to effect some reduction of these lines by a double coating of the bulb. The first coating is of magnesium arsenate, a red-emitting phosphor with a pale yellow body colour, and the second layer is a blend of phosphors. The first coating layer absorbs some of the near ultra-violet and violet-blue lines, producing a lamp with good colour rendering properties. A similar correction may be obtained by a single coating including the arsenate phosphor.

The Artificial Daylight lamp meets the requirements of BS 950 : Part 1 : 1967 for the assessment of colour. Its output contains the long wavelength ultra-violet radiation essential for colour matching operations normally done in natural daylight, as well as for the true comparison of fluorescent dyes now widely used in white materials.

From the many phosphors available it is possible to make lamps of a great variety of colour appearance and colour rendering properties. Some recent new types are lamps of colour temperature of about 5000 K (to meet BS 950 : Part 2 : 1967 for colour matching in the graphic arts), and 2700 K (to simulate incandescent tungsten light).

12.3.4   Effects of temperature and supply voltage

The maximum light output from a fluorescent lamp occurs when the temperature of the coolest part of the lamp is at about 40 °C. This temperature is usually maintained on the standard type of lamp when it is running in free air at an ambient temperature of 25 °C.

At these temperatures the mercury vapour pressure is at an optimum for the generation of ultra-violet radiation at 253·7 nm, but as the temperature of the lamp increases, the vapour pressure increases with the results described in Sect. 12.3.1.

Also, with increased temperature the arc voltage decreases and in a lagging circuit the lamp current increases sufficiently to keep the lamp wattage fairly constant. In a leading circuit changes in current are limited and the lamp wattage decreases.

Figs. 12.9 and 12.10 show how lamp current, voltage, wattage, light output and efficacy vary with fluctuations in the supply voltage. It will be seen that the variations are smaller in the leading circuit due to the presence of the capacitor.

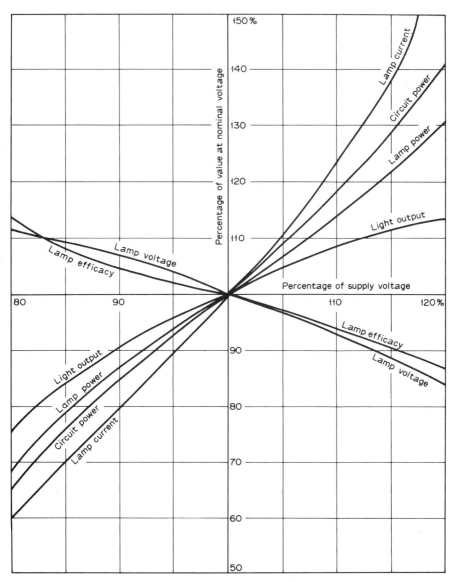

Fig. 12.9 Variation with supply voltage of 80 W lamp characteristics on a 240 V lagging switch-start circuit

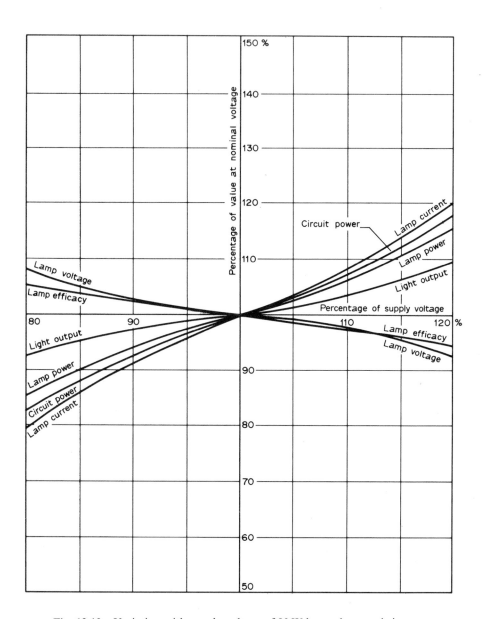

Fig. 12.10   Variation with supply voltage of 80 W lamp characteristics on a
240 V leading switch-start circuit

12.4   SPECIAL LAMP TYPES

Reflector lamps.   The usual radially symmetrical light distribution from a fluorescent lamp may be modified by including a reflecting surface in the lamp itself. The first reflecting coat usually consists of titanium dioxide and extends the length of the lamp and about 225° round the circumference. The whole tube is then coated with the phosphor layer on top of the reflecting layer, thus leaving the reflecting coat sandwiched between the glass and the phosphor. Consequently a certain amount of light control occurs in the lamp itself, the coating reflecting much of the incident light falling on it through the uncoated area.

These lamps are 10% to 15% less efficient than standard lamps but have about 70% more light directed in the downward direction. They may be used with advantage in (a) dirty locations which are difficult to reach for cleaning purposes, (b) rooms with poor reflecting surfaces or with unfavourable proportions, (c) ceiling lighting where the ceiling has a poor reflecting surface, and (d) lighting installations where, due to space limitations, reflectors are not practicable.

A disadvantage from the use of these lamps may be the high brightness of the 'window' which will give rise to more glare than the standard lamp.

Aperture lamps. The aperture lamp is similar to the reflector lamp except that the two layers inside the lamp (reflector and phosphor) coincide leaving a clear glass window of only 30° or 60°. This aperture runs the whole length of the lamp and has a luminance about four times that of a standard lamp, although the total light output is less because the window is not coated with phosphor.

These lamps give a narrow beam of light, which may be concentrated by the use of a lens or reflector to allow the light to be delivered to a small area. They may be used for lighting aircraft landing strips, bridge lighting and sign lighting.

Lamps for high ambient temperatures   With the increased use of enclosed luminaires, many at ceiling height, large numbers of standard lamps are running at temperatures in excess of those which give the maximum light output, in fact the loss in light output can be as much as 30% in some cases (Sect. 12.3.4).

A number of methods have been used to reduce the mercury vapour pressure in the lamp. One such method is to have a bar of metal pressed against the lamp by means of a spring; the top of the bar is in a cool part of the luminaire and heat is conducted away from the lamp.

A number of lamp designs have been used, one being a 'blister' blown into the lamp bulb to act as a cool spot where mercury may condense, with consequent control of the vapour pressure at the temperature of the mercury in the blister. Specially shaped non-circular tube sections have also been used for the same purpose, the best-known being the American Powergroove. More recently designs have been directed towards the use of an indium amalgam within the lamp in place of mercury, using the principle that the change in mercury vapour pressure with temperature is smaller with an amalgam than with mercury alone.

The relative light output versus temperature curves for a standard and a typical amalgam lamp are shown in Fig. 12.11a.

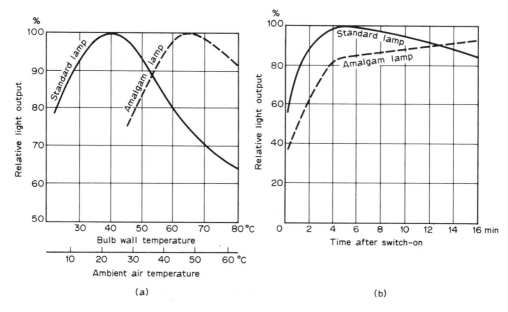

Fig. 12.11   (a) Light output versus temperature for standard and amalgam lamps
(b) Change of light output with running time for amalgam and standard lamps

This lamp type should only be used where high ambient temperatures are experienced, as under low temperature conditions a lower than standard light output will be given. The cross-over point is at an air temperature round the bulb of about 36 °C. An amalgam lamp takes a little longer than a standard lamp to reach maximum light output when switched on from cold (Fig. 12.11b), owing to the slowly produced equilibrium between the amalgam and mercury vapour as the tube gradually warms up.

Lamps for low ambient temperatures.   As can be seen from Fig. 12.11a the light output from fluorescent lamps falls when the wall temperature is either below or above the optimum of 40 °C. In order to maintain the temperature of the bulb wall jacketed lamps may be used. These have a clear glass jacket 45 mm in diameter fitted round the lamp with about 4 mm clearance of the lamp in all directions. This is sufficient under most conditions to increase the bulb wall temperature and consequently produce a much higher light output. There is approximately 2% reduction in maximum light output due to the enclosing tube.

Applications for this lamp type are where conditions are cold or windy, as in refrigerator rooms, outdoor installations, tunnels and subways. To assist the starting of lamps which are used under very cold conditions, lamps filled to a lower pressure with argon are sometimes used, but these lamps will have a somewhat shorter life and worse maintenance than standard lamps (Sect. 12.1.4).

Circular lamps.   These are available in three ratings, 210 mm diameter 22 W, 305 mm diameter 32 W, and 406 mm diameter 40 W. They fit concentrically within each other and are used where the length of the standard lamp may be a disadvantage, as in domestic installations. The construction of these lamps is difficult and costly.

U-*shaped lamps.* A range of U-shaped lamps is made in ratings from 10 W to 65 W, the 40 W lamp being the most popular. These lamps fit the inside a standard luminaire of the traditional 2 ft × 2 ft size. The 40 W lamp is made in two leg-spacing sizes measured between the centre points of each leg, 152 mm and 92 mm. It is possible to fit three of the 92 mm lamps in the 2 ft × 2 ft luminaire whereas with the larger size only two lamps are possible. Against this it is claimed that the lamps with the legs at wider spacings are cheaper and have a higher light output, also a lower weight owing to the use of thinner glass.

Germicidal lamps. The principal radiation which is generated in a low pressure mercury discharge has a wavelength of 253·7 nm which prevents the growth of moulds and bacteria. The soda-lime glass used in the manufacture of normal fluorescent lamps absorbs this radiation, but if a special ultra-violet transmitting glass, fused silica or Vycor (96% silica), is used and this glass is not coated with phosphor, the radiation emitted from the lamp will have germicidal properties. It is dangerous and can cause severe blistering of the skin and acute conjunctivitis. Therefore these lamps should not be directly viewed when lit and over-exposure should be prevented (Sect. 1.3.3).

Erythemal lamps. Radiation between the wavelengths of 290 nm and 320 nm is present in ordinary sunlight and is responsible for skin tanning and sunburn. Fluorescent 'sun lamps' used in 'solaria' have a special phosphor with an emission peak at about 300 nm and a band extending from 270 nm to 370 nm. A suitable glass to transmit this radiation is used.

Care should be taken that these lamps should be used only under medical supervision. They have been used to simulate outdoor sunlight conditions in under-cover installations (Sect. 1.3.3).

Ultra-violet lamps. These lamps are coated with a special phosphor which gives a peak output at about 370 nm. There is a small amount of visible light from the discharge of the lamp added to the ultra-violet radiation. This visible light can be almost completely eliminated if the lamp is made in Wood's glass instead of soda-lime glass. Wood's glass contains oxides of nickel and cobalt and is of a dark purple-blue colour. It absorbs almost all visible radiation but transmits the ultra-violet. Lamps made from this glass are often referred to as 'blacklamps'.

Lamps for horticultural purposes. Many conditions are necessary for the growth of strong healthy plants, including correct soil conditions, humidity, temperature and ir-radiation, and it is the latter which will be considered, the other conditions being taken as satisfactory. Plants and seeds need light to grow and flower; red and blue radiation is particularly useful in photosynthesis, the conversion of water and carbon dioxide into carbohydrates by means of chlorophyll. Lamps are now available which emit mainly in the blue and red ranges of the spectrum. Fig. 12.12 shows the spectral power distribution, together with the curve for chlorophyll synthesis. By limiting the green radiation in the lamp (largely reflected by chlorophyll) more power can be directed into the useful regions of the spectrum.

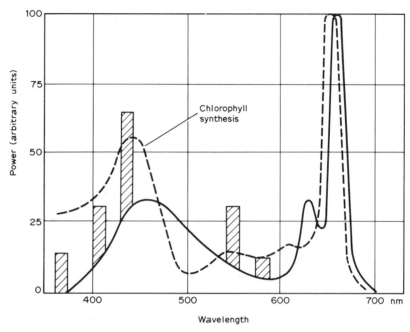

Fig. 12.12   Spectral power distribution of a Grolux lamp, and spectral activity for chlorophyll photosynthesis

Lamps for printing. Fluorescent lamps are used in various printing processes such as making photo-copies. In the diazo process the printing paper has a maximum sensitivity just below 400 nm (Fig. 15.8) and lamps ('actinic blue') are available which have an emission peak near this wavelength with a spread of from 300 nm to 500 nm. Other lamps, some of them aperture lamps, are available for printing processes which require maximum sensitivity at wavelengths in the visible spectrum (Fig. 8.1b). Like the other special purpose lamps these are not made in the normal full range but in suitable sizes for particular applications.

Coloured lamps.   A range of coloured lamps is available for decorative applications. Green and blue lamps are made simply with a suitable phosphor. If no phosphor provides an emission of the desired colour a pigment coating is used between the phosphor and the glass wall, for instance in red and gold lamps.

Cold cathode lamps.   Cold cathode fluorescent lamps emit light in the same way as standard fluorescent lamps (hot cathode lamps). Whereas the latter have electrodes of formed tungsten wire coated with alkaline earth oxides, the electrodes of cold cathode lamps consist of uncoated hollow cylinders of nickel or iron. In these lamps the cathode fall is high due to the uncoated electrodes and in order to obtain reasonable efficacy for general lighting purposes they must be made fairly long, say 3 m with a diameter of 20 mm or 25 mm.

About 2000 V is required to start the lamp, and about 900 V to 1000 V when running to maintain the arc. A leakage transformer is usually provided to start the lamp, the output falling to the lower running voltage when the lamp has lit (Sect. 18.2.3). Lamps filled with neon with or without phosphor provide a variety of colours used in sign lighting.

The advantages of cold cathode lamps compared with the hot cathode types are:

(a) They have a very long life, usually 15 000 h or more, in consequence of their rugged electrodes and low current consumption
(b) They start immediately even under cold ambient conditions
(c) Their life is unaffected by the number of starts
(d) They may be dimmed to very low light output.

Their main disadvantage is that the luminous efficacy is only about two-thirds of that of the hot cathode type because of the power loss at the electrodes.

13 Sodium lamps

Like mercury, sodium can act as a light producing vapour in discharge tubes. It has much lower vapour pressure, ionization potential and excitation potentials, which lead to very different requirements for efficient lamp designs. The extreme chemical activity of ionized sodium introduces acute problems in the selection of lamp-making materials. In the case of the high pressure sodium lamp some of these problems have only been solved comparatively recently.

The low pressure lamp is characterized by its nearly monochromatic radiation, its relatively large size and high luminous efficacy which may be in excess of 150 lm/W. It is therefore a very economical source when colour discrimination is unimportant, particularly in street lighting where its main applications are to be found.

Under comparatively high vapour pressure conditions the sodium discharge has much improved colour rendering properties, and for lamps above the 250 W rating the efficacy can exceed 100 lm/W. The physical size of the lamp is comparable with that of high pressure mercury types, and it can be accommodated in street and area floodlighting. Indoor schemes have also been carried out where imperfect colour rendering is acceptable.

Appendix I gives details of the more commonly used sodium lamps.

13.1 LOW PRESSURE LAMPS

13.1.1 Design requirements

Gas and vapour pressure conditions for the highest lamp efficacy dictate a relatively low arc voltage per unit arc length. Lamps therefore tend to have long narrow arc tubes. The temperature of the arc tube must be maintained in the region of 270 °C in order to secure the desired sodium vapour pressure of about 5 mTorr (1 Torr = 133·3 N/m^2). This necessitates an outer envelope coated with an infra-red reflecting film and evacuated in order to reduce heat losses.

In order to cope conveniently with a long arc tube a range of lamps is made where the arc tubes are bent back on themselves in the form of a tight U-shape. Further conservation of heat loss is obtained in this case by mutual heating of the limbs of the U.

It is possible to increase the voltage drop per unit length of arc by distorting the arc tube from a circular section. In this case arc tubes do not need to be bent and a range of lamps known as linear lamps are available. Fig. 13.1 shows examples of the two types for which the characteristics are given in Appendix I.

It will be seen that the U-shaped lamp has a single bayonet cap: it has an outside diameter of from 50 mm to 65 mm dependent on rating. The linear lamp has the general dimensions of a fluorescent lamp and uses two similar caps in the same way. Its opera-

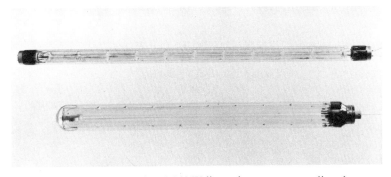

Fig. 13.1   135 W U-shaped and 140 W linear low pressure sodium lamps

tional wattage is changed by length and by changes in the infra-red reflective coating on the outer envelope.

An electrode is required at each end of the lamp to support the arc discharge. These electrodes may take different forms in order to suit different lamp designs, but all basically employ fine tungsten wire coiled or woven into a form suitable for holding a quantity of alkaline earth oxides which are electron emitters when heated. During lamp operation the electrodes are heated by electron bombardment when the electrode acts as an anode, and by ion bombardment when it acts as a cathode. Electrode temperature is self-regulating in that too little emission leads to increased bombardment and vice versa.

Sodium metal is solid below 98 °C and has a very low vapour pressure. It is therefore necessary to use an inert gas filling in the arc tube in order to start the lamp and allow it to run it up to working temperature. Neon is used for this purpose at pressures in the region of 5 Torr to 10 Torr. It is usual to include up to 1% argon with the neon in order to assist starting the arc. The argon produces a Penning mixture (Sect. 6.1.4) which lowers the starting voltage requirement by as much as 50% in some lamp designs.

Sodium vapour is very reactive at elevated temperatures and chemically attacks most glasses. A special type of glass has been developed to resist this attack but it is expensive and difficult to work. It is therefore coated on the inside of a cheaper and much more workable soda-lime glass (Sect. 7.1.1). The resultant glass called 'ply tubing' is used for the manufacture of all types of low pressure sodium lamps. Besides being chemically very active at elevated temperatures, sodium vapour is readily transported through vitreous material by electrolysis. Special care has therefore to be taken in mounting the arc tube inside the outer envelope. Ceramic insulators are necessary for holding the ends of U-shaped arc tubes in a mounting frame, and care must also be taken to isolate the infra-red reflective coating of tin oxide, indium oxide or gold which is quite conductive. It is also necessary to use a very high resistivity glass around the lead wires to prevent concentration of electrolysed sodium at the glass-metal interface which may cause cracked seals. The lead sleeving glass is itself protected at its high temperature end near the electrode by a ceramic bead. These features are illustrated in Fig. 13.2. The problems are not quite so acute with the linear lamp for opposite polarities are well apart, and the reflective coating is electrically connected at one end only. The small capacitance between the open end of the coating and the adjacent electrode acts rather like an earthed strip near a fluorescent lamp, reducing and stabilizing the lamp striking voltage.

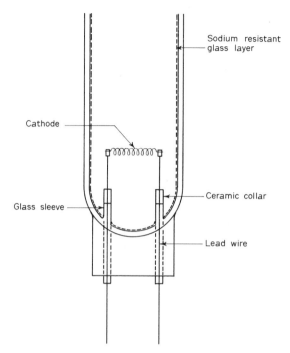

Sodium resistant glass layer

Cathode

Ceramic collar

Glass sleeve

Lead wire

Fig. 13.2 Low pressure lamp seal design

13.1.2 The sodium discharge

The low pressure sodium lamp is unique among discharge lamps for the severity of a process called ionic pumping that takes place at each half cycle within the arc tube. Ionic pumping is characterized by a tendency for the more readily ionizable gas, namely sodium vapour, to migrate towards the wall as current increases and thereby completely modify the electrical and radiation characteristics of the lamp. To explain the effect in more detail a complete half-cycle of a steadily burning lamp is considered.

Once each half-cycle, current ceases to flow in the lamp but a small and rapidly diminishing quantity of sodium ions remains in the discharge path. It is primarily the presence of these residual ions that enables the current to resume as a moderate voltage is re-established in the succeeding half-cycle. Fig. 13.3 shows the current in the lamp following a near sinusoidal curve. The arc voltage however falls to a lower value in 2 ms to 3 ms rising to a peak at 5 ms. It will be noticed that little light output occurs in the first 4 ms and that peak light output is not achieved until 6 ms have elapsed. The efficacy curve is interesting, particularly the small peak in the centre.

These curves were taken with a 'Dewar' type lamp, now obsolete, in which the arc tube was thermally insulated in a separate vacuum flask with clear glass walls. They are used here for explanation for they are more clearly defined than in modern lamp types. The shape of the curves is determined by the characteristics of the discharge, which can be explained in the following way.

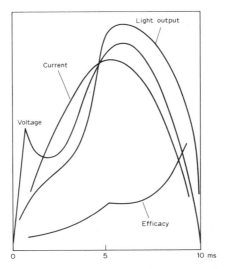

Fig. 13.3   Half-cycle performance of fully run up low pressure lamp on 50 Hz supply

By stroboscopic observation it is seen that the current builds up from the centre of the arc tube. As the current initially increases the tube voltage falls, which is typical of an unrestricted discharge. During this early period light output is low and the discharge visible swells to fill the whole tube. Free electrons are generated and being much more mobile than equally charged positive ions, will reach the wall and set up a negative wall charge. A radial field will result causing a migration of positive ions towards the wall. The ions will re-combine with electrons at or near the wall giving rise to heat losses and an increase in sodium vapour density near the wall. This process is common to most low pressure discharges where it passes unnoticed, for pressure equilibrium is maintained by rapid gas diffusion within the arc tube. In low pressure sodium lamps however the neon pressure may be of the order of 5000 times that of the sodium vapour. Under these conditions the diffusion rate of sodium is effectively slower than sodium ion migration in the radial field.

With the Dewar lamp at about 3 ms after the start of each half-cycle this process results in a small but very significant increase in sodium vapour density near the wall, where the excitation and ionization of sodium atoms takes place more frequently than in the rest of the arc tube. The effect is cumulative to such an extent that virtually the whole light output of the lamp is emitted from within 1 mm of the wall. The effect is most noticeable in a lamp of crescent-shaped cross-section when the inner wall of the indentations is viewed stroboscopically.

By implication most of the arc current must flow in the region near the wall, resulting in a reduction of the effective cross section of the discharge and an increase in arc voltage drop. From Fig. 13.3 it is seen that the arc voltage rises to over twice its minimum value at 2 ms to 3 ms, and that most of the light output of the lamp is emitted during the period when the arc vacates the centre of the arc tube.

The reason for low light output and efficacy in the early part of the half cycle is due mainly to losses within the discharge and absorption of the D line resonance radiation, which may be regarded as gas losses. When the arc vacates the centre of the arc tube the main losses are likely to be at the wall. The small peak in the centre of the efficacy curve, which is calculated from the other three, indicates that during the arc transit period from centre to walls an optimum low loss condition is traversed. Efficacy increases rapidly towards the end of the half-cycle indicating that while the arc should be restricted to the walls the effective current density should be low. It is also apparent from the curves that if the arc can be established near the wall earlier in the half-cycle then the efficacy of the lamp could be improved.

A further factor affecting lamp efficacy is that of the neon filling pressure. The extent of arc restriction will be affected by the rate of diffusion of atoms of sodium away from the walls of the lamp. A lower neon pressure will increase the diffusion rate and therefore reduce the effective current density and improve efficacy. In practice it is found inadvisable to lower the neon filling pressure much below 5 Torr, dependent on lamp type, for the neon and argon filling may become ionized resulting in efficiency losses and absorption of the already low percentage of argon in the sodium-resistant glass of the arc tube. A substantial argon loss will eventually result in failure to start the lamp. The dilution or substitution of other gases such as hydrogen or helium for neon is not found to be practical for although they increase the diffusion rate they increase the starting voltage substantially, and are readily lost by absorption in and diffusion through the arc tube walls. This discussion shows that the desirable conditions for high efficacy are low gas pressure, low current density, and a maximum diffusion of sodium vapour.

13.1.3   Design improvements

The now obsolete Dewar type lamp with its best efficacy about 70 lm/W showed the way in which improvements could be made. These improvements had to wait for the advancement of glass technology and improvement in glass working and treatment techniques.

It took many years to develop sodium-resistant glasses that did not discolour with sodium attack and still longer to remove the tendency of these glasses to absorb argon at low filling pressures. Modern glasses do not discolour and permit neon-argon filling pressures of the order of 5 Torr with an acceptable argon life.

The modern U-shaped (SOX) lamp employs a large diameter arc tube and is filled at a low gas pressure. These two changes result in an early establishment of ionic pumping in each half-cycle, a reduction of arc restriction to the wall and an increase in wall surface area. A considerable increase in efficacy is obtained at the expense of a reduction in lamp voltage drop.

For an improved lamp to be a direct replacement it must operate on existing control gear and be physically interchangeable. The existing gear can be used with lower arc voltages for the output current of the high reactance transformer remains substantially the same with a lower arc voltage. A reduced lamp wattage requires better heat retention than with the Dewar vacuum flask in order to maintain the sodium vapour pressure, and it is necessary to seal the arc tube in an outer jacket pumped to a high vacuum which is maintained by gettering. Heat loss is then almost entirely by radiation and this can be reduced by coating the outer jacket with tin or indium oxide. These oxides are reasonably transparent to the light from the arc tube and can be made to reflect a large percentage of its infra-red radiation. Improvements in these infra-red reflective coatings are a possible source of reduced lamp loadings for the same lumen output in all types of low pressure sodium lamps.

The maintenance of lamp efficiency during life is assisted by the provision of small round protrusions on the outside of each limb which, because they are slightly cooler than the remainder of the arc tube, act as reservoirs for sodium metal. Here the metal is preferentially retained against possible axial temperature gradients and mechanical shock or vibration which can result in a loss of sodium and thus of its vapour pressure at points along the arc tube.

The alternative to the U-tube design is a straight tube of non-circular cross section, shaped in order to increase the ratio of surface area to volume.

This shaping of the arc tube in the 'linear' lamp (Fig. 13.4) places parts of the wall surface nearer the centre of the arc tube and increases the total surface area compared with a circular cross section. Arc restriction to the walls therefore takes place earlier during each half-cycle and the effective current density is reduced.

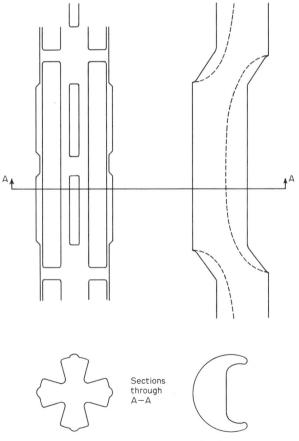

Sections
through
A–A

Fig. 13.4   Modified arc tube shapes for linear lamps

239

The crescent-shaped cross section is capable of a considerable improvement on the Dewar lamp performance while the four leaf section, with its increased surface area, can give a doubled luminous efficacy, as in the 140 W lamp. There is a great variety of mould shapes that can be used, some only produced at present by laboratory techniques, and the required effect can also be obtained by sealing suitable glass plates radially within an outer tube. A limit to efficacy improvement is reached when the ionic pumping effect is so degraded that resonance radiation absorption and gas losses become predominant.

Commercially available lamps use the four leaf mould (Fig. 13.4) which is designed for ease of manufacture and physical strength. As it is possible by variation of mould shape to reduce the effective current density in the discharge as required and establish arc restriction early in each half-cycle, there is no need to use low filling pressures of neon-argon to improve efficacy. Linear lamps therefore have a virtually infinite argon life. Sodium is held against mechanical forces and temperature gradients by capillary action in the tips of the crescent cross section and by the moulded protrusions on the outer diameter of the four leaf section.

The use of relatively high neon-argon filling pressures and the particular mould shape result in an arc voltage per unit length 25% higher than would be the case with an equal diameter SOX lamp arc tube. There is therefore little need to bend the lamp for dimensional convenience and a 200 W lamp can be less than 1·0 m long. As with the SOX lamp the linear types require a high vacuum outer jacket coated with a suitable infra-red reflecting metal oxide coating.

Various ratings of the linear lamp have been manufactured in Europe; manufacture in UK includes the 60 W, 140 W and 200 W versions.

13.1.4   Operating characteristics

Starting and run-up.   Sodium lamps in general operate with a high reactance transformer (Sect. 18.3.1), providing a high voltage for starting; in some cases the transformer can be used for more than one lamp rating. Some of the U-shaped designs have incorporated external probe-starting aids, which, in the case of the Dewar lamp, also served as a support member.

One feature of the sodium lamp is the independence of starting voltage with respect to ambient temperature which is in marked contrast to the behaviour of the mercury lamp. The starting voltage is largely determined by the Penning mixture of neon and argon which cannot be separated at any normal ambient temperatures, as mercury can from the argon-mercury Penning mixture in mercury lamps. Once started the lamp requires between 8 min and 15 min, depending upon design, to attain full light output and during this time the electrical characteristics change slightly (Fig. 13.5). To some extent these curves are affected by the gas content. In some lamps a small amount (0·2%) of xenon is added to control the tube voltage during run-up.

Supply voltage variation.   With increase of current in a lamp of SOX type the wattage increases slowly. As a result the peak of luminous efficacy is reached before the lamp reaches its maximum lumen output. The same effect is seen in Fig. 13.6, giving the variation of parameters of a linear lamp with supply voltage. It can be seen that the lamp is designed to operate initially between the maximum efficacy and maximum output points, and that a slight increase in mains voltage will raise the light output but lower the efficacy.

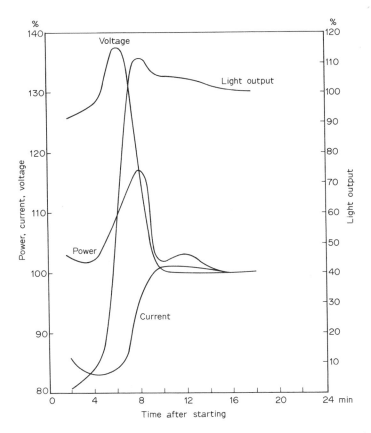

Fig. 13.5 Variations of light output, lamp power, voltage and current after switching on, shown as percentages of stable values; for 200 W SLI lamp

Operating position. The permitted orientation of lamps in operation is limited by the movement of sodium. The metal will condense in the coolest region but vibration and gravity cause the molten sodium to fall to the lowest point. In U-shaped lamps, cap-down burning can result in lamp failures due to the sodium collecting behind the cathodes, causing electrolysis and cracked seals.

Cap-up burning can result in sodium collecting in the bend and with all but the shortest lamps will produce 'red burners', caused by a shortage of sodium in the upper portion of the discharge tube. Lamps with no sodium-retaining facilities are thus limited to horizontal burning within 5° cap-down and 20° cap-up; though the lower wattage ratings can, with little loss of light, be burned vertically cap-up. Modern integral U-shaped lamps and the linear lamps can be operated within 20° of the horizontal.

Radiation characteristics. The spectral power distribution of a low-pressure sodium lamp is shown in Fig. 13.7a. Although other sodium lines are evident, with some SOX lamps 99·5% of the visible radiation is concentrated in the yellow 589·0 nm and 589·6 nm

241

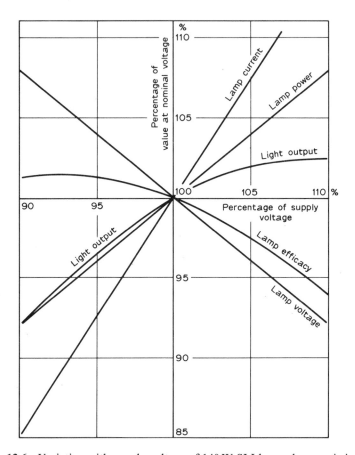

Fig. 13.6 Variation with supply voltage of 140 W SLI lamp characteristics

resonance lines of sodium. The nearly monochromatic radiation of sodium lamps and, as a result, the almost complete lack of colour discrimination are compensated by the fact that the wavelength of the light is close to that at which the human eye has its maximum sensitivity, thus giving the lamp a very high luminous efficacy. There are applications where colour rendering is unimportant, and even some instances where the emission of only yellow line radiation may be advantageous, in improving visual acuity by avoiding chromatic aberration in the eye.

13.2 HIGH PRESSURE LAMPS

As the power loading in W/m of arc length is raised, lamp temperature and sodium vapour pressure increase. Interaction between excited and ground state atoms produces broadening of the excitation levels and wide bands of radiation develop on either side of the resonance wavelength (Sect. 6.1.5). Little radiation is emitted at the resonance wave-length owing to absorption, except for a portion of that emitted within the mean free path of a photon from the outer limit of the discharge. In addition, other individual spectral lines become more marked due to relaxation from higher levels of excitation. The spectral power distribution of sodium discharges at different pressures is shown in Fig. 13.7.

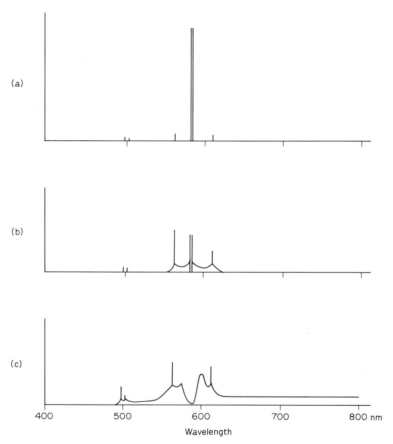

Fig. 13.7 Spectral power distribution of the sodium discharge at (a) 5 μ Torr (b) 30 Torr (c) 240 Torr

The colour appearance of the discharge improves as the pressure increases but efficacy reaches a maximum of over 100 lm/W between 100 Torr and 200 Torr and then declines. At maximum efficacy the colour appearance can be described as a golden white, the light having sufficient colour rendering properties to allow easy identification of other colours, so that it may be used successfully in certain indoor applications. Its chromaticity is about x 0·52, y 0·418. Higher vapour pressures result in further improvement in appear-ance and colour rendering until at about 450 Torr to 500 Torr it resembles a tungsten halogen lamp but with a much reduced efficacy (60 lm/W). Further pressure increases are undesirable for efficacy continues to fall and the colour worsens.

13.2.1   Materials and construction

The need for a special glass envelope to resist the extreme chemical activity of sodium has been described in Sect. 13.1.3. The problem becomes increasingly acute as lamp operating temperatures rise: even the best glasses discolour badly at temperatures under 400 °C. It is necessary to have a minimum arc tube temperature of 700 °C in order to obtain a pressure of 100 Torr of sodium. The high pressure sodium lamp therefore had to await the development of translucent ceramic material before even experimental lamps could be produced. There are now a number of translucent metal oxide ceramics with varying characteristics, and single crystal materials such as sapphire which are transparent, at least at low temperatures, and can be grown in tubing form.

The ceramic which has found favour for the high pressure sodium lamp contains over 99% aluminium oxide. The product called Stellox is described in Sect. 7.1.2. There were several basic problems concerning the material.

(a) Initially material costs were very high. At the present time they still are, but increasing quantity use should see the history of fused silica prices repeated and an acceptable cost obtained. Aluminium oxide is very abundant in the earth's crust but the processing problem is severe.

(b) Stellox is completely different from glass in that it cannot be softened or worked. It has a sharp melting point but when it freezes a different crystal structure is produced with a different expansion coefficient, and the melted material is liable to crack away from the parent body.

(c) It has a moderately high expansion coefficient and can be readily cracked by thermal shock.

(d) Being translucent and not transparent, strain and its effect on lamp life cannot be assessed by polarized light.

(e) It is very hard and can only be cut successfully with diamond tools.

Manufacturing techniques.   In order to produce a reliable lamp from this material lengthy research was required and a new manufacturing technique had to be developed. At the time of writing all the major companies marketing the lamp make the arc tube in different ways, and each has its own advantages.

A 400 W arc tube requires a piece of Stellox tubing 115 mm long with an 8·0 mm bore and 0·75 mm wall, with an electrode support and lead wire hermetically sealed into each end. The seal must withstand cycling between ambient temperature and above 700 °C and the seal materials must not be attacked by sodium to any deleterious extent. The manufacturing process must include the ability to exhaust unwanted gases and vapours and charge the arc tube with quantities of sodium, mercury and xenon. Sodium is added in considerable excess, to give saturated vapour conditions when the lamp is running and allow for loss by absorption on the internal surfaces. Excess of mercury is also present, providing a buffer gas (Sect. 13.2.2). Xenon at a low pressure is required to allow the lamp to start.

It is possible to use various sealing materials in order to attach end closures to polycrystalline alumina tube: glasses, other ceramics and metals may all be used. It is now the general practice to use niobium for exhaust tubes and metal parts sealed to the ceramic tube, for niobium has an expansion coefficient near that of alumina.

The end closure may take various forms:

(a) During the manufacture of the ceramic tube it is possible to place close fitting ceramic plugs in each end so that during the final sintering process, crystal growth seals the plug to the tube.

   This process provides ready-made end caps but metallic leads and exhaust tubes have still to be sealed to holes in the caps. At least one lamp at present marketed uses this form of end closure with niobium tubes to support the electrode assembly. The tubes are sealed in with a glassy material, the process ensuring that a minimum of sealant is left on the sealing surfaces and very little penetrates into the arc tube (Fig. 13.8a). The exhaust of unwanted gases and final filling of the arc tube with sodium, mercury and xenon is carried out during the sealing process.

(b) A second method of manufacture uses an entirely different approach. The ends of a plain ceramic tube are closed by a disc of niobium which may have a small annular indentation for strain relief and location. At one end the disc carries a tab to hold the electrode while at the other end it holds both an electrode and an exhaust tube.

   This lamp is assembled using a metal brazing material composed of metals such as titanium, vanadium and zirconium. These metals are highly reactive at high temperature and etch the lamp parts as they seal, producing a very strong joint. This lamp is separately exhausted (Fig. 13.8b).

(c) Another method of arc tube construction uses a ceramic tube closed by metal end caps which in this example are turned up at the edges by about 3 mm (Fig. 13.8c). The cap to ceramic tube seal is again made with a brazing material similar to that in example (b) but with lower melting point and reduced reaction with the lamp components. This type of seal can be designed so that only compressive stresses exist in the seal region giving adequate life expectancy.

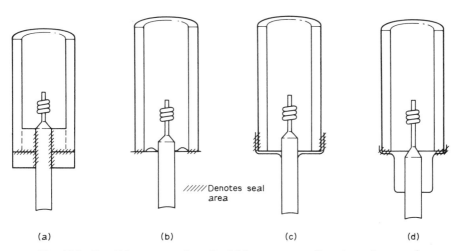

////// Denotes seal
area

(a)   (b)   (c)   (d)

Fig. 13.8   Possible constructions for high pressure sodium lamp in ceramic
arc tube

(d) A last example of a production lamp is similar to the construction in (c), but a ceramic frit is used as a seal material and the metal cap is domed mainly for strain relief (Fig. 13.8d). Successful ceramic frits may be made either in binary or ternary form from the oxides of aluminium, calcium and magnesium.

There are obviously other possible end closures, for instance a metal braze may be used with examples (a) and (d) and a ceramic frit or glass may be used with example (c).

The use of niobium seems to be a common feature for all metal seal parts. Its ductility and high melting point are valuable properties and it has a suitable expansion coefficient; it is not attacked by sodium and can easily be made in the required forms. A weakness however is that if it absorbs even small quantities of gas, particularly hydrogen, it will become brittle and unsuitable.

The seal-making processes that may be employed are determined by the protection required for the electrode assembly and the niobium parts, the enclosing atmosphere being limited to pure inert gases or high vacuum. Seals may be made and in some cases the exhaust and dosing of the lamp carried out in small bell jar enclosures using resistance or r.f. susceptor heating; alternatively seals may be made in bulk in large vacuum furnaces. When exhaust and dosing is required this can be done on separate machines and the arc tube finally sealed by cold welding, when the exhaust tube is pinched with extremely high pressure applied by suitably shaped jaws.

The finished arc tube has external niobium surfaces and must be protected from the atmosphere, it is therefore mounted and sealed in an outer envelope similar to that used for mercury lamps. Mounting details differ only slightly, but the arc tube with a temperature between the electrodes of over 1100 °C expands considerably at its maximum tempera-

Fig. 13.9   Outer envelopes for high pressure sodium lamps (400 W SON)

ture and therefore requires one end to be free for axial movement. There is no striking electrode but a suitable getter is mounted and fired to ensure the maintenance of a high vacuum in the outer envelope during life.

Outer envelopes may take two basic forms (Fig. 13.9), either clear tubular or elliptical coated with a diffusing layer. The diffusing layer, usually of powdered glass or silica ensures optical characteristics similar to MBF lamps and enables the same lantern to be used.

13.2.2 Operating characteristics

The production of light by the discharge is discussed in Sect. 6.1.5. The operation of the electrodes is basically similar to that in high pressure mercury lamps (Chap. 14). The vapour pressure of the mercury-sodium dose in the arc tube is very low at ambient temperatures, consequently xenon is necessary in order to start the discharge and run it up to working temperature. It will be noticed that there is no mercury radiation in the light output of the lamp despite the fact that the weight of mercury used is about four times that of sodium. This arises from the comparatively low temperature required for the excitation of sodium vapour in the discharge owing to its low excitation and ionization potentials. Some light emission occurs at temperatures as low as 1250 K. Rising temperature increases the radiation until at about 3000 K any further increased power input to the arc results in an equal increase in radiation and a gas temperature limit is reached. Mercury vapour with its high excitation and ionization potentials requires at least 4000 K in order to emit light and in a high pressure sodium lamp this temperature is not achieved in the arc.

The mercury vapour therefore acts as a buffer gas and increases the electrical impedance of the discharge which would allow an arc voltage drop of only about 50 V to 60 V without it. Higher voltages than this are required for economical control gear design. The saturated vapour condition of operation means that the temperature of the coolest spot on the lamp will control the vapour pressure and hence the arc voltage. In this design the coolest parts are behind the electrodes and heated mainly by them. As in the case of the low pressure lamp, electrode temperature is largely self-regulating depending on the required emission. As the emission varies according to the square of the temperature, cathode temperature does not vary greatly with lamp current and lamp voltage drop may be expected to remain reasonably constant over a mains voltage change of 10%. The arc discharge does however have some effect on cool spot temperature, the actual extent depending on seal and cathode geometry and materials. Each lamp construction (Fig. 13.8) will have its own characteristic variation with supply voltage but Fig. 13.10 is typical. Ambient temperature also affects lamp operation to a small extent, but more serious effects may occur in an enclosed luminaire. The outer envelope of the lamp absorbs the long wave radiation from the lamp and remains at a fairly constant temperature (275 °C to 465 °C according to its size), but it transmits more than half the lamp output (at wavelengths less than 2500 nm). If this is partly returned to the lamp by reflecting surfaces in the lantern it may raise the temperature of the seals, resulting in rise of sodium vapour pressure and rise of arc voltage. The lamp will eventually be extinguished by this process.

A striking electrode is not included in the lamp. It would raise considerable design problems on account of possible electrolytic effects with sodium, and the risk of short circuit to the probe by liquid metal would cause difficulties. Furthermore, for a third

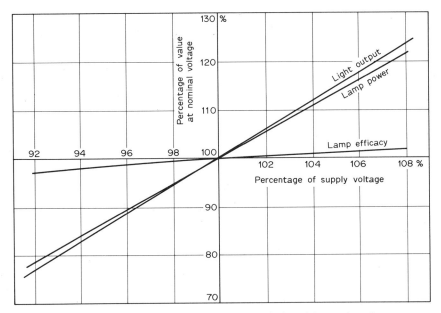

Fig. 13.10 Variation of SON lamp characteristics with supply voltage

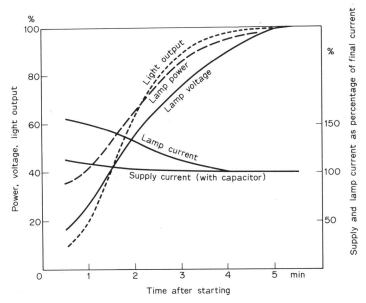

Fig. 13.11 Variation of SON lamp characteristics and mains current during run-up

electrode to be completely effective a Penning gas mixture would be required in the arc tube in place of xenon. As the mercury vapour pressure is greatly decreased when the lamp is cold a neon-argon mixture as used in low pressure lamps would be necessary. This mixture would result in considerable losses in the discharge and lamp efficacy could be impaired by as much as 20%.

It is generally accepted that in order to obtain the best life and light output the lamps should be operated with a starting pulse of 2 kV or more, applied for a few ms to ionize the xenon filling and allow a mains voltage derived arc to start. There are numerous ways of obtaining the required pulse voltage such as thermal or glow switches or the use of semiconductor devices (Sect. 18.3.1).

Once the arc has been started the high loading in W/m^2 of the arc tube surface, together with the low thermal inertia, give a reasonably quick run-up performance (Fig. 13.11). If switched off the lamp cools quite rapidly, and assisted by the electronic ignitor will restart within one minute.

Future possibilities.   The high pressure lamp is by no means in its final form, and developments are possible in several directions. There are other ceramics that may be used, and single crystal transparent alumina tubing is becoming available. Halogen additives are possible if corrosion problems can be solved. Higher temperatures for the seals would allow the use of other metals than sodium with increased loadings in the arc tube, and a highly efficient source of white light might become possible.

14   Mercury lamps

Mercury lamps as a general description covers a wide range of light sources. They are all based on the operation of an electric discharge tube generally made of fused silica and containing mercury vapour at a pressure of some atmospheres. In most cases no liquid mercury is present in the lamp when it is in full operation.

The colour and luminous efficacy of mercury lamps primarily depend on the vapour density within the lamp. They can be modified by the use of phosphors (Sect. 8.4), by the addition of other elements to the discharge (Sect. 15.1.1), and by adding light from an incandescent filament. Lamps within the range are used in general lighting, light projection and special applications.

Mercury lamps can be classified by the nomenclature used in this chapter, but it should be remembered that other countries have other systems. Operating data for the most common types are given in Appendix I.

14.1   PRINCIPLES OF OPERATION

The operation of electric discharge lamps is based on the collision processes between electrons, atoms and ions within the discharge tube (Sect. 6.1.3). Ionization of atoms by electron collision is necessary to enable current to flow in the lamp. Excitation of atoms or molecules is necessary for the subsequent emission of the characteristic line or band spectra. Light is also emitted as a spectral continuum chiefly due to ion and electron recombination. The principal resonance wavelengths of mercury are in the ultra-violet, the other main spectral lines being in the blue, green, and yellow regions (Fig. 6.4). The effect of vapour pressure can be seen when a mercury lamp is switched on. Initially the voltage across the lamp is low, about 20 V. The discharge fills the tube and appears blue. At this time the discharge is similar to that in a fluorescent lamp and a relatively high proportion of the emitted radiation is ultra-violet. With time the temperature of the discharge tube rises and with it the pressure of mercury, the discharge itself constricts to a narrow band along the axis which gradually becomes brighter. As the pressure further increases the radiated energy is concentrated progressively towards the spectral lines of longer wavelengths, and a small proportion of continuous radiation is introduced so that the light from the discharge becomes whiter. When fully run-up the discharge tube of the MB lamp has a pressure of mercury vapour of some 2 atm to 10 atm (1 atm $= 1 \cdot 013 \times 10^5$ N/m^2) depending on the lamp rating. At higher pressures of 10 atm to 100 atm reached in ME and MD lamps the spectral lines are progressively broadened and the continuous radiation increases relatively to the lines. These effects result in the emission of radiation over wider areas of the spectrum and an improved colour of light.

Perhaps the best known mercury lamp has an ellipsoidal outer envelope coated internally with phosphor. Fig. 14.1a shows the construction including the arc tube with its electrode structures, the internal connections and the general assembly. The lamps are often described as mercury fluorescent or MBF/U. The discharge tube emits the greenish-white light typical of the mercury discharge together with some ultra-violet. The phosphors on the inside of the bulb absorb this ultra-violet and convert it to visible light. The phosphor normally emits red light between 600 nm and 750 nm, because the discharge itself emits little in this range. The combined light is of reasonably good colour rendering suitable for street lighting, industrial high-bay lighting and some commercial interiors. Lamp efficacy is about 50 lm/W depending on the phosphors used and the lamp rating.

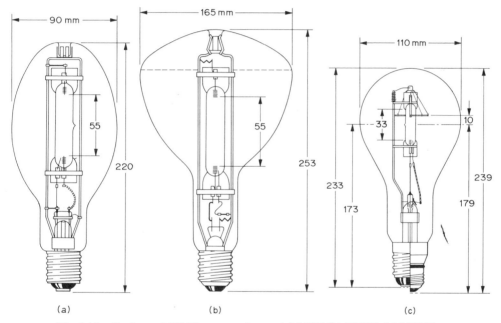

Fig. 14.1   Designs of 250 W mercury lamps (a) MBF (b) MBFR (c) MBTF

One of the earliest forms of mercury lamp was the MA. The discharge tube was made of aluminosilicate glass and could only operate at a pressure of about 1 atm. The lamp is now obsolescent and has been replaced by the MB/U lamp with its improved colour, luminous efficacy and versatility. These improvements are due to the use of fused silica for the discharge tube, which can withstand higher temperatures. To be an effective replacement the MB/U was introduced to the same overall dimensions as the MA, with a tubular envelope, but it is also available in a clear ellipsoidal envelope.

A simple variation of the MBF/U is the MBFR/U or reflector version. The construction is shown in Fig. 14.1b. The bulb is shaped to produce a particular polar distribution of light intensity. This enables a simpler luminaire to be used for high bay and industrial lighting.

The tungsten-ballasted or blended lamp (MBT) is a combination of a mercury discharge tube and a tungsten filament operating in series (Fig. 14.1c). The filament not only controls the current through the discharge tube so that no external control gear is required, but it also contributes to the light output by providing the red emission which the mercury discharge lacks. Modern lamps include on the inner surface of the outer envelope a coating of phosphor which further improves the spectral energy distribution (Sect. 14.3.4).

Several other varieties of lamp based on the MB discharge tube are available for specific applications and a selection of these is shown in Fig. 14.2. The MBW/U is a

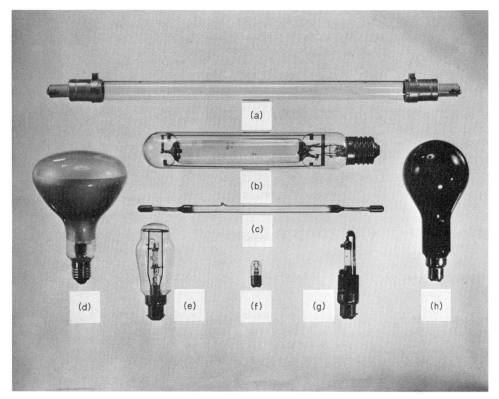

Fig. 14.2   Various mercury lamps (a) Blue printing lamp (b) 400 W MA/H (c) 1000 W Industrial photochemical lamp (d) 300 W Sun lamp (MBT) (e) 40 W MB used with compressed air generator for mine lighting (f) 4·5 W Miniature lamp (type M2) (g) Laboratory ultra-violet lamp (MBL) (h) 125 W Blacklight lamp, Wood's glass envelope (MBW)

standard discharge tube, usually 125 W, inside a Wood's glass envelope which reduces the amount of visible light emitted, but allows most of the 365 nm ultra-violet to pass through.

Miniature low pressure mercury lamps (M1, M2) were developed to provide a small cheap source of ultra-violet and some visible radiation: they are used in spectrographic applications, in biological and entomological investigations, and in the excitation of fluorescent materials. The M1 operates on 24 V d.c. with a resistance ballast while the M2 is for use on mains voltage a.c. supply with a series inductance.

Since mercury discharges are rich in ultra-violet and blue radiation, they have many applications in photo-printing and other photochemical processes. They are also useful in erythemal and germicidal applications. Each purpose has particular requirements in lamp dimensions and rating, and several examples exist in ratings from a few watts to a few kilowatts. The wavelength range of the emitted radiation is important, for example the peak wavelength for germicidal activity is about 260 nm, for erythemal activity it is about 297 nm (Sect. 1.3.3). In photo-printing there are many ranges of spectral sensitivity, chiefly in the long wave ultra-violet, blue and green regions, and while mercury lamps are still useful in specific cases, a new versatility is being found in this field using metal halide lamps (Sect. 15.1.5).

14.2   CONSTRUCTION AND MANUFACTURE OF MB TYPES

This section describes the various parts of a typical MBF lamp as shown in Fig. 14.1a and discusses some of the considerations involved in its construction and the ways in which it is manufactured.

14.2.1   Discharge tube

The central feature of the lamp, the discharge tube with its component parts, is shown in Fig. 14.3. The tube itself is fabricated from fused silica often loosely referred to as quartz. This material can be used satisfactorily up to about 800 °C, but above this temperature phase changes are likely which could result in devitrification and lamp failure. The devitrification can be aggravated by contamination particularly by alkali metals, and it is essential in lamp making for the fused silica surfaces to be clean. Contaminants and moisture content within the material can affect lamp parameters such as lumen maintenance and starting voltage, and it is normal to wash, and then heat the tubes at about 1100 °C for several hours prior to lamp fabrication. In MBF lamps the fused silica operates well within its temperature limitations, the centre tube wall temperature being in the range of 600 °C to 750 °C depending on the rating and operating position.

Seals.   The hermetic seal at each end of the tube must allow for the passage of electrical energy to the discharge. A suitable current-carrying seal can be made by using molybdenum in the form of a thin foil of elliptical cross section (Sect. 7.1.3). The seals are made by welding the components together as shown in Fig. 14.3 and inserting this structure into the end of the discharge tube which is heated to about 2000 °C and pressed. The metal parts are meanwhile protected from oxidation by a flow of inert gas.

Main electrodes.   These are fabricated from tungsten but contain some additives of lower work function. The design and processing of electrodes is crucial to lamp performance in terms of starting, lumen maintenance and life. The general form consists of a tungsten central rod which carries fabricated forms of tungsten as shown in Fig. 14.4:

253

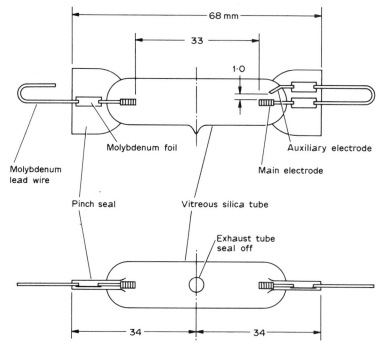

Fig. 14.3   125 W Discharge tube

in some designs the rod does not extend to the end of the coil and in such cases the rod may be made of molybdenum, which is cheaper than tungsten and more easily welded to the coil.

The electrodes are generally impregnated with electron-emissive materials. Thorium metal has also been used as an electron emitter, but lamps are more difficult to start and end darkening occurs more readily. The electrodes are designed to achieve easy starting of the discharge and optimum operating temperature of the tip of the electrode, where the arc normally runs, and of the portion retaining emissive material (Sect. 14.3.1). The rod diameter, the length of protruding tip, the size and weight of the surrounding wire structure all affect the temperature profile of the electrode, and this in turn affects lumen maintenance and factors such as stability, extinction voltage and flicker. In general if the temperatures are too high emissive material evaporates, darkens the tube wall and obscures the light output, particularly in small lamps. Low temperatures produce arc instability, poor emission and may also lead to wall darkening. Electrode tip temperature during operation is typically between 1500 °C and 1900 °C with temperature of the over-winding between 1000 °C and 1400 °C. Generally the emissive material consists of a slurry of barium and strontium carbonates with thoria and other additives. This mixture is usually applied to the electrodes by a dipping process although the precise coating method varies. The emissive material is retained in the spaces between the wire coils or in the braid but the outer surfaces of the electrode are cleared of emitter to avoid its evaporation to the walls.

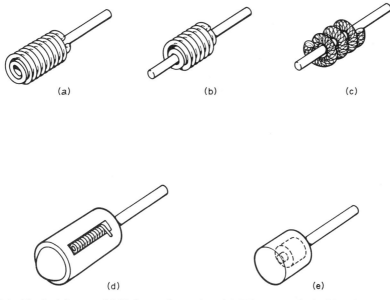

Fig. 14.4   Typical forms of MB lamp electrodes (a) Wire overwinds (b) Wire overwinds with protruding tip (c) Braided wire overwind (d) Sintered tungsten with side coil retaining emissive material (e) Sintered tungsten with annulus of emissive material

Subsequently the electrodes are heated in a reducing atmosphere to a temperature between 1500 °C and 2200 °C for converting the carbonates to oxides. This treatment also produces some free barium to facilitate electron emission. After heat treatment the electrode coatings are easily contaminated by air and moisture, and they are protected by means of inert dry gases during subsequent processing. The amount of emitter included on each electrode must be adequate for the life of the lamp and amounts to a few milligrams depending on the lamp rating. If too little is used then later in life the work function and consequently the temperature of the electrode will rise, leading to tungsten evaporation and poor lumen maintenance.

The electrode formed from wire is derived from the techniques developed for incandescent lamp filaments. A more direct and economic method of manufacture is by powder metallurgy. Porous, sintered slugs of tungsten with selected additions make effective discharge lamp electrodes. In these cases a source of alkaline earth emissive material is located or generally distributed within the electrode body.

Starting electrode and resistor.   To enable a mercury lamp to start on a 200/250 V supply a starting electrode of molybdenum or tungsten is mounted adjacent to one of the main electrodes but connected to the opposite main electrode through a resistor usually of 10 000 Ω to 30 000 Ω. When the lamp is switched on the full supply voltage appears across the gap between the main and adjacent starting electrode; this breaks down into a glow discharge creating a supply of ions and electrons which is adequate to cause the breakdown of the main electrode gap. The resistor limits the glow discharge.

If the resistance is too high a higher supply voltage is required to strike the main discharge. If the resistance is too low then energy is lost when the lamp is running due to the shunting effect across the discharge.

14.2.2   Exhaust and filling

The discharge tube after fabrication is exhausted of air and contaminants and filled with several Torr ($1\,\text{Torr} = 133\cdot3\,\text{N/m}^2$) of argon and a controlled quantity of mercury. In some manufacturing methods the discharge tubes are baked at several hundred degrees Celsius and the cathodes are heated to complete the exhaust process. A simpler and effective method is to transfer the discharge tubes directly from sealing-in, in which operation they are raised to a higher temperature than in any other operation, to the exhaust stage where they are alternatively evacuated and flushed with inert gas several times before being finally filled with gas and sealed off. The gas used is normally $99\cdot95\%$ argon and the filling pressure can be between 15 Torr and 50 Torr depending on the lamp type. Argon has been found to be the best inert gas for this purpose. Krypton and xenon are weakly excited in a mercury discharge and reduce its efficiency, whereas neon and helium give higher starting voltages and lower light output. The control of filling pressure is important: lower pressures aid starting and higher pressures improve lumen maintenance.

The amount of mercury added varies with the lamp rating and construction but typical values are about 15 mg for an 80 W lamp and 60 mg for a 400 W. These quantities are accurately predetermined and are such that all the mercury is vaporized in operation. The vapour density is then essentially constant provided the coldest point of the discharge tube is above a certain temperature, and the lamp characteristics are less affected by temperature and loading. The mechanism for automatically dosing mercury is normally based on dispensing constant volumes, measured either by a predetermined length of capillary tubing or by a fixed volume cavity.

14.2.3   Outer envelope

Although MB/U lamps are often seen in clear tubular envelopes the most common form of envelope is essentially ellipsoidal. This shape was introduced with the use of phosphors for modifying the colour of mercury lamps. Phosphors such as magnesium fluorogermanate and yttrium vanadate are not greatly limited by temperature and the envelope has become smaller than for sulphide coatings (Sect. 8.4) and shaped for appearance and optical performance. Temperatures of about 270 °C round the middle of an ellipsoidal envelope are normal whereas the maximum temperature of tubular envelopes operating horizontally can reach about 500 °C. The envelopes of lamps of 250 W and above are normally in hard borosilicate glass which is more resistant to thermal shock and atmospheric deterioration, while the smaller ratings are more usually in soda-lime glass.

Phosphor coating.   A typical process is to prepare a suspension of the phosphor powder in an organic binder, such as nitrocellulose, with selected solvents and diluents. Suspensions in water with an appropriate binder are also used. The suspension can be applied to the inside of the envelope by a jet directed to the top of the envelope, or by a spray or an electrostatic deposition method. After coating the solvents are evaporated using heat and air flow to leave a uniform dry coating of phosphor in the binder. Subsequently the binder has to be removed by baking the envelope to 600 °C in an oxidizing atmosphere, without leaving residues which could reduce the light output.

Frame construction. The method of location of the arc tube within the outer bulb is important mainly in aspects of transport, and vibration in operating conditions. Normally the frames are made of nickel-plated iron, nickel or stainless steel (Fig. 14.1). It is essential to good lumen maintenance that metal parts are clean and free from grease. Prior to final assembly the frames are degreased and washed to eliminate possible contaminants.

Filling and capping. The discharge tube in its frame is sealed into the coated envelope by heating the neck of the envelope and collapsing the glass on to the stem flare (Fig. 14.1). This join is usually moulded to a shape suitable for capping. After sealing the lamps are exhausted of air and filled with inert gas which protects leads and seals from oxidation during life. The gas is normally nitrogen or a nitrogen/argon mixture at a cold filling pressure of 200 Torr to 500 Torr.

The cap is fixed to the neck of the lamp using a cement or a mechanical locking method. A commonly used technique is to mould the seal in the form of a screw thread so that the cap can be screwed on the lamp and retained by adhesive or mechanical lock.

14.3 DESIGN AND PERFORMANCE OF MB TYPES

14.3.1 Electrical characteristics

The MB lamp like most discharge lamps has a negative resistance characteristic (Fig. 18.1) and some circuit element is needed to control the current. In addition a discharge lamp requires a higher voltage to start than to operate and the external circuit must accommodate this difference.

The choice of control gear depends on the supply voltage but in UK and Europe it usually takes the form of a series choke with a capacitor in parallel with the supply for power factor correction (Sect. 18.3.2).

MB and MBF lamps can be run in any position, although the electrical and luminous characteristics may be slightly different between vertical and horizontal operation.

Starting and run-up. The starting of a lamp is affected by many parameters including discharge tube length and diameter, gas filling and pressure, and auxiliary electrode spacing. The longer and narrower the lamp the more difficult starting becomes. Since at ambient temperatures the vapour pressure of mercury is very low, an inert gas is necessary to initiate the discharge. One reason for choosing argon is that it forms with mercury a Penning mixture (Sect. 6.1.4) which ionizes at a lower voltage than either of the constituents alone. At lower temperature the mercury vapour pressure falls much more quickly than the pressure of argon and the relative concentrations for minimum breakdown voltage no longer exist. This results in high starting voltages at lower temperatures as illustrated in Fig. 14.5.

The auxiliary electrode is necessary for reliable starting on a 200/240 V supply. At room temperature and without the starting electrode a lamp may require over 240 V to start.

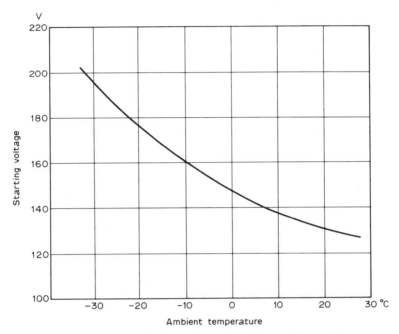

Fig. 14.5 Typical variation in starting voltage of MB lamp with ambient temperature

The gap between the main and auxiliary electrode is important especially for lamps of shorter length, and is objectively 1 mm. In an 80 W lamp at room temperature a 2 mm gap could raise the starting voltage by 10 V and a 3 mm gap by 25 V. For very low temperature conditions lamps with an auxiliary electrode at each end are often used.

The starting of a lamp takes place in stages: the breakdown between the main and auxiliary electrodes, the breakdown between the main electrodes, and the run-up to full temperature. During the first stages sputtering of electrode material may cause darkening at the ends of the discharge tube and adversely affect lumen maintenance. The effects can be reduced by increased gas pressure and by low thermal inertia electrodes such as those having braided wire coils. Breakdown between the main electrodes establishes a diffused low pressure mercury discharge which originates from points on the overwindings. As the pressure increases the discharge constricts and localizes on the tips of the electrodes. The time taken to run-up can be reduced by the shape of the discharge tube behind the electrodes and the electrode positioning. Sometimes this area behind the electrodes is covered with a heat-reflecting paint to speed run-up and to ensure that all the mercury is evaporated. The gas in the outer envelope has a cooling effect on the discharge tube. Gases of high molecular weight such as argon have less cooling effect due to their lower mobility; on the other hand the gas must also prevent flash-over between connections within the lamp and nitrogen is usually included (Sect. 7.3). Fig. 14.6 shows how the characteristics of a lamp vary through the run-up period.

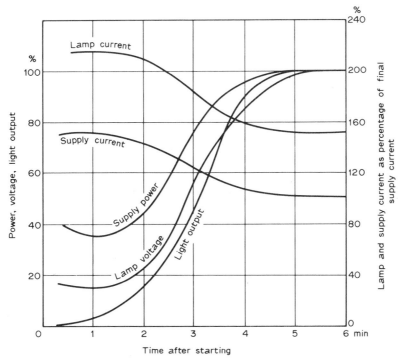

Fig. 14.6   Variation in MB lamp characteristics during run-up

Lamp restarting.   When running normally the pressure in an MB lamp is of several atmospheres. When the lamp is switched off this pressure falls gradually as the discharge tube cools. The voltage necessary to restart the lamp at its operating pressure is several kilovolts but as the discharge tube cools below about 400 °C the voltage necessary rapidly decreases, until at about 200 °C the lamp is capable of restarting on a 200/240 V supply. The time taken to cool depends on the ambient conditions and the outer gas filling but generally it is of the order of 3 min to 6 min for a lamp in free air.

The use of semiconductor or glow discharge ignitors (Sect. 18.3) which supply pulses of several kilovolts can reduce this restarting time but the limit in conventional lamps is the possible breakdown within the lamp or in the cap. Special double-ended lamps may be designed which with the use of fairly expensive high voltage equipment can be restarted within a few seconds of extinction.

Supply voltage variation.   Since the mercury lamp operates with all the available mercury vaporized, pressure variation with temperature is small, and the tube voltage remains sensibly constant with variations of mains supply. The current however is controlled by the choke and Fig. 14.7a shows the change of various lamp parameters with varying supply voltage. These curves relate to slow changes. Rapid reductions in supply cause the current to fall initially and the lamp voltage to rise. The lamp voltage may then be too great for circuit stability on the new supply voltage and the lamp may

259

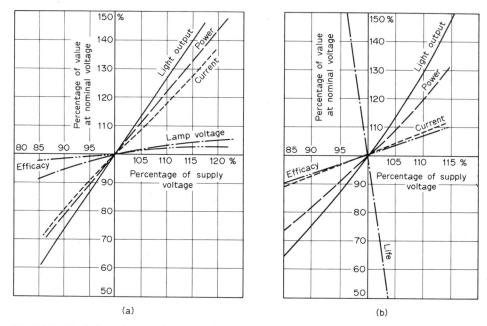

Fig. 14.7   Variation of lamp characteristics with varying supply voltage (a) MBF (b) MBTF

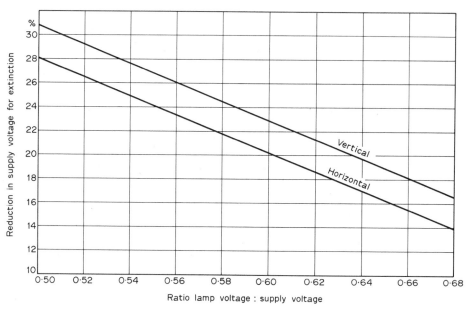

Fig. 14.8   Lamp extinction as a function of the ratio of lamp to supply voltage for 400 W MBF lamp

extinguish. The ability of a lamp to withstand rapid voltage reductions is primarily related to the ratio of lamp voltage to supply voltage. Fig. 14.8 shows a typical relationship for a 400 W lamp on a 200/240 V supply.

14.3.2 Light output

In designing a lamp the prime requirement may be a particular lumen output or a particular power consumption. The designed tube voltage should be about 0·6 of the supply voltage, a compromise between being as high as possible for good circuit efficiency and yet low enough to avoid discharge instability with supply voltage variation. The values of tube voltage and wattage decide the nominal lamp current, taking into account the voltage fall at the electrodes (about 15 V) and the waveform factor which for a mercury lamp is approximately 0·9. This factor is the ratio of real to apparent wattage resulting from the non-sinusoidal waveforms of lamp current and voltage.

To achieve high luminous efficacy the power loading needs to be high, but the total power in the tube is limited by the permitted temperature of the fused silica which should not be above about 800 °C, or 10 W/cm^2 to 20 W/cm^2 of tube surface, the loading being a little higher for lamps of small diameter due to greater convection cooling. The discharge tube length and diameter are also limited. Although short discharge lengths increase the W/cm loading they necessitate higher doses of mercury to maintain the tube voltage and this can give rise to an unsteady discharge. Increases in tube diameter also improve efficacy particularly during life, but high values can induce instability. The amount of mercury added is a direct function of the required tube voltage, the tube length and diameter. Power loadings are normally in the range 30 W/cm to 80 W/cm of tube length. Luminous efficacies are between 40 lm/W and 60 lm/W, being higher for higher wattage lamps.

The maintenance of light output during life is determined primarily by the electrodes and the absence of contaminants in the lamp. Generally lamps of lower wattage are poorer in maintenance, chiefly due to the effects of end darkening on short tubes and the proportionately larger effect of included contaminants. While depreciation of light output is more rapid initially the average rate throughout life is typically 2% to 3% per 1000 h, but the figure varies with lamp rating and operating conditions.

When lamps are operated on a.c. supplies there is a cyclic variation in light output of twice the fundamental supply frequency. On 50 Hz supplies the effect is a 100 Hz flicker which can be visible in individual cases under some conditions. The flicker index is defined as the ratio of the area of the light output versus time curve which lies above the mean value of the light output ordinate, to the total area of the curve above the base line. The value for mercury lamps is about 0·24 varying with phosphor coating. Fluorescent lamps give values of 0·08 to 0·17, and GLS incandescent lamps 0·03. Partial rectification of the lamp current in a mercury lamp can superimpose a 50 Hz modulation on the light output, to which the eye is more sensitive than to 100 Hz. The amount of 50 Hz component can be controlled by electrode design, and to avoid perceptible flicker the difference in light output between adjacent (100 Hz) peaks divided by their mean value should not exceed a few per cent.

Spectral power distribution.   The emission spectrum of the MB lamp is shown in Fig. 14.9a and consists of the line spectrum of mercury with some continuous radiation. The

261

rendering of colours under this lamp is poor because of its restricted spectral power distribution, particularly in the red region: the 'red ratio' is only 1% to 2%. This ratio is defined by BS 3677:1963 as the proportion of the luminous flux transmitted by a red filter (Wratten 25). The colour of the lamp is bluish-green. Phosphors used in MBF lamps modify the colour by utilizing the ultra-violet radiation as in fluorescent lamps, but not all the phosphors found suitable for fluorescent lamps are useful in MBF, where the operating temperatures are much higher and there is proportionately

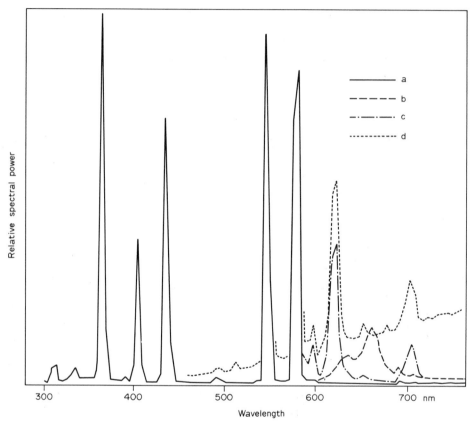

Fig. 14.9 Approximate spectral power distribution of MB lamp   (a) with clear envelope (b) with magnesium fluorogermanate: Mn   (c) with yttrium vanadate: Eu, the °Kolorlux lamp (d) with yttrium vanadate and tungsten ballast (MBTF)

more 365 nm radiation than 253·7 nm. Until a few years ago the commonly used phosphors were strontium magnesium phosphate, and particularly magnesium fluorogermanate, the spectral power distribution of which is shown in Fig. 14.9b. The lamp coated with magnesium fluorogermanate renders red colours well but has a greenish-white appearance. Its luminous efficacy is about the same as that of the uncorrected MB lamp.

The more recently introduced yttrium vanadate activated by europium is also a red-emitting phosphor which has a spectral power distribution shown in Fig. 14.9c. The emission near 700 nm ensures a good response in the deep red but the 620 nm peak, which is closer to the peak of the $V(\lambda)$ curve than the emission band of magnesium fluorogermanate, gives a higher lumen output and a warm colour appearance to the lamp. The colour rendering of the lamp can be further improved by phosphors emitting light in other gaps in the spectrum.

Invariably an MBF lamp is used in a luminaire which directs the light. The phosphor layer, apart from emitting light, also diffuses the light from the discharge tube and determines the luminance across the lamp. With increased thickness the luminance distribution is more uniform but the amount of light is slightly reduced. Thinner layers give a sharper image of the discharge tube in the optical system and facilitate control of the light distribution.

14.3.3   Lamp life

Failure to light is normally due to loss of emission from the electrodes and on this criterion alone individual lamps can burn for tens of thousands of hours. Useful life is primarily dependent on the depreciation of light output and the rate of failure of lamps in an installation. Because of the cost of replacing individual lamps, bulk replacement at about the rated life is usually more economic.

14.3.4   Other forms of MB lamp

Reflector lamps (MBFR).   An MBFR lamp (Fig. 14.1b) is made in a similar manner to an MBF, the only difference being the shape and treatment of the outer envelope. The shape depends on the polar distribution of light required but it is generally designed to produce a BZ 5 distribution (Sect. 5.1.1).

The conical surface is coated inside with a fine titanium dioxide powder which has a reflectance throughout most of the visible region of about 95%. On top of this is a layer of phosphor. In some lamps the front face is coated with a thin layer of silicon dioxide or is acid-etched to give a diffusing surface.

The polar distribution for a reflector lamp shows that about 90% of the light output is emitted below the horizontal, so although the total lumen output is only 85% to 90% of the MBF lamp of the same rating more light is directed downwards. Because of the small proportion of upward light, dust deposited on the lamp has little effect on the total light output. These lamps are normally used in installations at high mounting heights (High bay, Sect. 24.1.2).

Blended lamps (MBT and MBTF).   The construction of an MBT lamp is shown in Fig. 14.1c. The filament is designed to contribute light and to control the current. It is mounted round the discharge tube to achieve mixing of light and to reduce the run-up time which is detrimental to light output and life.

MBT lamp making includes techniques familiar in incandescent lamp manufacture. Getters are used for contaminant gases, while the gas filling for the envelope is normally a nitrogen-argon mixture at nearly 1 atm to give low thermal losses and minimize filament evaporation.

263

Since the filament is in effect a resistor giving a more distorted lamp voltage waveform than an inductance, the r.m.s. lamp voltage is usually 10 V less than for an MB lamp of equivalent size to ensure stability. Modern lamps are designed to give a ratio of about 4 to 1 of mercury to incandescent light, in order to achieve a high luminous efficacy and a life of 6000 h. They usually incorporate a phosphor coating giving additional red light.

On starting when the tube voltage is low, the voltage across the filament constitutes the majority of the supply voltage while in stable operation, when the tube voltage is much higher, the filament voltage is 40% to 50% less. Clearly the design of the filament must be a compromise between the required luminous efficacy in steady operation and the effect on life of the increased voltage during starting and run-up. The filaments are designed to operate at about 5 lm/W to 7 lm/W. Because of the filament the MBTF lamp characteristics with varying supply voltage are slightly different from those of MBF lamps (Fig. 14.7b). The effect on life is more severe than in incandescent lamps since the same change in supply voltage is a greater proportion of the voltage across the filament (Sect. 9.4).

The average luminous efficacy of MBTF lamps is between 12 lm/W and 25 lm/W; the lumen maintenance depends on the same factors which affect mercury lamps, and also those affecting filament lamps such as filament evaporation and gas contamination. The spectral output is a combination of the contribution from the discharge tube, the yttrium vanadate phosphor and the filament. Fig. 14.9d shows the effect of the filament on emission at longer wavelengths.

The main application of tungsten-ballasted lamps has been as alternatives to incandescent lamps in industrial and commercial lighting where the increased efficacy and longer life are advantageous, or for low initial cost installations. Lamps have been available in traditional pear-shaped envelopes but they are now appearing in envelopes similar in shape and size to MBF lamps. A special form of the MBT is the 'Sun Lamp' normally available in a 300 W rating, which incorporates a reflector-shaped bulb of special glass transmitting the erythemal radiation near 300 nm.

Long wave ultra-violet lamp (*MBW*).   This is available in a 125 W rating. The discharge tube and methods of assembly are identical to those used in MBF lamps. The envelope, which can be pear-shaped or ellipsoidal, is made of Wood's glass which transmits radiation between 290 nm and 420 nm with a peak transmission of about 70% at 360 nm. Over 95% of the emitted radiation from the lamp is in the mercury lines near 365 nm, with negligible visible or erythemal radiation.

These lamps are used to excite fluorescent materials in a variety of lighting applications, including identification and detection in industry and commerce.

14.4   VERY HIGH PRESSURE MERCURY LAMPS

In lighting applications such as projection, theatre and studio lighting and many industrial and commercial tasks high intensity beams of light are required. To achieve these with relatively cheap optics it is necessary to make lamps of small size and high luminance. Using the MB discharge tube as a starting point two important design methods can be followed.

(a) The length of the discharge is reduced while maintaining the voltage. To prevent the tube surface becoming too hot the diameter is increased and the shape becomes nearly spherical. Such lamps are referred to as compact source lamps (type ME).

(b) The voltage gradient in the discharge is increased. This results in a narrow tubular lamp, of high surface temperature, that has to be cooled by air or water flow (type MD).

The main use of ME lamps is in projection systems where colour fidelity is not of prime concern. Lamps from 100 W to over 5000 W have been made for various applications, such as thread illuminators in weaving, detectors in float-glass manufacture, and in several copying and image-projection systems. Fig. 14.10a and b shows two typical ME lamp designs.

Contrasting with the short arc ME lamp which provides a very small source of high luminance, the MD lamp is a linear source of high luminance. Fig. 14.10c shows a typical discharge tube and a complete lamp where the discharge tube is enclosed in a

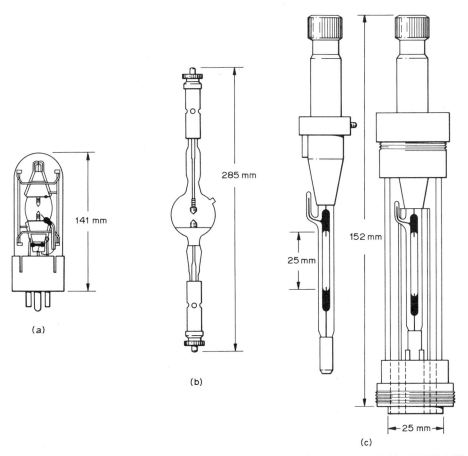

Fig. 14.10   High luminance mercury lamps (a) 250 W ME (b) 1000 W ME (c) 1000 W MD

265

double-layered glass envelope through which the cooling water is passed, and which also provides electrical connections. These lamps are used in optical marking, profile projection and photochemical applications. They provide high light intensities with minimum rise in the ambient temperature since most of the heat generated is removed by the water.

14.4.1   Compact source lamps (ME)

Basically the same principles apply as in the manufacture and design of MB lamps, but currents are higher and the mercury vapour pressure is in the region of 20 atm to 40 atm.

Bulb.   A good quality of fused silica is essential to avoid blemishes which could show in the projected light beam. The bulb is basically spherical, but it may be pear-shaped or ellipsoidal to provide more uniform surface temperatures. The loading in watts per unit area of surface must be limited to avoid overheating and possible devitrification and short life. Smaller bulbs cause poor lumen maintenance since the material sputtered from the electrodes will be deposited over a smaller area. Larger bulbs lengthen the run-up time of the lamp and this can cause increased electrode evaporation and inconvenience in operation. The bulb around the seal area, which is the coolest portion, may be covered with a heat-reflecting paint or a metal reflector to conserve heat and aid run-up. For wattage ratings between 100 W and 5 kW bulb diameters range from 10 mm to 120 mm with wall thicknesses of 1·5 mm to 5 mm.

If a lamp should fracture in operation or when it is cooling down considerable explosive energy is dissipated. A lamp should only be used in a suitable housing to ensure safety.

Seals.   Seals are formed using molybdenum foil (Sect. 7.1.3). Higher wattage ratings utilize the multi-foil or cup seal techniques (Sect. 15.2.1). In some lamps the discharge tube is enclosed in an outer envelope which is filled to about half an atmosphere pressure of nitrogen to protect the seals from oxidation, thus extending the life of the lamp (Fig. 14.10a).

Electrodes.   Because of the higher currents the electrodes for ME lamps are more massive than those for MB. The principles of design however are similar (Sect. 14.2.1). Generally the electrode consists of a machined tungsten rod carrying a coil of tungsten wire. The tungsten may contain a small proportion, about 3%, of thoria to reduce the work function and lower the lamp starting voltage. The gap between the electrodes is normally just below the mid-point of the bulb, in order to improve temperature uniformity over the bulb and seals. When a lamp is designed for a.c. operation both electrodes are similar. For d.c. operation the anode is usually larger than the cathode since the voltage fall is higher at the anode and the power dissipation is higher.

Usually electron-emissive materials are not used in these lamps as they are very rapidly evaporated from the electrode causing excessive and premature bulb blackening. As a lamp ages the shape of the electrodes is modified by local melting and pip growth affecting the discharge characteristics and stability. This is largely a function of electrode temperature but it can be improved by the choice of raw material and processing.

Some lamps have a tungsten auxiliary electrode carried by a third seal to facilitate starting on mains voltages. This complicates lamp construction but the two-electrode lamp without the auxiliary requires more complicated control gear.

Gas filling.   Normally the gas used is a Penning mixture of neon and argon at a pressure of approximately 60 Torr. In some lamps (MEX), xenon at pressures between 0·5 atm and 2 atm is used. Although these lamps require special circuits for starting, the initial discharge in xenon provides sufficient light of good colour while the full mercury vapour pressure is being established. The addition of xenon also increases the speed of run-up with improvement in lumen maintenance and life.

Starting and run-up.   The starting procedure of ME lamps is similar to that described for MB (Sect. 14.3.1). The time taken is a function of the lamp current and gas filling; it may also be extended by excessive cooling of the bulb. If the lamp is extinguished it will take 15 kV to 50 kV to restart it immediately. With only mains voltage available the lamp will normally take 5 min to 10 min to cool and restart. Several circuits have been devised which compromise between these two extremes.

Operating characteristics.   Alternating current circuits are normally cheaper and more economic but d.c. is often used where the application requires improved discharge stability. Because of the lower lamp voltage and higher current of the ME compared to the MB the control gear is usually much heavier and more expensive. The changes in lamp characteristics with varying supply voltage depend on the lamp rating and operating conditions, but in general terms the trends are similar to those for MB lamps (Fig. 14.7a).

Generally ME lamps are intended for vertical operation. If lamps are burnt horizontally the wall above the discharge may overheat due to the convected stream of hot ionized vapour and this can cause devitrification and short lamp life.

Light output.   The luminous efficacy of ME lamps is about 40 lm/W to 50 lm/W. Since these lamps are used for projection it is more important to know the luminance of the discharge and the luminous intensity. The luminance distribution along the discharge length is almost constant except in the regions adjacent to the electrodes, but the distribution across the discharge at its centre is near Gaussian with a peak of 4×10^4 sb (cd/cm^2) for a 1000 W lamp; at 1·25 mm from the axis the luminance is 2×10^4 sb.

Since the vapour pressure is higher in the ME lamp than the MB the spectral lines broaden and the continuous emission is increased in relation to the line emission, especially at the short wavelength end. Fig. 14.11 shows a typical spectral power distribution for the ME type. The red ratio of the lamp is about 4%.

Metals such as cadmium can be added to mercury discharges to improve the red ratio. The effect in MA and MB lamps is rather small and it is achieved with a marked reduction in luminous efficacy. In higher wattage ME lamps the use of cadmium can double the red ratio at no loss in luminous efficacy. A more elegant method of improving both colour and efficacy of a compact source lamp is by the addition of metal halides to the discharge (Sect. 15.1).

Lamp life.   As the lamp ages the emissive properties of the thoriated tungsten electrodes deteriorate and the bulb progressively darkens due to tungsten evaporation. Eventually either too little light is emitted or the lamp fails to start. Both these effects are accelerated by frequent switching. Rated life is between 500 h and 2000 h depending on loading and mode of operation.

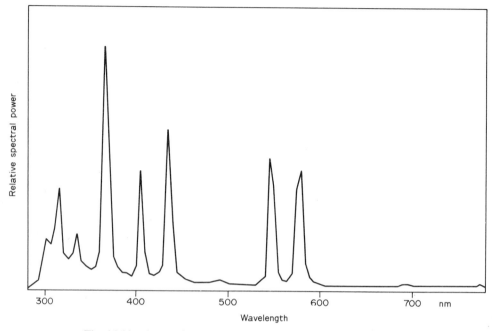

Fig. 14.11   Approximate spectral power distribution of ME lamp

14.4.2   Water-cooled lamps (MD)

In operation the inner surface of the discharge tube is about 1000 °C while the outer surface which is in contact with the water is about 50 °C; the wall thickness therefore must be designed to withstand thermal stresses, as well as high internal pressures in the range of 50 atm to 200 atm of mercury vapour. Typically the tubes are of 2 mm bore with a wall thickness of 1 mm to 2 mm. Despite forced cooling the fused silica is operated above the temperature at which devitrification begins to take place so that lamp life is short.

One form of the discharge tube is shown in Fig. 14.10c. A graded seal is made between the tungsten wire lead and the fused silica tube. The electrode is a tungsten rod and the spacing between the electrodes is set during sealing. The tube is exhausted in the normal way, filled with an excess of mercury and approximately 40 Torr of argon, and sealed. The mercury is retained in a pool behind each electrode, which protrudes some 0·5 mm beyond the mercury surface. If the final lamp voltage is low more mercury can be forced into the discharge tube by shortening the seal-off tip. The presence of liquid mercury in the lamp when operating distinguishes this type of lamp from the usual high pressure mercury discharge.

Another method of construction uses the molybdenum foil to fused silica sealing technique together with a shaped electrode and no back spaces. These lamps can be dosed with a controlled volume of mercury, all of which is vaporized, so that the voltage is predetermined and varies little with changes in loading. The high pressures within the lamp demand sound construction.

The water jacket is normally made of two concentric glass tubes (Fig. 14.10c). The water passes between the discharge tube and the inner tube and returns between the inner tube and the outer tube. The water flow is high (60 ml/s) to avoid boiling and to remove bubbles which could affect the optics of the system.

For a.c. circuits the control gear normally takes the form of a high reactance transformer, and for d.c. operation similar equipment is associated with a rectifier network.

Lamps are generally run horizontally. The high loading of the MD lamp results in a short run-up time of some 5 s and due to the water cooling the restarting time is of a similar duration. When fully run-up the lamp dosed with excess mercury operates in saturated vapour pressure conditions and transient variations in voltage and light output may occur. When extinguished the mercury must be evenly redistributed before the lamp is restarted.

Light output.   The initial luminous efficacy of an MD lamp is about 60 lm/W to 65 lm/W. The luminance increases with loading and with reduced discharge tube diameter and wall thickness. These parameters also affect the rated life of the lamp and a compromise is necessary. As in the case of the ME lamp the spectral output of the MD is composed of the mercury lines, broadened due to the high concentration of mercury atoms, and a continuum which is a considerable proportion of the output on account of the high pressure within the lamp. Although the colour rendering is improved over the MB the red ratio is only about 6%.

Use can be made of the improved colour and efficacy at high loading by using current pulses a few milliseconds in width with peak currents five to ten times the effective steady current. This mode of operation is possible only with the controlled-dose lamps and the life is much reduced.

The light output also falls off more quickly due to increased tungsten evaporation but the effect of this can be reduced by using halogen additions to the discharge tube to control darkening.

As a lamp ages the brightness falls due to devitrification and tungsten evaporation. The tube voltage increases due to cathode erosion and tube deformation. Wattage dissipation and light intensity changes with life are affected by the type of control gear used (Chap. 18).

Life.   The end of life is generally due to devitrification, which normally starts around the electrodes and spreads along the tube. Devitrification is accelerated by repeated heating and cooling of fused silica so that life varies greatly with frequency of switching. On duty cycles of a few switches per hour a lamp life of 30 h to 100 h is achieved. Failure is normally due to bursting of the tube but the water acts as a buffer and no external damage is caused. Since failure is not predictable lamps are often mounted in multiple units so that another may be brought into use as one fails.

15 Metal halide, xenon and neon lamps

This chapter considers a number of types of discharge lamp which are either in an active state of development (the metal halide lamps), or have specialized uses (xenon and neon lamps). The first group has been derived from the long-established high pressure mercury lamp (Chap. 14) by a development process which has some similarity to the use of halogens in tungsten incandescent lamps, in that elements of very high boiling point can be brought into the vapour state as halides. The other lamp types discussed use the inert gases instead of mercury as the light-producing element, but at very different pressures and power loadings.

15.1 METAL HALIDE LAMPS

Metal halide discharge lamps, the first group to be considered in this chapter, are not dissimilar in appearance to high pressure mercury lamps, the arc tubes being of fused silica with electrodes of pure tungsten, or thoriated because any oxide-coated emissive type electrode is destroyed in the presence of halogen additives.

The addition of metal halides has almost doubled the lumen output compared with mercury lamps and there is also a substantial improvement in the colour appearance and rendering qualities. Although there are about seven metal halides now in common use, either singly or in mixtures, there still remains considerable scope for research and development to exploit other elements, either to produce visible light, or radiation in the near ultra-violet and infra-red parts of the electromagnetic spectrum.

The glass envelope type lamps are providing a new stimulus to the indoor lighting of supermarkets and large stores where these sources offer improved colour quality. As lamp power is increased the bare linear types are being used for the lighting of large areas, car parks, city centres and sports stadia. With the compact source metal halide lamps, because of their high luminance and excellent colour quality, applications are diverse in high speed photography, mobile searchlights, optical instruments, sports stadia (Chap. 33) and theatre spotlights. Electrical and light output data for the lamps are given in Appendix I.

15.1.1 Principles of operation

In the high pressure mercury lamp a considerable portion of the cross-section of the arc tube is not effectively used to emit light. This non-productive space is required to reduce energy dissipation at the wall of the arc tube to a value compatible with long lamp life. If, however, another element of low excitation potential can be introduced, without interfering too much with the basic mercury discharge, then this element can be excited in the otherwise non-productive space. Its characteristic spectrum will be added to the mercury spectrum so improving colour, while the additional light output should contribute to increased lamp efficacy.

Unfortunately, some of the elements having suitable radiation characteristics also possess excitation levels similar to mercury and hence would make little contribution to better space utilization in the arc tube. The use of these elements, for example thallium and indium, has to be carefully controlled in order to obtain colour and efficacy benefits without detriment to the basic mercury discharge.

A further point which must be considered when designing for good colour and efficacy, is that 1 W of electromagnetic radiation of 555·0 nm in the yellow-green visible spectrum will give 680 lm, while at 715 nm in the deep red it will give only 1 lm of light. The proportioning of the radiation from elemental additions must therefore be designed to give an acceptable combination of colour and efficacy.

Only the excitation and radiation effects of elemental additives to a high pressure mercury discharge have been considered. When the practical question as to how other elements may be maintained in vapour form in the arc tube is examined, it is found that while the maximum arc temperature of 6000 K is adequate for the purpose, the minimum wall temperature (behind the electrodes) is inadequate for all desirable elements except, perhaps, the alkali metals. The alkali metals would in practice discolour and destroy the silica of the arc tube by chemical attack in a very short time.

It has been established that the temperature problems arising from very low vapour pressures of many desirable elements may conveniently be overcome by introducing them in compound form, with iodine. Moreover when the alkali metal iodides are used, chemical attack on the silica can be eliminated. It has also been established that in the iodide form large proportions of the elements of the periodic table may be successfully added to the mercury discharge. Their visible spectra are thereby included in the light output of the lamp. Iodine itself, in moderate quantities in the arc tube, has little or no effect on the characteristics of the discharge.

In order to obtain maximum benefit in colour and light output, iodides are included in the arc tube filling in proportions determined by their vapour pressures and desired contribution to the total spectral radiation. During lamp operation the individual iodides exert partial vapour pressures within the arc tube. In regions of moderate temperature, between the core of the arc and the walls, the iodides will dissociate, liberating iodine and metal atoms. The iodine and metal elements will also have partial vapour pressures and will diffuse through the volume of the arc tube. When the metal atoms and iodine atoms meet in regions of the relatively cool walls of the arc tube they will again combine to form iodides and this is of particular significance in the case of the chemically active metals, in preventing attack on the walls. Compare the halogen cycle with tungsten as the volatile metal (Chap. 10).

15.1.2 Glass envelope lamps (MBI and MBIF)

These are made in several ratings, the 400 W and 1 kW lamps being physically interchangeable with mercury types having elliptical outer envelopes, also others of 2 kW and 3·5 kW in tubular glass envelopes. A 400 W lamp is shown in Fig. 15.1 and differences will be noted in the arc tube mounting from that of a mercury lamp (Fig. 14.1a). The lead wire from the arc tube, remote from the stem, is spaced away to reduce photoelectric currents, which otherwise can lead to sodium loss by electrolysis through the arc tube

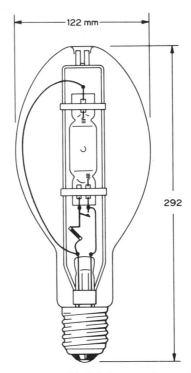

Fig. 15.1   400 W metal halide lamp and arc tube assembly

wall into the outer jacket, with possible arc tube failure. The thermal switch in the starting probe lead has a similar purpose: when closed it removes the potential difference between the adjacent electrodes while the series resistor minimizes power loss.

As previously discussed, the arc tubes of mercury lamps contain a low pressure filling of argon, which forms a Penning mixture with mercury vapour at temperatures in the range $-20\,°C$ to $+30\,°C$, enabling the lamps to start satisfactorily from a supply of 200/250 V. In metal iodide lamps the argon pressure is 35 Torr (1 Torr $= 133\cdot3\,N/m^2$) but the starting conditions for mercury lamps no longer apply due to the presence of free iodine, which raises the necessary striking voltage. There are alternative ways by which a suitable starting aid may be provided, for example, by the inclusion of a starter switch integral with the lamp, by a starter switch positioned across the choke ballast, or by the provision of a transformer winding to provide an adequate peak voltage (Sect. 18.3.3).

The Metalarc lamps, enclosed in a clear elliptical envelope, contain the iodides of scandium, sodium and thorium in addition to mercury, while the °Kolorarc lamps have the outer envelope internally coated with yttrium vanadate phosphor (Sect. 8.4). These lamps provide very good colour rendering combined with good colour appearance in the region of 4000 K. The spectral power distribution is shown in Fig. 15.2. The inclusion of a tin halide has been shown to provide an almost continuous spectrum, and while colour rendering is reasonably balanced the efficacy is only equivalent to

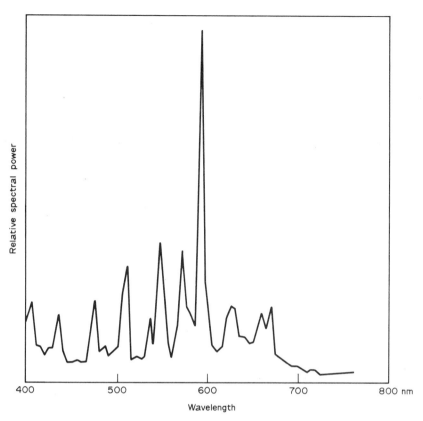

Fig. 15.2   Spectral power distribution of metal halide lamp with phosphor coating (°Kolorarc)

that of a mercury lamp. There will no doubt be many further developments as other additives are examined.

Some of the larger lamps do not contain sodium but thallium, indium and dysprosium iodides to give greater flexibility in lamp design and overcome some of the problems associated with the sodium iodide. A typical spectral power distribution is shown in Fig. 15.3. Even closer approximations to daylight distributions have been made in lamps containing mercury with thallium, dysprosium, holmium and thulium, with high colour rendering indices (Sect. 3.4.1). On the other hand, strongly coloured light sources, of possible use for signal purposes, have been made by single additions (thallium or indium).

15.1.3   Linear source silica lamps (MBIL)

The linear source lamps, made in ratings of 750 W, 1600 W and up to 10 kW enable compact luminaires to be designed giving very good optical light control. Containing similar metal halide additives to the glass-jacketed types, the arc tube loading is increased

273

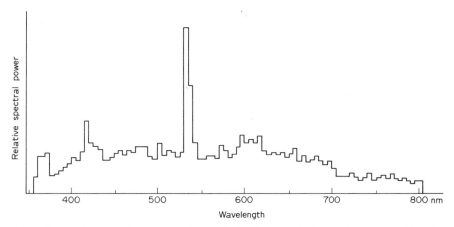

Fig. 15.3   Spectral power distribution of metal halide lamp with dysprosium and thallium iodides

and the luminaire itself forms the outer envelope so that the replaceable bare lamp is kept to a low cost.

The arc tubes are long and narrow (Fig. 15.4), and they become essentially horizontal burning lamps to ensure a thermal equilibrium along their arc path. The arc voltage is also increased and a high reactance transformer is used to ballast the lamps and to provide

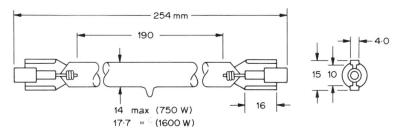

Fig. 15.4   Linear metal halide lamps (750 W or 1600 W)

sufficient voltage to make them self-starting. This type of lamp construction permits high ignition voltages to be applied should this be considered desirable to provide hot restriking.

15.1.4   Compact source lamps (CSI)

In the compact source iodide lamp the discharge takes place between tungsten electrodes spaced 9 mm or 14 mm apart in an almost spherical bulb (Fig. 15.5). The construction is single-ended, unlike most compact source lamp designs, making the lamp itself very small and convenient for efficient use in a mirror or lens optical system.

These lamps contain halides of sodium, gallium and thallium as well as mercury, and with their higher current density and pressure a considerable background continuum

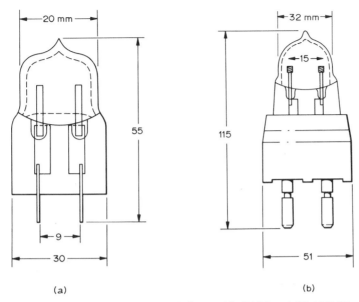

(a)   (b)

Fig. 15.5   Compact source iodide lamps (a) 400 W and (b) 1000 W

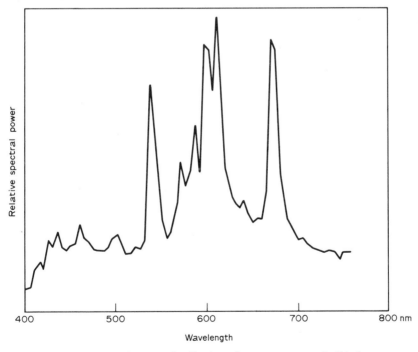

Fig. 15.6   Spectral power distribution of compact source iodide lamp

is developed to give excellent colour rendering with a spectral power distribution shown in Fig. 15.6. This may be compared with the other lamp types previously discussed.

In Fig. 15.7 is shown a sealed beam lamp enclosing a 1 kW CSI lamp, making a very

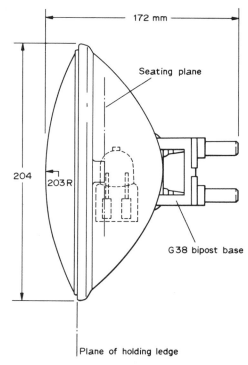

Fig. 15.7   1000 W CSI lamp in PAR 64 reflector bulb

compact unit having a peak beam output of 1.5×10^6 cd with an $18°$ wide beam. Because of the fully enclosed and sealed lamp and reflector the light output maintenance is high with a much longer life than in the air-burning type.

15.1.5   Photochemical lamps

In photochemical, photo-reproduction, and photo-resist processes it is desirable to increase the ultra-violet content from a discharge light source, not only to obtain a shorter exposure time but also to reduce the heating effect on photo-responsive materials which can thus suffer a lowering of their sensitivity.

Mercury lamps have provided a useful alternative to the carbon arc, rich in the longer wave ultra-violet, and clean in operation, though of lower actinic efficacy. Following the inclusion of metal halides in discharge lamps to improve lumen efficacy, other metal halide additives provide a two-fold gain over mercury to give at least 19% of the radiated power in the 360 nm to 450 nm band. A 1200 W photochemical lamp, having the same physical size as the 1600 W lamp previously described, contains halides of gallium as

276

well as mercury; other materials like indium and bismuth can result in a suppressed mercury emission but the total amount in the ultra-violet region is increased. The spectral energy distribution of the 1200 W lamp is shown in Fig. 15.8 with response curves of some photo-resists and diazo material.

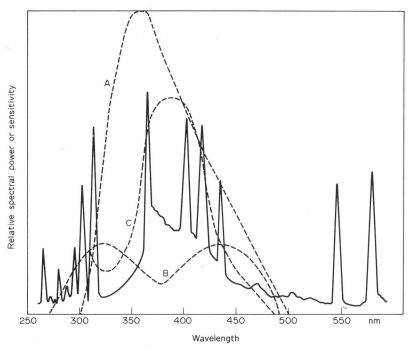

Fig. 15.8   Spectral power distribution of 1200 W MBIL photochemical lamp and graphic arts materials requiring this spectral range
                      A. A photopolymer resist film (Riston)
                      B. A photosensitive lacquer for photoelectro-forming (KPR2)
                      C. A diazo photocopy material

The use of ultra-violet radiation for catalytic processes and curing of resins and polyesters will no doubt result in the development of more powerful and actinic sources.

15.2   XENON LAMPS

The xenon lamp is the most important example of a discharge in which the radiation is emitted primarily as a continuum, unlike the sodium lamp where the resonance radiation is excited at low pressure.

Optimum conditions for the production of radiation in a continuum are high specific power, high current density and high gas or vapour pressure leading to small, bright, highly-loaded sources. The efficacy increases with specific loading and is not sharply

277

dependent on operating temperature. Because of the high specific loading, operating temperatures are high and fused silica is normally used in the construction. The inert gas xenon, having few strong lines in the visible region and heavy positive ions of low mobility, is one of the more suitable gases to use as a filling for such a light source.

The major use of compact source xenon lamps particularly in ratings of about 2 kW is in cinema projectors, and in lighthouses where, because of the small high luminance source, the large rotating optics are now replaced with elements of only 100 mm to 300 mm diameter. Larger lamps of 10 kW to 25 kW or more have uses in solar simulators, arc-imaging furnaces and numerous specialized aids to scientific investigations. The smaller compact source lamps find many optical uses while the linear sources up to 6 kW rating are used for colour matching and fadeometers. Higher power linear source lamps of up to 65 kW are applied to sports stadia and city centre lighting. Lamp data are given in Appendix I.

15.2.1   Operating characteristics

Xenon lamps consists of an arc burning between solid tungsten electrodes, in a pressure of pure xenon, contained in a fused silica envelope (Fig. 15.9). They may be designed to operate from a.c. or d.c., and be of compact (XE) or linear (XB) form. The arc of the compact source is a few millimetres in length, is electrode-stabilized, and is located at the centre of a relatively large bulb of approximately spherical shape. The shape of the electrodes has a marked effect on the stability of the arc, and as 'pip-growth', leading to deformation of the electrodes, is more likely to occur with a fluctuating current, the lamps are usually designed to operate from a smoothed d.c. supply. Because of the short arc length the lamp voltage is low and the current is high. The fused silica-molybdenum foil hermetic seals are described in Sect. 7.1.3; wider and thicker foils may be arranged to form an annular seal to carry currents of 100 A or more, some seals being shown on lamps in Fig. 15.9. Substantial advantages in increased lamp voltage, luminous efficacy and, more particularly, arc brightness accrue from the higher specific power loading as the filling pressure within the bulb is increased. Cold-filling pressures up to 12 atm are commonly used and as a result there is a potential hazard from explosive failure of the lamp. The arc of the compact-source xenon lamp is extremely bright and it is the only known source from which radiation approximating to sunlight in spectral power distribution, intensity and collimation can be obtained.

The linear form of xenon lamp has a wall-stabilized arc contained within a long, tubular, fused silica envelope. The lamp is of a simpler design than the compact-source form, and since the assembly can be partially mechanized it is somewhat less costly to produce. Electrode shape does not have a serious effect on arc stability and the lamps are usually designed to operate from an a.c. supply. The longer arc length gives a higher voltage drop for a given power and the lamp current is correspondingly less. Limitations imposed by the maximum operating temperature of fused silica restrict the specific power loading of the wall-stabilized arc and high filling pressures are not used. The specific power loading is considerably less than in the compact-source lamp, say $9 \cdot 0 \, \text{W/cm}^2$ of the arc tube against $19 \cdot 0 \, \text{W/cm}^2$ for the compact type, and while the higher arc voltages imply a higher ratio of arc wattage to electrode losses, similar luminous efficacies can be achieved only in lamps of very much higher power ratings.

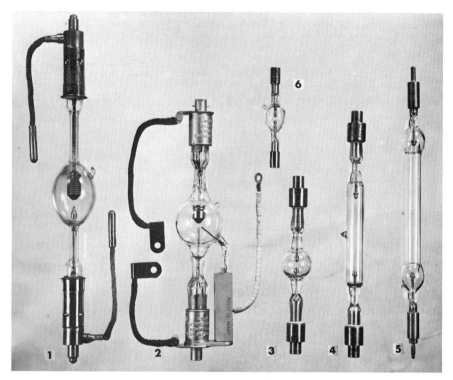

Fig. 15.9   Xenon lamp constructions
(1) 2500 W XE   (4) 1000 W XB
(2) 2000 W XE   (5) 1500 W XB
(3)   500 W XE   (6)   250 W XE

The source size is too large for projection purposes though it is compact when compared with other linear sources of similar light output. The very high power ratings in which the lamp can be made can also be an advantage, and for area floodlighting with un-collimated light the linear lamp in a simple trough reflector has much to recommend it. Lamps are commercially available in ratings from 150 W to 2 kW in the compact source form. Ratings up to 500 W can be made to operate from a.c., with a shorter life than the equivalent d.c. form. Above 500 W, a reasonable life can be achieved only on d.c., which must be smooth with a ripple content less than 5% r.m.s. Other compact sources rated at 5 kW, 10 kW and 30 kW have been described in the literature. Linear lamps are rated at 1 kW upwards, and are used most in ratings up to 20 kW. Larger types have been made up to a 300 kW rating.

In both forms of the lamp, compact and linear, the permanent gas filling ensures that the full light output is available immediately at switching on: there is no run-up period as with mercury lamps. A high voltage, high frequency pulse starter is used to initiate the arc, which requires a pulse of the order of 30 kV to 40 kV though a lower voltage of 10 kV to 15 kV is used for lamps with a starting probe (Sect. 18.3.3).

Typical spectral power distribution data are given in Table 15.1 and graphically in Fig. 15.10. With higher spectral resolution the lines can be separated more definitely from the continuum.

Table 15.1   Spectral power distribution of xenon lamps

Lamp rating	250 W XE/D	500 W XE/D	2 kW XE/D	1 kW XB
Efficacy	18·6	22	35	22 lm/W
Spectral band (nm)	Radiated power per 30 nm band (W)			
250 to 280	0·48	1·40	8·4	2·20
280 to 310	0·74	1·87	9·3	2·20
310 to 340	1·02	2·53	12·5	3·08
340 to 370	1·28	2·97	17·8	4·50
370 to 400	1·54	3·74	22·5	7·00
400 to 430	1·63	4·07	26·0	7·70
430 to 460	1·82	4·29	28·1	8·55
460 to 490	2·15	5·28	33·9	11·0
490 to 520	1·85	4·55	28·5	8·75
520 to 550	1·85	4·40	27·4	8·75
550 to 580	1·90	4·50	29·2	8·97
580 to 610	1·93	4·50	29·0	9·10
610 to 640	1·97	4·40	28·7	9·30
640 to 670	1·93	4·18	26·3	9·10
670 to 700	2·12	4·60	27·6	10·0
700 to 730	2·07	4·55	27·9	9·80
730 to 760	2·25	4·95	30·8	10·6
760 to 790	2·08	4·73	27·9	9·83
790 to 820	2·70	5·85	35·0	12·7
820 to 850	4·55	10·3	68·3	21·5
850 to 880	2·80	6·60	35·5	13·2
880 to 910	5·60	12·0	77·0	26·4
910 to 940	3·75	8·90	56·9	17·6
940 to 970	3·17	7·05	47·0	14·9
970 to 1000	3·45	8·36	52·5	16·3

A typical arc luminance distribution for a 2 kW compact-source xenon lamp is illustrated in Fig. 15.11. The correlated colour temperature of xenon lamps is normally in the region of 5000 K to 6000 K, but the chromaticity is located slightly below the Planckian locus. To correct for this slightly purple colour compared with natural daylight, for example in colour matching applications, various filter combinations have been used, generally including a pale greenish heat-absorbing glass which also reduces the unwanted infra-red radiation.

15.2.2   Comparison with other light sources

The xenon lamp has a moderately high luminous efficacy (20 lm/W to 50 lm/W depending on the type) and a usefully high luminance. In compact source lamps the usable areas

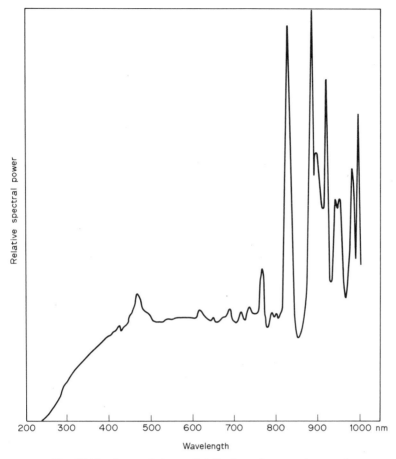

Fig. 15.10   Spectral power distribution of compact xenon lamp

of source approach the sun's luminance (2×10^5 stilb), and in some lamps of 10 kW or above the cathode spot may exceed this value and reach 10^6 stilb in lamps with water-cooled electrodes. It is this combination of good colour appearance and rendering, reasonable luminous efficacy and high luminance which makes the xenon lamp so outstanding.

In comparison with compact source mercury lamps the instant availability of full light output with xenon is a real practical advantage. Xenon provides a very powerful source of continuous ultra-violet radiation and, compared with a hydrogen discharge lamp or the efficient radiation of wavelength 253·7 nm from a low pressure mercury vapour lamp, its radiance and power rating are much higher.

In the infra-red region there is a pronounced peak at about 900 nm and a continuum up to 3000 nm which radiates about twice as much in proportion as in sunlight. Its

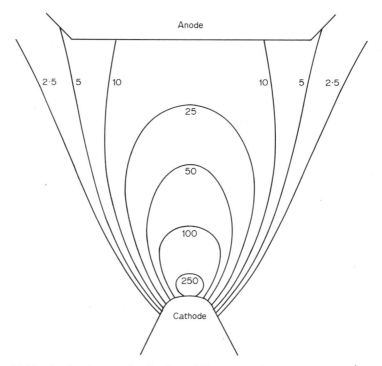

Fig. 15.11   Arc luminance distribution of 2 kW xenon lamp; values in 10^3 cd/cm^2

radiance in comparison with an incandescent source or other infra-red radiator is again high because of the power concentration in an arc gap of only a few millimetres.

Certain disadvantages have limited the more widespread use of xenon lamps, mainly their cost and the bulky and heavy control gear. While the cost per lamp is high, lamp life is long compared with other projector sources and running costs are competitive. Precautions are necessary to safeguard against the high voltage starting pulse, the copious ultra-violet radiation and the potential explosion hazard when using compact source lamps. Linear lamps are cheaper and for a given power the current is lower, a.c. operation is more applicable, and there is no explosion hazard. In practice explosive failures of compact source types are rare.

15.3   XENON FLASHTUBES

The xenon flashtube is a light source for producing a flash of very high intensity from electrical energy stored within a capacitor. It was used extensively during the second world war for aerial night photography and today there are many general and specialized applications. The spectral output is very similar to daylight in the visible region but the presence of high ultra-violet and infra-red radiation extends its range of application.

There are many differing requirements for flashtubes and any design of tube may perhaps be suitable for only one of these modes of operation:

(a) Aerial or studio photography and photochemical work require high power dissipation.
(b) Amateur and studio photography, general industrial and scientific uses, marine and airport beacons, medical research and the graphic arts require medium power dissipation and a reasonably short flash.
(c) Some scientific applications require a flash of the order of microseconds only.
(d) Use with lasers requires a short arc, highly loaded.
(e) Stroboscopic applications need lamps working at low power and high frequencies, as in the inspection of moving parts, ignition timers, and wheel balancers.

15.3.1   Construction

Most flashtubes are fabricated from borosilicate glasses except for very high loadings when fused silica is used. The electrodes and seals must be designed to carry high peak currents which may be several thousands of amperes, the energy dissipation being limited by the crazing or melting of the surface of the arc tube. To maintain a high current density in the positive column, the tubes are of small diameter to constrict the arc. To form a more concentrated light source the tube is wound into a helix or other configuration without affecting performance significantly. The tube dimensions, gas filling pressure, electrode design and emitter coatings all have a controlling influence on tube efficiency, flash duration and life. Pure xenon provides a radiation quality suitable for most photographic applications in monochrome and daylight colour film, but for high speed photographic events where motion is to be arrested, mixtures of argon and trace amounts of hydrogen provide light flashes only microseconds in duration. The shorter arc gap lamps contain 1 atm to 2 atm of gas while the linear or helical sources with a long positive column have pressures of 50 Torr to 200 Torr.

There are many and varied shapes, sizes, power ratings and light output characteristics of xenon flashtubes. Power loadings vary widely up to at least 10^4 J per flash.

15.3.2   Single flash operation

A typical circuit for the operation of a flashtube is shown in Fig. 15.12 where the energy stored in the capacitor is given by $\frac{1}{2}CV^2$. The voltage to charge the main capacitor C_1 is provided from some convenient d.c. source, while the smaller capacitor C_2 derives its charge from a potential divider. The energy released from C_2 by closing the switch S promotes a high voltage pulse which is applied to a wire round the flashtube, or to a third electrode. This pulse ionizes the gas and allows the dissipation of the energy stored in C_1 in the flashtube.

For reliable operation trigger voltages of 4 kV to 16 kV are required, with energies of about 5 mJ having a pulse rise time corresponding to a natural frequency of about 40 kHz. In total darkness triggering of a tube is difficult but irradiation of the tube by photons, or increased trigger energy and voltage, ensure positive firing.

The charge resistor R_1 has two important functions. It limits the current drawn from the power supply and where a long recharge period is of no consequence, allows a high power output from a low current-rated power supply. Secondly, it must limit this charge

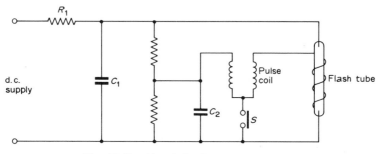

Fig. 15.12   Circuit for flashtube operation

current, so that when capacitor C_1 has discharged, the flashtube can de-ionize and extinguish without 'burn on' occurring. Burn on occurs when the voltage on C_1 rises above a critical value before de-ionization takes place. This is of major importance in stroboscopic circuit design and for satisfactory operation the time constant of the circuit should be chosen so that

$$\frac{1}{fRC} \approx 4$$

where f = maximum frequency (flashes/s)

R = charge resistance (ohms)

C = capacitance (farads)

Some circuits circumvent this limitation by automatically disconnecting the capacitor from the charge circuit for a short period after each flash. Electrolytic capacitors are generally used for low voltage tubes ($\not> 1000$ V) because of size and weight considerations. Paper capacitors have a lower internal impedance, giving rise to a shorter flash duration and consequently higher luminous efficacy. The d.c. supplies may be from any convenient source, batteries or rectified a.c. Pulse coils are generally air-cored, Tesla-type transformers, sometimes with isolated primaries. They are of low primary resistance to enable rapid discharge of the trigger capacitor. The coil should be located near to the tube to prevent high frequency losses in long leads. For safety in photographic applications the voltage on the trigger capacitor is generally limited to a maximum of 150 V since this appears on the camera contacts; similarly, to prevent damage at the contacts the continuous current is restricted to 500 µA.

Like other discharge sources, flashtubes cannot be operated in parallel. Each requires its own discharge capacitor, charge resistor, and usually, for reliable operation, a trigger coil. They can be used in series by a suitable increase in operation voltage, and are then triggered by applying the trigger pulse, either to both tubes in the normal way, or to the common point.

Flashtubes are generally designed to operate within a range of voltage to allow for decrease in battery voltage and variables in equipment design. BS 3205:1969 specifies a tolerance of $+10\%$ to -20% from the nominal voltage. The tube itself gives operational limits somewhat wider than these tolerances, the maximum being the hold-off voltage, above which stray ionizing radiation may trigger off the tube spasmodically. The lower limit is set by the minimum striking voltage below which the tube becomes erratic, or fails to fire. In practice this is not a fixed figure and depends on the ionization produced by the trigger pulse (effectively the voltage and energy of the pulse).

15.3.3   Stroboscopic applications

In stroboscopic applications the basic circuit is not dissimilar to single flash operation but the time constants of the circuits become of greater importance. The triggering switch is usually a cold cathode valve of the Neostron type driven by a multi-vibrator circuit. A basic circuit is shown in Fig. 15.13 where the frequency range varies from a few flashes/s up to 300 flashes/s.

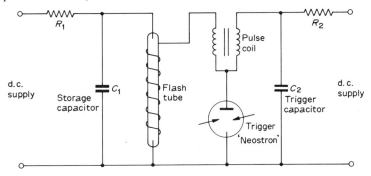

Fig. 15.13   Circuit for stroboscopic use

For high speed stroboscopic repetition rates ($> 1000/s$) series control valves are normally used where the flashtube is 'overvolted'. Above the 'self-flashing voltage' the tube will flash spontaneously whenever this voltage is applied, for example, by a thyratron, or a triggered spark-gap in the discharge circuit, so dispensing with the flashtube trigger (Fig. 15.14). On switching the thyratron the capacitor discharges through valve and flashtube, some of the energy being lost in the valve. The high pulse currents involved often means that the valve is working outside the manufacturer's limits, but experience has proved these circuits and they are invaluable for high-speed stroboscopic work.

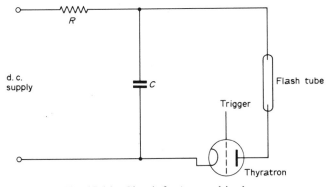

Fig. 15.14   Circuit for 'overvolting' use.

15.3.4 Light output

Fig. 15.15 shows a plot of light flux versus time for a typical flashtube. The parameters usually quoted are total quantity of light, which is the area under the curve in lumen seconds; peak lumen output P; and flash duration t. Because of the long persistence of the flash, the duration is quoted at $\frac{1}{2}$, $\frac{1}{3}$ or $\frac{1}{10}$ of the peak value. The quantity of light is approximately equal to the product of P and t (at $\frac{1}{3}$ peak). This quantity divided by the energy per flash in joules gives the efficacy in lm/W. If intensities are measured, then the quantity of light is taken as 10 times the candela second value, rather than 4π times. For fully loaded tubes the efficacy is about 40 lm/W. Compare Fig. 11.2.

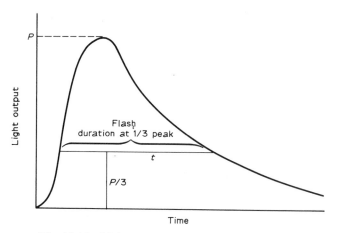

Fig. 15.15   Light output curve for a flash discharge

Flash durations of xenon flashtubes range from several microseconds to approximately 10 ms. For short durations in the microsecond region, short arc-gaps are required, also minimum values of the external resistance and the inductance of leads and capacitor. Operation at high voltage contributes to shortening of the flash duration. Longer flash durations may be obtained by including an inductance in the discharge circuit. The duration is then given approximately by $t = \pi\sqrt{(LC)}$ where L is in henries, C in farads and t in seconds.

Since flash duration is roughly proportional to the capacitance for a given loading, small changes in flash duration may be accommodated by variation of operating voltage. Maximum ratings are however given for the nominal operating voltage, and shortening the duration will increase the peak current and have an adverse effect on life. This applies particularly to 'overvolting' operations, where the peak current may be several orders higher, thus necessitating either considerable reduction in loading from stated peak values, or artificial lengthening of the flash.

Tube life for single flash operation is generally stated at 5000 to 50 000 flashes whereas for stroboscopic use the average life is given as 100 h to 200 h burning life. Life of a tube depends very much on the circuit and tube combination, and by suitable adjustments to these most performance criteria can be satisfied.

Spectral power distribution.   Most flashtubes have pure xenon as the filling gas, and at the high current densities involved the characteristic broad continuum is produced (Fig. 15.16). Higher operating voltages will shift the spectrum towards the blue, and low energy or under-loaded tubes fall off more than usual in the red end of the spectrum.

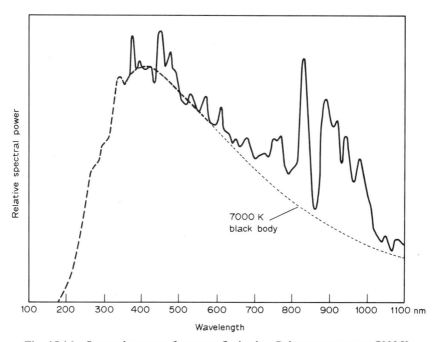

Fig. 15.16   Spectral output of a xenon flashtube. Colour temperature 7000 K

At the ultra-violet end the nature of the envelope, or cover, determines the cut-off, approximately 180 nm for bare silica and 300 nm for glass tubes. In the infra-red there are superimposed peaks in the 850 nm to 1000 nm region and the radiation ceases at approximately 2000 nm. The colour temperature of tubes for most photographic work falls into a range of 6000 K to 7500 K, though in some tubes with xenon-hydrogen mixtures and an arc not confined by the tube walls, colour temperatures as high as 40 000 K may be reached.

15.4   PULSED XENON LAMPS

The pulsed xenon lamp follows the same basic principle of light generation as the flash-tube but in addition it is designed to operate with a high mean power dissipation, giving light flashes at each half cycle from normal a.c. supply. Not only is the arc tube body made from fused silica but in addition it is forced air-cooled. Made in linear and helical forms these tubes dissipate power from 500 W up to 10 kW each from special electronic control units.

As with other xenon discharges, full light output is obtained at once when a pulsed xenon lamp is switched on. With this characteristic, and a reasonably high luminous efficacy, combined with daylight spectral quality, it is widely used for many applications in the graphic arts. Light output maintenance is good with a long life, and because it can be switched readily to make photographic exposures the lamp is widely applied to copy-board lighting and printing down applications in colour and monochrome processes.

15.4.1 Design and construction

Unlike the flashtube, the pulsed xenon lamp has to support a mean current as well as a higher peak current, so that the electrode and seal design are significantly different. The fused silica seal has to carry a mean current of about 15 A to 25 A with a peak current limited to about 70 A to 100 A. Such a seal would, if a lamp were to be used as a high power flashtube, fail like a a fuse due to the much higher peak current reached in a flashtube.

The electrode design, having to support a mean current of about 15 A, follows very closely designs used in mercury lamps where a solid tungsten rod with a helical tungsten overwinding supports an emissive coating.

The arc tube of fused silica is varied in length with a loading of about 50 W/cm, the tube bore remaining substantially constant. The gas filling of xenon is adjusted to provide a maximum arc voltage compatible with the ability to trigger the tube on each half cycle. Again, like the xenon flashtube, a variety of shapes can be made but the more popular types are linear or wound into a helix to provide a compact light source. Linear tubes are often used in a rectangular format operating 2 in series, or with smaller tubes 4 in series.

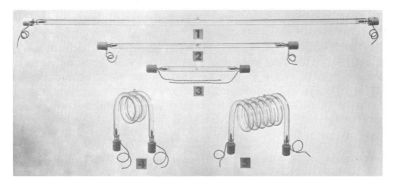

Fig. 15.17 Some linear and helical pulsed xenon lamps
(1) 3 kW (2) 1·5 kW (3) 750 W (4) 4 kW (5) 8 kW

As the lamps are fitted within a reflector system, through which air flows, they are supported from refractory caps, the electrical connection being made by a flying lead. Adequate cooling, particularly adjacent to the electrode system, is important to obtain a good tube life. A range of lamps is shown in Fig. 15.17.

15.4.2   Operation

The lamp is started by a driving circuit (Fig. 15.18) producing in the pulse transformer a pulse of 10 kV to 15 kV which ionizes the xenon; energy stored in the capacitor is then released to produce a light flash whose duration is dependent upon the inductance and capacitance of the circuit. On the next half cycle of the supply voltage the capacitor will be recharged and the pulse transformer will again trigger the lamp. After a few seconds the trigger pulse can be stopped and the tube becomes self-operating giving light pulses 100 times per second from the 50 Hz supply.

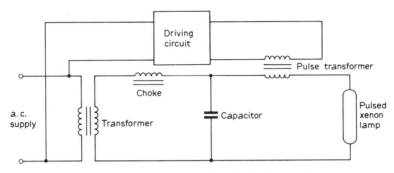

Fig. 15.18   Circuit for operation of pulsed xenon lamps

Other circuits make use of triacs where the voltage to the tube is switched on and off during the half cycle to control lamp power, the lamp having been started initially by a voltage pulse.

Peak lamp currents vary between 20 A and 70 A and the pulse duration between 2 ms and 5 ms. The arc tube voltage and the volt-ampere characteristic vary and depend upon peak current and duration, controlled by the circuit design. The open circuit voltage provided by the circuit is normally about twice that of the lamp or the total of lamps used in series. Efficacy is about 25 lm/W for linear types, 30 lm/W for helical.

15.5   NEON LAMPS

Most discharge lamps use the positive column as the source of light. If the arc-gap is shortened until the positive column disappears it is found that the phenomena at the electrodes are unchanged, and the light emanates from a glow discharge surrounding the cathode. Neon glow lamps make use of this effect. They are used for many purposes such as indicator lamps and advertising signs. They differ mainly in the electrode form, the bulb shape being chosen to accommodate the dimensions used. For example, the familiar beehive indicator lamp uses the conventional pear-shaped lamp bulb, while a sign lamp having a cathode in the form of letters would be in a tubular bulb. The electrodes of iron or nickel are unheated except by the discharge. Small quantities of argon are often included in the gas filling to lower the striking voltage; neon pressure is about 8 Torr. A resistance ballast is used to control the lamps, although the larger ones may have this included inside the lamp cap. For indicator lamps both a.c. and d.c. types are made, mostly requiring a current of less than 2 mA. The beehive lamp takes 25 mA and dissipates 5 W.

Neon lamps using the positive column as the light source are also available. For high efficacy, as high a proportion of the lamp voltage as possible must appear in the positive column. Lamps are therefore of long arc length and require an operating voltage of several kilovolts. Efficacies are less than 5 lm/W and this, together with inconvenient dimensions and the high operating voltage, restricts the application to advertising signs and displays.

Use of a hot cathode increases electrode emission and the associated decrease in cathode voltage fall allows use at normal voltages. It also allows a greater lamp current, and results in a lamp of more reasonable proportions operating on normal supplies with an efficacy of 10 lm/W to 15 lm/W. One form of this lamp uses similar components to a 200 W linear sodium lamp but having a low pressure filling of neon; it has found application as a flashing hazard beacon.

16 Electroluminescent devices

Electroluminescence is the emission of light from phosphors under the direct action of an electric field, the light-emitting process being identical with that operating when the phosphor is excited by ultra-violet radiation, cathode-rays, etc. Most practical lamps and other devices make use of 'intrinsic' or 'Destriau' electroluminescence, and their construction is essentially that of a flat-plate condenser in which the phosphor material is the dielectric medium, and one electrode is transparent to allow the light to be emitted externally. The commercially important phosphors are all based on zinc sulphide, suitably activated to give yellow, green, or blue emission. The emission bands closely resemble those of sulphides excited by ultra-violet radiation, but the method of preparation is different.

Electroluminescent lamps can be divided into two main types, *organic* and *ceramic*, according to the type of binding material used for the phosphor powder. These groups can be further sub-divided, according to the substrate upon which the lamp is built. Development of the general principle, with more complicated constructions, has led to two different types of image storage device.

16.1 CONSTRUCTION

All electroluminescent devices rely on some form of electrically conducting transparent electrode as an essential part of the lamp. Where glass is the substrate, the electrode is formed by spraying the glass, heated to its softening point, with a solution of a tin salt. This forms a tough adherent layer of tin oxide on the surface of the glass, having an optical transmission better than 90%, and an electrical resistance of the order of 1000 Ω per square measured from one edge to the opposite edge. A similar tin oxide film can be formed on vitreous enamel layers by the same technique. Plastic substrates can be coated with other metal oxide layers (for example, indium oxide) deposited by vacuum evaporation techniques, and having similar properties to those of tin oxide films.

16.1.1 Ceramic lamps

A diagrammatic representation of the coatings involved in the preparation of a ceramic electroluminescent lamp is shown in Fig. 16.1.

After suitable surface preparation, a thin sheet of enamelling iron is coated with a layer of a vitreous enamel frit, which is then fused to the plate at red-heat to form a perfectly adherent layer about 0·05 mm thick. This layer must possess a high dielectric constant but low electrical conductivity, and it must be white to act as a light reflector. A typical composition is a zinc titanium borosilicate containing small amounts of

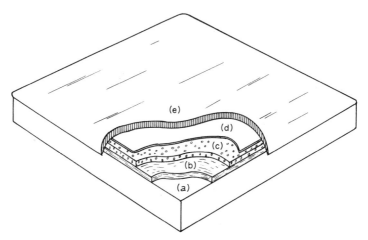

Fig. 16.1 Construction of a ceramic electroluminescent lamp
(a) Metal plate   (d) Transparent conducting film
(b) Ground coat   (e) Transparent overglaze
(c) Phosphor in ceramic layer

potassium fluoride and the oxides of potassium, barium and aluminium. It must be free from traces of lead, iron, nickel, cobalt and other impurities.

The phosphor layer, about half as thick as the ground coat, is now applied to the coated plate in the form of an enamel frit containing the required proportion of powdered phosphor. This frit must have a lower fusion temperature than the ground coat. While still hot from the fusion process, the plate is sprayed with a tin salt solution to form the transparent conducting tin oxide second electrode. At this stage the panel can be illuminated, if connected to a suitable a.c. supply.

Finally, the plate is coated with a clear protective glaze, which again must fuse at a lower temperature than the preceding layers. This overglaze is electrically insulating so that at least the front surface of the lamp is electrically safe. A small area of the transparent conducting film is not overglazed and is used for making one of the electrical contacts on the front surface of the lamp, usually at an edge where it is not obvious or where it can be hidden by a frame or surround.

The ceramic electroluminescent lamp can be made in a variety of plane shapes, including circular and angular forms. The panel can have holes and slots in it, but these must be formed in the metal plate before processing, and cannot be made in the finished lamp. As the cost of the panel is largely dependent upon its shape and the number of holes, it is advisable to use simple rectangular shapes wherever possible, and standard sizes of rectangular Panelume lamps are available, up to 250 mm × 200 mm. The electroluminescent surface can be made to extend to about 1 mm from any edge or hole, but if holes or slots are used for accommodating fixing bolts, it is often unnecessary to have the luminous surface so close to the edge.

16.1.2 Organic lamps

In the construction of lamps using organic dielectric materials, the phosphor and a light-reflecting powder are bonded in organic resins on a glass sheet having a transparent conducting tin oxide film on the surface. This conducting surface is first coated with the phosphor layer, followed by a layer of barium titanate to scatter light forwards and increase the overall dielectric constant, so that more power can be applied to the lamp. Finally, an electrode of either evaporated metal or conducting paint is applied to the back. This *organic-on-glass* type of lamp requires careful sealing to prevent the entry of moisture, as this can cause dielectric breakdown, hence the back is usually coated with paraffin wax and aluminium foil or other moisture barriers. A comparison of this type of construction with a *ceramic-on-glass* type of lamp is shown in Fig. 16.2.

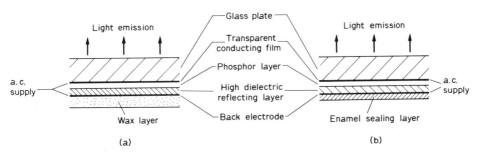

Fig. 16.2   Sections through (a) an organic-on-glass and (b) a ceramic-on-glass electroluminescent lamp

Light is only emitted from those areas of the lamp where the phosphor is subjected to an alternating electric field, that is between the two electrodes. If the back electrode is suitably shaped, an illuminated legend or pattern is displayed when the panel is switched on, but it remains completely invisible when the panel is off. The organic electroluminescent panel is especially suited to this type of application, as opposed to the *ceramic-on-metal* type where the transparent electrode must be shaped, making the legend partially visible even when the lamp is off, and giving rise to difficulties in connecting up isolated areas of the front electrode.

16.1.3   Other types of electroluminescent lamp

The ceramic-on-glass lamp, Fig. 16.2b, is similar to the organic-on-glass construction, except that the component layers are vitreous enamels instead of organic resins; this type of panel is therefore more resistant to moisture penetration than the organic-on-glass type. However, because the front conducting glass sheet is used as the structural member upon which the subsequent layers are fabricated, the phosphor layer undergoes several heating cycles before the lamp is completed: as a result the finished lamp is often less bright than the other types.

   The most recently developed electroluminescent lamp is the *plastic* type, the construction of which is similar to that of the organic-on-glass lamp, except that in place of the glass a transparent flexible sheet of plastic, with a transparent conducting layer of metal oxides evaporated on to one surface, is used as the structural member. Instead of protecting the back of the lamp with wax, the basic panel is encapsulated in a transparent envelope, to give a semiflexible lamp about 1 mm thick. With this construction it is particularly difficult to prevent the ingress of water vapour, therefore plastic lamps tend to have a relatively short operating life.

16.1.4   Lamps for d.c. operation

All the electroluminescent lamps described so far have operated from an alternating supply. A number of techniques are known whereby d.c. electroluminescence may be obtained, these falling broadly into two groups (a) vacuum-evaporated continuous films of zinc sulphide (suitably activated), and (b) constructions enabling a direct current to flow through a layer of powdered phosphor.

Vapour-deposited films of zinc sulphide operate at low voltages, from a few volts up to about 80 V and the luminance values claimed are often in excess of those for conventional lamps. There are constructional difficulties leading to non-reproducible results, while the devices require an initial electrical forming process to develop the full light output; furthermore the life is very short compared to that of conventional electroluminescent lamps.

Devices employing the usual powder phosphors have been made for d.c. operation employing both ceramic and organic constructions. In the latter case, it is usual to produce a conducting layer of copper sulphide around each phosphor particle by treatment with copper salts. Suitable binding media for the phosphor are required to enable d.c. to pass through the lamp. As with evaporated layers, an initial forming process is often required, and the layers are unstable and of short life, although the luminance compares very favourably with that of conventional lamps.

These types of d.c. electroluminescent lamps will not assume commercial importance until the stability and life have been improved. Because of the relatively low operating voltage, they would then have a potential application in connection with modern transistorized electronic equipment.

16.2   CHARACTERISTICS AND APPLICATIONS

16.2.1   Operating conditions

The commercially important electroluminescent phosphors emit in the yellow, green and blue regions of the spectrum. A few red-emitting materials have been found, but their brightness is not comparable with the three main phosphors. The phosphors tend to show small variations in colour, depending on the frequency of the supply. The green phosphor usually shows a marked shift towards the blue end of the spectrum when operated at frequencies over 1000 Hz, because the emission spectrum of this phosphor contains both green and blue bands, and as the supply frequency is increased, the blue band increases in relative intensity. Intermediate colours and white can be obtained from mixtures of phosphors though ranges of colours, including whites and reds, can be obtained in a more satisfactory manner by using the cascade excitation of certain organic fluorescent paints, applied to the exterior surface of the lamps.

The luminance and life, as well as the colour, also depend on the operating frequency. The luminance is proportional to the frequency, while the life of the panel has the inverse relationship. In practice, at high frequencies there is a decrease in light output due to electrical losses in the panel.

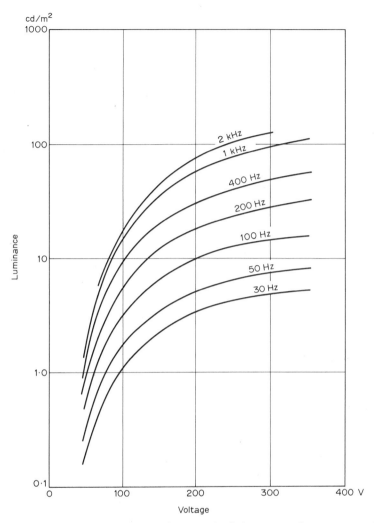

Fig. 16.3   Effect of frequency and voltage on the light output of a green ceramic lamp

In operation, the panels achieve full light output after a few cycles of the applied voltage. During their long life they do not usually undergo catastrophic failure but merely show a decrease in light output. For this reason the operating life is defined as the time taken for the luminance to fall to 50% of its initial value. Most panels show a slight increase in luminance during the first few hours of life, followed by a roughly exponential decay over several thousand hours, depending on the supply frequency used.

By way of example, the initial luminance of a green ceramic lamp, operating at 240 V, 50 Hz, is about 8 cd/m^2 at a current density of about 1 A/m^2. In aircraft applications, green ceramic panels operating at 115 V, 400 Hz have a luminance of about 15 cd/m^2, while the organic-on-glass type at 350 V, 400 Hz produces about 80 cd/m² at 1·5 A/m². For comparison, the fluorescent lamp has a luminance of the order of 5000 cd/m². Temperature has little effect on a green ceramic lamp between 0 °C and 100 °C but the luminance decreases to about 10% at − 196 °C.

Fig. 16.3 shows the effects of both applied voltage and frequency on the light output from a typical ceramic lamp. Electroluminescent lamps may be easily and smoothly dimmed to extinction by varying the applied voltage. A typical efficacy is 0·5 lm/W, but the exact value varies considerably with the type of construction used and the operating conditions, as does the power factor for which a typical value is 0·25; the lamp behaves essentially as a capacitor in parallel with a leakage resistor.

16.2.2   Uses of electroluminescence

As mentioned earlier, each method of constructing electroluminescent panels has its own particular merits, and the various types are suited to different applications.

The organic-on-glass structure is ideal for panels of simple general shape, such as rectangles and discs, on which a complicated legend is to be displayed, often with parts separately switched. Typical applications include alpha-numeric indicators and aircraft panels described later. Because the organic type of lamp does not lend itself as readily to mass production techniques as the ceramic type, it is more expensive requiring skilled hand operations in its construction.

A particularly interesting application of the plastic construction is for luminous markings for personnel engaged in hazardous situations, such as police on traffic control duty at night. This type of use is possible because of the light-weight and flexible construction, and because it can be operated from a transistorized invertor driven by portable batteries.

The ceramic construction is especially suited to the mass production of panels giving a surface of uniform but low luminance where little or no maintenance is required; their long life and robust nature are an added advantage, for example in illuminated electric clock faces, light-switch surrounds and self-luminous instrument dials and scales. In such applications the power consumption is negligible, and the thin planar nature of the panel does not usually involve appreciable design changes in the article. The ceramic construction is essential in one of the methods of lighting aircraft instruments.

Other possible applications of ceramic panels include cine-projector control panels, radio and television tuning scales, exit signs, markers for stair-risers and dark-room safe-lights. Electroluminescent lighting of motor vehicle instrument panels has been used in USA. A suitable alternating supply is obtained from the car battery by a transistor-oscillator. Also in USA, large panels have been used for road and motorway signs.

Alpha-numeric indicators.   Many modern instruments and display systems use digital read-out systems, and electroluminescent digital indicators have the advantage that all the illuminated elements are in one plane, giving a wide viewing angle. The panel carries a number of separate strips, combinations of which are illuminated to give the digits 0 to 9 in a slightly stylized but quite readable form (Fig. 16.4).

Alphabet indicators, based upon the above idea, can also be used in display systems. In this case, the minimum number of bars required is 14. By increasing this number to

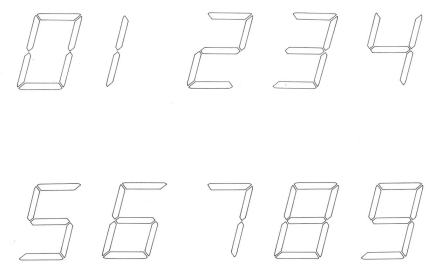

Fig. 16.4   Digits for an electroluminescent digital indicator using seven component elements

16, 20, or more, successive improvements can be made in the style of letter presented.

Alpha-numeric indicators can be made in a range of sizes from 15 mm to over 1 m high. Both ceramic and organic constructions have been used, depending on the size and complexity of the indications.

Aircraft lighting.   One of the first commercially important applications of electro-luminescence was in aircraft lighting, and there is still a constant demand. Most aircraft electrical systems operate at 400 Hz, which gives adequate brightness even for day-time viewing, while low power consumption, lightness and the inherently slim form of the panels are further advantages. The principal uses are in cabin signs, and the illumination of control panels.

The organic-on-glass construction is particularly suited to the manufacture of No Smoking and Fasten Seat Belts cabin signs, the legend being invisible when the panel is off, while the power consumption of about 1 W per panel is minimal. These have been used in a wide range of passenger aircraft.

Ceramic panels are used in the Panelume system for lighting the instrument panels in aircraft. The light from the panel is piped through a clear transparent plastic, the external surface of which is opaque; light emerges only where the exterior of the panel has been engraved through the opaque layer into the transparent layer, and markings on the control panel thus become illuminated. The complex panel shape is pressed out of sheet enamelling iron before the ceramic layers are fired on. The edges of some of the holes are also re-shaped slightly to redirect light for instrument illumination, these being behind the Panelume panel. The system can be adapted for all forms of instrument and control panel illumination. A further application of ceramic panels is for aircraft map-reading devices. As with the Panelume system the light output may be smoothly dimmed to suit night-flying conditions.

There seems little prospect of any immediate improvements in the brightness and efficiency of electroluminescent panels, which means that they should not be considered as alternatives to high intensity incandescent and discharge lamps used for space lighting, but used for their unique properties. They are, by virtue of their planar form, ideal for subdued uniform illumination of surfaces where the spatial requirements of the lighting system must be kept to a minimum.

16.3   IMAGE STORAGE DEVICES

16.3.1   The image retaining panel (IRP)

The image retaining panel resembles a conventional ceramic-on-metal panel in construction and appearance, except that a special phosphor (ZnCdS:Mn) is used, and the device is usually operated at 100 V d.c. In the dark no luminescence occurs until the panel is exposed to some form of radiant energy, when, provided the d.c. potential is maintained, it emits a yellow glow over the regions of its surface which were irradiated. The panel is sensitive to gamma and X-rays, ultra-violet, and the near infra-red, to visible light except in the region of its own emission band, also to electrons of energy greater than about 5 keV. If the d.c. potential is removed, the emission disappears and after a few seconds the panel is ready to receive another radiation exposure following re-application of the d.c. potential. If, having formed an image, the radiation is switched off, the image will remain for about 30 min, or until the d.c. potential is switched off.

If a photographic negative is projected on to the panel, a positive image will be formed, showing a range of half-tones as in the original negative. In fact, the IRP performs many of the functions of a photographic plate without the need for a development process, and can be used many thousands of times. An interesting application is the detection of the red and near infra-red emission from pulsed lasers during the setting up of the device. The IRP also has integrating properties for low-intensity electron beams, and can be used in electron microscopy, where it functions as the screen upon which appears the image of the specimen under examination.

Another application is its use with X-rays, because the image can be studied at leisure after the X-rays have been switched off. The image resolution of about 8 line pairs/mm is not sufficient for many non-destructive testing applications, but is quite adequate for routine examination of assembly faults. The relatively high X-ray dose required to excite the panel, compared with photographic film, prevents use of the panel in the medical field.

16.3.2   The image storage panel (ISP)

Electroluminescent panels are particularly suitable for incorporation into image display panels. The image is formed in this case by local variations of the voltage across the electroluminescent phosphor, producing corresponding variations in the luminance of the lamp. The basic image intensifier or converter panel consists of an electroluminescent lamp with an additional photoconductive layer. This layer has a high resistance in the dark, which decreases by several orders of magnitude when suitably irradiated. According to the photoconductor used, the device can be sensitive to bands in the infra-red, visible or ultra-violet spectrum, and to alpha, beta, gamma and X-rays. A former image panel contained a cadmium sulphide photoconductive layer, sensitive to red light and

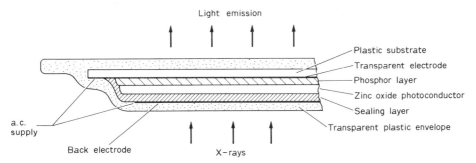

Fig. 16.5 Construction of an X-ray image converter

near infra-red, and to X-rays and gamma rays. The resolution and sensitivity of this device were not high enough to make it commercially important.

The ISP is a recently developed image converter using zinc oxide as the photoconductive material, which has the great advantage of storing the image for a considerable period of time after the incident exciting radiation has been removed. This device is sensitive to long wavelength ultra-violet and to X-rays. The construction shown in Fig. 16.5 is based on the organic-on-glass or the plastic methods of fabrication.

The zinc oxide photoconductor has the fundamental property of suffering a change of electrical impedance when irradiated and retaining this lowered impedance for a very long time. A good quality image can be retained for a period of the order of 30 min at room temperature, and much longer at lower temperatures. The image can be removed by allowing natural decay over about a day, or by heating the panel at 100 °C for 20 s when the device will be ready for another image.

The ISP operates from an a.c. supply, in the frequency range 50 Hz to 100 Hz, the voltage being adjustable up to 250 V according to the image contrast required. In contrast

(a)   (b)   (c)

Fig. 16.6 Photographs of a circuit-breaker (a) under normal light; and under X-rays using (b) the image retaining panel (c) the image storage panel

to the IRP the application and removal of the panel voltage has no effect upon the storage properties of the photoconductive layer. This means that the panel can be exposed to X-rays, and then removed to a convenient viewing area for the application of voltage to reveal the impressed image.

The main application envisaged for this device is in the inspection of complex mechanical and electronic assemblies and the examination of metal structures for gross defects, where the cost and time of processing X-ray film are a serious encumbrance to the inspection process. The definition is about equal to that of the unaided human eye, but at present the sensitivity to X-rays is not high enough for medical applications.

Fig. 16.6 illustrates the application of image storage devices to the examination of assembly faults in a miniature circuit-breaker. The superior contrast and definition obtained with the ISP is apparent from the photographs.

17   Semiconductor lamps

Although junction electroluminescence was first observed by Round in 1907 when he obtained faint yellow emission in silicon carbide crystals, it was not until 1962 when it was noted that a gallium arsenide junction diode biased in the forward direction was an efficient emitter of radiation, that a renewed effort was made into exploiting this phenomenon. In the past ten years there has been an increasing effort in the development of new materials to obtain efficient visible radiation and also on the theoretical interpretation of the operation of these devices.

Electroluminescent p–n junctions are identical in electrical characteristics to the more conventional silicon and germanium diodes and, in principle, could be used as a replacement. However, the mechanism which sets them apart from the normal rectifier is that when biased in the forward direction they convert some of the energy dissipated into radiation rather than into resistive heating. This factor makes possible a completely new type of lamp to which this chapter is devoted.

17.1   SEMICONDUCTOR THEORY

In an ideal crystalline semiconductor at absolute zero, the unoccupied conduction band is separated from the valence band, which is completely filled with electrons, by a 'forbidden gap'. At room temperature some of the electrons in the valence band have sufficient thermal energy to move into the conduction band, leaving available states at the top of the valence band for the motion of valence electrons. This can be conveniently described by the notation of *holes*, where a hole has a positive charge equal to that of an electron and a positive effective mass similar to that of an electron. Normal crystals, in addition, have defects which give permitted localized electron levels in the forbidden gap.

The two most important types of levels in the forbidden gap are donor and acceptor levels, which are situated very close to the conduction and valence bands respectively. These are created when certain foreign atoms replace some of the host atoms in the crystal. The atom of a donor impurity has one more valence electron than the host atom and this extra electron, which is only lightly bound to the parent atom, can readily escape into the conduction band. Thus the addition of donor impurities increases the density of conduction electrons with a consequent suppression of the hole density under thermal equilibrium. In a similar manner, the presence of an acceptor impurity, which has one valence electron less than the host crystal creates an increase in hole density.

A semiconductor in which the majority of the free carriers are electrons is termed *n-type*; in such a semiconductor the holes are the *minority carriers*. Conversely if the majority carriers are holes and the minority carriers are electrons, then the semiconductor is termed *p-type*. In an n-type semiconductor the electron density is primarily dependent on the donor impurity concentration and in a p-type semiconductor the hole density is dependent on the acceptor impurity concentration.

17.1.1   P–n junction at equilibrium

Consider a filamentary semiconductor of uniform area which has a constant density of donor atoms up to a specific cross-sectional plane from where the impurities become acceptor atoms. At absolute zero there will be no free carriers, since all the electrons will be attached to the donor atoms and all the holes at the acceptor sites, but at room temperature the thermal energy will be sufficient to ionize the impurity atoms. The charge carriers will now no longer be associated with a specific impurity atom, which will carry a net charge equal and opposite to that of the released carriers. As long as there is no net drift of carriers, charge equilibrium will be maintained. This condition holds well away from the junction of the n and p-type materials.

Close to the junction there is an imbalance of both electrons and holes: the electrons will diffuse into the p-type material leaving behind a net positive charge of uncompensated donor atoms. This positive charge, together with a corresponding net negative charge caused by the diffusion of holes near the junction into the n-type material, causes a field to be set up. The direction of this field is in such a direction as to oppose further carrier flow. At equilibrium, the diffusion forces on the carriers are exactly balanced by the field forces and no net flow occurs.

17.1.2   Forward biased p–n junction

When an external voltage is applied across the semiconductor filament containing a p–n junction in such a direction as to reduce the field at the junction (a positive voltage on the p-type side) then there will be a net flow of current across the junction. The holes flow into the n-type side and electrons into the p-type side. As these injected carriers diffuse into the opposite side of the junction they recombine with the majority carrier, but before recombination the injected carriers may be trapped at defects where they lose some of their energy. When the injected carriers eventually do recombine, they release potential energy less than or equal to the energy gap of the semiconductor, depending on whether they have been trapped at a defect or not. This energy may take the form of resistive heating or appear as a photon.

The electroluminescent p–n junction may, therefore, be described as one in which recombination of injected carrier occurs with an appreciable fraction of the recombination energy being converted into electromagnetic radiation. For the application as semiconductor lamps, interest is particularly directed to the production of radiation in the visible part of the spectrum.

17.1.3   Photon emission

The simplest recombination mechanism is band-to-band recombination, or the direct recombination of a free electron with a free hole. This type of recombination leads to the emission of a photon with an energy closely equal to that of the energy gap of the semiconductor. This is the highest energy photon which under normal circumstances can be emitted from a semiconductor, although there is no similar limit on the low energy emission: this indicates the minimum energy gap of a semiconductor which is required to give the possibility of visible emission. Taking the long wavelength limit of the red spectrum at 760 nm the corresponding energy gap is 1.63 eV (1 eV $= 1.602 \times 10^{-19}$ J).

Recombination may also take place by way of shallow or deep electronic states in the forbidden gap when impurity atoms are incorporated into the lattice. One advantage of generating radiation with energy less than the energy of the band gap is that this radiation is not attenuated in passing through the semiconductor. This situation occurs in the generation of red emission from gallium phosphide, which is due to recombination at a zinc-oxygen complex.

Minority carriers injected in a forward biased p–n junction may undergo either radiative or non-radiative recombination with the majority carriers. Obviously the ratio of these two competing mechanisms determines the efficiency of electroluminescence. One of the major influences on this ratio can be related to the detailed band structure of the semiconductor. The 'direct band' structure allows free electron-hole recombination without the participation of lattice vibrations (*phonons*). In the 'indirect band' structure, phonon participation is required which reduces the probability of radiative recombination. Thus, in general, a semiconductor with a direct band gap will produce a more efficient electroluminescent device.

It should be noted that the change from direct to indirect transition is a gradual process. For instance, gallium arsenide which is a semiconductor with a direct band gap of 1.41 eV is an efficient infra-red electroluminescent emitter. Gallium phosphide on the other hand has an indirect gap of 2.25 eV. Fortunately, gallium arsenide and gallium phosphide form a solid solution over the entire arsenic/phosphorus range, and the composition of gallium arsenide-phosphide can be adjusted to give any particular band gap between the extreme values of arsenide and phosphide. The phosphorus-rich alloys have an indirect band gap. By choosing a composition of GaAs$_{0.4}$P$_{0.6}$ it is possible to preserve the direct transition but enable visible red radiation to be produced at 660 nm.

17.1.4 Choice of semiconductor

Many of the semiconductors which promise efficient electroluminescence have not been grown in single crystal form and little is known about their physical properties. The fabrication of p–n junction also requires the availability of high purity material so that controlled doping can be made. The important properties of the better known semiconductors are given in Table 17.1.

It is of interest to consider in more detail those factors which have an influence on the choice of a semiconductor for efficient electroluminescence.

Crystal growing. The action of a p–n junction requires single crystal material. In addition the material should exhibit a minimum of defects and the possibility of controlled doping to less than 10 ppm. It is found that many of the III–V semiconductor compounds, which could be used for junction electroluminescence, have very high melting points and a high vapour pressure at this temperature. This disadvantage has been overcome to some extent by the use of crystal pulling under high pressure, and by the use of solution growth and epitaxial growth, both of which can be performed at temperatures considerably below the melting point.

303

Table 17.1   Characteristics of semiconductors for visible electroluminescence

	Band gap energy at 25 °C eV	Conductivity type	Transition type	Melting point °C
II–VI compounds				
Zinc telluride	2·2	p	direct	1240
Zinc selenide	2·6	n	direct	1600
Cadmium sulphide	2·4	n	direct	1475
Cadmium selenide	1·7	n	direct	1240
III-V compounds				
Indium nitride	2·5			
Gallium phosphide	2·26	n/p	indirect	1465
Gallium nitride	3·3	n/p	direct	2000
*Gallium arsenide phosphide	1·95	n/p	direct	
*Gallium indium phosphide	2·2	n/p	direct	
*Gallium aluminium arsenide	1·90	n/p	direct	
Aluminium phosphide	3·0	n/p	indirect	1500
Aluminium arsenide	2·16	n/p	indirect	1600
*Aluminium indium phosphide	2·1		direct	
IV–IV compound				
Silicon carbide	3·1	n/p	indirect	

* Energy gap given corresponds to value at crossover between direct and indirect.

Amphoteric conduction.   The technique of carrier injection at a p–n junction assumes that the semiconductor can be doped both n and p type. Many semiconductors, particularly those from the II–VI group, exhibit only one type of conductivity, either n-type or p-type. On attempting to produce the other type of carrier by impurity doping, a mechanism of vacancy compensation takes place which resists this change. Fortunately this does not occur in the III–V compounds to which most research effort is being directed.

Energy gap.   As previously mentioned, the energy of photon emission from a forward biased p–n junction has an upper limit equal to the energy gap of the semiconductor. To obtain devices which will cover the full range of the visible spectrum to 400 nm therefore requires semiconductors with an energy gap up to 3·1 eV. This is strictly true for radiation generated at the p–n junction. However, a new class of device is being developed in which a phosphor is coated on the surface of the semiconductor chip. The action of the phosphor is to convert into the visible region the radiation from the semiconductor, which is typically infra-red. The phosphor is of anti-Stokes type (Sect. 8.1.1).

Table 17.1 shows that the high band gap semiconductors tend to have high melting points and associated high processing temperatures. This increases the difficulty of fabricating devices.

Internal efficiency.   As previously indicated, the band structure of the semiconductor has a strong influence on the efficiency of radiative recombination. In many cases detailed measurements are required to verify the predicted band structure.

Absorption and refractive index.   Although a semiconductor may be an efficient producer of radiation a high percentage of this is lost by absorption before it reaches the
semiconductor surface. Also, because of the relatively high refractive index of the semiconductor only a small fraction of the generated light will be transmitted at the air
interface, the remainder being internally reflected. Gallium arsenide has a refractive
index of 3·6 at its emission wavelength, gallium phosphide 3·33 at 700 nm and 3·6 at
550 nm.

Mobility.   The flow of current across the junction is required to be as uniform as
possible to ensure uniform brightness of the lamp. This implies that the conductivity
of the top surface should be adequate and this is in turn related to the carrier mobility.
High carrier mobility assists in obtaining uniform emission.

17.2 DESIGN AND CONSTRUCTION OF LAMPS

Electroluminescent p–n junctions are being used for two types of display. By mounting
a single chip of an electroluminescent p–n junction in a suitable lamp package a long-life
single spot indicator can be manufactured. More complex indicators are also possible.
By using an insulating substrate an array of chips may be mounted, so that by energizing
the appropriate junctions a range of alpha-numeric characters can be displayed. The
two types of device differ only in the final stages of construction.

At the present time there are three different materials being used for commercially
available semiconductor lamps. Red indicators are being made from both gallium
arsenide-phosphide and gallium phosphide, while green indicators use gallium phosphide
or a phosphor-coated gallium arsenide diode. This latter type of lamp with anti-Stokes
phosphor is commercially available in one device, but considerable improvement in
the performance and range of colours is expected with further development.

Fabrication details will be confined to the single spot indicator with two kinds of
electroluminescent material, gallium phosphide and gallium arsenide-phosphide. The
flow chart (Fig. 17.1) shows that there is considerable divergence in the initial processing.

Crystal growth.   The most satisfactory method of crystal growth is to withdraw a seed
crystal slowly from a saturated melt to form a rod of single crystal material. This is the
Czochralski technique, by which it is now possible to pull both gallium arsenide and
gallium phosphide single crystals. An alternative method of producing gallium phosphide
platelets, which does not require an expensive high pressure puller, is the solution
growth process. The substrates are heavily doped to give low resistivity n-type material
which minimizes series resistance.

Epitaxial growth.   This is the addition of a layer of crystalline material to a similar or
foreign crystal by liquid phase or vapour phase growth, the lattices of layer and substrate
being conformable. It has been found that epitaxial layers grown by the liquid phase
technique tend to produce more efficient electroluminescent devices than those grown
from the vapour phase. The method is to allow the compound to crystallize on the
substrate from a saturated solution in a metal of low melting point.

Gallium phosphide devices are normally produced by two consecutive liquid phase

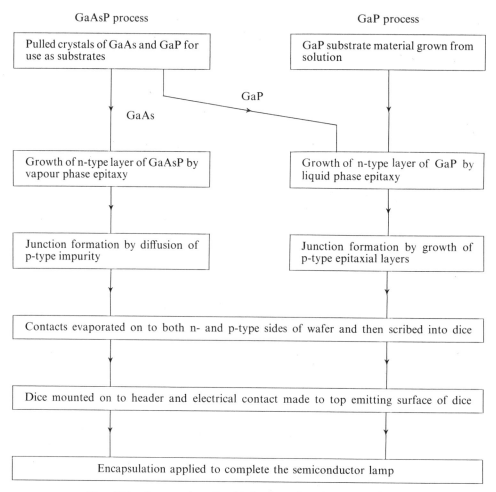

GaAsP process

GaP process

| Pulled crystals of GaAs and GaP for use as substrates | GaP substrate material grown from solution |

GaP

GaAs

| Growth of n-type layer of GaAsP by vapour phase epitaxy | Growth of n-type layer of GaP by liquid phase epitaxy |

| Junction formation by diffusion of p-type impurity | Junction formation by growth of p-type epitaxial layers |

Contacts evaporated on to both n- and p-type sides of wafer and then scribed into dice

Dice mounted on to header and electrical contact made to top emitting surface of dice

Encapsulation applied to complete the semiconductor lamp

Fig. 17.1   Process chart for fabrication of semiconductor lamps

epitaxial layers. The layer first grown is doped n-type and the junction formed by growing a subsequent layer of p-type material. Depending upon whether red or green emission is required, oxygen or nitrogen respectively is also incorporated into the lattice. For gallium arsenide-phosphide devices this mixed binary compound is grown by vapour phase epitaxy on to gallium arsenide substrates. To reduce strain due to lattice mismatch the phosphorus content is slowly increased to its final value during the course of the process.

Diffusion.   The standard method for diffusion of impurities into III–V compounds is the closed ampoule technique. For gallium arsenide-phosphide lamps this is a necessary process step in which the p–n junction is formed. The p-type impurity, zinc, together with a small amount of arsenic, is placed in an ampoule with the gallium arsenide-phosphide epitaxial wafer which is about 0·2 mm thick. After evacuating, the ampoule is sealed and annealed to produce a junction at about 3 μm below the surface.

Contacts. From this point onwards the processing of the gallium arsenide-phosphide and the gallium phosphide wafers are essentially the same. Before scribing the wafers into individual chips (or 'dice'), contacts have to be made to the top and back faces of the chips. Particular effort has to be paid to the design of the top contact which must serve to minimize the effects of current spreading but still only occupy a small fraction of the top emitting surface. Complicated patterns can be achieved by evaporation and photolithographic techniques.

Scribing. In addition to using a photolithographic method to optimize the shape of the top contact, some manufacturers use this technique to define a junction area which is then 'mesa-etched' to leave the centre of the junction as a plateau. This process has the advantage that the junction is not touched by the scribing tool and any possible high field spots are avoided.

Mounting and bonding. The following operations depend upon the final packaging intended. Although diode headers of the type known as TO-18 are the most popular package (Fig. 17.2), other types will undoubtedly be developed for specific applications.

Fig. 17.2 Gallium arsenide-phosphide lamp

Mounting of dice can be achieved either by solder or by heating to form a eutectic with the gold-plated Kovar header. The top contact of the diode is now connected by a thin gold wire to the insulated wire lead passing through the glass frit which fills the header. This connection is normally achieved by a thermo-compression bond.

Encapsulation. The encapsulation of a device has a dual purpose. It serves to protect the delicate bond between the chip and the lead from breakage and also reduces the reflection at the semiconductor surface, thus increasing the light output. At present the most commonly used encapsulants are silicone epoxy resins which have a maximum refractive index of approximately 1·6.

17.3   CHARACTERISTICS AND APPLICATIONS

Although the optical and electrical characteristics of electroluminescent diodes are similar, the variation in material and the processing procedure introduce differences in characteristics, making certain devices preferable to others for specific applications.

17.3.1   Electrical characteristics

The characteristics of electroluminescent diodes are very similar to those of the normal rectifying diode. The increased band gap of the electroluminescent semiconductors results in a slight increase of the 'knee' voltage in the forward low-impedance direction. It should be noted that when used as a lamp the device needs to be operated from a current source; alternatively the current must be limited by a series resistance. In the reverse direction the lamps present a high impedance up to the breakdown voltage which ranges typically from 5 V to 25 V. If the reverse voltage is limited to below this value, no adverse effect will ensue from connecting it in the wrong direction.

The forward current limitations are normally caused by the temperature rise of the device. It can readily withstand forward current surges of short duration or be used in a pulsed repetition mode. When a tungsten filament lamp is energized, there is an initial surge current which is many times the normal operating current. The only comparable effect with the electroluminescent diode would be related to the junction capacity but because of the low value of this capacity it would probably decay within a microsecond.

The rectifying characteristic of a semiconductor lamp enables it to be used as a logic element. This could be a considerable advantage in the design of circuitry used for process warning indicators.

17.3.2   Optical characteristics

The light output from an electroluminescent diode is primarily determined by the diode current. For gallium phosphide it is proportional to the square root of the current, for the arsenide-phosphide to the current, and for anti-Stokes phosphors to the square of the current. Thus for the first two cases the intensity is relatively stable for small variations in the power supply. In comparison the light output from a tungsten filament lamp is much more strongly dependent on the supply voltage, with the emission proportional to the 3·6 power of the voltage.

Colour.   Electroluminescent diodes are basically emitters of monochromatic radiation. This is a strong advantage in comparison with the tungsten filament lamp used as an indicator, since this lamp requires a colour filter which reduces the visible output by about 90% for red and green emission and by 99% for a blue emission.

The red-emitting gallium phosphide diode has an emission peak at 690 nm and a band width at half peak height (or 'half width') of 100 nm, whereas the gallium-arsenide-phosphide emission is not such a deep red at 660 nm but has a narrower half width of 40 nm. The amber emission from the gallium arsenide-phosphide is centred at 610 nm. Green emission is obtained both from gallium phosphide, where the emission peak is at 565 nm with a half width of 35 nm, and from the anti-Stokes phosphor device at 540 nm which in addition has a subsidiary broader peak at 660 nm.

Luminance. The luminance of electroluminescent junction diodes depends on the current density. Many of the commercial red-emitting devices operate at $3500 \, \text{cd/m}^2$, although for the stud mounted device which gives better heat removal $17\,000 \, \text{cd/m}^2$ is attained. These values are more than adequate for use as indicators in indoor applications even under the highest level of office lighting. By comparison a representative luminance of a fluorescent tube is about $5000 \, \text{cd/m}^2$.

Efficacy. It is instructive to consider first the efficacy of the filtered tungsten filament indicator lamp. For a miniature lamp operating at a colour temperature of 2300 K, the efficacy for luminous emission is about 4 lm/W. With the use of a red or green filter this is reduced to about 400 mlm/W.

Gallium phosphide red-emitting devices have an overall efficiency of about 1%. The luminous efficacy of this emission is about 20 lm/W so that the lamp efficacy is 200 mlm/W. For the green emission from gallium phosphide the overall efficiency is only 0·1% at present, but with emission close to the peak of the eye sensitivity the corresponding lamp efficacy is over 600 mlm/W. The red emission from gallium arsenide-phosphide lamps has a luminous efficacy of 40 lm/W so that with a typical conversion efficiency of 0·2% the lamp efficacy is only 80 mlm/W.

Life. The normally quoted life of these devices is in excess of 100 000 h. Thus if the devices are used on a 40 h/week basis this would mean a life of 50 years, probably well in excess of the equipment in which they are incorporated. This life is largely independent of the operating current of the diode so long as the maximum dissipation is not exceeded. By comparison the expected life of a miniature tungsten filament lamp is about 1000 h, and though increases in the life of the incandescent lamp can be made by reducing the voltage supply, it is difficult to extrapolate the expected life by a factor of 100.

Temperature. One of the major disadvantages of the electroluminescent junction diode is the dependence of emission and permissible dissipation on junction temperature. Typically an increase in junction temperature of 50 K gives a reduction in output by 30%.

17.3.3 Application as indicator lamps

Current consumption. Since it is the current density at the semiconductor junction which determines the luminance, it is possible for a specified current to adjust the luminance by altering surface area. At present, a luminance of $300 \, \text{cd/m}^2$ can be achieved for a current of 5 mA with a junction diameter of 0·4 mm. The effective emitting area can be magnified by suitable lens design.

Devices which are designed for this type of characteristic are useful where many indicators are to be energized from a single supply. In particular, it has been suggested that incandescent dial lights used on push-button telephones could be replaced by such lamps. With their low current consumption these lamps could then be energized by power through the telephone line.

Low current devices are also required for use in portable equipment where battery life is of major importance. In this context there are possible applications in electronic test equipment and also for domestic uses, such as illumination on the control knobs of television and radio sets. The use of opto-electronics in computers is also a potential mass market for low current devices.

Size.   As mentioned previously the most popular package for the semiconductor lamp is the TO-18 header which has a diameter of 4.2 mm. This small size allows a high density of indicators to be used where space is at a premium, and since the chip used is normally only 0·5 mm square, considerable further reduction in package diameter is possible.

Extensive use has been made of arrays of gallium phosphide lamps in film-making where information is printed on the film margins during aerial reconnaissance flights. A requirement for small indicators in the cockpits of modern aircraft can also be foreseen.

Compatibility with integrated circuitry.   This is believed, by many people, to be the real advantage of semiconductor lamps over the incandescent lamp. Their speed of operation and electrical characteristics make them ideal for use as indicators with integrated circuits. Coaxial packaging allows them to be mounted directly on to printed circuit boards, so that they could be used as a diagnostic tool in the repair of expensive and complex equipment.

Efficacy.   The inherent capability of high efficacy makes semiconductor lamps attractive to the automobile industry not only as panel indicator lamps, but eventually as possible replacements for rear and brake lamps with the advantages of long life and robustness.

17.3.4   Application to displays

To display an alpha-numeric figure, semiconductors are mounted on ceramic substrates, either in a 5 × 7 array of square dice or by rectangular dice forming a 7-segment array. Fig. 17.3 shows both arrangements. These devices, as with the majority of semiconductor displays, are fabricated from gallium arsenide-phosphide because of the more convenient technology. Moreover, the linear dependence of the emission on the current enables pulsed operation to be used.

(a)   (b)   (c)

Fig. 17.3   Semiconductor alpha-numeric displays
(a) 5 character, 7 × 5 array
(b) 4 character, 7-segment array
(c) Single character, 7-segment array

310

One of the difficulties associated with a semiconductor array is that of energizing the correct diodes to form the required display. To keep leads to the 7×5 array to a minimum (Fig. 17.3a), they have been connected in an X–Y array so that only one column at a time can be energized. This means that the array has to be associated with a purpose-built addressing circuit which scans the array and repeatedly energizes it. A similar technique applies to the 4 characters formed in a 7-segment array shown in Fig. 17.3b. By using only one character on a 14-lead package, as shown in Fig. 17.3c, individual segments can be simultaneously energized which dispenses with the necessity for pulsed operation.

The above types of display have an advantage over the neon discharge numeric displays in that it is possible to drive semiconductor displays with conventional micro-circuits using low voltage d.c. supply. Neon displays on the other hand require a.c. voltage for tube operation. A high luminance and small size of semiconductor displays suggests their possible use in digital clocks and watches.

Future prospects.   A natural development of the present position will be an extension of the range of colours to blue and yellow, and also a gradual increase in the luminous efficacy until these lamps become a serious competitor to all indicator lamps. There will probably be an increasing use of phosphors with the lamps so that the emission will eventually expand from narrow spectral bands to a variety of spectral distributions including white light. As with any new lamp its eventual widespread use will depend upon the economics of mass production in comparison with established lamps.

PART THREE

Luminaires and circuits

18   Electrical circuits for lamps

In previous chapters the electron-atom collision processes leading to the production of light in gas and vapour discharges have been explained and a variety of different lamps using this principle have been described. This chapter considers further the electrical characteristics of the discharge and practical methods used to start and stabilize the different lamps. Circuits and electrical components are described, together with new developments based on semiconductor devices which are used for operating and controlling lamps.

18.1   LAMP CHARACTERISTICS AND CIRCUIT COMPONENTS

18.1.1   Electrical characteristics of lamps

Operation.   Fig. 18.1 shows the relationship between the voltage across and the current through a self-sustaining gas discharge as the direct current is slowly increased from a low value. In the arc discharge region the characteristic has a negative slope due to the cumulative effect of electron-atom collisions producing ionization (Chap. 6): it is in

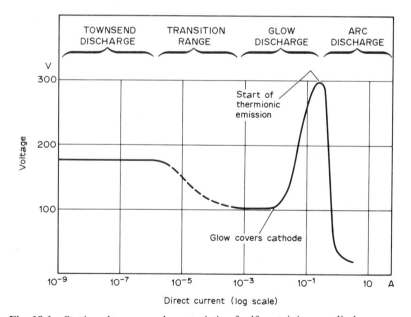

Fig. 18.1   Static volt-ampere characteristic of self-sustaining gas discharge

315

this mode that most discharge lamps operate. To ensure stable operation from a constant voltage supply the negative characteristic must be counterbalanced by a circuit element or component having a positive characteristic. This element is called a stabilizer or ballast.

The r.m.s. voltage-r.m.s. current characteristic of a fluorescent lamp on an a.c. supply is shown in Fig. 18.2, also the characteristic of a choke ballast. The addition of the two voltages, allowing for the phase difference, produces the supply voltage-current

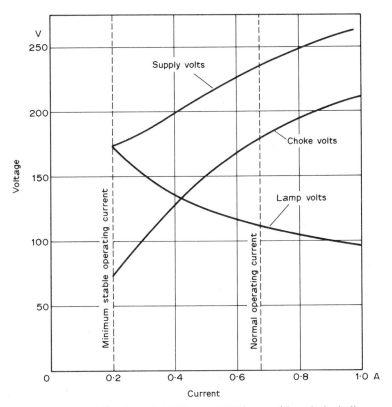

Fig. 18.2 Stabilization of a 1500 mm 65 W lamp with a choke ballast

curve shown. Stable operation of the lamp is obtained when the uppermost curve has a positive slope. It should be noted that the instantaneous value of the supply voltage (or sustaining voltage) must always exceed the instantaneous value of lamp voltage at any instant in the cycle otherwise the discharge will extinguish. This means that all discharge lamps can withstand only a limited drop in supply voltage before operation becomes unstable. This is further discussed in Sect. 18.1.2.

The lamp voltage-current characteristic shown in Fig. 18.2 is non-linear as well as being negative. This is because the effective resistance of the discharge varies with current and hence plasma density (Chap. 6). The non-linear characteristic results in waveform

316

distortion and operation with a sine wave shape current will give a lamp voltage having approximately a square wave shape. For this reason most discharge lamp circuits operated on a.c. take a current having a wave shape which is non-sinusoidal, that is, the input current contains a proportion of harmonics (Sect. 34.1). Because of waveform distortion, the design and evaluation of lamp circuits is complex, and simple equivalent circuit analysis cannot be used; for this reason circuit design is partly theoretical and partly empirical.

At higher operating frequencies the ionization state of the lamp can no longer follow the rapid changes of lamp current during each half cycle and this results in near constant plasma density and constant effective resistance throughout the cycle. The dynamic lamp voltage-current characteristic (Fig. 18.3) therefore tends to become linear as

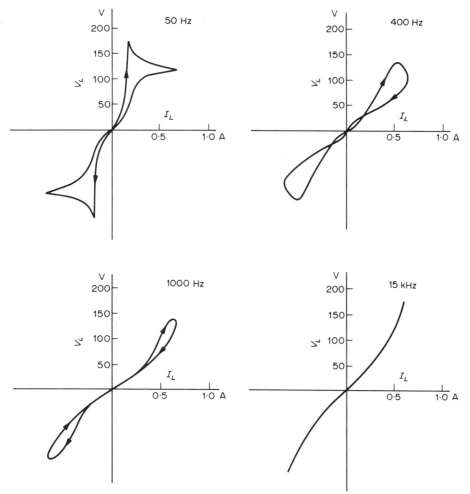

Fig. 18.3   Dynamic volt-ampere characteristics for a 1200 mm 40 W fluorescent lamp operated on various frequencies with a choke ballast

operating frequency is increased, waveform distortion is thereby reduced, and there may be a gain in light output (Fig. 18.17).

Lamp starting.   The process of starting a discharge has been explained in Sect. 6.1, where it was noted that a voltage higher than the normal lamp operating voltage is usually required. To make economical circuits it is often necessary to reduce the required lamp starting voltage by means of starting aids. One or more of the following may be used:

(a) Preheating of the cathodes to produce electron emission
(b) A starting conductor placed on or near the surface of the discharge tube to produce an electric field
(c) An auxiliary starting electrode placed inside the discharge tube close to one of the main electrodes to produce a local glow discharge
(d) Superimposed high voltage pulses to assist breakdown and reduce the r.m.s. starting voltage required from the circuit
(e) Radioactive materials inside the discharge tube to assist ionization and starting.

Lamp starting voltage depends upon a number of external factors; temperature, electric fields, and humidity (Sect. 12.3). To ensure reliable starting the circuit and control gear must be carefully designed and chosen to meet lamp starting requirements and these external ambient conditions. It should be noted that the hot reignition voltage of many high pressure discharge lamps is much greater than the cold starting voltage and it is therefore necessary to wait for these lamps to cool before they can be restarted.

Starter switches.   Starter switches are devices often used to start fluorescent lamps using both methods (a) and (d).

The glow starter switch is cheap, simple and reliable and is used for most fluorescent lamp switch-start circuits. It consists of a small glass bulb (Fig. 18.4) having two bi-metallic contacts and is filled with a mixture of helium, hydrogen and argon at a low pressure and a radioactive material to assist ionization. The bulb is mounted in a small metal or plastic canister which has two connecting pins. The starter switch is fitted into

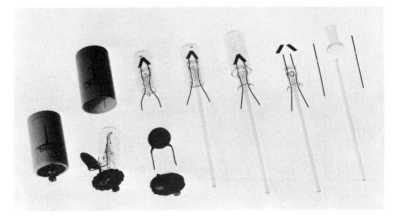

Fig. 18.4   Construction of a glow starter switch

a plastic socket and can easily be removed for replacement. During manufacture the switch is checked to ensure that the contacts will close at minimum lamp starting voltage (the test voltage) and that they do not close at the maximum lamp running voltage (the non-reclosure voltage). The thermal switch starter which has four connecting pins is also sometimes used. The operation of starter switches is described in Sect. 18.2.1.

Lamp run up. Discharge lamps containing metallic vapour require a short period to warm up before full vapour pressure is reached (Chaps. 13, 14, 15), during which time the electrical characteristics of the lamp change. The time of run up depends upon the circuit and the ballast. Fluorescent lamps run up in a very short time and give full light output almost immediately after starting. High pressure lamps require a few minutes run up, during which time the lamp current drops and the lamp voltage increases. Low pressure sodium lamps require about fifteen minutes' run up period, during which time the lamp current increases slightly and the lamp voltage falls. Discharge lamps containing only rare gas require no run up time and the electrical characteristics do not change after starting.

18.1.2 Ballasts

To ensure stable operation, discharge (including fluorescent) lamps must be used in conjunction with ballasts or stabilizers. The prime function of the ballast is to limit lamp operating current to its rated value. In addition the ballast should be efficient, simple, ensure proper lamp starting, have no adverse effect on lamp life, and ensure stable operation over a change in input voltage of $\pm 10\%$.

Stable lamp operation is determined mainly by ensuring the following:

(a) The overall supply current-voltage characteristic must have a positive slope which in turn is usually related to the ratio of lamp voltage to ballast voltage. In a simple series ballast circuit, greatest stability is obtained when the lamp voltage is low and voltage across the ballast is high.

(b) Sufficient sustaining voltage must be available throughout the cycle when the lamp is used on an alternating supply to reignite and maintain lamp operation. A lamp with a high voltage drop may extinguish if sufficient voltage cannot be provided by the circuit at the beginning of each half cycle. It may be noted that lamp reignition voltage is sometimes greater when the arc tube is operated in a horizontal position. Metal halide lamps sometimes exhibit voltage waveform peaks during run up and may extinguish if sufficient sustaining voltage is not available from the ballast circuit.

Resistor ballasts. A simple resistor can be used as a ballast, but the disadvantage of this arrangement is that considerable power is wasted as heat in the resistance and thus overall efficiency is low. The use of a resistor on an alternating supply also results in greater distortion of the current waveform since a delay in reignition causes near-zero current periods at the beginning of each half cycle.

An incandescent filament is used as a ballast for MBT mercury lamps (Sect. 14.3.4). The positive temperature coefficient of resistance of tungsten results in small variations of total power with changes in supply voltage, but changes in supply voltage cause large variations in filament temperature and life. When a filament ballast is used, the ratio of arc voltage to supply voltage must not be too large otherwise difficulties will occur with reignition and extinction may result if the supply voltage drops. In applications where large supply voltage variations occur, MBT or MBTF lamps are unsuitable especially if mounted with the arc tube horizontally.

Choke or inductor ballasts.   A choke has two main functions. It must deliver correct power and current to operate the lamp, and in certain circuits must also allow correct run up or starting electrode preheat current to flow. In addition a choke has to be silent, have a long life, absorb the minimum of power, withstand supply voltage variations, and have no harmful effect on lamp performance or life.

The power loss in a choke is low and the overall circuit efficiency is usually 80% to 95%. Losses occur in the winding due to coil resistance, increasing with ballast temperature, and in the core due to hysteresis and eddy currents.

Like many engineering products, the design of a choke is a compromise between size, shape, performance and cost. The size and weight of a choke is largely determined by its volt-ampere rating and high power lamps operating at high currents require larger chokes. Optimization of choke design involves choosing optimum values for many variable parameters: the large number of mathematical calculations necessary can be carried out by a computer programme. Very often the dimensions of the choke are limited from the outset by the size and shape of the luminaire. It is often necessary to manufacture chokes which have small width and height so that they can easily be mounted in shallow reflectors or channels. Such slim designs confront the ballast designer with a number of problems.

A choke ballast (Fig. 18.5) consists of coils of enamelled copper wire insulated and assembled on to a high permeability core of silicon-iron laminations. The laminations are insulated from each other to reduce eddy current losses in the core. An air gap is provided in the core to obtain satisfactory electrical characteristics and reduce magnetic flux saturation: more than one air gap may be necessary. To improve insulation, electrical strength, thermal conductivity, and to reduce noise level, it is necessary to impregnate the choke with varnish compounds, or alternatively fill the choke with resin or

Fig. 18.5   Construction of a fluorescent lamp choke

bitumen mixtures. Chokes are often enclosed in sheet steel cases or boxes and fitted with terminals or connecting wires.

Chokes are constructed using either a shell type (one coil) or core type (two coil) configuration. Coil windings may be placed transversely or longitudinally in relation to the longest dimension. The coils are wound on plastic bobbins or on formers with layer interleaving. The coil and wire insulating materials determine the permitted rated operating temperature (t_w) of the ballast winding. To improve the space factor of coils and reduce the layer-to-layer electrical stress, some chokes have either 'precision' or 'orthocyclic' windings. With these types of winding the turns of wire are wound very accurately to form a compact coil without layer insulation.

The three basic materials used in choke construction are silicon-iron laminations, enamelled copper wire and insulation, and it is necessary to ensure that these materials are worked within the limits of their capabilities if satisfactory performance is to be obtained. Core flux density and copper current density together with surface area and thermal transfer determine the temperature at which the choke will operate.

Capacitor ballasts. On a 50 Hz supply, capacitors are unsuitable ballasts, since at the beginning of every half cycle the inrush of energy to charge the capacitor causes harmful heavy peak current pulses of short duration through the lamp together with considerable flicker. On higher frequency supplies rapid current fluctuations do not occur and capacitor ballasts can then be used.

Series choke-capacitor ballasts. Although a capacitor cannot be used alone as a lamp ballast on power supply frequencies, a capacitor in series with a choke provides an acceptable ballast arrangement having a number of useful features. The voltages across capacitor and choke differ in phase by nearly 180°; if the capacitive reactance is made about twice the inductive reactance the current waveform is satisfactory even though the resulting ballast impedance is capacitive. The circuit also provides sufficient re-ignition voltage to enable a longer fluorescent lamp with a higher lamp voltage drop to be operated stably. A 2400 mm fluorescent lamp cannot be operated from a 240 V supply with a simple choke ballast, but is satisfactory with a series choke-capacitor ballast. A further feature of this circuit is that it has a nearly constant current characteristic and is therefore less sensitive to variations in supply voltage. It should be noted that the power factor of such circuits has a value about 0·7 leading.

Capacitors. Capacitors consist essentially of two electrically conducting plates or electrodes separated by a thin dielectric insulating material having high permittivity. To form compact capacitors, the electrodes and dielectric are rolled up into a cylinder and usually sealed into a metal case having two connections.

As shown in Table 18.1 several forms of construction are used, and some are impregnated with suitable materials to improve dielectric strength and permittivity. The permitted operating temperature of a capacitor depends on its construction and is usually marked upon the case. It is important to ensure than capacitors are not operated above rated temperature or voltage otherwise life will be shortened. Drastic over-temperature operation will cause local thermal instability and eventual short-circuiting. Capacitors often receive heat from lamps and other components, and care must be taken to keep them as cool as possible.

Table 18.1   Capacitor materials

	Foil type		Metallized type		
Electrodes	Aluminium		Aluminium		Zinc
Dielectric	Paper		Paper	Polypropylene or polycarbonate	
Impregnant	Chlorinated diphenyl liquid	Chlorinated napthalene wax	Mineral oil	None	None

Power losses in capacitors are very small and vary between $0.2\,W/\mu F$ for paper capacitors to $0.05\,W/\mu F$ for plastic film types. To reduce danger from electric shock, capacitors are fitted with discharge resistors so that the terminal voltage is reduced to less than 50 V one minute after switching off. Some capacitors are fitted with internal fuses to give protection against internal failure, the case then being marked 'F' or 'fuse fitted'.

Leakage-reactance transformer ballasts.   Normal a.c. supply voltages are not sufficient to start and operate certain types of lamp. A transformer is therefore required to step up the voltage to a suitable value. The ballast impedance required to stabilize the lamp can often be incorporated in the transformer design by deliberately introducing leakage reactance. Such a device is known as a 'stray-field' or 'leakage-reactance' transformer.

In a power transformer, the voltage and current taken by a load connected to the secondary winding is transformed or reflected into corresponding volts × amps which have to be supplied to the primary winding. This transfer of energy from one winding to another can simply be considered as taking place through the magnetic field which links the two separate windings. In a conventional transformer the mutual magnetic field which links both windings must be kept as high as possible so that maximum energy is transferred. For this reason an iron core is provided to increase and guide the magnetic flux and the two windings are placed close together so that the same flux links both.

In the leakage-reactance transformer (Fig. 18.6) mutual magnetic flux linking the two windings is deliberately reduced, and only a limited amount of energy is allowed to be transferred to the load. In order to reduce the mutual flux and increase leakage flux the two separate coils are spaced apart and sometimes magnetic shunts are used to provide an easy path for the flow of leakage fluxes. Flux which links only one winding and does not therefore contribute to transfer of energy is known as leakage flux. As a load is taken from the transformer, leakage flux associated with primary and secondary coils increases and output voltage drops. The output characteristic (Fig. 18.6) of a leakage-reactance transformer depends upon the leakage coefficient which is defined as the ratio of Xsc to Xoc. Xsc is the total short circuit leakage reactance, obtained by short-circuiting the secondary coil and allowing rated current to flow in the primary coil; Xoc is the open-circuit reactance measured on the primary side. The primary and secondary windings of leakage reactance transformers are sometimes auto-connected.

Ballast noise.   Any electromagnetic device such as a transformer or ballast operating

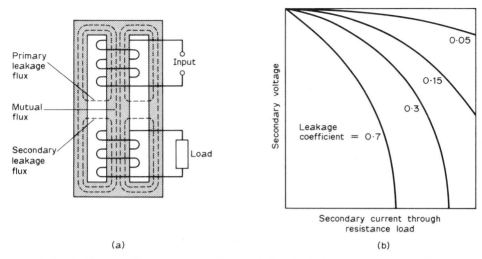

Fig. 18.6   Construction and output characteristics of a leakage-reactance transformer

on alternating current is inherently noisy, to a degree depending upon its size and design. Lamp voltage waveforms contain harmonic components ranging from 100 Hz up to 3000 Hz or more, so that ballast noise may vary from a low pitched hum to a high pitched 'rustle'. Noise can be generated in several ways: by cyclic magnetostrictive changes in the dimensions of the core, by vibration of the core and by stray magnetic fields causing vibration of the ballast case or even of the luminaire in which the ballast is mounted.

Magnetostriction noise cannot be entirely eliminated but it can be reduced by using short magnetic circuits and avoiding high flux densities and uneven flux distribution in the core. It follows, therefore, that units such as leakage-reactance transformers and some kinds of ballast which rely upon special core configurations and flux distributions must be more noisy than simple chokes. In general, ballast noise tends to be amplified by the luminaire. To minimize this effect, control gear should be securely fastened and luminaires designed without loose parts which might vibrate. Mounting luminaires on thin panels or boards which may act as sounding boards is best avoided.

The ambient noise level of the location in which the luminaire is used should dictate the level of noise from the luminaire that can be tolerated (Chap. 21). The British Standard Specification (BS 2818) requires the choke to be suspended in an echo-free chamber and readings to be taken at various positions at a distance of 25 mm from the surface of the ballast: the r.m.s. summation of the noise levels measured must not exceed 30 dBA. Various proposals have been made for alternative test methods and specifications involving a system of ballast noise grading.

Temperature limitations.   The insulation materials used in choke and ballast construction slowly deteriorate at an increasing rate as temperature is increased. To obtain satisfactory life it is necessary to place upper limits on the permitted operating temperature of the windings.

323

The relationship between temperature and life is

$$L = Ke^{\frac{D}{T}}$$

where L = Life of the insulation system,
         T = Absolute temperature of the insulation
         D = Constant which depends on the insulation materials
         K = Constant which depends upon the units chosen and insulation materials

If $1/T$ is plotted against log L, a straight line relationship is formed between life and temperature. This relationship is shown, with the ordinate converted to degrees Celsius and inverted, in Fig. 18.7.

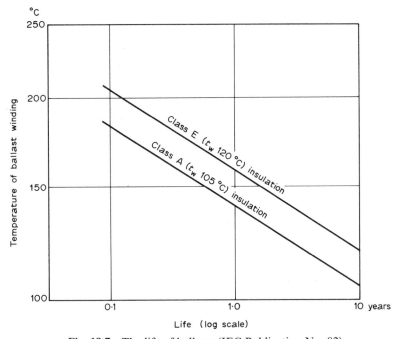

Fig. 18.7   The life of ballasts (IEC Publication No. 82)

If chokes are endurance tested for a short time at an elevated temperature, it is possible by extrapolation to predict the working temperature which will give a continuous life of 10 years. The permitted working temperature of a ballast winding is designated t_w and this value forms the basis for thermal tests on luminaires to IEC Specifications 82 and 162 (Chap. 19). Various values of t_w may be obtained by using insulating materials with different thermal ratings.

It should be noted that the enclosure of fluorescent lamps inside diffusers will considerably increase lamp temperature, and this in turn will reduce light output and increase lamp and ballast current. Unfortunately this aggravates the heating problem still further, and luminaire designers must use care and ingenuity in locating and mounting control gear to ensure acceptable ballast temperatures.

The normal temperature rise of a ballast winding (under specified test conditions) is designated Δt; the margin of heating permissible when the ballast is built into a luminaire is indicated by the amount its t_w value minus the room ambient temperature exceeds its Δt value.

18.1.3   Power factor correction and radio interference

Power factor is defined for sine wave shapes as the ratio watts/volts × amps. A low value of power factor is undesirable for the following reasons:

(a) It unnecessarily increases the kVA demand from the supply.
(b) The useful load that can be handled by cables and wiring accessories is reduced.
(c) Special tariffs and penalties may be imposed on the consumer taking a load with a low lagging power factor.

All lamp circuits using chokes (Fig. 18.8a) or leakage-reactance transformer ballasts have a low lagging power factor, usually between 0·3 and 0·5.

A lagging power factor can be corrected quite simply by connecting a suitable capacitor in shunt across the a.c. supply. The capacitor takes a current which is leading in phase, and this partly cancels the lagging current taken by the lamp circuit. Fig. 18.8b shows the vector diagram of a lamp circuit in which the shunt capacitor improves the power factor from 0·5 to 0·85 lagging and reduces the supply current by 40%.

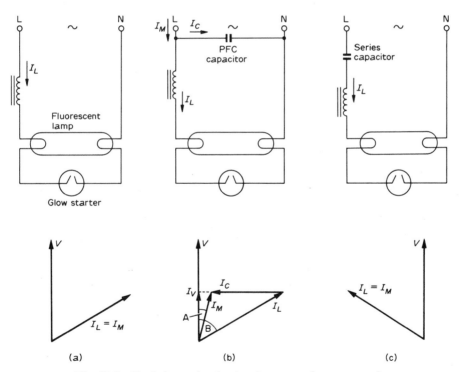

Fig. 18.8   Single lamp circuits showing power factor correction

The shunt capacitor value necessary to obtain a required power factor can be calculated as follows:

In Fig. 18.8b. V = supply voltage I_M = supply current
          W = load power in watts I_C = capacitor current
          I_L = lamp current f = supply frequency
          I_v = useful or active component of load current
     cos A = required corrected power factor
     cos B = uncorrected power factor of load (lagging)

$$I_v = \frac{W}{V}, I_C = I_v(\tan B - \tan A) \quad \text{and} \quad C = \frac{I_C \times 10^6}{2\pi f V} \, \mu F$$

Combining these three equations:

$$C \text{ (in microfarads)} = \frac{W}{V}(\tan B - \tan A)\frac{10^6}{2\pi f V}$$

$$= \frac{W(\tan B - \tan A)\,10^6}{2\pi f V^2}$$

and for 50 Hz the required capacity in μF to correct power factor

$$= \frac{3180\,W\,(\tan B - \tan A)}{V^2}$$

If the lamp and choke in Fig. 18.8b take a total power of 80 W from a 240 V supply at a power factor cos $B = 0.5$, the capacitor needed to correct the power factor to cos $A = 0.85$ is

$$\frac{3180 \times 80 \times (1.732 - 0.620)}{240 \times 240} = 4.9 \, \mu F$$

Another way of changing the power factor of a lamp circuit is to connect a suitable capacitor in series with a choke ballast: a vector diagram is shown in Fig. 18.8c.

If a choke controlled circuit with a lagging power factor of 0.5 is combined with a series capacitor circuit operating at a leading power factor of 0.5 the overall power factor of the two circuits will be nearly unity. This arrangement is called a lead-lag twin circuit.

In UK it is usual to correct lamp circuits to give a power factor of 0.85, but circuits below 30 W rating are often uncorrected. It is possible to obtain higher power factors by increasing the size of the capacitor but this is not usually justified.

The harmonic distortion of the supply current waveform has an important effect upon the power factor obtainable. This is because on a supply with a sinusoidal voltage waveform the power factor capacitor can only correct or compensate the fundamental component of the lamp circuit current waveform: the harmonic components in a distorted current waveform cannot be corrected or reduced by the capacitor current. Table 18.2 shows how the maximum possible power factor is related to the percentage of harmonic distortion in the current waveform. In some sodium lamp circuits it is impossible to obtain a power factor greater than 0.85.

Table 18.2 Relationship between maximum possible supply power factor and percentage of current harmonics

Current harmonics as per cent of fundamental	0	33	48	62	75
Maximum possible power factor	1·0	0·95	0·90	0·85	0·80

When a capacitor is switched on to an a.c. supply, a momentary inrush current will flow for a few microseconds. The magnitude of the inrush current is limited only by the impedance of supply at the capacitor terminals and may be as high as several hundred amperes if the circuit is switched on at the peak of the voltage wave. Care must be taken with selection of fuses to ensure that this high surge of current does not blow the fuse in the capacitor or the luminaire. Switching transients and harmonic distortion are both discussed further in Sect. 34.1.2.

Radio frequency interference. Discharge (including fluorescent) lamps, particularly towards the end of their life, generate radio noise signals which may interfere with radio and television reception. The r.f. interference signal is modulated at twice the power supply frequency and this causes a low pitched hum in the loudspeaker.

Lamps cause interference over a wide frequency spectrum from 100 kHz to 10 MHz covering the long, medium and short wave broadcasting bands. Interference reaches the radio receiver by four paths:

(a) By direct radiation from the lamp to the aerial.
(b) By conduction along the mains wiring to the receiver.
(c) By conduction along the mains wiring and subsequent radiation to the aerial.
(d) By radiation to, conduction along, and then re-radiation from wires, etc., not directly connected to the lamp.

In practice most interference is caused by route (c) and is reduced by small suppressor capacitors often fitted in starter switches and lamp circuits as an integral part of the control gear. In troublesome cases interferences can be reduced by fitting r.f. line filters in the supply or by repositioning the radio aerial. Chokes with two symmetrical windings are used where a low level of mains-borne interference is required, particularly on systems without an earthed neutral. To reduce direct interference by route (a) an earthed mesh screen may be fitted round the lamp, but this is only necessary when sensitive apparatus is within a few metres of the lamp.

Phase controlled dimmer circuits using semi-conductor devices may also cause r.f. interference even when used with incandescent lamps.

18.2 FLUORESCENT LAMP CIRCUITS

As noted in Chap. 12, many types of fluorescent lamp are available and many different circuits are used. Lamps can be divided into three broad categories. Preheat types with high resistance (HR) cathodes, preheat types with low resistance (LR) cathodes and cold-start types with instant-start (IS) cathodes. Circuits for these lamps can be divided into three types:

(a) Switch-start circuits, which provide preheat for the cathodes (HR or LR).
(b) Resonant-start circuits, which also provide preheat (HR or LR).
(c) Transformer circuits which fall into two groups; one group providing preheat (Quickstart circuits for lamps with HR cathodes, rapid-start circuits for lamps with LR cathodes) and the other group for cold-start lamps (instant-start circuits for lamps with IS cathodes, straightforward transformer circuits for cold cathode lamps).

18.2.1   Switch-start circuits

Glow starter switch circuit.   Fig. 18.4 has shown the construction of a glow starter switch: the upper part of Fig. 18.9 shows its operation during the starting period.

V_S is the striking voltage needed to start the lamp.
V_L is the voltage available across the lamp for starting.
I_L is the lamp operating current.
I_H is the current through the cathodes or heaters.
T_H is the time during which cathode preheating current flows.
T_T is the total time needed to start the lamp.

The bimetal contacts of the glow switch are separated by a small gap and when the circuit is energized the supply voltage is sufficient to initiate a glow discharge through the gas filling: this slowly heats the contacts and they bend towards each other due to the differential expansion of two metals. When the contacts touch, after one or two seconds, a series circuit is made through the choke and the lamp electrodes and a relatively heavy current (preheat) rapidly warms the cathodes to red heat for a time T_H. When the bimetal contacts touch the glow discharge is extinguished since there is no voltage between the contacts. The contacts now begin to cool and after a short interval they spring apart and open the main series circuit. Because the circuit is highly inductive, a high voltage pulse of between 800 V and 1500 V lasting for about a millisecond is produced across the ends of the lamp.

The pulse rapidly ionizes the gas and vapour filling inside the lamp and a current flows between opposite emissive electrodes. The voltage between the ends of the lamp in the running condition is now reduced and is not sufficient to reignite the glow in the switch. Thus, the glow starter switch consumes no current or power when the lamp is running. If the switch opens near the zero part of the alternating cycle very little back e.m.f. will be produced and the switch will automatically make a second attempt to start the lamp.

When a lamp fails at the end of life the cathodes may remain intact but have insufficient emission to maintain the arc current. Under these conditions the glow starter will continuously attempt to start the lamp, causing flashing and blinking until the starter itself fails.

Thermal starter switch circuit.   The central part of Fig. 18.9 shows a second type of circuit also using an automatic starter switch. The thermal starter switch has bimetal

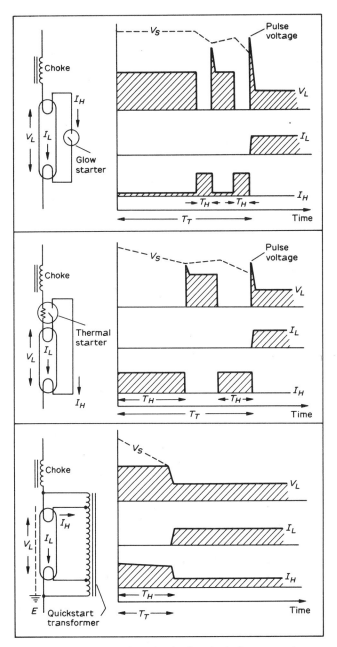

Fig. 18.9 Three starting circuits for single fluorescent lamps

contacts which are actuated by heat from a small resistance heater coil. The contacts are normally closed and are kept open during lamp operation by flow of current through the heater coil. The starter is housed in a canister having 4 connecting pins.

18.2.2   Resonant-start circuits

The necessary preheat current and starting voltage obtained in switch-start circuits can also be obtained from resonant circuits using combinations of inductance and capacitance. Such circuits are often economical since the capacitor can also be used to correct power factor. Some circuits of this type do not produce voltage pulses to assist starting and it is often necessary to provide an additional starting aid in the form of an earthed conductor placed on or near the outside of the glass tube of the lamp in order to create a high potential gradient between one cathode and earth: this assists ionization and starting. The earthed metal reflector or channel of the luminaire serves this purpose. It is also necessary to ensure that circuits of this type are used on single-phase a.c. supplies having an earthed neutral.

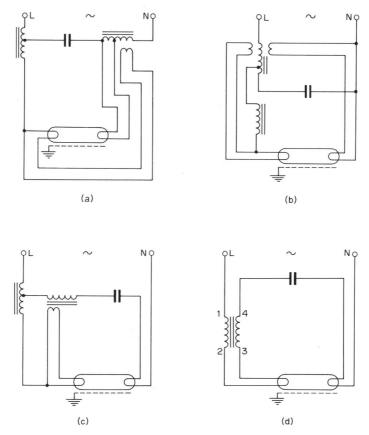

Fig. 18.10   Resonant-start circuits for fluorescent lamps

There are three main types of resonant start circuits for fluorescent lamps:

(a) The single choke type, in which a capacitor is connected to a tapping on the choke. This enables a step-up of starting voltage to be obtained, and preheat current can be provided for the cathodes from windings on a separate transformer (Fig. 18.10a).

(b) The twin choke type, in which resonance between one choke and the capacitor produces a high voltage for starting and the second choke is used as a ballast (Fig. 18.10b). Cathode preheat is obtained from windings on the first choke. Several variations of this circuit are possible by rearrangement of the two chokes and the tappings thereon (18.10c). These circuits usually have very low supply current harmonic distortion.

(c) The semi-resonant type (SRS) which has a single choke ballast with an additional over-winding in opposition to the main winding. Both windings are connected in a series circuit with the two lamp electrodes and a capacitor (Fig. 18.10d). The two windings on the ballast may be either tightly or loosely magnetically coupled. The latter arrangement usually gives lower harmonic distortion but is more difficult and costly to manufacture.

When the SRS circuit is switched on the lamp cathodes are preheated by a current through the series circuit. The preheat current does not depend upon the cathode resistance and so the SRS circuit can be used with lamps having either LR or HR cathodes. The starting voltage across the lamp is the vector sum of capacitor and over-winding voltages: this is usually higher than the input supply voltage.

When the lamp has started the main winding acts as a ballast to stabilize the lamp and the over-winding carries a capacitive current which corrects the overall power factor. The current through the main winding is thus the vector sum of lamp current and capacitor current. SRS circuits are widely used for operating single fluorescent lamps on a 220/240 V a.c. supply and give satisfactory starting without the need for a starter switch.

18.2.3 Transformer-start circuits

Cathode-preheat lamps. The lower part of Fig. 18.9 shows the operation of the Quickstart circuit used for operating lamps with HR cathodes (lamp types MCFA/U, MCFE/U, MCFR/U). As in some resonant-start circuits, an earthed starting aid is required near the lamp. A feature of the Quickstart transformer circuit is that cathode voltage and heating are reduced after the lamp has started and the transformer only consumes a small amount of power.

The basic Quickstart circuit is shown in Fig. 18.11a. A rearrangement of the cathode heating windings on the transformer as in Fig. 18.11b enables a step up of starting voltage to be obtained. A further modification in Fig. 18.11c enables two short fluorescent lamps to be operated in series.

Lamps with LR cathodes are widely used in America in rapid-start transformer circuits. Fig. 18.12a shows a single-lamp circuit using a small heater transformer connected directly to the supply. It should be noted that the cathode voltage does not drop after a lamp has started. Fig. 18.12b shows a twin-lamp circuit using a leakage reactance auto-transformer with heater windings supplying 3·6 V to each lamp cathode. A series capacitor is included to enable the transformer to operate with a high ratio of lamp

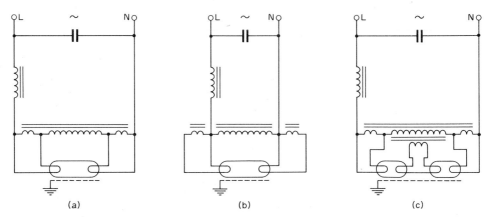

Fig. 18.11   Quickstart transformer circuits for fluorescent lamps

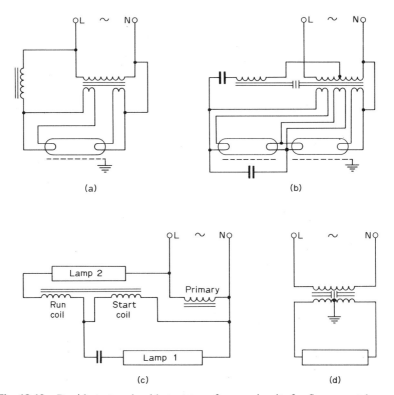

Fig. 18.12   Rapid-start and cold-start transformer circuits for fluorescent lamps

voltage to open circuit voltage. The leading power factor of the capacitor compensates for the lagging current otherwise taken by the transformer primary. Air gaps have to be provided in the core under the secondary winding to prevent undue flux saturation and waveform distortion. Such circuits are widely used in USA for RS, VHO and Power-groove lamps, and enable compact ballast units to be provided.

Cold-start lamps.   Some fluorescent lamps (Slimline, MCFB/U, TL-X, TL-S) have cathodes which do not require preheat before starting. These lamps are therefore cold-started with a high potential usually supplied from a leakage-reactance transformer. Fig. 18.12c shows a twin Slimline lamp circuit using a special leakage reactance transformer which has three coil windings. The start coil provides a high voltage to start each lamp in sequence. The lamps are stabilized by the reactance of the run coil and the series capacitor.

Some low pressure discharge tubes used for lighting and 'neon-signs' have large hollow cylindrical cold cathodes. These lamps must again be cold-started, and require a very high voltage which is provided from leakage-reactance transformers. As shown in Fig. 18.12d the transformer has isolated windings, and the centre tap of the output is usually earthed for safety. The cold cathode lamp usually operates at low current, about 120 mA. Suitable safety precautions must be taken with these circuits, since the output voltage usually exceeds 1000 V.

18.3   DISCHARGE LAMP CIRCUITS

18.3.1   Sodium lamp circuits

Low-pressure sodium lamps (Chap. 13) are cold-started, using an applied voltage of 460 V to 650 V supplied from leakage-reactance autotransformers. A typical circuit is shown in Fig. 18.13a. Because the ratio of lamp voltage to open-circuit voltage is low, most sodium lamp circuits have a low lagging power factor of 0·3 to 0·4 and this is corrected by connecting a large capacitor across the supply input. It should be noted that the operating current of 35 W and 55 W SOX lamps is similar and these two lamps can be used on the same ballast. A similar situation exists with the 135 W and 180 W SOX lamps and with the 140 W SLI and 90 W SOX lamps. The maximum permissible time for momentary interruption of the electrical supply to prevent extinction of low pressure sodium lamps is between about 6 ms and 15 ms: reignition of a hot lamp takes place within one minute.

High pressure sodium lamps have similar operating electrical characteristics to the long-established high pressure mercury lamp but the more rapid de-ionization gives a delay in reignition every half cycle and leads to a poorer lamp power factor and a lower arc tube voltage than with high pressure mercury lamps: a much higher voltage is required for starting. The lamp can be choke-ballasted but requires (at present) an additional starting device to provide high voltage, low energy, starting pulses. Mechanical-type starter switches can be used, but electronic solid-state starters are often preferred. Fig. 18.13 shows three high pressure sodium lamp (SON) circuits using electronic ignitors. High voltage pulses are produced once or twice per cycle by the sudden charge or discharge of a small capacitor into the primary winding of a pulse coil via a semiconductor switching device which is controlled by a trigger circuit. The high voltage

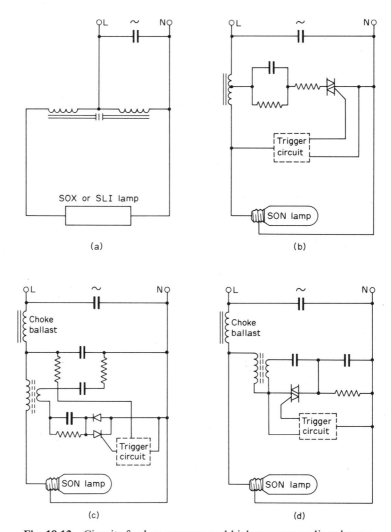

Fig. 18.13 Circuits for low pressure and high pressure sodium lamps

generated in the secondary winding is applied to the lamp terminals to ensure starting. In Fig. 18.13b the main choke is used as a pulse coil and its high inductance enables high energy pulses to be obtained. In Fig. 18.13c the pulse is generated in a series-connected pulse transformer and in Fig. 18.13d a small parallel-connected transformer is used to generate the starting pulse voltage. The ignitor circuits stop working after the lamp has started because of the reduced voltages on the trigger circuits.

With all circuits the high frequency starting pulse is reduced or attenuated by the stray capacity of the wiring between the ignitor and the lamp: an upper limit for the length of wiring is therefore usually specified. Reignition of a hot lamp takes place within

1 minute. The maximum permissible time for interruption of the electrical supply to prevent extinction of high pressure sodium lamps is 10 ms to 12 ms. The shell or screw thread of the lamp cap should always be connected to neutral because of the high voltage pulses on the line side.

18.3.2   Mercury lamp circuits

Mercury lamps (Chap. 14) can be divided into high pressure and very high pressure types.

European high pressure lamps (types MA, MB) have lamp voltages between 110 V and 135 V and are usually designed to start and operate on a 220/250 V a.c. supply using a choke ballast. The circuit shown in Fig. 18.14a is simple, efficient and of low cost. Choke ballasts for use out of doors have drip-proof construction and are cubic in shape to reduce power losses. Some American lamps require higher circuit voltages which are usually obtained from leakage-reactance transformer ballasts. All lamps have built-in starting electrodes. The lamp starting voltage increases at low temperature.

On a 220/240 V supply the maximum permissible time for interruption of the electrical supply to prevent extinction of MB lamps is 10 ms to 15 ms. Lamps must cool for at least 5 min before they will re-ignite. Circuits are normally designed to only allow about 15% reduction in supply voltage before instability and extinction occur. Towards the end of life mercury lamps may tend to rectify during starting and cause higher surge starting currents lasting a few cycles. Where cable ratings are adequate it is recommended that fuses rated at 2 or 3 times the normal steady running current should be used to allow for starting conditions.

Lower wattage mercury lamps may generate perceptible 50 Hz flicker (Sect. 14.3.2). This can be eliminated by operating the lamps on d.c. using a simple silicon bridge rectifier in conjunction with a normal choke ballast, or by operating the lamp on a.c. in a series choke-capacitor circuit.

Very high pressure mercury lamps (types ME, HBO) have short arc length and low arc voltage. They are available in 50 W to 1000 W ratings and may be operated on d.c. or a.c. supply in conjunction with appropriate control gear. Some lamp types require starting circuits and components in addition to the ballast. For a.c. operation the lamps are operated from a 200/250 V supply using choke ballasts. For d.c. operation a resistor ballast is required, and an increased voltage is required for lamp starting. It is possible to operate some lamps on d.c. by using choke-bridge rectifier circuits fed from a.c. supply. When used on d.c. supply it is important to ensure that the lamp electrodes are connected to the correct polarity. Type MD lamps operate on an a.c. supply from a leakage reactance transformer giving about 1000 V for starting.

18.3.3   Metal halide and xenon lamp circuits

Metal halide discharge lamps have similar electrical characteristics to high pressure mercury lamps but require higher voltages for starting. During run up, high reignition lamp voltage peaks can occur, and the lamps will extinguish if insufficient sustaining voltage is provided by the ballast circuits.

Circuits for operating the 400 W MBI lamp are shown in Fig. 18.14b to d. The additional starting voltage is obtained from transformers, from resonant circuits or from

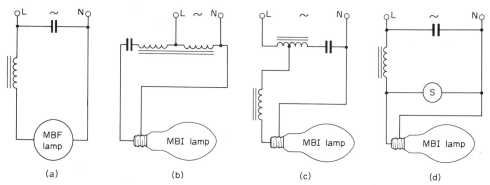

Fig. 18.14   Circuits for high pressure mercury and metal halide lamps

switching devices which produce transient or regular pulses. The voltage pulses must have high energy to enable the transition from glow to arc discharge to be made quickly.

At the present time, circuits have not been finalized and it is likely that future lamp and circuit development may enable metal halide lamps to start and operate on normal mercury lamp control gear.

Compact source iodide lamps are operated at high pressure and have short arc length and low arc voltage. They can be operated on a.c. circuits using choke ballasts, but require pulses of up to 9 kV to ensure satisfactory starting. The pulses are obtained from a vibrator circuit in conjunction with a series connected ferrite-cored pulse transformer.

Xenon lamps have very high gas pressures and require extra high voltages to start. The control gear required is very large and expensive. The high starting voltage is obtained from high frequency spark-gap oscillator circuits. Lamps for an a.c. supply use heavy-current choke ballasts; lamps for d.c. use resistor ballasts or choke-bridge rectifier units. Some xenon lamps are flashed or pulsed at a repetitive frequency from special circuits (Chap. 15).

18.4   SOLID STATE CONTROLLERS

18.4.1   Lamp dimming

A number of methods can be used to dim an incandescent lamp on an a.c. supply:

(a) A variable resistor connected in series with the lamp. This method is inefficient and requires a large graded resistor having moving parts.

(b) A variable inductor (transductor) connected in series with the lamp having d.c. control windings which are used to vary the flux saturation of a magnetic core. This method is more efficient, but the components are large and expensive if a wide dimming range is required.

(c) A variable autotransformer having a commutator track from which the output voltage can be varied by a movable carbon brush which is driven through a mechanical clutch by a variable speed electric motor. This method is efficient but has now been superseded by electronic thyristor dimmers.

(d) A solid state semiconductor switch connected in series with the lamp to give phase control dimming so that the conducting period of each half cycle of the lamp current can be varied.

This last method is now widely used and gives high efficiency and compact dimming equipment. Fig. 18.15 shows the circuit of a small domestic dimmer switch for lighting.

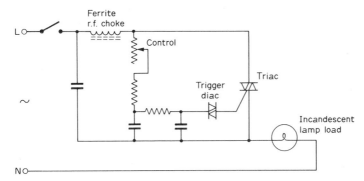

Fig. 18.15 Circuit for a small domestic dimmer switch having 85% conduction period, used to control up to 500 W lamp load

The Triac is a silicon semiconductor device which can be made to conduct between its main terminals when a small positive or negative control current is fed into a third 'gate' terminal. The device can only be restored to its off (blocking) state by externally reducing the load current to zero. In an a.c. circuit this is achieved automatically twice each cycle at each zero of the load current. The on (conducting) period is controlled and varied by a phase control circuit in which the application of a gate signal is delayed by a solid state four layer trigger device known as a Diac. This device conducts only when the potential across it exceeds a certain value.

In simple circuits of this kind only a limited phase angle conduction period is obtained and full control is not possible. Modifications to the trigger circuit and the use of two thyristors connected in reverse parallel enables better performance to be obtained. Solid state dimmer circuits of this type generate r.f. interference due to the fast rise time of applied voltage every half cycle, and special suppression filters may be necessary.

Hot cathode preheat fluorescent lamps can be dimmed using phase control if the control gear is modified. It is necessary to heat the lamp cathodes continuously from windings on a small heater transformer and provide an additional starting voltage pulse at each half cycle through the series choke ballast to assist reignition and obtain a wide dimming range. Power factor correction capacitors must not be connected to the output side of the semiconductor dimmer.

Photoelectric control. There are many applications, street lighting for example, where lamps are only required to be switched on during hours of darkness. Switching control can be automatically obtained by using photoelectric relays. In these devices, the switch contacts are actuated by a small cadmium sulphide cell which is light-sensitive. Small plug-in photoelectric relays are available to handle currents up to 10 A and are usually fitted on the top of each lantern.

337

18.4.2   Solid state ballasts and inverters

The advent of semiconductor devices has led to the consideration of new methods and new circuits to operate discharge lamps. The conventional ballast can be replaced by a transistor chopper circuit in which lamp current is regulated to a constant average value by controlled switching at high frequency through the action of a single power transistor. The new circuits are expected to be smaller, more efficient, give better lamp stability and eliminate flicker. At present these circuits are costly and introduce power supply waveform distortion but future development may overcome these problems.

Transport and portable lighting.   The high efficiency, long life and more uniform illumination provided by fluorescent lamps make this form of lighting as attractive for the interiors of vehicles, aircraft, ships and trains as it is for the interiors of buildings. The electrical supply available for such applications is usually low voltage d.c. from a battery and to operate fluorescent lamps it is necessary to convert the d.c supply into an a.c. supply at a higher voltage. Semiconductor inverters are used for this. The output frequency is often made higher than 50 Hz to achieve improvements in inverter performance, size and cost. Battery drain is an important consideration and the light output per unit current drain from the battery is three or four times higher for inverter-driven fluorescent lamps than for filament lamps.

Group or bulk inverters.   In this type of system the low voltage d.c. from the battery is converted into a.c. at a frequency of 400 Hz to 3000 Hz or more by a large central transistor or thyristor inverter. This supplies individual fluorescent lamp circuits and luminaires, which are provided with starterless ballasts adapted for high frequency operation. A typical bulk inverter used on British Rail operates at 1100 Hz and drives six 40 W fluorescent lamps from a 24 V battery.

Individual inverters.   In this system the d.c. battery voltage is fed to each fluorescent lamp luminaire which contains a small transistor inverter operating at 5 kHz to 20 kHz and feeding a built-in ballast for each lamp.

There are two basic small inverter circuits each using a single transistor:

(a) Class C inverter giving a sine wave output.
(b) Blocking oscillator inverter giving a quasi-square wave output.

Fig. 18.16 shows a simple class C inverter circuit to operate a small fluorescent lamp from an 11 V to 15 V battery. Such a circuit has an efficiency of about 60% and is inaudible because of the high operating frequency, usually 20 kHz. Other inverter circuits are available to operate fluorescent lamps of rating between 4 W and 40 W on d.c. supplies up to 200 V.

The operation of the circuit is as follows: transistor VT_1, which acts as a switch, is driven by a feedback winding on the transformer T_1, Automatic base biasing is derived from capacitor C_3, and the rectifying action of the emitter-base junction of VT_1 builds up a charge on C_3 which is allowed to leak away via starting resistor R_1. VT_1 switches on and excites the resonant circuit formed by the primary winding and the parallel tuning capacitor C_2. This forms an oscillatory circuit which generates sine wave shape high frequency oscillations. The loosely coupled secondary winding on the transformer

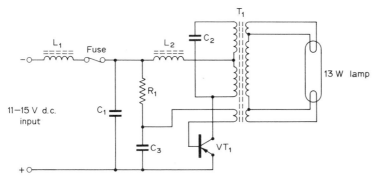

Fig. 18.16   Inverter circuit for operating a small fluorescent lamp from a battery

has two cathode heating windings and provides a high voltage to start the lamp. When the lamp starts, the secondary voltage falls due to leakage reactance, thus stabilizing lamp current. The charging choke L_2 limits the in-rush current to the capacitor and enables the transistor to function more efficiently as a switch. The filter choke L_1 and smoothing capacitor C_1 serve to limit transient interference.

Emergency lighting.   To overcome a power supply failure in public buildings, shops, etc., a d.c. battery supply can be used to drive bulk or individual inverters to supply emergency power for fluorescent lighting. Automatic changeover switching can be arranged so that the emergency system is immediately operated when power supply

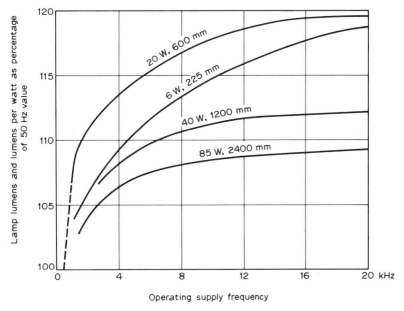

Fig. 18.17   High frequency characteristic of fluorescent lamps for sine wave current

failure occurs. Several different emergency lighting systems are available and the choice depends upon individual economic and technical factors.

High frequency lighting.   Large thyristor inverters are now available to convert 50 Hz power into 3 kHz to 5 kHz power, and future operation of large fluorescent lighting installations on a high frequency supply may become attractive if an overall cost saving can be made. The advantages of high frequency lighting are:

(a) Lamps operate more efficiently (Fig. 18.17).
(b) Control gear is smaller, cheaper and more efficient.
(c) Lamp flicker is negligible.
(d) The total heat from a lighting system is reduced, thereby reducing the load on air conditioning equipment.

Suitable thyristors to handle 10 kW of high frequency power are now available and new circuit techniques enable three-phase 50 Hz power to be converted into single-phase high frequency power without an output transformer. It is likely that high frequency lighting will be used in future for large industrial buildings where the additional expense of inverter equipment is more than offset by the lower cost of luminaires and lower electricity costs due to higher efficiency. A number of trial installations are already working.

19 Design and manufacture of luminaires

Luminaires can be divided into two categories: those which are essentially decorative and those which are essentially functional.

Decorative luminaires are usually in the form of an assembly of decorative components around a light source, ranging from a simple pendant to the large, one-off, prestige chandelier for a building entrance.

Functional luminaires are those where the light needs to be controlled to meet the high efficiency and low glare requirements necessary in commercial fluorescent luminaires, street lanterns, interior and exterior floodlights and display units.

In this chapter those aspects of design and manufacture (design procedure, specification and testing, materials and production processes) which apply to both categories of luminaire are examined, leaving the optical design of functional luminaires to be discussed in Chap 20.

19.1 DESIGN PROCEDURE

An important attribute of any product is its appearance: a good appearance is achieved by assessing the functional requirements and integrating them with the aesthetic requirements. Whether the appearance is good or bad is dictated by a variety of factors: shape, colour, a sense of completeness and balance. A good appearance can create confidence and acceptance of a product. If the first impression is good, a user will be disappointed if the performance is found to be inferior, but a faulty appearance may lead a prospective user to expect a poor performance. From this it can be deduced that the appearance should be a true expression of the function and quality of the product; it tells us what the object is and how well it is likely to perform.

19.1.1 Design function and plan

There are four main design functions requiring integration in the design of any luminaire:

(a) Industrial design: the creation of a design suitable for the most efficient means of manufacture at the lowest cost consistent with the required quality.
(b) Optical design: the means of controlling light into the required zones at the maximum efficiency.
(c) Technical design: the technology of materials, techniques and machines.
(d) Mechanical design: the assembly of technological requirements into a working function.

The tungsten halogen floodlight shown in Fig. 19.1 exemplifies well the integration of these four functions. The early involvement of optical designers in the project (Sect.

Fig. 19.1   Haline floodlight

20.3.1) led to the realizable concept of using an extruded aluminium section as both body and reflector. This enabled a very accurate contour to be maintained and produced a unit which is both attractive and economical.

It is very difficult to abide by a set procedure for designing any luminaire but Fig. 19.2 indicates the general plan that is followed. In certain projects some of these stages will be undertaken concurrently; in some cases they will be consecutive; in others there will be a series of overlapping recurrent events leading towards a final solution. It follows therefore that there must be constant communication between the designer and those concerned with the other aspects as work proceeds.

The first requirement for a designer is that he takes a logical approach to problem solving and this must be supported by a capacity for intuitive judgment. A great deal of muddled thinking is responsible for what is an impracticable approach to a design problem: a great deal of time and money can be spent finding relatively useless solutions. The product design problem includes everything appertaining to the product, ranging from market information, invention, cost and manufacture, through to packaging and literature.

19.1.2   Design concept and brief

The designer should have a clear idea of the use for which the luminaire is required and the conditions which will apply to its manufacture. There is usually a choice of manufacturing methods which must be matched to the resources available and also to the

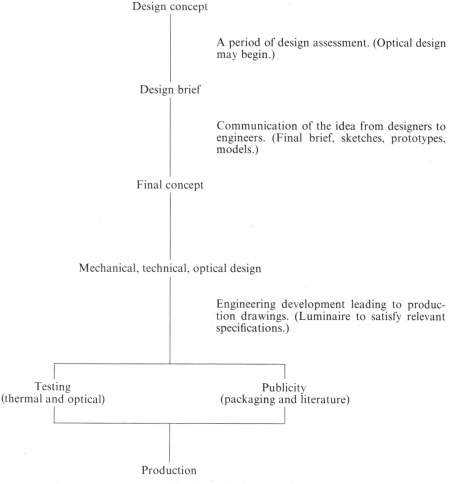

Fig. 19.2   Design plan

functional requirements and cost. The quantity and rate of manufacture are very often governing factors in the choice of design method and in production allocation. The ultimate objective is to produce a balanced and fully integrated design which not only functions correctly but is suitable for economic manufacture.

Invention and ideas for new luminaires often originate from other sources than designers—from a marketing requirement to compete with an established concept, from a completely new light source or a new item of control gear developed in the laboratories. Examples of this diversity in the origin of ideas are the luminaires shown in Fig. 19.3. A range of tungsten halogen floodlights of the type shown in Fig. 19.3a started with an American concept that was changed to meet British market requirements and conditions. A range of fluorescent luminaires of the type shown in Fig. 19.3b was conceived as a result of a completely new choke ballast: for the first time it was possible to relate the

343

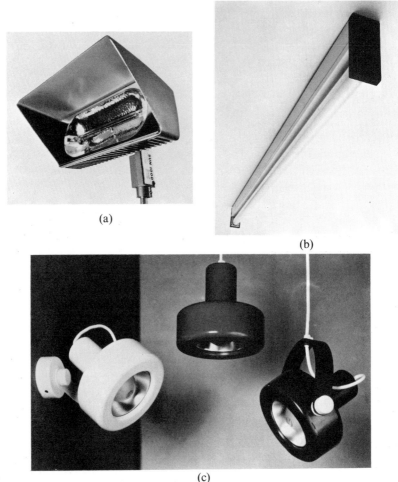

Fig. 19.3 (a) Sunflood luminaire (b) Arrowslim luminaire (c) Versatile spotlights

ballast cross-section to the tube section and hence produce a neat rectangular form. The versatile range of domestic spotlights, shown in Fig. 19.3c, originated from a designer's idea.

Design brief. A design brief is a statement of the requirements and conditions of the design project. It is both useful and necessary at the outset of any design to specify the design requirements of the product and the extent of responsibility of the designer. Since a brief is drawn up at the commencement of work, it cannot specify accurately every detail of the final product. Some factors, such as optical and thermal performance, will be to some extent unknown until a considerable part of the work is done. For this reason the initial specification in a brief must allow for some variation as the work proceeds.

344

Typically a design brief will contain four main sections:

Objective: The objective defines the general parameters of the product to enable a logical design method to be applied.

Technical specification: Photometric requirements, environmental conditions, lamp and control gear to be used. At the brief stage it is particularly important that the technical information available is assessed and studied in order to evaluate the degree of risk in producing an incorrect design.

Standards: Home and export market. All luminaires are required to comply with the relevant standards (Sect. 19.3.1).

Marketing specification: Target costs, quantities and construction. Production and design methods are largely dictated by the cost and quantity requirements: if the quantity is small emphasis must be on methods which are less specialized and which carry a lower investment than methods used for larger scale manufacture.

Following the establishment of a design brief comes the development and engineering of the luminaire. At this stage, co-operation with production engineers becomes essential: in parallel with the later stages of the designers' work (Fig. 1.2), the following activities are necessary from the production standpoint:

(a) Consultation on the possible production methods and materials.
(b) Initial considerations of tooling requirements.
(c) Initial costing.
(d) Production planning.
(e) Tool design and manufacture.
(f) Carton design.
(g) Final costs.
(h) Production samples.

19.2 ENGINEERING AND PRODUCTION

The production processes involved in luminaire manufacture are entirely dependent on the materials selected. Many factors influence this selection but the usual objective is to produce an end product that gives satisfactory service in its intended usage, at an economic price.

The designed life expectancy of a luminaire varies depending upon its type and application. For example, the metalwork and control gear of a fluorescent luminaire designed for use in a normal dry atmosphere, would have a life of at least ten years. It is such expected life values, allied to the needs of mass production requirements and the requirements to comply with the relevant British Standards, that determine the choice of materials and their finishes.

19.2.1 Metals and finishes

Fluorescent luminaires for use in normal indoor atmospheres are usually constructed from sheet metal, shaped to form an enclosure or spine into which is mounted the control gear and accessories necessary for the operation of the fluorescent tube. Sheet steel is the most commonly used material in the manufacture of the spines, due to its mechanical strength, cost and adaptability to manufacturing methods. The steel can be supplied either in standard size sheets, which are cut into blanks of the required size by means of a manually operated power guillotine, or in non-standard sizes ordered specifically for maximum utilization. An alternative method of producing blanks is from coils which are up to 1·5 m wide. The coils are slit by shearing wheels and rollers into narrow strips and recoiled on to mandrels. These slit coils are then fed into a powered automatic shearing machine which crops the steel to length.

Although it is possible to pierce holes in a spine section after it has been formed, it is usually more practical to carry out this operation in the flat stage before the section has been formed. The cut blanks are manually fed into a power press, known as a 'brake press' because it is possible for the operator to stop the action of the press at any point during its operating stroke. There are two distinct types of tooling which can be used in the press for piercing operations, a one-piece purpose-made piercing tool which is the full length of the blank to be pierced, or a tooling system (such as the well-known 'Redman' type) consisting of a series of standard tools, one for each hole or group of holes, which is set up in the press to a template and operated simultaneously by the upper member of the press. Tools of this latter type can be broken down and repositioned to allow for modifications, or even a different design of fitting.

The most common method of producing the required section from the flat pierced blank is to form each bend or group of bends separately with a succession of operations. The blank is fed manually into a brake-press set up with a standard vee block and blade, the vee block being fixed to the bed of the machine and the blade to the upper moving member. By adjusting the stroke of the press, the desired angle of bend is formed. A more advanced method is the cold rolled forming process in which the pierced blank is fed through a series of powered rollers, which together with a system of guides form it into the required section.

The most advanced method of piercing and forming sections is one which the piercing operation is linked to the roll-forming operation by means of a transfer mechanism to give continuous production from coiled strip (Fig. 19.4).

The finishing of sheet steel parts is important to give degrees of protection against corrosion. Of the many finishing processes available, stoved-enamel painting is the most economical method of protecting large areas. Before the metalwork can be painted it has to be subjected to a chemical process which removes any oil from its surface and gives a thin coating of iron phosphate: phosphating can be done by either spraying or dipping.

As soon as possible after phosphating, the metalwork is painted, either with a hand spray gun or an electrostatic spray system. With electrostatic spraying the metalwork is suspended from a continuous conveyor which carries the components round a spinning disc, the disc travelling up and down a predetermined stroke to suit the size of components. Paint is fed on to the spinning disc to be sprayed off by centrifugal force: it is charged to a positive potential of 90 kV and attracted to the metalwork which is at earth potential. This method gives a 50% saving in paint when compared with conventional hand spraying and ensures an even coating without runs.

On leaving the spray booth the metalwork continues on the conveyor for a short distance to give time for the solvent in the paint to evaporate before entering the stoving oven. The configuration of the conveyor system inside the oven is arranged to give a period of 30 min to 35 min for stoving to be completed.

346

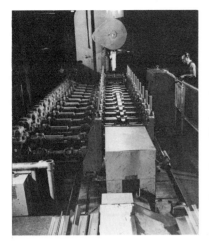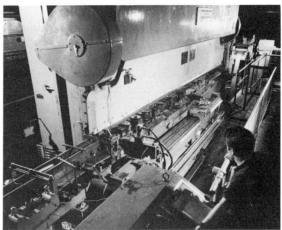

Fig. 19.4 Luminaire metal forming

Standard stoved-enamel finish, based on alkyd resin, is used extensively on metalwork intended for use indoors where the atmosphere is comparatively dry (up to 80% relative humidity), free from chemical contamination and where condensation is unlikely. In conditions of high humidity or heavy condensation, water can penetrate this enamel at the edges of the metalwork or other weak spots and rust is likely to occur.

Acrylic stoved-enamel finish is a comparatively recent development and is generally used on the more expensive ranges of luminaires. Acrylic enamel can withstand short term exposure to conditions of high humidity and condensation to a greater extent than alkyd base enamels, because of its more impervious nature. Having a harder finish than alkyd, acrylic withstands abrasion better and therefore maintains its surface gloss and finish longer: resistance to attack from chemicals is also superior.

Luminaires for corrosive atmospheres. It is not possible to be categorical about corrosion resistance without knowing the specific conditions. However, it is a reasonable assumption that the term 'corrosion-resistant' applied to luminaires indicates that they would provide satisfactory service under adverse atmospheric conditions, but not so adverse that people working there would need special masks or breathing apparatus. Many different types of luminaires can be classified as corrosion-resistant, for although their intended applications differ widely, the materials used in their construction have been chosen because of their acceptability to exposure in chemically-corrosive as well as high-humidity atmospheres.

The choice of materials used in the construction of these types of luminaires is usually governed by economics, quantities and manufacturing techniques available. If a reasonably-priced mass-produced luminaire is required for general use, the choice of body materials would probably be either glass reinforced plastic (Sect. 19.2.2) or plastic-coated steel.

The finishing of steel constructed luminaires with a protective coating of plastic is a technique which is of particular interest, allowing the designer to take advantage of standard sheet metal manufacturing processes without investment in expensive special-ized tooling. The most popular method of applying a coating of plastic to steel compo-nents is the fluidized bed process. The part is heated and then immersed into a specially designed tank containing the plastic in a powder form. This powder is fluidized by an upward air current which both separates and suspends it. In this condition the powder looks and acts as a liquid. As the powder particles contact the preheated metal compo-nents they fuse and adhere to its surfaces, forming a uniform film of plastic. Many different coating materials are available, the most popular types being PVC, nylon and polythene.

Exterior luminaires.   Such units as floodlights and street lanterns present the engineer with problems of structural rigidity and strength, together with positive sealing against the ingress of moisture. The problems associated with corrosion-resistant and exterior luminaires are related in that they are both exposed to similar adverse conditions, but because of market requirements, exterior luminaires need to be more robust and frequently need to withstand far greater temperatures because they house more compact discharge lamps. The material most commonly used for the manufacture of exterior luminaires is aluminium, and because the majority are comparatively compact in design they lend themselves to the technique of casting.

The casting method adopted is dependent upon the size and quantity requirements, but generally the choice is limited to two processes, gravity or pressure die-casting. Both employ metal split moulds often referred to as dies, into which the molten aluminium is cast: the basic difference is the method employed to force the molten metal into the mould. Gravity die-casting relies on the pressure from a head of metal above the cavity, whilst in pressure die-casting the molten metal is injected into the die at high pressure. The latter method of casting gives a greater degree of precision and allows thinner sections to be produced, but because more expensive dies are necessary it is an uneconomic process unless long production runs are required. The grade of aluminium alloy usually selected is LM6. This has excellent corrosion resistance, high ductility and is suitable for all shapes of die castings, including those with thin sections. Generally it is not necessary to apply a protective finish because of the corrosion-resistant properties of LM6: paint finishes are only used for aesthetic purposes.

It should be noted that corrosion will occur due to electrochemical reaction if alumin-ium is in contact with a dissimilar metal such as brass, nickel, copper or phosphor-bronze. This means that all non-aluminium accessories, such as support brackets, should be plated with a metal of an intermediate potential, a cadmium plated finish being com-mon for steel accessories.

19.2.2   Plastic materials

The major application for plastic materials is in opal diffusers, prismatic controllers and protective enclosures. The choice of a specific plastic material depends on the properties required, quantity-cost factors and the manufacturing processes available. Plastics technology, both of materials and production processes, is developing rapidly and all that can be given here is a brief synopsis of the major types of materials and the most common manufacturing processes currently used in the lighting industry.

Plastic materials fall into two main groups, thermo-plastic and thermo-setting. Thermo-plastic materials can be softened to a pliable mass by heating and then shaped to the desired form which is retained on cooling: this softening process can be repeated a number of times without changing the material. Thermo-setting materials are produced by the application of heat to certain polymers, normally with applied pressure: this curing process results in an irreversible chemical change taking place and further heating will not re-plasticize the material.

Polystyrene is the plastic generally adopted for the manufacture of diffusers or controllers for fluorescent luminaires intended for use in normal atmospheres. General purpose polystyrene in its basic form is an unsuitable material because of the premature yellowing caused by heat and ultra-violet radiation. This limitation can be overcome by the addition of ultra-violet stabilizers to produce a low-priced material which is suitable for general use indoors.

Acrylic is a higher-priced alternative material to polystyrene which has excellent resistance to chemical attack and is suitable for outdoor use. Acrylic diffusers and controllers are therefore used in corrosive atmospheres and for outdoor enclosures where lamp reflectors have to be protected from the prevailing atmosphere.

Cellulose acetate butyrate (CAB) and ultra-violet stabilized polycarbonate are two materials having a higher impact strength than acrylic and equally good weathering properties. These two materials are used as protective enclosures for exterior luminaires requiring the prevention of damage by vandalism. Polycarbonate, because of its extremely high impact strength and its high resistance to distortion from heat is becoming the standard material for this application.

Glass-reinforced plastics (GRP) are finding increasing application as an alternative to plastic-coated steel for the bodies of luminaires for use in corrosive atmospheres or out-of-doors. The type of GRP generally used is epoxy or polyester pre-impregnated glass fibre material supplied in sheet form. The mouldings of this material are light in weight and have excellent impact strength and rigidity as well as good corrosion resistance.

Phenolics and urea formaldehydes are inexpensive thermo-setting resins used for electrical accessories in luminaires, such as lamp-holders, terminal blocks, fuseholders, etc. They possess excellent electrical and flame-resistant characteristics.

Processing. Extrusion is the most common manufacturing method for producing polystyrene diffusers. The material is fed into a heated barrel containing an Archimedean screw, where it is plasticized and forced by the screw through a die. The die can be either annular—producing a tube which is then split and formed to the required shape while still in a soft state—or a profile die which produces the finished required section. The process is a continuous one and there are no length limitations other than those of handling and transporting.

Thermo-forming is the normal method of producing controllers and enclosures for corrosion-resistant and outdoor luminaires. The basic material arrives in the form of a sheet instead of a powder. The sheet is clamped in a frame and softened by radiant heaters. The softened sheet is then sucked into a female mould by vacuum or a bubble is blown in the soft sheet, a mould introduced inside it and the sheet drawn closely to the mould by vacuum.

Injection moulding of thermo-plastic materials is a production technique which is being used increasingly in the manufacture of luminaires and electrical accessories. Generally the thermo-plastic material is heated to plasticity in a cylinder and forced by a ram through channels into a split mould, which is prevented from opening by an external clamping pressure: the article is then allowed to solidify before the mould opens. The high cost of these moulds usually limits the process to components requiring relatively large production runs, but the process can sometimes be economically viable for smaller quantities if alternative production methods involve a large amount of hand fabrication.

Compression moulding is the usual technique for thermo-setting materials. The moulding compound, in either a powder state or in the form of a heated pellet, is placed in a split mould which is closed at high pressure and heated. The material softens and flows to fill the mould cavity and then the irreversible chemical reaction takes place. The material hardens and may be removed without waiting for the mould to cool. This process is used for the production of electrical accessories and for GRP luminaire bodies using a sheet rather than powder or pellet.

19.2.3   Glass

The development of various plastics suitable for diffusing and protective screening has led to the replacement of glass in the construction of fluorescent luminaires, long diffusers and large panels in plastic being so much lighter and less liable to breakage.

The traditional craftsmanship of glass-blowing is still utilized fully in the decorative incandescent field and offers the designer the opportunity of introducing subtleties of design impossible to reproduce by mass production techniques. Although in recent years the use of clear coloured glass has increased, following modern design trends, the most popular type of glass is still ply opal. This is constructed with a layer of pot opal which is skinned with a layer of clear glass. The pot opal is a very dense diffusing material consisting entirely of particles of calcium fluoride and is extremely brittle unless coated with a layer of glass. The outer glass skin can be given a satin finish by applying a light acid etch, which prevents specular surface reflections.

When glass is selected as an alternative to plastic in functional luminaires, this usually arises from temperature considerations, sometimes because of ultra-violet degeneration. Most commonly this selection is made when compact high pressure lamps are encountered in streetlighting lanterns or in floodlights: the glass is usually there to provide a protective screen for the lamp and reflector systems against the ingress of dirt and moisture, but prismatic optical control can be provided. Two types of glass are generally available—soda lime, which has a temperature limit of 250 °C, and borosilicate which can withstand far higher operating temperatures (Chap. 7). Both soda-lime and borosilicate glasses are normally treated with a toughening process to overcome possible breakages caused by thermal shock when exposed to adverse weather conditions.

19.2.4   Cables

At the same time as the change of standard sizes of wiring to metric dimensions there has been a change from the use of stranded conductors to single solid conductors: the latter are invariably used currently for the internal wiring of luminaires. The standard conductor material is copper, often tinned or nickel plated, the latter where high operating temperatures increases the likelihood of oxidation. In extreme temperature conditions, where nickel plating would not provide sufficient protection against oxidation, pure nickel conductors are employed.

The development of plastic insulating materials has led to the replacement of rubber, which for many years has been the accepted cable insulation material, PVC being the most generally used insulating material. PVC has a high dielectric constant, so that a small cross-section area suffices; it is impervious to moisture and does not degenerate when used in general lighting luminaires. Of the two types of PVC insulation material available, general purpose and high temperature, the latter is the one most commonly used. Under the more demanding temperature conditions of floodlights and street lanterns, cable insulation materials withstanding a higher temperature become necessary. Asbestos insulation may be used but it is not recommended for use outdoors or in high humidity atmospheres because of its hygroscopic nature. The temperature ratings for cables used as internal wiring in a luminaire under unstressed conditions are as follows:

General purpose PVC	70 °C
High temperature PVC	105 °C
Glass braided silicone varnished	180 °C
Silicone rubber	200 °C
PTFE	260 °C

19.3   SPECIFICATIONS AND TESTING

19.3.1   Specifications

Specifications are laid down to govern the design and construction of luminaires such that they conform to agreed requirements of safety, reliability, durability, performance and ease of maintenance.

In UK the British Standards Institution is the recognized authority for the issue of these specifications and they are compiled as a result of committee and liaison work between the lighting manufacturing industry, major users of lighting equipment and the BSI. Some large user organizations have their own specification requirements but these usually involve only minor deviations from the basic BSI specification. The main British specification for luminaires has been BS 3820 but this will be superseded by BS 4533 which, at the time of writing, is in preparation.

In view of potential markets for the supply of lighting equipment outside UK, designers and manufacturers must also consider the particular requirements of other countries. To this end, BS 4533 is being brought into line wherever possible with IEC recommendations and the requirements of CEE (International Commission on Rules for the Approval of Electrical Equipment). This will, to a large degree, ensure international uniformity of requirements when designing to BS 4533.

Mechanical requirements.   The actual constructional requirements of luminaires are laid down by specifying such things as the minimum mechanical strength of the components to ensure reasonable durability in handling and in use, and the strength of the suspension used to mount the luminaire. Metal components must be adequately protected against corrosion, and attention must be paid to dissimilar metals in contact that could cause electrolytic action in the presence of moisture and thereby cause the onset of more serious corrosion.

Enclosure requirements.   Luminaires for street lighting and other outdoor uses must satisfy very rigorous weatherproof requirements, and indoor luminaires for some special applications must provide protection against the entry of water or dust. The requirements depend on the classification of the luminaire, such as drip-proof, rain-proof, jet-proof, water-tight, submersible, dust-proof or dust-tight. Table 24.2 outlines the hazards in industrial lighting.

Electrical requirements.   Luminaires are classified according to the method of protection they employ to protect the user from electric shock. Superior insulation materials have been developed over a period of years and are now commercially available at economic prices.

One of the classifications of a luminaire is that of Class O and, on this type, provision for earthing is not mandatory. There are many of this type in common use but they do not really provide adequate protection in the event of a breakdown in the insulation. The current Regulations for the Electrical Equipment of Buildings (known universally as the IEE Regs) have now barred this type from use. A luminaire in which all the metalwork is connected to an earth terminal, which is intended for connection to the earthing system of the premises power supply, is said to be Class I. Protection can also be provided on a pendant unit, to be operated on a conventional two-wire domestic lighting circuit with no earth conductor, by means of double insulation. If one layer were to break down, there would still be another layer of insulating protection: this would be deemed a Class II luminaire.

The electrical wiring of a luminaire is of importance for safe operation: specifications include such things as the types of insulated cable that can be used, the minimum size of cables for a particular type of luminaire, the method of connection to the supply and the protection against damage and chafing where the supply cable passes through apertures in the body of the luminaire. Another important factor specified is the minimum distance that must be maintained between live parts and adjacent earthed metalwork.

The various electrical components such as ballasts, lampholders, capacitors, have their own relevant specifications and must comply with these in order to be incorporated in a fitting that is to comply with BS 4533.

Thermal requirements.   One of the main problems in the design of a luminaire is limiting the temperatures which will occur during operation and to this end BS 4533 is quite specific on the maximum temperatures that can be permitted at various points and on various materials. A concise table is included that covers such things as the maximum temperature of windings, capacitors, painted surfaces, insulation of wiring and plastic materials used in the construction of the components and the fitting. In the case of luminaires for discharge (including fluorescent) lamps these temperatures are taken when operated at 10% over rated voltage. This will have the effect of generating more heat within the luminaire: if it operates satisfactorily under these conditions, it will have an inbuilt safety factor when running at normal voltage.

Any insulating parts protecting live parts of the circuit must possess self-extinguishing properties in the event of their overheating due to electrical malfunction.

Marking requirements. Another important factor governed by specification is the marking that must be applied to enable ready identification of the manufacturer, supply voltage, rated wattage, classification, etc.: this is essential for the installer and maintenance engineer. The marking must be durable and the manner in which it is applied is itself subject to a test.

19.3.2 Testing

Before a new design is passed to the production departments, the requirements of a very thorough testing programme must be satisfied and some of the tests are made many times during the development of a luminaire, particularly if it is for outdoor applications. It is necessary at an early stage in the design to make a detailed appraisal of a prototype sample and thus provide the data for subsequent modifications throughout later stages of development up to the final design when a formal test programme is carried out to the relevant specification. Virtually all the main requirements in a specification are covered by an associated test and the test procedures are clearly laid down.

Mechanical tests. The various components of a luminaire must be able to withstand the mechanical forces encountered in service: for example, screws which are used during installation or servicing and the mounting arrangements for outdoor luminaires are subjected to tests appropriate to the torques and forces occurring in practice.

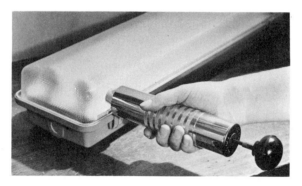

Fig. 19.5 Impact hammer

Luminaires must be reasonably proof against impact damage. Even indoors, luminaires can be damaged by accidental blows and those used outdoors are often subject to vandalism. It is particularly important that covers for live parts are robust but the weakest part of a luminaire is usually the bowl or diffuser covering the lamp chamber. For many years a pendulum impact hammer was used to test mechanical strength but this is being replaced in many specifications by a spring-operated impact hammer (Fig. 19.5). Sometimes a contract for the supply of luminaires may call for special tests in addition to these standard specification tests; for example, a particular requirement from a Middle East country is that any street lighting luminaire should withstand airgun pellets in order to be classified as vandal-proof.

Table 19.1   Testing of protective finishes

	Minimum requirements	Probable result	
		Standard stoved-enamel	Acrylic stoved-enamel
1. Hardness tests: Special pencils of increasing hardness grade are pushed across the enamel surface until a hardness grade is reached which cuts through the enamel before the pencil breaks due to excessive pressure.	F	2H	5H
2. Scratch resistance: Enamel subject to 'strokes' with a point load of 1 kg until the paint finish is broken.	35 strokes	40 strokes	200 strokes
3. Stain resistance: Not specified, but ink, mustard and lipstick are good test samples.	No test	Slightly stained	Unstained
4. Heat and humidity resistance: The test calls for four 12-hour test cycles at 35°C and 100% humidity on a sample where the finish has been cut with a razor blade. Corrosion shall not have penetrated more than 0·8 mm from the cut and reflectance shall not be less than 75%.		Passes	Passes

Additional tests are carried out at 100% humidity with a cyclic variation between 42 °C and 48 °C every half hour. This produces heavy condensation on the test sample, as the 'dew point' is passed on both the rise and the fall stages. Although both standard and acrylic finishes meet the test limits, the acrylic sample gives better resistance to corrosion penetration and maintains a high gloss and reflectance.

Materials and finishes are normally assessed by small samples but an additional check is made on the complete luminaire during long-term environmental tests. Table 19.1 indicates the manner in which paint samples are tested.

Enclosure tests.   The apparatus used for the rain-proof testing is shown in Fig. 19.6. A semicircular tubular hoop is fitted with many fine jets through which water is directed at the luminaire to simulate rain. The hoop oscillates 60° either side of vertical and the luminaire is rotated in the horizontal plane thereby ensuring that every relevant part is sprayed with water. The luminaires are switched on and operated for an hour before the test is made so that in addition to checking that no water enters them, they are subjected to thermal shock, a condition which will obtain during normal service. This is a particularly important test when external parts are made from glass or similar material. The rain-proof test is continued for 20 min and for the second half of this period the luminaire is switched off and cooled by the rain, thereby reducing the air pressure within the luminaire and providing an effective check on the ability of the luminaire to 'breathe' without drawing in rain.

Luminaires which are required to be dust-proof or dust-tight are tested in a special

Fig. 19.6   Rain-proof testing

Fig. 19.7   Cabinet for dust-proof tests

cabinet (Fig. 19.7) in which a fine dust such as talcum powder is agitated by means of a blower so that the air surrounding the luminaire is heavily laden with dust particles. During this test, which may last for between two and eight hours, a partial vacuum is maintained inside the luminaire to encourage the ingress of dust past any gaskets or seals. At the end of the test there must be no dust within a luminaire classified as dust-tight and for dust-proof luminaires the dust which has entered must not cause any danger or impair efficient operation.

Electrical tests.   A safety requirement is that no live parts should be able to be accidentally touched, and this is checked by using a standard test finger (Fig. 19.8). Electric lighting luminaires must satisfy many other safety requirements such as minimum creepage distance across the surfaces of insulating materials; minimum clearance distances between live parts and between live parts and earth or touchable metal parts. Luminaires must also pass high voltage flash tests and insulation resistance tests after several days in humid conditions.

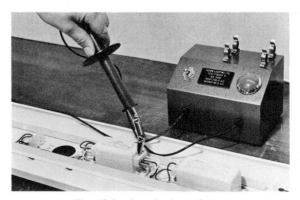

Fig. 19.8   Standard test finger

Thermal tests.   Luminaire temperatures are usually measured in a standard draught-free room (Fig. 19.9). The luminaire is fitted with many fine wire thermocouples and it is then operated under specified conditions until the temperatures indicated by these thermo-couples are stable. In the case of fluorescent or discharge lamp luminaires with built-in ballasts, the operating temperature of the ballast winding is determined by the change in resistance of the winding.

During the thermal measurements the luminaire is usually mounted in the most unfavourable position which it is likely to encounter in use: for example, a fluorescent luminaire for indoor use would be mounted on the underside of a large sheet of block-board to simulate ceiling-mounted conditions.

In addition to the measurements in the thermal test room, luminaires are subjected to long-term environmental tests. Street lighting and other outdoor luminaires are mounted outdoors so that the effect of the elements may be observed. Some of them are operated almost continuously with only short off periods to accelerate any thermal effects, while others are operated on their normal switching cycle or by photo-electric cells to simulate street lighting conditions.

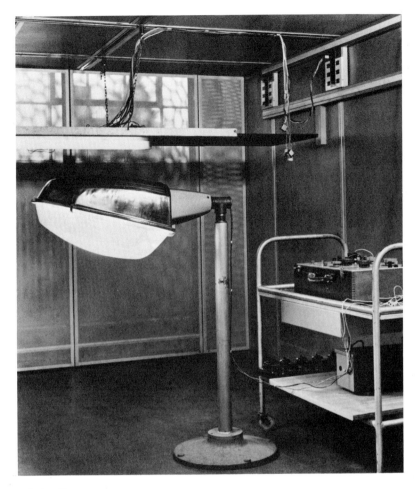

Thermocouple locations

 1 Bulb wall
 2 Inside canopy*
 3 Outside canopy*
 4 Lampcap
 5 Lampholder
 6 Terminals of lampholder
 7 Ballast case
 8 Capacitor case
 9 Terminals of capacitor
10 Terminals for external wiring
11 Terminal block
12 Terminals of ballast
13 Outside diffuser*
14 Inside diffuser*
15 Gasket*
   *Several positions

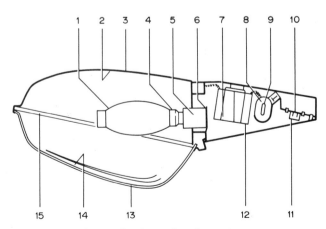

Fig. 19.9 Draught-proof room for thermal testing

357

20 Optical control in luminaires

An important element in the design and development of luminaires which has been omitted from Chap. 19 is optical design.

The purpose of optical design is to re-direct the light from a bare source to the areas where it is needed, to reduce the light in those zones where it may cause glare, and to provide a housing that is pleasing in appearance while, if necessary, protecting the lamp.

The fundamental laws of refraction and reflection have already been discussed in Chap. 1; in this chapter it will be shown how these laws are applied to the design of optical control systems for luminaires. Several examples are given of practical reflective and refractive systems for luminaires described in Chap. 19 as functional, as opposed to decorative.

20.1 INITIAL DESIGN CONSIDERATIONS

Before any optical design work can be undertaken, the objective light distribution must be determined. This will depend on the use to which the luminaire will be put, but the two factors which most usually enter into its determination are the efficient use of the flux available from the light source and the control of glare. The light distribution required from luminaires used as signals will depend on a third factor, that of visibility.

20.1.1 Light source

Once the photometric performance of the luminaire has been decided upon, the requirements of the light source can be determined.

Flux.   The first requirement of the light source is that should emit sufficient flux. If the luminaire distribution is specified in terms of intensity distribution over defined angular zones or illuminance levels over defined areas, then the total luminaire flux can be found using methods described in Chap. 5. To find the required lamp flux, the luminaire flux has to be multiplied by a factor to allow for the light lost in the luminaire. If the defined zones or areas do not cover all directions in which light is emitted, the factor must allow for the light falling outside the zones or area of interest. The factor may vary from 3 for a floodlight to $1\frac{1}{2}$ for a fluorescent luminaire used in a room with walls and ceiling of high reflectance. Whilst this factor could be predicted by calculation it is simpler and perhaps surer to refer to the performance data for similar types of luminaire.

Size.   The size of the source has also to be considered as this will affect the size of the luminaire. As the surface area for a given lumen output is decreased the luminance of the luminaire will be increased and glare may then become a problem. Also the location of a small source in the luminaire is more critical than is a large one and the optical components of the controlling system may have to be made more accurately.

Luminance. The luminance of any optical system cannot exceed that of the lamp (when in the luminaire) and at the best will be somewhat less owing to losses. Since intensity is the product of luminance and projected area it follows that the maximum intensity of a luminaire is fixed for a given luminaire size and source luminance. This is a fundamental limitation in optical design which cannot be overcome. Source luminance can be increased by reflecting light back on to the source or putting one source behind the other, but the fundamental limitation still holds with the increased value of luminance.

Colour. Another requirement to be met by the light source is that its colour should be suitable for the lighting application of the luminaire. For certain applications, such as street lighting, the colour of the light source is not important, but the colours of lights used for signalling have to lie between close limits (Sect. 31.1).

20.1.2 Optical system

An important initial consideration in optical design is whether to use reflection, refraction, diffusion or a combination of these.

Reflector systems using specular reflecting materials have the advantage over refractor systems that very much more of the light flux can be controlled with a simple optical system. They are particularly useful where the light has to be concentrated into a beam as for projectors. Generally speaking they are not used for general purpose indoor luminaires except in cases where stringent glare control is needed.

Refracting systems utilizing prisms or lenses are generally used in systems where several beams are needed from one source, as in beacons. They are also used in street lanterns where beams are required but there is a need to keep the lantern narrow. Sheets of refracting prisms (prismatic controllers) are also used in general purpose indoor luminaires for fluorescent lamps: these give less stringent glare control than reflectors, but are capable of giving higher light output ratios, and their more lively appearance is preferred by some.

Where light control is not critical, sheets of transmitting opal material (opal diffusers) can be used. Since the intensity in any direction is approximately equal to the projected area multiplied by the luminance of the diffuser, some light control can be achieved by shaping the diffuser to have large projected areas in the directions in which the greatest intensities are required.

The final system of control is provided by obstruction. For this purpose matt white reflecting surfaces can be used which direct the light in certain directions as well as providing obstruction in other directions. Tight beam control cannot be obtained by this method but glare control can be good. For very stringent glare control black surfaces are sometimes used but result in inefficient luminaires.

20.1.3 Materials for optical control

Table 20.1 shows the optical properties of materials commonly used in optical systems. The terms used for measuring optical properties are defined in Sect. 1.4.7 but two kinds

Table 20.1   Optical properties of materials

Material	Finish	Diffuse reflectance %	Regular reflectance (normal incidence) %	Transmittance (normal incidence) %	Refractive index	Critical angle °
Aluminium commercial grade	Anodized and polished	0	70			
Aluminium super-purity	Anodized and polished	0	80			
Aluminized glass or plastic	Specular	0	94			
Chromium	Plate quality	0	65			
Stainless steel	Polished		60			
Steel	White paint glossy	up to 75	5			
Flint glass 3 mm	Polished	0	8	92	1·62	38
Soda glass 3 mm	Polished	0	8	92	1·52	41
Clear acrylic 3 mm	Polished	0	8	92	1·49	42
Opal acrylic 3 mm	Polished	10–15	4	50–80		
Polystyrene 3 mm	Polished	0	8	92	1·60	39
Polyvinylchloride (PVC) 3 mm	Polished	0	8	88	1·52	41
Polycarbonate (LS) 3 mm	Polished	0	8	88	1·58	39
Cellulose acetate butyrate (LS) 3 mm	Polished	0	8	85	1·47	43

of reflectance are distinguished in the table: regular reflectance, which includes only the light that is reflected in accordance with the laws of optical reflection, and diffuse reflectance, which includes all the reflected light. The values of transmittance given are for normal incidence of a parallel beam: for diffuse incidence (as from a sky of uniform luminance) the values are somewhat lower, for example 85% for clear acrylic. The absorptance is sometimes of interest and is equal to the sum of the transmittance and reflectance subtracted from unity. In selecting a material for optical control not only must the optical properties be taken into account but so must also the suitability of the material as regards strength, durability, resistance to heat and ultra-violet radiation, and ease of manufacture of the final product (Sect. 19.2).

The most used specularly reflecting material is aluminium. This has taken the place of silvered glass because it is lighter, not fragile and easier to form. To obtain the best specularity (that is to form a sharp image as opposed to a diffuse one) the aluminium has to be polished electrically or mechanically. Higher reflectances can be obtained with super-purity aluminium but this material is soft. A compromise alternative is commercial grade aluminium clad with super-purity aluminium. Glass surfaces which have been aluminized give a high reflectance, but are seldom used except on lamp envelopes. Aluminized plastic with a protective coat of lacquer is used for some indoor luminaires, but the process tends to be expensive. Chromium plate and stainless steel, although of good specularity, have a low reflectance and are not used for reflectors.

White paint on metal provides diffuse reflection. For ease of cleaning, the paints used are usually glossy, but the specular component due to the gloss is of no practical significance in designing optical systems for luminaires.

Glass as a refracting material is used where resistance to heat is required. Polymethyl methacrylate (acrylic) is extensively used for refractors for both indoor and outdoor luminaires. Polystyrene is cheaper than acrylic but is not suitable for exterior use. Polyvinylchloride (PVC) can be used out-of-doors: it has good impact resistance but is more expensive than acrylics. When high impact strength is required, as in vandal-proof street lanterns, polycarbonate or cellulose acetate butyrate (CAB) can be used: light stabilized (LS) grades should be chosen though these have the disadvantage of having low values of transmittance.

Acrylic, PVC, polystyrene and glass are available in opal grades and these are used where the source is to be hidden or where a bowl having a substantially even luminance is required.

20.2 STANDARD ELEMENTS FOR OPTICAL CONTROL

20.2.1 Reflective elements

Plane surfaces. A plane specular surface forms an image of an object which appears to be behind its surface. The exact location of the image can be found by ray tracing. In Fig. 20.1a O is a point object: it can be shown geometrically that since the marked angles of reflection and incidence are equal, the rays of light will appear to diverge from

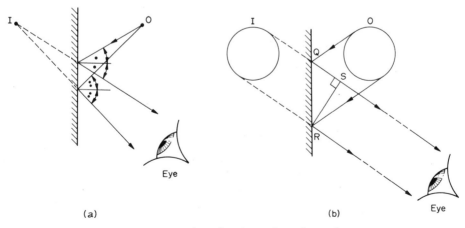

Fig. 20.1 Location of an image in a plane mirror

361

an image I, located at a distance behind the mirror equal to the distance that O is in front of it. To locate the image of an object of finite size, the image of a number of points on the object can be located enabling the position of the complete object to be found.

To find the intensity of the image it is necessary to find the projected area of the mirror that appears bright or *flashed*. In Fig. 20.1b I is the image and O is the object, a source of light of uniform luminance for simplicity. To an eye at a great distance from the mirror (so as to receive nearly parallel light) the part of the reflector that will appear flashed is QR, and the projected area is proportional to SR. If the luminance of the source is L, the luminance of the flashed part of the mirror will be ρL where ρ is the reflectance of the mirror. This relation also holds for curved mirrors, and if transmittance is substituted for reflectance, for lenses and prisms.

The intensity of the optical system can then be calculated from the relation:

$$\begin{array}{cc} \text{Intensity of optical system} \\ \text{in a particular direction} \end{array} = \begin{array}{c} \text{Luminance in} \\ \text{that direction} \end{array} \times \begin{array}{c} \text{Projected area that is} \\ \text{flashed in that direction} \end{array}$$

Spherical and cylindrical surfaces.   The rays of light from a small source placed at the centre of curvature of a reflector will be reflected back on to the source as shown in Fig. 20.2a. This element is useful where the source is small and as much light as possible from it has to be collected for redirection by a lens or another mirror. Since in practice the source itself will block the rays it is usually necessary to displace it somewhat from the centre so that the path of the rays is not obstructed.

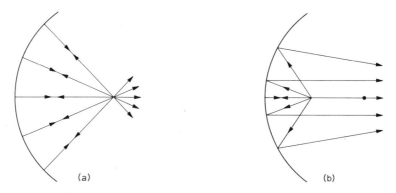

(a)   (b)

Fig. 20.2   Reflection from a spherical or cylindrical mirror

If the source is placed at a distance equal to one-half the radius of curvature from the back of the reflector (Fig. 20.2b), rays from the source that do not deviate more than 10° from the axis of the system will be reflected into a substantially parallel beam.

If the source is linear a cylindrical surface with its axis parallel to that of the lamp is more appropriate than a spherical surface. Once again for nearly parallel light the lamp centre should be placed at a distance from the reflector equal to one-half the radius of curvature of the reflector.

The parabola. The parabola is the most commonly used reflector contour: it is defined by the equation $y^2 = 4ax$ (Fig. 20.3) where a is the shortest distance of the focal point to the reflector. The most important optical property of the parabolic reflector is that if a point source is placed at its focus a parallel beam of light is obtained.

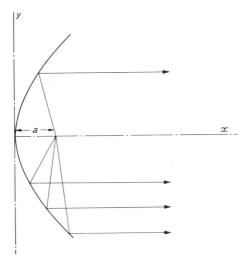

Fig. 20.3 Parallel beam produced by point source at focus of parabola

In practice the shape of the distribution curve depends on the size of the source in relation to the focal length and mouth width of the reflector. Fig. 20.4 shows how the intensity distribution in a vertical plane can be predicted for a cylindrical source of uniform luminance located centrally at the focus of a horizontal parabolic trough reflector. By finding the flashed area at selected angles of elevation the intensity distribution can be found. To demonstrate the principles involved the difference in luminance between the bare lamp and the flashed reflector will be ignored.

In Fig. 20.4a the rays from the source to the edge of the reflector are shown diverging over an angle of $\pm\theta_1$ from the axial direction. The innermost rays intersect at G, the crossover point. If the reflector is viewed from beyond this point in any direction not deviating more than an angle θ_1 from the axis, the whole of it will appear fully flashed, since cones of rays emanating from other points of the reflector (closer to the source) will have a greater angle of divergence. Up to an angle θ_1 the intensity will therefore be proportional to $\cos\theta$. At angles greater than θ_1, the reflector will be incompletely flashed. For instance, when the reflector is viewed at an angle θ_2 (Fig. 20.4b) the flashed area is proportional to LM. At angles greater than θ_3 (Fig. 20.4c) light ceases to be reflected and only the bare lamp contributes to the intensity. The bare lamp will contribute its full intensity until the angle θ_4 (Fig. 20.4d) is reached, when the edge of the reflector begins to obscure it. At θ_5 the lamp will be totally obscured and the intensity will be zero.

Fig. 20.5a shows the resultant idealized intensity distribution. If a larger lamp of the same luminance were used the peak intensity would be the same but the angles θ_1, θ_2,

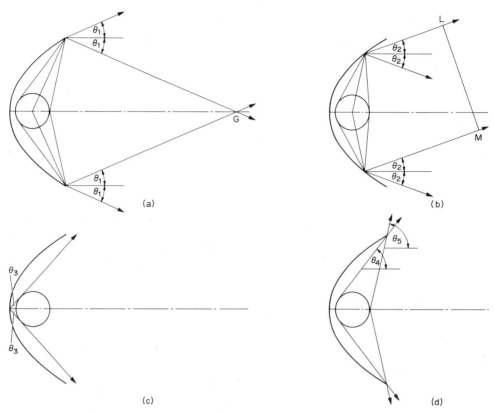

Fig. 20.4   Reflection of light from large source at focus of parabola

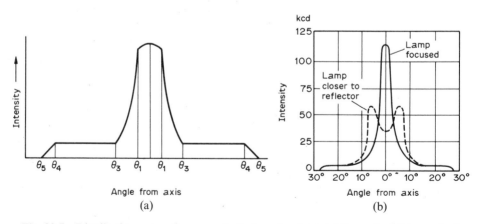

Fig. 20.5   Distribution curves from parabolic trough mirror (a) theoretical (b) practical

etc., would be increased, giving a wider beam. Fig. 20.5b shows a curve obtained from an actual test: the sharp boundaries in the idealized distribution do not appear because of geometrical imperfections.

Fig. 20.5b also shows the effect of defocusing the lamp in an attempt to control the beam width: a dip is produced in the intensity distribution. Wider beams are more usually obtained by using a patterned or matt material for the reflector: in this way wide and narrow beam distributions can be obtained from the same reflector contour and a common housing can be used for each type of floodlight.

The uncontrolled light from the source itself is a disadvantage when it is emitted outside the beam and liable to cause glare. This can be reduced or eliminated by putting a baffle in front of the lamp. If the baffle is spherical or cylindrical it can be used in either of two ways. It can form an image of the source adjacent to the source itself: this in essence would extend the source size and therefore the beam width. (Should the flashing of the parabola be incomplete owing to inaccuracies in manufacture, the beam intensity may also be increased because of the fuller flashing resulting from the larger effective source size.) Alternatively the image of the source could be formed on the source, increasing the maximum intensity while retaining the original beam width. In the case of a filament lamp, this would result in the filament being heated to a higher temperature and the life of the lamp being shortened.

The ellipse.   The ellipse is a contour with two foci such that if a source is placed at one focus all the rays of light will be reflected through the other. This is a useful property when light from the source has to be directed on to a slot or a gate of a projector.

Sharp cut-off reflector for tubular sources.   In some applications a sharp cut-off above the beam is desirable to reduce the glare as much as possible. The action of such a reflector giving this control is shown in Fig. 20.6a where it can be seen that in contrast to the parabola all the upper bounding rays of the reflected beams of light are parallel.

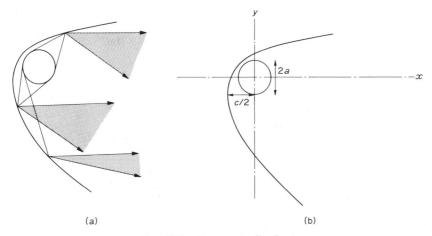

(a)   (b)

Fig. 20.6   Sharp cut-off reflector

365

The curve is described by the parametric equations (Fig. 20.6b)

$$x = \frac{1}{2}\left[y\left(p-\frac{1}{p}\right)-a\left(p+\frac{1}{p}\right)\right]$$

$$y = p(c-2a\varphi)-a$$

where a = the radius of the tube,

$p = dx/dy = \tan\varphi$,

$c/2$ = the distance of the back of the reflector from the y axis.

Direct light from the tube tends to spoil the cut-off so it is necessary to use a baffle in front of it.

20.2.2   Transmissive elements

Prisms.   Prism systems or banks have to be specially designed for the job they are intended to do: the individual prisms may be used for refracting or reflecting and refracting. When a ray of light enters a refracting prism (Fig. 20.7) it is deviated towards the base: the following equations can be used, where the letters refer to the angles marked in Fig. 20.7:

$$D = (i-r)+(i'-r')$$

$$A = r+r'$$

$$i' = 90° + C - Q$$

$$i = 90° + B - P$$

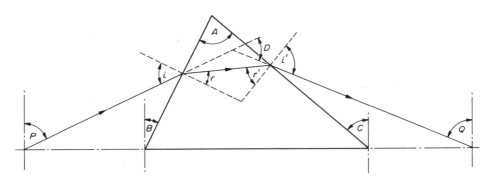

Fig. 20.7   Trace of ray through refracting prism

To obtain complete flashing of the prism from the direction of the emergent ray, the base of the prism should be made parallel to the path of the ray in the prism or these should converge on the right-hand side of the figure.

The chart in Fig. 20.8 evaluates the angle between the two refracting surfaces of a prism, made of a material having a refractive index of 1·49, for different directions of incident and emergent light.

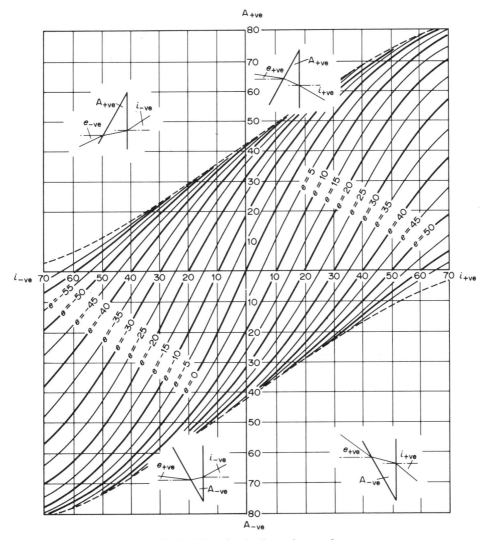

Fig. 20.8 Chart for finding prism angles

An important property of refracting materials is that their reflectance increases with the angle of incidence. For a material of refractive index of 1·5, this means that angles of incidence greater than 60° for rays entering the material and 35° for rays leaving the material should be avoided. This limits the deviation that can be obtained by a refracting prism to 50°. For greater deviations reflecting prisms have to be used.

Fig. 20.9 shows the trace of the ray through a reflecting prism UVW, X and Y axes being inserted for reference. The ray leaves the source at an angle P to Y_1Y_1 and enters the face UV at the point L. It is reflected from the face UW at the point S and leaves the prism through the face WV at the point M, making an angle Q with Y_3Y_3.

367

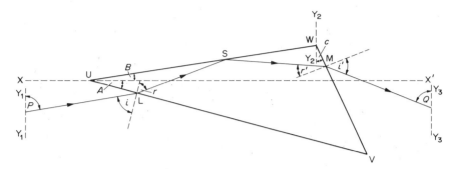

Fig. 20.9   Trace of ray through reflecting prism

Since the angles LSU and WSM are equal, the following relations exist between the various marked angles:

$$i = P - A$$
$$i' = C - Q + 90°$$
$$B = \tfrac{1}{2}(C - A + 90° - r - r'),$$

If the face UV is sloped above XX', A has to be taken as negative.

These relations enable B to be found once C and A have been set. The work can be most conveniently set out in a table.

To achieve complete flashing of the face WV in the direction of the emergent ray, UV must either be parallel to SM or converge towards SM on the right-hand side of the figure. If UV is made parallel to SM, WV will be completely flashed for rays making a smaller angle than P with Y_1Y_1, and will be incompletely flashed for rays making a larger angle than P with Y_1Y_1. The condition for UV to be parallel to SM is that $A = r' - C$.

In all these calculations, it should be checked that the angle of incidence of the reflected ray is in fact equal to or greater than the critical angle of the prism material.

Prisms mask each other when they are made into a bank. It is very useful, as in all prism design, to draw the prisms to find the extent of the masking. At the same time, the effect of light inter-reflected from parts of the optical system other than the light source can be found.

Lenses.   Convex lenses provide a means of obtaining a narrow beam and are particularly useful where more than one beam is needed. Fig. 20.10a shows a convex lens with spherical surfaces, which would give a near-parallel beam of light from a small source placed at its focus. However, as the collection angle of the lens is made greater by increasing its size it is found that the periphery of the lens does not flash in the axial direction (owing to spherical aberration) and there is no further gain in beam intensity. This limitation can be overcome to a certain extent by using lenses having specially calculated contours. One commonly used is shown in Fig. 20.10b: this has the surface nearest to the source spherical and the other parabolic.

In optical systems for large sources, the lens would tend to be thick, making the luminaire too heavy and too costly, and it is therefore better to use a stepped or Fresnel lens (Fig. 20.10c).

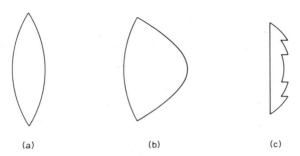

(a)   (b)   (c)

Fig. 20.10   (a) Biconvex lens (b) Parabolic lens (c) Stepped lens

Diffusers and controllers.   Diffusers are made from opal materials and are used to increase the light emitting area of a luminaire in order to decrease its luminance and improve its appearance. To achieve a reasonably even luminance over the surface of a diffuser, there must be a sufficient separation between it and the light source, and the diffusing effect of the opal (which usually increases as the transmittance decreases) must be great enough. In a fluorescent luminaire, the diffuser of which is usually extruded, the opal can be reeded to enhance its appearance, or opal sides can be extruded with a clear patterned base to give glare control.

Controllers embody prisms or lenses and are used where more precise optical control than can be obtained by diffusers is required.

20.3   EXAMPLES OF DESIGN

20.3.1   A floodlight with faceted reflectors

One drawback of some of the standard reflective elements already described is that the images of light sources are sometimes in front of the elements and this often results in undesirable striations. Reflectors formed of flat facets overcome this difficulty, since the images are always formed behind the reflector. They also have the advantage that the slope and size of each facet can be calculated and specified exactly so that a template or tool can easily be made with the exact dimensions. Although the facets can be made separately and held together with an end template, a better method of manufacture is by extrusion, using aluminium. In this way any movement of the facets with respect to each other due to uneven heating from the lamp is prevented.

Fig. 20.11 shows a design for a linear floodlight with a 15° square-topped beam with a sharp run-back (reduction of intensity) above and below the peak. Lines OL_1, OL_2, OL_3, etc. are drawn from the source O at 15° to each other: OX is the axis of the reflector which bisects the angle L_2OL_1. The first element AB is made perpendicular to OX and set at a distance from O to give a convenient size of drawing. The next element BC is put at such an angle that the ray OB is reflected in BC at 7·5° to OX below the horizontal: the ray OC will then be reflected in BC at 7·5° to OX above the horizontal. The positions of CD and the succeeding elements are deduced similarly.

An adaptation of the above construction can be made to enable a sharp run-back

369

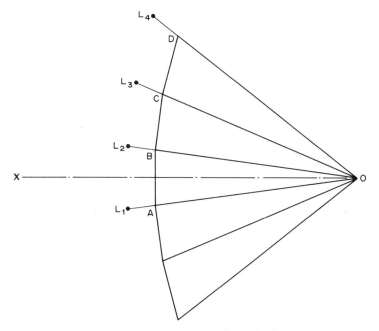

Fig. 20.11   Construction of faceted reflector

above the peak and a slower one below the peak to be achieved. This asymmetry is useful in certain applications such as stadia lighting, where an even illuminance over a large area is required.

20.3.2   A cut-off street lighting lantern, using a linear source

The main features of the photometric performance required are that the peak intensity should be as near to 65° as possible, the intensity at the horizontal should be very nearly zero, and the intensity in the 0° to 30° zone should not exceed 80 per cent of the peak intensity.

The severe limitation of the intensity at the horizontal precludes the use of prisms on the side of the lantern for beam control, since the scattered light from these would be too great. Therefore the lantern must rely on reflector control, with no part of the lamp visible from the horizontal.

The first detailed part of the design work is to determine how deep a reflector is needed to provide a peak having sufficient intensity. The required peak intensity is specified in terms of its ratio to the average intensity of the lantern in the lower hemisphere (MHI): this must lie between 2·0 and 4·0 so that an acceptable uniformity of luminance of the road surface is achieved.

Let the lumen output of the lamp be Φ. Then the intensity of the lamp at right angles to its surface will be Φ/π^2 cd, approximately 0·1 Φ cd.

Suppose that the downward light output ratio of the lantern is to be 0·7, then the downward flux will be 0·7 Φ. The MHI will be then 0·7 $\Phi/2\pi$, since the solid angle subtended by the hemisphere is 2π and intensity is equal to flux divided by solid angle. If I_{peak} is the peak intensity then the

$$\text{peak intensity ratio} = \frac{I_{peak}}{MHI} = \frac{I_{peak} \times 2\pi}{0.7\,\Phi}$$

which must be equal to at least 2·0. Hence

$$I_{peak} = \frac{0.7\,\Phi}{\pi} = 0.2\,\Phi$$

approximately.

Since this is twice the value given by the bare lamp, the reflector will have to give a flashed area equal to the bright area of the arc tube, but to allow for losses $1\frac{1}{2}$ times the area is a more realistic target.

A drawing of the lantern can now be made as in Fig. 20.12. A line XX is drawn representing the bottom limit of the reflectors and the arc tube is drawn in to touch XX at Q. Four lines are drawn tangential to the arc tube at 65° to the downward vertical, the

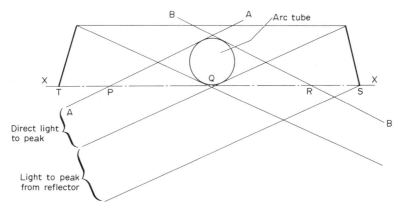

Fig. 20.12   Optical system of cut-off street lantern

desired angle for the peak intensity. The two upper lines AA and BB cut XX at P and R respectively. The lantern cannot be narrower than PR otherwise the reflectors would cut off the view of the bare lamp at 65°.

The tilt of the reflectors has now to be determined. If the reflectors were vertical, they would produce a horizontal beam, but the beam has to be at 25° below the horizontal and it is therefore necessary to tilt the reflectors by half this angle, that is 12·5°. Since the reflector depth is to be $1\frac{1}{2}$ times the arc tube diameter the reflectors need to be further out than R and P; at S and T as shown in the diagram. To ensure complete flashing they should be given a radius of curvature equal to twice QS.

The reflectors would be housed in a white canopy. If a flat bowl were used underneath, the peak intensity ratio might be reduced below 2·0 because of the angle of incidence on the bowl being such that a considerable amount of light in the beam would be reflected back into the canopy. It might be necessary to use a bowl having sides sloped at right angles to the beam direction as shown in the photograph (Fig. 20.13). Care has to be

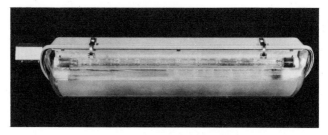

Fig. 20.13   Cut-off street lantern

taken that the lensing effect of the bend in the bowl does not spoil the smoothness of the light distribution or reflect too much light out at the horizontal. If the white canopy reflects too much light into the 0° to 30° zone, where the intensity is limited in the current lantern specification, it might be necessary to design a suitable spreading pattern for the bottom of the bowl.

20.3.3   A prism bank for a semi-cut-off street lighting lantern

Suppose a prism bank is required for a street lantern using a linear sodium lamp. Suppose also that the bank is to shield the lamp at 90° to reduce glare, but that at the angle of maximum intensity, 75°, at least two images of the lamp, as well as the lamp itself, are to be seen. Fig. 20.14 shows the lamp with a line HH tangential to its bottom surface

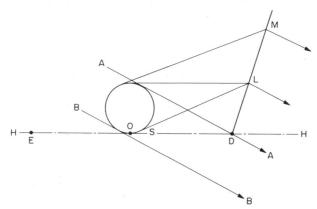

Fig. 20.14   Lamp and prism bank in semi-cut-off street lantern

at O: the prism banks must then come down to this line. Two parallel lines AA and BB, tangential to the lamp, are drawn in the direction of the required beam. The upper line cuts HH at D and this is the closest point to which the prism bank can be brought to the lamp without cutting off the direct beam from the lamp: a similar point E can be found on the left hand side of the lamp.

It has next to be decided whether to have the prisms facing towards or away from the lamp. This decision governs the shape and to a large extent the construction of the lantern.

If the prisms face away from the lamp the prism bank will be tilted with its bottom edge towards the centre line of the lantern. Fig. 20.15a shows a bank of prisms that bends the light down, as is required in the lantern. If the left hand surfaces of the prisms are to be made common, the bank will slope as shown in Fig. 20.15b: with the prisms facing away from the lamp complete flashing of the bank is impossible since the non-working faces are not flashed.

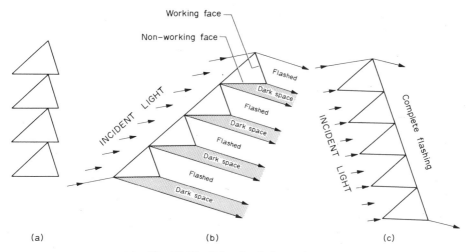

Fig. 20.15 Prism bank formations

If the prisms face the lamp the bowl must widen towards its bottom as shown by Fig. 20.15c. The bank can be designed to give complete flashing in the peak direction. Light falling on the non-working faces tends to cause a small peak above the horizontal and although this is not detrimental as regards glare control, it does represent a small reduction in the light flux directed on the road surface.

It is possible to design each prism individually to bend the light rays from the lamp into the beam. If a part of the lamp is of much higher luminance than the rest of the lamp, this is a wise procedure, because it ensures the maximum luminance of the prism bank is achieved. However, if the variation of luminance across the source does not vary significantly then the prisms can be designed in banks, each bank having a width equal to the lamp diameter. This makes tooling somewhat easier. Referring to Fig. 20.14, the first bank DL bends the light into the beam. It is then checked that ray SL emerges at an acceptable angle. The procedure is then repeated for the second bank LM, and so on if necessary: the limit is reached either when the diagonal ray (the equivalent of SL) emerges at too high an angle or else it is impossible to design the prisms to bend the light rays sufficiently. Reflecting prisms may then have to be used if more flashed area is required.

20.3.4 A bi-directional inset runway luminaire

This luminaire is used to mark the centre of runways for pilots landing and taking off (Sect. 31.2.2). It is inserted into a hole about 300 mm in diameter in the runway and has to be robust enough to allow aircraft to run over it. So as to minimize the possibility of damage to the tyres of the aircraft, it must not protrude more than 17 mm above the level of the runway and there must be a gradual slope up to the highest part of the luminaire.

The precise photometric requirements are laid down in a specification issued by the International Civil Aviation Organization. Two beams at 180° in azimuth must be provided, each with a peak intensity of 7500 cd at 3° above the horizontal. Other intensity requirements relating to the width of the beam are stipulated: from these it can be calculated that 400 lm is required in each beam.

The simplest way of obtaining two beams in opposite directions is to use two lenses with the lamp between them (Fig. 20.16). The designer has first of all to select a lamp

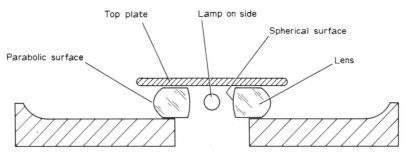

Fig. 20.16   Optical system of bi-directional inset runway luminaire

and using this, find whether it is possible to meet the photometric requirements. If the ultimate performance falls short then it will be necessary to scale the wattage up accordingly, and conversely if the intensity values are very much greater than specified and this better performance is not required then the wattage can be scaled down.

A tungsten halogen lamp would be ideal for this application as it can be switched on without any warming up time (which would not be the case with discharge lamps) and it is a compact source. Also the shape of the filament can be altered to give the best performance for the selected lens. The highest possible rating of this source would be about 200 W because of the difficulty of dissipating the generated heat. A suitable source has an intensity of 400 cd broadside-on to the filament and its luminance is 18 cd/mm². With a required intensity of 7500 cd it follows that the area of the lens must be $7500/18 = 420$ mm², but to allow for transmission losses and incomplete flashing of the lens this value must be increased by 20%, giving an area of 500 mm². From the height limitations of the luminaire and from the fact that the whole of the lens must be visible at 3° for it to contribute to the intensity in that direction, it can be determined that the effective height of the lens will be 10 mm, giving a lens width of 50 mm.

The distance (d) of the filament from the back of the lens can now be calculated taking into account the fact that the lens must emit 400 lm in the beam. The first step is to estimate the flux the lens has to receive in order to emit 400 lm. A transmission factor of 20% has already been used but an extra allowance has to be made for the fact that some light will fall outside the beam. Assuming that 30% of the flux received by the lens will be lost, about 550 lm will have to be collected.

The flux to be collected by the lens equals the intensity of the filament multiplied by the solid angle that the lens subtends at the filament. Hence $550 = 400 \times (500/d^2)$ or $d = 19$ mm.

Since the distance of the filament from the back of the lens is short in comparison with the area of the lens, an uncorrected convex spherical lens would not give the required intensity owing to spherical aberration. A lens with one surface parabolic and the other spherical (Fig. 20.10b) would be necessary for this application.

It will be appreciated that these are only rough calculations: they are given to show the general lines of reasoning in the optical design of such a unit. Further calculations would be needed to determine the exact contours of the lens. Experimental work would then be needed on a mock-up to determine the precise positions of these components and the shape of the lamp filament giving the best performance in relation to the lens.

PART FOUR

Lighting

21 The interior environment

A comfortable interior environment hinges primarily on the proper control of the visual, thermal and aural environment stimuli. Although the primary concern of this book is with lighting, it is important to understand all three types of stimuli and the techniques used to control them in interiors. Many of the solutions to individual environmental problems conflict in performance with each other and can result in costly compromises and unsatisfactory conditions. Integration of the building services can reduce or even eliminate these conflicts and offer better and more flexible spaces with considerable saving in capital and fuel costs.

21.1 PERCEPTION OF THE ENVIRONMENT

Man in his environment requires comfortable conditions and a knowledge of what is going on around him. Information is channelled through the sensory pathways, primarily through the senses of sight, hearing and to a lesser extent smell, touch and the thermal nerves. Perception also makes use of the information which has been stored in the memory bank from previous experiences: recognition of new information relies on a satisfactory comparison with that memorized.

The route to perception starts in the environment with stimuli which are absorbed by receptors in the ear, the eye, etc. and are converted into a series of neural impulses and transmitted to the central nervous system. These signals are processed in the cortex and sub-cortex and often give rise to response signals which are conveyed to the muscles. The overall response time to a stimulus is very short, but it is dependent on adaptation, fatigue, acclimatization, the arousal level and on environmental comfort.

21.1.1 Visual stimuli and lighting criteria

Light is a form of energy which stimulates the sensation of vision. The characteristics of light and its units have been outlined in Chap. 1 and the visual mechanism and its behaviour described in Chap. 2. The stimulus conveyed by the visual environment through the eye is dependent on the lighting system and on what has been revealed by lighting the space. Satisfactory vision not only relies on a sufficient quantity of light but also on its quality. The recommended illuminance levels for visual tasks are based on the degree of visual performance needed (Sect. 2.3) with due attention to economics. The limiting glare index (Sect. 2.2.2) is the only generally recognized criterion for quality in interior lighting but there have been attempts to formulate criteria for a good visual environment which take into account preferred distributions of luminosity, the colour quality of light and space, modelling, the directional flow of light and spatial as well as planar illuminance, but none of these has been fully established to date (Chap. 22).

21.1.2   Aural stimuli and noise criteria

Sound is a form of energy produced by the vibration of an elastic medium: it stimulates the sensation of hearing.

The vibration of an object sets up a succession of waves of compression and expansion in the air and is propagated through it. Sound in air travels at about 340 m/s but the precise speed depends on the air temperature and humidity. In denser media such as water it travels many times faster: it cannot be propagated through a vacuum.

In producing sound, very little mechanical energy is required since the generating process is merely to transfer vibrational energy from source to receiver. The amount of sound a source generates is termed the sound power, measured in watts. An orchestra playing full blast will generate about 90 W of sound power. The sound from a source spreads over an increasing area and the intensity of sound is the rate of flow of sound energy per unit area, measured in W/m^2. In general the sound intensity decreases as the square of the distance from the source.

The presence of sound in air can be detected by a cyclic increase and decrease in atmospheric pressure. The r.m.s. value of this alternating pressure, which is related to the intensity, is known as the sound pressure, measured in N/m^2. The relationships between power (P), intensity (I), and pressure (p) are:

$$I = \frac{p^2}{\rho c} \text{ where } \rho \text{ and } c \text{ are the density and sound velocity of the medium}$$

$$P = 4\pi I r^2 \text{ where } r \text{ is the distance from the source at which } I \text{ is measured.}$$

Sound intensity and pressure are traditionally specified in decibels (dB) of level, by evaluating the ratio of the quantity to a reference value near the threshold of hearing ($I_t = 10^{-12}$ W/m^2, $p_t = 2 \times 10^{-5}$ N/m^2).

$$\text{Sound level} = 10 \log_{10}\left(\frac{I}{I_t}\right) \text{dB} = 20 \log_{10}\left(\frac{p}{p_t}\right) \text{dB}$$

A decibel scale is also used for generated sound power using a reference power of $P_t = 10^{-12}$ W.

$$\text{Sound power level} = 10 \log_{10}\left(\frac{P}{P_t}\right) \text{dB}$$

The rate of repetition of vibrations of a sound determines the frequency of the sound, also referred to as the tone of sound. The human ear only responds to sounds having frequencies between 20 Hz and 20 kHz, and within this audio band its response varies. The dotted curve in Fig. 21.1 shows the minimum audible level of sound at different frequencies.

The variation of response with frequency suggests that to give components of low and high frequency equal weighting to those of mid frequency in defining sound level is unfair. 'Weighted' sound level measures have been devised, the most commonly used one being dBA where the components of a noise are reduced by the ordinate of the 40 phon curve in Fig. 21.1 before being combined to give the level.

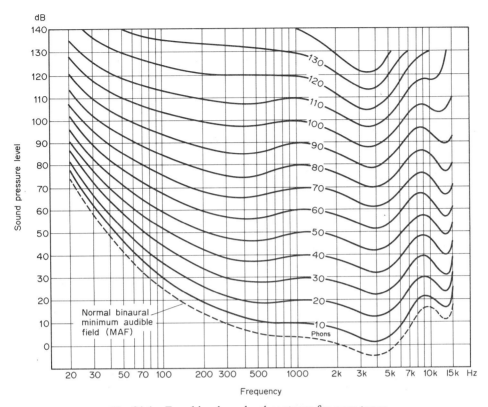

Fig. 21.1 Equal loudness level contours for pure tones

Loudness is a technical term to indicate the subjective effect of sound. The loudness level of a sound, in phons, is the sound level (dB) of a 1000 Hz tone which sounds subjectively as loud. Thus the 'equal loudness contours' of Fig. 21.1 are labelled with a number in phons which is the value of the ordinate when the abscissa is 1000 Hz. Unfortunately 2 phons are not twice as loud as 1 phon, and a second unit for loudness has been invented—the sone. The sone scale is designed so that a sound of 2 sones is twice as loud as one of 1 sone. The phon scale may be converted into sone scale by the relationship:

$$\text{Loudness level in phons} = 40 + 10 \log_2 (\text{loudness in sones}),$$

or
$$\text{sones} = 2^{\frac{\text{phons} - 40}{10}}$$

Criteria for noise control. Human reaction to noise can be assessed as to whether it causes damage to hearing, interferes with speech communication or causes annoyance.

The upper limit is set by the risk of damage to hearing. Levels of 140 dB will cause pain at any frequency. Continuous exposure to noise levels of 95 dB at frequencies more than 500 Hz can cause damage inside five years.

In most commercial buildings the permissible noise level is governed by the ability to carry out speech communication easily. Speech contains frequencies between 100 Hz and 5000 Hz but intelligibility remains if the lower frequencies in this range are cut out. Speech interference level (SIL) is a measure of the masking effect of a noise on speech and is given as the arithmetic mean of the sound levels of the interfering noise in dB in the three octave bands 600 Hz to 1200 Hz, 1200 Hz to 2400 Hz and 2400 Hz to 4800 Hz.

SIL is a fairly crude criterion which makes no allowance for the relative masking of different frequencies within the chosen band nor the effect of frequencies outside it. A more sophisticated measure of the interfering effect of a noise is obtained by comparing the spectrum of the noise with a set of reference spectra, known as the Noise rating (NR) curves, shown in Fig. 21.2. Each curve is classified by a number, roughly corresponding to SIL. NR 0 is below the threshold of hearing and NR 130 is on the threshold of pain. Alongside the curves in Fig. 21.2 is a table showing the maximum NR values recommended for a range of interiors.

NR curves can also be used as criteria for annoyance. The louder the noise the greater the annoyance it will cause, but its frequency and duration is of equal importance. High frequency noise is more annoying than its loudness indicates whilst an intermittent noise is generally more annoying than a continuous one. The degree of annoyance will also depend on the physical condition of the listener, where he hears it and who caused it, why and when. Suitable corrections which can be applied to the NR curves for some of these effects are given in Fig. 21.2.

21.1.3   Thermal stimuli and criteria

Heat is the most common form of energy and it cannot be destroyed: it can only be transferred from one object to another. Heat exchange between man and his surroundings stimulates the thermal nerves under his skin to produce thermal sensation.

The human system generates a certain amount of heat all the time, the exact amount depending on the activity of the individual. The assimilation of food, and the production of water, gases and heat is called metabolism. The human blood temperature has to be maintained very near to 37 °C for both comfort and health. This temperature will vary between individuals but for any individual a variation in excess of ± 0.2 °C will cause discomfort, ± 2.5 °C could cause death. In order that the human body can maintain this constant internal temperature the metabolic heat must be rejected at the same rate as it is generated. The loss in heat is mainly by conduction, convection, and evaporation. It can take place externally from the skin or internally by the lungs. The efficiency of heat shedding depends on the local conditions of the air and the temperature of the environment.

The surface temperature of the body will be somewhat less than the blood temperature but still very much higher than the surrounding air temperature. Therefore there will be a heat loss from the skin to the ambient air, dependent on the temperature difference, the insulation of clothing and the rate at which air impinges on the body surface.

Veins and capillaries near the surface of the skin will expand and contract according to the stimulus received by the nerves. If the blood temperature drops, indicating an excessive loss of body heat, the capillaries will contract, allowing less blood to flow to the skin. Therefore the skin temperature drops thus reducing the heat exchanged by conduction or

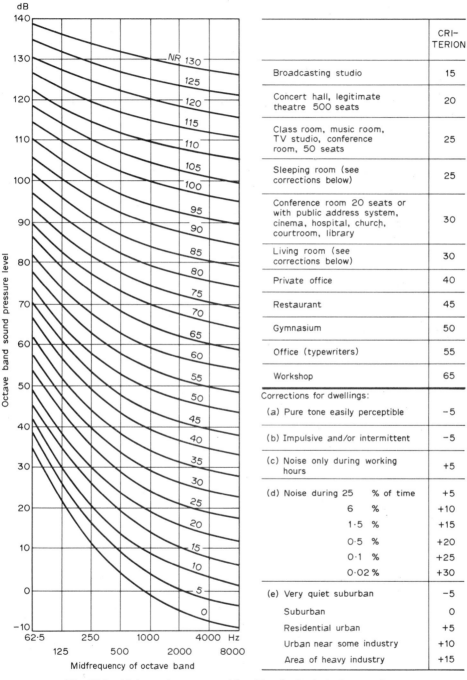

	CRI-TERION
Broadcasting studio	15
Concert hall, legitimate theatre 500 seats	20
Class room, music room, TV studio, conference room, 50 seats	25
Sleeping room (see corrections below)	25
Conference room 20 seats or with public address system, cinema, hospital, church, courtroom, library	30
Living room (see corrections below)	30
Private office	40
Restaurant	45
Gymnasium	50
Office (typewriters)	55
Workshop	65
Corrections for dwellings:	
(a) Pure tone easily perceptible	−5
(b) Impulsive and/or intermittent	−5
(c) Noise only during working hours	+5
(d) Noise during 25 % of time	+5
6 %	+10
1·5 %	+15
0·5 %	+20
0·1 %	+25
0·02 %	+30
(e) Very quiet suburban	−5
Suburban	0
Residential urban	+5
Urban near some industry	+10
Area of heavy industry	+15

Fig. 21.2 Noise rating curves with table of criteria and corrections

convection. If further losses occur from the skin, involuntary shivering or goose pimples occur to induce activity and generate more heat.

If in a hot situation the body heat loss by conduction and convection is insufficient to keep the internal temperature from rising, heat is rejected by sweating—moisture is produced which is evaporated by the air. Evaporation can offer a great deal of cooling but its effectiveness is dependent upon the humidity and the rate of movement of air near the body. If heat cannot be rejected at the rate it is generated the body temperature will rise. A lassitude follows which tends to reduce the heat produced and attempts to balance the heat production with loss. If it cannot balance, heat exhaustion or heat stroke can occur: other effects could be dehydration and excessive loss of body salts.

Radiant heat has a great effect on skin temperature. Radiant heat exchange can take place provided there is a temperature difference. With large areas of heat-radiating surfaces, comfortable conditions can be maintained at low air temperatures since they can supply sufficient heat to keep skin temperature at comfort level. Equally, large areas of heat-absorbing surfaces, such as cold windows, can cause discomfort even in high ambient temperatures.

Clothing has a major effect on body heat gain or loss. It can function as an insulator and offer protection against heat loss or gain.

Comfort criteria.   The factors which influence thermal comfort and discomfort are air temperature, surface temperature, fresh air level, air movement and humidity.

The air temperature in a room should be as cool as is compatible with comfort. The range of comfortable air temperature is from 18 °C to 22 °C, the upper values generally enjoyed by women and people over 40, the lower limit being widely used where heating is by radiant means. The gradation of air temperature vertically should not exceed 3 °C, and the air at head level should not be distinctly warmer than that near floor level. Severe changes in temperature between areas or between incoming and room air need to be avoided and limited to 10 °C difference.

The average temperature of the walls should not be more than 3 °C lower than that of the air and preferably higher: mean radiant temperature (m.r.t.), as measured with a black bulb thermometer, should be lower than the air temperature. If the surface temperature is very much lower than the air temperature a sensation of stuffiness will be experienced.

Fresh air should be supplied at a minimum rate of about $18 \text{ m}^3/\text{h}$ per occupant of a room. This rate of change is sufficient to prevent high concentrations of bacteria and carbon dioxide. In crowded or smoky areas the rate should be doubled. There should be adequate air movement, variable rather than uniform. A general movement of 0·1 m/s is acceptable, increasing up to 0·2 m/s to achieve a sense of freshness.

A relative humidity of between 30% and 70% is desirable. A high humidity produces a feeling of chill at low air temperature and oppressiveness at high air temperature, while a low humidity causes a sensation of parchedness and allows a significant build-up of static electricity on many objects.

Numerous single number indices for scales of comfort have been proposed, of which three are notable:

(a) Equivalent temperature, which combines the effects of air temperature, radiation and air movement.

(b) Effective temperature, which takes into account the air temperature, air movement and humidity.

(c) Environmental temperature, combining the effect of radiation and air temperature.

21.2 INDIVIDUAL ASPECTS OF ENVIRONMENTAL DESIGN

21.2.1 Lighting

The visual environment, in which lighting plays a direct part, is more immediately apparent to most people than are the thermal or aural aspects of the environments, at least until they have to work in it.

The first aim of lighting is to provide adequate visibility without causing excessive discomfort glare to the occupant. The source may be electric light or daylight. Daylight is restrictive since it is only available in short periods and mainly through windows in side walls. The techniques used to predict daylight are described in Chap. 23. Electric lighting can provide a more controlled light distribution and permit a more flexible use of space. Electric lighting design, covering more than just the first aim, is examined generally in Chap. 22 and in its more particular aspects in the remaining chapters of the book.

21.2.2 Acoustics

Noise in buildings may be internally generated sounds or intruding sounds from the outside. Internal noise can arise from heating, ventilating, air conditioning, water supply, drainage, transformers, lighting and lifts. Other sources may be work aids or tools such as typewriters, telephones, trolleys and business machines. Noise is also produced by people talking, walking, shutting doors and handling paper or furniture.

The amount of noise experienced due to an internal source is governed by the sound power of the noise source and the acoustic properties of the room. This implies a two-fold approach to its control: firstly by a reduction of noise at source and secondly by reducing the spread of noise from it. Reduction of the noise at source can be achieved by proper design of the equipment and its installation, whilst the spread of noise calls for the acoustic treatment of the room.

The behaviour of sound in rooms is very similar to that of light. It can be reflected, transmitted, absorbed or even diffracted.

Sound radiated from a source will diminish in strength with the square of the distance but because the source is enclosed by a finite sized room, the sound will be reflected each time it strikes a bounding surface. The total sound level will be the sum of the direct and reflected sound.

The sound pattern in a room is governed by the shape and size of the room and by its surface finishes. Certain frequencies of sound are emphasized in a room in the same way that organ pipes have natural frequencies. These frequencies are called modes or eigentones and can be evaluated for a rectangular room of dimensions L, W and H from the expression

$$f = \frac{c}{2}\sqrt{\left[\left(\frac{x}{L}\right)^2 + \left(\frac{y}{W}\right)^2 + \left(\frac{z}{H}\right)^2\right]} \text{ Hz}$$

where c is the velocity of sound and x, y, z are positive integers 0, 1, 2, etc.

Except at low frequencies, where the eigentones are separated, it can be shown that if an omnidirectional source has a sound power level of L_W the total sound level L_P at a distance of r from the source will be

$$L_P = L_W + 10 \log \left(\frac{1}{4\pi r^2} + \frac{4(1 - \bar{\alpha})}{S\bar{\alpha}} \right)$$

where $\bar{\alpha}$ is the average absorption coefficient of the surfaces, and S is the total surface area of the room.

If $\bar{\alpha} = 0$ the sound level becomes infinite. Fortunately this cannot happen in practice since no known material is totally reflective. It must be noted that a doubling of the average absorption coefficient of an interior only gives a 3 dB reduction in noise level. Room surface materials absorb different amounts of sound depending on the frequency. Acoustic tiles commonly used have absorption coefficients ranging from 0·2 to 0·8.

If the sound source in a room is suddenly cut off the sound level in the room will decay gradually: the time taken for the sound level to fall by 60 dB is called the reverberation time of the room. Reverberation time is the physical correlate of the subjective acoustic quality of an interior described by such words as dead or echoing. The approximate formula relating the reverberation time T (seconds) with room volume V (m³), surface area S (m²), and absorption coefficient $\bar{\alpha}$ is $T = 0·16\ V/S\bar{\alpha}$. For maximum effectiveness in noise reduction, absorbing materials should be placed close to the noise source. In large rooms like offices the best location is on the ceiling or the floor, but for small rooms it can also be put on the walls. In large classrooms or lecture rooms the ceiling should not be treated as this surface needs to be reflective to reinforce the speaker's voice.

Up to now the problem examined has been that of internal noise sources. The subject of noise due to an external source introduces a further important concept in acoustics, that of insulation and sound transmission. Noise generated outside a building or in an adjacent room can penetrate the room walls. The amount of noise experienced depends on the sound power of the source and the transmission loss of the intervening wall: the absorption within the room itself is of less significance. This transmission loss, a measure of the sound insulation of a partition, increases for building materials with the frequency of the sound and with the mass of the partition. In theory the sound insulation increases by 6 dB for a doubling of mass or frequency. In practice, stiffness and damping play a part as well as mass, and the theoretical 6 dB becomes 4 dB to 5 dB. Buildings do not consist of homogeneous partitions: in a composite structure where sound can travel by two alternative paths the effectiveness of the insulation will be largely governed by the weaker of the two.

21.2.3 Heating and air conditioning

The control of an indoor climate is partly the function of the building, which modifies the outdoor climate, and partly the job of the internal heating and ventilation services. Much of any success in providing thermal comfort indoors will depend on the shaping, siting and orientation of the building and on its insulation. The main function of insulation is to make the coarse adjustment of the external climate, the remaining fine control being achieved by the services.

Heating and ventilation. The design of these services cannot commence until the flow of heat within the building is assessed. The steady state heat flow out of a structure is given by $H = UA(t_i - t_o)$ where H is the rate of flow of heat (W), A is the area (m^2), U is the thermal transmittance coefficient (W/m^2 °C), t_i and t_o are the air temperatures inside and outside (°C). The rate of flow is constantly changing depending on outside conditions and on the storage characteristic of the building.

Heat flow in and out of the building also takes place through cracks, openings and ventilation air. This is called the infiltration load and is made up of a sensible and a latent heat load. A sensible load is where only changes in temperature are occurring, while latent heat involves a change of state, such as humidification.

The infiltration load, representing an outflow of heat, is given by

$$H_S = Qds(t_i - t_o) \quad \text{and} \quad H_L = Qdh(l_i - l_o)$$

where H_S and H_L are rate of heat flow, sensible and latent respectively (W), Q is the rate of flow of air (m^3/s), s is the specific heat capacity of air (J/kg °C), d is the density of air (kg/m^3), $(t_i - t_o)$ is the temperature difference (°C), h is the latent heat of vaporization (J/kg) and $(l_i - l_o)$ is the change in humidity ratio (kg/kg). Calculations are usually based on an outside design temperature of $t_o = 28$ °C for summer and $t_o = -1$ °C for winter, while the inside design temperature t_i lies between 18 °C and 22 °C.

Heat gains can be produced by many sources (Fig. 21.3). The main source of heat gain is due to solar radiation penetrating the building. This may be direct radiation through windows or roof lights or re-radiation from the opaque surfaces of the building. The rate

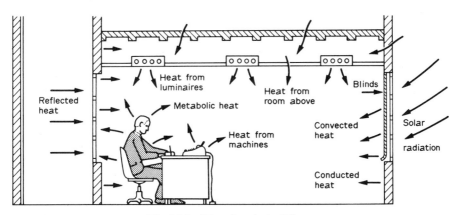

Fig. 21.3 Heat flow in buildings

of heat gain from solar radiation depends on many factors such as the area, orientation, location, shading, surface finish as well as the sun position and cloud density. The calculation and the data needed for this are enormous: details for computing it are given in the IHVE guide.

Other internal gains are from people (100 W/person to 150 W/person), lighting (20 W/m^2 to 60 W/m^2) and other electrical appliances, business machines and motors which can amount to as much as 30 W/m^2.

To maintain a satisfactory thermal environment a net loss has to be met by heating: a net excess has to be removed by cooling the room.

The simplest form of thermal conditioning is a heating system operated locally or centrally, the source of fuel being electricity, coal, gas or oil. Heat is generated in boilers, carried by hot water or steam in pipes and distributed by radiators, where heat is transferred to the space by radiation and convection. The best place to site radiators is under windows where the highest heat losses will usually occur and where the radiators will compensate for the cold radiation effect of the window. During the summer the heating is switched off and cooling is traditionally introduced by partial opening of the windows. Natural ventilation can only be induced into relatively small areas: in deeper buildings forced ventilation is required.

Forced ventilation can be produced by a local or a central plant. A local plant usually consists of a fan unit bedded into an outside wall or the roof and supplies fresh air locally: the air may be heated before it is discharged into the room. A central plant consists of a fan taking in outside air and distributing it along ducts to the various areas where it is discharged into the room through outlets. Ventilation may provide some cooling although its effectiveness largely depends on the outside air temperature and humidity.

It is not uncommon to find buildings where the summer cooling loads are very much greater than that which could be reduced by a simple ventilation system. In such cases the supply air has to be cooled well below room temperature in order to absorb some of the heat in the room. This process calls for refrigeration, which is a major component of an air conditioning plant.

Air conditioning.   This is the process of treating the air so as to control simultaneously and automatically its temperature, humidity, cleanliness, distribution and movement in the conditioned space. Air conditioning equipment can control the thermal conditions on an all-year-round basis with the exception of the mean radiant temperature or the cold radiation effect of a window: the ill-effects of these can be minimized by the design and layout of the system. An air conditioning system may consist of self-contained packaged units but these are not suitable for large areas. More usually a system consists of a central plant (filter, cooler, heater, humidifier, fan) with distribution ducts and outlets. In addition to distributing the air into the space these outlets may be active in mixing air or providing additional temperature control. Central plant systems are categorized according to the manner in which they distribute the air to the conditioned space:

(a) Single duct all-air systems: These systems rely on the conditioned air being supplied to the room via a single duct from a central plant, this air being returned back to the plant (Fig. 21.4). Some local cooling or heating can take place to meet the demand of different zones.

(b) Dual duct systems: Hot air and cold air are conveyed from the central plant at a high velocity to a terminal unit located in each zone. The terminal unit mixes the two air streams to obtain the conditions required by the room.

(c) Air water systems: A minimum amount of air is supplied by ducting to a number of terminal units incorporating water coils in which the water may be hot or cold. Conditioning is achieved by inducing secondary air into the unit for cooling or heating.

(d) Water systems: Individual fan coil units (a water coil with its own fan and filter) are located in the areas requiring conditioning. Fresh air is allowed to enter locally through an external wall or the roof.

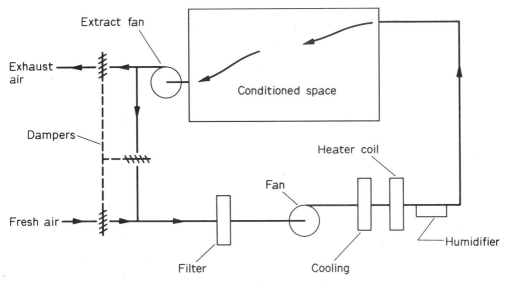

Fig. 21.4   Low velocity single duct all-air system

21.2.4   Interaction in environmental design

There is a great deal of interdependence in the individual services of lighting, acoustics, heating and air conditioning.

The first consideration must be the building envelope which serves functionally to produce a difference between the external and internal climate. The commonly used lightweight structure with large areas of glazing can be particularly troublesome since it reflects the external conditions almost instantly indoors with no thermal lag, little screening for solar radiation, and low noise insulation. Large windows can provide plenty of working light but also produce excessive solar heat in the summer and uncomfortable radiant cooling and heat loss from the room in the winter. Opening windows in summer can provide adequate ventilation, but at the expense of admitting dirt, excessive noise and uncontrollable air movement. Techniques for overcoming some of the drawbacks of windows are examined in Sect. 23.4.

The increasing cost of land has led to an increase in deep buildings—buildings with large floor areas. In these deeper rooms the lack of natural light has meant that more electric light is needed and for longer periods of time (Chap. 23). Perimeter heating, needed to replace heat losses in the perimeter areas, retards the flow of heat from the core areas. These then become too warm and stagnant because the heat generated by the lighting and the occupants is trapped. The building therefore requires simultaneous heating and cooling, which can best be provided by air conditioning. The increased lighting load for core areas in deep buildings implies an increased cooling load for the air conditioning system which in turn implies more air supplied by larger ducts and distributed by more supply outlets. This has led to a competition for ceiling space between luminaires, supply and extract air outlets and acoustic absorption material.

389

It is all too obvious from these interactions that co-ordination between services is essential: integration of services can lead to a saving on equipment and running cost as well as creating a better interior environment.

21.3   INTEGRATED ENVIRONMENTAL DESIGN

Integrated design can be defined as the interdisciplinary treatment of a building construction with all its services to optimize the interior environment to suit the many activities which the occupants are likely to want to perform.

While integrated design is not limited to open plan design, this latter offers the maximum space flexibility since it reduces the structural obstructions, partitions and passage ways and it provides a low ratio of perimeter to floor area with consequent low fabric heat loss. The essential feature of an open-plan design is a coherent yet flexible arrangement of the different work groups for ease of communication: the occupants can be provided with high environmental standards for lower costs than in a cellular design.

Only air conditioning can provide simultaneous cooling and heating and it also lends itself to a heat recovery system—one in which energy in a building, which is otherwise wasted, is collected and re-used.

Carpets, free standing screens and the suspended ceiling provide acoustical control: recessed luminaires provide the high level of illuminance which is part of the required environmental standard. The desire to integrate service equipment has involved further developments in air conditioning and ceiling systems as well as in luminaire design. Suspended ceilings not only conceal equipment but can also be used as return air ducts. The luminaires not only provide a good quality of light but also handle air and can offer additional acoustic control.

21.3.1   Conservation of energy

In well-insulated buildings the heat gain from occupants, motive power and lighting are mostly retained within the building envelope. The outside temperature at which these internal heat gains equal the heat loss is called the balance point. Above the balance point cooling is required, while below it heat should be supplied. The balance point is governed by the efficiency of the thermal insulation and the heat gains.

The function of a heat recovery system is to collect the heat liberated within a building and redistribute it by an automatically controlled process. No heat should be discharged from the building if it can be economically reclaimed for re-use and no heat should be added to the system unless it is absolutely necessary.

To accommodate such a system the building is divided into various internal and perimeter zones. The air conditioning plant is designed to transfer heat from zones where there is a surplus of heat to zones where there is a deficit. When re-heating is necessary, it should be based on the utilization of low grade heat, that which is generally wastefully rejected from the refrigeration condenser to atmosphere and also that which is available from the lighting when air-handling luminaires are used.

The technique for reclaiming low grade heat from the refrigeration plant necessitates the use of two water circuits in the condenser: one is used for heat reclaim and the other circuit for heat rejection. The heat emitted by the lighting system can be collected by air directed to flow through the luminaires. At levels of only 500 lux the heat gain will be between 20 W/m^2 to 50 W/m^2 and can reduce the balance point below 0 °C in an adequately insulated building. The heat can be either used or disposed of by the air conditioning system: if it is not needed it may be stored in water tanks rather than rejected. A thermal storage tank can provide extra heat for the building for use after an unoccupied period: if necessary it can be supplemented by additional heating using gas, electricity or an external source heat pump.

21.3.2 Air-handling luminaires

The electrical energy consumed by various light sources is dissipated by convection, conduction and radiation (Table 21.1). This energy dissipation is modified by the lumi-

Table 21.1 Energy dissipation in lamps

Energy	Fluorescent tube (%)	Tungsten lamp (%)	High pressure discharge lamp (%)
Convected and conducted	55	19	28
Radiant	45	81	72

naire body and optical controller. White enamel paint which is widely used as a light-reflecting finish on the body absorbs a substantial part of the ultra-violet and infra-red radiation. The optical controllers also absorb a large part of the emitted non-visible radiation. It should be noted that not all the energy emitted is dissipated in the occupied space: a large quantity is directed into the plenum void, especially by recessed luminaires (Table 21.2).

Table 21.2 Measured energy distribution of recessed luminaires using fluorescent tubes

Luminaire type		Energy up (%)	Energy down (%)
	Open	38	62
	Louvre	45	55
	Prismatic or opal diffuser	53	47

A substantial part of the energy emitted downward is radiant. Part of this is the required light: the remainder is very difficult to control even by the use of air conditioning and it can cause discomfort. The acceptable level of irradiance is inversely proportional to the ambient air temperature and in general should not exceed 12 W/m^2.

An increasing number of air-handling luminaires are in use either to overcome thermal problems or to promote integration in design. Although most currently available air-handling luminaires are for fluorescent tubes, luminaires are being developed for other sources. In early luminaires the air-handling functions were carried out by units attached to the luminaires. In these, the air was passed through slots in the trim (Fig. 21.5a) without entering the lamp compartment: negligible heat transfer took place, although sometimes the air was allowed to flow around the ballast. More recently luminaires involving significant heat transfer have become available (Fig. 21.5b). The return air is allowed to pass

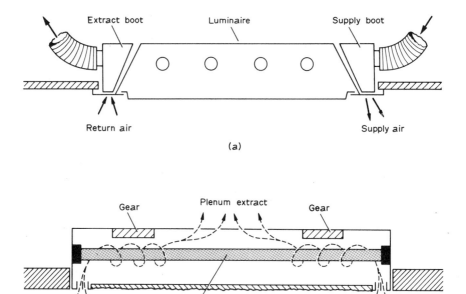

Fig. 21.5   (a) Air-handling luminaire with supply and extract boots (b) Air flow path through prismatic luminaire

through the lamp compartment, giving more efficient removal of the heat generated since this heat can be removed before it enters the occupied space. With fluorescent tubes, the removal of the heat from the lamp compartment results in the tube operating at its optimum temperature, maintaining its efficiency and designed colour.

There are four major criteria governing the design of these luminaires. Physical requirements determine its shape, size, position and method of fixing. Lighting requirements involve the utilization factor, glare rating and the number and wattage of lamps. Air-handling requirements include the amount of heat to be extracted, the resistance to air flow, and the change in light output at specified flow rates. Acoustic requirements concern the maximum noise level produced by the ballast and the flow of air, also the degree of cross-talk acceptable when luminaires are to be installed in adjacent rooms having a common plenum. Many of these requirements conflict and compromise is necessary.

To meet the air-handling performance the air flow through the luminaire has to be regulated. The inlet and extract slots have to be positioned so that air is directed along paths which give the greatest heat transfer. The air flow pattern needs careful control so that dust and dirt in the air is trapped or allowed to pass through the luminaire. A number of luminaires are in use where the supply and extract air are handled by the same unit: in these it should be ensured that no short-circuiting between supply and extract air can take place.

Noise generation by air flow can be minimized by ensuring that there are no sharp edges facing the air stream and no constrictions or rapid changes in the air flow path. Cross-talk attenuation can be improved by changes in the directions of the air flow paths, since at each change in direction some reduction in sound transmission will occur. Further improvement can be made by acoustic treatment of the air flow path in the luminaire.

As well as photometric data, information is required for any air-handling luminaire showing its air-handling performance, noise generation, and cross-talk attenuation. Fig. 21.6 shows a typical method of presenting air-handling data. Heat extraction of up to 80% can easily be attained with noise generation below NR 25 and a cross-talk attenuation of 35 dB.

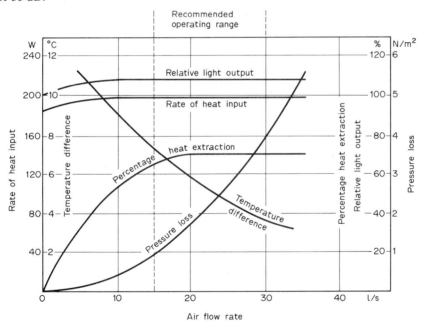

Fig. 21.6 Air-handling data for a typical plenum extract luminaire

21.3.3 Suspended ceilings

A suspended ceiling may have a suspension depth of anywhere between 100 mm and 1000 mm. Ceilings may be translucent or louvred, with lamps above them, in which case the general term luminous ceilings is applied. Most erected ceilings form a sealed cavity, called the plenum void, into which most of the building services can be accommodated, and carry individual luminaires. Such ceilings can be heated by hot water or electric cables. As well as concealing the services and the unfinished structure, they provide a surface for decoration, acoustic control and thermal insulation: they also contribute to the overall fire resistance of the structural floor.

Suspended ceilings are capable of providing sound absorption and to a less extent sound insulation. Most materials used for sound absorption tend to be fragile and liable to damage and are therefore best used on the ceiling. Porous materials offer the best control for high frequency noise, membranes or panel absorbers for low frequency noise: cavity resonators, usually absorbing over a narrow band of frequencies can be tuned to the dominant frequency of the noise source. Panel materials in general use are mineral wool, fibre, perforated metal and plastic.

In most buildings the suspended ceiling has to fulfil the role of sound insulation. For reasons of space flexibility the dividing partitions do not extend beyond the suspended ceiling level, and so sound transmission by way of the plenum above the partitions has to be reduced by the ceiling panels. The reduction of sound transmission is mainly dependent on the mass of the ceiling: efficient insulation can be obtained with a uniformly distributed mass of $20 \, \text{kg/m}^2$ to $25 \, \text{kg/m}^2$. In terms of a suspended ceiling this is very heavy. The most effective type of tiles are metal or screeded plaster boards, or sandwiched layers having at least a 50 mm air gap. There are usually many items such as luminaires, air diffusers and loudspeakers which are bedded into a ceiling. The overall insulation is governed by the weakest item and there is little point in having a massive ceiling if it is full of slots, cracks and equipment having poor insulation.

The absorption of an acoustic ceiling tile can largely be established and adjusted by its porosity, but a porous tile also allows air to flow through it. In many integrated systems the plenum acts as a return air duct and therefore is at a lower air pressure than the room. The degree of airtightness of the ceiling has to be limited to a leakage rate of 10% to 15% at the specified plenum pressure when air-handling luminaires are used.

Suspended ceilings are constructed on a secondary framework, the most common type being the jointless ceiling (Fig. 25.2). This construction consists of a framework supporting the ceiling tiles which can be an exposed T-section grid or a concealed fixing system. The exposed system permits easy access into the void but has the higher leakage rate for plenum extract systems. The concealed system provides an unbroken ceiling appearance and is less liable to leakage under negative pressure. Airtightness of the ceiling has to be considered during erection. As well as tile-sealing, special treatment may be necessary around the ceiling perimeter or around any equipment to be positioned in the ceiling.

21.4   INTEGRATED SYSTEMS IN USE

21.4.1   A store: Boots (Sunderland)

The lighting in the sales area (Fig. 21.7) is by 600 mm-wide prismatic troffers in six continuous rows using three 2400 mm 85 W Warm White tubes. The luminaires are an integral part of the ceiling and provide an illuminance of 1400 lux, a power loading of $45 \, \text{W/m}^2$.

The sales area is served by a low velocity air conditioning system to provide thermal

Fig. 21.7 Lighting arrangement in the heat-from-light system at Boots (Sunderland)

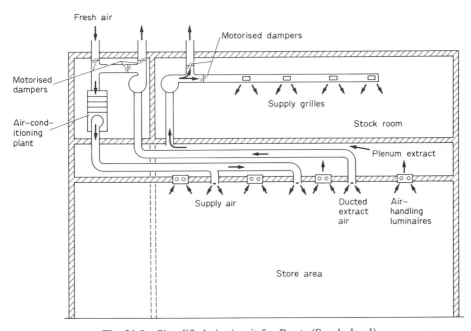

Fig. 21.8 Simplified air circuit for Boots (Sunderland)

conditions of 22 °C (with no humidification) for external temperatures between −1 °C and 24 °C. $5{\cdot}2\,m^3/s$ of conditioned air is supplied to the area by perforated supply diffusers and of this air $1{\cdot}8\,m^3/s$ is always fresh air. This fresh air volume is increased when the outside temperature drops below 11 °C to make use of free cooling. The extract air is returned by two circuits (Fig. 21.8), $1{\cdot}8\,m^3/s$ through the luminaires into a common plenum and $3{\cdot}4\,m^3/s$ through extract grilles and ducts back to the plant.

Each luminaire handles $17\,l/s$ of air at a plenum depression of $5\,N/m^2$ and extracts about 65% of the heat generated in the fitting. When needed for re-use as background heat, this heated air is distributed by ducts into the stock area, otherwise it is discharged to the atmosphere.

The heat extraction from the luminaires has enabled the air conditioning plant to be reduced by 20% and the heat reclaim arrangement has enabled the gas boiler plant to be reduced to 75% of that necessary for a conventional system.

21.4.2   An academic building: University of Surrey (Guildford)

The lighting design in the academic buildings is based on 1200 mm × 300 mm recessed luminaires with prismatic controllers housing two or three 1200 mm 40 W White tubes (Fig. 21.9). The luminaires have a *DLOR* of 49%, a BZ3 light distribution and provide an average illuminance of 450 lux with a glare index of 18.

The perimeter rooms are naturally ventilated but the core area is mechanically ventilated using air-handling luminaires. The ventilation system uses a plenum extract and is designed to control the room temperature at 20 °C, the luminaires passing the return air into the plenum. Up to $90\,l/s$ of air is handled by a luminaire at a plenum depression of $3{\cdot}7\,N/m^2$. Each pair of luminaires achieves a room-to-room cross-talk attenuation of more than 30 dB and the maximum generated noise is below NR 25.

The basic luminaire is designed to take additional boxes to allow the required volume of air to be handled (Fig. 21.10). $23\,l/s$ of air is passed through the lamp compartment,

Fig. 21.9   Air-handling and non-air-handling luminaires at the University of Surrey (Guildford)

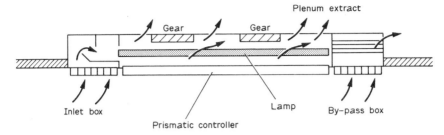

Fig. 21.10 Longitudinal section of the University of Surrey luminaire

taking 70% of the lighting heat with it, and 67 l/s is handled by the other box which can be volume controlled. The return air from the void is discharged to the atmosphere, taking away the surplus lighting heat, since most of these areas are laboratories where corrosive or obnoxious fumes could occur. Not all the luminaires handle air and so ventilation slots are incorporated in the back of non-air-handling luminaires to avoid a noticeable colour shift between two adjacent luminaires.

21.4.3   An open office : MANWEB (Chester)

This building has the first large-scale totally integrated heat-from-light air conditioning system in Britain.

Much of the building consists of 15 m × 30 m open-plan offices having 40% glazing on the external walls. Shading and heat reflecting curtains are employed to minimize solar heat gains.

The lighting is by individual 1800 mm × 600 mm recessed prismatic luminaires (Fig. 21.11) equipped with three 1500 mm 65 W White tubes providing an illuminance of 1000 lux with a glare index of 19. The total lighting load is about 45 W/m².

The heat reclaim scheme is designed and based on a patent system by Carrier Engineering Limited (Fig. 21.12). The air conditioning plant maintains the offices at

Fig. 21.11   Air-handling luminaires in the landscaped offices for MANWEB (Chester)

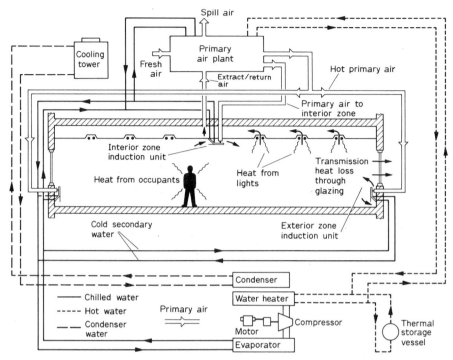

Fig. 21.12   Water and air flows in the heat recovery system at MANWEB (Chester)

21 °C at an RH of 50% for an outside temperature of −4 °C to 27 °C. The whole heating load needed to maintain this internal temperature at the minimum outside temperature is normally met by heat reclaimed from lighting (45%), from office equipment and air conditioning plant (40%) and from the occupants (15%). The system includes a thermal storage vessel and makes use of a refrigeration plant, used in the air conditioning system as a heat pump to convert the low grade heat at between 21 °C and 27 °C to re-usable heat at 49 °C, with a split condenser system.

Fresh air is supplied by a single high velocity duct to induction units under the windows and in the ceiling. All the return air is extracted through the luminaires from a common plenum. Each luminaire handles 14 l/s of air at a plenum depression of 2·5 N/m² and at this rate more than 60% of the lighting heat is removed.

A special feature of the lighting system is its control by photoelectric switches. During the day full use is made of the vast amount of daylight. The lighting is switched by three photocells placed on the side of the building when the illuminance there exceeds 9000 lux. When this occurs the outer row of fittings and one tube in each inner row are switched off. This arrangement affords a considerable saving in running cost.

22 Electric lighting of interiors

Electric lighting is provided indoors:

(a) to permit safe circulation,
(b) to permit the performance of tasks, and
(c) to reveal the structure and the contents of the room.

For any interior the subject can conveniently be considered under the two broad headings of criteria (what is to be achieved) and design methods (how to achieve the objectives).

The desirability of separating criteria and method is becoming more obvious with the increasing tendency on the part of lighting designers to allow their calculation methods, or their lack of alternative methods, to dictate the criteria to be specified. Thus horizontal illuminance is the most common criterion for the amount of light required simply because it can be calculated more easily than vertical or inclined plane illuminance: one of the latter values would be a more valid design objective in underground stations, in drawing offices, in shop windows, in industrial machine shops.

Criteria and design methodology are examined generally in this chapter: the application to specific types of interior is taken up in Chaps. 24 to 30.

22.1 LIGHTING DESIGN CRITERIA

The lighting of a work space involves the proper specification of task illuminance, direct glare, reflected glare and the spectral distribution of the source. These may be regarded as the functional aspects of lighting as opposed to the aesthetic aspects, and for every lighting installation designed a balance must be found between these two aspects, although their requirements may sometimes be mutually exclusive. The criteria selected must accept the constraints imposed by the site, the structure, the internal services, and the eventual use of the room.

For sustained working interiors such as offices and factories the balance of design effort, or cost, between function and effect lighting would average about 95% to 5% at present, although many lighting authorities would like to see a progression to a balance of 80% to 20%.

In general interiors with no sustained visual task for the majority of occupants (airport buildings, public spaces in banks, department stores) the average balance between function and effect is probably about 60% to 40% and this produces reasonably good installations.

Specialized interiors vary so widely that average figures would be meaningless but a cathedral might well work out at 20% function to 80% effect and a private house at 10% function to 90% effect.

22.1.1   Working interiors with sustained visual tasks

If the prime objective of enclosing a space is to provide housing for people to undertake specific sustained work, then the satisfactory lighting of that work is generally the prime lighting objective.

Illuminance.   Work lighting is usually specified by a minimum value of illuminance required on the task, as quoted by the IES Code. The recommendations in this document are very often misquoted and it should be clearly understood by the specifier and the designer of lighting installations that illuminance values given in the Code are minima and not design objectives. The same illuminance on two very different tasks such as black type on white paper and pencilled writing on blue paper would not provide the same ease of seeing. The IES Code cannot be specific enough to cover every possible variation in tasks or circumstances and it is therefore the responsibility of the lighting specifier or designer to interpret the Code recommendations in the light of his own skill and experience.

In selecting the design value of illuminance, due note must be taken of Statutory Instruments that affect lighting conditions. The lighting of all factories is subject to the provisions of the Factories Act 1961. The lighting of commercial premises is subject to the requirements of the Shops, Offices and Railway Premises Act 1963, which gives guidance on sufficiency and suitability of lighting. While sufficiency could be equated to task illuminance, suitability could well include direct discomfort glare, reflected glare, the spectral properties of light sources and directional properties of the lighting.

Direct discomfort glare.   Since 1961 it has been possible to compute a figure predicting the degree of direct discomfort glare (Sect. 2.2.2) to be expected from a general lighting installation using conventional fittings. This figure is the glare index, and the IES Code specifies an upper limit for various work situations. The specified limit varies with the difficulty of the visual task, it being assumed that the more critical the task, the lower the limiting glare index should be.

The point of view has been expressed that the lower the glare, the better the installation will be. This is tantamount to suggesting that the absence of luminance contrasts is desirable. Many lighting people consider that this could lead to a visual monotony as unsatisfactory as excessive glare.

When seeking to control discomfort glare, designers should aim to achieve the limiting glare indices recommended by the IES and not the lowest possible glare index. This approach offers reasonable opportunities for a satisfactory compromise between the conflicting demands of glare control on the one hand, and variety and interest on the other.

Reflected glare.   This is experienced when a light source is reflected in glossy room surfaces, desk tops or in the task itself. Occasionally a degree of reflected glare is desirable: for instance in reading a micrometer one produces a bright image in the polished metal thus permitting easy reading of the dark engraved scale. Normally, however, reflected glare is undesirable; it can occasionally cause discomfort, but more often affects adversely the ability of the eye to see. It can be minimized by suitable orientation and positioning of desks relative to luminaires, and also by choice of luminaire distribution or by polarization (Sect. 22.3.2). The contrast rendering factor (*CRF*) referred to in Chap. 2 is a parameter likely to be used in the future to specify the reflected glare potential of different lighting systems.

Lighted appearance of interiors.   The most useful way to express a desired lighting appearance is by specifying the amount of flux needed on each of the bounding surfaces of an interior, and in addition specifying the amount and direction of flux needed on objects or people within the room. For some years research has sought to establish those ratios of flux—expressed either as ratios of illuminance and reflectance, or as ratios of luminance, which would result in observers approving the scene. The results of this work have generally been published as one range of values. Experience of lighting design tells us that the same luminaires, if used in two interiors differing widely in their surface reflectances or in their proportions, would produce very different appearances (Fig. 22.1). For this reason it appears that a more detailed specification for a satisfactory lighting effect is needed than one set of ratios.

This specification would usually be expressed in the form of ratios of luminances of the room bounding surfaces, and would be drawn up to produce the desired effect from the most important viewing position for the room. The specification produced should be

Fig. 22.1   Contrasting effect produced by using similar luminaires in different interiors

checked by considering the view presented to all other relevant viewpoints in the room. In many rooms the occupants and furniture may be more important visually than the bounding surfaces, and due note should be taken of this when establishing the flux distribution required.

From recent appraisal work carried out by lighting engineers some general rule-of-thumb guides to planning for pleasantness appear to be emerging:

(a) If any room surface has a reflectance of 15% or less the amount of light put on the surface is unlikely to affect the perception of the surface.
(b) A room with pleasant colour contrasts will generally look good under a wide variety of lighting systems.
(c) A room without acceptable colour contrasts needs brightness contrasts introduced by the lighting.
(d) Subtle lighting contrasts are not generally noticeable.

Colour appearance and colour rendering.   The spectral quality of the light may be particularly important in circumstances where the visual tasks involve critical colour matching or colour discrimination. In other working situations the creation of satisfying cosmetic effects, or the provision of lighting giving acceptable visual clarity, involves a careful consideration of the merits of different light sources.

22.1.2   General interiors with few sustained visual tasks

It was suggested earlier in this chapter that the proportions of cost or effort devoted to functional and effect lighting averages 60% to 40% in non-working areas. It is certainly accepted that interiors of this type require more attention to the effects of lighting than do sustained working interiors. In these circumstances probably the least effective way of lighting the interior is by the regular layout of general lighting luminaires used in working areas to ensure that a reasonably uniform illuminance is provided throughout the interior. This last requirement does not hold for such places as an airport concourse, a department store or a foyer. For these interiors it is highly desirable that the lighting should be interesting and attractive, while ensuring that the few specific working points in the interior are well illuminated.

The first objective would be the required value of task illuminance at working positions. In an airport terminal, a task illuminance would be required on the check-in desks, which could be equated to the recommended minimum value for office lighting. By the same reasoning the direct discomfort glare, from the working positions only, should be no greater than would be acceptable for a general office.

The objectives set for lighting the remaining part of the area will depend largely on the structure: for example it would be futile to specify a high vertical illuminance on the bounding surfaces if the walls were completely glazed.

There is no single criterion of interest that can be adopted as a design objective. Usually, however, interest in lighting can be equated to contrasts in brightness and colour. Contrasts in brightness can be expressed by using light sources of higher intrinsic brightness than usual—for example, crystal chandeliers. Contrasts in colour will usually be the responsibility of the interior designer and it will be the lighting designer's responsibility to guarantee the colour scheme, sometimes to complement it. For example interest can be created by the use of different light sources, such as a mixture of colour-corrected mercury in downlighters and tungsten filament spotlights illuminating one of the room walls.

In interiors of the type we are considering, the lighting of people is very often not given much attention, yet in a large open space it is the people within that space who will be most prominent to any observer. This would seem to be an excellent reason for designing any lighting system to show people off as pleasantly as possible. As a general guideline it can be suggested that side lighting is preferable to top lighting (Fig. 22.2), a view that will be supported by any observer who has witnessed in a top-lit building the brilliance of reflections from polished foreheads that appear to intensify the deep vertical shadows on the face.

(a)   (b)

Fig. 22.2   Lighting effects on human face (a) side lighting   (b) top lighting

In any building with fixed seating positions or a fixed direction of view it would be simple to design a side lighting system to produce the desired effect. The latest work carried out on this subject suggests that light should be incident between 15° and 45° in elevation.

A completely different situation presents itself when considering a building, such as an airport terminal, where there is no fixed direction of view for the majority of occupants. For the multiview interior the aim should be to create soft shadows on the face, and as economics tend to favour top lighting systems it would be practicable to specify the average horizontal illuminance required from top lighting, and also to specify the average vertical illuminance to be provided, possibly by a secondary lighting system. A proposed range of ratios of vertical to horizontal illuminance for producing favourable judgements of faces is 0·5 to 0·3. An alternative term for average vertical illuminance is mean cylindrical illuminance (Sect. 1.4.10).

Work carried out in USSR and UK has shown a correlation between mean cylindrical illuminance and scalar illuminance. As scalar illuminance can be calculated very simply (Sect. 1.4.9), a reasonable criterion to adopt for the lighting of people would be scalar/horizontal illuminance ratios: the suggested range of value for this ratio is 1·0 to 1·7 for any installation directing light predominantly downwards.

22.1.3   Circulation areas

In the main these would be corridors, but circulatory elements could be found as parts of larger areas. Wherever they occur, circulation areas should be illuminated in the most appropriate manner to aid movement in the desired direction. Design objectives could be an enhanced illuminance on the floor of a large area to indicate key directions of movement, but this is not effective if large numbers of people are expected to follow the indications. Enhanced illuminance of vertical surfaces, contrasting with ceiling and floor can assist in the visual determination of boundaries and directions. Internally illuminated signs are an obvious way of indicating directions and locations: these can often form part of a general or a local lighting system, but the ambient lighting must be such that traffic along and across the circulation area can move safely. This is particularly important in industrial locations where small electric-powered vehicles share circulation routes with pedestrians.

The limitation of glare must be a prime objective in the lighting of stairs, also in the lighting of hospital corridors where patients are wheeled on stretchers flat on their backs. In the latter case, it is meaningless to calculate a glare index from the IES glare tables as this method assumes a horizontal line of vision: the BRS formula (Sect. 2.2.2) must be used.

Emergency lighting is often a requirement for interior traffic routes, and the location of luminaires providing this is determined by the doors and other possible exits from the building. Due to the time needed for the eye to adapt from full illumination to very low illumination the emergency lighting should produce at the critical points illuminances of at least 1% of the normal value.

22.2   GENERAL DESIGN METHODS

In a general lighting scheme the luminaires are arranged in a regular array where the spacing of the luminaires along the rows is substantially the same as the spacing between the rows, and the spacing between the walls and outer rows of luminaires is approximately half the spacing between the rows. In the case of long linear sources the spacing along the rows may be less than between the rows, or continuous runs of luminaires may even be employed.

The appropriate spacing will be determined by the light distribution from the luminaire, the value of illuminance required, the height of the building and other practical considerations, such as the available roof structure members to which luminaires can be easily attached.

22.2.1   The 'lumen' method of design

The most frequently used method of lighting installation design depends upon a determination of the total flux required to provide a given value of working plane illuminance
and is generally known as the 'lumen' method.

Basically, the procedure is to determine the quantity of light flux which the sources
must emit to obtain the required value of task illuminance extending over the whole of
the working plane, allowing for the flux which is lost by absorption in the luminaires and
the room surfaces.

The lumen method can be expressed using the formula:

$$\Phi = \frac{E_{av} \times A}{UF \times MF} \tag{22.1}$$

where Φ = total flux required in lumens
E_{av} = average working plane illuminance
UF = utilization factor
A = the area of the working plane
and MF = maintenance factor, which takes account of losses due to the accumulation
of dirt in the luminaires and on the room surfaces (Chap. 34).

Utilization factor.   The British Zonal Method for determining the *UF* (given in IES
Technical Report No. 2) considers separately the contributions from the downward and
the upward components of flux from the installation. Flux from the luminaires is divided
between the lower and upper hemispheres. The ratio of the downward flux emitted from
the luminaires to the total lamp flux, is known as the downward light output ratio
(*DLOR*). Similarly the ratio of the upward flux emitted from the luminaires to the total
lamp flux is known as the upward light output ratio (*ULOR*).

The total flux reaching the working plane consists of that part which is directly incident
on the working plane plus that part which reaches it after inter-reflection. The lower
hemisphere flux which is utilized contains a direct component and an inter-reflected
component, while the upper hemisphere flux which is utilized will consist entirely of
inter-reflected flux within the space between ceiling and walls (Fig. 22.3).

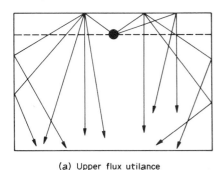
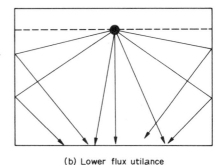

(a) Upper flux utilance   (b) Lower flux utilance

Fig. 22.3   Flux utilization

The distribution of light in the lower hemisphere is expressed in terms of the direct light incident on the working plane: that proportion of the total downward flux from a conventional installation of luminaires which is directly incident on the working plane is known as the direct ratio (*DR*) and forms the basis of the BZ classification of luminaires (Sect. 5.1.1).

The proportion of the total downward flux from the luminaires which reaches the working plane, some directly and some after inter-reflection, is known as the lower flux utilance (*LFU*). Similarly the proportion of the total upward flux which finally reaches the working plane after inter-reflection is known as the upper flux utilance (*UFU*).

The basis of the BZ method can be stated by the equation

$$UF = LFU \times DLOR + UFU \times ULOR \qquad (22.2)$$

Values of *DLOR* and *ULOR* are included in manufacturer's data for luminaires. Values of *LFU* and *UFU* are obtained from tables given in IES Technical Report No. 2.

For the calculation of both the direct and inter-reflected components in these IES tables certain assumptions are made and conventions adopted. It has been found that the inter-reflected components calculated for a square room will apply, with sufficient accuracy, to a rectangular room of the same height and surface reflectances, provided the ratio of working plane area to wall area is the same. This leads to the concept of a single-number index to define the room shape, known as the room ratio or *room index*

$$k_r = \frac{LW}{(L+W)H_m} \qquad (22.3)$$

where L and W are the length and width respectively, and H_m is the mounting height of the luminaires above the working plane. Conventionally the room dimensions are taken for L and W, but care must be exercised in ensuring that the dimensions used are clear of obstructions. For example, in a warehouse with storage racks extending to truss height a room index based on the room dimension would be too high, and the dimensions used should be those between adjacent racks.

The distance of the outer rows of luminaires from the walls of a building affect both the distribution of the available light flux and its utilization. There will be occasions when it is desirable to locate the outer rows of luminaires closer to the walls than the conventional half-spacing distance, so as to increase wall luminance and work-plane illuminance near walls. If the wall to outer row spacing is reduced to less than half the spacing in the rows, then the overall utilization will be smaller and the number of luminaires may need to be increased over the value obtained from utilization factor calculations. It should be noted that in these circumstances, although the utilization factor is lower, the quality of an installation may well be enhanced.

For those installations in which the luminaires are suspended from the ceiling, the inter-reflected light calculations are made only for the space between the working plane and the plane of the luminaires. The space above the plane of the luminaires is replaced by an equivalent ceiling which has an effective reflectance less than that of the actual ceiling (Fig. 22.4). In general, where the suspension length H_s is less than one-sixth of the ceiling height above the work plane, the luminaires may be regarded as ceiling mounted.

It can be shown that the light lost by absorption within the space above the luminaires, known as the ceiling cavity, is the same as that which would be lost on an imaginary

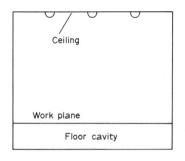

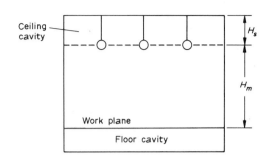

(a) Ceiling mounted luminaires   (b) Suspended luminaires

Fig. 22.4   Ceiling cavity

ceiling at the same height as the luminaires, when this equivalent ceiling has an effective
reflectance ρ_e given by the formula

$$\rho_e = \frac{A_c \rho_a}{A_c \rho_a + A_t(1 - \rho_a)} \qquad (22.4)$$

where A_c = plan area of the ceiling
A_t = total area of all surfaces within the ceiling cavity
ρ_a = average reflectance of all surfaces within the ceiling cavity

$$= \frac{A_{s_1}\rho_1 + A_{s_2}\rho_2 + \cdots A_{s_n}\rho_n}{A_{s_1} + A_{s_2} + \cdots A_{s_n}}$$

This average reflectance ρ_a can be expressed for a rectangular room in terms of ceiling
and upper wall reflectances and the *ceiling cavity index* k_c

$$k_c = \frac{LW}{H_s(L + W)} \qquad (22.5)$$

where H_s is the luminaire suspension length.
    Using this concept the average reflectance of the ceiling cavity is given by

$$\rho_a = \frac{k_c \rho_c + 2\rho_w}{k_c + 2} \qquad (22.6)$$

where ρ_c = ceiling reflectance and ρ_w = upper wall reflectance.
    The steps in applying the cavity method are:

(a) Determine room index (k_r) from Eq. 22.3.
(b) Determine ceiling cavity index (k_c) from Eq. 22.5.
(c) Determine average reflectance of ceiling cavity (ρ_a) from Eq. 22.6.
(d) Determine effective reflectance of equivalent ceiling (ρ_e) from Eq. 22.4.
(e) Determine *LFU* and *UFU* from tables.
(f) Determine utilization factor (UF) from Eq. 22.2.

    Any change in the effective working plane reflectance will affect the installation
utilization factor. Published utilization factors are for a specific effective working plane

407

reflectance and it is necessary to use a correction factor (Table 22.1) where the value differs from this.

Table 22.1   Correction factors for UF when effective working plane reflectance differs from 10%

% Reflectance		Room index									
Ceiling	Wall	0·6	0·8	1·0	1·25	1·5	2·0	2·5	3·0	4·0	5·0
		Factors for 20% effective working plane reflectance									
	50	1·03	1·03	1·04	1·04	1·05	1·05	1·06	1·06	1·07	1·07
75	30	1·01	1·02	1·02	1·03	1·04	1·04	1·05	1·05	1·06	1·07
	10	1·01	1·01	1·02	1·02	1·03	1·04	1·04	1·05	1·05	1·06
	50	1·02	1·02	1·03	1·03	1·03	1·04	1·04	1·04	1·04	1·05
50	30	1·01	1·01	1·02	1·02	1·02	1·03	1·03	1·04	1·04	1·04
	10	1·01	1·01	1·01	1·02	1·02	1·02	1·03	1·03	1·04	1·04
30	30	1·01	1·01	1·01	1·02	1·02	1·02	1·02	1·02	1·02	1·03
	10	1·00	1·01	1·01	1·01	1·01	1·02	1·02	1·02	1·02	1·02
		Factors for 30% effective working plane reflectance									
	50	1·05	1·06	1·07	1·09	1·10	1·11	1·12	1·13	1·14	1·15
75	30	1·03	1·04	1·05	1·06	1·07	1·09	1·10	1·11	1·13	1·14
	10	1·01	1·02	1·03	1·05	1·06	1·07	1·09	1·10	1·12	1·13
	50	1·04	1·05	1·05	1·06	1·07	1·08	1·08	1·09	1·09	1·10
50	30	1·03	1·03	1·04	1·04	1·05	1·06	1·07	1·07	1·08	1·09
	10	1·01	1·02	1·02	1·03	1·04	1·04	1·06	1·06	1·07	1·08
30	30	1·02	1·02	1·03	1·03	1·03	1·04	1·04	1·05	1·05	1·05
	10	1·01	1·01	1·02	1·02	1·02	1·03	1·03	1·04	1·04	1·05

Example of installation design for a large general office in a clean situation:

Required task illuminance	400 lux
Dimensions	8 m wide × 20 m long × 4·5 m high
Height of desks	0·8 m
Surface reflectances	Ceiling 0·70
	Walls 0·30
	Floor 0·10
Luminaire	Twin 1800 mm 85 W, prismatic BZ3
	DLOR 0·48, *ULOR* 0·10
Suspension distance of luminaire from ceiling	0·5 m

Calculation of utilization factor:

(a) Room index

$$k_r = \frac{L \times W}{H_m(L + W)}$$

$$= \frac{8 \times 20}{3·2 \times 28}$$

$$= 1·8$$

(b) Ceiling cavity index

$$k_c = \frac{L \times W}{H_s(L \times W)}$$

$$= \frac{8 \times 20}{0 \cdot 5 \times 28}$$

$$= 11 \cdot 4$$

(c) Average reflectance of ceiling cavity

$$\rho_a = \frac{k_c \rho_c + 2\rho_w}{k_c + 2}$$

$$= \frac{(11 \cdot 4 \times 0 \cdot 7) + (2 \times 0 \cdot 3)}{11 \cdot 4 + 2}$$

$$= 0 \cdot 64$$

(d) Effective reflectance of equivalent ceiling

$$\rho_e = \frac{A_c \rho_a}{A_c \rho_a + A_t(1 - \rho_a)}$$

$$= \frac{160 \times 0 \cdot 64}{(160 \times 0 \cdot 64) + (188 \times 0 \cdot 36)}$$

$$= 0 \cdot 60$$

(e) From Tables 7.3 and 8 in IES Technical Report No. 2

$$LFU = 0 \cdot 81$$

$$UFU = 0 \cdot 41$$

(f) Utilization factor

$$UF = LFU \times DLOR + UFU \times ULOR$$

$$= 0 \cdot 81 \times 0 \cdot 48 + 0 \cdot 41 \times 0 \cdot 10$$

$$= 0 \cdot 43$$

With a utilization factor of 0·43 and an assumed maintenance factor of 0·72 the total lamp flux required is:

$$\Phi = \frac{\text{Illuminance required} \times \text{Area}}{UF \times MF}$$

$$= \frac{400 \times 8 \times 20}{0 \cdot 43 \times 0 \cdot 72}$$

$$= 207\,000 \, \text{lm}$$

With Natural tubes the number of luminaires needed to produce the illuminance is:

$$N = \frac{207\,000}{4350 \times 2}$$

$$= 24 \, \text{luminaires}$$

Quite separately from the calculations so far, it is now necessary to establish the maximum spacing between the centres of luminaires. The maximum spacing is that distance apart at which the distribution of light will ensure that the minimum illuminance is not less than 0·7 of the maximum illuminance. The spacing/height ratio recommended for the luminaire is 1·1 : 1. With a mounting height of 3·2 m from desk top to luminaire the maximum spacing is 1·1 × 3·2 m = 3·5 m

$$\text{Minimum number of luminaires} = \frac{L}{\text{Maximum spacing}} \times \frac{W}{\text{Maximum spacing}}$$

$$= \frac{20}{3·5} \times \frac{8}{3·5}$$

$$= 13 \text{ luminaires}$$

This is the minimum number of luminaires permissible, and as the illuminance calculation gave 24 luminaires there is no uniformity problem. It is necessary to space the 24 luminaires evenly within the space: a reasonable layout would be 3 rows of 8, with $\frac{8}{3}$ m spacing between rows and $\frac{20}{8}$ m spacing between centres of luminaires.

22.2.2 Predicting discomfort glare ratings

It will be evident that the lumen method of lighting installation design is a limited one in that it does not give any indication of the brightness of the work surfaces, or whether there may be objectional contrasts which could be a cause of discomfort. This limitation may be overcome, in part, by assessing the discomfort glare index for the installation. The procedure for doing this is set out in IES Technical Report No. 10, based upon the empirical formula developed by the Building Research Station (Sect. 2.2.2).

In a practical installation the glare assessment is made for an observer who is sitting at the mid-point of one side of the room, looking straight ahead along a horizontal sight line, and the total glare is taken to be the sum of that due to each source taken separately.

The glare index can be derived from the basic formula, but the procedure is lengthy and so the IES Report includes tables of glare index for installations covering a selected range of room dimensions, light distributions (BZ classification), and room surface reflectances. The selected ranges are chosen so as to cover the range of lighting installations generally met in practice.

Certain factors have fixed values in the tables:

(a) The downward flux per luminaire = 1000 lm
(b) The height of the luminaires above a 1·2 m (4 ft) eye level = 3·05 m (10 ft).
(c) The luminous area of a luminaire = 645 cm² (100in²). This is defined as the area seen from beneath the luminaire for BZ1 to BZ8 luminaires, and as the area seen from the side for BZ9 and BZ10 luminaires.

Conversion terms are provided to correct for these factors in a particular installation.

The values of initial glare index in the tables are computed for a basic installation using each of the ten defined light distributions (BZ1 to BZ10), four defined luminaire flux ratios, 0, 0·33, 1·0 and 3·0, and selected combinations of room dimensions and reflectances. There is one table for each of the classified distributions.

The glare index for a particular installation is obtained by reading from the appropriate table, opposite the room dimensions and surface reflectances, the initial glare index and then applying the appropriate conversion terms taken from another table.

Having determined the installation glare index, it can then be compared with the value of the limiting glare index which has been assessed as appropriate for that type of location, these limiting values being given in the IES Code.

When planning an installation in which luminaires having non-symmetric distributions are used it is sometimes possible to reduce the glare index by re-orientating the luminaires.

If a particular type of luminaire is found unsuitable for one installation it does not follow that it is necessarily unsuitable for another. Also, if a particular luminaire in a given installation produces a glare index very much lower than the recommended limiting value, it is not necessarily a better lighting installation than that in which some other luminaire gives a glare index just below the recommended limit: there is no great virtue in a glare index considerably lower than the recommended limit.

Example of glare calculation.   A sheet metal works has dimensions: 42 m long, 21 m wide, with luminaires mounted at 8·2 m above the floor. Room reflectances: ceiling 0·50, walls 0·30, effective working plane 0·14. Luminaires: fluorescent BZ4 classification mounted in rows parallel to the longer side of the factory. Flux fractions: 0 up, 100% down. Total downward flux: 6000 lm. Luminous area: 0·476 m².

Height above eye level $H = 8·2$ m $- 1·2$ m $= 7$ m.

Room dimensions in terms of H: $Y = 6H$, $X = 3H$.

Initial Glare Index from IES tables $= 23·6 + 1·3$ for endwise viewing.

Conversion terms from IES tables:

$$F = +4·7 \text{ due to downward flux}$$
$$A = -7·0 \text{ due to luminous area}$$
$$H = +1·2 \text{ due to mounting height}$$
$$\text{Total} = -1·1$$

Installation glare index 23·8.

The limiting value recommended for a sheet metal works is 25 and therefore the designed installation will be satisfactory.

If the factory were a woodworking shop where the recommended limit is 22, the condition could be met by adjusting the height of the luminaires to 11·7 m, for then $H = 10·5$ m, $Y = 4H$, $X = 2H$.

Initial index from tables $= 20·7 + 0·5 = 21·2$.

Conversion terms: $F = +4·7$ as before
$A = -7·0$ as before
$H = +1·9$

giving an installation glare index of $21·2 + 4·7 - 7·0 + 1·9 = 20·8$.

22.3   UNCONVENTIONAL DESIGN METHODS AND LUMINAIRES

Lighting design is constantly evolving due to the introduction of new lamps and luminaires and due to changes in the accepted ways of using light.

At any one time it is possible to draw a distinction between, on the one hand, accepted design methods, and on the other hand, unconventional methods. Sect. 22.2 has covered the former, and this section considers the latter.

22.3.1   Appearance design

The 'apparent brightness' method of design was first proposed to permit an orderly calculation of the lighting needed to produce any proposed visual effect. The effect is specified by allotting a brightness value to each surface in the interior, in arbitrary units. Standard curves produced by Hopkinson, Waldram and Stevens enable these brightness values to be converted to luminance values. Using these luminances, the reflectances of the surface and inter-reflection calculations, the required direct illuminance on each surface can be obtained.

This method has often been used for cathedrals and churches, for which it is particularly suitable, and has produced many fine installations (Fig. 22.5), but is not generally considered suitable for working interiors as the brightness scales used are inadequate at higher levels of illuminance.

There are a number of other methods of design used since the Waldram method was conceived which involve a consideration of luminance. These vary from the industrial

Fig. 22.5   Church lighting by 'apparent brightness' method

412

task, where contrasts in the luminance between the task and its background are important, to the private office where the ratios of the luminances of the room surfaces are more important. Luminance may itself be considered, or it may be considered indirectly by taking illuminance and reflectance. Both methods have their protagonists but as very few lighting installations are reported that have been designed in terms of luminance, more experience is needed before firm proposals can be made.

Fig. 22.6   Bank lighting by 'luminance design' method

The following step by step procedure has been followed in a luminance design scheme for the banking hall shown in Fig. 22.6:

(a) Obtain full drawings showing interior furnishing and reflectances of all surfaces.
(b) Select one viewpoint on plan for which total effect will be designed.
(c) Note working positions and allot appropriate illuminances to each.
(d) Using average task reflectance establish task luminance.
(e) From typical working position specify luminance of desk top in relation to task.
(f) Specify floor luminance if this appears in field of view.
(g) Specify luminance of facing wall.
(h) Specify luminances of other walls in relation to those values already specified.
(i) Review all luminances in relation to each other to avoid undue contrasts or to create contrasts.
(k) Review all luminances from selected viewpoint for effect and adjust as necessary.
(l) Calculate direct flux required on each surface.
(m) Calculate flux distribution of luminaire needed to produce specified flux distribution.
(n) Check to see if luminaire is satisfactory from glare and economic viewpoints. If not, determine where direct flux needs to be provided by local or localized lighting to permit use of standard luminaire with overall satisfactory performance.
(o) As all calculations up to this point are for average values, assess gradations of luminance of each surface for suitability and adjust as necessary.

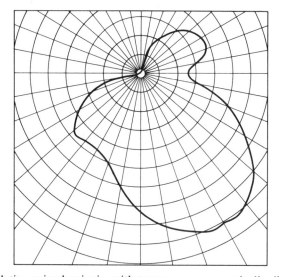

Fig. 22.7   Installation using luminaire with transverse asymmetric distribution (shown)

Ideally the brief to the lighting designer should be given by an architect or an interior designer, and the lighting should be designed to harmonize with and enhance the total effect. The job of the lighting engineer is then to persuade the specifier to verbalize his design objectives in detail. Whatever his objectives, if expressed in basic terms they can be met either by selecting colour and reflectances to produce the various effects, in which case the lighting need is for a constant value of illuminance over all surfaces; or they can be met by an unrelated choice of colour and reflectances, which would require the lighting man to use his skill in adding light where necessary and reducing it where low key effects are needed.

22.3.2   New types of luminaire distributions

The 1961 IES Code emphasized the British Zonal Method for classifying luminaire distributions, and gave impetus to the development of prismatic controllers to meet the requirements of the Glare Code. Inevitably the mathematical curves in the BZ system became accepted as the only design objectives for general lighting luminaires. Standardized intensity distributions led inevitably to lighting installations having a standardized appearance. To break away from this, and for reasons connected with the flow of light, a fluorescent luminaire with a transverse asymmetric distribution was developed in 1967 (Fig. 22.7). This gave a more effective lighting of working points due to reduced obstruction on the part of the worker, a higher proportion of light on vertical surfaces, and a different pattern of shadowing on people.

Appraisal of lighting installations using this asymmetric luminaire showed that the functional aspect of the design was good, but opinion was divided on the total effect; some opining that the glare was excessive, and few observing any effect of the flow of light.

A logical development from the asymmetric luminaire is the back-to-back asymmetric, or batwing distribution (Fig. 22.8). This type of distribution has all the advantages claimed for the asymmetric distribution except for the so-called coherent flow of light.

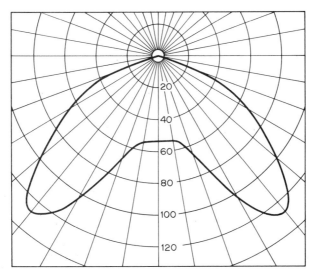

Fig. 22.8   Polar distribution of batwing luminaire

When used in an installation where workers are facing in the direction of the axis of the luminaire, reflected glare is reduced below that of any conventional luminaire and so visual performance for a given illuminance value is greatly improved. The distribution also enables a greater spacing/mounting height to be used for a given uniformity of illuminance.

Where the batwing distribution is inappropriate, such as an open-plan office with the occupants liable to face any direction, the use of a multi-layer polarizer in the luminaire will result in a reduction of reflected glare in horizontal visual tasks. Intensity distributions for such luminaires tend to be conventional, but the polarizers reduce the fraction of horizontally polarized light emitted to an increasing extent with angle from the downward vertical: horizontally polarized light accounts for most of the specular reflections in horizontal tasks which give rise to reflected glare.

23 Daylight in interiors

The design of lighting for interiors has to take account of the variation of natural lighting throughout the 24 hour day and throughout the year. The time of day when natural lighting ceases to be adequate for users of buildings to perform tasks, or pass through with safety, will determine the time when artificial lighting must take over from daylight. The time at which this will occur is determined not only by the level of daylight outdoors but also by the extent of the penetration of daylight, at adequate intensities, into the building. To design the lighting so as to satisfy the users of a building throughout the year three aspects of design have to be considered:

(a) The design of windows to provide as high a level of natural lighting as possible consistent with other design parameters, such as solar heat gains and losses, sky glare and the penetration of noise.
(b) The supplementing of daylight, during daylight hours, in areas of buildings remote from the windows.
(c) The lighting during hours of darkness using artificial light sources.

23.1 CHARACTERISTICS OF DAYLIGHT

23.1.1 Sunlight

The illuminance due to direct sunlight, at any point on the earth's surface varies, with the time of day and the season of the year and also the prevailing atmospheric conditions. Atmospheric absorption is an important factor in determining the illuminance and in addition to the meteorological conditions it depends on the distance through which the sun's radiation travels, which is determined by the sun's altitude.

The precise altitude for any time and place may be calculated using the formula:

$$\sin \theta = \sin \lambda \sin \delta + \cos \lambda \cos \delta \cos h \tag{23.1}$$

where θ is the altitude of the sun, λ is the latitude, δ is the declination and h is the hour angle. The angle of declination may be read from Fig. 23.1 and the hour angle h, in degrees, is obtained by multiplying the number of hours after the sun crosses the meridian plane by 15.

The time at which the sun crosses the meridian is not precisely 12.00 by local clock time; the difference is known as the equation of time (Fig. 23.1). A correction to GMT allows for irregularities in the actual length of the solar day.

$$\text{Local apparent time} = \text{GMT} + \text{Equation of time} \pm 4L$$

where L is the longitude of the locality in degrees. Where an hour of 'daylight saving' is in operation, one hour must be added to give clock time.

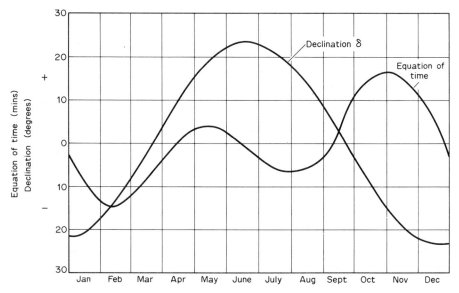

Fig. 23.1 Variation of angle of declination and of the equation of time throughout the year

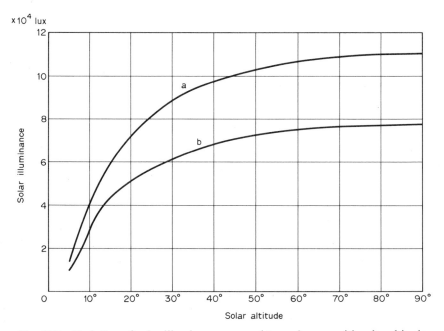

Fig. 23.2 Variation of solar illuminance, normal to sun's rays, with solar altitude
(a) for sunny climates   (b) for less sunny climates

Values of solar illuminance perpendicular to the sun's rays in Britain may be obtained from Fig. 23.2, derived from measurements made at Teddington, in which curve (a) applies to places in sunny climates and to particularly clear skies such as those in UK, and curve (b) applies to average clear skies in less sunny climates.

23.1.2 Skylight

Because of the variations in daylight it is impossible to determine precisely the illuminance to be expected at any given time or place. However, measurements taken at a number of places over prolonged periods have enabled average values to be established. For lighting designers it is generally of more value to know how much light will be available from some aspect than from the whole sky; therefore, the variations of daylight for each of the

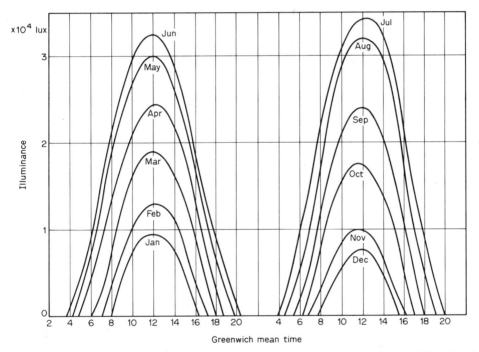

Fig. 23.3 Horizontal illuminance due to the whole sky (sun excluded) at the middle of each month (Teddington)

four quadrants of the sky centred on the four cardinal compass directions have been measured in addition to that for the whole sky (Fig. 23.3). Records of measurements made at Teddington during the years 1933 to 1939 have established values of daylight which may be used for lighting design for any place in UK.

When planning daylighting it is often of importance to know the times of day throughout the year when the illuminance falls below some given value. Curves of these data are given in Fig. 23.4 for the whole sky.

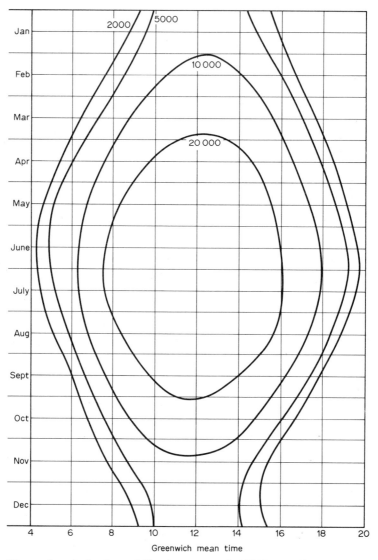

Fig. 23.4   Times when the horizontal illuminance equals 2000 lx, 5000 lx, 10 000 lx and 20 000 lx (Teddington)

The daylight illuminance at a point inside a building will be determined by the luminance of that area of the sky visible from the point, which may be a small part of the whole sky. The variation of luminance from one region of the sky to another will greatly influence the daylight illuminance at the point. Sky luminance, except for the densely overcast sky, is highest in the region of the sun and lowest at about 90° from it.

Because it is of considerable interest to the designer of buildings the overcast sky condition has particularly been extensively studied. The steady overcast sky represents for the designer the worst conditions for which he has to cater: a relatively simple expression defining the luminance distribution for this condition can simplify daylighting calculations. For this condition an empirical formula has been agreed by the CIE for international use:

$$L_\theta = \tfrac{1}{3}L_z(1+2 \sin \theta) \qquad (23.2)$$

where L_θ is the luminance of the sky at an angle θ above the horizon and L_z the luminance of the sky at the zenith. The relative luminance distribution is shown in Fig. 23.5.

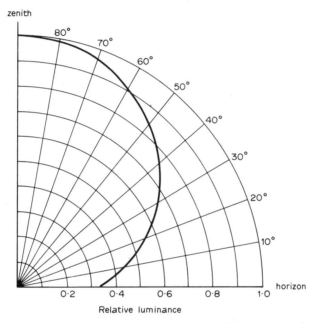

Fig. 23.5   Relative luminance distribution of CIE overcast sky

23.1.3   Spectral distribution

The light-producing processes of the sun, the absorption in the outer layers of the sun, the absorption and scattering of the upper layers of the earth's atmosphere, the absorption and scattering of water vapour, clouds and industrial haze, all contribute in varying proportions to the spectral power distribution of daylight, which is given in Fig. 23.6.

In the passage of sunlight through the atmosphere a great deal of light is scattered. It was shown by Lord Rayleigh that the proportion of the radiation scattered by minute particles (in this case air molecules) is proportional to λ^{-4}, where λ is the wavelength of the radiation. Larger suspended particles (aerosols) also scatter light in a similar way though less selectively. The consequence of this is that more blue light and near ultraviolet is scattered than red, and therefore direct sunlight appears distinctly yellow. When the path traversed by the radiation through the atmosphere is long, such as at sunrise and

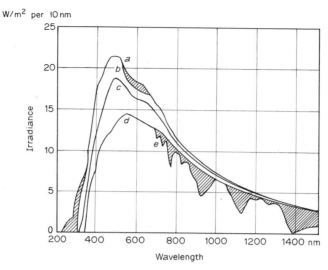

W/m² per 10 nm

Fig. 23.6   Spectral power distribution:
(a) extra-terrestrial radiation
(b) after passing through ozone layer
(c) after Rayleigh scattering
(d) after aerosol absorption and scattering
(e) after water vapour and oxygen absorption

sunset, the sun appears red. Some light which is scattered is completely lost, but some reaches the ground and therefore the sky appears blue. Light from clouds is a mixture of direct sunlight and sky-scattered light. Hence the spectral power distribution of daylight at any given place will depend upon the relative proportions of direct sunlight, scattered light and light from the clouds. When the sky is completely overcast the diffusion by the clouds is complete and the spectral power distribution is similar to that which would be obtained if there was no atmospheric scattering.

Measurement of spectral power distribution for various sky conditions has shown that, to a close approximation, the distribution can be equated to that of a full radiator at a given colour temperature, and it is often the practice to define a given sky condition by reference to its colour temperature. For example Fig. 3.9 gives the spectral power distribution for one phase of daylight (radiation from the whole sky, including direct sunlight) which has a spectral power distribution similar to, but slightly more green than, a full radiator of colour temperature 6500 K.

23.2   DAYLIGHT IN BUILDINGS

The daylight illuminance inside a building is subject to the same variation as daylight outdoors; to a first approximation the illuminance at a given point inside a building is a constant fraction of the illuminance at the same instant at a point outside. This approximation serves as a basis for the calculation of daylight at any given point within a building. The ratio of the illuminance indoors to that at the same instant outdoors is known as the daylight factor.

23.2.1 Daylight factor and its components

The daylight factor is defined as the ratio of the daylight illuminance at a point on a given plane due to light received directly or indirectly from a sky of assumed or known luminance distribution to the illuminance on a horizontal plane due to an unobstructed hemisphere of this sky. Direct sunlight is excluded from both values of illuminance.

The daylight at a point in a building may be considered to be made up of three components:

(a) Light reaching the point directly from the sky.
(b) Light reaching the point after reflection from external surfaces.
(c) Light reaching the point after reflection from the surfaces of the room and its furnishings.

(a) The *sky component* is defined as the ratio of that part of the daylight illuminance at a point on a given plane which is received directly from the sky of assumed or known luminance distribution to the illuminance on a horizontal plane due to an unobstructed hemisphere of this sky. Direct sunlight is excluded from both values of illuminance.

(b) The *externally-reflected component* is defined as the ratio of that part of the daylight illuminance at a point on a given plane which is received directly from external reflecting surfaces illuminated directly or indirectly by a sky of assumed or known luminance distribution to the illumination on a horizontal plane due to an unobstructed hemisphere of this sky. Contributions of direct sunlight to the luminances of external reflecting surfaces and to the illuminance of the comparison plane are excluded.

The externally-reflected component is an 'equivalent sky component' of the external obstructions at the reference point and is a function of the luminance of these obstructions relative to the sky which is obscured. The luminance of the external surfaces visible from inside a building averages about 10% of the sky luminance and therefore the externally-reflected component is taken as being equal to the sky component of the equivalent area of sky multiplied by 0·1.

(c) The *internally-reflected component* is defined as the ratio of that part of the daylight illuminance at a point on a given plane which is received from the internal reflecting surfaces, the sky being of assumed or known luminance distribution, to the illuminance on a horizontal plane due to an unobstructed hemisphere of this sky. Contributions of direct sunlight to the luminances of internal reflecting surfaces and to the illuminance of the comparison plane are excluded.

23.2.2 Daylight factor contours

Windows are generally divided into two main classes as far as daylighting of interiors is concerned, those situated in a side wall and those in the roof. With a vertical window in a side wall the sky component of daylight factor falls off rapidly with increasing distance from the window, especially over the first metre of this distance. This is illustrated in Fig. 23.7 (curve A), which shows how the sky component varies along a line perpendicular to a window, 1·5 m high and 0·9 m wide, with an unobstructed outlook. The line for which the sky component is drawn is that passing through the middle point of the window sill, distances being measured from the outer face of the window.

It will be seen that at 0·3 m the sky component is approximately 23% and that it

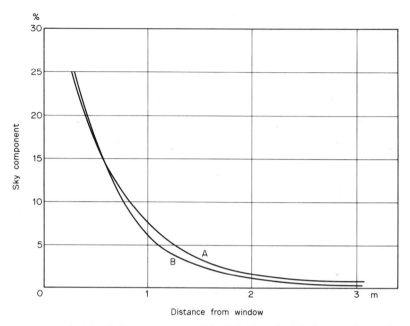

Fig. 23.7   Variation of sky component of daylight factor with distance from window

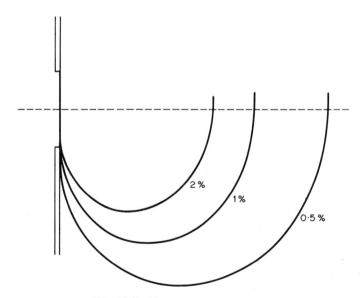

Fig. 23.8   Sky component contours

reduces to 3% at 1·6 m and to about 1% at 2·4 m. The influence that window height has on the sky component is also shown in Fig. 23.7. Curve A is for a window 1·5 m high and width 0·9 m and curve B is for a window height of 0·9 m and width 1·5 m. At a short distance from the window the sky component is approximately the same for both windows, but for all points greater than 0·6 m from the window, the sky component for the taller window gives a higher illuminance, almost twice as much at a distance of 3 m.

Additional information regarding the illuminance on an interior horizontal plane can be provided by a map of contour lines corresponding to different values of sky component, such as 2%, 1% and 0·5%. An example is given in Fig. 23.8 for the plane passing through the lower edge of window A referred to above. It will be seen that the contours are approximately ellipses passing through the outer edge of the window opening. The area enclosed within a given contour of s per cent is the area of the working plane which has a sky component of s per cent or more.

The amount of light provided by a window is sometimes specified by one or both of the following: (a) the area enclosed by a particular sky component contour, (b) the maximum distance from the window at which the particular sky component is realized.

23.2.3   Measurement of daylight factor

The most direct method of measuring daylight factor is to make measurements at the same instant of time at the indoor position and somewhere out of doors with an unobstructed horizon. It frequently happens that an unobstructed sky is difficult to obtain and use is sometimes made of the fact that for an overcast sky the illuminance of a horizontal surface exposed to a whole sky is the same as it would be if the sky was of uniform luminance equal to that of the overcast sky at an angle of elevation of about 42°.

A recently developed instrument (Fig. 23.9) enables daylight factors to be measured by either of these methods. (The instrument can also be used to measure illuminance or the luminance of a 15° field). Three photocells A, B and C are incorporated in the instrument. If an unobstructed sky is available, cell A is placed at the position where daylight factor is to be measured and cell B under the sky: the instrument reads directly the ratio of the two illuminances. Cell C, at the left hand side of Fig. 23.9, accepts light from a 15° field and can be set to sample the sky at a mean elevation of 42°: this is used in conjunction with cell A when the second method of measuring daylight factor is to be used.

Fig. 23.9   Daylight factor meter

23.3   DAYLIGHT FACTOR PREDICTION

The component of daylight factor which can be determined most precisely is the sky component and the method adopted may be used to calculate the externally-reflected component, but the determination of the internally-reflected component requires a quite different approach.

23.3.1   Sky component due to an element of an overcast sky

Graphical methods of determining the sky component of daylight factor at a point depend upon the relationships linking:

(a) The illuminance on a horizontal plane due to a small element of sky.
(b) The luminance of that element.
(c) Its angle of elevation at the point where the illuminance is measured.

In Fig. 23.10, representing a sky of radius r, is a small element of sky at angle of elevation θ and azimuth angle α, of luminance $L_{\theta\alpha}$.

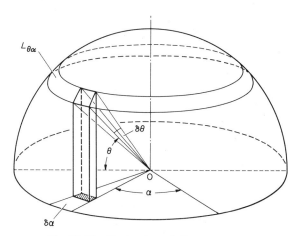

Fig. 23.10   Derivation of sky component

The illuminance at 0 due to this element of sky

$$\delta E = \frac{L_{\theta\alpha} \cdot r \, \delta\theta \cdot r \cos\theta \, \delta\alpha}{r^2} \cdot \sin\theta$$

$$= L_{\theta\alpha} \sin\theta \cos\theta \, \delta\theta \, \delta\alpha \qquad (23.3)$$

(independent of sky radius)

For an overcast sky $\qquad\qquad L_{\theta\alpha} = \tfrac{1}{3}L_z(1 + 2\sin\theta) \qquad (23.2)$

and for the whole sky

$$E = \int_{\alpha=0}^{2\pi} \int_{\theta=0}^{\pi/2} \tfrac{1}{3}L_z(1+2\sin\theta)\sin\theta\cos\theta \, d\theta \, d\alpha$$

$$= \tfrac{2}{3}\pi L_z[\tfrac{1}{2}\sin^2\theta + \tfrac{2}{3}\sin^3\theta]_0^{\pi/2}$$

$$E = \tfrac{7}{9}\pi L_z \tag{23.4}$$

Therefore the sky component due to an element $\delta\theta$, $\delta\alpha$ at θ, α

$$= \frac{9}{7\pi L_z} \cdot \tfrac{1}{3}L_z(1+2\sin\theta)\sin\theta\cos\theta \, \delta\theta \, \delta\alpha$$

$$= \frac{3}{7\pi}(1+2\sin\theta)\sin\theta\cos\theta \, \delta\theta \, \delta\alpha \tag{23.5}$$

23.3.2   Graphical method of determining sky component

Using the above results, if a network is constructed with abscissae proportional to α and with ordinates proportional to $(\tfrac{1}{2}\sin^2\theta + \tfrac{2}{3}\sin^3\theta)$, so that δx is proportional to $\delta\alpha$ and δy is proportional to $(\sin\theta\cos\theta + 2\sin^2\theta\cos\theta)\,\delta\theta$, then a window aperture plotted on the network will have an area proportional to the sky component for an overcast sky. Such a network, shown in Fig. 23.11, is known as a *Waldram diagram*.

The Waldram diagram can be used to find the sky component at any given point in an interior; all that is required is to trace on the diagram the outline of the patch of the sky visible from that point.

For example, if the reference point is 2 m from the centre of the sill of a window which is 1·52 m high and 0·91 m wide, the outline of the window is of the form shown in

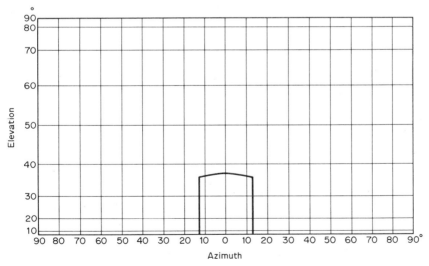

Fig. 23.11   Waldram diagram for CIE overcast sky, unglazed window

Fig. 23.11. The angle of elevation at the centre of the window head is the angle whose tangent is 1·52/2, that is 37·2°; and at either end is the angle whose tangent is $1·52/\sqrt{(2^2 + 0·455^2)}$, that is 36·5°. The horizontal angle at either side of the window is $\tan^{-1} 0·455/2$, that is 12·8°, as shown in Fig. 23.11.

The area enclosed by the trace of the window edge, divided by twice the area of the whole diagram and expressed as a percentage, is a measure of the sky component. The whole diagram represents only half of the sky hemisphere, hence the need to divide by twice the area of the diagram.

A further factor which must be taken into account is that there is a loss of light due to reflection at the glass surfaces. This loss is not constant but varies with the angle of incidence of the light. Because of this variation with angle of incidence, the lines of constant elevation on the Waldram diagram which allows for glass absorption are no longer straight lines but are curved (Fig. 23.12).

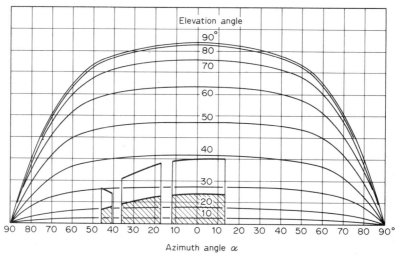

Fig. 23.12   Waldram diagram for CIE overcast sky for vertical glazed window with trace of 'box window' and outside obstruction

The trace of a vertical line is always vertical on either of the two Waldram diagrams described and the trace of a horizontal line is a curve, for example the upper edge of the window shown in Fig. 23.11. If this window were plotted on Fig. 23.12, the upper edge would be even more curved because of the curvature of lines of altitude when allowance is made for glazing absorption. *Droop lines*, tracing horizontal lines perpendicular to the direction of viewing (and sometimes at right angles to this) are often included on Waldram diagrams to assist in tracing windows and external obstructions.

The Waldram diagrams described above are for sky components at a point on a horizontal plane, but a similar diagram can be constructed to give the sky component on a vertical plane at a reference point facing towards the window wall. Such a diagram has been produced for a uniform sky and used for determining the sky component on a horizontal plane beneath rooflights. Diagrams for a CIE sky are not immediately inter-changeable for these two applications.

The plan of part of a room containing a 'box' window, shown in Fig. 23.13, is used to illustrate the procedure for determining the sky component at a point P on a horizontal plane which coincides with the lower edge of the window glazing. The upper edge of the window is 2·5 m above its lower edge. The lines 1 to 7 are drawn through P and the seven points which represent the effective sides of the window. The angles which these lines make with PR as reference line, corresponding to 0° on the diagram, are values of α for the

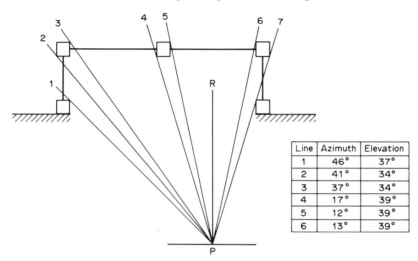

Line	Azimuth	Elevation
1	46°	37°
2	41°	34°
3	37°	34°
4	17°	39°
5	12°	39°
6	13°	39°

Fig. 23.13 Plan of box window showing azimuthal sight lines and corresponding angles of elevation

sides of the windows. The corresponding angles of θ are found by measuring the lengths of the seven lines. It should be noted that it is the outer edge of the window head that limits the view of the sky from the point P. The lengths are, therefore, measured to the outer edge of the window wall and the height taken as 2·5 m in each case. The angles θ may be found graphically or by calculation so that the points representing the top corners of the window can be plotted on the diagram as shown in Fig. 23.12. It should be noted that the droop line used to draw the side window is different from that for the far facing windows.

If there is an obstruction outside the window its outline can be traced in the same way from a knowledge of its dimensions and from a plan showing its position relative to that of the window.

For example, consider the outline of a building of height 10 m above the horizontal plane containing the lower edge of the window and at a distance of 20 m. On the Waldram diagram the droop line for the obstruction will be 27° since 10/20 = tan 27°.

The Waldram diagram may be used to determine the externally reflected component of daylight factor, using the same diagram as that used to determine the sky component. The part of the diagram which outlines that part of the sky obscured by external structures gives a measure of the reflected light. It is obtained by expressing the obscured area as a percentage of twice the area of the diagram multiplied by the ratio of the luminance of the obstructions to that of the sky.

Alternative graphical methods for determining the sky component are available; for example, the radial diagram. If on the hemisphere of Fig. 23.10 lines of latitude and longitude are drawn and then projected on to the base, a radial diagram is obtained in which lines of longitude are straight and lines of latitude are circles. If the outlines of a window are traced on to this diagram by means of a series of pairs of angles (θ, α) then the sky component at the reference point is equal to the area enclosed by the trace divided by twice the area of the diagram.

Other diagrams are also used, in which the sky component produced by a given patch of sky is not proportional to the area of the patch as represented on the diagram. A pattern of dots can be used on these diagrams, the spacing of the dots being a measure of how large an area is needed to make a particular contribution to the sky component. The value for a given patch of sky is found by counting the number of dots enclosed within the representation of the patch on the diagram. Generally these diagrams are designed to be superimposed on a photograph taken at the reference point or on a scale drawing of the window as seen from the reference point.

23.3.3   BRS protractors and tables

Another method of determining the daylight factor is the use of the BRS protractors which are applied to the scale drawings, plan and elevation, of a building. Ten different protractors have been designed to allow measurements to be made for a uniform sky or a CIE overcast sky, for window glazing at various angles of slope.

Each protractor is in two parts. One part is applied to the sectional elevation of the building: it measures the angles of elevation of the top and bottom of a window and evaluates the sky component as if the window were infinitely long. The other part of the protractor is applied to the plan of the building and provides correction factors for windows subtending less than 180° in plan. Absorption due to the glazing is allowed for in the scale values.

The application of Protractor No. 2 is illustrated in Fig. 23.14 for the evaluation of the sky component for a vertically glazed window under a CIE overcast sky. Sight lines are first drawn from the reference point (P) in the interior to the edges of the window or visible part of the sky on both sectional elevation and plan. The centre of the appropriate protractor is placed over the reference point on the sectional elevation with the centre line of the protractor in the reference plane. The intercepts of the sight lines to the upper and lower edges of the window (or obstructions) with the sky component scale are read. The difference between the two readings gives the 'primary' sky component at the reference point for a vertically glazed window of infinite length in both directions. The angles of elevation of the sight lines are also noted. The protractor is now placed on the plan drawing with its centre at the reference point and with the base diameter parallel to the window. A semicircle on the correction factor scale corresponding to the average angle of elevation of the window is deduced and the intercepts with the sight lines to the edges of the window (or obstructions) are then read from the curves. The value of the 'primary' sky component for the infinitely long window is then multiplied by the correction factor to obtain the sky component for the window of finite length.

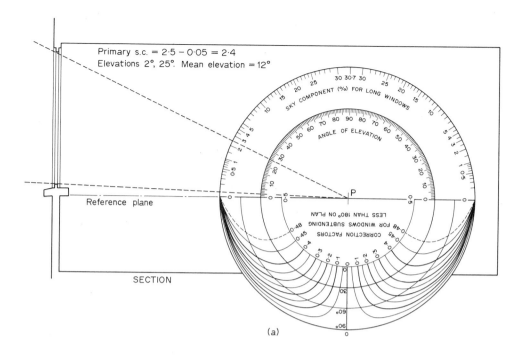

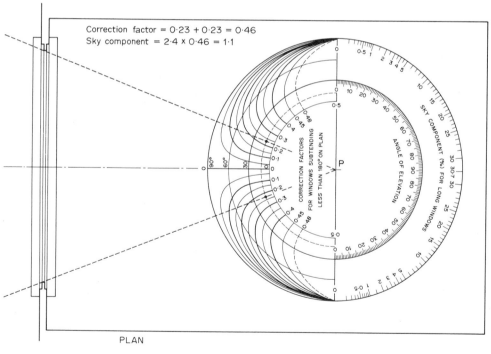

(b)

Fig. 23.14 Application of BRS Protractor No. 2 to measurement of sky component for vertically glazed window under CIE overcast sky

431

Table 23.1   BRS sky component table.

Ratio W/D = Width of window to one side of normal : Distance from window

Ratio H/D = Height of window head above working plane : Distance from window

H/D	0·1	0·2	0·3	0·4	0·5	0·6	0·7	0·8	0·9	1·0	1·2	1·4	1·6	1·8	2·0	2·5	3·0	4·0	6·0	∞	Angle of obstruction
∞	1·3	2·5	3·7	4·9	5·9	6·9	7·7	8·4	9·0	9·6	10·7	11·6	12·2	12·6	13·0	13·7	14·2	14·6	14·9	15·0	90°
5·0	1·2	2·4	3·7	4·8	5·9	6·8	7·6	8·3	8·8	9·4	10·5	11·1	11·7	12·3	12·7	13·3	13·7	14·0	14·1	14·2	79°
4·0	1·2	2·4	3·6	4·7	5·8	6·7	7·4	8·2	8·7	9·2	10·3	10·9	11·4	12·0	12·4	12·9	13·3	13·5	13·6	13·7	76°
3·5	1·2	2·4	3·6	4·6	5·7	6·6	7·3	8·0	8·5	9·0	10·1	10·6	11·1	11·8	12·2	12·6	12·9	13·2	13·2	13·3	74°
3·0	1·1	2·3	3·5	4·5	5·5	6·4	7·1	7·8	8·2	8·7	9·8	10·2	10·7	11·3	11·7	12·0	12·4	12·5	12·6	12·7	72°
2·8	1·1	2·3	3·4	4·5	5·4	6·3	7·0	7·6	8·1	8·6	9·6	10·0	10·5	11·1	11·4	11·7	12·0	12·2	12·3	12·3	70°
2·6	1·1	2·2	3·4	4·4	5·3	6·2	6·8	7·5	7·9	8·4	9·3	9·8	10·2	10·8	11·1	11·4	11·7	11·8	11·9	11·9	69°
2·4	1·1	2·2	3·3	4·3	5·2	6·0	6·6	7·3	7·7	8·1	9·1	9·5	10·0	10·4	10·7	11·0	11·2	11·3	11·4	11·5	67°
2·2	1·1	2·1	3·3	4·1	5·0	5·8	6·4	7·0	7·4	7·9	8·7	9·1	9·6	10·0	10·2	10·5	10·7	10·8	10·9	10·9	66°
2·0	1·0	2·0	3·1	4·0	4·8	5·6	6·2	6·7	7·1	7·5	8·3	8·7	9·1	9·5	9·7	9·9	10·0	10·1	10·2	10·3	63°
1·9	1·0	2·0	3·0	3·9	4·7	5·4	6·0	6·5	6·9	7·3	8·1	8·5	8·8	9·2	9·4	9·6	9·7	9·8	9·9	9·9	62°
1·8	0·97	1·9	2·9	3·8	4·6	5·3	5·8	6·3	6·7	7·1	7·8	8·2	8·5	8·8	9·0	9·2	9·3	9·4	9·5	9·5	61°
1·7	0·94	1·8	2·8	3·6	4·4	5·1	5·6	6·1	6·5	6·8	7·5	7·8	8·2	8·5	8·6	8·8	8·9	9·0	9·1	9·1	60°
1·6	0·90	1·7	2·7	3·5	4·2	4·9	5·4	5·8	6·2	6·5	7·2	7·5	7·8	8·1	8·2	8·4	8·5	8·6	8·6	8·6	58°
1·5	0·86	1·6	2·6	3·3	4·0	4·6	5·1	5·6	5·9	6·2	6·8	7·1	7·4	7·6	7·8	7·9	8·0	8·0	8·1	8·1	56°
1·4	0·82	1·5	2·4	3·2	3·8	4·4	4·8	5·2	5·5	5·9	6·4	6·7	7·0	7·2	7·3	7·4	7·5	7·5	7·6	7·6	54°
1·3	0·77	1·4	2·3	2·9	3·6	4·1	4·5	4·9	5·2	5·5	5·9	6·2	6·4	6·6	6·7	6·8	6·9	6·9	6·9	7·0	52°
1·2	0·71	1·3	2·1	2·7	3·3	3·8	4·2	4·5	4·8	5·0	5·4	5·7	5·9	6·0	6·1	6·2	6·2	6·3	6·3	6·3	50°
1·1	0·65	1·1	1·9	2·5	3·0	3·4	3·8	4·1	4·3	4·6	4·9	5·1	5·3	5·4	5·4	5·5	5·6	5·6	5·7	5·7	48°
1·0	0·57	1·1	1·7	2·2	2·6	3·0	3·3	3·6	3·8	4·0	4·3	4·5	4·6	4·7	4·7	4·8	4·8	4·9	5·0	5·0	45°
0·9	0·50	0·99	1·5	1·9	2·2	2·6	2·8	3·1	3·3	3·4	3·7	3·8	3·9	3·9	4·0	4·0	4·1	4·1	4·2	4·2	42°
0·8	0·42	0·83	1·2	1·6	1·9	2·2	2·4	2·6	2·7	2·9	3·1	3·2	3·3	3·3	3·3	3·3	3·4	3·4	3·4	3·4	39°
0·7	0·33	0·68	0·97	1·3	1·5	1·7	1·9	2·1	2·2	2·3	2·5	2·5	2·6	2·6	2·6	2·6	2·7	2·7	2·8	2·8	35°
0·6	0·24	0·53	0·74	0·98	1·2	1·3	1·5	1·6	1·7	1·8	1·9	1·9	2·0	2·0	2·0	2·1	2·1	2·1	2·1	2·1	31°
0·5	0·16	0·39	0·52	0·70	0·82	0·97	1·0	1·1	1·2	1·3	1·4	1·4	1·4	1·4	1·5	1·5	1·5	1·5	1·5	1·5	27°
0·4	0·10	0·25	0·34	0·45	0·54	0·62	0·70	0·75	0·82	0·89	0·92	0·95	0·95	0·96	0·96	0·97	0·97	0·97	0·98	0·98	22°
0·3	0·06	0·14	0·18	0·26	0·30	0·34	0·38	0·42	0·44	0·47	0·49	0·50	0·50	0·51	0·51	0·52	0·52	0·52	0·53	0·53	17°
0·2	0·03	0·06	0·09	0·11	0·12	0·14	0·16	0·20	0·21	0·21	0·22	0·22	0·22	0·22	0·23	0·23	0·23	0·23	0·24	0·24	11°
0·1	0·01	0·02	0·02	0·03	0·03	0·04	0·04	0·05	0·05	0·05	0·06	0·06	0·06	0·06	0·07	0·07	0·07	0·07	0·08	0·08	6°
0																					0°

The externally-reflected component is obtained in the same way as described previously, one tenth of the equivalent sky component. More detailed information on the use of the BRS Protractors is contained in a booklet entitled 'BRS Daylight Protractors', published for the Building Research Station and Ministry of Public Buildings and Works by HMSO in 1968.

The sky component of daylight factor at a point illuminated by a rectangular window of given dimensions can also be obtained by the use of tables in which values of sky component are expressed in terms of the ratios of window width (W) and window height (H) to the distance of the window from the reference point. These tables apply to windows with vertical sides and vertical glazing, one of whose lower corners is at the projection of the reference point in the plane of the window. The sky component for a rectangular window, however situated with respect to the reference point, can be found by addition or subtraction of values given in the tables. A sample table (Table 23.1) is given for an overcast sky with allowance for glazing. As in the case of the methods already described, these tables can be used for obstructed windows, the clear position and the obstructed portion being treated separately.

Internally-reflected component of daylight factor. The precise calculation of the internally-reflected component of daylight factor is very difficult and therefore, in general, an approximate method is used. This method considers the interior as an enclosure in which light entering the window is repeatedly reflected at the ceiling, walls and floor. It is known as the *split-flux* method and is derived from the principles of the integrating sphere. It is expressed by the formula

$$\text{IRC} = \left[\frac{0.85\,W}{A(1-\rho)} \right] [40\rho_f + 5\rho_c]\% \qquad (23.6)$$

where W = area of the window,

$\quad$ A = area of all the room surfaces including the window,

$\quad$ ρ_f = average reflectance of all the surfaces receiving light directly from the window and situated below the horizontal plane through the middle of the window,

$\quad$ ρ_c = average reflectance of all surfaces above this plane excluding the window wall,

and $\quad$ ρ = average reflectance of all surfaces in the room including the window wall.

Using this formula, values of internally-reflected component have been calculated and presented in terms of the ratio of actual glass area to floor area. In Table 23.2 an example is given of values of internally-reflected component for rooms with side windows.

23.4 DAYLIGHT AND THE INTERIOR ENVIRONMENT

Windows. The size and number of windows in our older commercial buildings arose from considerations of elevational proportions rather than from daylighting requirements; the total net area above first floor level seldom exceeded one third of the total external wall area. Window size was restricted, by the Metropolitan Act of 1885, to half the wall area to ensure stable structures. However, the fact that more light is desirable in

433

Table 23.2   Internally-reflected component (Minimum IRC (%))

Ratio of actual glass area to floor area	Actual glass area (% of floor area)	Floor reflectance (%)											
		10				20				40			
		Wall reflectance (%)											
		20	40	60	80	20	40	60	80	20	40	60	80
1:50	2	0	0	0·1	0·2	0	0·1	0·1	0·2	0	0·1	0·2	0·2
1:20	5	0·1	0·1	0·2	0·4	0·1	0·2	0·3	0·5	0·1	0·2	0·4	0·6
1:14	7	0·1	0·2	0·3	0·5	0·1	0·2	0·4	0·6	0·2	0·3	0·6	0·8
1:10	10	0·1	0·2	0·4	0·7	0·2	0·3	0·6	0·9	0·3	0·5	0·8	1·2
1:6.7	15	0·2	0·4	0·6	1·0	0·2	0·5	0·8	1·3	0·4	0·7	1·1	1·7
1:5	20	0·2	0·5	0·8	1·4	0·3	0·6	1·1	1·7	0·5	0·9	1·5	2·3
1:4	25	0·3	0·6	1·0	1·7	0·4	0·8	1·3	2·0	0·6	1·1	1·8	2·8
1:3.3	30	0·3	0·7	1·2	2·0	0·5	0·9	1·5	2·4	0·8	1·3	2·1	3·3
1:2.9	35	0·4	0·8	1·4	2·3	0·5	1·0	1·8	2·8	0·9	1·5	2·4	3·8
1:2.5	40	0·5	0·9	1·6	2·6	0·6	1·2	2·0	3·1	1·0	1·7	2·7	4·2
1:2.2	45	0·5	1·0	1·8	2·9	0·7	1·3	2·2	3·4	1·2	1·9	3·0	4·6
1:2	50	0·6	1·1	1·9	3·1	0·8	1·4	2·3	3·7	1·3	2·1	3·2	4·9
Conversion factor to obtain average value of IRC		×1·9	×1·5	×1·3	×1·2	×1·8	×1·4	×1·3	×1·2	×1·6	×1·4	×1·2	×1·1

some buildings than would suffice in others was recognized and taken into account in planning fenestration. Examples of this are the early roof-lighted weaving sheds and artists' studios.

The domestic architecture of the Georgian period suggests also an awareness that ample daylight in dwellings was a desirable amenity. Daylighting technology has made considerable progress in the past 50 years, and developments in building construction techniques, such as the framed structure, have made possible the thinner glass curtain wall.

The UK has been regarded as having a climate which causes no overheating problems in buildings due to excessive solar heat gains, but radiation intensities admitted through large window areas can cause overheating in spite of comparatively low external air temperatures. Furthermore, the newer buildings have less structural mass and so warm up more quickly and the difficulties are often accentuated by poor ventilation, especially where traffic noise discourages window opening. In traditional buildings, with massive structure, the heat gains and losses did not occur to the same extent and therefore the gain in daylight penetration, made possible through the new freedom to build large windows, caused the problem of solar heat gain, and another important factor, that of discomfort due to sky glare, to be overlooked in many designs.

Control of solar heat gain can be carried out by various means such as the use of solar radiation reflecting and absorbing glasses or by internal or external screens. Solar heat gains comprise radiation transmitted through the window glass together with a proportion of radiation absorbed by the glass which is re-transmitted to the interior by convection and re-radiation from the inner glass surface. For glasses with a high absorptance the solar transmittance alone will significantly underestimate the solar heat gain.

As windows are primarily provided to admit daylight to a building, it is necessary in assessing a particular window glass to take account of the transmission of light as well as of solar heat, the relative values of these transmittances being different for different types of glass. Heat-absorbing glasses reduce the transmission of solar heat without greatly reducing the transmission of light. This absorption of unwanted infra-red radiation is brought about by introducing ferric oxide into the glass. These glasses are not as effective in reducing solar heat gains as would appear from solar transmittance data because, as already mentioned, part of the absorbed heat is re-transmitted.

Grey and coloured glasses which have been introduced to control glare by effectively reducing sky luminance without reducing daylight penetration, reduce the transmittance of solar heat mainly by absorption of the visible radiation in the sun's spectrum. Table 23.3 shows the characteristics of solar heat and light transmission for a selection of different window glasses.

Heat-reflecting glasses obtained by the deposition of a semi-transparent metallic coating or by firing metallic oxides on to the glass surface, preserve an undistorted view. By using a coating which selectively reflects the unwanted infra-red radiation, glasses can be made which have a smaller solar heat transmission than light transmission. In theory these glasses, for a given light transmission, are most effective in reducing solar heat gain because the problem associated with heat absorbing glass (re-transmission) is largely eliminated. Many of the coatings available, however, are not completely non-absorbing nor do they provide total selective reflectance.

The sound insulation of windows is generally accomplished using specially designed, accurately built windows with double or multiple glazing, with all joints carefully sealed:

Table 23.3   Characteristics of window glasses

Type of glazing	Solar trans- mittance %	Solar absorp- tance %	Solar * heat gain %	Light trans- mittance %	Heat: † light ratio
Single, $\frac{1}{4}$ in, vertical					
Clear (Pilkington's float)	74	19	80	88	0·91
Lightly heat-absorbing					
(Pilkington's Antisun)	42	53	58	73	0·79
Densely heat-absorbing					
(Pilkington's Calorex)	20	75·5	43	47	0·91
Grey (anti-glare) (Glaverbel)	42	53	58	37	1·56
Grey lacquer on glass (Sun-X)	38	57	55	36	1·53
Double, $\frac{1}{4}$ in, vertical					
Heat-reflecting double glazing					
(Glaverbel's Stopray Thermo-					
pane)	24	32	27	38	0·71
Heat-absorbing double glazing					
(Pilkington's Calorex: Clear plate)	17	77	29	42	0·70

* Solar heat gain   = Solar transmittance + 0·3 × Solar absorptance
  (single glazing)

† Heat:light ratio = $\dfrac{\text{Solar heat gain}}{\text{Light transmittance}}$

the elimination of cracks has a significant effect on insulation. Increased insulation can be achieved by increased weight of the glass in both single and double glazing systems. The improvement which this gives is, however, small compared with the noise admitted through cracks in the window or its surround. Where the window construction is of a high standard, doubling the weight of glass in single glazing will provide approximately a 5 dB increase in overall insulation: with double glazing, a greater or smaller increase results, depending upon the size of the air space. Spaces less than 5 cm provide a slight benefit for high frequency sounds but the overall insulation of such a window will be little more than that of a window glazed with a single glass of the same weight as the combined weight of the two glasses of the double glazed window. A 10 cm air space will give a reasonable improvement at medium and high frequencies and is about the minimum worth having. The optimum air space width is about 30 cm, but 20 cm space is commonly found to be acceptable.

PSALI.   The optimum shape and size of a window is a function of the adaptation conditions and the resulting luminosity distribution. The illuminance on the working plane and the degree of freedom from sky glare are other factors which should influence the shape and size of a window.

    Side-lit rooms often appear poorly lighted because of the contrast between the areas near to and remote from the windows. Though the level of illuminance in those areas remote from the windows may be adequate for a visual task to be performed, dissatisfaction with the lighting may be experienced. This dissatisfaction can be lessened by careful window design. Where conditions permit, the use of windows in two side walls can relieve the problem.

In rooms with unobstructed windows on one side only, the ratio of daylight illuminance between the front and back of the room may frequently be of the order of 10 or 20 to 1 (Fig. 23.7). If the window area is increased to raise the illuminance at the back of the room, the illuminance near the window also increases and it does not appear to bring about any improvement.

For rooms which are deep compared with their width, the solution is to provide permanent supplementary artificial lighting—PSALI. There may be two problems to be solved by PSALI: the need to provide additional light to supplement inadequate daylight and the need to brighten those parts of the room which, because of a view of the bright sky, are subjectively depressed.

Supplementary lighting to be fully effective must be designed so as to achieve a correct visual balance with daylight. The apparently darker areas should be brightened by the supplementary lighting to appear as bright as the rest of the room without destroying the essential character and direction of the dominant daylight. Fig. 23.15 shows one solution to the daylighting problem in a large office.

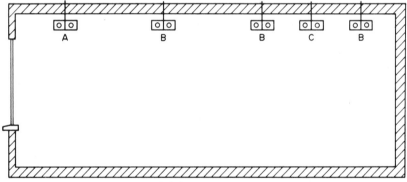

Fig. 23.15 Lighting arrangement for PSALI
Daytime: B and C on.   Night-time: A and B on.

Psychological factors.   It has been claimed that better, more comfortable lighting can be installed and maintained more economically with electric lighting than with daylighting. To eliminate daylight entirely would make easier the control of building heating, ventilation and noise. However, most people have come to expect that the fullest use be made of daylighting within the prevailing structural possibilities and economic conditions. Also, most people consider that windows have another important function to fulfil, to maintain visual contact with the outside, an instinctive desire which is concerned with freedom and the need to escape from a sense of complete enclosure. The total exclusion of daylight, it is felt, would lead to a sense of deprivation, a loss which cannot be measured in economic terms.

A further factor, probably of biological origin has been revealed by experiments on people's preferences for levels of task illuminance. Higher illuminances are preferred in windowless buildings than are normally required for night-time lighting.

24 Industrial lighting

The lighting requirements for industrial interiors can be considered as two basic and inter-related functions designed to suit the tasks of manufacture and inspection.

In some instances the requirements of the two tasks will be very similar whereas in others, particularly where the manufacturing process is automated, the inspection task may require the use of separate lighting facilities.

This chapter examines the lamps and luminaires suitable for both general and localized lighting of industrial interiors, gives guidance on general lighting design, and provides information on the more specialized lighting techniques which can be applied to some visual inspection processes.

24.1 SOURCES AND LUMINAIRES

24.1.1 Selection of light source

Table 24.1 gives details of the major characteristics of light sources used for industrial lighting. The selection of the light source for a specific task will be based mainly on efficacy, life, cost (both initial and operating) and colour. Additionally the physical size of the source may be important as this will affect the degree of light control possible. The amount of heat generated by the source and reaching the task area may be important; freedom from flicker and from stroboscopic effect may also be desirable.

Information on all of these lamps is given in earlier chapters but the following comments are applicable to their use for industrial lighting:

(a) Incandescent lamps, particularly the low voltage types, offer a small source area, and therefore are capable of accurate optical control. Efficacy is rather low and their use for general lighting is therefore rarely economic although the linear tungsten halogen types can be used effectively for side lighting applications in large buildings. Localized lighting using incandescent lamps to supplement general lighting from other sources is often used, and where the heat generated adjacent to the task from this arrangement is not acceptable dichroic-coated reflector lamps, which reflect light in the desired direction but transmit heat away from the task, can be used.

Where possible the use of low voltage types is desirable for localized lighting for increased safety.

Incandescent lamps are often used for emergency lighting, particularly in installations where general lighting is provided by high pressure discharge sources.

(b) Fluorescent tubes are very widely used, their high efficacy and long life providing very economic lighting installations. The source size is large and accurate optical control is therefore difficult to achieve. The large-area low-brightness source reduces direct glare and shadows. The higher efficacy tubes have colour properties which are acceptable for

Table 24.1 Light sources for industrial lighting

Light source	Output range lm/lamp	Control gear losses %	Rated life h	Lamp efficacy lm/W	Relative source size	Relative lamp cost	Colour rendering
GLS incandescent	200– 27 500	Nil	1000	8– 18	Small	Low	Fairly good
Tungsten halogen incandescent	200– 33 000	Nil	1000–2000	15– 22	Small	Medium	Good
Low voltage incandescent	100– 800	Nil	350–1000	15– 18	Very small	Low	Fairly good
High efficacy fluorescent	800– 8 700	20	7500	55– 80	Large	Low	Fair
Improved colour fluorescent	400– 6 500	20	7500	25– 55	Large	Low	Good
Miniature fluorescent	100– 700	80	5000	25– 60	Large	Medium	Fair/good
Colour-corrected mercury	1 800– 54 000	7–30	7500	36– 54	Medium	Medium	Fair
Tungsten-ballasted mercury	2 500– 11 500	Nil	6000	16– 23	Medium	Medium	Fair
Metal halide	24 000–280 000	14–22	7500	60– 80	Small	Fairly high	Fair
Phosphor-coated metal halide	27 000– 85 000	14	7500	68– 85	Medium	Fairly high	Good
Low pressure sodium	4 500– 27 500	20–80	6000	105–160	Large	Medium	Very poor
High pressure sodium	19 500– 38 000	12–20	6000	78– 95	Medium	High	Fair

many industrial applications, but where more accurate colour rendering is required, tubes of lower efficacy but better colour properties are available.

Miniature tubes are useful for localized lighting.

In enclosed luminaires, where the lamps operate in high ambient temperatures, amalgam tubes should be used.

(c) Mercury lamps are available with colour-correcting phosphor-coated envelopes in both standard and integral reflector forms: since the introduction of the improved colour phosphors these are being used extensively, particularly in areas where the luminaires are mounted at high level. The lamps have reasonable colour performance and efficacy; the source area is not too large and luminaires are consequently small. The use of the integral reflector type is particularly recommended in dirty atmospheres, but it is important that the luminaire used should provide some screening for the lamp if glare is to be kept to tolerable levels.

Tungsten-ballasted mercury lamps have longer life and higher efficacy than incandescent lamps, and do not require external control gear as the arc tube is ballasted by the internal incandescent filament. These lamps are used principally as replacements for incandescent types.

(d) Metal halide lamps have been introduced relatively recently and are becoming available in an increasing range of sizes both with and without phosphor-coated envelopes. The lamps without phosphor-coated envelopes offer high efficacy with reasonable colour and small source size, and should be used where accurate optical control is desired. The linear types used in luminaires with fan-shaped asymmetric distribution are very useful for high level side-lighting installations.

The phosphor-coated types have similar source dimensions to equivalent wattage conventional mercury lamps, but have higher efficacy and better colour performance.

(e) Sodium lamps are available in both low and high pressure types. The low pressure lamps have very high efficacy, but monochromatic colour, and are only of use industrially for specialized applications. The recently introduced high pressure sodium lamp has much improved colour performance, and can be used either alone or blended with high pressure mercury lamps for the general lighting of industrial interiors, particularly where high mounting heights are involved.

When selecting a lamp for industrial applications consideration should be given to the possible risk of the stroboscopic effect, causing rotating or reciprocating machinery to appear to be running at speeds other than their actual speed, or in extreme cases to appear to be stationary. Fluorescent tubes incorporate phosphors with relatively long afterglow which helps to reduce stroboscopic effect, but wherever possible the luminaires should be connected electrically such that they are distributed over the three phases of a star-connected supply with adjacent luminaires on alternate phases. Where this is not possible fluorescent tube control circuits of the lead-lag type can be used. High pressure discharge lamps when used in these applications should always be distributed over a three-phase supply.

24.1.2 Selection of luminaire

The selection of the luminaire for an industrial interior will usually follow and be largely influenced by the selection of the light source to be used. Also influencing the choice is the required light distribution, the degree of glare control and such physical considerations as the method of fixing, ease of maintenance and compliance with the requirements of relevant standards.

Light distribution is usually defined by the British Zonal classification and the flux fraction up and down. The degree of glare resulting from an installation of luminaires can be assessed by calculation of the glare index, the result being compared with the limiting recommendation contained in the current issue of the IES Code.

Luminaires should be capable of withstanding use in the conditions in which they are to be located. This will involve consideration of localized ambient temperature and humidity, the possibility of dust or chemical attack, the ability to withstand a proposed method of cleaning (for example, a jet-proof fitting may be required) and compliance with relevant safety standards. BS 4533 defines standards for luminaires for general indoor lighting applications, and also provides test procedures to ensure minimum standards of proofing for some specialized applications.

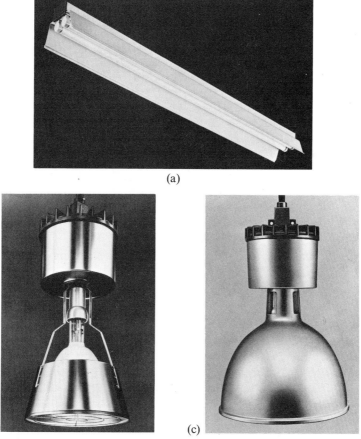

(a)

(b)   (c)

Fig. 24.1 (a) Industrial fluorescent luminaire   (b) High bay luminaire for mercury reflector lamp
(c) High bay mercury/metal halide/high pressure sodium luminaire

441

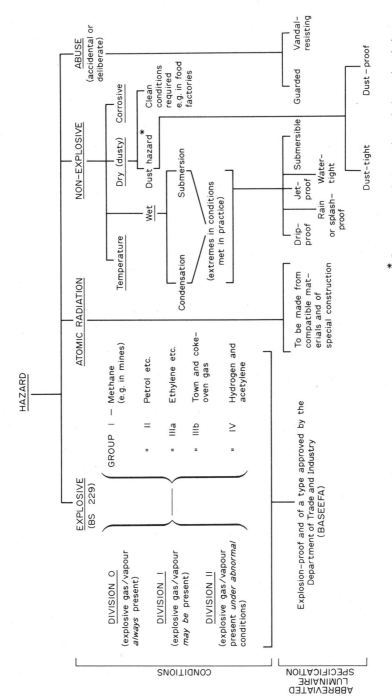

Table 24.2 Luminaire hazards

442

Table 24.2 specifies the hazards to which luminaires may be subjected and indicates the description usually applied to equipment designed for use in such locations.

Typical general lighting luminaires are illustrated in Fig. 24.1. It should be noted that the luminaires for fluorescent tubes and for mercury reflector lamps allow some degree of upward lighting which prevents the ceiling and upper parts of the walls becoming too dark and producing an unpleasant 'tunnel' effect. The slots in the reflecting luminaires allow for convection and thus help to reduce the accumulation of dirt on the reflector surfaces.

Localized lighting luminaires, if intended to be adjustable by the operative, should preferably employ low voltage sources for increased safety, and should be so designed that adjustment can be easily carried out without necessity to touch parts of the luminaire which have been heated by the lamp.

24.2 LIGHTING FOR MANUFACTURE

24.2.1 General lighting

The IES Code gives recommended minimum levels of illuminance and limiting glare index values for general lighting for a large number of manufacturing processes. Where industrial areas are being used for a variety of tasks the lighting provided must be capable of meeting the requirements of that task which requires the highest value of illuminance, the lowest limiting glare index and the best colour rendering.

The illuminances recommended in the 1968 IES Code (Table 24.3) are the minima to be maintained in service: information on the depreciation of light output through the life of an installation is given in Chap. 34.

Table 24.3 IES recommendations (1968) for industrial lighting

Class of visual task	Examples	Illuminance (lux)
Casual seeing	Locker rooms	100
Rough tasks with large detail	Heavy machinery assembly; stores	200
Ordinary tasks with medium size detail	Wood machining; general offices; general assembly	400
Fairly severe tasks with small detail	Food can inspection; clothing, cutting and sewing; business machines; drawing offices	600
Severe prolonged tasks with small detail	Fine assembly and machining; hand tailoring; weaving silk or synthetic fibres	900
Very severe prolonged tasks with very small detail	Hosiery mending; gauging very small parts; gem cutting	1300–2000
Exceptionally severe tasks with minute detail	Watchmaking; inspection of very small instruments	2000–3000

Adherence to the limiting glare index value in the IES Code will ensure that direct glare from the lighting installation is kept within limits which are satisfactory to the task being performed, but will not necessarily reduce reflected glare to an acceptable level. Reflected glare will occur when bright objects, usually luminaires or windows, are reflected in polished or partly polished surfaces and can only be reduced by elimination of polished surfaces within the visual field, or by the re-orientation of either the operator, the task, or the reflected bright area, such that the reflections occur outside the normal line of the operator's vision.

The lighting installation must be capable of allowing colour to be distinguished to a degree suitable to the processes involved. In some cases the ability of the selected light source to allow accurate assessment or matching of colour will be more important than the efficacy of the source, but it should be noted that if accurate colour appraisal is to be made the provision of a value of illuminance of at least 1000 lux is essential. The usefulness of light sources with high colour fidelity will be lost if large areas of strong colour are permitted within the visual scene, as the resulting lighting will be distorted by the selective reflection properties of such areas. An indication of the colour rendering ability of lamps generally used for industrial interiors is given in Table 24.1.

General lighting for industrial interiors is most often provided by near-symmetrical arrays of overhead luminaires: the number required can usually be calculated by the well-established lumen method and the glare index of the proposed installation checked as described in Sect. 22.2.

The layout of the luminaires should be such that the uniformity of illuminance on the work plane does not fall below 0·7:1. To achieve this the spacing/mounting height ratio for fluorescent and mercury reflector luminaires will usually need to be 1·5:1 or less and the corresponding ratio for narrow distribution luminaires 1:1 or less. If necessary, the uniformity ratio can be checked by a series of point illuminance calculations.

Installations comprising symmetrical layouts of overhead luminaires with conventional light distributions produce predominantly horizontal illumination with vertical surfaces lit mainly by inter-reflected light. This arrangement is suitable for many industrial applications but proper assessment of the task must be made to determine the suitability for each application: in some instances the illumination of vertical surfaces

Fig. 24.2   Factory general lighting, using 1 kW °Kolorlux high bay reflector luminaires

may be more important. Careful choice of the reflectances of building surfaces can help to provide higher values of spatial illuminance which will improve visibility on vertical surfaces.

Where strong vertical illumination is required, luminaires will need to be wall mounted or to incorporate optical control providing a light distribution which is not predominantly vertically downward, for example luminaires with an asymmetric or a batwing distribution (Sect. 22.3.2). Wall-mounted luminaires with asymmetric fan-shaped distribution, usually employing linear tungsten halogen or metal halide lamps, are worth consideration for interiors with high mounting heights where vertical illumination is important: the direct illuminance provided by such units can be calculated by the floodlighting techniques described in Chap. 33.

The visual design of an environment includes not only the parameters of illuminance and glare, but also the distribution of luminance within the total visual scene. The practice of the principles of luminance design given in Chap. 22 has been largely ignored for industrial interiors: the visual demands of industrial processes are often both critical and prolonged and therefore merit no less attention than the commercial tasks which have enjoyed the benefits of more complete lighting design techniques for some time.

24.2.2 Localized, emergency and stand-by lighting

Localized lighting should be used where necessary to supplement general lighting but never as a substitute for it. Careful assessment of the purpose of localized lighting is most important to determine whether incandescent luminaires capable of providing strong modelling effects will be more appropriate than miniature fluorescent luminaires having larger source areas.

Emergency lighting may be required to enable personnel to vacate the premises safely in the event of a failure in the mains electrical supply. This may be particularly important where high pressure discharge lamps are used, as a short break in the supply will extinguish the lamps, not to re-strike until the arc tube has cooled. Luminaires for incandescent lamps with integral battery systems are available: alternatively low voltage tungsten filament lamps can be supplied from a bank of remote batteries. Fluorescent tubes can be operated from battery supplies using transistorized inverters. Emergency lighting should provide illuminances of about 1% to 2% of those provided by the main installation.

Stand-by lighting is sometimes required where it is necessary for work to continue following an interruption of the main electrical supply. The necessary illuminance is considerably higher than for emergency lighting, 5% to 20% of that provided by the main scheme. In most cases stand-by lighting is best provided by a battery-fed transistorized inverter, controlled by a mains-held relay, feeding an appropriate fraction of the luminaires in the main installation.

24.3 LIGHTING FOR INSPECTION

The inspection of manufactured articles may require special lighting techniques and equipment. The application of the basic principles of lighting design, described in this and other chapters, following detailed analysis of the inspection task, will usually provide an adequate solution to visual inspection problems. However, some brief notes describing the more widely used solutions to specific inspection problems may help to suggest solutions to other inspection tasks.

The accurate assessment or matching of colour is one of the inspection problems most often encountered. BS 950, Part 1, specifies the performance of light sources for accurate colour appraisal in industrial inspection and manufacture. Fluorescent tubes complying with this specification are available but unfortunately their efficacy is rather low and their use for general lighting is often economically prohibitive. The use of inspection booths (Fig. 24.3a and b) obviates the need for general lighting to comply with the

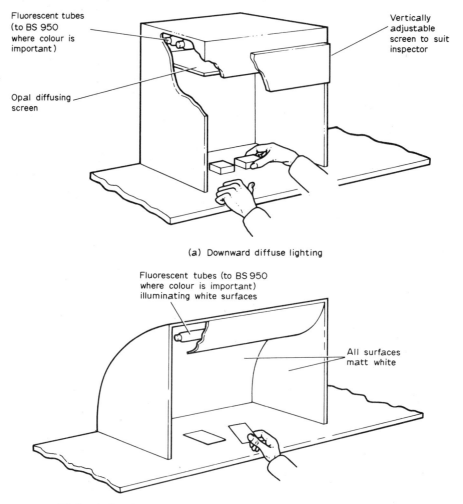

(a) Downward diffuse lighting

(b) Omni–directional lighting for components with specular finish

British Standard, and additionally isolates the inspection task from other possible extraneous influence. Booths for colour assessment should be illuminated to at least 1000 lux, using diffuse lighting: the surfaces of the booth should have a neutral matt finish.

Inspection booths can be usefully employed for other inspection tasks which may not involve critical colour appraisal (Figs. 24.3c, d and e). It must be remembered that some inspection (and manufacturing) tasks are beyond the ability of unassisted vision, and in such cases the eye must be assisted by an appropriate visual aid. This may be as simple as a magnifying lens or as complicated as a profile projector capable of projecting a very much enlarged image of the object being inspected with great accuracy.

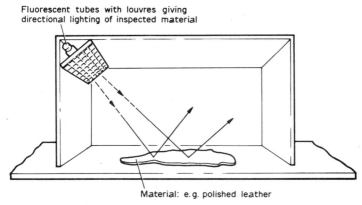

Fluorescent tubes with louvres giving directional lighting of inspected material

Material: e.g. polished leather

(c) Directional lighting for semi-polished materials

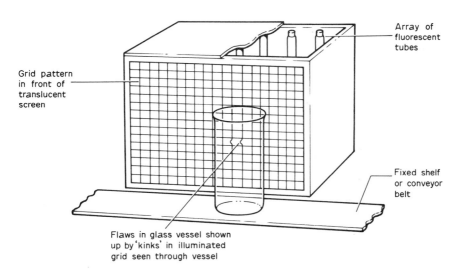

Array of fluorescent tubes

Grid pattern in front of translucent screen

Fixed shelf or conveyor belt

Flaws in glass vessel shown up by 'kinks' in illuminated grid seen through vessel

(d) Inspection of regular transparent objects

Fig. 24.3 Five examples of inspection lighting techniques

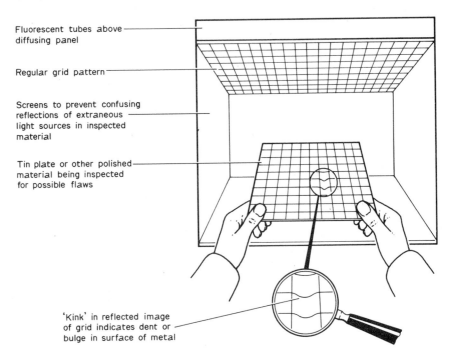

Fluorescent tubes above diffusing panel

Regular grid pattern

Screens to prevent confusing reflections of extraneous light sources in inspected material

Tin plate or other polished material being inspected for possible flaws

'Kink' in reflected image of grid indicates dent or bulge in surface of metal

(e) Inspection of specular materials

Polarized lighting has been successfully applied to the inspection of transparent glass and plastic products. Any strain in the product will cause non-uniform transmission of the polarized light causing colour fringes which are visible to the inspector.

Stroboscopic devices providing pulses of light at controlled frequency can be used to check the speed of rotating or reciprocating machinery, or to slow the apparent movement of the mechanism so that a more detailed examination can be made.

The colour properties of a light source can assist with other inspection problems. For example, monochromatic light provided by low pressure sodium lamps or specialized mercury lamps can improve visual acuity and can therefore be useful where details in the task approach the limit of size detectable by the eye. Also monochromatic lighting in conjunction with optical flats can be used to check the flatness of precision-finished surfaces. The reflections from the test surface interfere with the light reflected from the optical flat and set up bands or fringes which are observed through the optical flat. The number and contour of these bands indicate the degree of error in the test surface.

Colour contrast can assist in the inspection process. For example, a coloured dye is often applied to the surface of steel so that scribe marks can be more easily seen: increased contrast results from the use of coloured light which would be absorbed by the coloured dye but reflected by the base material.

Lighting having radiation predominantly in the ultra-violet wavebands can be used to make fluorescent or phosphorescent objects visible: materials which look alike under visible radiation can show marked differences under ultra-violet radiation and substances which are imperceptible in visible light can be revealed by ultra-violet radiation. For example, fluorescent tracers are often added to coolant fluids, and examination for possible leaks is made by searching for signs of the tracer with ultra-violet emitting lamps. As has been noted in Chap. 6 short wave ultra-violet radiation is dangerous to eyes and skin and should only be used where long wavelength radiation is incapable of exciting the fluorescent material being considered.

The number of lighting techniques which can be applied to specific tasks is almost limitless: as new problems are found, so will new solutions be devised, the only requirements being a detailed analysis of the task, and a subsequent reference to the basic principles of light and lighting.

25 Office lighting

The lighting alone cannot provide the necessary pleasantness so important to office workers; the decor, furniture, temperature, air change and acoustics also have an important part to play. The success of any lighting installation depends upon its integration with the structural and functional elements of the building. Thus the lighting designer should be equipped with as much information as possible about the interior before starting his design work.

The advent of deep-plan offices, where the majority of the occupants are located away from the windows, requires a close study of the visual field within the office area. It is even more important than in shallow offices to create a pleasant visual atmosphere so that what ever the task might be, the employee has a sense of well-being and pleasure in working in his surroundings.

25.1 LIGHTING CRITERIA

The visual tasks in offices are quite diversified, ranging from those which are spasmodic and easy to those which are continuous and exacting. Generally, the more exacting work is undertaken by the more experienced worker, who is older and therefore has a reduced visual performance capability in comparison with the younger person.

Many office occupations involve the reading of type, either printed or type written: the severity of the visual task (assuming a normal reading distance) depends upon the type size and its clarity, the reflectances of the type and paper on which the message appears. Management can therefore ease the visual tasks of their employees by paying attention to the choice of type and typewriter, by ensuring that staff are not regularly required to read poor carbon copies, and by choosing papers of appropriate reflectance and colour (it should be borne in mind that some men suffer some deficiency in their powers of colour discrimination).

Many office tasks have a number of areas of interest. For instance the typist needs to look at her notebook or copy, the typewriter keys and the script in the machine. Generally it is the notebook or copy which receives the most attention: some typists prefer to have the notebook on an incline and some punch-card machines involve a vertical visual task. Specular reflections from typewriter keys and the surfaces of office machinery should be avoided whenever possible.

The most exacting visual tasks are usually to be found in the drawing office where critical detail must be seen with precision and contrasts are often poor; for example, pencil lines when seen through tracing paper or cloth. Further difficulties arise through the possibility of shadows thrown by drawing instruments. Reflected glare can also be experienced since the board often occupies a large proportion of the visual field and is often of high reflectance: a matt backing medium of about 40% reflectance can help to reduce this glare.

In contrast, private offices embrace less exacting visual tasks. The appearance of the occupants and their surroundings are often more important since discussions and dictation are the prime functions, with work akin to that in the general office being performed spasmodically. However, there are certain classes of senior staff in private offices who do have critical visual tasks and care must be taken to ensure that their requirements are satisfied.

Conference rooms are similar to private offices in their demands, except that a more relaxing atmosphere is generally required since usually only intermittent reading is involved. Care must be taken to avoid distracting specular reflections in the tables, which often have polished surfaces.

The provision of lighting in offices is subject to legislation under the Offices, Shops and Railways Premises Act 1963. Table 25.1 specifies the illuminance and glare index

Table 25.1 IES recommendations (1968) for offices

	IES recommended illuminance (lux)	IES recommended limiting glare index
General offices:		
general	400	19
desks	400	19
Typing rooms:		
general	400	19
desks	400	19
Conference Rooms, executive and clerical rooms	400	19
Business machines and computer rooms:		
general	600	19
machines	600	19
Drawing offices:		
general	400	19
boards and tracing	600	16

recommendations given by the 1968 IES Code, the illuminance values being the minimum to be maintained in service. Meeting these recommendations, while satisfying the 1963 Act, will not necessarily create satisfactory visual conditions. As has been indicated in Chap. 22, there are a number of inter-related factors which contribute to the satisfactory lighting of any interior: the luminance of the major room surfaces and of the luminaires, the revealing of form and texture, colour appearance and colour rendering.

25.2 LIGHTING EQUIPMENT

25.2.1 Sources

Economics generally dictate the use of sources having a high efficacy, acceptable colour rendering, long life and minimal flicker. The source which satisfies these requirements is the fluorescent tube, although high pressure discharge lamps and luminaires are being developed for use in commercial interiors and will no doubt require consideration in the very near future.

The fluorescent tube is produced in a variety of colours and those generally considered for offices are White, Warm White, Natural and °Kolor-rite. The basic differences between these four types of tube are in luminous efficacy and colour rendering. The first two have a high efficacy with only fair colour rendering, tending to give a yellowish tinge to the visual scene: this is quite acceptable if the lighting is not expected to blend with natural lighting. The last two types have good colour rendering properties with a luminous efficacy of about 70% of the White tube. The colour rendering and appearance of the Natural and °Kolor-rite tubes make them suitable for blending with daylight.

25.2.2   Luminaires

The required illuminances in offices can be provided efficiently and without causing excessive glare by choosing from a wide variety of lighting equipment currently available. A few examples of these luminaires are given in Fig. 25.1, having different methods of flux control.

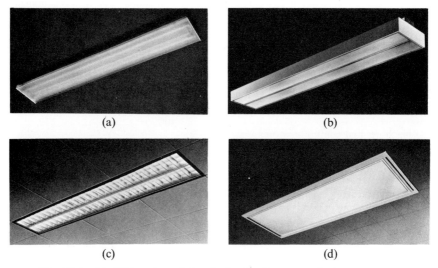

(a)   (b)

(c)   (d)

Fig. 25.1   (a) Wide prismatic luminaire (surface mounting)
(b) Low brightness luminaire (surface mounting)
(c) Recessed air-handling low brightness reflector luminaire
(d) Recessed prismatic air-handling luminaire with air slots

Luminaire (a) is a surface-mounted totally-enclosed diffuser unit having a wide prismatic controller with linear side prisms and pyramidal base prisms. The function of these prisms is to redirect light from the tubes either above the horizontal or below 60° from the downward vertical, thus ensuring the least amount of light being emitted in the zone most likely to give rise to discomfort glare.

Luminaire (b) meets the demand for a design that can provide high illuminance with a very low glare index. This is achieved by using a combination of longitudinal extruded aluminium reflectors and a base panel with moulded transverse prisms. This not only diffuses the light from the tubes when viewed along their length but also provides sufficient luminosity to avoid the dull effect that can occasionally be produced with low glare luminaires. The transverse light distribution is of the batwing type (Sect. 22.3.2) which gives a more even spread of light over the horizontal plane than the more conventional concentrating optical systems.

Luminaire (c) is a recessed design, also of the low brightness type. The optical system is a one-piece unit assembly per lampway, made from figured aluminium sheet and extruded aluminium baffles with a specular anodized finish.

Luminaire (d) is a recessed modular unit with a prismatic controller for use in a wide range of suspended ceilings. Both (c) and (d) are air-handling luminaires (Sect. 21.3.2): in (c) the air is drawn through the whole length of the louvre assembly, and in (d) the air is drawn into the luminaire through carefully designed slots in the end trims. In both designs the air can pass either through the slots in the back of the luminaire and into a ceiling plenum or into a hood for ducting directly to the air controlling plant. In addition to lessening the load on an air-refrigeration plant by taking away heat at source, the passage of air over the fluorescent tubes within a luminaire increases the efficacy of the source; it is possible to obtain up to 15% more light output from an air-handling luminaire as compared with an equivalent non-air-handling unit.

25.2.3 Suspended ceilings

The modern building generally involves the installation of false ceilings, primarily to give a clean and pleasing appearance to this surface. This also facilitates the concealment of ugly structural elements and the mechanical, electrical and plumbing services, as well as offering acoustical and thermal control. Further it permits the use of recessed luminaires, ensuring a clean appearance to the ceiling and minimizing the interruption of forced air flow.

Though the detailed mechanical structure of a suspended ceiling varies from manufacturer to manufacturer it is generally made up of a series of main bearers, running parallel to each other at about 1 m to 2 m centres, supported from the underside of the structural slab by either steel straps or wires. Secondary bearers for the ceiling tiles run across the main bearers, the distance apart being dependent on the chosen module of the lining, usually based on a factor of 300 mm, the most popular sizes being either 300 mm × 300 mm or 300 mm × 600 mm. Bearers are made from a wide range of materials, the detailing of the jointing being dependent upon whether an exposed or a concealed grid system is used (Fig. 25.2). The lining panels take the form of tiles or trays and may be of plasterboard, fibreboard, plaster, mineral wool or asbestos: these have little mechanical strength and are susceptible to damage by moisture. Others are of steel or aluminium perforated trays or planks lined with sound-absorbent or insulating material.

The planning of a recessed lighting installation has to be related to the ceiling module and any mechanical services. If air-handling luminaires (Sect. 21.3.2) are used with a ceiling plenum air-extract system, attention has to be given to the points at which luminaires join the ceiling and to the choice of ceiling tile and suspension: little or no air should be drawn through anywhere but the luminaires, otherwise pattern staining of the tiles can readily occur by dirt and dust being entrained into the moving air.

Access into a suspended ceiling must be provided when plant or other building services within the ceiling plenum needs periodic attention. Most ceiling systems are either

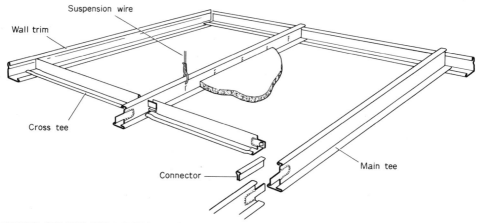

JOINTED CEILINGS WITH EXPOSED GRIDS

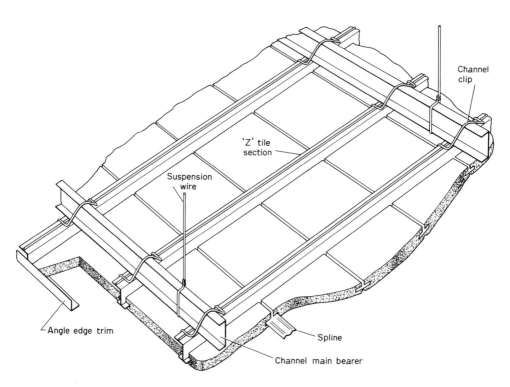

JOINTED CEILINGS WITH CONCEALED GRIDS

Fig. 25.2 Suspended ceiling systems

totally demountable or make provision for access at specific points: such points may be sources of air leaks in a sealed plenum system, as the effectiveness of the seal will tend to deteriorate with use.

25.3   LIGHTING DESIGN

The luminance design method (Sect. 22.3.1) is particularly applicable to offices. The task luminance gives a reference for the average luminance of the other major surfaces of the interior: the immediate background should be between 0·3 and 0·5 of the task luminance, general surroundings between 0·1 and 0·9. These ranges may seem to be rather wide but are so in order to achieve variation in design to prevent monotony.

25.3.1   General offices

Current building techniques often provide offices with little or no daylight so the use of artificial light is paramount. Windows are provided primarily for visual contact with the outside world to satisfy ever-enquiring minds as to the state of the weather and other exterior happenings. These recurring enquiries can be satisfied in a moment even by comparatively small areas of glazing. The provision of such information generally promotes longer periods of concentration than if there were no windows. However, it is necessary to provide a compensation in the standard of artificial lighting to avoid a sense of deprivation of natural light. In such circumstances the minimum illuminance of 400 lux recommended by the IES is generally regarded as inadequate and 700 lux to 1000 lux is usually the design target.

The quantity of light cannot be divorced from its quality, and the fluorescent tube, because of its high luminous efficacy and considerable area, facilitates the provision of uniform illumination without hard shadows. The planning of lighting installations usually requires the use of multi-tube luminaires either recessed or surface mounted. The choice is dependent upon the nature of the ceiling, the desired lighting effect, and the relationship of the lighting to other building services. The brightness contrasts between luminaires and ceilings should be at a minimum: where decorations are light in colour and where there is a lightly coloured floor, the need for upward light from the fitting is not vital as the ceiling receives sufficient light by inter-reflection.

The layout of luminaires, particularly in large open areas, has to be related not only to the working area but also to the ceiling module of the building and that of the windows. The external appearance at night is often of importance and in multi-storey offices it is preferable to ensure that the lighting layout follows a consistent regular pattern on all floors.

Rather than use a series of individual luminaires it is worth considering a continuous run as shown in Fig. 25.3. This gives a more unified appearance to the ceiling and facilitates wiring. However, very long continuous runs can be monotonous: this can be overcome by the introduction of regular gaps which can be used to accommodate loudspeakers or decorative tungsten lighting features or air-extracting louvres.

The boundaries of the visual scene should always be carefully considered. As stated earlier, buildings are tending to have smaller windows which means that an external wall has comparatively large solid surfaces which if not adequately illuminated could be too

455

Fig. 25.3   General office, SWEB

dark by contrast with the windows. It is worth considering placing the first row of luminaires comparatively close to this wall in order to provide it with a satisfactory luminosity and perhaps obviate supplementary lighting which might otherwise be necessary.

Although economics do not always allow flexible lighting trunking systems, they can be introduced to enable supplementary lighting to be applied to the occasional features such as rest and conference areas or visual relief points such as indoor plants: should these areas be moved then so can the lighting.

25.3.2   Business machine offices

Much of the equipment has the visual task in the vertical plane and it contains small detail. Since the majority of this equipment has intricate electrical circuitry it is unlikely to be moved once installed, thus the lighting designer can provide lighting for a particular layout.

As described in Sect. 22.3.2, luminaires having an asymmetric light distribution have been developed to provide economically a high standard of horizontal and vertical illuminance. Fig. 25.4 shows a business machine office illuminated by this type of luminaire and it can be seen by the variation in the luminosity of the vertical surfaces that the modelling is quite pronounced. The location of this type of luminaire differs from that having a conventional symmetrical distribution in that the luminaires are arranged complementary to the windows, with the first row sited immediately adjacent to the window wall, thence the conventional spacing of the rows is applied. The adoption of this layout maintains the simulation of natural light flowing across the room as well as ensuring a satisfactory uniformity in the horizontal illumination at task level. Since this

Fig. 25.4 Business machine office, using asymmetric luminaires

form of design is closely linked with natural lighting the colour rendering quality of the light sources must be considered and should blend well with that of daylight.

25.3.3 Private offices and conference rooms

Whilst occupants of a general office are usually engaged for long periods in such activities as reading, writing, calculating and typing, the occupant of the private office spends most of his time in discussion and dictation. Uniformity in the lighting is not called for and may in fact be undesirable. It is necessary to light the desk area to a minimum illuminance of 400 lux; if the office is close to a general office having 1000 lux then a level of 600 lux or 700 lux should be considered to prevent a sense of deprivation. This may be provided by special lighting features. The lighting of the general surroundings should provide a comfortable but stimulating atmosphere, and it should be remembered that the predominant sightline is likely to be nearer the horizontal than for a worker in a general office.

The principles of lighting a private office also apply to conference rooms. Whilst it is often necessary to make notes at the conference table much of the time is taken up with discussion and an evenly lit room rarely helps to create an appropriate atmosphere. The area of the table should be lit to 400 lux with equipment which will offer the minimum of specular reflections in the surface of the table. The peripheral areas generally allow scope to the lighting engineer for the application of decorative and imaginative lighting treatment.

25.3.4 Drawing offices

The lighting of drawing offices has always been a controversial topic, particularly the choice between a modest general lighting installation supplemented by local lighting and a more ambitious general lighting scheme.

457

Fig. 25.5   Drawing office, using continuous prismatic troffers

A draughtsman often prefers the former, since local control is at his disposal and psychologically he feels this gives him a degree of privacy. However, such systems can cause luminosity differences throughout the office which may be distracting or even uncomfortable especially when the local light used by one draughtsman becomes a source of glare to another. General lighting in excess of the 400 lux recommended by the IES Code is currently very common, and under these conditions the need for local lighting is greatly diminished.

General lighting is best achieved by fluorescent luminaires running parallel with the major axes of the boards (Fig. 25.5). This minimizes the creation of disturbing shadows along the edges of drawing instruments.

26 Shop lighting

Over the last ten years, trends in the design of shops and in selling methods have appeared which have transformed the shopping streets of our towns and to a large extent the habits of customers. The most outstanding of these are:

(a) Most food shops have been converted to self-service. This tendency extends throughout the trade and is no longer limited to the multiples.
(b) Boutiques, which originally catered mainly for teenagers, are now appearing among the better class of clothing shops.
(c) Large departmental stores no longer cater exclusively for middle-class and upper middle-class customers and have been much influenced by the boutique idea.
(d) Specialist shops are fewer and most shops sell a wide variety of goods.
(e) There are fewer individually owned shops and a marked increase in the multiples, especially in the shoe, clothing and food trades.

All this can be summed up in the ideas of self-selection and self-service: point of sale lighting is of paramount importance in modern shops, and both the colour and quality of the light must be chosen to suit the merchandise displayed.

26.1 PRINCIPLES OF SHOP LIGHTING

A shoplighting installation has one main purpose, to help the shopkeeper sell his goods. The lighting must attract the customer's attention to the goods, help him to appraise them and provide an atmosphere conducive to sales. How this is done will vary according to the goods displayed, the trading methods used, the design of the shop and the class of customer expected: not only the windows but the whole shop must be considered. It might be concluded that all that is necessary is to provide enough light at the point of sale (displays and counters) and rely on 'spill' to light the rest of the room, but this is not necessarily the case: general lighting is often needed.

Shops can be divided into four main categories, each of which has its typical form of lighting:

(a) Boutiques and small specialist shops: lighting at the point of sale and on displays, spill lighting providing general illumination, decorative luminaires may be used for atmosphere.
(b) Selling floors in department stores, furniture stores and similar larger specialist shops: general lighting from fluorescent tubes in diffusing luminaires with local lighting on counters and displays, decorative filament lighting may be used to give atmosphere.

459

(c) Self-selection stores in the medium price range: general fluorescent lighting from diffusing luminaires, supplemented by display lighting in selected areas (towards the
back of the shop or for special and seasonal displays).
(d) Supermarkets and self-selection stores in the lower price range: general lighting from
rows of bare tubes, sometimes supplemented by special lighting over meat counters
(usually at the back of the shop).

26.2   GENERAL LIGHTING

The 1968 IES Code recommends a general illuminance of 200 lux for circulation areas
and 600 lux on counters. This clearly implies localized lighting on the latter but the values
are rather low by present-day standards and the average illuminances found in practice
are much in excess of those recommended.

The choice of fluorescent luminaires for general shop lighting is little different from
that of similar equipment for an office, but a higher glare index (22) is acceptable. In large
selling floors, the cumulative glare of an array of diffusing fittings can be rather over-
powering, and fittings of a lower BZ classification may be used. Ventilation of large
selling floors presents a serious problem and many stores would benefit from the use of
air-handling luminaires: this technique has been used effectively with continuous rows of
recessed luminaires handling the extract air (Fig. 21.7).

A very important factor in the choice of luminaires in stores and shops is ease of maintenance. Cleaning staff is almost always unskilled and luminaires which cannot easily be
serviced by one man should be avoided. Where floors are carpeted a good deal of fluff is
always present in the air and terrazza floors produce dust. Luminaires may have to be
cleaned at rather shorter intervals than in an office where there is less movement and a
smaller number of people in the room.

Boutiques and small specialist shops.   The lighting can be localized at the point of sale
and the spill lighting used for circulation areas. Lighting wall displays from open-topped
canopies makes the shop look wider and provides some indirect lighting to soften shadows
in gangways. The back part of the shop should be given special lighting treatment to draw
customers in and make full use of the floor area.

Since the position of counters is usually fixed, downlighters can be arranged over them:
this eliminates the heat build-up inside an internally lit counter and ensures that goods
taken out of the counter and put on the top of it are even better lit than they were before.
Care must be taken to align the luminaires with the front edge of the counter to avoid
annoying reflections in the glass (Fig. 26.1a).

Department stores and larger specialist shops.   These are almost always lit by an array of
fluorescent luminaires unrelated to the counters below them. It is difficult to provide
display lighting from ceiling level because of the length of throw and the difficulty of
aiming the equipment; consequently the majority of stores use internally-lighted counters, often arranged around lighted shelves or showcases enclosing what is virtually a
supplementary stock-room. Lighted canopies are often provided on island displays in
department stores, and almost always on wall shelves or display areas (Fig. 26.1b).

460

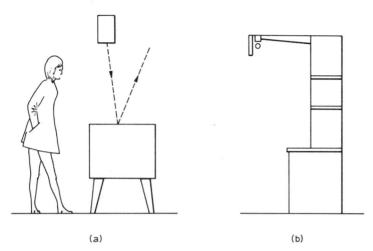

Fig. 26.1 (a) Luminaires mounted over glass counter
(b) Lighted pelmet for wall display or for island site

Attempts to concentrate lighting exclusively on merchandise and to rely on spill lighting for general illumination can only work reasonably well if the area is not too big. Where the technique is used with a dark-painted ceiling in a larger area, the effect can be rather depressing.

Self-selection stores and supermarkets. General lighting is always used, supplemented by canopy lighting around the walls. In self-selection stores selling good quality goods at reasonable prices, the display is kept at counter level to facilitate customers' appraisal and to allow a clear view across the room. Such stores are normally lighted to at least 500 lux using multilamp luminaires: display lighting is confined to the window area.

The lower-priced self-selection stores and almost all supermarkets are lit by rows of bare fluorescent tubes. These are oriented end-on to the check-out positions and in line with the gondolas: they should be sited above the gangways to facilitate maintenance. Although enclosed fittings are now beginning to be used, it is claimed that bare tubes give a busy bustling appearance to the shop, and discourage loitering. They suggest a 'no nonsense' place where money is not wasted on frills and where customers can appear in overalls without exciting comment: this idea is also seen in roadside cafes where bare fluorescent tubes are invariably used. Bare tubes reduce maintenance to an absolute minimum: all that has to be done is to wipe the tubes. In almost all supermarkets there is a meat counter at the back and here tungsten filament lamps may well be used; alternatively fluorescent tubes of a warmer colour appearance may be mounted above diffusing or louvred panels.

26.3 LOCAL LIGHTING

26.3.1 Counter and showcase lighting

Internally-lighted showcase counters usually house fluorescent tubes, although in a few cases doubled-ended tubular filament lamps are used. The usual method of concealing

461

the lamp is to mount it in a metal reflector behind a strip of mirrored glass on the customers' side of the counter (Fig. 26.2a) giving good light distribution but making the counter look rather clumsy. Glass counters are often made with only a slender metal frame to hold the glass, or the glass is butted together without any frame at all, and so it is preferable to mount the lamps at the back of the showcase (Fig. 26.2b). The control gear

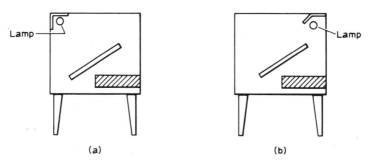

Lamp

Lamp

(a)   (b)

Fig. 26.2   Two ways of lighting a counter showcase. Control-gear is mounted in a drawer (shaded area)

is mounted in a ventilated drawer at the bottom of the counter. Shopfitters use standard counter units, traditionally 4 ft or 5 ft (1·25 m or 1·5 m) long which can be built up in sets, consequently the 1200 mm 40 W tube is commonly used, °Kolor-rite being recommended.

Wall showcases and shelf displays are usually lit from the top. Glazed wall showcases are commonly used to display small valuable goods or those which can be spoiled by handling. Individual lighting under shelves is sometimes used or fluorescent tubes mounted vertically behind glazing bars. Both techniques have been used successfully on open shelf displays.

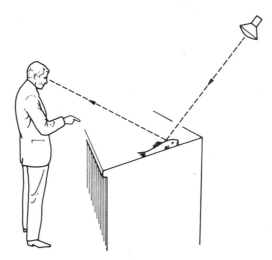

Fig. 26.3   Bouncing the light off the surface of the display helps to make the fish look fresh

Some types of merchandise respond to special lighting. For example, blown and engraved glass looks extremely effective against a softly lighted and lightly textured neutral-coloured background: cheap moulded glass can look most effective if light is shone through it from below. Cut glass looks its best lit strongly from above and standing on a black or dark velvet plinth. Silverware and jewellery should be shown under filament lamps. The disadvantage of filament lamps is their comparatively short life, necessitating more frequent changing of lamps. Where space is limited and a lively lighting effect is wanted, miniature (12 V 50 W) reflector lamps can be used.

Modelling and 'flash' have a marked effect on the appearance of the merchandise. Goods with a strongly textured surface, such as deep-pile carpets, knitwear and some furnishing fabrics, need directional lighting to bring out their qualities: usually this is done by adding tungsten spotlights to the general lighting. In some types of merchandise 'flash' or glitter is equally important: thus when lighting fresh fish a mixture of a cool fluorescent (Northlight or °Kolor-rite) and filament lamps should be arranged so that their light is reflected into the eyes of the observer, increasing glitter and making the fish look wet and therefore fresh (Fig. 26.3).

26.3.2 Window lighting

The shop window is the main link between the shopkeeper and the public, and its design is perhaps more important than any other part of the shop. The shopkeeper may use his window as a catalogue of the goods to be found inside the shop. Display men call this a 'stocky' window and it is found in shoe shops, many clothing shops, ironmongers and similar shops, jewellers and those food shops that use a window display. The high-class draper or department store uses his windows to put over the ideas of luxury or of good value, boutique windows may be as 'kinky' as the goods they sell, while most supermarkets, motor-car dealers and quite a number of specialist shops make use of open-backed windows which allow a view of the shop interior over or through the display.

The window may be glazed on any number of sides and lighting equipment has to be arranged so as to avoid glare to customers. Complete concealment of luminaires is no longer regarded as essential but it is still necessary to screen the actual source of light from view. From this it will be clear that there is no single solution to the problem of the choice of lamps and lighting equipment: this depends not only on the shape and size of the window but on the display technique favoured by the management, the class of customer and the district in which the shop is found.

Single aspect windows are found almost exclusively in large department stores. One side only is glazed, and the lighting equipment can easily be concealed behind baffles (Fig. 26.4). Both fluorescent and tungsten filament lighting are used in this type of window. Background lighting may be provided by coloured fluorescent tubes and may be dimmer controlled: if white light from the luminaires in the front of the window falls on the background the effect will be spoiled.

It is recommended that whenever practicable reflectors should be used: mounting fluorescent tubes behind baffles without reflectors results in overlighting the upper part of the window display (Fig. 26.5). Filament spotlamps may be mounted on trunking so as to give maximum flexibility to the installation, and low voltage spotlighting is often used to highlight individual items of the display.

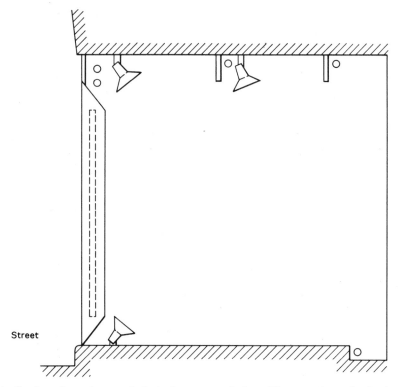

Fig. 26.4   Section through a typical single aspect window. The trough at the back conceals
coloured background lighting equipment

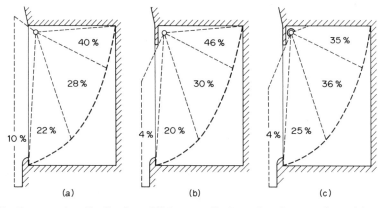

Fig. 26.5   Comparative distribution of light on a display using the same lamp (a) unshielded
(b) behind a white-lined pelmet   (c) in a specular reflector

Double aspect windows occur in the majority of shops which have a window to one side of the entrance or two windows flanking it. They are commonly found in small shops, and are usually lighted by two or more rows of fluorescent tubes mounted behind a pelmet and supplemented by two or more 150 W reflector lamps. Since the re-entrant side of the window is only the depth of the entrance lobby, there is no need to screen the lamps further, but where there is a deep re-entrant or an arcade window, cross baffles or louvres are often used. The usual method is to mount fluorescent tubes above a louvred or diffusing panel and position filament lamps in fixed or adjustable reflectors on or in a strip of solid soffit inside the window glass (Fig. 26.6a). In shoe-shops the window often takes the form of a large show-case with its floor at about waist level and the soffit only just above eye level.

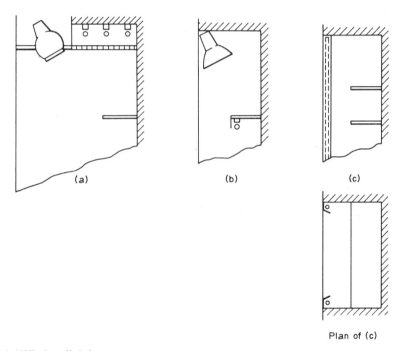

(a)   (b)   (c)

Plan of (c)

Fig. 26.6   Window lighting:
(a) Fluorescent tubes above louvred soffit, with glass shelves
(b) Top lighting with miniature fluorescent tubes mounted behind pelmets underneath the shelves
(c) Screened fluorescent tubes mounted vertically at the sides of the window

Where there is adequate headroom an alternative to the use of conventional lamps is to recess 750 W tungsten halogen shop window floodlights in the ceiling. The chief advantages of this method are that the number of luminaires is reduced, the lamps give excellent colour rendering and a lively play of light and shade, and that the lamps have a life of 2000 h thus doubling intervals between lamp replacements.

Island and open-back windows.   The first are usually found in the entrance arcades of old-fashioned departmental stores and are best lit by concentrating spotlights which do not appear glaring unless one is directly in the beam. Lighting equipment in open-backed windows can constitute a glare source when seen from inside the shop, so the same method is recommended: fluorescent tubes can be screened from view by means of pelmets or mounted above louvres.

Very shallow windows.   Jewellers and confectioners commonly display their goods on shelves mounted very close to the window glass or in shallow window-showcases. Both these types of window are difficult to light from the top only. Extra lamps mounted under the shelves are sometimes effective, and miniature fluorescent tubes can be used (Fig. 26.6b). In jewellers shops, miniature reflector spotlamps (12 V 50 W) are often mounted at the sides of the window, and the use of well screened fluorescent tubes mounted vertically at the sides of the window is also common (Fig. 26.6c). Small spotlamps or fluorescent tubes on the stall-riser can also be effective.

Brightness of window displays.   It is customary to classify the light required according to the expected brightness of the adjacent shop windows, but the enormous increase in the number of multiples has resulted in most shopping centres being almost uniformly brightly lit. Shops in side streets can afford to use lower illuminances than those in the main shopping centre of a town. Overheating of window displays can be a serious matter: some diminution of the heating effect of filament lamps can be obtained by using dichroic reflector lamps, an important consideration in windows displaying perishable goods. Typically the watts of light power per metre run of window when tungsten reflector lamps are used range from 600 W/m for main shopping areas to about 150 W/m for side streets: these figures should be halved for wholly fluorescent installations.

Calculation of illuminance by the lumen method of design is misleading, partly because of the directional nature of the light and the large areas of glass involved, partly because the method determines the average illuminance on a horizontal plane while in a shop-window vertical surfaces should be more brightly lit than horizontal ones. Mean horizontal illuminance is only useful as a means of deciding whether the window is brightly enough lit to compete with its neighbours. Because two or more sides of a shop-window may be glazed, it can be considered as a room with one, two, three or four black walls: consequently a very low utilization factor (0·2 or less) applies.

Photometric data are not always available for display lighting fittings, and the lighting engineer may have to combine several different methods to find what his final result is likely to be. Where a line of fluorescent luminaires is installed behind a pelmet, a good idea of the illuminance on a display can be had by estimating the proportion of the total lamp lumens cast in that direction. This can most easily be done by means of a scale drawing: it can be checked by comparison with the published polar curve of the luminaire. It is important to remember that while the illuminance at points opposite the middle of the tube will be roughly proportional to the inverse of the distance from it, those opposite the ends will be more nearly proportional to the inverse of the square of the distance. Few display artists understand a polar diagram, so most manufacturers publish 'light in the beam' or 'target' diagrams for display lighting equipment which can be used to calculate the illuminance to be expected.

26.4 DISPLAY LIGHTING EQUIPMENT

The techniques of display lighting closely resemble those employed in stage lighting, but the equipment is very different and to follow stage lighting practice is unlikely to be satisfactory. Stage lighting equipment is bulky but it is easily concealed and the powerful lamps are used for short periods with quite considerable throws. Display lighting equipment must be compact as there is little room available, the power of the light source can be lower as throws of more than ten feet are unusual, and the lamps must last at least 1000 h in order to reduce maintenance and replacement costs. The equipment must be robust enough to stand rough handling by unskilled labour.

Almost all display spotlamps make use of parabolic reflectors either spun in super-pure aluminium and used with a separate lamp or in the form of a reflector lamp. Where a tight beam is essential it is necessary to use low voltage lamps in order to make the filament as nearly as possible a point source.

Narrow beam spotlights. Very compact reflector lamps working at 12 V and rated at 50 W are especially useful where space is strictly limited. They give a tight beam, but about 50% of the light is uncontrolled 'spill' light: where this must be avoided it is better to use a crown-silvered lamp of equivalent rating in a spun aluminium reflector. The latest development is the use of tungsten halogen lamps in similar reflectors. These give still better light control, and the lamps have a higher light output and twice the life of conventional crown-silvered lamps: the transformer is usually housed in the luminaire, allowing it to be used on a lighting track system. Conventional low-voltage units may use a separate transformer and it is then important not to reduce the length of the low tension lead or the lamps will be over-run.

Mounting reflectors. Display lighting equipment must be capable of being pointed in any direction and be provided with a cable entry which is electrically and mechanically safe. Swivel attachments through which the lead-in wires are fed may not hold the unit firmly in position, may pinch the cable or have no provision against twisting it off. In the majority of well-designed spotlights the cable is now taken in separately through the back of the housing and the swivelling device is separate from it.

Trakline systems. These allow the display artist to move spotlights about in the window at will, and thus to achieve effects impossible with fixed lighting equipment. It is recommended that Trakline should be installed at the sides and base of the window as well as in the window head: a line at the back of both floor and ceiling level can be most useful as it saves the cost of installing switch-sockets at these places.

Heat dissipation. Heat is reflected with the light in the beam of a spotlight and can lead to a severe build-up of heat on the display. Inside the shop too, customers may suffer discomfort and since this heat is radiated it cannot be dispersed by ventilation or the use of fans. Cool-ray lamps are recommended in all situations where heat creates problems (displays of shoes, food and other perishable goods), but it must be remembered that the total amount of heat emitted is no less than that from a conventional lamp of the same wattage, so provision must be made to disperse the heat radiated through the back of the lamp.

The heat build-up in fluorescent luminaires, discussed in previous chapters, is equally applicable to shops and stores where the high proportion of filament lighting to fluorescent aggravates the thermal problem. The deterioration of the colour of tubes running in too high an ambient temperature is more important in sales areas than in offices. Where banks of fluorescent tubes are used in shop windows, it is recommended that wherever possible the gear is mounted remote from the lamps and that the window should be ventilated.

Coloured filters and reflectors may be standard glass filters designed to slip on to the front of a spotlight housing, or frames holding coloured Cinabex or similar plastic material. PAR reflector lamps can be used with a coloured skin on their front glass or with dichroic filters (Sect. 9.2). Glass filters have the advantage of neatness and robustness, and can be used again and again, but they are only available in a limited range of colours, as are the coloured PAR and dichroic lamps. If subtle colour effects are wanted it may be necessary to use Cinabex screens, although they are rather untidy and deteriorate with use. Coloured anodized aluminium reflectors may also be used with crown-silvered lamps to produce a beam of coloured light.

27 School and hospital lighting

For both schools and hospitals the necessity of providing the correct environment is as much a building design problem as one of mechanical and electrical services, and no one aspect can take precedence. Naturally the overall design brief must be centred around the requirements of the welfare of the occupants, staff efficiency and overall economics. In respect to lighting, there is a fundamental difference of approach between the relevant Ministries: for schools there has for many years been legislation on lighting levels, luminaire performance and daylight, whilst the Department of Health and Social Security have relied on codes of practice, not always enforced at Hospital Board level. Such codes have had little or no influence on building design and have in most cases been diluted in interpretation in the face of economic considerations. For schools, however, the statutory daylight requirement has probably been the predominant single factor influencing school building design and it is clear that the Department of Education and Science will need to co-ordinate the many varying aspects which together produce the environmental problem, especially in teaching areas.

27.1 SCHOOL LIGHTING

27.1.1 Lighting requirements and trends in school design

Good lighting is an essential part of a successful school building, this being recognized by the then Ministry of Education in the first Statutory Building Regulation made under Section 10 of the Education Act of 1944. This act incorporated improved standards both of daylight and artificial lighting and was the first statutory lighting standard outside the Factory Act of 1941. These regulations, the current version published in 1959 as Statutory Instrument No. 890, require that 'In all teaching accommodation and kitchens the level of maintained illumination and the daylight factor on the appropriate plane in the area of normal use shall not be less than $10 \, \text{lm/ft}^2$ (108 lux) and 2% respectively. In such areas no luminous part of any unit or mirrored image thereof, having a maximum brightness greater than 1500 ft lamberts ($5140 \, \text{cd/m}^2$) or an average brightness greater than 1000 ft lamberts ($3430 \, \text{cd/m}^2$), shall be visible to any occupant in a normal position within an angle at the eye of 135° from the perpendicular from the eye to the floor. A sufficient part of the light emitted from the light fitting shall illuminate the ceiling and upper part of the walls so as to prevent excessive contrast between the fittings and their background.'

Although these instruments are still in force they were clearly conceived for use with tungsten filament lighting units which have to a large degree been superseded by fluorescent luminaires due to their higher efficacy and lower overall running costs. As far as the electric lighting aspect of the legislation is concerned, the IES Code (revised 1968) is the accepted standard in current use today.

469

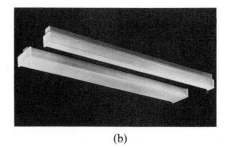

(b)

Fig. 27.1   (a) Tungsten filament luminaire complying with Ministry requirements but not economically viable in the light of present standards   (b) Fluorescent luminaires economically achieving IES Code requirements which can be used individually, or continuously on tracking, or in pairs end to end from a single electrical outlet

(a)

An important factor within the last few years with respect to the building of schools and their design has been the economic one. The cost of building and of available land is such that in many instances the building needs to be specially tailored to the plot on which it is to be built. In teaching areas perhaps the greatest problem has been to meet the increasing needs of modern education while at the same time adhering to the statutory requirement of a 2% daylight factor. In multi-storey schools this results in tall windows and high ceilings giving rise to higher building costs and problems of heat losses, etc. To meet the economic problems confronting the public authorities, the first move of significance was the formation by local authorities of purchasing groups (consortia). Initially these were for the purpose of economic contract buying of equipment, mostly for educational purposes. At a later stage some consortia expanded this concept to building materials and even to building systems. In modern times this concept has further expanded to development work on the total environment carried out by specialists and consultants on behalf of consortia, watched over, of course, by the Department of Education and Science. Working within stringent budgets there is constant pressure on local authorities to produce more and more available school places and better facilities at the most economical costs possible. The interim report of a feasibility study, issued by the County Architect's Department of the Gloucestershire County Council, 'Integrated Environmental Design of School Buildings', is a typical example of this work.

27.1.2   The lighting problem and typical solutions

The lighting problem for school teaching areas is to achieve an illuminance at desk level of no less than 300 lux, 400 lux on the blackboard, with a limiting glare index of 16. The stringent need for wall storage and display space together with ceilings of economic height sometimes means that the 2% daylight factor requirement is not always met and in such conditions some form of permanent supplementary artificial lighting (PSALI) may be necessary (Sect. 23.4). With some local authorities the provision of large deep windows is discouraged due to the distraction of young students and for reasons of economics. Experiments have taken place using vision slits, to maintain visual contact with the outside, combined with a PSALI lighting system, this being appropriate for large and deep teaching areas especially in primary schools where group teaching occurs. The daylight factor can sometimes be increased by the provision of roof lights.

A typical lighting layout is shown in Fig. 27.2a for a classroom of 11·3 m by 7·0 m and 4·3 m high, with standard windows providing a 2% minimum daylight factor. Based on the average sky luminance during a working day, only 110 lux is provided by daylight on desks remote from the window. The artificial lighting from twin 1500 mm fluorescent luminaires would give approximately 300 lux at desk level with the IES requirement of a limiting glare index of 16.

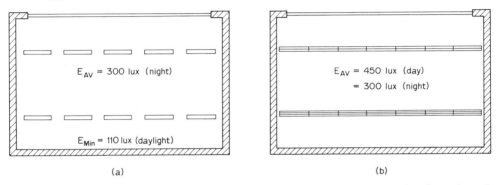

(a)   (b)

Fig. 27.2   (a) Typical classroom lighting layout   (b) A PSALI arrangement showing twin and 3 lamp 1500 mm diffusing luminaires

If the classroom had a reduced ceiling height of 3·5 m, a daylight factor of only 1·25% would be produced. Feasibility exercises indicate the economic advantages of adopting the lower daylight factor and in some cases the DES have waived the 2% requirement. A PSALI arrangement is shown in Fig. 27.2b.

Experimental schools are being built with coffered roof lighting ceilings on a 1·8 m module easily permitting a 2% daylight factor. This system has the advantage of providing the maximum wall coverage so necessary in education today. With such a system 125 W mercury lamps can be used with a simple louvred system (Fig. 27.3) to produce the lighting level and limiting glare index required.

The lighting of other school areas are well covered by the current IES Code, IES Technical Report No. 5 (Lecture theatres and their lighting), and IES Technical Report No. 7 (Lighting for sport). It should be remembered however that where canteens are utilized as examination rooms they should be lit accordingly.

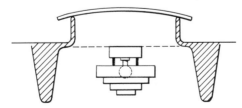

Fig. 27.3   Lighting arrangement using a louvred mercury lamp in a coffered ceiling system

27.2 HOSPITAL LIGHTING

There is no doubt that the trend in hospital design is for larger buildings, housing special-ization wards to a standard design. Much is being done by consultants and specialists to relate the building services to these special requirements both in respect of economy and efficiency. Standard layouts for General, Maternity and Psychiatric wards will soon be forthcoming and information is awaited from the Department of Health and Social Security. How this concept will influence the building design is not yet clear but it is likely that the 'racetrack' system will continue. In this system medical services are con-centrated in the core with wards around the perimeter having access to natural light (Fig. 27.4).

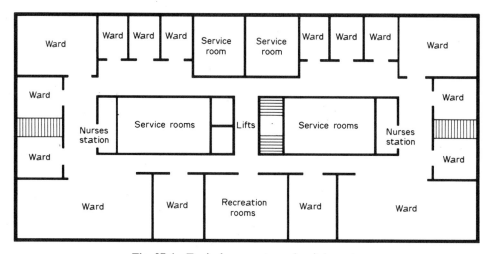

Fig. 27.4   Typical compact ward unit layout

These developments will not influence to any degree the lighting design, as the lighting requirements of the Ministry are clearly laid down and fully interpreted in IES Technical Report No. 12 (Hospital lighting). Since the issue of this report the Ministry have made available HSE Data Sheets DEI 31/53 'Standard Reference Lighting Fittings for Hospitals'. These sheets clearly indicate luminaire design, appearance and application over a large range.

The importance of the correct choice of light source is well appreciated and on the grounds of economic necessity and of colour rendering and appearance only two light sources are at present in use, fluorescent tubes and tungsten filament lamps. In respect to fluorescent tube colour the DHSS has recommended for clinical and nursing areas Colour 37 or °Kolor-rite, the authority for these specifications being covered by Memo-randum No. 43 of the Medical Research Council and DHSS Circular J/J5/01C dated July 8, 1970.

27.2.1 Hospital ward lighting

Ward lighting in general comprises:

(a) General lighting units, suspended or ceiling-mounted, with stringent glare control. General design and appearance is covered by DHSS data sheet type B.
(b) Bedhead lighting, intended primarily for reading and for occasional use by nurses, these units usually embodying a tungsten filament lamp. They have a wide angle of horizontal movement, but a restricted movement of 10° in the vertical plane in order that the lamp or a reflected image is not seen directly by other patients. The recommended mounting height of such wall units is 2 m: details are covered by DHSS data sheets type MI/NI. For use in children's wards a ceiling mounted 30° beam angle unit (type O) is recommended.
(c) Watch lighting, intended for use to observe critically-ill patients. This comprises a very low wattage lamp usually forming part of the bedhead unit.
(d) Night lighting, which is provided to allow safe movement after the general lighting is switched off. This is usually provided by small 15 W lamps within the general ward lighting units. The DHSS recommend that the value of illuminance at the bedhead should not exceed 0·1 lux from such units.
(e) Examination lighting is an extra requirement calling for a higher illuminance than can be provided by either the general or the reading light. These are often mobile or portable units, some of which can be plugged into a service trunking system running behind the bedhead.
(f) Nurse's station lighting, usually situated at strategic positions, should provide 300 lux by day and no more than 30 lux by night. This sometimes forms an integral part of the general lighting, in which case the limitations imposed on the ward lighting units also apply to those at the nurse's station.

The illuminances recommended in IES Technical Report No. 12 for these different lighting situations are shown in Table 27.1.

Table 27.1 Hospital ward lighting—IES illuminance recommendations

Situation	General lighting	Patient's reading lighting	Night lighting	Watch lighting
At bedhead	30–50 lux	200 lux minimum on book	0·1 lux (1 lux in children's wards)	5 lux
Circulation space	100–200 lux		0·1 lux	
Nurse's station	300 lux		30 lux	

It is clear that any ward lighting system must be as glare-free as possible. This must not only cover direct glare from any lighting unit but reflected glare from surfaces. The IES Code recommendation is for a limiting glare index of 13. This stringent requirement

473

Table 27.2 Hospital ward lighting—DHSS luminaire performance recommendations

Type of lighting unit	Performance recommendation
Pendant or semi-recessed ward luminaire	Maximum luminance 1000 cd/m² within 45° of any primary line of sight. Sitting position taken as standard
Surface-mounted or recessed ward luminaire	Maximum luminance 1000 cd/m² or 700 cd/m² (if upward lighting component is less than 20%) within 45° of any primary sight line
Wall-mounted luminaire	(a) Ceiling luminance directly above not to exceed 170 cd/m² at any point (b) Wall luminance not to exceed the ceiling luminance (c) Wall luminance diversity above the luminaires not to exceed a ratio of 10 to 1
Bedhead lighting	Minimum illuminance of 150 lux on the book at any sitting or lying position
Nightlighting	Maximum luminance of any equipment used as nightlighting not to exceed 3·4 cd/m² viewed from the bedhead. If low level units are employed the reflected image of the light source must not be able to be seen by recumbent patients

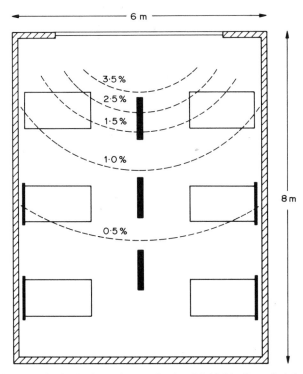

Fig. 27.5 Typical 6-bed ward necessitating PSALI indirect lighting units

applies to patients and others having widely-varying lines of sight: this makes glare so difficult to calculate and implement as to produce an impracticable standard. The recommendations by the DHSS (Table 27.2), although most stringent, are more practicable.

A typical 6-bed ward (Fig. 27.5) measuring approximately 8 m by 6 m by 2·5 m high on a racetrack service system would require a 1% daylight factor from the windows at one end. The central zone would need to be lit to a minimum value of 100 lux with 30 lux to 50 lux over the bed area, 1 m from floor level. The glare index would need to be no more than 13. Bedhead units for reading would also be necessary, perhaps incorporating watch lighting, and the general lighting would need to be lamped with °Kolor-rite or Colour 37 fluorescent tubes.

To meet these stringent requirements is not easy but a possible solution is shown on Fig. 27.5. It will be seen that a standard size of window does not produce the necessary daylight factor and four indirect wall lighting units, each with three 1500 mm tubes would be necessary to remove the gloom at the inner end of the ward. The general lighting would be achieved by 3 single-tube (1500 mm 65 W) luminaires of DHSS type B, having an upward flux fraction of 20%.

27.2.2 Lighting of other areas

Corridors need to be carefully lit as they receive little or no direct daylight. This is usually achieved by some form of wall lighting, sometimes concealed, and often forming part of a service trunking system. There should be as little glare as possible when viewed from a lying position (patients on trollies) and the general illuminance should be controllable to achieve comfortable conditions between core and ward. Recommended illuminance values are shown in Table 27.3.

Table 27.3 Preferred illuminance values for 24 hour period. System controlled either by dimmers or switching from a master solar clock.

Space	Illuminance (lux)		
	Day	Evening	Night
Bed areas assumed to be naturally lit	50–3000	30–300	0·01–0·1 (up to 1 for children)
Corridors open along their lengths to naturally lit rooms	300	100–200	5–10
Corridors with no natural light divided by partitions and doors from naturally lit rooms and other corridors	300	100–200	5–10
Internal rooms without natural light where specific visual tasks are performed	400	400	400
Other rooms	300	100	100

Operating theatres are areas having the most critical visual tasks. It is usual to provide general lighting from fully-recessed sealed fluorescent troffers, the actual task lighting being provided from specially designed units with multi-faceted reflectors which produce a very high value of illuminance over a local area, commonly between 2000 lux and 10 000 lux, with general lighting providing between 400 lux and 1500 lux.

Anaesthetic rooms, using sources of an approved colour, should be lit to a general value of 300 lux: there should be some upward component from the luminaires and dimming may well be required.

Recovery and intensive care rooms. The general value required in such areas is limited to between 30 lux and 50 lux, but provision should be made to raise the value to 300 lux at any bed position when necessary.

Emergency lighting.   DHSS Technical Memo No. 11 makes reference to three grades of lighting which should be provided in the case of mains failure—full lighting, 50% lighting and low lighting (to permit movement of staff and trolleys). In practice the whole matter is one of economics and requirement priorities. The general method is by the provision of stand-by generators: in one of the most recently-built hospitals the stand-by generator capacity is 15% of the normal connected load.

28   Library, art gallery and museum lighting

Libraries, art galleries and museums are institutions with superficially similar functions but with very different lighting problems. These range from the provision of lighting to permit the selection of books from racks and reading at study tables to the special conditions associated with the sequential viewing of objects or pictures in a series of galleries or rooms. Further complications are encountered with museums containing objects of high value which could be seriously damaged by exposure to light, either daylight or artificial: the designer has to take into account both the visual requirements and conservation aspects of the exhibits.

28.1   LIBRARIES

28.1.1   General lighting in libraries

There are two basic types of library: the public lending library, such as those operated up and down the country by local authorities, and the reference library, which can form part of a local lending library or may be a library in its own right such as that attached to the British Museum, or to a university, college or professional institution.

To understand fully the needs, and hence the requirements for suitable lighting for both types of library, it is necessary to look into the visual tasks involved. The major visual task in any library is reading either spines or covers to permit the correct selection of a book from the shelves or the study of printed pages in whatever form they may be presented. Several factors affect the efficiency of this reading process: the age of the person performing the task; the size, legibility and form of the printed matter; disability caused by glare from luminaires or windows or from specular reflections on the pages of the books under examination.

The recommendations for illuminance values in the various areas of either reference or lending libraries are given in the IES Code, as are the recommended limiting glare indices (Table 28.1).

Specific values for bookshelves in lending libraries are not included in Table 28.1: it is recommended that lighting systems specially designed for this purpose should be employed. Such a system should be capable of providing adequate illumination not only on the vertical spine surfaces, enabling titles to be easily read, but also in the horizontal plane at chest level: this is because many borrowers, having selected a book, then read part of it standing at the bookcase. Reliance on the illumination provided by the general lighting can be defeated by the combined screening effect of several borrowers looking for books in the same case at once.

The criteria for the lighting of lending libraries apply equally well to reference libraries, with one important exception. The primary user is now going to be seated at a study table instead of standing between the bookcases, and there is a need for a higher illuminance in

Table 28.1   IES recommendations (1968) for library lighting

	Recommended illuminance (lux)	Limiting glare index
Reading rooms (Newspapers and magazines)	200	19
Reading tables (Lending libraries)	400	19
Reading tables (Reference libraries)	600	16
Counters	600	19
Closed book stores	100 on vertical surfaces	
Binding	600	22
Cataloguing, sorting, stock rooms	400	22

such areas of study, including of course the librarian's place of work and any enquiry desks.

In addition to the IES Code recommendations for the artificial lighting of libraries, consideration should also be given to the utilization of daylight in providing satisfactory working illuminance values (Chap. 23). To enable the occupants to have some visual contact and release from the interior, windows are desirable: a minimum daylight factor of 1% is a reasonable recommendation as it produces a window area which is visually satisfying as well as giving adequate daylight penetration.

Associated with the daylight factor and the need to limit discomfort from excessive brightness contrasts, care is needed in the specification of the internal reflectances. For example, the window wall should have a high reflectance to reduce the contrast with the window, and also the ceiling, to reduce the contrast between that surface and any luminaire mounted on it or recessed into it. Ideally the reflectances of library interiors should be of the order of 80% for ceilings and walls and 30% for floors and furniture.

On the basis of economics the fluorescent tube is usually the most appropriate light source for general lighting. While the use of high efficiency tubes would seem to be the most suitable choice on cost grounds, their colour rendering may not be completely satisfactory: de luxe lamps, whilst having lower luminous efficacies, will provide a more pleasing and comfortable environment. The only possible disadvantage in the use of fluorescent tubes is the noise level produced by the control gear. This could be a nuisance in the reading room of a reference library, which usually has a low general noise level, but if good quality luminaires are employed and care is taken that the luminaires are not mounted directly on to a surface that will act as a resonator, no trouble should be experienced.

The design of the lighting within any new library interior will almost certainly meet with a ceiling height of between 1·75 m and 5 m and the size of luminaires for fluorescent tubes will preclude the use of suspended units if a satisfactory visual appearance is to be produced. Surface or recessed luminaires are to be preferred, but care must be taken in their selection to avoid excessive luminance contrast with the ceiling. A general diffusing luminaire will produce an evenly distributed and subjectively flat lighting condition, but if some additional local lighting is provided for certain areas, perhaps by means of tungsten spotlights directed on to notice and display boards, and with highlighting of the counters, a satisfactory interior luminance pattern can result.

28.1.2 Lighting of bookstacks and study tables

The addition of special lighting on bookcases has a two-fold effect. Firstly it increases the luminosity of the bookcase front and hence adds to the visual appearance of the interior and secondly, if correctly designed, it adds to the visibility of the book titles on display.

The main problems in bookstack lighting are getting light to the lower shelves and dealing with the obstruction caused by the borrowers: no perfect solution exists, but several methods are currently used to overcome the problems. One solution to the first problem is a change in the form of the stack: if the lower shelves are inclined outwards an immediate improvement in the visibility of the lower shelves becomes evident. Whether or not this is done, the most suitable solution to both problems is to use fluorescent tubes incorporated into a canopy affixed to the top of the stack. Ideally the lamps should be used in conjunction with reflectors designed to direct as much light to the lower shelves as possible.

To ensure that the whole case is evenly illuminated the tubes should be continuously mounted along the length of the bookcase. The distance by which the lamps can be offset will be determined by the aesthetic appearance of the case and its associated canopy:

Fig. 28.1   The lighting of bookstacks

with a stack 2 m in height, an offset of 0·5 m will be satisfactory, especially if the lower shelves are inclined (Fig. 28.1).

The fabrication of a canopy to house the tubes can, with advantage, have the front facia turned into an internally-illuminated sign, but the luminous sign must not be so bright as to make the reading of the legend difficult.

The individual illumination of bookcases sets the problem of the supply of electricity to free-standing units. The supply will have to come from the floor by means of flush-mounted outlet boxes, and will inevitably cause some difficulty if the layout of cases is changed. A system of ducts, with the usual removable covers, set into the floor provides for greater flexibility in the library layout.

The method of lighting study tables will vary with the architectural form of the building, but one or two general methods are used. If the study desks are large and shared by several readers, a system of general lighting related to the tables is most suitable. If the study tables are of the individual type, a more localized light source is appropriate.

A local lighting unit should provide a reasonably uniform distribution of light across the working areas and must not give rise to harsh shadows or to veiling glare by specular reflection from the glossy surfaces of text books. The unit should be located to one side of the reader, in line with or slightly to the rear of his head. The practice of placing a luminaire on the far edge of the desk eliminates shadows from the reader, but is liable to give rise to severe disability glare by specular reflection and will not illuminate any books other than those laid flat on the desk top. If individual control over a local lighting unit is to be given to the reader, only a restricted movement should be permitted so as to reduce the possibility of distracting glare to other readers.

28.1.3   Special lighting requirements

Gramophone libraries. A fast-expanding library service is the lending of long-playing gramophone records, usually as part of the main adult lending library. Two special visual problems arise: the identification of the record number on the sleeve and the close inspection of the record surface for damage on issue or return. The records are usually stored in racks similar to the general bookcases and therefore require a similar lighting treatment. Record inspection is a difficult visual task due to the dark surface and the fine surface scratches which have to be looked for: the most suitable examination unit will incorporate its own light source and some form of optical aid such as a magnifying lens.

Microfilm.   Microfilm storage systems are used for recording details of books lent and also for making available for reference purposes volumes which are either too valuable or in too poor a condition for general handling. The film-reading machines should be contained in a room or an area of the library where the lighting can be reduced to give good viewing conditions for the projected image. Special care must be exercised in the choice and placing of the luminaires so as to ensure that no unwanted reflections of the light sources are evident on the screens.

Mobile libraries.   In rural areas, where the density of population does not warrant the establishment of a permanent branch library, local authorities operate mobile library services from purpose-designed trailers. The same lighting problems exist here as in a permanent library and the solutions are similar. As the only power supply is likely to be from static batteries, the lighting load must of necessity be kept to a minimum and fluorescent luminaires are the only practical choice, the fluorescent tubes being operated on transistorized inverters (Sect. 18.4.2). The capacity of the batteries will probably define the illuminance levels rather than strict lighting requirements.

Special displays. These are often held in libraries, and rely on visual impact for their general effectiveness. It is advantageous to equip display areas with a lighting track installation, with a number of spotlights available. Special lighting can then be arranged with complete safety by electrically-unskilled library staff.

28.2 ART GALLERIES AND MUSEUMS

28.2.1 Lighting requirements

A visit to a museum or art gallery is basically a visual experience, and the visitor relies upon the lighting to enable him to see the exhibits: the lighting designer's skill will be needed if the communication between observer and observed is to be established and maintained. This would become a fairly simply exercise in lighting design if it were not for one significant factor, that no damage to the objects on display must occur from the lighting. The majority of exhibits in museums and art galleries are affected in one way or another by the presence of light, be it daylight or artificial (Sect. 28.2.2).

There has been a considerable change of late in the style and presentation of collections. At last it has been recognized that the assembly of a large collection of assorted items under one roof, as was current in Victorian times, is not the way to present objects to best advantage. The display has therefore become more concerned with the individual characteristics of the exhibit. The lighting has had to follow suit, taking into account the specific needs of individual objects as well as the physical comfort and well-being of the visitor.

In any museum interior the visitor is presented with a sequence of static visual pictures: museum design and lighting design must take this sequential viewing as a factor of paramount importance. A visit starts at the main entrance, and proper control must be applied right from this position and not only be confined to the display galleries themselves. The visitor upon entering and moving through the building must be given time and satisfactory ambient lighting conditions to enable him to adapt continuously to the different display lighting conditions for different exhibits.

The lighting of the exhibits and their backgrounds must be carefully adjusted so that the objects on display are seen to full advantage. With well-controlled conditions, relatively low levels of illuminance can be perfectly satisfactory, which may be necessary where the subject matter is liable to deterioration by the effect of light. Not all objects are light-sensitive and some will benefit from strong dramatic lighting to enhance their particular features, machinery and sculpture for example. Areas of highly-lit exhibits should not immediately precede areas of relatively dimly-lit objects, as the latter will then appear as gloomy.

28.2.2 Conservation

Most materials and their colours are damaged and faded by radiation. Museum objects of great value may be severely damaged or even destroyed when illuminated for normal display to the public. Even slight damage of materials and colours may produce changes in the overall appearance of objects such that confusion may arise in art scholarship circles. It follows that where these sensitive items are displayed, the lighting must not be chosen primarily for visual acuity and contrast discrimination but for conservation.

Any radiation (infra-red, visible or ultra-violet) which is absorbed by an object is liable to cause damage. Ultra-violet is the most dangerous because it is more likely to cause photochemical changes in organic materials, whereas the absorption of longer wavelengths promotes chemical changes only by the heating effect produced. High humidity accelerates these reactions and should therefore be an additional matter of concern in museums and art galleries.

The admission of daylight into a gallery will cause excessive fading in certain materials due to the relatively high quantity of ultra-violet radiation present. The same will apply to the use of fluorescent tubes, as these also produce ultra-violet radiation, in varying degrees dependent upon the colour selected. In many museums the quantity of artificial lighting is relatively small compared with the quantity of daylight, and most conservation effort has been directed towards the provision of ultra-violet filters for the windows and skylights rather than for the artificial lighting units.

Table 28.2, taken from IES Technical Report No. 14, gives details of fluorescent tubes from the viewpoint of their use in museums and art galleries. Colour rendering properties depend upon the spectral distribution of the source: providing these are reasonably smooth and balanced (high-fidelity) the colour rendering of objects will not change dramatically with the colour appearance of the source because of adaptation of the eye.

Table 28.3 gives the IES illuminance recommendations for art galleries and museums. When using the low illuminance of 50 lux, good control of the light together with correct display techniques become imperative.

28.2.3   Lighting techniques

In studying the use of artificial lighting in galleries, various techniques have been developed over the years, covering the two aspects of general and local lighting. General lighting must take into consideration the component of daylight to be expected from windows and roof lights. The study of daylight design has its foundations in the work of F. P. Cockerell, Hurst Seager and the National Physical Laboratory: it began as soon as the deficiencies of the nineteenth century public galleries became apparent. The trend at the present time is towards the exclusion of nearly all daylight and reliance on easily controlled and steady artificial light sources.

Wall lighting.   A system often used in the lighting of murals, tapestries and pictures is shown in Fig. 28.2. The fluorescent lighting unit would normally be offset so as to achieve the best possible distribution of light on the subject matter. A variation of 3:1 in illuminance could be called for under critical conditions, but often variations of 10:1 are found to be acceptable. Too great an offset distance will lead to specular reflection with glazed exhibits and those with glossy surfaces. A visual cut-off to the source is generally achieved by the lower edge of the reflector: this should never exceed 30° from the downward vertical in the direction of the observer. It is important in areas using this system not to over-illuminate the walls and leave the ceiling dark, making for undue contrast between the two surfaces.

482

Table 28.2   Colour rendering, colour appearance and ultra-violet content of fluorescent tubes

Colour appearance	Low fidelity (Colour rendering index 50–70)			Medium fidelity (Colour rendering index 70–85)			High fidelity (Colour rendering index 85–100)		
	Lamp designation	Ultra-violet content mW/100 lm	Relative light output per cent	Lamp designation	Ultra-violet content mW/100 lm	Relative light output per cent	Lamp designation	Ultra-violet content mW/100 lm	Relative light output per cent
Cool (6500 K approx)	Daylight	11–14	90–100	Natural	12–15	70–75	Artificial daylight {Colour matching; Northlight	60–65	40–45
							Trucolor 37	18–22	60–65
								3–5	55–60
							°Kolor-rite	12–15	65–70
Intermediate (4000 K approx)	White	10–12	100						
Warm (3000 K approx)	Warm White	8–10	95–100	De Luxe Warm White	10–15	65–70	Softone 27	1–3	55–60

Table 28.3   Illuminance recommendations for art galleries and museums

Object	Maximum service illuminance (lux)
Objects insensitive to light such as metal, stone, glass and ceramics, stained glass, jewellery and enamel	Unlimited, though in practice subject to display and radiant heat considerations
Oil and tempera painting, undyed leather, horn, bone, ivory, wood and lacquer (Oriental and European)	150
Objects specially sensitive to light, such as textiles, costumes, water colours, tapestries, prints and drawings, stamps, manuscripts, miniatures, paintings in distemper media, wallpapers, gouache, dyed leather. Many natural history exhibits, especially those including skins and botanical specimens	50

483

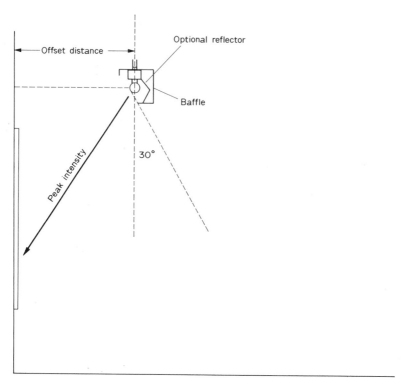

Fig. 28.2 Unit for lighting murals, tapestries or pictures

Cornice lighting. In many rooms where the ceiling may be painted or decorated, it is frequently desirable to be able to illuminate it. This technique will depend upon the availability of existing cornices, or if none, the design of a purpose-made cornice luminaire. The luminaire should be mounted as low as possible so as to spread the light across the ceiling evenly.

The addition of cornice lighting to a room with a wall lighting installation will help give the correct balance to the ceiling and wall luminosity, as well as providing circulation lighting by reflection. The design of the cornice must ensure that whilst maximum light output is obtained, no direct view of the lamps is possible from normal viewing angles.

Show-case lighting. The problems associated with the satisfactory illumination of objects displayed in glass cases are numerous and will range from the elimination of unwanted reflections to the careful control of the heat generation from internal incandescent lamps or fluorescent tubes. Descriptions of the techniques most usually used are given in Sect. 26.3.

29 Stage and studio lighting

It would be an over-simplification of a far from simple problem to say that the primary objective in stage and studio lighting is to light the actors and the set so that the audience can see them. Whether considering the stage or the television studio it is not sufficient for the audience to be able to see: the picture must be visually attractive. The objective of this chapter is to survey the principles involved in painting an attractive picture, the equipment involved and the techniques used.

29.1 LIGHTING PRINCIPLES AND CRITERIA

Direct frontal lighting, which we know to be unattractive for a building becomes quite unacceptable for a face. The same attention to lighting direction and quality is as necessary for the stage as for the photographic studio, with the added difficulty of a highly mobile subject.

Except for highly dramatic effects it is generally found that the main frontal lighting is required from above at both sides of the subject, at angles of 30° to 45° in plan and elevation, and not necessarily at the same intensity or quality from each side. In television, for example, the 'key' light from the one side is strongly directional whilst the 'fill' light from the other side is softer and frequently supported by carefully placed back-lighting. The effect on a face of varying combinations of lighting can be seen in Fig. 29.1. If lighting is to achieve more than the mere ability to see the actors it must be composed of elements not only from both sides but probably directly from the front as well. It should be borne in mind that the actor must not change in appearance as he changes position on the stage, hence the whole pattern of lighting must be carefully arranged to provide a series of overlapping beams.

In addition it is necessary to light the set, to a greater or less degree depending on the style of production, and great care is needed in placing the lanterns in such positions that those for the set do not conflict with those for the actors.

Frequently, almost invariably, the final lighting design for a stage production turns out to be a compromise between what the designer would like to see and what is physically possible within the limitations of scenery positions and the inflexible laws of light.

On stage the illuminance values employed vary tremendously from one production to another and the slide rule or photometer would be the last item of equipment likely to be used by the professional lighting designer. More than any other lighting expert he lights for effect and balances his lighting, in both intensity and colour, to transform in the most realistic manner possible a mass of painted canvas and wood to represent, say, a Mayfair flat or a mountain cave.

In the television studio, illuminance values are very important indeed, particularly for colour programmes, where the question of the colour temperature of the light source is

Fig. 29.1 (a) High-angle lighting from in front and on one side only
(b) Additional lighting from a similar position on the other side, at a slightly lower angle and at a lower intensity
(c) Back-lighting added
(d) Low-angle frontal lighting added to soften shadows under eye-brows and cheek-bones

also very much to the fore. Generally speaking television studios provide 1500 lux to 2000 lux for the production of colour programmes despite the fact that modern cameras can produce acceptable pictures from considerably less, as in the case of outside broadcast work where such levels would be extremely difficult to provide. The mean colour temperature is usually in the region of 3000 K but variations of ±150 K are quite acceptable, which means that a reasonable degree of dimming can be employed to provide pictorial balance. This is a very important point when it is remembered that the ratio of black-and-white to colour receivers must be of the order of 10 : 1 and the transmitted picture must be visually acceptable on both.

The use of colour media is of great importance to the stage, where it is used extensively in almost every production, in contrast to the television studio where it is used mainly for light entertainment. This is because of the need to create on stage, within the time scale of an evening, every shade of mood or climate which may occur from June to December in Manchester or mid-Sahara. The same applies when dealing with Son et Lumiere productions where historical buildings are used as settings for dramatized and recorded plays or scenes from their past. Colour, music and the spoken word are very carefully blended by the producer to create life, drama and atmosphere from the solid inanimate blocks of stone forming the walls of an historic castle.

29.2 LIGHTING EQUIPMENT

29.2.1 Sources

Although it is often assumed that all theatrical lighting is based on special types of lamps, a surprisingly large number of ordinary GLS (General Lighting Service) lamps are employed, particularly where precise optical control of the light is not important. This includes wide angle floodlights of various sizes from 150 W to 1000 W, compartment battens and floodlights (groundrows) and many other simple luminaires.

Projector lamps with accurately-positioned compact filaments are used where more precise optical control is needed. These suffer the disadvantages of a relatively short life and some limitation on the angles at which they can be operated, but nevertheless they are used very extensively both in stage and studio applications.

Tungsten halogen lamps became popular for this application immediately they were developed and it is significant that the lamp and lantern manufacturers now work more closely together than at any time in the past, with mutually satisfactory results. Perhaps the most striking example of this success is the range of dual-rated tungsten halogen lamps developed for television studio lighting, providing a greater flexibility for a given installation than could be obtained from lamps of a single rating. The most important advantage of the tungsten halogen lamp is its near-constant colour temperature throughout life. Linear tungsten halogen lamps are also used both for stage and studio, particularly in cyclorama floodlights and in the soft-light end of dual purpose luminaires (Sect. 29.2.2).

Discharge lamps, with their high efficacies, can rarely benefit the stage or studio because these lamps can only be dimmed by some mechanical means. Even switched applications are not really practicable because of the twin problems of warm-up time and restriking after extinction; hence discharge lamps are used very rarely and only for the creation of special effects. One exception is the recently developed compact source metal halide lamp (Sect. 15.1.4): this has made an immediate impact for special types of luminaire where the high intensity and good colour rendering meet the requirements of follow-spots. Because these luminaires are hand-operated there is no difficulty in controlling the light output of the lamp either by the shutter or the iris diaphragm which forms part of the normal controls.

Lamp 'sing' is a phenomenon of relatively recent significance, an unwelcome by-product of the thyristor dimmer (Sect. 29.2.3). If the electricity supply to a lamp is not only interrupted but the wave-form is distorted, magnetostriction takes place within the lamp leads and this becomes manifest in a high pitched and quite audible singing note. When the lamps are used in the open types of floodlight known as scoops this lamp sing is amplified, causing considerable trouble in direct pick-up microphones. Tungsten halogen studio lamps use lead wires of non-magnetic material which has been found to reduce the magnetostriction effect to negligible proportions.

29.2.2   Luminaires

Floodlights.   For many stage and studio applications simple floodlights (Fig. 29.2a) are used, having no more sophisticated optical control than a polished metal or silvered glass reflector and with no shielding of the direct light emitted by the lamp. Provision is normally made for carrying colour frames and the range of lamp sizes commonly used are 150 W, 200 W, 500 W and 1000 W.

Almost invariably the colour medium used is in the form of thin sheets, available in more than 50 colours, each given a name and a number for easy reference. These sheets are made of dyed plastic which must conform, in terms of flammability, to the requirements of BS 3944 (Specification for colour filters for theatre lighting). They suffer the disadvantage of fading or bleaching as well as buckling under the combined effects of heat and light, and for this reason coloured glass is sometimes used.

Banks of floodlights are sometimes mounted in long strips to form compartment battens or groundrows, usually wired with alternate units on separate circuits for 3- or 4-colour control. The PAR lamp (App. I) is growing in popularity for floodlighting, used either as a single unit or mounted in battens: the high efficacy of the lamp and its compact size make it particularly suitable for use in restricted spaces. In UK PAR lamps of 150 W and 300 W are available (PAR 38 and PAR 56) while in USA the 500 W (PAR 56) lamp is also used.

For cycloramas, floodlight battens and groundrows are commonly used, with the more powerful tungsten halogen lamps becoming more popular both for stage and television studios. Since these units employ lamps from 625 W to 1250 W there is a need for frequent changing of colour filters but the improved optical control allows extremely close spacing to be employed.

Profile spotlights.   Perhaps the most versatile and certainly the most widely-used lantern in the theatre is the profile spotlight (Fig. 29.2b) having a beam which can be controlled to produce a sharp-edged spot of any shape. An iris diaphragm is used to vary the diameter of circular spots, and fixed metal masks called gobos are used for the projection of irregular or special shapes. The lanterns in common use have ratings from 250 W to 2000 W and beam angles in the region of 20° to 30°. The lantern comprises a compact-source filament lamp, the light from which is collected by an ellipsoidal reflector and passed through a gate to an objective lens. Shutters and masks control the size and shape of the gate, whilst the beam can be brought to a hard or soft focus by movement of the objective.

Fresnel spotlights. These employ the stepped or Fresnel lens to provide a soft-edged beam of light. The optical system (Fig. 29.2c) comprises a spherical reflector and lamp housing, together with a short focus lens consisting of a number of annular prisms. Movement of the lamp (and reflector) towards the lens broadens the beam: because it is possible to make large diameter lenses commercially, the effective 'collection angle' becomes quite large. Thus the Fresnel spotlight is really a combination spot/floodlight and is regarded as an all-purpose lantern both in the theatre and the studio.

Beam angles can be adjusted within the range of about 15° to 60° and lanterns in common use utilize a range of lamps from 250 W to 5000 W. External flaps called barn doors are usually fitted and these can be separately adjusted or rotated to avoid spill light catching the edges of scenery. Colour frames are also fitted, but little used on the 5 kW size which is generally confined to the television studios. 10 kW lanterns are also used in television studios: there are 20 kW models as well, but their use is almost completely confined to film studios.

A special version of the Fresnel spotlight has become popular for television studios and comprises two lanterns in one, mounted back to back inside a common metal frame (Fig. 29.2d). One side is a 5 kW spotlight designed to take the dual-rated 2·5/2·5 kW tungsten halogen lamp with each filament separately switched. The other side is a 5 kW 'softlight', comprising 4 × 1250 W tungsten halogen linear lamps, switched in pairs to give 2·5/2·5 kW rating. Thus in one lantern are combined four basic units. Even greater flexibility is provided by carrying out the tilting, focusing and panning (traversing) adjustments by means of a pole.

Lantern adjustment. Considerable dissatisfaction is felt throughout the world of stage and studio at the need to go through the long and cumbersome procedure of climbing up to or lowering down the lanterns to carry out the adjustments of tilt, pan and focus which are essential parts of every production.

Several attempts to produce remote-controlled luminaires have been made and some successful systems are already in use, but at a cost which is regarded as prohibitive both for commercial theatre and television studio. A development from France uses five separate motors to carry out the operations of tilt, pan, focus, raise and lower, as well as to drive the complete unit and its supporting trolley along a special track arranged over the stage in the form of a grid. Another development, from UK, using a single motor and a system of magnetic clutches, is designed to deal with the tilt, pan and focus operations and to handle the individual adjustments of the four barn doors as well.

These latest innovations mark a considerable advance on the degree of remote control previously available, which consisted of changing colour filters either by means of a rotating wheel in front of the lantern or a semaphore operated magazine equipped with the requisite filters for the production.

The foregoing review of lantern types has, of necessity, omitted many of the specialist items such as follow-spots and effects projectors, but most manufacturers publish detailed catalogues containing full information on beam angles, lamp types, methods of mounting and adjustment. Descriptions vary from country to country but the CIE has recently issued a set of design symbols for use by architects, consultants and lighting designers: these are shown on Fig. 29.2.

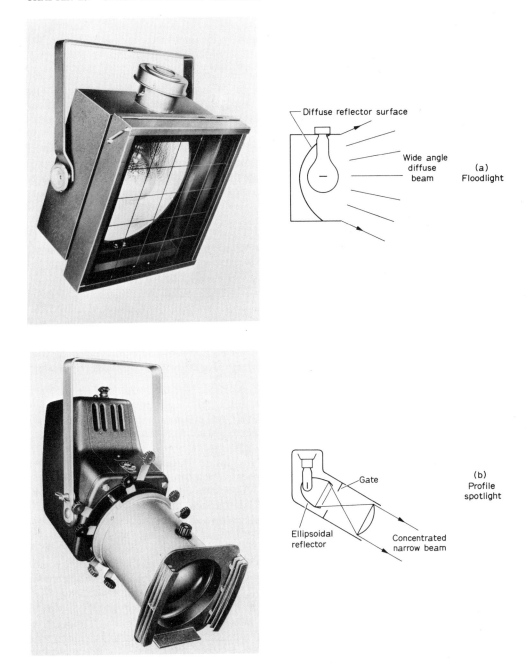

Diffuse reflector surface

Wide angle
diffuse
beam

(a)
Floodlight

Gate

(b)
Profile
spotlight

Ellipsoidal
reflector

Concentrated
narrow beam

Fig. 29.2 Photographs and drawings of stage lanterns together with CIE design symbols

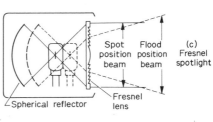

Spot Flood (c)
position position Fresnel
beam beam spotlight

Spherical reflector Fresnel lens

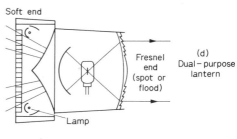

Soft end

Fresnel end (spot or flood) (d) Dual-purpose lantern

Lamp

CIE DESIGN SYMBOLS

Floodlight A lantern with a beam angle of 100 degrees or more and with a cut-off not less than 180 degrees.	**Lens spotlight** Lantern with simple lens and with or without reflector and capable of adjustment of beam angle by relative movement of lamp and lens	**Effects spotlight** Lantern with optics designed to give an even field of illumination of slide and well defined projection of detail using suitable objective lenses. The slide can be of moving effects type or stationary.
Special floodlight Unit with a specified beam angle (less than 100 degrees) and a specified cut-off angle.	**Fresnel spotlight** As a lens spotlight, but with stepped lens providing a soft edge to the beam.	
Reflector spotlight Lantern with simple reflector and adjustment of beam angle by relative movement of lamp and mirror.	**Profile spotlight** Lantern giving hard edged beam which can be varied in outline by diaphragms, shutters or silhouette cut-out masks.	**Softlight** A lantern of sufficient area to produce a diffuse light causing indefinite shadow boundaries. *For stage lighting purposes this is taken to cover batten flooding equipment, two such symbols being joined by a line.*
Sealed beam lamp		

491

29.2.3 Control equipment

Since the use of electricity first made it possible to control light simply and easily from remote positions, various forms of dimmer have been developed: a survey of world theatres would reveal an incredible variety, with the possibility that a few examples may still survive of the brine-filled pot and submersible electrodes with which dimmer history began. Developments moved relatively slowly until the period between the wars when a considerable number of dimming systems became available in various parts of the world. These included simple resistance dimmers, auto-transformers, saturable reactors, and an extensive range of control systems, many of which are in use today. The impact of electronics came in 1947 when thyratron valves were used for the first time as dimmers, but as in so many fields, the greatest advance came with the wide use of semiconductors in the last decade, when the thyristor dimmer (Fig. 29.3) was born.

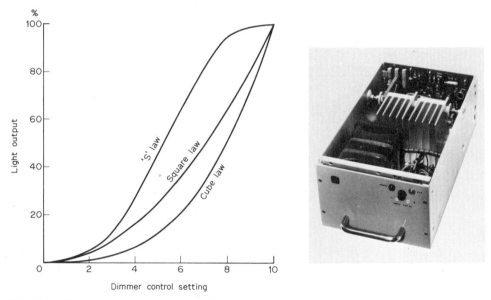

Fig. 29.3 Dimmer curves showing relationship between control lever setting and light output. Photograph shows typical modular thyristor dimmer of 5 kW rating

Practically all new installations use thyristor equipment, principally because of its reliability, high efficiency, variable load capacity and ease of remote control. For convenience, dimmers are usually made in modular form in sizes ranging from 2 kW to 10 kW and because of their very low heat dissipation it is possible to house 100 kW of dimmer capacity in a rack measuring less than 1 m square and 2 m in height. Many types are made where it is possible to remove or replace dimmers on load without affecting the remaining units in the same cubicle.

Probably this effective solution of the dimmer problem has prompted development in the control field and the past few years have seen more dramatic advances than in the 100 years or so that electric stage lighting has been available. Very few systems are made these days which do not provide at least one additional set of controls which enable the operator to set up a complete scene in readiness without disturbing the lighting in progress and to change over from 'live' to 'pre-set' smoothly and simply by means of a pre-set master control. Several pre-sets can be provided if required but most theatres are content, usually for financial reasons, to manage with a 2- or 3-pre-set system.

Full memory capacity became a reality in 1967 when a Q-File 100 memory system was installed in a BBC television studio. This system represented a complete break with tradition in that instead of individual control levers (or faders) for each lamp circuit, it employed a single lever associated with decimal-coded push buttons. After more than 40 systems have been installed in television studios and theatres, lighting operators have confirmed their acceptance of this system. Data processing techniques have provided a capacity of 100 or 200 separate memories each representing a complete lighting scene using up to 300 or more circuits, and adjusted to a variety of dimmer settings. Memories can be recalled in any required order, either as an instantaneous 'cut' or as a pre-timed fade and the system also provides many other operational features, including the ability to run several fades automatically and at different speeds. An added refinement is a tape-programming unit which permits a complete lighting plot for a play or an opera to be recorded on a tiny tape cassette and stored in readiness to 're-charge' the system the next time that production is needed (Fig. 29.4).

Other memory systems are also available, ranging from the German punched-card version to an alternative British system known as DDM (digital dimmer memory) and an American system which uses specially modified computer techniques and a unique

Fig. 29.4 Q-File intensity memory lighting control desk, complete with mimic panel and auxiliary controls

method of adjusting dimmer settings by means of a 'light-pen' operating directly on a picture display tube.

Fundamental differences exist between the general requirements of lighting control for the theatre and for the television studio: this has led to slight variations in the form of control equipment used. Because television cameras cannot operate at very low illuminances, dimmers are used primarily to balance the lighting, fades to low levels being very rare. By contrast, scenes in the theatre are sometimes played in almost complete darkness and dawn takes place very gradually and with the maximum awareness on the part of the audience. This implies very fine control at the bottom end of the dimming range, which is of relatively little importance to the television world. The relationship between dimmer lever position and light output, known as the dimmer law, is used as a convenient way of describing and comparing dimmer performance. Fig. 29.3 shows a family of curves known as square law, cube law and 'S' law, where lumen output is plotted against the dimmer scale setting. For television applications the square law is generally favoured, while for the theatre preference has been expressed for the 'S' law, which corresponds broadly with the performance of the simplest form of thyristor dimmer.

29.3   LIGHTING TECHNIQUES

Stage lighting is a generic term which must cover not only the proscenium stage but all other forms such as the thrust stage, theatre-in-the-round, the extended stage and any other form which might arise in the form of an experiment. Each form presents a different lighting problem: the more intimate the relationship between actor and audience, the more difficult it becomes to conceal the lighting equipment. Audiences now share the auditorium with the lanterns and become no more conscious of their presence than the football crowd of the floodlights once the play has begun. But the fundamental principles of lighting still remain and actors must generally be lit effectively from at least two-directions if they are to appear realistic. This means that for theatre-in-the-round, for example, it is necessary to install lighting-in-the-round and to remember that each section of the audience will get a completely different picture of each scene. The important task is to make each picture visually acceptable whatever the viewpoint or the stage form employed.

Against such a background of problems and the need to pre-plan and pre-set the lighting equipment to cover the entire action of an opera or a 3-act play without physical adjustment, the breed of lighting designer has emerged. His function is to plan and design not only the physical layout of the equipment, together with its focusing, adjustment and colour, but to prepare, in conjunction with the director, a fully detailed lighting plot with every cue detailed and timed.

Television lighting.   By contrast with the theatre, the television studio has little need to consider audience viewpoints or the general appearance of the interior, and it is common practice to cover the entire studio ceiling with a grid of steelwork supporting a large number of luminaires. These can be positioned almost anywhere over the entire ceiling and may be suspended by electrically-operated 'telescopes', individual hoists or hoist bars capable of carrying 3 or 4 separate lanterns. Thus whatever the lighting requirement, it is possible to lower into position, in readiness for final adjustment, those lanterns required for a particular scene. This technique, sometimes referred to as saturation lighting, is obviously expensive in outlay but provides a much higher utilization of studio time than could possibly be achieved by rigging every lantern as required for every scene. Even so, a considerable amount of additional lighting from lower levels has to be employed, particularly where the construction of the set or the required camera angle makes it necessary: this is usually provided by a spotlight mounted on a floor stand.

As with so many other aspects, the success of a stage or studio lighting scheme may well lie in the fact that nobody notices it. The lighting must never become an end in itself but must assist the director, the scenic designer, the actor, the camera operator or the author himself to create just the impression the audience is meant to receive, and which, without light, would be equally without meaning either on the stage or the television screen.

Son et Lumiere. Stage and studio lighting techniques extend far beyond the formal confines of the theatre and the studio suite—into the world of Son et Lumiere for example —where the auditorium may be a grassy bank and the set a stately home, a ruined castle or a majestic cathedral. Recorded voices, music and sound effects portray the story of the building itself, accompanied by dramatic lighting designed to suit the incident described or to match the mood of the story. Here the lighting problems are immense by comparison with formal stage or studio although the audience is confined to a set area and therefore viewing angles can be pre-established. Because there are no grids, spot bars, lighting slots or bridges, all the lighting must be provided from positions in front of, or on the building itself. Of necessity the greater part of the equipment is placed on the ground in concealed positions, frequently extremely close to the walls, which may rise 15 m or more above the lanterns. Since most Son et Lumiere subjects are also tourist attractions by day, the equipment must not only be positioned to avoid spoiling the appearance of the building but cables and floodlights alike must not provide a hazard to inattentive tourists. By the same token the equipment needs to be vandal-proof and extremely weatherproof, which precludes the use of most normal stage luminaires. Floodlights are used instead, both standard and narrow-beam types, or profile spotlights located in purpose-made weatherproof housings.

Light entertainment. By contrast to the scale and atmosphere of Son et Lumiere the requirements of clubs and discotheques, although theatrical in character, frequently demand the use of light for direct excitement, quite regardless of the form of stage presentation. Although much conventional stage lighting equipment is used, special multicolour flashing circuits and stroboscopic equipment are also employed. A high degree of sophistication is required in the control equipment and this is sometimes directly linked with the sound amplification system in such a way that selected light colours are associated with certain sound frequencies for the provision of linked audio-visual effects. As with Son et Lumiere, however, these are special cases of lighting for entertainment and bear little relationship to what we understand in terms of conventional stage lighting.

30 Domestic lighting

Domestic lighting is a unique subject which cannot be treated in the same way as a commercial or industrial installation. For most lighting schemes many calculations have to be made to determine the level of illuminance required for a particular activity or location; not only the amount of light needed but also its direction, its colour and the luminosities it produces are sometimes calculated to ensure that the task being lit can be performed safely and adequately. In home lighting, however, while all these considerations are perfectly valid, they are carried out completely subconsciously, if at all. The lighting of a home is generally selected by a non-professional in the lighting sense for reasons of aesthetic preference.

30.1 GENERAL PRINCIPLES OF DOMESTIC LIGHTING

'I bought it because I liked it' is invariably the motive given for a particular home lighting purchase, a valid motive as long as the selected lamp or luminaire performs its function adequately.

It is obvious that the lighting over a staircase should produce adequate illumination for safety: it is equally obvious that the lighting for a specific visual task such as sewing or reading should be suited to that task. These lighting criteria can be analysed numerically. But how does one calculate for attractiveness? What are the rules that determine a pleasantly lit room? Where is the table of figures that would tell a housewife she should have a 1500 mm Warm White fluorescent tube in the pelmet over her new curtains rather than a 1200 mm Daylight tube? If indeed there were such figures available, would she be able to use them? She would know the effect in her living room of changing the curtains but she would find it difficult to appraise subjectively the likely effect of a change in the source of light. It is only by advising her that her home would be more attractive if lit in another way and thereby creating a subconscious desire to alter her existing arrangements that the standard of domestic lighting in her home can be improved.

When considering specific visual tasks requiring to be lit in the home, this concept of 'attractiveness' must not be lost. This is best seen in terms of the overall created effect rather than in just the luminaire lighting the task.

It is convenient to consider the lighting techniques for the home under the two headings of work lighting and effect lighting.

Work lighting is the light required to permit safe walking around the house or garden. The light needed for sewing or reading is work lighting and can be provided by a table lamp or a floor standard. If, however, these luminaires are not being used specifically to light a task, then they are providing 'accent lighting'.

Effect lighting combines both accent and atmosphere lighting. If there is a picture on a wall and a spotlight is directed at it or if there is a floodlight on the branches of a tree in the garden, an accent is added to the lighting scene. Accent lighting provides the highlights and the shadows that turn a house and garden into an attractive and stimulating home. Lighting for atmosphere is more difficult to define and to judge as it is an aesthetic consideration that varies from person to person; one man's subdued lighting is another man's gloom. Lighting that causes glare is unsuitable for offices and factories, but crystal chandeliers with bare lamps can create a sparkling atmosphere in a Victorian pub.

30.2   DOMESTIC LIGHTING TECHNIQUES

30.2.1   Porches

Work lighting.   Functional lighting is necessary in a porch for three main reasons: recognizing a caller, locating a key-hole and identifying a house number or name. The requirement here is a 60/100 W filament lamp (or the lumen equivalent in small fluorescent tubes) in a weatherproof luminaire mounted on the wall or the canopy. It should be positioned so that light is thrown forward and downward on to the face of a caller and not shielded from the keyhole position by someone trying to insert a key.

Effect lighting.   The functional porch light can also be used to accentuate the texture of the building material used in the porch or to illuminate a feature that is visually attractive by day. It can also contribute to the general atmosphere surrounding a home by implying a warm welcoming environment.

30.2.2   Halls, stairs and landings

Work lighting.   The necessity for functional lighting in a hall is dependent upon its size and the adjacent areas. If the hall is large enough to invite callers to enter and work, perhaps enter insurance contributions in a book, a light is required to illuminate the table or shelf where such work would be done. If the hall or landing is adjacent to the stairs then the area should be lit to a similar level to the stairs so that the eye does not have to adapt to a different luminosity.

The lighting of a staircase must be such that each tread can be seen clearly without any confusing hard shadows. Many accidents in the home happen on staircases and generally these occur when one is going downstairs. Although more light should fall on the treads than on the risers some light should be provided from the front of the staircase so that shadows are softened and there are no great contrasts.

If a landing is between an elderly person's room and the bathroom, then it should be considered as part of a suite and lit to a level comparable to the adjacent rooms. The lighting on a landing outside a child's bedroom would ideally incorporate a dimmer. A child often needs a reassuring light at night and a low illuminance on the landing is more useful than a bedroom nightlight as it will also serve to light the way safely to the bathroom.

Effect lighting.   Decorative features such as paintings or tapestries in halls or on landings can be enhanced by accent lighting. Care must be taken that the light comes from the correct angle. Light falling directly on to the front of any object will tend to flatten it whereas light from an acute angle will enable texture or form to be discernible to the eye. Effect lighting can also help to create the right atmosphere in a hall which might be bright and colourful on some occasions, cosy and intimate on others. Well considered switching arrangements for functional and accent lights could ensure that the atmosphere can be easily altered.

Care must be taken, however, with effect lighting in the area immediately adjacent to the stairs and here such lighting should generally be avoided. The danger is that a brightly lit area will become a focus for the eye and will cause the surrounding areas to appear even darker by contrast.

30.2.3   Living areas

Work lighting.   At least one light source to provide lighting for circulation must be controlled by a switch adjacent to the door so that the room can be illuminated quickly and easily. Apart from this, which could double as a specific working or accent light, all luminaires should be chosen to suit the various specific visual tasks liable to be performed in the room.

Typical reading or writing tasks in a home encompass a very wide range of seeing difficulty. In general terms, a luminaire should be positioned above or behind the reader so that the light falls on the printed page without a shadow being cast on it and without reflected glare being experienced by the reader. It is particularly important when writing that the hand does not cause a shadow over the page and the light should, therefore, come from above and behind the left shoulder of a right-handed writer.

Sewing is one of the most difficult visual tasks carried out in the home, difficult because of the smallness of detail and the low contrast between the material and the thread. The illuminance must therefore be high (Table 30.1) and even if this is provided by the built-in light source of a sewing machine it is desirable to illuminate the im-

Table 30.1   Recommended minimum service values
of illuminance (1968) for domestic lighting

	lux
Living rooms	
General	100
Reading (casual)	200
Sewing and darning	600
Studies	
Desk and prolonged reading	400
Bedrooms	
General*	50
Bed-head	200
Kitchens (working areas)	200
Bathrooms*	100
Halls and landings	100
Stairs (at tread)†	50–100
Workshops (benches)	400
Garages	50

* Supplementary local lighting should be provided at mirrors.
† Luminaire should screen the lamps from view both when going up and down the stairs.

mediate surrounding area to an illuminance not less than a third of that being received on the task. It has to be remembered also that the user will be looking away from the machine from time to time: the part of the room visible from the sewing machine should be lit to a value not less than a tenth of that of the task illuminance.

Television viewing is frequently combined with another visual task, such as ironing or knitting. It is important to provide both lighting for the specific task and additional room lighting to balance the luminosity of the task with that of the television screen and other room surfaces in the field of view. Even when there is no other activity than watching television, it is still advisable to have additional lighting in the room to avoid excessive luminance contrasts between the screen and adjacent areas. No matter how absorbing the programme, the eye frequently wanders away from the screen.

Fig. 30.1   A rise-and-fall pendant lights the dining table, with adjustable spotlights to provide effect lighting

The working light in a dining area is obviously that which is needed to illuminate the table for dining, but a dining table has many other uses such as homework and letter-writing. A luminaire that can provide a good directional light for dining, adjustable in luminosity and mounting height, supported by perimeter lighting to give light behind and above the head of a writer is the most suitable and flexible answer for this situation (Fig. 30.1).

Effect lighting.   Most of the individuality, a large proportion of the cost and nearly all the pleasure in home lighting comes from the effect lighting used in the living area. Imagination, coupled with personal preferences and good advice are the only requirements needed to add the quality of attractiveness to an otherwise functionally lit area (Fig. 30.2).

Fig. 30.2   Effect lighting in a living room

The lighting of curtains increases the apparent size of a room and adds a focal area of high colour. A fluorescent tube concealed in a pelmet will give an even spread of light across the curtains while spotlights located in or on the ceiling directly above the curtains will create dramatic highlights and shadows, particularly good with plain, rich coloured drapes.

Pictures should be lit either by the working light or by additional spotlights or striplights located on the ceiling or wall adjacent to the picture. A tungsten striplight or fluorescent luminaire is very effective when used directly beneath a painting but care must be taken that the source of light is shielded from direct view.

When decorative glassware is on sale in shops it appears at its best because it is effectively lit (Sect. 26.3.1). When displaying the same glassware at home it is worth repeating the same lighting techniques, using concealed striplights or miniature fluorescent tubes built into display cabinets or shelves. Bowls of flowers are most effective when lit from above: downlighters, either surface mounted or recessed, will provide a satisfactory solution. The technique of downlighting, usually from a simple cylinder, is very effective for accentuating other features in the home or simply to add interesting pools of lighting in an otherwise dull area.

Whatever additional emphasis lighting is used it should be separately controlled by switches so that a selective balance of lighting can be achieved by the householder. If these switches are dimmer control units then the accent lighting can be used to create a variety of different atmospheres.

30.2.4   Kitchens

Work lighting.   The functional areas in a kitchen are the sink, the cooker and the working surface/table. The important design consideration is that tasks are generally carried out facing the walls of the room, and there is therefore little use in providing a luminaire in

Fig. 30.3   A kitchen, using fluorescent luminaires

the centre of a kitchen unless it is a large enough luminaire to throw light on to the task around the person performing it. A fluorescent luminaire is generally suitable and should be ceiling-mounted above the front edge of the sink or cooker (Fig. 30.3). If there are wall cupboards mounted above a working surface, then fluorescent or tubular incandescent luminaires should be mounted on the underside of the front edge of the cupboard so that light is thrown on to the rear of the working surface. This is the area where the cookery book is likely to be resting, and gastronomic catastrophes should not be caused by indifferent lighting installations. Low-mounted luminaires should incorporate diffusers or shields so that the bare light source is not visible. Lighting of the right colour is important in a kitchen and when fluorescent lighting is involved a de luxe tube colour such as Natural or °Kolor-rite should be used.

Effect lighting.   The inclusion of a decorative pendant low over a kitchen table can help to turn an austere functional area into a more pleasant and restful room. Spotlights on gay articles hung on the walls help to break up the visual dullness of an evenly lit room. Lighting units mounted on top of wall cupboards to illuminate the ceiling will help to increase the apparent size of a kitchen and create an interesting and unusual visual effect.

30.2.5   Bedrooms

Work lighting.   In a bedroom, light must be provided to enable the user to make a choice between clothes of similar colours, to attend to personal grooming and to read in bed.

Functional lighting should be provided in or adjacent to a wardrobe in such a position that the user does not shield the light with his body.

Personal grooming is a difficult task to light as it obviously involves a mirror. Because the apparent distance of the face or figure viewed in the mirror is twice its actual distance from the mirror and because the details to be seen are small and of low contrast to their background, a high illuminance is required on the face. Light must be directed on to the user and not on to the mirror. The most satisfactory mirror lighting system is probably that used in artists' dressing rooms—bare lamps extremely close together around the outside edge of the mirror. Although somewhat flamboyant for normal domestic use, the principle is sound. Side lighting is the most acceptable as lighting from directly above will produce unpleasant and confusing shadows on the face.

Bedside lighting should be provided mainly for people reading in bed. The luminaires should be positioned above eye level and preferably to one side so that they do not obstruct anyone sitting up in bed. If the luminaires are adjustable, they can be used to meet other functional requirements or as additions to the effect lighting scheme. A dimmer built into the switch that is used to extinguish the light last thing at night is a blessing, as this can be switched on at a low level in the morning and adjusted up to a normal level quite slowly.

The comments relating to adult bedrooms generally apply to a child's room but it should be noted that luminaires must not be placed where young children can touch them, remembering that the increasing use of bunk beds gives a small child a reasonable chance of reaching the ceiling. Surface-mounted ceiling luminaires, well away from the anticipated position of the bed, probably close to the centre of the room, are usually the best answer. In a child's bedroom it may also be necessary to provide lighting for play or study.

Effect lighting.   Many bedrooms have alcoves or recesses between cupboards that need not remain dingy and unused. A simple unit of glass shelves lit from beneath, or a picture framed by an alcove and lit from a spotlight hidden by a pelmet across the top of the alcove, will help transform an ordinary bedroom into a room worthy of spending a third of a lifetime in! Children love pin-up boards where posters or the latest drawings from school can be displayed: spotlights, recessed or surface mounted, will add emphasis to the area and create pleasing contrasts between adjacent wall surfaces.

It is always worth considering the occupant of the room when selecting luminaires. A pretty, frilly feminine lamp shade or a metal drum may both do the same lighting job, but the former may be more suitable for a young teenage girl, creating an atmosphere in which she feels comfortable. A simple change of lamp from pearl to pink will add a romantic atmosphere to any bedroom.

A child, particularly a young child, needs the security bred of familiarity. In lighting a child's room, therefore, the artificial source should create a similar night-time scene to the natural daylit scene. Luminaires should not be located in positions that cause unnatural shadows at night: even a nightlight can turn the silhouette of simple bed post into something quite alarming. Nightlights may not be necessary if a dimmed landing light is used but if extra night lighting is needed then decorative electroluminescent panels are very suitable: they need to have a very low luminance to avoid being glaring to the dark-adapted eye.

30.2.6   Bathrooms

Work lighting.   The specific functional area in a bathroom that needs special lighting is the mirror over the basin, the requirements being the same as those for bedroom mirror lighting. The luminaires used must be permanently fixed and preferably steamproof: luminaires that incorporate a shaver socket must have an isolating transformer built into them.

Effect lighting.   Bathrooms these days are often so small that the mirror light is sufficient to illuminate the whole room, but as taking a bath is such a pleasant exercise, at least for adults, the lighting can be arranged to suit the mood. One or two recessed incandescent luminaires with sparkle glass attachments mounted in the ceiling will give a touch of luxury. They are easy to install unless there is a solid floor above but must not be mounted directly over the bath.

30.2.7   Gardens

Work lighting.   For safety reasons, the entrance to drive-ways, especially if concealed and on unlit roads, should be lit, also the back porch area and any footpaths commonly used after dark, including fuel store areas. The luminaires used in external areas need only be simple tungsten or fluorescent lanterns, of the type designed for commercial applications.

Effect lighting.   The more able we are to extend our living area beyond the four walls of our house the more pleasure we can obtain from our total living space. Lighting our gardens so that the attractive areas are emphasized and the unattractive areas are concealed will add an extra dimension to our living area.

It is not necessary to locate light sources that will simulate the elevation of the sun, so dramatic modelling effects can be tried. A weatherproof coloured spotlight illuminating the foliage of a tree or the shrubs around a pond, a couple of low level spotlights lighting

Fig. 30.4   Garden lighting extends the living area of any home

flower-beds or bushes can give a very familiar garden an added quality of surprise and interest after dark (Fig. 30.4).

Effect lighting is also concerned with the special occasion out-of-doors. The barbecue, the firework party or just the more regular use of a terrace for supper on warm evenings are situations which, whilst embracing the concept of work lighting, also require consideration of the carnival atmosphere one is trying to create. Strings of coloured lamps are easily installed and removed after a special occasion and will add gaiety to the functional working light needed around the barbecue grill or the firework store.

The house itself, whether modern or traditional, can be enhanced by floodlighting (Chap. 33), but this is generally less effective than the selective highlighting of interesting contours or architectural features. A reasonably flexible installation system will allow minor changes to be made in the location of equipment which can provide a variety of changes in the effect achieved.

31 Transport lighting

There are many requirements for lighting in connection with land, sea and air transport. Light signals and illuminated signs are required on the ground to control the movement of all types of vehicle by day and night, and to provide guidance and information. Vehicles moving at night are required to carry specified lights so that they can be seen and can indicate intended manoeuvres: they also carry driving lights to illuminate the way ahead. Public transport vehicles have, in addition, their own interior lighting systems.

This chapter provides general information on all these aspects of lighting for transport, with the notable exception of street lighting systems, to which Chap. 32 is devoted.

31.1 SIGNAL COLOURS

The colours of transport signals, usually operated by incandescent sources (though also by oil lamps), are defined by areas on the CIE chromaticity diagram (Fig. 31.1). The essential requirement is not so much to control colours as to avoid confusion between similar colours. The permitted variation in a colour will therefore differ according to the number of colours in the system: if white and yellow are used as independent signals, for instance, a smaller tolerance for white would be specified than in a system where white did not have to be distinguished from yellow. There are also grades of red and green of different precision whose use varies with the type of transport concerned.

The subject is codified in BS 1376:1953: the table in Fig. 31.1 shows the specified restricted colour limits referred to in the colour ranges shown on the CIE chromaticity chart. However, complications are arising due to the use of self-coloured sources such as red neon beacons and yellow sodium airfield approach lighting, also due to the requirement for increased filter transmittance to produce higher signal intensities in conditions of poor visibility. Both CIE and BSI are currently preparing new documents: in all probability the green, white and yellow limits will be extended and the blue and red ones slightly contracted.

31.2 CONTROL AND NAVIGATIONAL LIGHTING

31.2.1 Roadway signals and signs

With the continuing increase in traffic on our roads, together with the tremendous amount of extraneous lighting (shop windows, advertising, etc.) traffic signals and signs can be very difficult to recognize and interpret. Because of this, the current recommendations and specifications for signals and signs ask for high sign luminances for those situations where difficulty in seeing has been evident in the past.

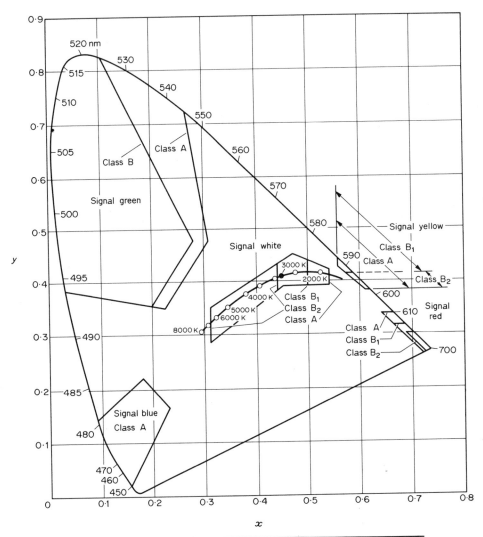

Signal colour	Red	Yellow	Green	Blue	White
Signal service	Class				
Road traffic	B_1	A	B	—	—
Aviation—airborne	A	B_1	A	A	B_1
Aviation—ground— general	A	B_1	A	A	B_1
Aviation—ground—high recognition	B_2	B_1	B	A	B_1
Railway—semaphores	B_1	B_2	B	—	—
Railway—lenses	B_2	B_1	B	—	A or B_2
Lighthouse	A	A	A	A	A
Ships' lights	B_1	—	B	—	A

Fig. 31.1 BS signal colours

506

Traffic lights. The usual traffic lights use rough service mains voltage 65 W lamps, housed in simple parabolic reflectors. A prismatic front glass is made from the correct colour materials and is designed to eliminate 'phantom' effects. Phantom is the term which describes the effect of the signal reflecting some external light (sunlight perhaps) and making the signal appear to be operating.

BS 505 : 1939 for traffic signals is soon to be reissued, and this will recommend that the signal will have the facility for much higher intensities. Some signals will be required to have two intensities, one for night use and one for use during the day, to eliminate any glare problems. The night intensity will be recommended to be between 1/5 and 1/12 of the day intensity, depending upon the particular conditions.

Peak intensities of 475 cd for red and green signals, 950 cd for amber, will be required, these values being increased to 800 cd and 1600 cd respectively when the speed of approach can be in excess of 80 km/h.

In order to comply with these recommendations, tungsten halogen lamps are being used for new units. A problem in using these lamps for this application is that the amber signal only remains alight for a short period: this means that the iodine cycle is restricted as the lamp may not reach its correct operating temperature. Special designs of lamp have been developed in order to combat this difficulty.

Road signs. The lighting of a road sign has to be a compromise. On the one hand, the sign should be easy to see, but on the other hand, it should not be too bright and give rise to glare. It should be illuminated as evenly as possible and must also be easy to see during the day when unlit.

The Traffic Signs Manual (1967) Chap. 11, describes the recommended lighting of signs. For signs illuminated externally, the Manual recommends a mean luminance of at least 10 ft L (34 cd/m²), with the maximum luminance not exceeding 100 ft L (342 cd/m²) and the ratio of maximum to minimum luminance not exceeding 10:1. The recommendations for self-illuminated signs are given in Table 31.1.

Table 31.1 Limits of luminance values for self-illuminated signs

Location	Area of sign face	Mean luminance of the white portions of the sign face cd/m²		Maximum luminance ratio over the white portions of the sign face	
		Max	Min	Inner area	Outer area
Sites where the ambient lighting is *not less* than that provided by Group A2 street lighting	Up to 1·5 m²	1000	350	5:2	5:1
	1·5 m² to 4·0 m²			3:1	8:1
Unlighted site or sites where the ambient lighting is *less* than that provided by Group A2 street lighting	Up to 1·5 m²	350	175	5:2	5:1
	1·5 m² to 4·0 m²			3:1	8:1

507

The choice of light source used to illuminate any sign will be somewhat dependent upon the size of the sign. Fluorescent tubes, in both normal and miniature forms, serve as good sources for both internally and externally illuminated signs. Their dimensions, luminous efficacy and long life are advantageous for this application: the Ministry recommendation for the colour of fluorescent tubes is Daylight (or Cool White). The selection of lamp and control gear has to allow for low temperature starting.

Belisha beacons.   One of the earliest flashing road signs to be put into general use was the Belisha beacon used at pedestrian crossings. Experimental evidence, obtained by the Road Research Laboratory in 1953, showed that amber beacons flashing at 60 times per minute were the most conspicuous. The conspicuity of beacons is not as great as it was, due to the rapid growth of adjacent irrelevant lighting, so there is a need to increase the luminance of the beacons or to floodlight the crossings.

Part-time and variable-legend signs.   There is an increasing demand for signs of this type—motorway warning lights, variable speed limit indicators and traffic control systems which are tidal or part-time.

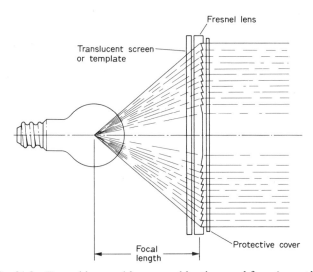

Fig. 31.2   Fresnel lens and lamp combination used for a 'secret' sign

They can be made 'secret' by use of the optical system shown in Fig. 31.2. When the lamp is not alight, the sign will appear completely featureless and only when the lamp is alight will the sign show.

31.2.2   Airfield lighting

Almost all aerodromes have to receive a Government licence before they can be operational. To obtain this licence they must comply with conditions stated in the Department of Trade and Industry Document CAP 168: the performance of luminaires to be used in aerodromes is specified in this document.

Most of the lighting on an airfield is there to convey information of one sort or another to flight personnel and this is particularly important as an aircraft is about to land. From the time the pilot first sees the airfield until he safely disembarks he will be helped by nine types of lighting units. In order of usage these are:

(a) Airport location beacons: these are often morse flashing lights mounted on the roof of a central building in the airport. They use conventional incandescent lamps (500/1000 W) housed in parabolic reflectors and are green.

(b) Approach lights: these are normally 300 W PAR 56 lamps arranged to give a pattern of lights leading into the runway. In USA, flashing lights are used in the centre-line of the pattern. The contour of the terrain may necessitate mounting approach lights on masts.

(c) Visual approach slope indicators (VASI units): a parallel corridor is defined down which the pilot should travel (Fig. 31.3). The pilot sees only white bars when he is too high, only red bars when he is too low and red on white when he is on the correct angle of approach. Twelve units are used, each unit containing three 200 W PAR 64 lamps housed in a special frame.

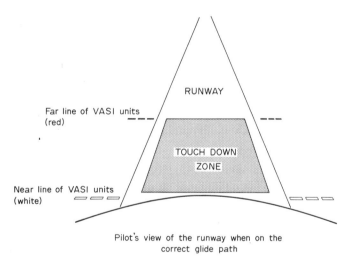

Pilot's view of the runway when on the correct glide path

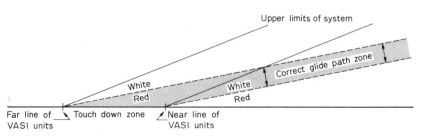

Fig. 31.3   The visual approach slope indicator (VASI)

(d) Threshold lights: these are usually green and mark the threshold of the runway: they are seen by the pilot as he approaches touchdown. They are normally flush fittings using conventional 200 W incandescent lamps with glass prismatic lenses.

(e) Touchdown zone lights: these mark the immediate area of landing. They are recessed into the runway, use 200 W tungsten halogen lamps and are white.

(f) Runway centre-line lights: these are recessed into the runway centre line at 30 m intervals. They use 100/200 W tungsten halogen lamps and are white: a photograph of one of these units is shown in Fig. 10.8 and its optical design is outlined in Sect. 20.3.4.

(g) Runway edge lights: normally these are surface-mounted units using conventional incandescent lamps (100/200 W) housed in glass prismatic lenses and placed at about 60 m intervals in lines at each side of the runway. The most modern type is recessed into the runway and uses tungsten halogen lamps. They are normally white.

(h) Taxiway lights: these guide the pilot, after completing his landing, to the disembarking area. They can be either surface-mounted (side) or recessed into the taxiway (centre line) or both. They use 45 W to 100 W lamps and are green (centre line) or blue (side). High intensity units, for the high speed taxiing currently desirable because of increased air traffic, will be recessed into the taxiway and use 45 W or 100 W tungsten halogen lamps.

(i) Apron floodlights: normal floodlighting luminaires are used at disembarking or unloading areas. The cut-off of these units has to be very sharp to avoid glare to pilots in approaching aircraft.

31.2.3 Lighthouses

The aim of a lighthouse is to provide a visible signal to shipping over a long range. The range under specified weather conditions should be large enough to cover the geographical range, which is limited by the curvature of the earth. When the required range has been established the necessary intensity of signal can be calculated. In the case of a flashing light the Blondel–Rey law is used to find the required intensity (Sect. 2.2.2). The signals sent out should be distinctive and easily recognizable as the signal from the particular lighthouse: its colour and flashing characteristic will be different from any other lighthouse and also distinct from other neighbouring signals.

Normally the flashing lights from lighthouses are produced by means of revolving screens or by revolving the entire optical system, where a narrow beam is produced, or by shutters. Recently, investigations have been made into the use of very intense flashtubes: a flashtube is very economical for lighthouse use but mariners seem to prefer the revolving spoke appearance of a conventional system to the somewhat glaring effect of the new flashtubes.

Small size and very high luminance combined with long life is what is required from the lamps used for lighthouses. These lamp characteristics enable the associated optics to produce the very high intensity, narrow-angle beam normally required for lighthouse applications. 2 kW compact-source xenon lamps have been used by Trinity House, but most existing lighthouses use high wattage incandescent lamps as their light source.

A current development is the use of gas lasers for lighthouse signalling. The very narrow, extremely intense monochromatic beam produced by a laser has excellent penetrative qualities which are very useful in bad visibility. With further development, a combination of laser and conventional systems could be used to great advantage.

31.3   DRIVING AND INDICATOR LIGHTS

31.3.1   Automobile lights

The lighting used by motor cars is very strictly regulated by law. Any vehicle used during the hours of darkness must be fitted with two white side lamps facing forward and these must be in working order at all times. Two red lamps with a minimum power of 5 W must be fitted to the rear of the vehicle, and the positions of both front and rear lights is subject to legislation.

Directional indicators of some type are obligatory for all vehicles, but for vehicles registered after September 1965 only flashing lights are permitted. These flashing indicators must be amber and their intensity for particular angles of view is also the subject of legislation. They should have a power of between 15 W and 36 W and should flash between 60 and 120 times a minute. By 1973, rear-facing directional indicators will be required to be dimmable. This will allow very bright signals to be used in daylight or fog, and less bright, non-glaring signals to be available for use at night. The luminous intensity for directional indicators must currently lie between 100 cd and 700 cd for front-facing indicators and between 50 cd and 200 cd for rear-facing indicators. Dual intensities for the latter will be 40 cd to 160 cd by night and 175 cd to 700 cd by day.

Headlamps of at least 30 W are obligatory, with certain exceptions, for all four-wheeled vehicles used on a road. They must be used at all times at night unless either a matched pair of fog lamps is being used or the vehicle is on a road where street lighting is in use. The driver must be able to select either a main beam or a dipped beam (Sect. 9.3.1). The required intensity of headlights is given in Table 31.2.

Table 31.2   Headlight intensity requirements

Headlight type	Main beam	Dipped beam		
	Min intensity cd	Min intensity cd	Max intensity above the horizontal cd	
Headlamps with prefocused filament lamps	25 000	6000	2000	
Sealed beam headlamps: 180 mm diameter, 12 V, 45/60 W 145 mm diameter, 12 V, $37\frac{1}{2}$/50 W	36 000 25 000	10 000 12 000	2000 2000	

From 1971, new vehicles must have two stop lamps, red or amber in colour and of minimum power 15 W. After 1973 these lamps will again have to be dimmed when the obligatory lights are switched on: when a fog lamp is used the brighter stop lights should be in operation.

31.3.2   Railway locomotive lights

In the past every locomotive was required to have four front lights, one at the top and three along the bottom just above the buffers. The way these lights were used indicated the type of train that the locomotive was pulling. This system is still occasionally used but the present system is that trains must carry an indicator board which must be illuminated at night, also in tunnels or fog by day. The number on the board consists of a figure indicating the type of train, a letter denoting its destination and two numbers which identify the train. At the rear of the train only one red light is necessary, which may be oil or electric, unless the train is carrying royalty when two rear lights may be used.

31.3.3   Aircraft lights

Flying aircraft are normally in radio contact with other aircraft but they are still required to show lights somewhat similar to those used by ships at sea: a red light on the port wing tip, a green light on the starboard wing tip and a white rear-facing light on the tail. Additional red anti-collision lights are also used and these are often made to be flashing.

The effective intensity of these lights is normally only about 200 cd, so fast aircraft in flight have difficulty in seeing them. Recently, high intensity flashtubes have been advocated for use as anti-collision lights, with a coding to indicate the direction of the aircraft, for example a double flash forward and a single flash aft. The DC 10 uses this system with two lights facing forward, one on each wing tip and one tail-mounted light: the effective intensity of each light is approximately 400 cd. Many different anti-collision systems are being experimented with and it is essential that more standardization takes place in this field.

31.3.4   Ships at sea

A whole variety of different signals are specified to be shown by different types of vessel doing various jobs, but for any power-driven vessel under way, the Admiralty Manual of Navigation states that it should have a white light on the mast, red and green lights on the port and starboard sides respectively, and a white light on the stern. The green and red lights have to be so designed that there is a sharp cut-off in the forward inboard direction.

The lights are required to be visible at a distance of at least 2 miles on a dark night with a clear atmosphere. Under these conditions an intensity of only 5 cd is adequate for a distance considerably greater than the specified 2 miles. Such an intensity would be useless in anything other than good conditions and there is a clear need for an increase in these intensity requirements.

31.4   INTERIOR LIGHTING FOR PUBLIC TRANSPORT

The lighting in the passenger areas of all the various systems of public transport should aim to give enough light to see by without excessive discomfort glare. People are required to remain in a confined space, sometimes for hours at a time: while there they should be made to feel comfortable and relaxed. Comfort is not limited to seat design: the passenger's visual comfort is a function of the overall design of the interior, of which the lighting is an important part.

Coach interior lighting.   In a long-distance train or bus, passengers tend to make themselves at home because they may be there for some hours: it is not inappropriate to consider the techniques of domestic lighting (Chap. 30) as applicable to this situation.

A satisfactory illuminance is needed to allow the passenger to read and to write, but at night facilities for dimming the lighting should be available so that passengers can sleep. Under these conditions, a spotlight to enable a passenger to read without disturbing his neighbour is a very useful addition to general lighting.

Too often in the past a carriage or coach interior has been designed and then, almost as an after-thought, the lighting added: this mistake has not been made in the existing standard British Rail carriage (Fig. 31.4). The main lighting is fluorescent, with incandescent reading lights recessed into the base of the luggage rack. A special 24/28 V 6 W lamp having a crown-silvered bulb was devised to reduce direct discomfort glare.

Fig. 31.4   The interior of British Rail Mk. II D passenger coach

The use of fluorescent lamps in vehicles where the main source of electricity is from low wattage batteries has been made a practical proposition with the development of the transistor inverter (Sect. 18.4.2).

For local trains and buses, and for the Underground, the length of journey is relatively short, and a simple overall system of lighting is adequate. An illuminance of about 150 lux enables people to read or move about with ease. Fluorescent tubes operated from transistor inverters are generally used.

Aircraft.   As with long-distance trains and coaches a combination of fluorescent tubes and incandescent lamps can be used to achieve good lighting, but the space restriction in an aircraft makes it more difficult to build in the lighting. There is also a strict weight limit: this raises the problem of the weight of gear to operate the fluorescent tubes. Fortunately the use of a 400 Hz power supply enables conventional control gear to be smaller than usual, even if transistorized inverters are not used. Considerations of economy in space and weight have led to special wedge-base reflector lamps being developed for use as individual reading lights for the passengers: these are now being used in the VC10 airliner.

32 Street lighting

This is a very important aspect of transport lighting: it involves the expenditure of public money but produces commensurate benefits in saving traffic accidents and reducing congestion by encouraging the use of the road system through the hours of darkness. But more than this, the quality of public lighting can enhance the quality of our environment if the lighting system and the equipment are wisely chosen.

After analyzing the requirements of street lighting in relation to the visual task of a driver, basic design principles are discussed and applied to different situations under the headings used in published British and International recommendations.

32.1 THE FUNCTIONS OF STREET LIGHTING

The MOT Report (1937) summarized the functions of street lighting under four main headings:

(a) The convenience and safety of road users.
(b) Police purposes.
(c) The convenience of residents.
(d) Special purposes in shopping areas and important urban centres.

The report recognized two classes of road. On traffic routes (Group A) lighting was to provide an ample margin of safety for all road users without the need for headlights except possibly in fog. On other roads (Group B) the level of illuminance would be materially lower and it might be assumed that headlights would be in general use. Between these a clear demarcation in mounting height was applied, about 8 m (25 ft) for Group A and 5 m (15 ft) or less for Group B. This was intended as guidance to motorists on the use of headlights, but Group A installations were rarely of such a standard that motorists could be told they need not use headlights. It has been the responsibility of the motorist himself to use headlights when he needs them, but in recent years there has been pressure to use headlights in all but the best lit streets, and headlights are now compulsory after lighting-up time wherever there is no adequate street lighting. They are not satisfactory for driving in town traffic, less because of their effect on the contrast with which objects are seen in silhouette than because high intensities are projected into the eyes of other drivers due to the geometry of roads and vehicle movements. The most dangerous condition is probably when some are using dipped headlights and others are not. Thus the performance of traffic route street lighting installations should be without doubt quite adequate for their purpose, namely to enable a driver with normal vision to follow his route and perceive any hazard on the road ahead without the use of headlights.

514

32.1.1 Visual task and requirements of the vehicle driver

There are considerable demands on a driver's attention and he does not usually scan the scene but as far as possible directs his gaze to the road some 100 m ahead. Especially at speed, he should be able to see considerably further to follow his route and be able to give indications in good time. His eyes take in the scene, but he gives fully conscious attention to only a limited amount of the visual information available. A process of subconscious selection, developed by experience, seems to focus his attention on any hazard and he may then look directly at it. Small objects on the road at moderate distances ahead, or larger objects a long way ahead, are first seen by parafoveal vision as silhouettes rather than by surface detail, with the road surface as a bright background. Making the whole of the road surface appear bright, to reveal its direction and show things up as silhouettes, can be achieved economically by directing beams of light on to the road at glancing angles towards the approaching motorist. Silhouette is not a poorer type of vision compared with direct vision by surface detail, but it exploits both the way in which objects ahead are seen and the higher reflectivity of road surfaces under these conditions of illuminance and view.

Adequate lighting in generally downward directions is needed for pleasantness and seeing nearby objects by surface detail. It is important for the motorist to be able to see adjacent kerbs, lane markings and even road texture. This enables him to judge his position across the road and his direction of travel, usually subconsciously. Footpaths and other backgrounds such as buildings often form the background against which objects are seen and these also need lighting.

The visual task of a driver is kinematic in that he does not fixate on features of the scene but lets their images stream across his retina, and also in that his viewpoint and the scene are changing as he travels. Anything in the scene which attracts his attention unnecessarily—glare from opposing headlights, over-bright stoplights or indicators, glare from street lanterns—is indirectly a hazard.

To meet the requirements of a driver, a lighting installation should produce the following:

(a) High and reasonably uniform road surface luminance.
(b) Good silhouetting contrasts of distant or small objects on the road ahead (revealing power).
(c) Adequate illuminance for pleasantness and seeing nearby features.
(d) Restrictions of luminance and intensities from lanterns in directions which can cause glare.

At first it would seem that for different traffic conditions different levels of illuminance, road surface luminance and control of glare from the lighting would be needed. But when weather or traffic is bad a driver expects to put extra effort into his driving. He may need to do so under other conditions, such as when lighting is poor. The community using and paying for the roads would not wish to put up with such conditions always: there is a balance between what it would like and what it is prepared to afford. As techniques, lamps and equipment improve, higher standards become practicable. Experience of what is possible and its cost must influence strongly what is judged to be necessary.

Table 32.1 Cost of accidents in UK

(a) Average cost, including subjective costs, of all accidents per personal injury accident 1968 (from *Road Research*, 1969)

Urban areas	Rural areas	Motorways	In daylight	After dark	All accidents
£1120	£1870	£2820	£1210	£1510	£1290

(b) Classified by severity, average for all areas 1968 (from *Road Research*, 1969)

Fatal	Serious	Slight	Damage only
£10 660	£1220	£220	£90

(c) Analysis of total economic costs of accidents 1969 (from *Road Accidents*, 1969)

Medical treatment, ambulance and funeral costs	£15 000 000
Police and administration costs	£26 000 000
Damage to vehicles and other property	£183 000 000
Lost output	£96 000 000
Total economic costs of accidents in 1969 (excluding pain and suffering)	£320 000 000

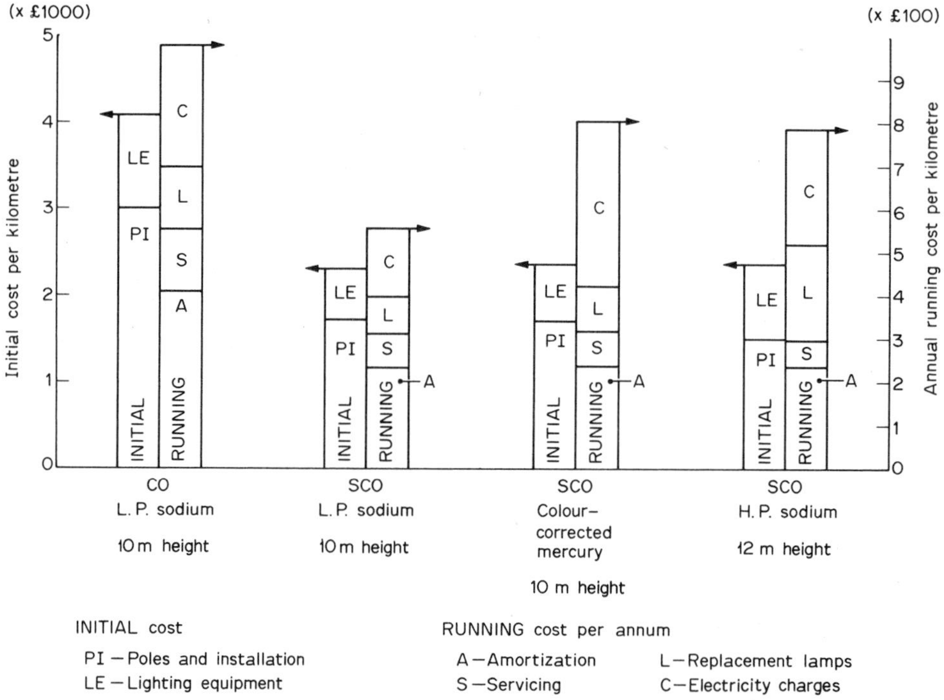
(x £1000)
(x £100)
Initial cost per kilometre
Annual running cost per kilometre
0
1
2
3
4
5
6
7
8
9
LE
PI
C
L
S
A
INITIAL
RUNNING
CO
L. P. sodium
10 m height
SCO
L. P. sodium
10 m height
SCO
Colour-corrected mercury
10 m height
SCO
H. P. sodium
12 m height
INITIAL cost
PI — Poles and installation
LE — Lighting equipment
RUNNING cost per annum
A — Amortization
S — Servicing
L — Replacement lamps
C — Electricity charges

Fig. 32.1 Relative costs of street lighting installations

32.1.2 Cost benefit evaluation

The installation of traffic route lighting up to the standard of the 1952 British code of practice and the improvement of poor lighting has been shown to reduce night-time accidents in towns by an overall 30%. The saving on rural roads may be as much as 40%. Of fatal and serious accidents in 1969, 24% occurred at night in urban areas and 14% in rural areas.

When the Government took over full financial responsibility for trunk road lighting a cost benefit analysis scheme was instituted in England and Wales for the purpose of assessing priorities for capital expenditure. The cost of a new installation was balanced against the saving of 30% of the accidents at night over the previous three years (Table 32.1). Dividing the saving per annum by the capital cost gave the Merit Rating on which priority was allocated.

Although capital cost was the criterion used, this is only one aspect of the total cost to the community. Evaluation of the cost of lighting systems is examined in Chap. 34 and the principle is established of amortizing capital costs and adding the costs of lamp replacements, electrical energy and servicing (cleaning, painting, patrolling and relamping). Fig. 32.1 shows typical costs of alternative code installations for a 13 m wide road.

32.2 GENERAL PRINCIPLES OF INSTALLATION DESIGN

Whether design is to a performance specification using road surface reflectivity data, or by using tables in a code based on experience, it involves the choice of light source, lantern light distribution and installation layout. For traffic route lighting these should be chosen so that from the viewpoint of a motorist driving through the installation the road surface appears reasonably uniformly bright. Siting is a question of matching the bright patches from the individual lanterns together economically. The extent of each patch depends on road surface reflectivity characteristics and lantern light distribution.

32.2.1 Reflection from the road surface

There are two modes of reflection even from rough surfaces.

With diffuse reflection, luminance is related to illuminance. The bright patch from a single lantern with a symmetrical intensity distribution is circular when seen from above but changes to an ellipse when seen in perspective along the road. If the light distribution is concentrated in any direction the patch is extended (Fig. 32.2). The spectral distribution of the light may be changed by the surface reflecting some wavelengths better than others.

Quasi-specular reflection depends on the directions of light incidence and viewing. Seen from above there is little contribution to the bright patch by this mode, but as the angle of view changes to that of a motorist a bright streak forms between him and the lantern. There is little change in the spectral distribution of the light. The streak commences in the region where the patch due to diffuse reflection begins to fall off in luminance. The length of the streak depends on the smoothness or shine of the surface and the intensities emitted by the lantern at angles between about 75° and 87° to the downward vertical. If either of these is low, the length of the streak is severely limited. The rougher the surface the wider the streak and the lower its luminance: the width depends also on

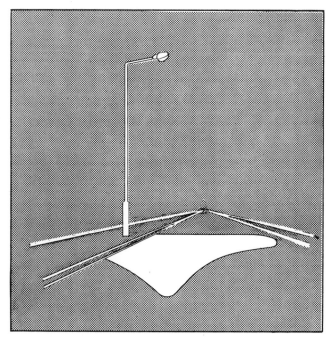

Fig. 32.2   Bright patch appearing on road by reflection of light from a single SCO lantern when the road surface is light and diffusing

the plan width of the beam from the lantern and its direction relative to the observer. For very shiny surfaces, or wet surfaces approaching what is called surface flooding, the width of the streak depends on the width of the lantern as seen (Fig. 32.3) and its maximum luminance is related to that of the light source. Fluorescent lanterns transverse to the road provide very effective lighting in such conditions.

The combination of the head produced by diffuse reflection and the streak or tail by quasi-specular reflection, forms a T-shaped bright patch. High angle light and smooth or wet road surfaces produce a long tail: if the lantern intensities above 70° are restricted or the road surface is rough, the tail is short. The head of the T depends on illuminance and lightness of the surface: if the road is dark and shiny there will be negligible head.

32.2.2   Light distribution from lanterns

For convenience these are described in terms of the degree of cut-off or the restriction of glare intensity. Since for practical reasons the beam angle is lower when the cut-off is stricter, this system of description is adequate.

Because of the length of tail on smooth surfaces, non-cut-off high-angle beam distributions could be used most economically at relatively long spacings, but glare would be excessive. Usually in UK the semi-cut-off (SCO) light distribution is used because this permits a reasonable spacing/mounting height ratio. Cut-off (CO) lighting, costing maybe 30% more, should be considered if the road surface is rough and light, or if the

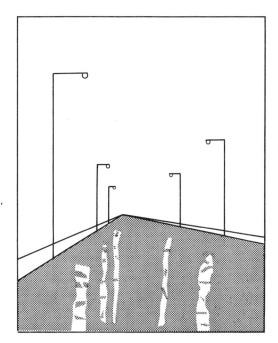

Fig. 32.3   Collapse of bright patches on a road which is wet to the extent of surface flooding

road undulates so that glare could be troublesome from high-angle intensities where lanterns appear to run down into the road over the brow of a hill, or if drivers on an elevated road see the lanterns at about eye level, or if the installation is small and isolated such as a roundabout with unlit approach roads. It may be better on wide roads, or where a dual carriageway is lit from the central reservation, or where a road is lit from one side, especially where trees may intercept high-angle light.

32.2.3   Arrangement of lanterns

On a single carriageway lanterns are usually staggered, that is, placed alternately on one side, then on the other. The semi-cut-off distribution is eminently suitable: as the luminance of the head of the T from one lantern falls off towards the far side of the road it is supplemented by the tail from the next lantern beyond it. Up to a certain road width the bright patches with commonly used road surfaces comfortably cover the whole width of road when lanterns are placed above or near the kerb. If the road is wider the bracket arm length can be increased to give a moderate overhang but if this is carried too far dark areas may be left near the kerbs. On even wider roads the mounting height can be increased, but before doing this it may be more economic to close up the spacing: a pairs-opposite arrangement may be preferred, but there is often little difference in appearance.

On a level curve of small radius (less than about 80 × mounting height) the staggered arrangement is replaced by a single-side arrangement with the lanterns on the outside of the curve. On sharp bends it may be necessary to close up the spacing as well.

519

On narrow roads a single-side arrangement is satisfactory; this may be used on wider roads to avoid overhead telephone wires or trees, but long brackets and cut-off lanterns should be used.

On dual carriageways with central reservations up to 5 m wide, the choice is between a pairs-opposite arrangement or twin lanterns on the central reservation. The latter is likely to offer considerable savings in columns, cables and electricity supply services.

32.2.4   Principles of siting

It is best to consider intersections and pedestrian crossings first. This may be done initially on a scale plan but a site survey is usually necessary for final planning.

A lantern is placed on the nearside some 15 m beyond a road entering from the left, to provide a bright patch revealing the mouth of the side road. Another is placed opposite the approach lanes of the side road to show the main road well ahead. When this conflicts with the need to place lanterns on the outside of a bend, the latter has priority but sometimes an extra lantern is justified. Similarly a lantern is placed on the nearside beyond a pedestrian crossing. Powerful floodlighting is being increasingly used on crossings, but it does need to be powerful or the pedestrian may have a false sense of being visible.

Having catered for these points, the distance between is divided up according to the design spacing. Then a visit to the site should be made for checking obstructions and any necessary adjustment made.

A siting gauge can be constructed and used to ensure that the separation between bright patches is not excessive, particularly at the changeover from staggered to single-sided on a bend, or from one side to the other on an S-bend. Progressing through the installation, first one way then the other, one end is set at the motorists' viewpoint and one edge laid through the plan position of each lantern to check that the angular spacing to the next is not excessive.

In roads where there are pedestrian footpaths or a speed limit of 30 mph (48 km/h) or less, columns should be set back at least 0·5 m from the kerb: otherwise the set back should be 1·5 m or more. Clear delineation of kerbs is desirable. A vertical kerb face shows up as a hard dark line when lanterns are mounted over the kerb or with a small overhang. Angled kerbs may show up as a light strip when the overhang is greater.

When an installation passes within 3 miles (4·8 km) of the boundary of an airfield, consultation with the authorities concerned is essential as these have power to restrict lighting which may be a danger to air navigation. Similar precautions are necessary on roads in the vicinity of railways, docks and navigable waterways to avoid confusing signals or excessive glare.

32.2.5   Choice of lamp

Street lighting operates from dusk to dawn (some 4000 h per year) or from dusk to about midnight, usually with an additional early morning period (some 2000 h or more per year). Because of the high cost of electric power and the high cost of labour for patrolling and lamp replacement, lamps of high efficacy and long life are required. In UK, in town streets as well as traffic routes out of town, the low pressure sodium lamp continues to be the most commonly used, the lighting of shop windows and such premises as cinemas often alleviating the poor colour rendering of the sodium light. Towards a town centre a better colour is desirable and colour-corrected mercury lamps are commonly used, although some fluorescent lighting remains from the post-war years and even some filament lamps: high pressure sodium lamps are being increasingly used in town centres and it is anticipated that metal halide lamps will find an increasing application here. In residential areas colour-corrected mercury is the most common alternative to low pressure sodium.

Sometimes one type of lamp and sometimes another has been claimed to be better in fog. Objects are usually seen in fog silhouetted against a surround of brighter haze, the contrast falling with distance and with fog density. There could be differences in apparent contrast with different source colour, but light fog is so variable that it is impossible to generalize. Lanterns can act as beacons to help traffic movement in dense fog, but since the particle size is then commensurate with light wavelengths, differential transmission effects are negligible: the luminance and the flashed area of the lanterns are certainly more important than colour, and shape can indicate usefully whether a lantern is on the left or the right.

32.3 BRITISH PRACTICE

Street lighting practice in UK is closely controlled by British Standards. The current issue of the Code of Practice on Street Lighting, CP 1004, consists of several parts: Part 1 (General Principles) and Part 2 (Lighting for Traffic Routes) were issued in one booklet in 1963. Other parts have followed, but some have not yet been completed, such as that dealing with high mast lighting where techniques are still developing. The main purpose of a code is to set standards to justify the expenditure of public money, avoiding waste due to either inadequate lighting or excessively lavish lighting. As higher standards become necessary due to more arduous driving conditions, and practicable due to improvements in lamps and equipment, standards need to be reviewed.

32.3.1 Traffic routes

The original installation design tables in CP 1004 Part 2 provide for three standards:

Group A1—for the more important routes.
Group A2—for the generality of main roads with considerable vehicular and pedestrian traffic.
Group A3—for main rural roads and minor urban roads not requiring Group A2 lighting.

There are four mounting heights, ranging from 7·6 to 12·2 m (25, 30, 35 and 40 ft). The permissible transverse distance between two rows of lanterns is related to mounting height, being 10% greater for Group A3 lighting than Group A2, and 10% greater for Group A2 than for Group A1. Maximum spacings are indicated and a minimum value for downward light flux (related to the square of the mounting height) both of these having a 10% differential between groups.

Road surface illuminance and luminance are therefore about 30% greater in Group A1 than Group A2. For any one road surface, a consistent average dry-road luminance results from the different recommended combinations of width and spacing for the different lantern arrangements for cut-off or semi-cut-off light distributions. But the difference in luminance between groups A1, A2 and A3 is small compared with the differences produced by different road surface reflection characteristics. The differentials are further blurred in practice by the use of the same available lamp and mounting height whether the target is Group A1 or A2, and also by the constraint on spacing by such factors as the distance between road intersections. For these reasons two simpler tables have been issued as Appendix B to CP 1004 Part 2.

These tables, one of which is given here as Table 32.2, are alternatives to the design tables in the body of the code, but in practice have largely superseded them. They produce

Table 32.2   Installation design recommendations for SCO lighting on traffic routes

Arrangement	Mounting height (H) m	Width between kerbs m														
		6	7	8	9	10	11	13	15	17	19	21	23	25	27	29
		Design spacing m														
Single side	8	35														
	10		47	41												
	12			56	53											
Single central, single carriageway	8					38	38	32								
	10							47	44							
	12									56	50					
Staggered	8	35	35	35	34	31	28									
	10	**44**	**44**	**44**	**44**	**44**	**44**	37	32	28	25					
	12							**53**	**46**	**41**	**37**	**33**				
Opposite, or off-set opposite	10							50	50	50	50					
	12									**60**	**60**	**60**	**60**	**56**	**52**	**48**
Twin central, dual carriageway (width between kerbs is per carriageway)	10		47	41	37											
	12		**56**	**56**	**53**	**47**	**43**									

Recommended design spacings are in heavy type.
It is assumed that lanterns are mounted over the kerb or within $\pm 0.1 H$ of the kerb line. When this limit is exceeded the lateral separation between rows of lanterns should be used instead of the width between kerbs.

lighting of generous Group A2 standard. Following international recommendations, three mounting heights are used of 8 m, 10 m and 12 m. Target or design values of spacing are given (as opposed to maximum spacing) on the assumption that one of three broad groups of lamp/lantern combination will be used.

Lamps of about 20 klm output give approximately 12 klm downward light flux in currently available lanterns; these are recommended for use at 10 m mounting height on the majority of roads. On wider roads where 12 m mounting height is used, 12 klm downward light may be adequate where traffic flows freely in the relative absence of conflicting traffic movements, but where it is considered necessary higher output combinations giving some 20 klm to 24 klm of downward flux are advised.

32.3.2 Specification of light distribution

In producing the tables of CP 1004 certain assumptions have been made about the intensity distributions of lanterns, namely that these conform to BS 1788:1964. Table 32.3 gives the requirements.

Table 32.3 Intensity distribution requirements of BS 1788:1964 for Group A lanterns

Type of light distri-bution	In plane of principal vertical polar curve				Limits of intensity ratio in any direction within the cone from downward vertical to 30° therefrom		In vertical plane parallel to street axis		
	Angle of elevation con-tained within the beam	Limits of peak intensity ratio (*PIR*)					Angle of elevation at which an intensity ratio of 1·2 occurs		Maxi-mum intensity ratio at hori-zontal
		min	max	min	max		min	max	
CO	65°	2·0	4·0	0·3	2·0	} maximum not to	72°	78°	0·15
SCO	75°	1·8	4·0	0·3	1·7	} exceed 80%	78°	84°	0·6
SCO(S)	75°	1·8	4·0	0·3	1·7	} *PIR*	80°	86°	0·7

To make the specification applicable to lanterns with a wide range of light output, most of the light intensity requirements are expressed in terms of the average intensity in directions below the horizontal. The mean lower hemispherical intensity (MHI) is equal to the downward light flux divided by 6·28 since the solid angle making up the lower hemisphere is 2π steradians. The ratio of any intensity to the MHI is the intensity ratio (IR) in the direction considered.

The beam is defined as the solid angle including directions where the intensity is not less than 0·90 of the peak intensity. The peak intensity is restricted to within certain limits: if too high it could cause glare, if too low the road luminance could be patchy at code spacings. The limits seem wide (from 1·8 IR to 4 IR for a semi-cut-off light distribution) because the specification has been made general. The upper limit is needed more for light sources of small size and high luminance with which excessive intensities could occur. The lower limit ensures adequate beam intensities from sources of lower luminance.

The run-back above the beam is controlled by restricting the intensity ratio at the horizontal and making the direction at which an intensity ratio of 1·2 occurs fall between certain angles. These requirements relate to the light distribution in the vertical plane parallel to the road axis as these are approximately the directions in which a lantern is seen by a motorist. Investigations have indicated that the light from low pressure sodium lamps is less glaring than that from mercury lamps and higher intensities above the beam are permitted when these lamps are used (SCO(S) in Table 32.3) but this relaxation is likely to be changed.

Finally, with a view to improving road surface luminance uniformity, there are limitations on intensities for angles up to 30° from the downward vertical. Wide limits are permitted for the value of the intensity ratio in this zone, but there is the proviso that it shall not exceed 80% of the peak intensity ratio.

It is probable that the next revision of this section of the specification will change the basis of intensity specification from intensity ratio to intensity per 1000 lm lamp output (cd/klm) to simplify the testing of groups of lanterns for compliance.

An amendment to BS 1788 in 1969 added a light distribution specification for Group B1 lanterns—the beam to contain the direction of 65° to the downward vertical, peak intensity to be not less than 110 cd/klm, intensities in the 0° to 30° zone not to exceed 0·8 times peak intensity, and the horizontal intensity not to exceed 100 cd/klm (150 cd/klm for sources of low luminance).

When a lantern is marked with the registered certification trade mark of the BSI, the *Kite Mark*, it is an assurance that the BSI is operating a system of supervision, control and testing during manufacture and that the lantern fully meets the requirements of the specification.

32.3.3   Lightly trafficked roads

CP 1004 Part 3 (1969) follows the Local Government Act of 1966 in its definition of Group B1 for lightly trafficked roads and Group B2 for footways. The Act made the Highway Authority responsible for Group B1 lighting.

Group B1 lighting is indicated where the road width and traffic do not justify Group A3 lighting and much of the benefit of the latter can be achieved with a less expensive installation.

Normally a mounting height of 5 m is used, but where the road width exceeds 8 m or lanterns are mounted on poles carrying overhead electric cables, and it is more economic, this may be increased to 6 m. Spacings of 33 m ± 10% and 40 m ± 10% are specified for 5 m and 6 m mounting heights respectively.

Instead of a range of lantern light output levels, target values are given, 3 klm or 5 klm for 5 m mounting height and 5 klm or 8 klm for 6 m. These values are total (not lower hemispherical) outputs for a clean lantern. This part of the code is not as realistic as others because there is no colour-corrected mercury lamp currently available which gives a 5 klm lantern output, only low pressure sodium lamps.

32.3.4   Junctions and roundabouts

CP 1004 Part 4 (1967) gives specific guidance on siting at road intersections, based on traffic flow patterns and the principles described above. The lantern directly in front of the traffic approaching the junction from the side road is particularly important so that the junction can be seen well in advance. The lantern should emit light in the direction of the side road but not so much as to be glaring.

In the lighting of a roundabout such lanterns are now omitted, because vehicles so often collided with them. Lanterns are placed round the outer perimeter, relying on the ring of lanterns to give warning of the roundabout in good time. Chevron screens are placed opposite the entry roads to promote visibility: lanterns on the outer perimeter are suitably placed to illuminate these. An average illuminance of about 20 lux is envisaged with nowhere along the kerb less than about 10 lux. On roundabouts the heads of the T-shaped bright patches are more important than the tails because of the shorter viewing distance when travelling round the island. Cut-off light distribution is indicated, except where approach roads are lit by semi-cut-off lanterns. Little is to be gained by changing the colour of the lamps to signal the presence of a roundabout island. An increasing number of roundabouts are being lit by one or more high mast units (Sect. 32.3.8).

32.3.5 Bridges and elevated roads

CP 1004 Part 6 indicates that elevated roads and many bridges can be lit by conventional traffic route lighting: the choice between pairs-opposite and central mounting is often determined by the structure. When there is a rise towards the centre, such as on a long bridge over a navigable river, a cut-off light distribution should be considered.

The more costly parapet lighting is sometimes used. The mounting height is usually below eye level, typically 1 m, and a high intensity beam is required at just below horizontal and across the road, with a rapid run-back above. Sometimes vertical louvres are used to reduce glare but these often aggravate flashing effects. Continuous lines of fluorescent tubes give the least uncomfortable lighting: separate compact sources are unpleasant and no advantage results from directing the beam diagonally following or towards traffic. This method is not suitable for roads wider than 12 m, and a light rough road surface with light parapets and central barrier is desirable when it is used. Performance is better when the road or bridge is curved in plan.

Bridges of architectural or historical interest need individual treatment such as specially designed lanterns mounted at 4 m or 5 m along the parapet or central reservation, or floodlight projectors on the structure or on masts at the ends.

32.3.6 Tunnels and underpasses

Short tunnels, which can be seen right through on approach, rarely need lighting by day or night as the length of darkened road is foreshortened in perspective.

If the length is less than 50 m or ten times the roof height, lighting by day is usually unnecessary. If a light well is provided near the centre, somewhat longer tunnels may be satisfactory without lighting. Lighting at night is not needed inside a tunnel if the traffic route lighting on the approaches illuminates all points on the road from both ends at not more than $75°$ incidence angle.

When daytime lighting is necessary, lighting of night-time standard in the entrance section is quite useless. The problems are the provision of adequate visibility when the approaching driver looks into the tunnel while still in sunlight and the maintenance of visibility as he passes beyond the entrance section to sections where, for reasons of cost, lighting is reduced.

Over a luminance range of 10 cd/m^2 to 100 cd/m^2, it has been found that if the luminance of a driver's general field of view does not fall by more than 50% within 3 s, he can see sufficiently well into a region where luminances are about 10% of those of his immediate surroundings.

In bright sunshine, luminances of 8 kcd/m^2 can occur and 800 cd/m^2 would be needed in the tunnel entrance, which would be exorbitant. High luminances on the approach can be avoided by the use of a dark road surface, a dark facade to the tunnel and the planting of trees. Wall and road luminances of 200 cd/m^2 and 100 cd/m^2 respectively will be then satisfactory.

525

Artificial lighting is not usually needed over the first 5 m because of daylight penetration, but beyond this a 50 m section of strong lighting is needed. For speeds up to 70 km/h the lighting can then be reduced by steps of 50% at the end of consecutive 50 m sections, until a luminance of about 5 cd/m^2 is reached. On a one-way tunnel this can extend to the exit but it is unnecessary to light the last 30 m to 40 m due to daylight penetration. A louvre system over the approach road can take the place of the initial section of strong lighting.

Full lighting is needed only in full daylight or sunlight. Luminances in the strong lighting sections can all be reduced by photoelectric cell control in steps (typically 200 cd/m^2, 50 cd/m^2, 12 cd/m^2, 3 cd/m^2) for night-time use.

Continuous lines of fluorescent luminaires are commonly used. These may be at the top of the walls in two-lane tunnels or centrally over the traffic lanes, one line to each lane. The latter probably gives the better lighting but the former may give easier access for maintenance. Light is projected mainly on the walls and road surface, the roof being left relatively dark. CP 1004 Part 7 gives guidance on simplified calculation methods appropriate for tunnel lighting.

32.3.7   Town centres

The aim should be to provide lighting which is outstanding compared with that of the approach roads, which can cater for heavy pedestrian traffic and which is suitable in appearance. In CP 1004 Part 9 (1969) two standards are envisaged for areas with vehicular traffic: Group G1 for thoroughfares of considerable importance, where at least 5 klm is provided per 100 m^2 of area to be lit, and Group G2 where at least 2·5 klm is provided.

There is a wide choice of lighting systems:

(a) Augmented Group A lighting (Fig. 32.4) with appropriate supplementary flood-lighting.
(b) Street lanterns or floodlights of a suitable type mounted on buildings (Fig. 32.5).
(c) High mast lighting.
(d) Large area, low luminance pole-top lanterns at 9 m to 15 m.

In all cases it is desirable that vertical surfaces are well lit to form bright backgrounds, and that footpaths are well lit.

In pedestrian and shopping precincts 20 lux should be provided on walking areas and 50 lux under canopies. The installations should be planned as part of the environment: where columns are used these will probably be of height 5 m to 6 m with symmetrical-distribution pole-top lanterns.

In public car parks a mean service illuminance of 20 lux should be provided, a mounting height of 10 m being most economical. Enclosed or multi-storey car parks need 50 lux mean service illuminance with 70 lux on ramps and corners: at entrances and exits 150 lux is needed by day.

Pedestrian subways up to 6 m wide can be lit by a single line of fittings along the ceiling or at the top of one wall, wider subways needing additional lines. A mean service illuminance of 100 lux should be provided with up to 200 lux on long or important subways, usually by recessed fluorescent luminaires.

526

Fig. 32.4 Conventional traffic route lighting (SON) augmented to suit important city road—
Charles Street, Leicester

Fig. 32.5 Wall mounted lighting (MBIL) in important city street—Princes Street, Edinburgh

32.3.8   High-mast lighting

This technique has become established for multilevel road complexes, city centre areas, motorway service areas, car parks, roundabouts, docks and industrial areas. It differs from high tower floodlighting in using slender, often elegant, masts (Fig. 32.6). Available mounting heights range from 20 m to 40 m, with three to six lanterns per mast, the lanterns being lowered for servicing.

Fig. 32.6   High mast lighting—approach to Clyde Tunnel

Cut-off, symmetrical-distribution lanterns are most commonly used but adjustable directional lighting with lamps of 24 klm and 36 klm is coming into use. In these the beam is at about 50° to the downward vertical, with a run-back to a low value by 70°. There is some oscillation at the top of the mast and highly directional light distributions are unsuitable.

With symmetrical-distribution lanterns, light utilization on the carriageway is low, but it is often considered that the lighting of the general surrounds is equally important, helping the motorist to relate the scene to advance-direction signs and his route plan. An important consideration is coverage of all parts of the area by more than one lantern, in case of lamp failure. Careful siting of the masts is important: they should be placed where there is least danger from vehicles running off the road.

32.3.9   Motorway lighting

The risk of an accident at night on an unlit motorway is about three times that by day, but lighting costs at least £8000 per km, and is only justified on the more heavily trafficked sections.

Lighting from columns on the central reservation is most economic, unless it requires substantial expenditure on guard rails that might not otherwise be incurred. Two arrangements used are the conventional twin bracket column with lanterns transverse to the road, and axial catenary with the lanterns strung at relatively close intervals along the central reservation. A cut-off distribution should be used with the conventional arrangement if low pressure sodium lamps are used, because the beam from these is substantially axial and there would be excessive build-up of luminance on the inner lanes. If compact light sources are used, the beam should be directed at an angle of between 20° and 40° from the road axis, and a semi-cut-off distribution with good glare control can be used. A mounting height of 12 m is required.

With the axial catenary system a transverse beam is used with low pressure sodium lamps at a spacing/mounting height ratio of about 1·5 : 1. With compact lamps a 20° to 40° toe-in beam can again be used with advantage at greater spacing. A mounting height of 10 m is common.

32.4 INTERNATIONAL RECOMMENDATIONS

Where there is less of a traffic problem than in UK the main requirement of street lighting is robust but inexpensive equipment which is easy to maintain: colour-corrected mercury discharge lamps in refractor bowl lanterns are used extensively. Codes become necessary where more sophisticated techniques are required, and therefore national codes are found in the more highly developed countries of the world.

The Australian and New Zealand codes are largely based on the British code, giving a similar recipe for a range of standards associated with a light distribution specification, but modified to suit local requirements.

The current American Standard Practice for Roadway Lighting recommends illuminance levels, classifies light distributions and gives detailed guidance on the choice of light distribution for different types of road. It has been adopted in Canada and many South American countries.

CIE Publication No. 12 (1965) 'International Recommendations for the Lighting of Public Thoroughfares' was intended for countries without a code but has been increasingly adopted by most countries other than the above, as a basis for a national code. These countries include those of Eastern Europe, the Middle East, Africa and Japan. The CIE recommendations are based on European cut-off lighting practice, although semi-cut-off and non-cut-off distributions are described. They indicate target levels of average luminance and uniformity for dry road conditions, and give guidance on the design of installations to achieve these targets and to control glare.

Public thoroughfares. The CIE recommendations are summarized in Table 32.4. The mean levels of luminance are service values and the design value should be 30% more. Good luminance uniformity is realized when in the roadway lying between 60 m and 150 m ahead the minimum luminance is not less than 0·4 times the average luminance. Very good luminance uniformity has been discussed in terms of the luminance gradient along and across the road, but has not yet been defined.

Mounting heights of 8 m, 10 m and 12 m are recommended, the latter for wide roads and powerful light sources. Guidance on the illuminance required for the production of

Table 32.4   International recommendations and guidance

(a) Requirements

Class of lighting instal- lation	Types of road		Luminance of dry road surface		Glare	Types of luminaire	
			Mean cd/m²	Uniformity		Preferred	Permitted
A1	Motorways (when lit)		2	Very good	Strictly reduced	Cut-off	Semi-cut-off
A1	Rural roads	Heavy traffic			Strictly reduced	Cut-off	Semi-cut-off
A2	Rural roads	Considerable traffic	1	Good	Strictly reduced	Cut-off	Semi-cut-off
—		Light traffic	Unlit				
A1	Urban roads	Through ways and by-passes	2	Very good	Reduced	Cut-off	Semi-cut-off
B1	Urban roads	Principal local traffic routes	1	Good	Moderate	Cut-off or semi-cut-off	Non-cut-off
B2	Urban roads	Secondary roads with local traffic	0·5	Satisfactory	Moderate	Cut-off or semi-cut-off	Non-cut-off

(b) Means of achieving the requirements

Type of light dis- tribution	Angle of peak intensity to downward vertical	Maximum intensity, candelas per 1000 lm from lamp		Maximum spacing in terms of mounting height†	Light flux required lux per cd/m²	
		At 90° to D.V.	At 80° to D.V.		Road surface	
					Light	Dark
Cut-off	0° to 65°	10*	30	3	12	24
Semi-cut-off	0° to 75°	50*	100	3·5	9	18
Non-cut-off	—	—*	—	4	7	15

* But never more than 1000 cd for any value of lamp output.
† Mounting height 8 m or 10 m, or 12 m for wide roads or high light output.

the recommended luminance is given for dark road surfaces (reflectances up to 0·15) and light road surfaces (reflectances above 0·15). It will be seen that non-cut-off and semi-cut-off distributions are rated more effective in producing luminance than is a cut-off distribution, but this is a generalization more valid with smooth surfaces.

The restriction on lantern intensity in certain directions for glare control, and the guidance given on the production of road luminance, are regarded as provisional and work has continued with a view to getting a more precise system.

Motorways.   Draft recommendations, in more detail than the general targets of Publication No. 12, are at an advanced stage and should be published in 1972. Cut-off lighting to produce an average service luminance of 2 cd/m² is recommended, with a high degree of uniformity. It is envisaged that colour-corrected mercury or low pressure sodium lamps will be used, and later high pressure sodium lamps. The economy of central mounting is recognized, but this is considered more inconvenient for access than the alternative of lines of lanterns along the outer verges, the latter being recommended for wide carriageways. Axial catenary lighting is recommended for good visual guidance and also as being economic in total running cost. Lighting from continuous lines at about 1 m height and along the outer verges is discussed: this has good appearance but is subject to heavy dirt depreciation and vandalism. Coverage of more than 12 m to 15 m width is difficult by this method and the expense is quoted as being 5 to 10 times that for conventional lighting.

Side lighting is recommended for access lanes, the mounting height depending on road width, but more than 15 m is not recommended because of cost. A spacing of 3 times mounting height is suggested, with a cut-off light distribution.

Tunnels. Again the draft recommendations are at an advanced stage and it is hoped they will be published in 1972.

Luminance in the entrance zone should be one tenth of that of the approach zone, or better, to avoid the 'black hole' effect. The tunnel entrance should be as high as possible to improve adaptation conditions. Within the entrance zone, 50 m in length when there is a speed limit otherwise 75 m to 100 m long, luminance must be constant: by day, non-cut-off lanterns can be used here to give visual guidance to approaching drivers. At the end of the entrance zone, luminance can be dropped in 3:1 steps according to a specified curve, to a daytime level of $10 \, cd/m^2$, or $5 \, cd/m^2$ for long lightly-trafficked tunnels. The lighting should be in continuous lines: if not, the gaps should be less than 1 m or greater than 10 m to avoid flicker effects. Luminances at night should be reduced to between $2 \, cd/m^2$ and $5 \, cd/m^2$ but not more than three times the approach road luminance. At least 200 m of the approach and exit road should be lit. The tunnel lighting recommendations are much more detailed than those of the corresponding part of the British code, but standards are much the same.

Although ideas may differ on design methods, and different light distributions are used, the standards of performance of new British and overseas public lighting installations are broadly comparable. In spite of the age of some urban installations, the overall standard of street lighting in Britain is by and large unmatched in any comparable area, as of course it should be with our traffic and population density.

33 Floodlighting

The general term 'floodlighting' defies precise definition as it is used widely by experts and laymen to describe any lighting which is not general interior illumination. Fortunately, definition is also unnecessary as this wide usage leads to no serious misunderstanding. This chapter is concerned with all forms of exterior lighting (excluding the substance of the last two chapters) which are intended to raise the luminosity of a surface or an object considerably beyond that of its surroundings. For some reason, the attitude towards floodlighting in this country is that it represents wanton extravagance. This is difficult to explain as there is hardly a form of floodlighting which does not represent a financial gain in one form or another.

33.1 APPLICATIONS AND PRINCIPLES

33.1.1 Applications

Floodlighting can be divided into three broad groups: industrial, commercial and recreational.

Industrial. This includes all areas where a visual task must be executed outdoors after dark: docks, marshalling yards, cargo terminals, airports, storage areas, civil engineering and building sites. Apart from allowing work to continue efficiently the lighting has an amenity value for pedestrian and vehicular traffic in both industrial and public areas. Good lighting also increases safety, and accident prevention can be a vital factor in maintaining production. There are also the security aspects where lighting acts as an effective deterrent to the thief and the vandal.

Commercial. Floodlighting also acts as a sales aid, whether the selling is direct, as in the case of petrol stations, used car lots and garden centres, or indirect as with advertising hoardings, office blocks and factories. As the expression of civic pride, floodlighting of historic buildings and town centres attracts visitors and tourists. Few holiday resorts exploit the possibility of modern floodlighting to the full and in most of our principal towns and cities effective installations are conspicuous by their absence.

Recreational. As with some of the other applications already mentioned, the lighting of parks and gardens gives scope for decorative effects with a combination of conventional floodlights and possibly street lighting equipment. Not all recreational floodlighting applications are decorative: there is now an increasing demand to extend the utilization of municipal and private sports facilities such as tennis courts, bowling and putting greens and golf courses. Many of these installations can be self-financing by the use of coin-in-the-slot meters. Soccer, rugby, hockey and all-weather playing areas can all be used after

532

dark with economical floodlighting systems. In fact any outdoor sport can be carried out under floodlights. For practice, training and recreational play, low illuminance values are sufficient, but higher values are required for tournament or competition play: with the new light sources now available even the exacting requirements of outside broadcast television in colour can be satisfied.

33.1.2 Lighting requirements

Mainly because it is easier to calculate, recommendations for illuminance values for floodlighting are usually given in the horizontal plane. The purpose of most area flood-lighting, however, is to make the vertical surfaces of objects clearly visible. For golf-driving and skeet shooting ranges, horizontal illumination becomes entirely meaningless as the observer requires only to see the flight of the ball or the target, and to do this it is only necessary to light the surface of the projectile towards the observer.

The designer must be aware of the importance of the vertical component and the ratio of horizontal to vertical plane illuminance provided by different systems. This is not too difficult to predict: if the angle of incidence at the surface is less than 45° then the proportion of illuminance on a plane at right angles to the surface will be low, whereas if the angle is greater than 45° then the proportion of vertical illuminance will be high. There is, however, a limiting factor in this. As the mounting heights become lower or the aiming angle of the floodlights increases, giving an increased vertical component, so glare can become a problem. Where there is excessive glare, light is usually being wasted, because

Table 33.1   Guide to illuminance requirements for area lighting

Illuminance range	Critical plane	Applications
1–10 lux	Horizontal	General amenity. Building and civil engineering sites. Docks. Cargo terminals. Marshalling yards. Storage areas.
	Vertical	Security. Casual night training for sports.
10–50 lux	Horizontal	Storage areas. Car parks. Non-critical working areas.
	Vertical	Aircraft aprons.
50–100 lux	Horizontal	Critical working areas. Sports practice. Recreational sports. Playgrounds.
	Vertical	Golf driving ranges. Aircraft service areas.
100–500 lux	Horizontal	Club and tournament sports. Advertising hoardings on unlit roads. Swimming pools. Car parks. Sales areas.
	Vertical	Spectator sports. Garage forecourts. Used car lots. Closed-circuit television security.
500–1000 lux	Horizontal	Advertising hoardings on lit roads. Town centres.
	Vertical	Sports lighting for colour television.

the flux at high angles rarely lights the area involved and the glare produced reduces the visual efficiency of the observer.

The diversity of illuminance for colour television or other critical applications should be better than 5:1, but usually a variation of 10:1 is visually acceptable and 20:1 or more for general area lighting is permissible. In some cases a deliberate fall-off is required and this would usually need to be of the order of 20:1 to be recognized as such. Smaller changes in illuminance will be more obvious on plain matt light-coloured surfaces than on dark, heavily-textured or patterned surfaces. Variations in the vertical illuminance on objects standing on, or moving across a surface are difficult to detect.

Table 33.1 gives a guide to illuminance requirements in critical planes for area lighting.

Although floodlighting requirements are generally specified in terms of illuminance, the eye in fact responds to luminosity or luminance patterns in the field of view. This is particularly significant in the case of building floodlighting. Table 33.2, based on IES Technical Report No. 6, shows the range of minimum average illuminance recommended for different surfaces. These values are dependent on the luminance required to make the building stand out from its surroundings or the 'district brightness'.

Table 33.2 Recommended illuminance values for building floodlighting

Based on reflectance for *white* light. When using coloured sources on areas of similar colour, such as sodium lamps for yellow brick, plan for 70%–50% of recommended illuminance. Values in lux.

Material	Condition	Low district brightness	Medium district brightness	High district brightness
White brick	Clean	15	25	40
	Fairly clean	20	35	60
	Fairly dirty	45	75	120
Portland stone	Clean	20	35	60
	Fairly clean	35	55	90
	Fairly dirty	65	110	180
Concrete	Clean	30	50	80
	Fairly clean	45	75	120
	Fairly dirty	90	150	240
Middle stone	Clean	35	55	90
	Fairly clean	50	90	140
	Fairly dirty	100	180	280
Dark stone	Clean	40	60	100
	Fairly clean	55	90	150
	Fairly dirty	110	180	300
Yellow brick	Clean	45	75	120
	Fairly clean	65	110	180
	Fairly dirty	130	220	360
Red brick	Clean	55	90	150
	Fairly clean	80	140	230
	Fairly dirty	160	280	450

33.1.3 Surface characteristics

The response of a surface to incident light, as well as being affected by colour and cleanliness, is also dependent on whether the surface is matt or specular, heavily textured or patterned.

Specular surfaces such as glass, gold leaf, aluminium, stainless steel, mosaic, glazed bricks and tiles present particular difficulties for floodlighting. In daylight the main source of light is from above the building so that specular reflections are projected downwards towards the eye of the observer: as a result these materials appear to sparkle and shine. When floodlights are installed at ground level the direction of light is reversed and the specularly-reflected component is now directed into the sky and away from the observer: the surfaces now look dull and lifeless and the building loses an essential element of its daytime appearance.

The spire on the building in Fig. 33.1 is covered with gold leaf and to give it an effective floodlit appearance it was designed with horizontal ribs to direct the light of the floodlights downwards. With all specular surfaces it is important to remember that the luminosity will depend on the source luminance rather than the illuminance, as well as varying with the direction of view.

Whatever the reflection characteristics of the surface may be, it is important to remember that floodlighting cannot duplicate the daytime appearance of a building or an object, as the main direction of light is usually reversed and the diffused component from the sky cannot be faithfully imitated. The best decorative floodlighting installations are those which exploit these differences rather than try to minimize them. For industrial and other types of strictly functional floodlighting the change between the natural and artificial lighting condition need not be a disadvantage. Sports floodlighting tends to concentrate the attention of the spectators on the area of play; carefully positioned projectors on a building site or refinery can increase visual awareness; the rails in a marshalling yard are clearly visible due to specular reflections although the illuminance level may be very low. On the other hand the edges of a dock or curb stones may be made more visible by painting them white rather than installing additional floodlights.

33.2 FLOODLIGHTING TECHNIQUES

33.2.1 Industrial floodlighting

Area lighting. There are two basic approaches to area lighting which can be differentiated by the intensity distribution provided by the luminaires. A generally downward distribution can be used in areas where obstruction from storage stacks and closely-parked vehicles must be minimized and where high values of vertical illuminance are not required. The second method uses projector floodlights on widely spaced poles or towers: a high vertical illuminance is provided but glare is sometimes a problem.

The luminaires used in the first case are mainly street lighting lanterns which perform a valid area-lighting function. Low wattage lanterns are used at heights of 5 m, intermediate wattages for up to 10 m and 1000 W units at heights of up to 40 m. The spacing of poles should not generally exceed three times the mounting height. Depending on the illuminance required, the highest possible wattage and mounting height usually provides the most economical solution for this type of installation.

Installations using projectors can be sub-divided again into rectangular areas, lit from the side using floodlights at heights of 15 m to 30 m with fan-shaped beams, and regular or irregular-shaped areas lit with symmetrical projectors on 25 m to 60 m towers mounted at the corners or within the area itself. Where areas are lit only from one side the depth of the area should not exceed five times the mounting height. Where bi-directional lighting is used, a spacing/mounting height ratio of 7:1 is acceptable. With side lighting using fan-shaped beam floodlights the lateral spacing should not exceed 3:1 and in cases where good diversity is essential 1·5:1 is preferred. Using symmetrical projectors with omnidirectional aiming of the luminaires on the headframes, a general spacing/mounting height of 7:1 in all directions is acceptable, provided all parts of the area receive light from at least two towers.

Exterior working areas.   In these areas, the floodlighting is usually designed to provide a low level of amenity lighting (Table 33.1) which is supplemented in specific areas to allow more exacting visual tasks to be carried out. The direction of the light is often important. It is usually convenient to mount the lighting towers or poles at the perimeter to avoid plant, machinery and vehicles within the working area.

Docks.   The dockside, where loading and unloading is carried out, is the most critical area, requiring a horizontal illuminance of 30 lux to 50 lux. Additional floodlights on crane jibs are often required to light the holds of ships. The remaining areas must be lit to enable heavy goods vehicles to manoeuvre safely. Large warehouse buildings can provide suitable mounting positions but they can also cause serious light obstruction, and mounting positions must be chosen carefully to avoid this. High masts and tower systems can also be used. The full range of tungsten and discharge lamps finds an application in dock lighting although colour requirements sometimes preclude the use of low pressure sodium lamps. The salt-laden atmosphere makes corrosion-resistant luminaires essential. Due allowance should also be made for atmospheric losses due to the misty conditions and air pollution.

Marshalling yards.   A low value of amenity lighting (5 lux to 10 lux) is generally provided from high towers with symmetrical projectors aimed omnidirectionally. Higher illuminances (20 lux to 50 lux) are provided in main working areas. Some tower sites within the area itself are required so that the floodlights can be aimed down the lines of trucks to minimize obstruction. Tungsten and discharge lamps are used and allowance for atmospheric losses and corrosive pollution should be made. Street lighting lanterns at lower mounting heights are used for smaller sidings and goods yards.

Oil refineries, tank farms and chemical plants.   These are generally classed as hazardous areas and all local lighting equipment must be in Division II or flameproof classes to suit the particular conditions. In view of this it is often preferable to provide general lighting of the area from projector floodlights on high towers which are outside the hazardous area. Due to the complicated form of the plant some local lighting is still required to relieve local light obstruction. Chemical plants have the added problem of considerable atmospheric absorption and pollution.

Building sites.   For large civil engineering projects, semi-permanent high-tower installations can be considered: floodlights with a wide fan-shaped distribution are preferred as these require less critical aiming than narrow-beam projectors. On building sites the lighting equipment is frequently moved as the building progresses, in which case robust lightweight tungsten halogen luminaires are favoured. Where safety requirements dictate, 110/120 V 500 W tungsten halogen lamps are available.

Security lighting. All the forms of area lighting discussed previously can also serve as security lighting, as a well-lit area has an understandably deterrent effect on the criminal. An intruder under security lighting will be more visible if the defenders see him illuminated against a dark background or in silhouette against a light background. Where the security system includes closed-circuit television the luminance of the vertical surfaces is the critical factor. Most camera systems will function adequately with a general field luminance of $60\,cd/m^2$.

Car parks. Any of the basic area lighting techniques can be used in these areas depending on local conditions and requirements. Low values of illuminance are sufficient in large industrial and municipal car parks (Sect. 32.3.7). Car parks associated with commercial establishments should be well illuminated in order to advertise the presence of the building and encourage passing motorists to pull in.

33.2.2 Commercial floodlighting

Building floodlighting. As with most things which involve aesthetic appreciation it is impossible to lay down hard and fast rules, but the following suggestions should be followed unless there are good reasons for not doing so:

(a) The appearance of the scene should be considered as a whole: areas of shade are just as important as highlights.
(b) The floodlights should be positioned to give a coherent flow of light and the main direction of light should not coincide with the main direction of view.
(c) Important parts of the building such as the roof line should be lit and the base of the building is also important unless a floating effect is required. In towns, the street lighting or even the interior lighting of the building can perform this function without additional floodlights (Fig. 33.1). End walls should be lit to give solidity to the building: these can be treated differently from the main face by providing colour or brightness contrast.
(d) Vertical features such as columns, towers and steeples will appear flat if equally illuminated from all directions.
(e) The random use of blinds and interior lighting is generally undesirable but it is very difficult to avoid in practice. Used deliberately, they can indicate a part of a building which cannot be lit externally.
(f) It is not necessary to achieve even lighting over the whole surface of a building: in fact a gradual fall-off can be used to accentuate height. If this effect is not required, light picked up by a projecting coping provides a clearly defined edge to the building and gives the impression of even lighting. Even the excessive diversity created by close offset floodlighting, where the floodlights are fixed to the face of the building, can be effective with spacings five to six times the offset distance, provided the windows or other dominant architectural features occur between the floodlights.

(g) Use should be made of special features such as trees, statues and fountains and these should be lighted in colour, seen in silhouette or used to produce shadows on the building: strong back-lighting of pinnacles or arches can be very effective.

(h) Lighting equipment should not be visible from any normal viewing direction, neither should their positions be betrayed by the presence of bright patches on the surface of the building.

Sales areas.   The primary requirement of such lighting is that it should arrest the attention of passers-by. Illumination of vertical surfaces is of prime importance, the amount required depending on the district brightness. The required impact is often achieved by using light sources of a different colour to the local street lighting. At the same time the source must provide suitable colour rendering of any merchandise. Sales areas are invariably situated on main roads in which case the floodlights must not cause glare to passing traffic.

Petrol filling stations.   Although the lighting on the forecourt must be adequate it is the vertical luminosity of the buildings which is seen from the roads. The colour of the light is important and low pressure sodium lamps are not recommended for lighting any point where money changes hands. All lighting equipment will need to satisfy the local Petroleum Officer.

Used car lots.   Strong front lighting is the main requirement here, providing very high values of illuminance relative to the district brightness. Tungsten halogen sources are generally preferred for the sparkle they provide to chrome and paint work. Some additional lighting at the rear of deep sites is also required.

Garden centres and nurseries.   The approach here is similar to parks and gardens, but since they are sales areas, a higher illuminance is justified. In stock areas an illuminance as low as 5 lux is adequate to allow customers to select plants. Colour rendering is important except where decorative colour effects are required.

Advertising hoardings.   The illuminance required depends on district brightness (Table 33.1). The colour rendering of the source is important and generally tungsten halogen lamps are the most suitable. Depending on site conditions and the illuminance requirements, these can be mounted at close offset distances at the top or the bottom of the hoarding or a single unit can be used at a greater offset.

33.2.3   Recreational floodlighting

Sports lighting.   It is necessary to analyse the visual requirements of each sport. For example, it is only strictly necessary for the archer to see the target, but for safety some general amenity lighting should be provided between the firing point and the target. In a large stadium the distance between the farthest spectator and the players is greater and therefore higher illuminance values are required. Neither club tennis nor bowls have a large spectator following but the fast-moving ball in tennis justifies higher illuminance levels. Where discharge lamps are used the equipment should be balanced over three phases, otherwise distracting stroboscopic effects may be produced.

Floodlighting for training or practice. Soccer or rugby practice pitches and all-weather games areas are quite satisfactory with a horizontal illuminance of 30 lux to 50 lux. Night training for these games and for athletics can be carried out successfully over a limited area from a single-side layout with mounting heights of 4 m to 5 m and illuminance values of only 5 lux.

Club and tournament sports areas and playgrounds. With higher standards of competitive play or where there needs to be a degree of supervision, horizontal illuminance values of at least 100 lux are required. Side-mounted area floodlighting techniques with luminaires providing fan-shaped beams from tungsten halogen or discharge lamps at a mounting height of 6 m or more are suitable. Where sports areas have spectator facilities, illuminance values of up to 500 lux are required, and glare control to the spectator areas becomes important: minimum mounting heights of 10 m are recommended.

Outdoor swimming pools. Area floodlighting techniques are required here using symmetrical post-top street lighting luminaires within the area or fan-shaped beam projectors at the perimeter. Tungsten filament lamps are preferred for pleasant colour rendering of flesh tones. Underwater lighting can be very effective, but floodlights submerged in the pool can be a hazard to swimmers and difficult to maintain: a low voltage supply is essential. Mains voltage projectors aimed through sealed ports in the side of the pool can be maintained from the pool side without draining. With either system an electrical loading of 50 W per square metre of pool area should be allowed.

Stadium floodlighting. For first-class grounds a system using four towers has become accepted practice: it gives minimum glare to spectators and players. The only disadvantage of this system is a high capital cost. Less expensive sidelighting systems are popular with smaller grounds: these usually employ eight 12 m to 20 m towers arranged along the sides of the ground, each carrying floodlights with linear filament or discharge lamps. A number of these installations use 1500 W tungsten halogen floodlights with a total of six or sometimes eight floodlights on each tower. Two 1600 W metal halide lamps per tower will provide similar results at lower cost: the quality of light is good, but glare is increased.

Colour television requirements. Table 33.3 shows a range of illuminance values against lens aperture, which defines picture quality: illuminances are measured normal to the camera lens axis. The lower illuminances quoted only allow for the use of wide-angle

Table 33.3 Colour television illuminance requirements (lux)

Picture quality	f2	f2·8	f4	f5·6
Studio quality	370	750	1500	3000
Acceptable for outside broadcasts	250	500	1000	2000
Poor quality, only just acceptable	180	370	750	1500

lenses: with higher values, telephoto shots with a reasonable depth of field become possible. The lower illuminance values also result in other picture quality problems for the television engineer.

The current BBC specification calls for average values of 800 lux to 1400 lux, which are intended to produce acceptable to excellent picture quality with a full use of zoom lenses. Allowance is made in these values for atmospheric losses in bad weather conditions. The illuminance quoted is measured towards the camera, but if a similar value is not available as a back-light, the pictures tend to be flat and lifeless. In the case of televised sporting events where the camera positions are not limited to one side of the stadium, as they are in football, the illuminance values quoted should be available towards all camera positions. The average illuminance on the front spectators should be one-third of the pitch illuminance.

Both high corner tower and sidelighting systems using metal halide lamps have been found suitable. The 1000 W compact source iodide lamp mounted in a PAR 64 sealed beam unit has been found particularly suitable for corner towers (Fig. 33.2) due to its excellent colour and light control characteristics. The compact size of the equipment allows it to be mounted on most existing tower structures to provide the maximum colour television requirement. For sidelighting, metal halide lamps from 1600 W to 10 kW have been used. Small lightweight floodlights to house the lower wattage lamps have a number of practical and economic advantages: by using a 1600 W unjacketed MBIL lamp in a luminaire providing an asymmetrical fan-shaped distribution the glare associated with sidelighting systems has been largely overcome (Fig. 33.3). There are greater lens flare problems for the cameras with this type of system but the lower initial cost makes it very attractive.

Decorative lighting of parks and gardens.   As with building floodlighting, it is difficult to lay down hard and fast rules, but the following general principles can be applied to good effect:

(a) No attempt should be made to floodlight everything. The main features should be selected and, where possible, visitors should follow a set route so that the lighted scene is revealed as a sequence of set pieces.

(b) The direction and colour of lighting should be chosen to enhance the appearance of trees or shrubs. Conifers only respond when strongly lit and are therefore frequently best treated in silhouette. On the other hand the copper-beech, beech, silver birch, willow and oak all respond well to floodlighting.

(c) Still water will not respond to direct lighting but should be used to mirror the floodlighting of bridges and trees or buildings at the water's edge. Waterfalls and fountains can be treated very effectively but since light is carried through the stream of water, lamps should be positioned just below the water level, either surrounding the jets or at the point where the cascade re-enters the water. Although some large waterfalls respond to front lighting the effect of direct lighting on to cascades from remote projectors is generally disappointing. Any luminaires submerged in water must, of course, be specifically designed for this application.

(d) Main pathways can be effectively illuminated by low wattage street lighting fittings on 4m to 5m columns. These columns can also be used to support 150 W PAR reflector lamps light flower beds and small shrubs. The use of these lamps at ground level among flowers and shrubs can also be very effective.

(e) All floodlighting equipment should be concealed from view both by night and day. Lighting equipment strapped to the boughs and the trunks of trees usually looks unsightly.

(f) Festoons of coloured lamps provide an atmosphere of carnival and are particularly effective when reflected in water. They can rarely produce an air of tranquillity or enhance the grandeur of nature and their use should therefore be tempered with restraint.

33.3   CALCULATION TECHNIQUES

Once the lighting requirements have been decided, floodlighting design falls into three stages. Firstly a practical assessment is made of where to locate the floodlights, the light distribution required, and the light source characteristics which suit the particular application. Secondly, a 'lumen calculation' is carried out to establish the number and the loading of the luminaires to achieve the design objectives. Thirdly, 'point-by-point calculations' are performed to determine the precise aiming of the floodlights to give a stated illuminance diversity: this in turn may necessitate slight modifications to the preliminary calculation.

The photometric performance of a floodlight can be represented in a large number of ways as no one form of data presentation suits all types of light distribution or calculation procedures.

One factor which can affect the final illuminance value in an installation is the atmospheric loss caused by airborne smoke, fog, etc. This will vary with the time of day and the season, as well as location, and needs to be taken into account when setting design values of illuminance.

33.3.1   Basic photometric data

The simplest form of photometric data indicates the width of the beam produced by a floodlight and the total flux within the beam.

The beam width or spread is most commonly referred to as 'beam angle' which is defined by the total angle over which the intensity drops to 0·1 of the peak value. For a symmetrical distribution one figure is quoted, for example 60° (or 2 × 30°). For asymmetric distributions the angles in the vertical and horizontal planes are given, for example: vertical 40°/horizontal 100°. In the case of floodlights giving a double asymmetric distribution the angle above and below peak are quoted in the vertical plane, for example: vertical above peak 10°, below peak 30°/horizontal 100°, or vertical 10° + 30°/horizontal 2 × 50°.

Beam flux is the figure of total flux contained within the beam angle. This can also be given as a beam factor, which is the proportion of lamp lumens contained within the beam. This data can be presented compactly in tabular form, including additional data such as peak intensity and the cut-off angles for the floodlight together with lamp performance data. Fig. 33.4 shows the data for a typical range of floodlights.

Lamp type	Lamp power (W)	Lamp flux (lm)	Beam angle to $\frac{1}{10}$ peak — Vertical Above peak	Below peak	Hor.	Beam angle to $\frac{1}{2}$ peak — Vertical Above peak	Below peak	Hor.	Beam flux (lm)	Beam factor	Peak intensity (cd)	Angle to cut off — Vertical Above peak	Below peak	Hor.
A. Symmetrical														
(i) GLS	500	7 700	34°			12°			2000	0·26	25 500	152°		
(ii) B2 proj	500	7 250	16°			8°			2100	0·29	95 000	148°		
(iii) MBF	400	21 500	56°			10°			7950	0·37	44 000	158°		
(iv) MBF	250	12 000	58°			22°			6480	0·54	26 500	156°		
B. Double asymmetric														
(i) Tung-	500	10 500	27°	32°	74°	6°	8°	44°	4 400	0·42	17 400	42°	49°	94°
(ii) sten	500	10 500	39°	48°	82°	18°	23°	50°	5 180	0·55	7 730	90°	90°	180°
(iii) halo-	1500	33 000	24°	30°	100°	5°	8°	68°	17 500	0·53	60 000	49°	53°	132°
(iv) gen	1500	33 000	37°	51°	112°	11°	16°	72°	22 100	0·67	34 000	90°	90°	180°
C. Double asymmetric														
(i) MBF	400	21 500	55°	84°	146°	32°	43°	75°	9 950	0·46	4 650	78°	108°	192°
(ii) MBIF	400	27 000	52°	88°	152°	28°	42°	60°	18 500	0·68	8 700	78°	130°	220°
D. Asymmetric			Vertical		Hor.	Vertical		Hor.				Vertical		Hor.
SLI	200	25 000	102°		138°	34°		102°	10 000	0·4	12 200	154°		166°

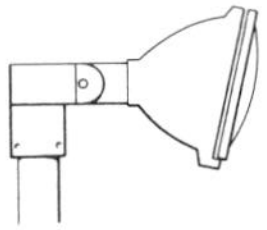

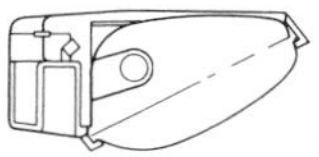

Fig. 33.4 Floodlight photometric data

544

Example to show the use of basic photometric data. It is required to illuminate the face of a warehouse 6 m high and 12 m long for security purposes from an existing pole 6 m away (Fig. 33.5a).

(a) The floodlight is located on the existing pole 3 m above the ground, in line with the centre of the building.
(b) The maximum angle subtended by the building at the floodlight is determined by drawing or by calculation.

$$\alpha = 2(\tan^{-1} 1\cdot0) = 2 \times 45° = 90°$$
$$\phi = 2(\tan^{-1} 0\cdot5) = 2 \times 27° = 54°$$

(c) From Fig. 33.4, floodlight type B(iii) has the required beam angles.
(d) The average illuminance is determined from the formula

$$E = \frac{\text{lamp lumens} \times \text{beam factor} \times \text{maintenance factor} \times \text{waste light factor}}{\text{area}}$$

$$= \frac{33\,000 \times 0\cdot53 \times 0\cdot9 \times 1\cdot0}{12 \times 6} = 220 \text{ lux}$$

The maintenance factor will depend on the local conditions and cleaning cycle: in this case it has been assumed that the lantern is operating in a fairly clean area or will be cleaned regularly. The waste light will be negligible.

The illuminance provided would enable security surveillance by closed-circuit television: if this is not required a lower illuminance could be provided by using two

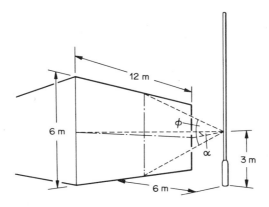

Fig. 33.5 Security lighting (a) Building geometry

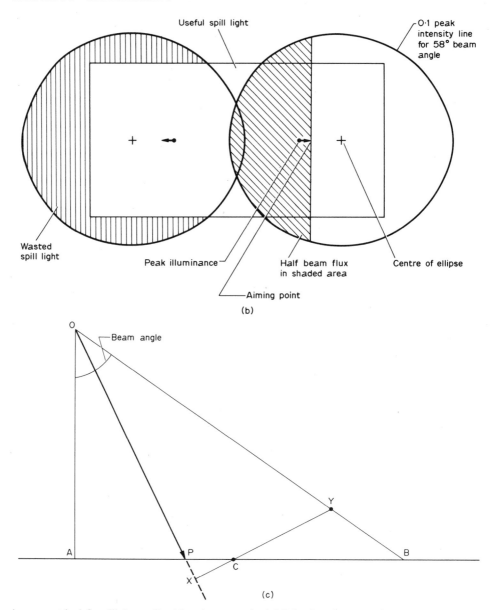

Fig. 33.5 Security lighting (b) Overlapping elliptical beams (c) Construction for finding ellipse axes

A symmetrical floodlight at O with a beam angle AOB is aimed at a surface so that the peak intensity at the centre of the beam reaches the surface at an angle OPA, which is less than 90°. The major axis of the elliptical area covered by the beam is length AB. Half the length of the minor axis is represented by a line XY which passes through the bisection of AB at C and is perpendicular to the extension of OP

546

floodlights of type A(iv) (Fig. 33.4). These would be aimed at the centre of each half of the building: Fig. 33.5b shows the coverage that would be achieved.

The average illuminance would be

$$\frac{2 \times 12\,000 \times 0.54 \times 0.9 \times 0.7}{12 \times 6} = 110 \text{ lux}$$

Fig. 33.5c shows a graphical method of determining the size of the ellipse produced by the beam. It should be noted that when a symmetrical floodlight is aimed other than normal to the surface the 0.1 peak isocandela line forms an ellipse and is not a line of equal illuminance. The centre of the ellipse moves away from the aiming point (or the main axis of the lantern) while the value of peak illuminance moves in the opposite direction.

In this example, when estimating the waste light, it should be remembered that half the beam flux is concentrated in 30% of the elliptical area shown shaded on the figure. Illuminance in the two central triangular areas will result from spill light outside the beam: in fact the illuminance here will be higher than at the extreme corners of the area.

33.3.2 Intensity distribution, isolux and zonal flux diagrams

Intensity distribution diagrams.   As has been stated in Sect. 5.1.1, intensity distribution diagrams in one plane are sufficient to define the photometric characteristics of symmetrical luminaires, but for asymmetric distributions diagrams in at least two planes are required. These may be given in cartesian coordinates for floodlights, and with these data it is possible to apply the inverse square and cosine laws for calculating point illuminance values.

Isolux diagrams.   Isolux diagrams can be used to show the variation of horizontal illuminance over the area illuminated by a floodlight at a specific mounting height. When more than one luminaire is used, diagrams can be superimposed to obtain the total illuminance. For different mounting heights but similar aiming angles, correction factors can be applied.

Zonal flux diagrams.   The need to calculate isolux diagrams for a whole range of aiming angles is a serious limitation even when the technique of adjusting for different mounting heights has been mastered. It is also usual to require information on the average horizontal illuminance achieved from a floodlighting design and this can only be obtained with difficulty from the type of data presented so far in this section. The zonal flux diagram is more adaptable as it allows any aiming angle in elevation to be investigated at will and it can be used at any mounting height without conversion factors.

A typical diagram is shown in Fig. 33.6a. This is divided through the plane of symmetry for the luminaire, with isocandela lines plotted on the angular grid on the left-hand-side, and figures indicating the total flux in each angular zone on the right. These angular zones are the zones referred to in Sect. 5.2.1, subdivided in azimuth. The diagram can be used to give either point values of illuminance or the total flux intercepted by the area to be lit.

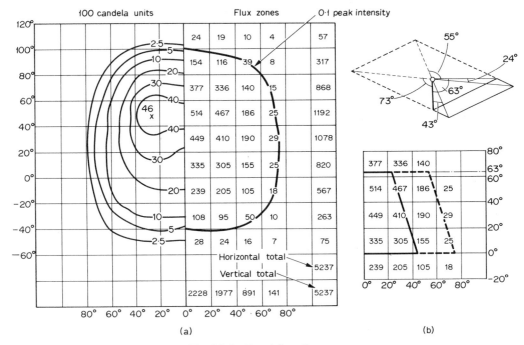

Fig. 33.6   Zonal flux diagrams

The sum of the flux values shown gives half the total light output of the floodlight and this should be doubled to take account of the flux from the other half of the diagram. The value of the total beam lumens is the sum of the flux within the single line which indicates the isocandela value of 0·1 peak intensity.

Any area to be illuminated can be drawn on the zonal flux diagrams using the same angular scale (Fig. 33.6b). Once the overlay showing the area is drawn, it can be moved up and down the vertical 0° grid line to account for elevational adjustments of the floodlight. It is necessary to redraw the overlay if the fitting aim is adjusted in azimuth.

33.3.3   Equal-area zenithal web

This has been introduced in Sect. 5.1.1 as a means of displaying the intensity distribution of an asymmetrical luminaire by isocandela contours. If the aiming point of a floodlight is taken as 90° in azimuth, the effect of tilting the lantern can be represented by a rotation of the isocandela contours around the centre of the diagram. This is a very useful characteristic for installation design, best illustrated by an example.

Example.   An all-weather sports area 86 m × 48 m is to be illuminated by floodlights mounted on six 18 m poles, three on each side at 30 m centres, 8 m back from the area (Fig. 33.7); the average horizontal illuminance is to be 100 lux.

There is little point in calculating the total number of floodlights required at this

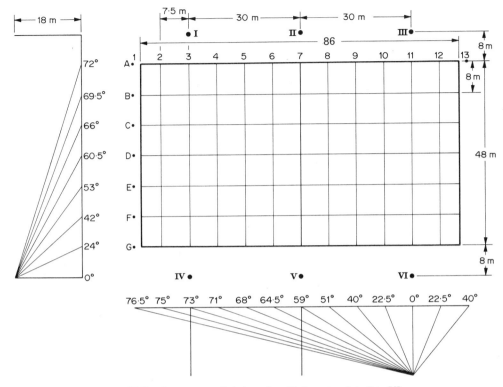

Fig. 33.7 Sports area lighting, floodlights at points I to VI

stage: it is more useful to examine the intensity distribution required to give coverage with one floodlight at each position and then adjust the final quantity to arrive at the illuminance specified.

(a) A grid is constructed over the area as shown in Fig. 33.7. The grid is on 8 m centres across the pitch, dividing the width into six strips: 7·5 m centres are selected along the pitch. As this divides the pole spacing equally into four, calculated illuminance values over the grid for a floodlight at one pole position can be applied easily to the floodlights at the other positions. The grid is labelled A to G in one direction and 1 to 13 in the other, so that each intersection point has a reference.

(b) By construction or calculation the angle from the downward vertical at the top of the selected pole (VI) is determined for each grid line. These values are shown on Fig. 33.7.

(c) It is now possible to construct this grid on the zenithal web, making use of the fact that lines perpendicular to the direction of aiming appear as radial lines on this projection: this should be done on a tracing paper overlay. Grid lines A to G are drawn as radial lines at the angular intervals shown on the left-hand side of Fig. 33.7 (Fig. 33.8a). To construct grid lines 1 to 11, the overlay is moved up 90° over the web and the grid lines traced off at the angular intervals shown on the bottom of Fig. 33.7 (Fig. 33.8b). It should

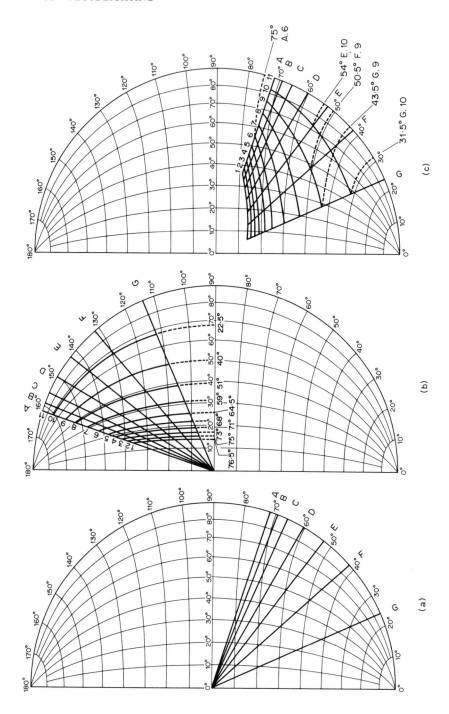

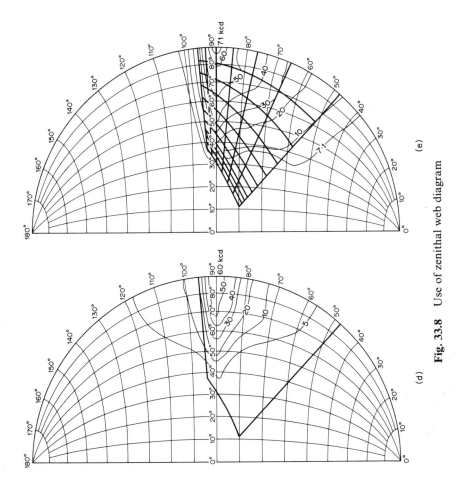

Fig. 33.8 Use of zenithal web diagram

be noted that grid lines 12 and 13 are equivalent to grid lines 10 and 9 on the diagram. The completed overlay can now be re-positioned over the lower quadrant of the web and the angles of incidence of the light at each grid intersection can be read off from the web (Fig. 33.8c). These values are then noted on a work sheet, part of which is shown as Table 33.4.

Table 33.4   Work sheet for zenithal web calculation

Grid reference	Angle of incidence (degrees)	Intensity from one fitting (kcd)	Pole VI Illuminance from one lantern (lux)	Pole III Illuminance from one lantern (lux)	Poles VI and III Total illuminance from one lantern per pole	Poles VI and III Total illuminance from three lanterns per pole
A 10	72	30	3·6	20·0	23·6	71
B 10	69·5	50	6·3	33·3	36·6	110
C 10	66	61	12·4	32·1	44·5	133
D 10	60·5	54	20·8	20·8	41·6	125
E 10	54	45	32·1	12·4	44·5	133
F 10	45	30	33·3	6·3	36·6	110
G 10	31·5	10	20·0	3·6	23·6	71
A 9	72·5	28	2·4	11·8	14·2	43
B 9	70	45	5·6	20·8	26·4	79
C 9	67	55	9·8	20·0	29·8	90
D 9	63	47	14·2	14·2	28·4	85
E 9	57	36	20·0	9·8	29·8	90
F 9	50·5	23	20·8	5·6	26·4	79
G 9	43·5	9·5	11·8	2·4	14·2	43

(d) To examine the suitability of alternative light distributions, the overlays are placed on isocandela diagrams drawn on the same web. Fig. 33.8d and Fig. 33.8e show this for a tungsten halogen and linear metal halide floodlight respectively. In both cases peaks have been aimed at 66° above the downward vertical: by rotating the overlay about the centre of the web the distribution can be examined at any aiming angle. From this inspection the metal halide floodlight is selected.

(e) The values of intensity are now read off Fig. 33.8e at each grid reference point and noted on the work sheet (Table 33.4).

(f) The illuminance at each grid point can be calculated using the formula

$$E = \frac{I \cos^3 \theta}{h^2}$$

where E = horizontal illuminance (lux), I = intensity (cd), θ = angle of incidence (degrees) and h = mounting height (m).

At this point the calculated values can be used to construct an isolux diagram which is necessary if the pole positions are on irregular centres or some floodlights are to be aimed at an azimuth angle other than parallel to the transverse grid line. In this example it is easier to continue by adding grid point values. The contribution from pole III can be found by reversing the column of figures for pole VI as shown on the work sheet. These are then added to give the combined result. These values can in turn be multiplied by the number of lanterns on the poles. This procedure is repeated for the remaining floodlights and Fig. 33.9 shows the illuminance produced over one quarter of the pitch using three floodlights on poles I, III, IV and VI and two on each of the remaining poles. This gives an average horizontal illuminance of 120 lux, thus meeting the requirements.

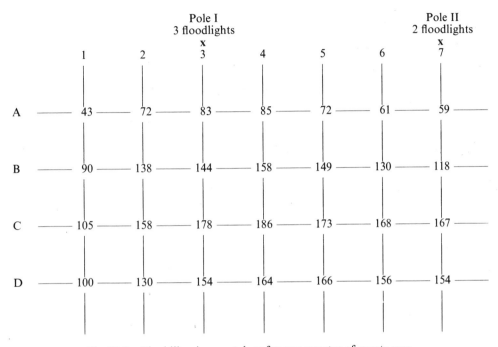

Fig. 33.9 Final illuminance values for one quarter of sports area

The zenithal web method represents the most convenient manual method available using two-dimensional projections for the solution of area floodlighting calculations. Its advantage over other methods of the same type is that the elevation aiming of the floodlights can be varied at will without re-plotting and it provides a convenient graphical solution to the three-dimensional trigonometry that is involved. However, like all other similar methods the azimuth aiming of the floodlights cannot be varied and this is a serious disadvantage when using projectors on high towers to floodlight sports stadia, marshalling yards and docks. The only way in which this can be done is to use a three-dimensional projection of the type described in July 1957 by G. K. Lambert in *Light and Lighting*.

33.3.4 Use of computers in floodlighting design

For the majority of floodlighting problems the use of a computer is difficult to justify, but on the more complex projects where many repetitive calculations must be carried out to ascertain the diversity of illuminance on the horizontal, vertical or inclined planes, the machine can be valuable. However, the computer can only act as a design aid in the limited sense that the final print-out of the results can tell the planner quickly and accurately whether his design works or not.

It is usual in these cases to define an XY grid covering the area. The steps in X and Y can be selected to give either a coarse or fine grid depending on the requirements. The positions of the floodlights are then defined in terms of X, Y and Z for altitude. Floodlight aiming can be noted either in degrees of elevation and azimuth or by using the X and Y co-ordinates of the point at which the peak intensity reaches the area. The photometric performance of the floodlights is then fed in in the form of an angular grid. The intensity values between grid points are handled in the programme either by curve fitting or by straight line interpolation. It is also necessary to define the format for print-out presentation. This can either be tabulated in the form of a chosen grid or a line plotter can be used to produce isolux diagrams. By introducing standard formulae into the programme, the print-out can be in terms of horizontal, vertical, inclined-plane, vector, scalar, mean cylindrical or any other form of illuminance for the whole or part of the specified grid.

The possibilities of the use of computers are endless and no doubt in the future the computer will be used in the initial design stages, but it will never knowingly make a building look beautiful or replace the designer's intuition. What it can do is calculate with great efficiency and so produce more information on a single project than its master can assimilate in a lifetime.

34 Installation, maintenance and economics

Previous chapters in this part of the book have examined lighting systems for specific situations. This chapter deals with three factors which are common to all lighting systems and which are of great practical importance; the installation of equipment, its behaviour throughout life and the real cost of the total system.

The first section covers practical installation factors affecting the wiring and protection of luminaires. The second section notes the progressive reduction in the light output of a lighting system and discusses maintenance, cleaning and re-lamping. The final section explains how cost evaluation can be used to assess alternative lighting systems, taking into account both capital and operating costs.

34.1 THE INSTALLATION OF LIGHTING EQUIPMENT

34.1.1 Wiring systems

The two most commonly used non-domestic interior wiring systems are screwed conduit with metric size PVC-insulated single-conductor cables or MICC (mineral insulated copper covered) solid cables, both used with fixed positions for the outlet boxes.

Greater flexibility can be provided by the use of continuous rows of trunking in place of conduit, since this permits the number of luminaires per row to be varied to suit changes in plant layout or the introduction of new light sources.

Fig. 34.1   Trakline, used for maximum flexibility in lighting installations

For maximum flexibility with minimum modification cost, particularly in display areas where frequent adjustment is made to the luminaires, the Trakline bus-bar system (Fig. 34.1) provides a PVC extrusion in which are embedded conductor and earth strips rated for a 30 A loading. The extrusion may be used on its own but a metal-clad version is available when greater strength and mechanical protection is required. Trakline can also be used in a metal trunking system, extruded aluminium alloy trunking for commercial applications or a larger cross-section rolled-steel trunking for heavier duty industrial application: this latter system provides duct spaces on each side of the insert, which can be used to carry cables segregated from the 30 A Trakline conductors. A wide range of accessories enable quick and simple connections to be made to the extrusion, including plug-in 3 A fused adaptor boxes with isolating polarity-controlled switches.

Apart from the recommendations on exterior wiring installation practice given by the IEE, the following may help to prevent problems arising when installing outdoor lighting equipment:

(a) Only galvanized steel or non-corrosive materials for cable risers should be used, avoiding electrolytic action between aluminium and steel connections.
(b) If conduit is used, venting drain-holes should be provided to prevent the build-up of condensed moisture inside the conduit and connecting boxes.
(c) For high tower floodlighting, PVC-sheathed SWA (steel wire armoured) multi-core cable should be used from the tower base to the floodlight headframe in order to overcome condensation effects. The final feeders to the floodlights should be in circular PVC-sheathed multi-core flexible cable, with a weatherproof gland entry into a weatherproof distribution box attached to the top of the tower or the headframe.
(d) Rubber cables should not be exposed to sunlight or other sources of ultra-violet radiation.
(e) A coat of paint over galvanizing will slow down atmospheric corrosion.
(f) Inspection and preventative maintenance against mechanical and electrical breakdown is necessary at least once a year.

34.1.2 Discharge lamp equipment

Special factors apply to the installation of discharge lamp equipment which do not apply to systems using incandescent filament lamps.

Switching transients.   As has been explained in Sect. 18.1.3, a momentary current surge (or transient) occurs when an a.c. supply is connected to a discharge lamp circuit: this can be 10 or 20 times greater than the steady circuit current. When the circuit is switched off, the sudden collapse of the magnetic field in the choke causes a transient voltage surge, which may be several thousand volts when using a switch-start fluorescent tube circuit.

The magnitude of these transient voltages and currents depends on the following factors:

(a) The type of fluorescent tube or discharge lamp.
(b) The instantaneous value of the alternating supply.
(c) The impedance of the mains distribution system back to the generator: much higher voltage and current transients will occur on a circuit which is connected close to a main sub-station than on a circuit which is at the end of a fairly long low voltage feeder cable.
(d) The nature of the switch mechanism that breaks the circuit.

Of the standard lighting switches in common use, the quick-make and quick-break type of switch deals adequately with the initial current surge of the capacitor but causes excessively high voltage surges when breaking the circuit. With the 'a.c. only' type of switch (slow-make and slow-break) there is a greater tendency for the contacts to weld together when making the circuit, but the transient voltage pulse when the circuit is opened is substantially reduced. For these reasons, the ideal switching arrangement for fluorescent tube circuits would be one comprising a quick-make and slow-break mechanism.

Experience has shown that 'all-insulated' switches are normally preferable for fluorescent circuits. Care should be taken when selecting switches which have a quick-break action, or switches with an earthed metal action or cover plate, since these may not withstand the switching transients produced by fluorescent lighting between line and earth.

Fuse ratings.   Because of switching surges, it is necessary to use a higher fuse rating than that of the steady running current taken by the circuit. Although satisfactory operation may be obtained with rewireable fuses when the fuse rating is only 1·25 times the steady circuit current, it may be necessary to use a higher fuse rating when HBC (high breaking capacity) cartridge fuses are employed. For example, a single 1500 mm 65 W tube circuit will have a steady running current of approximately 0·5 A, but because of the quick response of the fuse element in clearing an excess current load it is necessary to use a 2 A rated fuse in order to ensure that the element will not fail under transient conditions. Similarly, a 5 A cartridge fuse is needed for loads of up to four 1500 mm tubes (2 A steady load current).

This 'down rating' requirement with HBC cartridge fuses must be considered when planning the wiring installation, since if larger fuses are needed to overcome switching transients, then it may be necessary to increase the size of cables and accessories in order to meet the requirements of IEE Wiring Regulations, which state that all wiring must be at least equal to the rating of the fuse which protects the circuit.

Three-phase lighting circuits.   Because voltages in excess of 400 V exist between the phase or line conductors of a 3-phase supply, it is normally recommended that all lighting equipment in a given room should be connected to the same phase conductor, thus limiting the maximum voltage present to 250 V. The IEE Wiring Regulations also state that where medium voltages (in excess of 250 V) are present, then all conductors must be enclosed in earthed metalwork and not be readily accessible. Also, where it is necessary or desirable to install luminaires on different phases, the luminaires must be at least 1·8 m apart.

It is often desirable to use more than one phase in an area where there is rotating machinery, since it is then possible to run adjacent rows of luminaires on different phases to reduce the stroboscopic effect: this also helps to balance out the 3-phase load.

Earthed neutral supplies.   In the standard 3-phase 4-wire a.c. distribution system which is used in UK, the neutral conductor is bonded to earth throughout the distribution network. This means that the neutral conductor is at earth potential. In the case of fluorescent luminaires with switchless control gear, the best starting performance is obtained when the metalwork adjacent to the exterior glass tube surface is at the same potential as one of the internal end electrodes. This can be achieved in the case of an earthed-neutral supply by bonding the metalwork to earth, because this effectively connects it to the neutral electrode. Note that this bonding of the metalwork to earth will not provide efficient operation for non-switch-start circuits in the case of special supply systems where the 200/250 V input is obtained between the phase voltages.

Harmonics and neutral current in a.c. circuits.   A standard 50 Hz alternating voltage is normally produced by the power station alternators as a pure sine wave shape, but it is possible for the voltage wave shape to become slightly distorted by the time it reaches the final user. The waveform can be analysed into a pure 50 Hz sine wave plus a small percentage of harmonics. The presence of harmonics in the supply voltage will normally affect the larger and more important harmonic percentage in the load current, which is caused by the non-linear voltage/current relationship in a discharge lamp (Sect. 18.1.1). It is not possible to quote a precise value of percentage harmonic in the current of a particular discharge lamp circuit, since this will vary with the percentage harmonic in the supply voltage. In some circuits, a capacitor is connected directly across the main supply terminals to correct the lagging power factor created by the inductive choke ballast. The mains current is reduced as the power factor of the circuit is improved but the percentage harmonic will increase (Table 18.2).

Table 34.1 shows the range of percentage harmonics per phase and the average third harmonic current produced in fluorescent tube circuits when the supply voltage contains

Table 34.1   Harmonics in fluorescent lighting systems

Tube size	Type of circuit	Harmonics per phase %	Current per phase		Current in neutral	
			Mains A	Third harmonic A	Minimum A	Maximum A
2400 mm 125 W	Switch-start (leading p.f.)	14-15	0·94	0·135	0·405	0·97
2400 mm 125 W	Quickstart (high p.f.)	8-9	0·66	0·055	0·165	0·67
2400 mm 85 W	Quickstart (single tube unit)	7-8	0·42	0·03	0·09	0·43
1800 mm 85 W	Resonant-start (p.f. 0·86 lagging)	24-25	0·46	0·115	0·34	0·50
1500 mm 80 W	Switch-start (no p.f. capacitor)	6-7	0·85	0·055	0·165	0·86
1500 mm 80 W	Switch-start (leading p.f.)	14-15	0·85	0·12	0·36	0·88
1500 mm 80 W	Twin switch-start (lead-lag)	21-22	0·80	0·175	0·525	0·86
1500 mm 80 W	Switch-start (p.f. 0·85 lagging)	15-18	0·46	0·075	0·225	0·48
1500 mm 80 W	Quickstart (p.f. 0·85 lagging)	15-18	0·48	0·075	0·225	0·50
1500 mm 65 W	Switch-start (p.f. 0·85 lagging)	15-18	0·37	0·06	0·18	0·39
1500 mm 65 W	Resonant-start (p.f. 0·92 lagging)	24-25	0·36	0·085	0·255	0·39
100 W filament lamp for comparison		1-2	0·42	0·01	0·03	0·42

1% to 2% harmonic distortion. The third harmonic is particularly important, due to the fact that the neutral wire in a 3-phase 4-wire system, although carrying no fundamental current with a balanced load, will have to carry three times the third harmonic current per phase. This is therefore the minimum neutral current, shown in Table 34.1, which flows when the load is equally balanced across all three phases. Maximum neutral current occurs when full load is applied across two phases only and there is no load on the third phase.

34.2 THE MAINTENANCE OF LIGHTING SYSTEMS

34.2.1 Principles of maintenance

The illuminance initially provided by a lighting installation will decrease gradually throughout life, due to (a) a progressive reduction in lamp output and (b) the accumulation of dirt on the lamps, luminaires and room decorations. If the illuminance falls by 20% after a given period of use, then 20% of the total electric lighting bill is being wasted.

It can be shown that the most economic maintenance expenditure on cleaning or lamp replacement is when it is equal to the average of the light wasted as a result of dirt or depreciated lamp output respectively.

Most industrial and commercial lighting systems are designed to provide a uniformly illuminated interior; the 1968 IES code recommends that the minimum allowance should not be allowed to depreciate below 80% of the average service value, which is the average through-life value recommended for lighting design purposes and varies with the type of visual task and the interior. This means that the rate of light depreciation must be known before economic calculations can be carried out to assess the optimum frequency of cleaning and lamp replacement in a planned maintenance programme.

Sufficient life test data have been compiled to show that most light depreciation curves are non-linear for both dirt and lamp output: the initial loss of light due to dirt and lamp output depreciation combined is double or treble the average rate of loss. Thus if the total depreciation in light output is 40% over 10 months, giving an average rate of 4% per month, the rate of depreciation during the first month would be about 10%.

In practice, the effect of lamp output depreciation is taken into account by using the lighting design lumens for the lamps when planning schemes. For discharge lamps, this is normally the 2000 h value which is based on the average light output of the lamp over the first 5000 h of use. If fluorescent tubes or high pressure discharge lamps are to be retained in use after 5000 h, the lighting design lumens should be reduced by 2% to 4% per 1000 h of extra use, according to lamp type.

34.2.2 Maintenance factor

The depreciation due to dirt on lamps, luminaires and room surfaces is often allowed for in design (Sect. 22.2.1) by applying an arbitrary maintenance factor of 0·80: this assumes an average 20% depreciation below the initial performance produced when the luminaires are new and the interior has first been decorated. Apart from cleaning the lighting equipment and room surfaces at regular intervals, the 0·80 maintenance factor assumes that the interior is regularly re-decorated with a finish of equal reflectance.

There is no longer any need to use this arbitrary 0·80 maintenance factor, since the

Table 34.2   Classification of rooms and luminaires for maintenance

Premises	Location	Room category X = Particularly clean, Y = Average, Z = Particularly dirty	Bare lamp batten	Open ventilated reflector	Dust-tight, dust-proof or reflector lamp	Open non-ventilated reflector, enclosed diffuser	Open base diffuser or louvre	Recessed diffuser or louvre, diffusing or louvred luminous ceiling	Indirect cornice
Offices, shops and stores, hospitals, clean laboratories and factories, schools, etc.	All air-conditioned buildings	X	A	A	A/B	A/B	A/B	A	B
	Clean country area	X	A/B	A/B	A/B	B	B	A/B	C/D
	City or town outskirts	Y	B	B	B	C	B/C	B	E
	City or town centre	Y	B/C	B/C	B/C	C/D	C	B/C	F/G
	Dirty industrial area	Y	C	C	B/C	D	C/D	C	G
Factories, laboratories, manufacturing areas, machine shops, etc.	All air-conditioned buildings	X	A/B	A	A	C	B/C	B	B/C
	Clean country area	Y	B	A/B	B	C/D	C	B/C	D/E
	City or town outskirts	Y	B/C	B	B	D	C/D	C	F
	City or town centre	Y	C	B/C	B/C	D/E	D	C/D	G
	Dirty industrial area	Z	C/D	C	C	E	D/E	D	H
Steelworks, foundries, welding shops, mines, etc.	All air-conditioned buildings	X	B	A/B	A/B	D	C/D	C	—
	Clean country area	Y	C	B/C	B	D/E	D	C/D	—
	City or town outskirts	Y	C/D	C	B/C	E	D/E	D	—
	City or town centre	Z	D	C/D	B/C	E/F	E	D/E	—
	Dirty industrial area	Z	D/E	D	C	F	E/F	E	—

560

IES has produced its Technical Report No. 9: this contains a detailed evaluation of the various lamp and dirt depreciation effects and gives recommendations on the frequency of cleaning, lamp replacement and re-decoration. Table 34.2 is extracted from this report and shows how luminaires can be categorized (A to H) from a depreciation point of view when used in different room atmospheric conditions, also categorized (X to Z). Further tables appear in the report enabling maintenance factors to be determined for each luminaire and room category with different frequencies of cleaning: Table 34.3 has been compiled from these data. It shows three values of maintenance factor for each combination of luminaire category and room category: the values are for the most economical cleaning interval for low, average and high labour costs respectively, based on an average wall reflectance of 30% with annual cleaning or re-decoration of the room surfaces.

Table 34.3   Maintenance factors

Months per cleaning:		1	2	3	4	5	6	8	9	12	18
Luminaire category	Room category										
A	X	—	—	—	—	—	—	0·94	—	0·92	0·90
A	Y	—	—	—	—	—	—	0·92	—	0·90	0·88
B	X	—	—	—	—	—	0·88	—	0·86	0·85	—
B	Y	—	—	—	—	—	0·87	—	0·85	0·83	—
C	X	—	—	—	—	0·84	—	0·81	—	0·79	—
C	Y	—	—	—	—	0·83	—	0·80	—	0·78	—
C	Z	—	—	—	—	—	0·82	0·78	—	0·76	—
D	X	—	—	—	0·82	—	0·79	—	0·75	—	—
D	Y	—	—	—	0·81	—	0·77	—	0·73	—	—
D	Z	—	—	—	0·79	—	0·75	—	0·71	—	—
E	Y	—	—	0·78	—	0·73	—	0·68	—	—	—
E	Z	—	—	0·77	—	0·72	—	0·67	—	—	—
F	Y	—	0·77	—	0·71	—	0·67	—	—	—	—
F	Z	—	0·76	—	0·70	—	0·66	—	—	—	—
G	Y	—	0·73	0·69	0·66	—	—	—	—	—	—
G	Z	—	0·72	0·68	0·65	—	—	—	—	—	—
H	Z	0·75	0·68	0·63	—	—	—	—	—	—	—

For example, Table 34.2 shows that luminaire and room categories of B and Y respectively would apply to ventilated open base reflector luminaires used in a general factory located in the outskirts of a city. From Table 34.3 the B and Y categories give a recommended cleaning interval of 6 to 12 months with maintenance factors of 0·87 to 0·83 respectively. The normal 0·80 maintenance factor would therefore seem to be reasonable if the room surfaces were cleaned in accordance with the Factory Act requirement of at least once every 14 months. If alternative non-ventilated open reflectors were used in a steelworks in a dirty industrial area, Table 34.2 would give categories of F and Z and the corresponding maintenance factors from Table 34.3 would range from 0·76 to 0·66 with a cleaning interval of 2 to 6 months: for average labour costs a maintenance factor of 0·70 would be suitable for design purposes if the user agreed to a 4-month cleaning interval as part of a regular maintenance programme.

34.2.3 Group re-lamping

Whereas tungsten filament lamps with a 1000 h rated life are normally allowed to operate until the filament breaks, the longer life of 5000 h to 7500 h for discharge lamps and tubes make group re-lamping an economic alternative to individual replacement when lamps fail. The normal survival of discharge lamps is such that only 10% to 20% failures occur during the first 70% of average batch life and this makes it economical to re-lamp at about two-thirds of rated life. Group re-lamping should be carried out at the same time as the luminaires are being cleaned, because it takes no longer to change a lamp than to clean it.

Group re-lamping with systematic cleaning gives the following benefits:

(a) The maintained illuminance will be higher.
(b) The maintenance programme can be planned to minimize inconvenience. Work can be carried out in a factory during the annual shut-down period.
(c) Because the group lamps are from one batch, they are uniform in colour and brightness, giving a less patchy appearance to the interior.
(d) The saving on individual re-lamping labour costs more than offsets the extra group re-lamping costs. A few old lamps can be retained for spot replacements.

34.3 LIGHTING ECONOMICS

Many different lighting schemes can be designed to give a specified illuminance over a given area: a choice has often to be made between alternative schemes. In many cases, the scheme finally chosen may be based on the very simple basis of which has the lowest cost of luminaires and lamps. If all other factors are equal, then lowest cost is the right choice, but there may be very sound reasons for paying more in order to get better quality. For example, if a specially protected luminaire is used in a corrosive area where it lasts three times as long as a standard stove-enamelled luminaire then the first would certainly be an economic proposition, even if it costs twice as much as the second.

In most cases an economic comparison is based on two main factors, the initial cost of lamps and luminaires and the running costs due to the electricity consumed. A true comparison should, however, be based on the total annual lighting bill, which takes other cost items into account.

34.3.1 Annual lighting costs

The usual method used to calculate the total annual lighting cost for a given scheme is best introduced by means of a worked example.

A lighting scheme has been worked out for a factory workshop 30 m long × 20 m wide with a height of 5 m from floor to roof trusses. By using 4 rows of 8 twin-tube 2400 mm 85 W luminaires with slotted metal reflectors, an illuminance of just over 400 lux can be obtained. An alternative scheme is 6 rows of 8 twin-tube 1500 mm 65 W luminaires of a similar type suspended from the roof trusses.

Table 34.4 gives cost details for the two schemes being considered. They are compared for an equal period of use, 50 h of lighting per week or 2500 h per annum. The total annual lighting cost of each scheme will include seven separate items of cost, as follows:

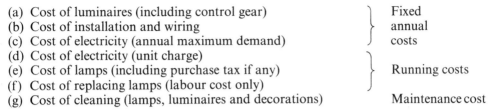

(a) Cost of luminaires (including control gear)   ⎫ Fixed
(b) Cost of installation and wiring   ⎬ annual
(c) Cost of electricity (annual maximum demand)   ⎭ costs
(d) Cost of electricity (unit charge)   ⎫
(e) Cost of lamps (including purchase tax if any)   ⎬ Running costs
(f) Cost of replacing lamps (labour cost only)   ⎭
(g) Cost of cleaning (lamps, luminaires and decorations)   Maintenance cost

Items (a) to (c) can be considered as fixed annual costs, since they are independent of the actual hours of use, whereas items (d) to (f) are called running costs because they vary in direct proportion to the hours of use.

Table 34.4 Cost comparison of workshop lighting systems

	1500 mm 65 W	2400 mm 85 W
Tube size		
Lamp lighting design lumens	4700	6800
Utilization factor × Maintenance factor	0·68 × 0·8	0·72 × 0·8
Number of luminaires required	48	32
Design illuminance provided	409 lux	418 lux
Nett price per luminaire	£7·68	£9·52
Total cost of luminaires	£368·64	£304·64
15% annual depreciation (luminaires)	£55·30	£45·70
Installation wiring cost per luminaire	£6·00	£7·00
Total cost of installation and wiring	£288·00	£224·00
10% annual depreciation (wiring)	£28·80	£22·40
Total watts per twin-tube luminaire	160 W	205 W
Total kilowatt load	7·68 kW	6·56 kW
Electricity MD cost at £10 per kW	£76·80	£65·60
Electricity unit cost for 2500 h at 0·6p per kWh	£115·20	£98·40
Nett price per tube	£0·51	£0·59
Total cost of tubes	£48·96	£37·76
Average tube life (h)	7500	7500
Tube cost per 2500 h	£16·32	£12·59
Replacement labour cost per tube	£0·30	£0·40
Cost of individual tube replacements	£28·80	£25·60
Tube labour cost per 2500 h	£9·60	£8·53
Cleaning cost per twin-tube luminaire	£0·25	£0·35
Number of cleanings per annum	One	One
Cleaning cost (luminaires and tubes)	£12·00	£11·20
TOTAL ANNUAL COST (2500 h)	£314·02	£264·42

Luminaire cost.   The assessment of annual luminaire cost is based on a given project life, with a gradual depreciation of capital value by the user. For example, if he proposes to spend £1000 on luminaires and is willing to accept a nominal life of 10 years, then he can allow one-tenth of his capital cost as an annual depreciation, i.e. 10% of £1000 = £100 depreciation. It is possible that the user may work on the basis of obtaining a loan for the capital expenditure involved and in this case it would be necessary to pay interest on the £1000 loan as well as repay the capital amount. Assuming that the sum of £1000 is to be repaid over a 10-year period, it is probable that the extra interest would amount to approximately £500. This means that a total of £1500 must be allowed for over a 10-year period and this is shown in the cost table as an annual depreciation of 15%. A more sophisticated assessment is obtained in Sect. 34.3.2, allowing for the effect of tax rebate on capital investment year by year together with changes in the annual operating costs.

Installation and wiring cost.   This varies widely according to the wiring system used, and also with the mounting height of the luminaires because the cost of installation will obviously be increased if expensive scaffolding is necessary to reach the roof trusses. A nominal value of £6 or £7 per outlet has been allowed in the cost table according to the size of luminaire involved. As with the luminaires, the installation and wiring cost is taken as an item of capital expenditure with an annual depreciation factor applied. A longer life is usually assumed for the wiring than for the luminaires and in the cost table it has been assumed that the normal life will be 20 years. It has also been assumed that the capital sum will be borrowed and that interest will have to be paid as well as capital repayment. Over a period of 20 years, approximately £1000 would have to be paid as interest in addition to each £1000 originally loaned. This means that a total of £2000 would be required over a period of 20 years and therefore 10% annual depreciation has been allowed in the table.

Electricity cost.   There are a number of different electricity tariffs in use throughout Britain. In some areas it may be found that a direct unit charge is applied for every kWh of electricity consumed. Another tariff may slightly modify this unit charge so that a higher price is paid for the first 100 units of electricity per quarter year, with a reducing price per kWh unit for subsequent consumption. The most common commercial and industrial tariff, however, is one based on a two part payment system. For the first part, the local electricity board assesses the power required for the complete installation and makes an annual charge for this maximum demand (MD). The charge may vary from £7 to £15 per kW per annum according to the size of the installation and the area involved, charges tending to be slightly lower in the north of England than in the south. For some very large users, special maximum demand meters are installed which measure kVA instead of kW to encourage the customer to maintain a high power factor. For installations where the MD charge is based on kW measurement, the power factor should not be less than a specified value, normally 0·85 lagging. In the cost table it has been assumed that the maximum demand charge is £10 per kW. The second part of the electricity cost is the charge made for the kWh units of electricity consumed: if the customer has already paid a maximum demand charge then the additional unit charge will vary between 0·4p and 0·8p per kWh. In Table 34.4 it has been assumed that the unit charge is 0·6p per kWh.

Lamp cost.   Although the cost of lamps may be considered as an initial cost item, and therefore subject to conditions of capital expenditure, the lamps are also expendable items which need replacing. In Table 34.4 only the replacement lamps have been considered, the initial batch being included as expendable items, and not as capital items. When arriving at the total cost of lamps, it is necessary to allow for any discounts to which the user may be entitled and it is then necessary to add purchase tax in the case of those lamps applicable. Once the total cost of a batch of lamps has been assessed, it is then necessary to take into account lamp life. General service filament lamps have a rated life of 1000 h, whereas fluorescent tubes and most discharge lamps have a rated life of 7500 h or 5000 h, the former being used in Table 34.4.

Lamp replacement labour cost. This item of annual cost may not always be applicable, for if group replacement of lamps is carried out after a specified period then it may be possible to arrange for this operation to coincide with one of the cleaning periods. If lamps are not replaced as part of a systematic maintenance programme, but allowed to

Table 34.5 Cost comparison of high bay factory lighting systems

Scheme reference	No. 1	No. 2	No. 3	No. 4
Luminaire type	Fig. 24.1b	Fig. 24.1c	Fig. 24.1c	Fig. 24.1a
Size and type of lamp	1000 W	400 W	400 W	2400 mm
				85 W
	MBFR	MBIF	SON	White MCF
Number of lamps per luminaire	One	One	One	Four
Lighting design lamp lumens	45 000	27 000	36 000	26 400
Total watts per luminaire	1070	460	455	410
Lamp lumens per circuit watt	42	59	79	65
Net price per luminaire c/w gear	£19·55	£21·75	£26·10	£17·00
Net lamp price per luminaire	£11·25	£6·67	£16·50	£2·22
Rated lamp life in hours	7500	7500	5000	7500
Light output ratio (up/down)	11/80%	0/77%	0/77%	6/77%
BZ distribution classification	BZ2	BZ1	BZ1	BZ5
Maintenance factor (dirt loss)	0·90	0·80	0·80	0·80

(A) Capital cost of lighting 100 m × 25 m factory with 15 m mounting height

	No. 1	No. 2	No. 3	No. 4
Useful lumens per luminaire (direct)	23 800	13 600	18 100	9900
Useful lumens per luminaire (reflected)	4100	900	1200	1700
Useful lumens per luminaire (total)	27 900	14 500	19 300	11 600
Number of luminaires required	36	69	52	87
Practical layout of luminaires	3 × 12	3 × 23	4 × 13	3 × 29
Average illuminance provided (lux)	402	400	402	404
Total net price of luminaires	£704	£1501	£1357	£1479
Price less 20% investment grant	£563	£1201	£1086	£1183
Total installation wiring cost	£1100	£1200	£1000	£1300
Price less 20% investment grant	£880	£960	£800	£1040
Price of initial batch of lamps	£405	£460	£858	£193
Price less 20% investment grant	£324	£368	£686	£154
Total luminaire, wiring and lamp cost	£2209	£3161	£3215	£2972
Price less 20% investment grant	£1767	£2959	£2572	£2377

(B) Annual cost of lighting 100 m × 25 m × 15 m factory for 2500 h per year

	No. 1	No. 2	No. 3	No. 4
15% of luminaire cost (less grant)	£84	£180	£170	£178
10% of wiring cost (less grant)	£88	£96	£80	£104
Lamp cost per 2500 h use	£135	£123	£343	£51
Electrical load (kW)	38·5	31·7	23·7	35·7
Electricity at £20 per kW per annum	£770	£634	£474	£714
Labour cost (annual maintenance)	£36	£69	£52	£100
Total annual cost (2500 h of lighting)	£1113	£1102	£1119	£1147

operate until they fail individually, then the labour cost of carrying out individual replacements can be extremely high and investigations have shown that the labour cost can be more than 75p per lampway. In Table 34.4 a nominal figure of 30p or 40p has been allowed per tube for each tube change. It is necessary, of course, to allow for the difference in lamp life when assessing annual labour costs for changing different lamp types.

Cleaning cost (lamps and luminaires).   The annual cost of cleaning the lamps and luminaires depends on the accessibility of the luminaire, the type of luminaire and the number of cleanings carried out per annum. If the luminaires are mounted at a considerable mounting height and scaffolding is necessary to reach them, then the cost per cleaning can be very high, possibly more than £1 per luminaire. Plastic diffusers must normally be cleaned with an anti-static fluid to prevent the electrostatic attraction of dust and thus the cost of cleaning luminaires incorporating diffusers is considerably more than for other luminaires. The frequency of cleaning is largely dependent on the nature of the working area (Sect. 34.2.2). In Table 34.4 it has been assumed that the reflectors will only be cleaned once a year at a cost of 25p or 35p.

Total annual lighting cost.   It can be seen from Table 34.4 that because of the smaller number of luminaires required, the 2400 mm 85 W scheme is cheaper than the 1500 mm 65 W scheme for all seven individual cost factors and is clearly the more economical proposition.

A similar exercise to that in Table 34.4 is carried out in Table 34.5, where a comparison is made between a multi-tube 2400 mm fluorescent lighting system and three high-pressure discharge lamp systems suitable for a high bay factory interior. The first of these high-pressure lamp systems uses an MBFR reflector lamp in the type of luminaire shown in Fig. 24.1b. The second and third use industrial reflectors of the type shown in Fig. 24.1c, incorporating metal halide and high pressure sodium lamps respectively. Capital costs in this example include the effect of an investment grant allowance but the full effect of tax and investment allowances can only be accurately assessed by using the method outlined in Sect. 34.3.2.

34.3.2   Discounted cash flow (DCF)

This section deals with the DCF method of appraising the profit return on capital invested in a lighting project for a given life period. To explain the principles involved, the data compiled in Table 34.4 have been used to prepare the DCF example in Table 34.6, but it is assumed that the 1500 mm 65 W system is already installed and consideration is being given to its replacement by the 2400 mm 85 W scheme. The existing wiring can be used and therefore only £32 installing cost need be added to the capital cost of luminaires and new tubes. Allowing for a project life of 12 years, the first part of Table 34.6 shows a very small difference between £2760 and £2726 total cost over 12 years, if no increase in annual costs are allowed for: it would not appear economical to invest £374 in new lighting equipment if the profit is only going to be £34 over a 12 year period.

The weakness in this static method of evaluation is that increases in annual operating costs and the effect of the actual times of payments are not taken into account: these

Table 34.6 Work sheet for DCF assessment

Scheme	1500 mm 65 W	2400 mm 85 W
Cost of luminaires	Nil	£305 capital
Cost of tubes	Nil	£37 capital
Cost of installation	Nil	£32 capital
Electricity cost	Annual = £192·0	Annual = £164·0
Replacement tubes	Annual = £16·3	Annual = £12·6
Maintenance labour	Annual = £21·6	Annual = £19·7
Capital + annual cost	Nil + £230	£374 + £196
12 years cost	£2760	£2726

Example of DCF net profit over 12 years

Based on 2500 hours use per annum and a 12 year project life allowing a 5% compound increase per annum in operating costs and a 10% interest rate

(a) Year	(b) (65 W–85 W) = cost difference	(c) Tax relief†	(d) Cash flow	Discount factor	(e) Profit or loss
0	nil − 374 = − 374	nil − nil	− 374	1·00	− 374
1	230 − 196 = + 34	130 − 14	+ 150	0·91	+ 137
2	241 − 206 = + 35	15 − 14	+ 36	0·825	+ 30
3	253 − 216 = + 37	11 − 15	+ 33	0·75	+ 25
4	266 − 226 = + 40	9 − 16	+ 33	0·68	+ 22
5	280 − 237 = + 43	7 − 17	+ 33	0·62	+ 20
6	294 − 249 = + 45	6 − 18	+ 33	0·565	+ 19
7	309 − 261 = + 48	4 − 19	+ 33	0·51	+ 17
8	325 − 274 = + 51	3 − 20	+ 34	0·465	+ 16
9	341 − 288 = + 53	2 − 21	+ 34	0·425	+ 14
10	358 − 303 = + 55	1 − 22	+ 34	0·385	+ 13
11	376 − 318 = + 58	1 − 23	+ 36	0·35	+ 13
12	395 − 334 = + 61	1 − 24	+ 38	0·32	+ 12
Total	3668 − 3482 = + 186	190 − 223	+ 153		− 12

† 1st figure = 40% of 60% of capital in year 1 (35% + 25%) then 40% of 25% in years 2 to 12 (reducing annual balance) plus write-off in year 1.
2nd figure = 40% of annual operating costs (plus or minus).

The overall % profit can be calculated from the 'cash flow' and 'net profit' totals as follows (approximate % profit per annum):

$$\text{Profit rate} = \frac{\text{£153 cash flow} + \text{£}(-12) \text{ net profit}}{\text{£153 cash flow} - \text{£}(-12) \text{ net profit}} \times 10\%$$

$$= 10\% \times \frac{\text{£141}}{\text{£165}} = 8\tfrac{1}{2}\% \text{ per annum}$$

factors can be assessed by using the DCF method shown in the second part of the table. This method also allows for the effect of tax relief on capital investment and the payment of interest on bank loans, assuming the expenditure of capital will increase the overdraft of the company. The following step-by-step procedure is used in compiling the columns in the lower half of Table 34.6:

(a) The life of the lighting equipment has been taken as 12 years, the project period.

(b) The cost per annum of the 85 W scheme has been subtracted from the annual expenditure of the existing 65 W system, thus giving a $-£374$ difference in year 0 as the capital investment against which annual savings (plus differences) are obtained in years 1 to 12. Note that the annual operating costs are increased by 5% per annum to allow for rising prices and labour costs: this increases the 12 year costs to £3668 and £3482 respectively. The overall gross profitability is therefore improved to £186 difference, before tax.

(c) Tax relief can be divided into profit and loss sections. The first amount given in the table is profit from capital allowances on the £374 investment plus an assumed £100 write-off of the book value of the existing 65 W equipment. From this is deducted the second amount given in the table, the loss of tax relief on the annual saving. The rate of tax relief has been taken as 40% of the allowances and operating costs (see † at the foot of the table for details of the 1970/71 tax allowances on capital investments).

(d) When tax relief has been taken into account, the true cash flow shows a reduction from £186 to £153 but it is important to note how the timing of the 'plus' savings have altered, with £150 cash flow in year 1. This means that almost half of the £374 investment is repaid in the first year and the interest payable on the bank loan is therefore reduced considerably. This is what DCF is all about: if profit can be made during the early years of the project life it is worth more than profit made at the end of the project period. For example, if the interest rate is 10% per annum, then £1 owed in year 0 will have become about £2 owed after 7 years. We can therefore discount half the value of £1 paid in year 7 when compared with its present investment value in year 0: the 10% discount factor is 0·51 when allowing for 7 years of added interest. The series of discount factors for the 12 year project life gives a reducing 'present value' relating the number of years of interest payable on each year of cash flow.

(e) The final column in the table shows the relative annual profit of the savings in years 1 to 12 compared with the value of money in year 0, and this gives a loss of £12 after allowing for 10% compound interest.

(f) The note at the foot of the table shows how the overall percentage profit can be calculated for the capital invested, giving a return of $8\frac{1}{2}$% per annum. This $8\frac{1}{2}$% profit figure is not particularly good, but this is because the 85 W scheme was compared with a fairly efficient 65 W existing system. If the comparison had been made between 2400 mm 85 W and the older type of 1500 mm 80 W system used in UK until about 1963, then the difference in annual operating cost could have been double that for the 65 W system and a DCF assessment would have shown a profit return of 17% on the 12 year investment: this would certainly have been a good return on capital.

568

The DCF method is dynamic in that the project life span can be varied to match the equipment life and that annual adjustments can be made to the operating costs and to the tax rate or allowances. It also presents lighting costs in financial terms of profit return on capital investment and allows for economic progress (Sect. 34.3.4).

34.3.3 Economics of incandescent filament lamps

As has been explained in Chap. 9, the effect of raising the temperature of the filament in an incandescent lamp is to give an increase in light output and luminous efficacy, with a decrease in the life of the lamp. The choice of the operating temperature is basically

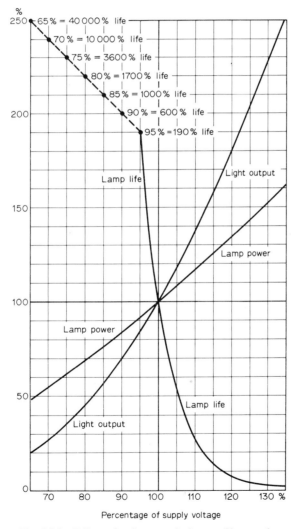

Fig. 34.2 Effect of voltage variation on filament lamps

a matter of economics: the temperature which gives a life of 1000 h has been selected in UK because this provides the cheapest overall cost of light, although 'double-life' lamps are also available.

A change in operating temperature can be accomplished by running a lamp at different voltages: Fig. 34.2 shows this effect quantitatively. A double-life lamp will be seen to have a lumen output of only about 84% of a standard lamp while taking 8% less power: thus to produce the same light output a double-life lamp will require 9% more power. A cost analysis is given in Table 34.7.

Table 34.7 Comparison of standard and double-life lamps

Rated lamp life (h)	1000	2000
Rated lamp output (lm)	1200	1200
Rated lamp power (W)	100	109
Total kWh per 1000 h	100	109
Electricity at 1p per kWh	£1·00	£1·09
Lamp cost per 1000 h	£0·10	£0·05
Total cost per 1000 h	£1·10	£1·14

This comparison shows that a double-life lamp can only be recommended where electricity costs are very low or the labour costs for re-lamping are fairly high.

34.3.4 Economic progress

Table 34.8 summarizes 50 years of lighting progress from 1920 to 1970. It shows why the fluorescent tube has largely replaced the filament lamp for general lighting in factories and offices and how the value of lighting (lumen hours per watt and lumen hours per penny) has steadily improved due to lower cost, improved efficacy and longer lamp life.

Table 34.8 Fifty years of lighting progress

Year	1920	1930	1940	1940	1950	1960	1970
Lamp type and rating	Filament lamp			Fluorescent tube			
	100 W	100 W	100 W	80 W	80 W	80 W	85 W
Average lamp lumens	1000	1100	1160	2160	3040	4320	6300
Lamp life (h)	1000	1000	1000	2000	3000	5000	7500
Lamp price (list)	37p	22p	10p	£1·97	95p	76p	70p
Kilolumen hours per watt	10·0	11·0	11·6	43·0	91·2	216	472
Kilolumen hours per penny	27	50	116	22	96	284	675
Cost of living (% of 1940 figure)	51%	72%	100%	100%	135%	200%	305%

Appendix I Lamp data

LAMP DESIGNATIONS

MB	High pressure mercury quartz arc tube in diffusing or clear outer bulb.
MBF	As for MB but outer bulb has internal fluorescent coating.
MBFR	As for MBF but outer bulb also has internal reflecting surfaces.
MBT	As for MB but with the arc in series with a tungsten filament.
MBTF	As for MBT but outer bulb has internal fluorescent coating.
MBI	High pressure mercury quartz arc tube with metal halide additives in clear outer bulb.
MBIF	As for MBI but outer bulb has internal fluorescent coating.
MBIL	As for MBI but in linear form and without outer bulb.
MBW	As for MB but with Wood's glass outer bulb.
MCF	Low pressure linear glass arc tube with internal fluorescent coating.
MCFA	As for MCF but with instant-start external metal strip connected to both caps.
MCFB	As for MCF but with instant-start internal strip connected to one electrode.
MCFC	As for MCF but with instant-start external metal strip not connected to either cap.
MCFD	As for MCF but with two instant-start internal strips connected to opposite electrodes.
MCFE	As for MCF with instant-start external water repellant (silicone) coating.
MD	High pressure mercury quartz arc tube but with forced liquid cooling.
ME	High pressure mercury compact source quartz arc tube with clear glass or metal box outer.
MEX	As for ME but with xenon filling.
NE	Neon linear glass arc tube.
SLI	Low pressure sodium linear arc tube in which arc tube and outer bulb are combined to form one unit with cap at each end.
SOX	Low pressure sodium U-shaped arc tube in which arc tube and outer tube are combined to form one unit.
SON	High pressure sodium sintered aluminium oxide arc tube in diffusing or clear outer bulb.
CSI	High pressure mercury quartz compact source arc tube with metal additives.
XE	High pressure xenon quartz compact source arc tube.
XB	High pressure xenon quartz linear arc tube.
U, H, V or D	Usual burning position: universal, horizontal, vertical cap up, or vertical cap down respectively.
PAR 38, 56 or 64	Parabolic aluminized reflector (sealed beam lamp), diameter $\frac{38}{8}$, $\frac{56}{8}$ or $\frac{64}{8}$ inches respectively.

LAMP CHARACTERISTICS

General lighting service incandescent filament lamps

(i) Pear shaped—240 V
Rated life 1000 h

Rating (watts)	Lighting design lumens	Class	Bulb finish	Cap	Nominal dimensions (mm)		
					Overall length	Bulb diameter	Light centre length
40	390	Coiled coil			As single coil see below		
60	665						
100	1260						
150	2040				125	68	90
25	200		Internally frosted	B22/25 × 26	105	60	75
40	325				105	60	75
60	575				105	60	75
100	1 160				105	60	75
100	1 160				125	68	90
150	1 960				160	80	120
200	2 720	Single coil		E27/27	161·5	80	121·5
300	4 300				233	110	178
500	7 700				233	110	178
750	12 400		Clear	E40/45	300	150	225
1 000	17 300				300	150	225
1 500	27 500				335	170	250

(ii) Mushroom shaped—240/250 V (245 V design)
Rated life 1000 h

40	380	Coiled coil	Internally white-coated	B22/25 × 26	100	60	78
60	640				100	60	78
100	1 220				100	60	78
150	1 860				121·5	75	95

Tubular fluorescent lamps

Rating (watts)	Operating volts	Operating current (A)	Cap	Nominal dimensions (mm)		Rated life (h)
				Overall length	Diameter	
15	57	0·34		450	25	5000
15	48	0·36		450	38	5000
20	57	0·37		600	38	5000
30	96	0·365		900	25	5000
30	81	0·405		900	38	5000
40	47	0·88		600	38	5000
40	103	0·43	G13	1200	38	7500
50	165	0·38	(Medium	1500	25	5000
65	110	0·67	bi-pin)	1500	38	7500
80	99	0·87		1500	38	7500
85	120	0·80		1800	38	7500
85	178	0·55		2400	38	7500
125	149	0·94		2400	38	7500
4	29	0·17	G5	150	15	5000
6	42	0·16	(Miniature	224	15	5000
8	57	0·145	bi-pin)	300	15	5000
13	95	0·165		525	15	5000
Circular				Maximum circle diameter		
22	55/69	0·40		215·9		5000
32	72/92	0·45	G10q	311·2		5000
40	100/120	0·42		412·8		5000

Colour designation and lighting design lumens

Rating (watts)		White	Warm White	Daylight	Natural	De luxe Warm White	°Kolor-rite	Northlight, Colour Matching	De Luxe Natural	Artificial Daylight
15	dia 25 mm	800	800	750	600	—	—	500	450	400
15	dia 38 mm	750	750	700	550	500	—	450	400	—
20		1100	1100	1050	800	750	750	700	600	500
30	dia 25 mm	2150	2150	2050	1600	1450	1300	1250	1100	—
30	dia 38 mm	1850	1850	1750	1400	1250	—	1050	900	—
40	600 mm	1700	1700	1600	1300	1200	1100	1050	900	—
40	1200 mm	2750	2700	2650	2100	1950	1800	1700	1500	1200
50		3300	3250	3200	2400	—	2200	—	1850	—
65		4700	4600	4450	3400	3100	3000	2700	2500	2100
80		5200	5100	4950	3900	3500	3400	3100	2700	2300
85	1800 mm	6300	6100	5750	4350	—	3850	3600	3200	2600
85	2400 mm	6800	6700	6500	5000	4700	4400	4100	3800	3000
125		8700	8600	8400	6500	6200	5700	5300	4800	3800
4		135	135	125	100	—	—	—	—	—
6		240	240	230	190	—	—	—	—	—
8		360	360	340	280	—	—	—	—	—
13		730	730	680	—	—	—	—	—	—
22	circular	—	850	—	—	—	—	—	—	—
32	circular	—	1600	—	—	—	—	—	—	—
40	circular	—	2300	—	—	—	—	—	—	—

Sodium lamps

(i) Low pressure sodium lamps
Rated life 6000 h

Rating (watts)	Type	Lighting design lumens	Operating volts	Operating current (A)	Cap	Max. dimensions (mm)	
						Overall length	Bulb diameter
35	SOX	4 500	70	0·60	BY22d	311	53
55	SOX	7 500	109	0·60	BY22d	425	53
90	SOX	12 500	112	0·92	BY22d	528	67
135	SOX	21 500	164	0·92	BY22d	775	67
60	SLI	6 400	82	0·80	G13	419	39·5
140	SLI	20 000	175	0·90	G13	909	39·5
200	SLI	27 500	145	1·55	G13	909	39·5

(ii) High pressure sodium lamps (SON)
Rated life 6000 h

Rating (watts)	Type of envelope	Lighting design lumens	Operating volts	Operating current (A)	Cap	Max. dimensions (mm)	
						Overall length	Bulb diameter
250	Elliptical	19 500	100	3·0	E40	227	91
250	Tubular	21 000	100	3·0	E40	257	53
400	Elliptical	36 000	105	4·4	E40	292	122
400	Tubular	38 000	105	4·4	E40	292	53

Mercury lamps

(i) Colour-corrected mercury lamps (MBF)
Rated life 7500 h

Rating (watts)	Lighting design lumens	Operating volts	Operating current (A)	Cap	Nominal dimensions (mm)	
					Overall length	Bulb diameter
50	1 800	85/105	0·61		125	55
80	3 350	100/130	0·80	E27	150	70
125	5 500	110/140	1·15		170	75
250	12 000	115/145	2·15		220	90
400	21 500	120/150	3·25	E40	280	120
700	38 000	125/155	5·40		320	140
1000	54 000	130/160	7·50		400	165

(ii) Tungsten-ballasted mercury lamps (MBTF)
Rated life 6000 h

Rating (watts)	Lighting design lumens	Operating current (A)	Cap	Nominal dimensions (mm)	
				Overall length	Bulb diameter
160	2 700	0·65	B22/25 × 26	173·5	88
250	4 840	1·05	E40	233	110
500	11 500	2·10	E40	267	130

Metal halide lamps

(i) MBI and MBIF

Rating (watts)	Lighting design lumens	Operating volts	Operating current (A)	Cap	Dimensions (mm)		Arc length (mm)	Rated life (h)
					Overall length (max)	Bulb diameter (nom)		
400*	24 000	120/150	3·3	E40	292	120	45	7500
400†	27 000	120/150	3·3	E40	292	120	45	7500
1000*	76 000	235/265	4·2	E40	400	165	80	7500
1000†	85 000	235/265	4·2	E40	400	165	80	7500
2000*	152 000	215	10·3	E40	430	100	100	—
3500*	280 000	215	18·0	E40	430	100	150	—

* Clear lamp (MBI)   † Phosphor coated lamp (MBIF).

(ii) Linear metal halide lamps (MBIL)

Rating (watts)	Lighting design lumens	Operating volts	Operating current (A)	Cap	Dimensions (mm)		Arc length (mm)	Rated life (h)
					Overall length (nom)	Bulb diameter (max)		
750	51 000	500	1·75	R7s	254	14	190	3000
1600	115 000	450	3·75	R7s	254	17·7	190	3000

(iii) Compact source iodide lamps (CSI)

Rating (watts)	Lighting design lumens	Operating volts	Operating current (A)	Dimensions (mm)		Arc length (mm)	Rated life (h)
				Overall length (max)	Bulb diameter (max)		
400	32 000	100	5	55	20	8/10	100
1000*	93 000	70/85	15	115	32	13/15	200

* In PAR 64 envelope—Beam intensity $1·5 \times 10^6$ cd. Rated life 1000 h.

Xenon lamps (compact source and linear)

Rating (watts)	Light output (lm)	Arc luminance (cd/cm²)	Operating volts	Operating current (A)	Dimensions (mm)		Arc length (mm)	Rated life (h)
					Overall length (nom)	Bulb diameter (max)		
150*	3 000	9 000	19	7·5	150	20	2·5	1000
250*	5 000	11 000	16	15	125	35	3	1500
500*	12 000	20 000	22	23	215	40	5	1000
2 000*	70 000	120 000	25	80	315	65	6/7	1000
1 000†	20 000	100	42	25	300	25	85	1000
1 500†	31 500	160	70	23	355	32	155	1500
10 000†	250 000	140	140	75	1150	35	750	2000

* Compact source (XE): dc supply greater than 65 V.
† Linear (XB): ac supply 240 V.

Appendix II Units and terms

The usual symbol is given in brackets at the end of the definition.

ABSORPTANCE (absorption factor)   Ratio of absorbed flux to incident flux (radiant or luminous). (α)

APOSTILB   Unit of luminance, that of a perfect diffuser emitting 1 lumen per square metre, equivalent to $1/\pi$ candela per square metre. (asb)

ASPECT FACTOR   That part of the illuminance equation for a line source relating to the angle subtended by the source at the point considered and to the intensity distribution of the source (AF, af)

ATMOSPHERE, STANDARD   Unit of pressure, equal to 760 Torr. (atm)

BREWSTER ANGLE   Angle of incidence of light at which it becomes linearly polarized by specular reflection.

CALORIE   Unit of energy, approximately 4·19 joule. (cal)

CANDELA   SI unit of luminous intensity, realized by a full radiator at the freezing point of platinum which has a luminance of 60 candelas per square centimetre. (cd)

CELSIUS   Correct name of the temperature scale commonly called Centigrade. The scale unit is the degree Celsius. (°C)

CHROMA   Subjective estimate of the amount of pure chromatic colour present in the sample observed. Quantitative parameter in the Munsell system.

CHROMATICITY   Colour quality of a stimulus defined by co-ordinates on a plane diagram; or by the combination of dominant wavelength and excitation purity.

CHROMINANCE   Product of luminance and a chromaticity difference; used in colour television to express a colorimetric difference.

COLOUR RENDERING INDEX   Applied to a light source. A measure of the degree to which the measured colours of objects conform to those of the same objects under a reference illuminant. (R)

COLOUR TEMPERATURE   Temperature of a full radiator which emits radiation of the same chromaticity as the radiator considered.

CONTRAST   Relating the luminances of two parts of a visual field by such a formula as $(L_2 - L_1)/L_b$ where L_b is the background luminance; also used to indicate the subjective assessment of a luminance difference. (C)

CONTRAST RENDERING FACTOR   The ratio of the detectable contrast in a task under a given lighting system to that under integrating sphere conditions. (CRF)

CONTRAST SENSITIVITY   Reciprocal of the minimum perceptible contrast.

CORRELATED COLOUR TEMPERATURE   Colour temperature corresponding to the point on the full radiator locus which is nearest to the chromaticity of a light source on a uniform chromaticity scale.

CRITICAL FUSION FREQUENCY   Frequency above which a succession of light stimuli appears to be a continuous light. (*CFF*)

DAYLIGHT FACTOR   Ratio of total illuminance at a point in a building, usually on a horizontal plane, received directly and indirectly from the sky, to the illuminance of a horizontal plane exposed to an unobstructed hemisphere of the same sky. Direct sunlight is excluded in both measurements.

DOMINANT WAVELENGTH   Wavelength of a monochromatic light stimulus which, combined with an achromatic stimulus, gives a colour match with the stimulus considered. (λ_d)

EFFICACY, LUMINOUS   For radiation, the quotient of the luminous flux by the radiant flux, in lumens per watt. (K, or $K(\lambda)$ for monochromatic radiation).
      For a source, the quotient of the luminous flux by the power consumed, in lumens per watt. (η_v)

EFFICIENCY, LUMINOUS   Ratio of the radiant flux, weighted according to $V(\lambda)$, to the radiant flux. (V)

EFFICIENCY, RADIANT   Ratio of the radiant flux to the power consumed. (η_e)

EFFICIENCY, SPECTRAL LUMINOUS   Ratio of the radiant flux at wavelength λ_m to that at λ such that they produce equal luminous sensations, λ_m being the wavelength at which the luminous effect is a maximum. ($V(\lambda)$)

ELECTRON-VOLT   Unit of energy, acquired by an electron when accelerated through a potential difference of 1 volt. (eV)

EMISSIVITY   Ratio of thermal radiant exitance of a solid to that of a full radiator at the same temperature. (ϵ)

E-VITON   Unit of erythemal radiant flux, producing the same effect as $10\,\mu W$ at 297 nm; in watts.

EXITANCE, LUMINOUS   Luminous flux leaving a surface element divided by the area of the element; in lumens per square metre. (M_v)

EXITANCE, RADIANT   As above, for radiant flux; in watts per square metre. (M_e)

FINSEN   Unit of erythemal dose rate, equal to 1 E-Viton per square centimetre, or 0·1 watt per square metre at 297 nm.

FLUX FRACTION   Ratio of the flux intercepted by a surface to the total flux emitted by another surface illuminating it. (i)

FLUX, LUMINOUS   Radiant flux weighted according to the spectral luminous efficiency function; in lumens. (Φ_v or Φ)

FLUX, RADIANT   Power emitted, transferred or received as radiation; in watts. (Φ_e)

FOOT-CANDLE   Obsolete unit of illuminance, equal to 10·76 lux.

FOOT-LAMBERT   Non-SI unit of luminance, that of a perfect diffuser emitting 1 lumen per square foot. (ft L)

FORM FACTOR   Ratio of the illuminance of a surface to the luminous excitance of another surface illuminating it. (f)

FULL RADIATOR   Thermal radiator having the maximum spectral concentration of radiant emittance at a given temperature; also called a black body to emphasize its absorption of all incident radiation, or a Planckian radiator.

GLARE INDEX   Number assessing the discomfort glare from a lighting installation.

GUIDE NUMBER   Number assigned to a given photoflash lamp, giving product of the subject distance and the lens stop number for photography under specified conditions.

HUE   Subjective attribute of a colour stimulus distinguished by names like blue, green, red.

ILLUMINANCE   Luminous flux on a surface element divided by the area of the element; in lumens per square metre or lux. (E_v or E)

ILLUMINATION VECTOR   Vector normal to a plane oriented so as to produce maximum difference of illuminance on its opposite sides. Vector value equal to the difference in illuminance. Vector direction may be considered either with or against the maximum light flux direction.

INTENSITY RATIO   Ratio of maximum intensity from a luminaire, in a downward direction, to the mean intensity over the lower hemisphere.

IRRADIANCE   Radiant flux on a surface element divided by the area of the element; in watts per square metre. (E_e)

JOULE   Unit of energy, equal to the work done when the point of application of a force of 1 newton moves through 1 metre. (J)

KELVIN   SI unit of temperature on both absolute and Celsius scales; or measure of temperature above absolute zero on absolute scale. (K, formerly °K)

LAMBERT   Obsolete unit of luminance, of a perfect diffuser emitting 1 lumen per square centimetre. [The millilambert is used more often, particularly by vision scientists. (mL)]

LIGHTNESS   Subjective estimate of the proportion of light diffusely reflected by a body.

LIGHT OUTPUT RATIO   Ratio of light output of a luminaire to sum of light outputs of the lamps it contains. (LOR)
May be divided into upward and downward components. ($ULOR$, $DLOR$)

LUMEN   Unit of luminous flux, emitted within one steradian from a point source of intensity of one candela. (lm)

LUMEN SECOND   Unit of quantity of light. (lm s)

LUMINANCE   Luminous flux from a surface element divided by the product of the projected area of the element perpendicular to the beam, and the solid angle containing the beam; in lumens per square metre per steradian, or candelas per square metre. (L_v or L)

LUMINANCE FACTOR   Ratio of the luminance of a body to that of a perfect reflecting diffuser identically illuminated.

579

LUMINOSITY   Subjective estimate of the amount of light emitted by an area; formerly known as brightness.

LUMINOUS INTENSITY   Quotient of the luminous flux leaving a source in an element of solid angle, by the solid angle; in candelas. (I_v or I)

LUX   Unit of illuminance, produced by a uniform luminous flux of one lumen on a surface of one square metre. (lx)

MAINTENANCE FACTOR   Ratio of mean illuminance on working plane after period of use of luminaires to mean illuminance for new installation with lamps aged as prescribed. (MF)

MEAN CYLINDRICAL ILLUMINANCE   Mean illuminance on the curved surface of a small cylinder with its axis vertical and located at the point considered. (E_c)

MILLIBAR   Unit of pressure, equal to 0·01 newton per square metre. (mbar)

MUTUAL EXCHANGE COEFFICIENT   Quotient of the flux (radiant or luminous) which one surface sends to another surface, by the excitance of the first surface; in square metres. (g)

NANOMETRE   Unit of length convenient for use in wavelengths of light; 10^{-9} of 1 metre. (nm)

NEWTON   SI unit of force, producing an acceleration of 1 metre per second^2 in a mass of 1 kilogram. (N)

PASCAL   SI unit of pressure, equal to 1 newton per square metre and generally referred to in this way. (Pa, N/m^2)

PURITY, EXCITATION   Ratio of the distance of a point on the 1931 CIE chromaticity diagram (representing a colour stimulus) from the achromatic point, to the distance of the latter from the dominant wavelength of the colour stimulus. (p_e)

PURITY, COLORIMETRIC   The above multiplied by the ratio of the luminance of the colour stimulus to that of the achromatic stimulus. (p_c)

PURITY, METRIC   As p_e, but measured on the 1960 CIE uniform chromaticity scale. (p_m)

RADIANCE   Radiant flux from a surface element divided by the product of the projected area of the element perpendicular to the beam, and the solid angle containing the beam; in watts per square metre per steradian. (L_e)

REFLECTANCE (reflection factor)   Ratio of reflected flux to incident flux (radiant or luminous). (ρ)

REFRACTIVE INDEX   Ratio of velocity of electromagnetic waves in vacuum to the phase velocity of waves of the wavelength considered in the medium. (n)

RELATIVE CONTRAST SENSITIVITY   Contrast sensitivity expressed as a percentage of the contrast sensitivity at a luminance of 10^4 cd/m^2. (RCS)

ROOM INDEX   Usually $LW/H_m(L+W)$ for a room of length L, width W and mounting height H_m of the luminaires above the working plane. (RI)

SATURATION   Subjective estimate of the proportion of pure chromatic colour in a sensation. Compare Chroma.

SCALAR ILLUMINANCE (mean spherical illuminance)   Mean illuminance on the surface of a small sphere located at the point considered. (E_s)

SPACING/HEIGHT RATIO   Ratio of spacing between centres of adjacent luminaires to their height above the working plane.

SPECTRAL DISTRIBUTION   Manner in which radiant flux or other quantity varies with wavelength (or frequency) over the spectrum.

STERADIAN   Unit of solid angle; $\frac{1}{4\pi}$ of a complete sphere. (sr)

STILB   Unit of luminance; 1 candela per square centimetre. (sb)

TORR   Non-SI unit of pressure; produced by 1 millimetre column of mercury. (Torr)

TRANSMITTANCE (transmission factor)   Ratio of transmitted flux to incident flux (radiant or luminous). (τ)

UTILIZATION FACTOR   Ratio of utilized luminous flux to that emitted by the lamps in the luminaires.

VALUE   Subjective estimate of lightness on a black to white scale. Quantitative parameter in the Munsell system.

VISUAL ACUITY   Reciprocal of the angular separation, in minutes of arc, between two points or lines just separable by the eye.

WATT   Unit of power; 1 joule per second. (W)

ZONE FACTOR   Factor by which the mean luminous intensity over a zone of given angular width is multiplied to determine the luminous flux in the zone, and equal to the solid angle containing the zone.

CONVERSION TABLES

Illuminance

The only factors now required are between the present unit and those units including Imperial measures of length which are now obsolete in UK and Europe.

$$1 \text{ lux} = 0{\cdot}0929 \text{ lumens per square foot}$$

$$1 \text{ lumen per square foot (1 'foot candle')} = 10{\cdot}76 \text{ lux}$$

Luminance

		cd/m^2	sb	asb	mL	ftL	cd/ft^2
1 candela per square metre	=	1	10^{-4}	3·14	0·314	0·292	$9{\cdot}29 \times 10^{-2}$
1 stilb (candela per square cm)	=	10^4	1	$3{\cdot}14 \times 10^4$	$3{\cdot}14 \times 10^3$	$2{\cdot}92 \times 10^3$	$9{\cdot}29 \times 10^2$
1 apostilb	=	0·318	$3{\cdot}18 \times 10^{-5}$	1	0·1	0·0929	0·0296
1 millilambert	=	3·18	$3{\cdot}18 \times 10^{-4}$	10	1	0·929	0·296
1 foot-lambert	=	3·43	$3{\cdot}43 \times 10^{-4}$	10·8	1·08	1	0·318
1 candela per square foot	=	10·8	$1{\cdot}08 \times 10^{-4}$	33·8	3·38	3·14	1

Pressure, energy, temperature

1 Torr = 133·3 newton per square metre = 1·333 millibar
1 standard atmosphere = 1013 millibar = 760 Torr
1 electron-volt = 1·602 × 10^{-19} joule
Energy of photon of wavelength λ nanometre = 1240/λ electron-volt
Temperature, kelvin (K) = 273·15 + temperature, Celsius (°C).

Appendix III Standards and technical reports

BSI Publications

BS52:1963	Bayonet lamp caps, lampholders and B.C. adaptors (lampholder plugs) for voltages not exceeding 250 volts.
BS88:1967	Cartridge fuses of voltage ratings up to 660 volts.
BS89:1970	Direct acting electrical indicating instruments.
BS98:1962	Dimensions of screw lamp caps and lampholders (Edison type).
BS161:1968	240 V tungsten filament general service electric lamps.
BS204:1960	Glossary of terms used in telecommunication (including radio) and electronics.
BS219:1959	Soft solders.
BS229:1957	Flameproof enclosure of electrical apparatus.
BS232:1952	Vitreous-enamelled steel reflectors for use with tungsten filament lamps.
BS233:1953	Glossary of terms used in illumination and photometry—overtaken by IEC Publication No. 50 and BS4727.
BS307:1931	Street lighting (withdrawn; see CP1004).
BS350:1959–	Conversion factors and tables.
BS354:1961	Recommendations for photometric integrators.
BS381C:1964	Colours for specific purposes.
BS398:1948	Classification of symmetrical light distributions from lighting fittings.
BS441:1954	Rosin-cored solder wire, activated and non-activated (non-corrosive).
BS469:1960	Electric lamps for railway signalling.
BS495:1960	Lamp caps and lampholders for double-capped tubular lamps.
BS505:1971	Road traffic signals.
BS535:1953	Bulbs for miners' electric lamps.
BS555:1962	Tungsten filament miscellaneous electric lamps.
BS559:1955	Electric signs and high-voltage luminous discharge-tube installations.
BS667:1968	Portable photoelectric photometers.
BS800:1954	Limits of radio interference.
BS816:1952	Requirements for electrical appliances and accessories.
BS841:1966	Lamp caps and lampholders for architectural lamps.
BS867:1939	Traction lamps (series burning).
BS873:1970	The construction of road traffic signs and internally illuminated bollards.
BS889:1965	Flameproof electric lighting fittings.
BS930:1962	Measurement of light output of cinematograph projectors for narrow gauge film.
BS941:1970	Filament lamps for road vehicles.
BS942:1949	Formulae for calculating intensities of lighthouse beams.
BS950:1967	Artificial daylight for the assessment of colour.

BS1015:1961	Exciter lamps.
BS1050:1953	Visual indicator lamps for use in telephone and telegraph switchboards and for allied purposes.
BS1075:1961	Studio spotlight lamps.
BS1164:1952	Dimensions of pre-focus lamp caps and lampholders (for voltages not exceeding 250 volts).
BS1259:1958	Intrinsically safe electrical apparatus and circuits for use in explosive atmospheres.
BS1270:1960	Schedule for electric discharge lamps for general purposes.
BS1298:1967	Lamp caps and holders for festoon lamps (for voltages not exceeding 50 volts).
BS1308:1970	Concrete street lighting columns.
BS1332:1960	Guide to civil land aerodrome lighting.
BS1376:1953	Colours of light signals.
BS1383:1966	Photoelectric exposure meters.
BS1404:1961	Screen luminance for the projection of 35 mm film on matt and directional screens.
BS1546:1963	Electric lamps for lighthouses.
BS1592:1958	Camera shutters.
BS1611:1953	Glossary of colour terms used in science and industry.
BS1615:1961	Anodic oxidation coatings on aluminium.
BS1650:1971	Capacitors for connection to power-frequency systems.
BS1788:1964	Street lighting lanterns for use with electric lamps.
BS1840:1960	Steel columns for street lighting.
BS1853:1967	Tubular fluorescent lamps for general lighting service.
BS1871:1952	Minimum requirements for silvering for glass reflectors for lighting purposes.
BS1875:1952	Bi-pin lamp caps and lampholders for tubular fluorescent lamps for use in circuits, the declared voltage of which does not exceed 250 volts.
BS1950:1953	Vitreous-enamelled steel reflectors for use with mercury electric discharge lamps (Types MB/V and MA/V).
BS1980:1953	Portable electric hand-lamps (open type with protective guard).
BS2063:1963	Studio spotlights for tungsten filament lamps for use in motion picture studios.
BS2135:1966	Capacitors for radio interference suppression.
BS2515:1954	Reflex reflectors for vehicles, including cycles.
BS2516:1954	Tail lights for vehicles, including cycles.
BS2560:1954	Exit signs for cinemas, theatres and places of public entertainment.
BS2660:1955	Colours for building and decorative paints.
BS2818:1962	Auxiliaries for operation of fluorescent lamps on a.c. 50 c/s supplies.
BS2833:1968	Schedule of expendable photographic flash bulbs.
BS2954:1958	Recommendations for screen luminance for the projection of 16 mm film.
BS2964:1958	Screen luminance in cinematograph laboratory and studio review rooms.
BS3042:1971	Standard test fingers and probes for checking protection against electrical, mechanical and thermal hazard.

BS3205:1969   Photographic electronic flash equipment.
BS3224:1960–   Lighting fittings for civil land aerodromes.
BS3232:1968   Safety requirements for medical treatment lamps.
BS3337:1961   Dimensions of plug part and lampholder for capless photo-flash lamps.
BS3456:1962–   The testing and approval of household electrical appliances.
BS3541:1962   Lighting fittings for general examination purposes in hospitals.
BS3648:1963   Cycle rear lamps.
BS3677:1963   Schedule of fluorescent mercury discharge lamps.
BS3720:1964   Torches for use in hospitals.
BS3767:1964   Schedule of sodium discharge lamps.
BS3772:1964   Starters for use with fluorescent lamps operating on a.c. 50 c/s supplies.
BS3820:1964   Electric lighting fittings.
BS3875:1965   Optical spectrophotometric cells.
BS3944:1965   Colour filters for theatre lighting and other purposes.
BS3989:1966   Aluminium street lighting columns.
BS4015:1966   Lighting fittings (luminaires) used for television production.
BS4017:1966   Capacitors for use in tubular fluorescent, mercury and sodium discharge lamp circuits.
BS4095:1970   Methods for the determination of photographic flash light output and guide numbers.
BS4099:1967   Colours and their meaning when used for indicator lights, annunciators and digital readouts in industrial installations.
BS4329:1968   Flash apparatus using expendable photographic flash bulbs.
BS4489:1969   Method for assessing black light used in non-destructive testing.
BS4533:1969–   Electric luminaires (lighting fittings).
BS4564:1970   Screen luminance for the projection of 70 mm film on directional screens.
BS4632:1970   Automatic exposure control equipment in cameras.
BS4647:1970   Lighting sets for Christmas trees and decorative purposes for indoor use.
BS4727 Part 4:1971–   Glossary of terms: terms particular to lighting and colour.
BS4782:1971   Ballasts for high pressure mercury vapour and low pressure sodium vapour discharge lamps.
BS AU40:1963   Motor vehicle lighting and signalling equipment.
CP3 Ch. 1 Part 1:1964   Code of basic data for the design of buildings: Daylighting.
CP1004 Parts 1–9:1963–   Street lighting.

CEE Publications

No. 3   Edison screw lampholders.
No. 11   Electric cooking and heating appliances for domestic and similar purposes.
No. 12   Fluorescent lamp auxiliaries.
No. 25   Lighting fittings for incandescent lamps.

CIE Publications

No. 2   Colour of light signals.

No. 8 Street lighting and accidents.
No. 12 International recommendations for the lighting of public thoroughfares.
No. 13 Method of measuring and specifying colour rendering properties of light sources.
No. 15 Official recommendations on colorimetry.
No. 16 International recommendations for the calculation of natural daylight.
No. 17 International lighting vocabulary.
No. 18 Principles of light measurements.

IEC Publications

No. 50 International electrotechnical vocabulary—Group 45 Lighting.
No. 61 Lamp caps and holders together with gauges for the control of interchangeability and safety.
No. 64 Tungsten filament lamps for general service.
No. 64A Tungsten filament lamps for general service—Lamps with a life of 2500 hours.
No. 81 Tubular fluorescent lamps for general lighting service.
No. 82 Ballasts for fluorescent lamps.
No. 155 Glow starters for fluorescent lamps.
No. 162 Lighting fittings for tubular fluorescent lamps.
No. 188 Schedule for high pressure mercury vapour lamps.
No. 192 Schedule for sodium lamps (integral type).
No. 238 Edison screw lampholders.
No. 240 Characteristics of electric infra-red emitters for heating purposes.
No. 259 Miscellaneous lamps and ballasts.
No. 262 Ballasts for high pressure mercury vapour lamps.
No. 357 Projector and floodlighting lamps.
No. 360 Standard method of measurement of lamp cap temperature rise.

IES Technical reports

No. 1 Lighting in corrosive, flammable and explosive situations.
No. 2 The calculation of coefficients of utilization—The British Zonal method.
No. 3 The lighting of building sites and works of engineering construction.
No. 4 Lighting during daylight hours.
No. 5 Lecture theatres and their lighting.
No. 6 The floodlighting of buildings.
No. 7 Lighting for sport
No. 8 Lighting of libraries.
No. 9 Depreciation and maintenance of interior lighting.
No. 10 Evaluation of discomfort glare.
No. 11 The calculation of direct illumination from linear sources.
No. 12 Hospital lighting.
No. 13 Industrial area floodlighting.
No. 14 Lighting of art galleries and museums.

IES Code 1968 (Currently under revision).

APLE Technical reports

No. 1   Lighting of traffic signs.
No. 2.   Computers in public lighting.

Miscellaneous UK lighting regulations

Statutory rules and orders No. 94. Factories (standards of lighting) regulations, 1941.
SI No. 890. Standards for school premises regulations, 1959.
SI No. 2168. The slaughterhouse (hygiene) regulations, 1958.
SI No. 1162. The food hygiene (general) regulations, 1970.
Offices, Shops and Railway Premises Act, 1963.
Traffic Signs Manual—Chapter 11. Illumination of signs, 1969.
Department of Trade and Industry Document CAP 168. Licensing of aerodromes, 1971.
Admiralty Manual of Navigation—Vol. 1, 1970.
IEE Regulations for the electrical equipment of buildings, 1970.

8   United Nations agreements

Regulation No. 2   Uniform regulations concerning approval of lamps for headlights emitting an asymmetrical passing beam or a driving beam or both.

Regulation No. 5   Uniform provisions for the approval of motor vehicle 'sealed beam' headlamps (SB) emitting a European asymmetrical passing beam or a driving beam or both.

Regulation No. 8   Uniform provisions for the approval of motor vehicle headlights emitting an asymmetrical passing beam or a driving beam or both and equipped with halogen lamps (H1, H2 or H3 lamps) and of the lamps themselves.

Regulation No. 20   Uniform provisions concerning the approval of motor vehicle headlights emitting an asymmetrical passing beam or a driving beam or both and equipped with halogen lamps (H4 lamps) and of the lamps themselves.

Appendix IV Suggestions for further reading

Fundamentals

Light. R. W. Ditchburn. Blackie 1963.
Principles of optics. M. Born & E. Wolf. Pergamon 1966.
Scientific basis of illuminating engineering. P. Moon. Dover 1961.
Physiology of the eye. H. Davson. Churchill 1963.
Eye and brain. R. L. Gregory. Weidenfeld & Nicholson 1966.
Light, colour and vision. Y. LeGrand. Chapman & Hall 1957.
Researches on normal and defective colour vision. W. D. Wright. Kimpton 1946.
Measurement of colour. W. D. Wright. Hilger 1969.
Colour science. G. Wyszecki & W. S. Stiles. Wiley 1967.
Photometry. J. W. T. Walsh. Constable 1958.
Design of optical spectrometers. J. F. James & R. S. Sternberg. Chapman & Hall 1969.
Light calculations and measurements. H. A. E. Keitz. Macmillan 1971.
Applied solid state science. R. Wolfe. Academic Press 1969.
Gaseous conductors. J. D. Cobine. Dover 1958.
Electric discharge in gases. F. M. Penning. Macmillan 1957.
Ionized gases. A. von Engel. O.U.P. 1965.
Electroluminescence. H. K. Henisch. Pergamon 1962.
Luminescent materials. G. F. J. Garlick. Clarendon Press 1949.
Introduction to masers and lasers. T. P. Melia. Chapman & Hall 1967.

Lamps and circuits

Glass Engineering Handbook. E. B. Shand. McGraw-Hill 1958.
Technical Glasses. M. B. Volf. Pitman 1961.
Introduction to ceramics. W. B. Kingery. Wiley 1960.
Tungsten. C. J. Smithells. Chapman & Hall 1952.
Fluorescent lamps. W. Elenbaas. Macmillan 1971.
Fluorescent lighting manual. C. L. Amick. McGraw-Hill 1961.
Gas discharge lamps. J. F. Funke & P. J. Oranje. Cleaver-Hume 1951.
High pressure mercury vapour lamps. W. Elenbaas. Cleaver Hume 1965.
High pressure mercury vapour discharge. W. Elenbaas. North Holland 1951.
Discharge lamps for photography and projection. H. K. Bourne. Chapman & Hall 1948.
Physics of electroluminescent devices. P. R. Thornton. Spon 1967.
Fundamentals of discharge tube circuits. V. J. Francis. Methuen 1948.
A.C. devices with iron cores. P. F. van Eldik. Cleaver Hume 1962.
J. and P. transformer book. S. A. Stignant, H. Lacey & A. C. Franklin. Iliffe 1961.

Luminaires, lighting and the environment

Theory and design of illuminating engineering equipment. L. B. W. Jolley, J. M. Waldram & G. H. Wilson. Chapman & Hall 1930.

Lighting fittings, performance and design. A. R. Bean & R. H. Simons. Pergamon 1968.

Lighting of buildings. R. G. Hopkinson & J. D. Kay. Faber 1969.

Ergonomics of lighting. R. G. Hopkinson & J. B. Collins. Macdonald 1970.

Lighting. J. W. Favie *et al.* Cleaver Hume 1962.

Daylighting. R. G. Hopkinson, P. Petherbridge & J. Longmore. Heinemann 1966.

Principles of natural lighting. J. A. Lynes. Elsevier 1968.

Daylight and its spectrum. S. T. Henderson. Hilger 1970.

Lighting. D. Phillips. MacDonald 1966.

Home lighting. A. Byers. Pelham 1970.

Lighting. R. Freeth. Studio Vista 1970.

Architectural physics—lighting. R. G. Hopkinson. HMSO 1963.

Lighting in schools: Building Bulletin 33. HMSO 1967.

Public lighting. J. B. de Boer. Cleaver Hume 1967.

Visual considerations of man, vehicle and highway. Society of Automotive Engineers 1966.

Basic principles of ventilation and heating. T. Bedford. Lewis 1964.

Acoustics, noise and buildings. P. H. Parkin & H. R. Humphreys. Faber 1969.

Environmental technologies in architecture. B. Y. Kinzey & H. M. Sharp. Prentice Hall 1963.

Index